MKV Sedan Page 7

JAGUAR
SPORTS CARS

Paul Skilleter

 **Haynes** **G T FOULIS**

First published November 1975

© *Paul Skilleter 1975*

ISBN 0 85429 166 0

*Printed in England by J H Haynes and Company Limited
for the publishers
G T FOULIS & CO LTD (Haynes Publishing Group)
Sparkford Yeovil Somerset BA22 7JJ
England*

*Distributed in the USA by
HAYNES PUBLICATIONS INC
9421 Winnetka Avenue,
Chatsworth Los Angeles
California 91311 USA*

*Bound by The Pitman Press Bath
Editor Tim Parker
Jacket Design Edward Piper*

CONTENTS

Foreword

by W M Heynes, CBE

People seldom bother to read the foreword of a book, and I myself am often an offender in this respect. Nonetheless, I was delighted when Paul asked me if I would perform the task of writing one for this particular book.

The Jaguar Sports Cars is a book written by an enthusiast for other enthusiasts, and it is, I believe, the most complete and authentic history of its subject that has been produced; perhaps the most surprising thing is that it is also written as a story, or saga, in a most readable way.

The fact that you have picked up this book at all indicates that you are Jaguar minded, maybe connected with racing or rallying, or possibly connected with the factory itself, perhaps through a dealer or agent; but most probably you are 'just' a Jaguar owner - the company's most treasured possession, and who has given us such marvellous support over the years. Which-ever catagory you belong to, I believe that in reading this book you will feel the same nostalgia that I experienced when I first scanned through the pages.

Jaguar Cars Ltd and Sir William Lyons - the names are synonymous. It was Sir William's enthusiasm, which he had the ability to transmit to his staff and colleagues, and his singleness of purpose, that made the whole thing tick. It was his ambition, as he told me when I was inter-viewed for the job of Chief Engineer in April 1935, to build one of the finest cars in the world - and who is to say that he did not succeed?

Sir William was not only a brilliant stylist who purely by eye, produced a series of body shapes which as a group have never been surpassed, but he was also a true economist; every penny that could be saved without effecting quality was saved, and the economy passed on to the customer. His argument was that for every £10 on the price of a car you lost so many customers - and through the years we walked alone, this policy always enabled the company to show a reasonable profit.

S.S. Cars Ltd, as the company was originally known, was made public in 1935. There were only two working Directors, Sir William as Managing Director and Arthur Whittaker, General Manager - Arthur played an important part in the build-up and success of the company, though he was always better known in the industry than to the general public; a man of great integrity, he became my closest friend and ally in all our mutual problems throughout the years we were together.

It has been said that in the development of the aeroplane, the only time progress was truly made was in time of war, and it is an indisput-able fact that anyone's best work and efforts are produced under conditions of urgency and stress. With Sir William at the helm, these conditions were rarely absent at Jaguar! The most typical example of this was the design and development of the C-type.

Sir William had agreed at the 1950 Le Mans race that we could build a car that would win the following year. But it was not until the Motor Show in October that he actually gave me the OK to go ahead, and we had about seven months to design, make and prove a new car from a clean sheet of paper and to complete three cars for the race. It was a very small team of designers, development engineers and builders who worked on this project, and it was a supreme effort on the part of everyone concerned, the meeting of a challenge that we had determined must not fail.

Had I been asked to name this book I would

7

have called it the 'Alpha & Omega of the Jaguar Sports Car', as with the finish of E-type production it seems unlikely that another true sports will emerge - although the engineering experience and ability is still available at Jaguar.

A sports car is an individualistic and personal thing, like fine jewellery or hand-made furniture, produced by people to whom achievement as well as profit is a major motive. We shall have to wait and see what the future holds.

W M Heynes, CBE
Snitterfield,
September 1975

Introduction and Acknowledgements

WHILE I'VE been engaged on this book, more than one person has asked me if I really thought there was room for *another* work on Jaguars, knowing as I did that there have been five or six published already. My answer was, of course, an unequivocal 'yes'. Virtually all previous works have been general histories of the marque, and in the past, as a Jaguar sports car enthusiast myself, I had often longed for greater detail and the answers to a number of questions relating solely to the sports cars. In fact, if I had to sum up my thinking in going about writing this book, I would say that I have written it in a way which would have satisfied all my unanswered curiosity years ago when I was already enthusiastic about Jaguar sports cars, but lacking the knowledge which research and enquiry have since accumulated. I sincerely hope and believe that the Jaguar neophyte reading this book today agrees with my choice of answered questions!

The fact of there being such a comparatively large number of words already in print about Jaguars sets another problem - to what extent does one traverse ground which has been well trodden before? Inevitably there must be some repetition otherwise the continuity of the story is lost, and of course, there is also the argument that it is very convenient to have in just one volume all the information one is likely to need on a particular subject. So, besides enlarging upon already well-known facts where possible, I have always tried to include information rather than leave it out, when in doubt as to what to do - bearing in mind that there may still be many readers to whom virtually everything concerning Jaguar will be fresh. I trust, therefore, that the 'old hands' will tolerate reading once more a few of the rather well-worn passages of Jaguar lore, in exchange for what I believe is the high proportion of new material appearing for the first time.

Motor cars, particularly those made by such companies as Jaguar, are not simply a list of components and statistics but possess characters all of their own, with faults, foibles and delights. Therefore in describing individual cars I have not only tried to include all the relevant technical details but also have attempted to convey what it is actually like to be behind the wheel of that particular car, and how it relates to our experience today; so that, if like me you cannot afford to own all the Jaguar sports cars of your choice, you at least have an idea of what you're missing!

So far as the Jaguar sports cars' competition activities are concerned, these have been so widespread and numerous that another book, at least the length of this one, would be necessary to do the subject justice; thus I have outlined most of the cars' major achievements, plus a few of the more interesting or unusual successes (or even failures!), without attempting to convey more than an overall picture. I have, however, devoted one chapter to the XK 120 in competition as the car's record in that field deserves rather more coverage than it has so far received.

In illustrating this book I have tried to use pictures which will be fresh to most readers, and wherever possible pictures which have never been published before at all; in this respect I have been greatly aided by having the negative archives of *Motor* and *Autocar* at my disposal, much of which has never been printed before, let alone reproduced in a journal or book.

When it comes to acknowledging help and advice received while writing such a book as this, it becomes a question of when to stop - over a period of years, the total number of people who have kindly donated time and material reaches surprising proportions; also memory fails to recall everyone even though their assistance is truly appreciated. But as for naming names, no-one will, I feel sure, object if I begin with those who are, or were, with Jaguar themselves, of whom Sir William Lyons must of course come first. I am very deeply indebted to Sir William for most patiently answering my many questions, some of which must have seemed very obscure at times, and especially for volunteering fascinating information which otherwise I might well have failed to discover on my own (I have in mind particularly the XK 120 replacement prototype). Mr FRW England, Mr WM Heynes MBE, and Mr W Hassan also suffered my interrogations willingly, Mr Heynes for a whole weekend at his delightful farm near Stratford-on-Avon. Phil Weaver of Jaguar's experimental department helped with many details relating to prototypes and competition models, while Jaguar's chief photographer Roger Clinkscales interrupted his very full routine to assist me with picture research.

Then how can any Jaguar researcher fail to be indebted to Andrew Whyte, for a number of years head of Jaguar's highly efficient public and press relations department; on behalf of the factory he extended to me every facility at the 'works' that I asked for, and gave generously of his own vast fund of knowledge whenever I called upon it. This is besides the invaluable spade-work which he has accomplished in his XK, C- and D-type *Profiles,* which were of enormous help. My

thanks must also go to Alan Hodge and other members of the PR department at Browns Lane who have spent long hours on my behalf in dusty company archives.

Turning from the factory, I must express my gratitude to my employers, IPC Business Press Ltd, who as custodians of *Autocar, Motor* and *Thoroughbred & Classic Cars* have kindly allowed me to quote much from the former two journals, and to use many photographs from their photographic libraries. I would also like to add my personal thanks to the editors under whom I have worked at IPC, namely Roger Bell of *Motor* and latterly Michael Bowler of *Thoroughbred & Classic Cars,* for tolerating over the past two years my occasional preoccupation with this book during working hours! In this I would also include my long-suffering colleague when I worked on *Motor,* Maurice Rowe.

Needless to say I have called upon the resources of the Jaguar Drivers' Club and its branches to the utmost, the *Jaguar Driver* magazine and the *XK Bulletin* both being most useful. The Registrar of the XK Register, Edward D. Walker, has been of enormous assistance to me and I have dipped deeply into his personal library of Jaguar literature, which must be amongst the most comprehensive in the world; Ted was also kind enough to read through the manuscript and point out a number of errors, and suggest various additions - though in all cases the liability for any mistakes which may remain, and for the various interpretations that I have made over the length of the book, must rest on my shoulders.

I would also like to thank a number of overseas Jaguar clubs, including the Jaguar Clubs of North America Inc. and the Classic Jaguar Association based in the same country. The latter's News & Technical Bulletins and S.S.90 and SS 100 Registers were of considerable assistance to me. I also extend my thanks to a number of individual members of overseas clubs, in particular Tom Hendricks of the Nation's Capitol Jaguar Owners' Club who helped me piece together various aspects of XK and E-type competition activities in the States, John Elmgren of the Australian Jaguar Drivers' Club, and Heinz Schendzielorz of the Jaguar Car Club of Victoria. Returning home, I am indebted to Mr and Mrs Christopher Jennings for allowing me to use pictures and contemporary material on the E-type prototype, Brian Lister for spending a morning answering questions on Lister history, Peter Sargent (now Chairman of the JDC) and Peter Lumsden, Joss Davenport (Chairman of the XK Register), Ken Mayfield (Chairman of the SS Register), Col. Rixon Bucknall, Stewart Laws, John Bolster, Jonathan Heynes and AF Rivers Fletcher. I should like to thank Anthony Bamford, John Harper, Bryan Corser and Phil Porter (past-Chairman of the E-type Register) for clearing up many points concerning the 'competition' E-type. For expert assistance on all matters pertaining to SS cars I thank David Barber, who also read through the first two chapters and added many interesting details. I also acknowledge the help given me, at some considerable length, by David Lethbridge mainly on the subject of XK 140 and E-type cars, and by Ron Beaty who supplied me with details on the modification of six and twelve cylinder Jaguar engines. I would like to express my appreciation too at being able to use material from Robert Danny's extensive collection of SS and Jaguar catalogues and other literature.

I openly acknowledge the value to me of various other one-make car histories, and thank their authors who have thus been of assistance to me in detailing parallel episodes of Jaguar history. Also, the more one delves into the subject, the more one appreciates the accuracy and meticulousness of Michael Sedgwick's researches, as evidenced by Lord Montagu's book, *Jaguar - A Biography* (Cassell) - which still stands as the only serious reference work on the overall history of Jaguar.

To Miles Marshall, formerly of GT Foulis & Co and now retired, I would like to extend my thanks for originally entrusting me with this book, and to his successor, Tim Parker I would like to express my appreciation of his knowledgeable assistance and the latitude he has extended to me in respect of deadlines.

Two final acknowledgements remain: firstly of my wife's patience while enduring the first year of our married life a poor second to this book, and for assembling the Index meanwhile, and secondly, of the help given me by Grant McMillan, friend and fellow enthusiast. If ever the aphorism including the words "without whose help..." can be truly applied, it is to this book and Grant, whose painstaking research and assistance over many months is the foundation on which a good proportion of this work has been built.

Paul Skilleter
Enfield, Middlesex
1975

Chapter One   The early S.S. days

The long low lines of the first SS attracted more interest and criticism than I have ever known before when an entirely new car was staged. It struck a new note

The Motor
September 24 1935

No-one would call the SS1 open tourer a dyed-in-the-wool sports car

W H Charnock
The Motor August 17 1945

The story of Jaguar and its creator Sir William Lyons is, perhaps, the best known of any British motor manufacturer. To the enthusiast it has almost the quality of a well-loved fairy story in its familiarity, and certainly the evolution of the back street Swallow Sidecar Company into Jaguar Cars, Coventry, makers of one of the fastest and most sought-after luxury cars in the world, has a magical quality about it; and in order to savour the full mystique of the Jaguar sports car, it becomes essential to re-visit those early years once more, and to see exactly how the young William Lyons embarked upon his historic career.

Born in 1901, the son of William Lyons senior, there was it seems little chance that William Lyons junior would follow his father into the family piano business in their home town of Blackpool. He was far too interested in motorcycles - he raced Nortons, Brough Superiors and Harley-Davidson vee twins in the Southport sand races - and cars - he found employment for a time at Crossley Motors in Manchester, also trying his hand at car sales-manship - for the piano business ever to be a serious possibility. Finally, a meeting with William Walmsley decided the course ahead. Ten years Lyons' senior, Walmsley was engaged in making a sidecar for the war-surplus Triumph

motorcycles he was reconditioning and selling, using a chassis from Haydens of Birmingham. Of polished aluminium and with a pleasing octagonal shape, Walmsley's sidecar caught Lyons' eye.

It is probably at this point that we see for the first time William Lyons' gift for first divining an opportunity, and then pursueing it without deviation until the full potential is realised; for he saw in the 'Swallow' sidecar a product that would sell, and sell very well, to a much larger market than Walmsley envisaged catering for, if production could be put on a more commercial footing and greatly expanded. Thus on September 4th 1922, Lyons' 21st birthday, the Swallow Sidecar Company was officially formed by Lyons and Walmsley in partnership, with finance provided by a £1,000 overdraft guaranteed on a 50/50 basis by their fathers. Although the business, initially established on two floors of a rather old building in Bloomfield Road, Blackpool with a workforce of the proverbial three men and a boy, soon began to flourish, the £1,000 proved rather inadequate at first and Lyons had to rely quite heavily on the bank manager's indulgence to pay the wages each Saturday morning!

The Swallow sidecar sold on style and quality; it had a dashing air about it which made many of its rivals appear unrefined and unimaginative, and notwithstanding the gathering Depression which was to culminate in the general strike of 1926, the Swallow Sidecar Company forged ahead, with increased production forcing the acquisition of two further Blackpool sites, one in Woodfield Road and the other in John Street. Its reputation was growing too, and the company had its own stand at the 1923 Motor Cycle Show. By mid-1926 the need for centralising manufacture was very much apparent and so there followed a move to a considerably larger factory in Cocker Street, Blackpool - organised with a later-to-be- familiar Lyons efficiency, all materials and the thirty staff by then employed, were transferred from the old premises to the new in two days, with only a pantechnicon and its driver being brought in from the outside to assist.

At a time when many companies in the sidecar and coachbuilding trades were fighting to survive, let along expand, growth was William Lyons' firmly set target. He was intrigued by the possibilities inherent in the little Austin Seven he had bought secondhand, if its strictly utilitarian lines could be exchanged for coachbuilt curves embodying style, colour and just a touch of exclusiveness. This concept gave birth to Lyons' first venture on four wheels - the Austin Seven Swallow, which was announced in May 1927 from the Cocker Street premises. The car was given a rather delightful little two-seater open body (the Sports), with rounded tail and nose, panelled in aluminium on a wooden frame, and with an optional hard top (which was hinged at the back, it sometimes being difficult to get in and out without lifting it up!). Mechanically, the Austin Seven Swallow was exactly as it left the Austin factory, except that pieces of angle-iron were added to the rear of the 'A' frame chassis, which otherwise didn't extend past the rear wheels. Virtually nothing identifiable as Austin remained visible externally, while inside gone was the austere dashboard, replaced by a fully instrumented Swallow version.

The little car sold well, appealing strongly to those who wanted a 'different' small car which combined a certain elegance with a very reasonable price-tag - £174, plus £10 extra if the detachable hard top was wanted. Within three months another two-seater was announced, the Morris Cowley Swallow, though the later arrival didn't remain in production long and in fact was the only Morris-based car to be catalogued by Swallow. The following year came the Austin Seven Swallow Saloon, which Lyons drove up to London and showed to Bertie Henly and Frank Hough who were running a new and dynamic motor sales business at 91 Great Portland Street. Lyons badly needed a reliable retail outlet for up until then customers had to go through the rather clumsy procedure of ordering their Swallow Seven from an Austin dealer, who passed it on to the Austin Company, who then in turn sent down the chassis to Cocker Street. The little Swallow saloon made an immediate impact with Henlys and the two partners gave Lyons an order for 500 at once, the only stipulation being that they should have exclusive distribution rights south of a line drawn from Bristol to the Wash. This was a far better deal than Lyons had ever expected although he was a little taken aback at the number of cars he would have to supply: "I did not know how on earth we were going to make 500 but I accepted the order with alacrity, and indeed considerable amazement!" he wrote later.

Needless to say, increased production was the by-word from then on, but the size of the Cocker Street workshops were by now completely inadequate - rather like the Blackpool railway yard which was full of chassis that Cocker Street just could not process, now that they were arriving in batches of 50 from the Austin works; the station master was raising hell! The right sort of labour was also in short supply so there was nothing for it but to make another move. The industrial Midlands seemed the obvious area so Lyons made a sortie to Coventry, where after several days searching he found a disused shell-filling factory at Foleshill;

after persuading the owners to lease it to him (they actually wanted to sell it), the Swallow Sidecar and Coachbuilding Company as it had become, moved in during September 1928, and had room to breathe at last.

Not that the pressure was in any way relaxed. The production target for Austin Swallows was now 50 a week, an increase of some 38 units over the Cocker Street weekly output, and to achieve this new figure Lyons used some quite revolutionary coachbuilding methods. Instead of making each body-maker responsible for the entire construction of each body frame, the new method adopted was the relative mass-production of the wooden frame pieces in special jigs, with the body frames then being assembled on a 'jigsaw puzzle basis'. A great many man-hours were saved this way and after some initial teething troubles, the output of bodies was indeed 50 a week by Christmas 1928. Lyons even initiated a time-study of sorts on the various operations involved, almost unheard of in 1928, and operated a voucher system of paying the workforce according to the type and amount of work done by each man - a novel method not altogether approved of by the locally recruited labour who were new to it, and who made quite plain their objections by invading the stores and emptying the contents of the parts bins all over the floor! But Lyons remained unmoved and after a week or two, having received good money under the Swallow system, the Coventry men were working as enthusiastically as the old hands from Blackpool.

It must not be forgotten that sidecar manufacture was continuing apace all the while, building up to some 100 - 150 units a week. With the Swallow sports and saloon selling well too, the company acquired an adjacent factory and began to extend their range of special bodies on proprietory chassis. Over the next few years quite a number of rather ordinary cars had their skirts raised and their hair let down - the Fiat 509A (990 cc, 1929), Standard 9 (1287 cc, 1929), Swift 10 (1190 cc. 1929), Standard 16

(2054 cc, 1931), Wolseley Hornet two-seater (1271 cc, 1930), Wolseley Hornet four-seater (1271 cc, 1931), and the Wolseley Hornet Special two- and four-seaters (1271 cc, 1932). All were processed according to the same broad formula - a re-bodying of very ordinary, box-like offerings typical of the late 1920s, in a way that suggested speed and individuality, and in which colour and fashion played a leading part. Today it would be called creating an image, and William Lyons was one day to become perhaps the supreme image - builder in the British motor industry.

Although the Swallow Hornets had six cylinder (ohc) engines in their spidery Wolseley chassis, it was undoubtedly the Standard Swallow 16 hp that pointed the way ahead more surely. It too had a six cylinder engine, and it was this tough, seven-bearing 2054 cc unit that was to play an important part in Swallow's transition from coachbuilder to car manufacturer - for William Lyons was about to take the young company on yet another leap forward. He had for some time been dissatisfied by the limitations on body design imposed by the use of someone else's chassis, and during 1930 had been busy negotiating with R W Maudslay, then chairman and managing director of the Standard Motor Company, for the supply of an exclusive chassis frame (made by Rubery Owen) complete with Standard engine and running gear which would give him much greater freedom.

Thus on October 9th 1931, a few days before the Motor Show was due to open at Olympia, the S.S.1 made its appearance, in what might fairly be termed a blaze of publicity - Harold Pemberton of the *Daily Express* had called in at the works for a preview of the new car a couple of days beforehand and the result was front page banner headlines announcing 'The car with the £1,000 look for £310', reinforced by a large picture of a low, long, and rakishly proportioned car of distinctive appearance. Lyons was as surprised as anyone by this incredible piece of publicity as Pemberton certainly hadn't led him to suspect that the S.S.1 would be given the front page treatment!

But the *Daily Express* had not misjudged public interest in the new car. Swallow's stand at the Motor Show was crowded and the S.S.1 Coupe was an undeniable sensation, its unorthodox proportions - the bonnet was half the length of the entire vehicle - prompting either acclaim or criticism according to the taste of the individual. A few of those who viewed it from the outside were of the opinion that visibility would be appalling, and that there wouldn't be room for two people inside, let alone four. Those who were actually able to put these points to the test found that there was in fact considerably more room inside than appearances suggested and that visibility also was very good - by the standards of the day one presumes!

Body design apart, the most important features of the S.S.1 lay under the skin, for no other coachbuilding firm could boast of using a chassis specially designed for them. It was based on the Standard Ensign 16 hp frame, a double-dropped design, but with the wheelbase increased and the semi-elliptic springs repositioned outside the frame instead of underneath it, which allowed the floor of the S.S. to be no less than 5 inches lower than the that of the corresponding Standard. Furthermore the engine was moved back in the chassis 7 inches and the radiator lowered. These modifications combined to give the S.S.1 its long low look, and its overall height was an impressive 13 inches lower than the Ensign derivative.

An alternative to the 16 hp unit was the Standard 20 hp engine, although the option was not initially publicised; with the smaller unit the car's top speed was 71 mph, but the bigger engine (also side-valve of course) increased this by some 4 mph. By the present day meaning of the word, the S.S.1 was certainly not a sports car, but in 1931 the term was applied so loosely that anything with a slightly above average performance or racy appearance could be, and usually was, described as such. Certainly this was the description headlined by *The Motor* in its first review of the new car, in which we find looks, "there is nothing resembling freakishness

in appearance", visibility, "we have never sat in a car in which visibility was better", and handling, "a sensation of tautness and correctness", were all praised. Some nice little details were appreciated too - the sycamore cabinet-work, the instrumentation which included an 80 mph speedometer and an Empire electric clock, and a lady's vanity set with its own mirror in the passenger's dashboard cubby-hole - a pleasing touch carried over from the original Austin Swallow.

The 7 feet 7 inches wheelbase S.S.II was announced at the same time as its larger sister. Based on the Standard Little Nine, it managed 60 mph and was in many ways an endearing little car although *The Light Car* in its road-test felt moved to offer at least one piece of advice. "To the designer of the S.S.II we would make one suggestion. A tendency for the front wings to flap when one car is traversing uneven road surfaces should be attended to."!

By Autumn 1932, the S.S.I had come under quite drastic revision. Gone were the cycle-type mudguards, replaced by curvaceous sweeping wings incorporating running boards in which is to be seen the basic 'Lyons line' which was to be carried through all subsequent S.S. and Jaguar designs up to the XJ series. The chassis too was much improved, now being underslung at the rear and with an increase in wheelbase and track of 7 inches and 2 inches respectively which allowed a re-proportioning of the body that did a great deal for the car's looks - besides turning into a full four seater rather than a slightly doubtful plus-two. Rather more significantly so far as we are concerned, the first open S.S. was offered in March 1933.

THE S.S. OPEN TOURERS

The four seater open tourers came on the S.S.1 and S.S.II chassis which incorporated the improvements made for the 1933 season, the S.S.1 tourers having a 9 feet 11 inches wheelbase and a track of 4 feet 3 inches. Then in October 1933 the entire S.S. range was again revised; the S.S.1 Open Tourers, like the saloon and coupe versions, were given an extra 2 inches in track, and the cruciform cross member on the chassis was moved forward slightly to provide more room for the rear passengers, whose footwells were enlarged. The S.S.II's wheelbase was increased by no less than 13 inches which made it greatly more habitable. Important engine changes were made too, which in fact amounted to a redesigning of the 16 and 20 hp units. The latter's capacity was enlarged from 2,552 cc to 2,663 cc by increasing the stroke from 101.6 mm to 106 mm, the bore being left at 73 mm; the 16 hp engine underwent a similar change of stroke which brought its capacity up from 2,054 cc to 2,143 cc. The breathing on both engines was drastically altered for the better; previously, the single RAG carburettor had been mounted on the offside of the power unit, with the inlet manifold feeding a tract which passed between cylinder numbers 3 and 4 inside the block, and led to a gallery on the nearside of the engine which supplied the valves! For 1934 this tortuous route was discarded, the carburettor being transferred to the nearside where the inlet manifold fed two holes in the block, an internal passageway still supplying the valves. The exhaust manifold, on the nearside as before, was now swept forward in an arc away from the bulkhead, in order to keep the heat away from the passenger compartment. The cylinder head design was changed too and the cooling system, formerly worked mainly by thermo-syphon, was now given a proper water pump.

Undeniably handsome, these two door tourers displayed more than a hint of the future S.S.90's lines, and were found to be really quite fast, good handling cars. *The Motor* tried a 20 hp example over 10,000 miles during which time the only departure from reliability was one broken fan belt, and the impression remaining with the testers was of "effortless performance and comfort which have made really long journeys untiring and rapid". Positioning of controls was approved of "with the racing type central handbrake a model for position", and the clutch and brake pedals were found to be positive in operation although obviously not light. The Marles-Weller steering was labelled "an excellent compromise" though ideally needing higher gearing, while the Andre shock absorbers were reckoned to need careful adjustment for best results. Absolutely no mention was made of the cable-operated Bendix brakes but one presumes that they were deemed efficient.

The performance figures taken by *The Motor* underlined the fact that this S.S. could not be scorned on the road. With the screen folded flat and the (standard equipment) aero-screens erected, a maximum speed of 84.5 mph was recorded on the 4.25:1 rear axle ratio, third giving 60 mph and second 40 mph. Sixty miles an hour was attained in 23 seconds from rest, with the standing ¼ mile coming up in 22.1 seconds.

Cruising speed was reckoned to be an easy 70 mph on good roads, and creature comfort had not been neglected either, as it was reported that "the bump is taken right out of Lancashire cobblestones". Inside the car, the rear seats were as low as the front ones which gave the rear passengers a degree of protection against the elements when the hood was down, and they were also given permanent arm rests in the usual Swallow/S.S. tradition. The weather equipment itself was described as "well fitting and rigid" and could be stowed away neatly when it wasn't in use. The price of the 20 hp S.S.1 Tourer was £340, the 16 hp model being £5 less and of course, subject to less road tax.

For an interesting personal view of what it was like to drive an S.S.I in contemporary conditions, extracts from *The Autocar* of August 17th 1945, in which W H Charnock wrote in typically candid terms of his experiences with the 20 hp tourer he bought new in 1933 can be quoted. The seven weeks' delivery is only one of several interesting points!

I have always felt that it was a most likeable vehicle, giving a lot of fun for its original list price of £335, and after well over twelve years' ownership I have exactly the same likes and dislikes over HV 2848 that I had when it had been in my possession a few weeks. This, it must be admitted, indicates consistency of behaviour, if nothing else!

The 2½ litre side-valve engine had the feature, unusual in this price class, of a seven-bearing crankshaft, and it was this which, to my mind, absolutely 'made' the whole car. It gave great smoothness at all engine speeds and that indefinable untiring feel after many hours of hard driving.

Against this the sump capacity of just over 1½ gallons was hardly in keeping, and an oil temperature of 95 degrees C was usual after a few hours on a hot day.

The small diameter Bendix brakes have given excellent results, but have demanded constant attention. There are two separate adjustments to each pair of shoes, and, in addition to fiddling with these, one needs to remove the drums and rough up the linings pretty frequently. A larger braking area would probably have rendered most of this unnecessary, but at any rate there has never been any question of the power of the brakes. My efforts at adjustment, through all these years, have been directed not towards improving braking distances, but to preventing the whole car from trying to wrap itself around the front axle. The 5.50 x 18 tyres make the high-geared steering very heavy at low speeds, and one could do with a little more caster action, but above 20 mph the steering is as good as any I have known. The very low build, of course, gives excellent cornering and road-holding, inspite of the 9 feet 11 inches wheelbase.

The coachwork was, and is, a thoroughly sound job and does not 'date' like most closed cars of around 1930. The seating is unusual for an open four-seater, in that the rear seats are lower than the front, and also in the provision of two bucket seats at the rear instead of the more usual bench type. I have improved visibility by raising the driving seat about two inches, but, even without this, one could see both front wings when seated normally.

I am afraid I have no phenomenal exploits with this car that I can put on record, but it has climbed Wrynose, Hard Knott, and the 'old' Honister, together with countless lesser-known pieces of rough stuff. These climbs dispose of the frequent criticisms I have heard concerning the ground clearance and steering lock of this car.

The true top speed of HV 2848 with the screen folded was reckoned by Charnock to be around 75 mph, but the car did have the lower 4.66:1 rear axle ratio of the very earliest examples. Its major fault was a sustained reluctance to start from cold, thought possibly

to have been an unfavourable starter pinion and flywheel gear ratio, but almost certainly due to the RAG carburettor which was badly designed in this respect.

While Charnock was perfectly correct in denying the S.S. tourers a sports car status (which of course the factory never claimed either), they have an important role as being the first S.S. model to have been seriously campaigned in competitions, and its exploits, whilst resulting in mixed success, must have inevitably encouraged the building in 1935 of William Lyons' first true sports car, the S.S. 90. Swallow's first venture into competition had probably taken place in 1932, when three S.S.1 Coupes were entered in the first RAC Rally held in March of that year, but this event compared poorly in scope and prestige to the Continental trials of the period, and anyway, the S.S. 1s didn't bring back any awards. This did not deter Lyons from entering a team of three S.S.1 Open Tourers in the 1933 International Alpine Trial however.

While in recent years the Alpine Trial (or Rally) has lost some of the status in once commanded, in 1933 it was one of the toughest endurance tests in the calendar. Three 20 hp S.S.1 Tourers were entered by the factory, an adventurous international debut for S.S., who unfortunately gave themselves a further handicap by deciding to raise the cars' compression ratios at the last minute, in a search for extra power; this was done by "taking a large slice" off the cylinder head. In fact, the three tourers were only just ready in time for the event and were, recalls Mrs Christopher Jennings, "collected from the factory only the night before the rally" - as Miss Margaret Allen, she was one of the three drivers chosen by S.S. for the rally, the other two cars being driven by Charles Needham and Humfrey Symons. The result was endless head gasket trouble and overheating, only Needham's car finishing, in 8th place in the 3-litre class after being nursed home. This was a pity, because otherwise the cars went well and their drivers liked them inspite of the steering gear tightening up if not often greased. One of the two private S.S. entries did rather better; George Hans Kock, the Austrian S.S. distributor, drove his S.S.1 Tourer to 6th place in the same 2-3 litre class, and was the driver of the highest placed British car in that class into the bargain - the only cars ahead of him were five Bugattis, all except one supercharged. While Count Orssich's S.S.1 Coupe managed 11th in the class.

A further assault on the Alpine Trial was mounted by Swallow the following year, when another team of three S.S.1 Tourers were entered supported by two other S.S.s, another S.S.1 Tourer and an S.S.11 Tourer, both listed as individual entries. The result so far as the 'works' cars were concerned is somewhat anomolous - inspite of Sydney Light's tourer dropping out of the Trial after its second crash, Swallow somehow managed to gain a team award, bringing home a Silver-Gilt Plaque. A similar award came the way of F W Morgan's privately entered S.S.1 Tourer, but as for the little S.S.11, its crew were excluded when they missed their morning call after a night stop!

The increasingly disturbed political atmosphere in Europe prevented the Alpine Trial being held in 1935, and by 1936 a very much more competitive S.S. would be keeping the flag flying for Lyons. Meanwhile there had been important developments within the company; for at the end of 1934 S.S. Cars Ltd had been floated as a public company (the issue yielding £85,000) while the Swallow Coachbuilding Company was left to continue making sidecars. Thus Lyons now headed a full-blooded car manufacturing concern in its own right, and was rapidly to leave behind the 'special builder' image which had hitherto remained in the background. Already an astonishing amount had been achieved - in less than eight years the business had progressed from placing slightly bijou coachwork on propriety chassis to building exceedingly good looking, pleasant handling 80 mph saloons and tourers which could more than hold their own in international competitions. Shrewd management, an eye for the market, and straightforward financial ability had enabled Lyons to pull far ahead of his competitors in the coachbuilding industry; in fact he was now in a totally different class, building well over 1,500 cars of his own a year. From this solid platform of success, and from the valuable lessons learned in the building and rallying of the S.S. Tourers, the company was ready to launch its first sports car. As the new year of 1935 dawned, the S.S. 90 was imminent.

Chapter Two   The S.S.90 and SS Jaguar 100

If anyone imagines that they have experienced all the thrills to be had from modern motorcars, they should acquire one of the latest 3½-litre two-seater Jaguars

The Motor

THE S.S. 90

The S.S.90 Sports Car made its debut in March 1935, rather over-shadowing the new S.S.1 Drop-head Coupe which was announced simultaneously, and although it may have been a marked departure from anything produced by Lyons and Walmsley before, its lines were identifiably S.S. as the motoring press was quick to point out. Built on a short chassis version of the S.S.1 frame, it carried close-coupled two-seater bodywork which was undoubtedly the most beautiful to have emerged from S.S. Cars Ltd up to that time, and many of its features were to be carried over to the SS 100 - the low, wide radiator shell, the big Lucas headlights, the long multi-louvred bonnet, and the supremely elegant wings - "given a considerable flare at both front and rear, the object being to provide efficient protection from mud with, at the same time, a reduction in wind resistance and weight", as *The Autocar* described these slightly controversial appendages. The original prototype S.S.90 was built with a neat rounded tail into which was set the spare wheel, hiding the fuel tank, but even the earliest press reviews noted that this arrangement would probably be altered for the production models. This in fact was the case, and all further examples were produced with the spare wheel mounted vertically against an exposed and upright slab tank. The bodywork construction was the traditional aluminium panelling on an ash frame, the same alloy being used for the hand-beaten wings.

The S.S.1 chassis, as adapted for the S.S.90, had some 15 inches removed from its centre portion; the cross bracing was removed for this operation, shortened at the rear, and replaced after the chassis had been welded together again and plated. Otherwise all its essential features remained substantially unaltered - the downsweep from behind the engine, the cross bracing amidships, and the underslung rear. The post-operative wheelbase was 8 feet 8 inches, or the same as the S.S.II, but the track was as wide as the S.S.1 at 4 feet 6 inches. The long and flat semi-elliptic springs front and rear which carried the beam axles used Silentbloc bushes in the shackles, and damping was by Andre Telecontrol shock absorbers which could be adjusted from the cockpit. The Bendix duo-servo brakes had 12 inch drums and as on the big saloons, they could be operated on all four wheels by the fly-off handbrake. The knock-off Rudge-Whitworth wheels were 18 inches in diameter and carried 5.25 or 5.50 x 18 Dunlop '90' tyres, and the steering gear was the usual S.S. choice of Marles-Weller cam and lever type - the turning circle was described as 'only' 35 feet 6 inches, but at least that was better than the 38 feet of the S.S.1 Saloon!

There was no choice of engine, a slightly modified version of the 20 hp 73 x 106 mm, 2,663 Standard six cylinder engine as used in the S.S.1 being standardised, with its chrome-iron block, seven bearing crankshaft, and light alloy pistons and connecting rods. The valves were still at the side, though a high compression version of the alloy head was used to give a cr of a little over 7 : 1, and a modified overlap cam was installed. Twin RAG carburettors provided the mixture. The cast aluminium sump held 2½ gallons of oil, a useful increase in capacity as the engine was inclined to suffer from high oil temperatures. The gearbox too followed the pattern of the saloons, being mounted as a (detachable) unit with the engine and with four speeds, synchronized on second, third and top. Ratios and the standard final drive were shared with the 20 hp S.S.1 Tourer, first, second and third gears being 15.3, 8.98 and 5.83 : 1 with a direct top gear of 4.25 :1. An optional rear axle ratio of 3.75 : 1 was available for 'for speed trials'.

For anyone who liked the 'straight arm' driving position, there was little chance for them to adopt it in the driving seat of the S.S.90. The big 18 inch sprung steering wheel (which also carried ignition and lighting control levers at its centre took up most of the space and the distance between it and the seat back was somewhat minimal. However, the 'elbows out' style was still heavily in fashion which is no doubt why *The Autocar* praised the driving position in their March 1935 description of the new car; though as no demonstrators were released by Lyons for full press road testing one wonders how they made up their minds so positively! The bucket seats were rather narrow too, though neatly upholstered in leather. But the central remote control gearlever and handbrake were nicely positioned, and the lower bonnet line permitted a better view of the road than the tourers, despite its length. Instrumentation included a revolution counter and a 100 mph speedometer, both with 5 inch dials.

The Autocar emphasised the sporting nature of the S.S.90 from the very start, headlining its entry in the forthcoming 1935 RAC Rally. The maximum speed of 90 mph implied by its name certainly indicated sporting potential, although this figure was never verified at the time in an independent road test; nor did S.S. publicly state the brake horsepower of its engine, although this was in fact around 75 - 80 bhp. Actual performance cannot therefore be stated in precise terms, although in general one could expect it to have been somewhere between the 20 hp S.S.1 Tourer and the soon-to-be announced SS Jaguar 100 - as the former was capable of nearly 85 mph and was substantially larger and heavier than the similarly powered S.S.90, it is quite likely that the sports car could approach 90 mph under favourable conditions, at least on the higher optional 3.75 : 1 final drive ratio. Speeds in the intermediate gears would have been much the same as the 20 hp tourer, gearing (4.25 axle), tyre and wheel sizes all being similar; thus 65 mph could be seen in third gear, and 40 mph in second. Flexibility of the Standard engine was a good point too, even in its higher compression S.S. specification, and the car would pick up cleanly in top gear from 8 or 10 mph. The original quoted weight of the S.S.90 was 18 hundred weight, which seems rather light even 'dry' - particularly as the virtually identical 2½ litre SS 100 of a few months later was all of 23 hundredweight.

Once again the Lyons' value-for-money factor was present and for this performance one did not have to pay a great deal; fully equipped, the S.S.90 retailed at £395. A reasonable comparison might be the 2-litre Frazer Nash BMW 319 of similar straight line performance announced by AFN Ltd a few months later at £460, or even the Aston Martin Type C Speed Model at something over £700! Only 22 (plus the prototype rounded tail car) S.S.90s were built, and the SS 100, by virtue of its vastly improved power unit and greater numbers, has rather relegated the earlier cars to a secondary status. But it remains the first sports car ever to have been built by Lyons (disregarding the 'one-off' two-seater S.S.1 built for Walmsley in 1934, of which not even a photograph survives), and whatever its performance might have been to the nearest fifth of a second, it was also faster than any other previous S.S. This fact was very soon proved by William Lyons himself, when at an S.S. Car Club rally at Blackpool, he drove the newly announced S.S.90 on a demonstration run over a set speed course along the sea front. Posting a time of 64 seconds, the new car was 7 seconds faster than the nearest official competitor!

As threatened by *The Autocar*, the Hon. Brian Lewis (now Lord Essendon) did indeed enter the prototype S.S.90 in the RAC Rally, although one is forced to add that the car's competition debut did not go altogether smoothly. Reported *The Motor* on one of the tests:

Hon. Brian Lewis made a demonstration run, set off rapidly, pulled up for the first reverse very neatly, shot backwards through the first gap very swiftly, and then, unfortunately, travelled in reverse with one wheel the wrong side of the curb for several yards, spoiling an excellent show.

Neither did the other special tests go sufficiently well to place the S.S.90 in the results table on that occasion. But other well-known trials experts were beginning to use the S.S.90, Douglas Clease forsaking his S.S.1 Tourer for an S.S.90 in the Scottish Rally of June 1935, and "making a good showing" in some of the tests. The car was also admired in the supplementary Concours d'Elegance and was placed second in the £250 - £500 class. Shortly afterwards E J Boyd's dark blue S.S.90 was adjudged to have been "outstanding" in the Appearance Competition incorporated in the MCC Torquay Rally of July, coming first in the Open Cars over £350 class. But this was rather too akin to the numerous but slightly meaningless beauty-parade successes of the original S.S.1 of 1932 and 1933 to be comfortable, and it was quite obvious that more power was required before anything of note could be expected in the competition sphere - although S H Newsome, E H Jacob and

a few others did win awards in S.S. Car Club and local events during the next year or two, driving the S.S.90.

At Foleshill nobody had any illusions about the power output of the side-valve Standard engine - years later Sir William commented that it "just wouldn't pull the skin off a rice pudding!" - so to make up this deficiency in brake horse power, Harry Weslake was asked to design a new head for the basically sound seven-bearing six cylinder Standard engine in use (it is said that Weslake's name was actually suggested to S.S. by a customer, who was commiserating with Lyons about the lack of real punch delivered by the Standard engine in his car). This Weslake did, hoisting the valves upstairs and, of course, reshaping the ports and combustion chambers. An increase from about 75 bhp to 90 bhp was needed from the 2½ litre engine to give the newly planned saloon the sort of performance that Lyons envisaged, so when in the event the new ohv head actually gave 105 bhp at 4,500 rpm on the test-bed, everyone was highly delighted. Even now, Harry Weslake considers the 2½ litre ohv cylinder head one of his finest achievements, and Lyons himself remembers the occasion as "one of the best breakthroughs we ever had".

The original 2,663 cc block was retained, the valve chest being covered by a plate, and as before the Standard Motor Company continued to produce the engine as a complete unit - Lyons having arranged with Capt. John Black, who was by then effectively running the company, to put in the new plant necessary. This suited S.S. Cars very well, as they were still not ready to build up a machine shop of their own.

It was at this juncture that William Heynes joined the company, also as it happened, through Lyons' Standard contacts. Both Ted Grinham and Les Dawtrey of Standard recommended to Lyons that he should interview the 32 year old Heynes when they heard that the head of S.S. was looking for a Chief Engineer, as they had been much impressed by Heynes' abilities when he had worked for them at 'The

Humber', their previous company. Heynes had joined Humber Ltd as an apprentice in 1923, and under Dawtrey's encouragement progressed to the point that when Grinham transferred to Standards, Heynes replaced him as head of the Stress Office in the design department. Not that the ever-careful Lyons made a hasty decision - Heynes remembers that a number of interviews took place before the chief of S.S. Cars was completely persuaded that here was the man with the exceptional engineering capability and the faculty for original thinking that he required to carry through successfully the plans already afoot for a new range of cars.

Heynes joined in April 1935, with a task in front of him at S.S. Cars that he recognised as "formidable." Although the new ohv engine was essentially ready, and a body for the new saloon had already been decided upon, a complete new chassis, suspension and steering had to be designed and made in less than six months; an awe-inspiring task but one which was accomplished by Heynes and his small staff (which included only one draughtsman) in the time allowed, helped by his old friends Grinham and Dawtrey of Standard. The new range of S.S. cars was to include a 1½ and a 2½ litre saloon, and a new sports car, the 2½ models being powered by ohv engines with the Weslake head. The 1½ litre 1936/37 saloon car used the 12 hp side valve unit.

THE 2½ LITRE SS JAGUAR 100

Thus the SS 100 was announced concurrently with the new SS Jaguar saloons, in September 1935; and with the new cars had come a new name - Jaguar. How the name was selected makes quite an interesting story in itself, and anyway it would be a good idea at this juncture to examine the derivation of the *marque's* nomenclature up to the War.

The use of the initials 'S.S.' with the advent of Lyons' first car in 1931 may well have been inspired by George Brough's motorcycles, models of which included the S.S. 80 and S.S.

90 Brough Superiors; Tommy Wisdom certainly claimed that this was the case, and went on to say that George Brough never really forgave his friend and customer William Lyons for this plagiarism! Whatever was the actual truth, this was the name which Lyons put forward to Standards, and "which was agreed upon after a long argument with Maudsley and Black, which resulted from my determination to establish a marque of our own. There was much speculation as to whether S.S. stood for Standard Swallow or Standard Special - it was never resolved". This was a very happy arrangement, as those at Standards no doubt firmly believed the letters stood for Standard Swallow, while at Foleshill those who wanted to could feel that they really meant Swallow Sports.

When it was decided to give the new 1936 ohv cars a model name, Lyons asked his publicity department (headed by E W Rankin, who had become Publicity Manager in 1934) to draw up a list of animal, fish and bird names.

I immediately pounced on 'Jaguar' for it had an exciting sound to me, and brought back memories of the stories told to me, towards the end of the 1914 - 1918 war, by an old school friend who, being nearly a year older than I, had joined the Royal Flying Corps as it was called in those days. He was stationed at Farnborough and he used to tell me of his work as a mechanic on the Armstrong Siddeley 'Jaguar' engine. Since that time, the word Jaguar has always had a particular significance to me and so SS 'Jaguar' became the name by which our cars were known.

If one wants to be correct, all the side-valve cars on the specially made chassis with Swallow bodywork are termed 'S.S.' (ie S.S.1, S.S.11 and S.S.90), while all the new models introduced from September 1935 until the war are named SS Jaguar - note also that the full-stop was omitted between the two letters from the 1936 season onwards, "as the letters no longer stand for anything" according to *The Motor* of March 1st 1938 in answer to a reader's query on the point. That magazine had indeed used the later style since the end of 1935, as had the factory on its own letterhead and publicity material after the same date.

It was not the SS 100 but the new SS Jaguar saloon cars that received the most column inches when the press came to review the 1936 SS range, which was only to be expected as the saloons were, and are, always the factory's main concern, being built in greater numbers than the current sports model and contributing by far the largest share of the profits. But it soon became clear that here was a British sports car with real performance, capable of out-running most of the opposition on this side of the Channel at least. For the same money that had bought a side-valve S.S.90 - £395 - one could now get a un-disputed 90 mph plus, and reach the magic mile-a-minute in 12.8 seconds from rest, as *The Motor* discovered when it put a 2½ litre '100' through its Rationalised Road Test routine - though it had to wait 20 months after the car's initial announcement before being able to do so. In fact actual production of the SS 100 did not really start until the beginning of 1936, although development had been well under way "almost before the S.S.90 was completed and put into production, as it was decided it was superior in every way", Sir William recalls. The models did overlap to an extent, S.S.90s leaving the factory up to November 1935 by which time the 1935 Show car (18002) and a few others SS 100s had been built.

The SS 100 had what was virtually the S.S.90 chassis, but incorporating some of the features of the new SS Jaguar saloons. Thus the actual SS 100 *frame* was still a derivative of the original S.S.1 frame, and the wheelbase and track were identical to the S.S.90's, but steering, brakes and to a certain extent the suspension, were all different, and shared with the new saloon cars. Thus instead of the Marles-Weller steering arrangements of the '90', the '100' had Burman Douglas worm and nut type, and the Bendix cable operated brakes were exchanged for the Girling rod-operated system - this employed a wedge and roller design which remains about the most efficient form of mechanical braking to this day. The brake shoes with their Ferodo BZ linings rubbed an effective surface of 13 inches x 1½ inches inside deeply ribbed Millenite brake drums, the outside diameter of which was 15 inches. Properly adjusted, the brakes worked extremely well even by modern standards and neither did they need constant attention; while the fade problems which were to affect the post-war XK 120 simply didn't exist with the SS 100 - the large diameter wire wheels and the absence of enshrouding bodywork allowed an ample supply of cool air to carry away unwanted heat.

The SS 100's suspension was essentially that of the S.S.90, except that the rear ends of the half elliptic springs on the front axle now slid in trunnion bearings as opposed to the S.S.90's shackles; this practice was adopted on the SS Jaguar saloons too. Damping was slightly un-usual in that both hydraulic and friction (Luvax and Hartford) shock absorbers acted on the front axle; Luvax CMP type hydraulic shock absorbers only were fitted at the rear, and were definitely a little inadequate for the job.

Dunlop splined hubs were now used in place of Rudge Whitworth, although the wheel diameter remained the same at 18 inches, with a rim width of 4½ inches. Either 5.50 or 5.25 x 18 Dunlop tyres appear to have been fitted.

Ignition and electrical equipment was 12 volt, and of Lucas manufacture, except for the twin SU electric petrol pumps which were mounted horizontally on the engine bulkhead. Manually controlled advance and retard was still offered, and the sparking plugs were 14 millimeter. External chrome-plated Lucas blended-tone horns were standard equipment too. Lighting was fairly minimal by today's standards - although P100 headlights have found their way onto quite a number of SS 100s, these were never fitted by the factory and the cars left Foleshill with Lucas QK596 items (sometimes called 'P90's). The only illumination to the rear was a single 'fly's eye' lamp of the familiar triple lens pattern, mounted on the offside rear wing (one on each side was fitted to export models). It incorporated stop and reversing lights too.

Although the SS 100 was an improvement over the S.S.90 in almost every department, it was of course the Weslake-designed ohv head on the 2,663 cc six cylinder Standard engine which brought about the biggest increase in performance and appeal. As installed it gave about 104 bhp at 4,600 rpm with smoothness and flexibility, breathing through two 1¼ inches SU carburettors - the 1936 cars had a manual choke but from 1937 onwards an electrically controlled enriching device was fitted.

As for appearance, the SS 100 might at a glance be taken for the S.S.90, but a closer examination of its features reveal quite a number of differences between the two cars. The immediate give-away is in the shape of the 'Le Mans' petrol tank, the rearward face of which is inclined at an angle instead of being of constant width and vertical as on the S.S.90. Thus the tank mounted spare wheel (the weight of which is actually borne by a tubular member which passes down to a chassis cross-member) is also at an angle from the vertical. The SS 100's body and wings are virtually identical to the S.S.90's but there are further dissimilarities at the front of the car. The headlamp tie-bar has '100' cast into it instead of '90', and the headlights themselves are as previously mentioned QK596 units, not the S.S.1 QBD166S type (minus the motif on top) that were worn by the S.S.90. The SS 100's radiator shell also differs from the earlier car's, having its grille recessed rather than bolted to the outer edge of the shells. The '100' also carries the winged motif containing the words 'SS Jaguar' which was brought in with the 1936 cars; this was mounted on the radiator shell in front of the filler cap, whereas - usually - the S.S.90 carried no badge or motif.

The interior of the SS 100 again followed the S.S.90 in general principles, only minor differences in instrumentation being at all obvious. Narrow by today's ideas on the subject, the SS 100's cockpit was described by *The Motor* as being "quite comfortable" with room enough for "two bulky persons" in the bucket seats.

Providing that the bulky driver could indeed squeeze himself behind the big Bluemel wheel, he had a good view over the long, many louvred bonnet through either the folding windscreen with its Giltedge safety glass or the standard equipment aero-screen mounted behind it. Directly in front of him on the painted aluminium dashboard (the usual finish) were a "galaxy" of instruments, namely a 100 mph speedometer (incorporating trip and mileometer records) and a matching revolution counter (red-lined from 4,500 rpm to 5,000 rpm), each on either side of the steering column, an oil pressure gauge, a petrol gauge (calibrated in both gallons and litres), an ammeter, and a water temperature gauge. A clock was set into the revolution counter. All the instruments had silver finished dials, with blue lettering and 'SS' insignia.

Dashboard controls were a large windscreen wiper knob, ignition (key), lights and panel light switches, fog light switch (when fitted), starter button, and, to the far right of the facia, a large chromium plated fuel-reserve tap (the petrol tank capacity was 14 gallons including two gallons reserve). A cigar lighter was given a central position on the facia between driver and passenger, although it could be replaced by an oil temperature gauge at extra cost. Ignition and headlight dipper controls were set around the steering wheel boss which itself sounded the horns; the steering wheel was adjustable for for-and-aft movement from the drivers' seat, but rake could only be altered by slackening the column mounting bolt and under-scuttle brackets - a slightly longer operation. Under the scuttle lurked the hand throttle and 'choke'.

The rather narrow bucket seats had Dunlopillo and spring cushions, and were covered in plain (ie non-quilted) leather and could be adjusted for reach; the doors were trimmed in leathercloth to match, and the whole compartment was carpeted including the luggage recess behind the seat backs - into which a surprising amount could be stowed, in front of the sidescreens if they were in their storage position.

The neatly fitted hood and tonneau cover enclosed this space, and unlike the equipment in some modern-day open vehicles, the SS 100's hood was easy to erect or take down. When folded, the hood could be covered by the hood envelope supplied with the car.

However, it was not just the quality of the SS 100's equipment or the car's potential performance that was attractive. It probably sold just as much on its looks as anything else, and in this one must bracket the similarly good-looking S.S.90. William Lyons had produced a car which can be described as being both beautiful *and* classic - perhaps a rare combination in an offering from Great Britain during the mid-Thirties. The SS 100's famous sweeping wing line has been criticised for being 'flambouyant' - but surely it is no more extravagant than, say, the fragile and beautiful 1½ litre Squire, or even the 1750 Zagato Alfa Romeo?

Lyons certainly introduced no innovations when he designed the SS 100, in fact he stuck very closely to the traditional British sports car mould, but the end result was rather better looking than most other sports cars of that period. While the SS 100 makes absolutely no concessions towards streamlining, there are some surprising subtleties in its execution which makes the car pleasing to look at from *any* angle. Very few cars indeed of that period - or dare it be suggested, not all that many from the Vintage period either - have quite the superb proportions and sense of balance that are immediately obvious in the SS Jaguar 100.

The actual construction of the SS 100 was on basically very traditional lines too, although Lyons may have speeded-up the process a little. Each chassis had its own body built up on it individually, the ash frame of the main section being assembled in situ and then skinned in aluminium. This becomes very apparent if body parts from one car are offered up to another - often they won't fit! It has been known for a bonnet to be an inch longer on one side than the other, and the windscreen mountings and other fitments were stamped with a certain number to match a certain car. This causes problems to the painstaking SS 100 restorer! The workmanship though was of a very high order throughout and about the only evidence of Lyons' cost-consciousness is the fact that a minimum amount of wood was used in the car's frame. This economy went a little too far sometimes and one of the SS 100's few bodywork deficiencies - scuttle shake on poor surfaces - can be blamed not so much on a flexible chassis as upon the lack of strength in the scuttle frame - all the weight (which includes the battery and the heavy brass windscreen frames and pillars) bears down on one very small wooden member in front of the door. Even the doors themselves were given only a very flimsy wooden frame, and required a cross-bracing of steel.

The SS 100's aluminium wings were 'bought out', being made by H H Cooke & Sons of Nottingham. Amazingly enough one can still purchase brand new sets of SS 100 wings from this company, the jigs having been kept to this day. They are even made by one of the men who did the job before the war! The complete car weighed just over 23 hundredweight ready for the road, its overall length was 12 feet 6 inches, width 5 feet 3 inches, and the height from the ground to the top of the screen was 4 feet 6 inches - although there are discrepancies of an inch or so in contemporary listings of the length and width data. Or in other words, a light and compact design with a very good power to weight ratio by the standards of 1935 - the XK 120 when it entered production weighed a good hundredweight more, and was over two feet longer, although possessed of rather more horsepower of course.

THE 2½ LITRE SS 100 ON ROAD TEST

The performance promised by these statistics was recorded by *The Motor* in its road test of the 2½ litre SS 100 in May 1937. A best top speed of 96 mph was recorded, and besides an excellent 0 - 60 mph time of 12.8 seconds, the standing quarter-mile was covered in 18.6

seconds, a real achievement for a sports car of those times and one which was rated as "outstanding". In normal driving this represented an easy 75 mph cruising speed with a generous reserve for climbing hills (the preoccupation with which was still being exhibited in road tests of the period, the testers being of the generation which remembered the time when it was sometimes an achievement to actually get to the top of some hills at all!). The gearbox was approved of (it was the same old double-helical Standard box, soon to be updated by Heynes as there were problems with teeth breaking), "the lever for which is very short but not heavy to operate"; and if desired it was possible to change down without double de-clutching through the top three gears, providing one took it slowly.

Of the steering: "Light and easy to handle when manoeuvering the car, it also has that quality of directness which gives confidence and pleasure at high rates of travel. Although on many occasions during our 600 mile test we encountered bumpy roads, there was never the slightest indication that wheel wobble, tramp or shimmy might develop".

These attributes were credited to a correct steering geometry and good damping - no comment was made though on a rather extravagant turning circle of 36 feet, even if only 2 1/3rd turns were required to achieve it. It was possible to improve the lock, however by judicious filing and bending, as Ian Appleyard discovered when he was preparing his SS 100 for the Alpine Trial after the war. As for handling, the SS 100 had on smooth roads what we would now term a gentle, final oversteer with power on. Or in The Motor's phraseology of the date, "when we cornered very fast, the rear wheels execute a mild skid which can be controlled very easily by an experienced driver". If the SS 100 does indeed have a reputation for spinning on twisty circuits (not altogether deserved), then it is far more likely due to the back end's inclination to hop out of line if cornered on anything bumpier than a billiard table surface, rather than any vicious final oversteer. No roll at all was noticed by the test staff during cornering.

The Motor found the SS 100's brakes to be as good as one would expect from such a specification, and were "in keeping with the performance characteristics" of the car, and the handbrake operated on all four wheels still.

The same 2½ litre SS 100 (chassis no. 18057, registered CHP 402, a car which also had a busy life rallying as one of the team cars) was the subject of The Autocar's 1,125th road test a little later on in 1937. By this time, July, the '100' had already been making its mark in trials, and the new SS Jaguar 2½ litre Saloon (which did 88 mph) had also established an excellent reputation. The journal therefore expected "something striking" of the sports car it was to test for the first time, and neither was it disappointed; while the car's performance was slightly down when the figures are compared with The Motor's, its top speed was still an impressive 94 mph best, the mean being 91.84 mph and 60 mph came up in 13.5 seconds from a standing start.

These figures indicated that "there is obviously real 'urge' when the engine is opened up on the lower gears, so much so that the rear wheels can be spun on a dry surface"; but The Autocar didn't overlook the flexibility of the power unit and the '100' was also described as a top and third gear car too. Thus: "one of the striking things is that it provides a valuable mixture of the sports car's and the ordinary car's qualities."

The writer of the road test discovered yet another facet of the SS 100's character; while its handling, cornering roadholding and brakes were certainly appreciated right from the outset, the car still grew on him:

...as closer experience is obtained of the machine, a still higher opinion is formed of these features. The car can be got into a balanced swing on bends and corners, and taken around extremely fast without heeling over, though, with the standard 'touring' pressure, there was tyre scream on the more extreme occasions. With its rapid acceleration and hill climbing, it is a vivid car not easily equalled from point to point when suitably handled.

So great was this impression that the same writer was to elaborate upon it still further some six years later, in a series obviously intended by *The Autocar* to cheer up those dreary war years by 'Talking of Sports Cars' even if they couldn't be driven:

> An outstanding feature recalled of the SS was that, whilst one felt sufficiently at home in it from the beginning, there came a stage, after perhaps a couple of hundred miles, where one suddenly found a great deal more in the car than there had seemed to be at first - not so much in sheer performance as in confidence in it.

Thus William Lyons had managed, with what was really his first production sports car, to achieve that 'thoroughbred' feel which was to remain present in all successive Jaguar sports cars; a certain quality whereby a personal relationship can be established between car and driver. Then as now, this knack was shared by only a handful of cars, most of them Italian.

To return to cold statistics, *The Autocar* found that second and third gears gave maximas of 50 mph and 78 mph respectively, the engine reaching the red band on the tachometer at 4,500 rpm "in a live and efficient way"; the unit also had the pleasing feel of appearing to work less at approaching 80 mph than at 60 mph. At the car's maximum of virtually 95 mph, the revolution counter showed 4,400 rpm on the standard 4:1 final drive ratio - the well-spaced intermediates were 5.48, 8.45 and 14.40:1 (although when CHP 402 was in *The Motor's* hands it apparently had a 13.6:1 bottom gear). Incidentally, exactly 90 mph was recorded with the main screen raised.

The Autocar also found the SS 100's brakes satisfactory, their reassuring nature when slowing the car down from high speed and their soft pedal pressures while touring being points singled out for praise. Similarly, the suspension "strikes a good compromise for a sports machine. It is firm, but not of the very hard, jarring variety over normally inferior surfaces or at low speeds in town" - remembering that the age was not long past when for the privilege of riding in

a sports car for a given period of time one had to pay by standing up for an equal length of time afterwards. Mind you, by today's standards the SS 100's ride over bumpy surfaces is poor to say the very least, and in retrospect it is not unfair to state that the SS 100 contributed little to eugenics of the sports car so far as ride comfort went; it certainly did not create the near-revolution in this field that the XK 120 and E-type Jaguars did in their eras.

Likewise, *The Autocar's* description of the cockpit ("there is ample width across the body") underlines changing standards - at a bare 43 inches from door to door it is decidely narrow, the seats being kept within the chassis frame, unlike the driver's right elbow which spends much of its time over the cut-away door and out in the elements, especially when a corner comes up and the wheel has to be turned. *The Autocar* volunteered that "good leg room and very fair space for the feet are found" which may or may not have been a veiled dig at *The Motor's* tester who complained about the battery box projecting into the front compartment "in such a manner as to cause a certain amount of inconvenience to a driver who happens to have big feet".

Mention should be made at this stage of saloon car developments at S.S. Cars Ltd, the four seaters being as they were the mainstay of the factory, and without which there would have been no SS 100. Preceding the new SS Jaguar saloons announced with the '100' in 1935, the company had marketed several further variations on the full length S.S.1 chassis, while continuing to sell the S.S.1 and S.S.11 in their later forms up until 1936. Most handsome of the S.S.1 variations was probably the Airline saloon, its styling a concession to the new 'fast back' look (a sort of embryo streamlining) which had become quite fashionable at that time, although it was never a favourite of Sir William's. It was introduced in 1934 and continued in production for two years. The drophead coupe S.S.1 with its beautifully designed disappearing hood was produced into 1936 but only nine of that very rare model were built that year, out of a total production of a little over 100.

The S.S.1 Open Tourer on the other hand survived as late as 1937, called the SS Jaguar Tourer and equipped with the ohv pushrod 2½ litre 'SS Jaguar' engine and using the same chassis as the SS Jaguar saloons. Only 105 of these ohv S.S.1 Tourers were made, and they are distinguishable by their SS Jaguar type radiator shells.

With the advent of the SS Jaguar saloons for 1936 it was obvious to all that SS Cars had grown up; there was not a hint of gimmickry in the lines of the new cars, and style was at last combined with performance now that the Weslake designed ohv head was available. The chassis of the 1936/37 saloons were very similar to that of the S.S.1, but wider and with different spring mountings; these chassis were bought directly from Rubery Owen and not through Standards as previously. *The Autocar* noted towards the close of 1936 that the SS Jaguar saloon was actually the fifth fastest British built closed car, and that all those that went more quickly were of considerably larger capacity and from twice to four times the price! So at £385 the 2½ litre SS Jaguar (and its smaller 1½ litre sister) became established as firm favourites and provided a strong foundation for Lyons' future plans.

THE 3½ LITRE SS JAGUAR 100

These saloons and the 2½ litre SS 100 continued in production until the end of 1937, when in September a new range of cars was announced by SS Cars. The 1938 saloon cars although of fairly similar appearance to the previous models, were in fact substantially different. They were given stiffer chassis, the side members being boxed in to provide greater rigidity, and an entirely new body shell featuring all steel construction (previously the steel panels had been mounted on a largely wooden framework) was standardised for all engine options, 1½ litre, 2½ litre, and a completely new 3½ litre unit. A new range of drophead coupes

was also launched. The 3½-litre engine was hailed by the press as something entirely new, although in fact its Standard ancestry was still apparent despite a good deal of redesigning by Heynes. Of 3,485 cc swept volume, it had a bore and stroke of 82 x 110 mm and a cylinder head which followed the pattern set by the Weslake-designed 2½ litre head, with overhead valves operated by pushrods. Twin SU carburettors supplied the mixture and two triple branch exhaust manifolds were now employed, which collected the gasses individually from each exhaust port; a practice which was from then on adopted on the 2½-litre engine too. The bottom end of the engine, with its seven-bearing, counter-balanced crankshaft, remained much as before apart from a little stiffening of the crankcase, but the steel connecting rods were an innovation for SS as previously an alloy had been the material used for these. This resulted in a more reliable oil pressure, especially under hot running conditions when the Dural rods were inclined to expand, with a consequent drop in oil pressure. With a 7.2:1 compression ratio and a peak rpm of 4,500, the new 3½ litre engine developed something approaching 125 bhp, so that when it was seen that the SS 100 would also be offered with that engine, joining the 2½ litre model, it was obvious that an already fast car would now be a great deal faster.

When the 3½-litre SS 100 came up for test, the motoring press was quite staggered by the car's performance under the stopwatch. *The Motor's* staff confessed to not believing the evidence of their own eyes, while *The Autocar* proffered the only slightly more restrained comment that the figures were "a striking set." For once both journals recorded very similar times, acceleration from 0 to 60 mph being 10.4 seconds (*The Motor*) and 10.9 seconds (*The Autocar*); the same top speed of 101.12 mph was recorded by both magazines, to two places of decimals - a highly unusual state of affairs in view of the many variables involved in maximum speed testing. All the more peculiar is the fact that *The Motor* recorded its maximum speed with the windscreen up, while *The Autocar's* men adjusted their goggles and ran with the screen down. When they tried it with the screen raised, 96.77 mph was the car's maximum.

From individual owners' experiences and the author's own part in an investigation into the subject (which included duplicating *The Motor's* original road test with a 3½ litre SS 100 rebuilt to exactly original condition, a project carried out for the same magazine some 32 years later) it would seem that in fact *The Autocar's* maximum speed figures are more representative of the average 3½ litre SS 100.

The increase in brake horsepower of some 25% did not mean that the power unit had outgrown its chassis, even though this continued in completely unchanged form for both the 2½ and 3½ litre SS 100s. Similarly, the car's character remained unaltered with the larger unit, being enhanced rather than changed, and *The Autocar* confirmed that the driver/car relationship was still there:

At increasing speeds as acquaintance is gained with the machine, it goes round bends close to the left--hand side, in an exact swing, and the feeling experienced at all times of positive connection between the steering wheel and the front wheels is worth more than even exceptional performance.

The 'exceptional performance' - the 3½ litre SS 100 was little slower than the post-war XK 120 up to about 60 mph and was only .2 second down over the ¼ mile - came with what was rapidly being accepted as a Jaguar trait - great flexibility and docility of the power unit. *The Autocar* again:

It can be driven quietly and not attract undue attention, and it is not a machine that calls for any trick methods of control. A driver who uses the indirect gears will obviously obtain the most from it, when it is seen that third can give over 80 mph, and second over 50 mph, but it is surprisingly flexible in top gear...

Possessed of high maximum speed and terrific acceleration, the S.S.100 is still a real pleasure for gentle motoring, not only because the engine is docile, but also because the car is under definite control in every way and the driver has first-class visibility. He is seated comfortably behind the wheel placed at the correct height and angle for confidence.

The Motor echoed its contemporary's findings:

It is not merely that the car provides an exceptional performance through the gears, that the road-holding is up to the speed of the car and that the brakes are among the best ever tested, but the fact that a complete absence of temperament and very great flexibility are also amongst the assets. This car will pull away in top gear, with the engine ticking over at 500 rpm, and there is no trace whatsoever of pinking or transmission snatch during the operation. The acceleration in top gear is so very rapid that the lazy driver may retain this ratio almost indefinitely.

Translated into seconds, this meant a top gear acceleration time of 7.3 seconds from 30 mph to 50 mph - or .8 second quicker than today's MGB V8 of similar capacity.

The same magazine found that wet and slippery roads did not inhibit the free use of the car, it being "commendably stable" in these conditions - poor weather also produced nothing but praise for hood and accoutrements, which "did not attempt to disintegrate at speed and gives sufficient headroom to obviate any suggestion of being shut in". Nor did the side panels rattle.

As the '100's chassis and suspension had changed not at all since its introduction in 1935, the car's general behaviour so far as handling and ride were concerned had similarly not altered much - and were still well thought of by the two magazines, although no-one pretended that the SS 100 rode like a big saloon. Said *The Motor*:

The shock absorbers would probably need to be slackened off on pave because the car normally has a very stiff feeling, which settles down into a pleasant motion when higher speeds are reached.

The writer summed up the SS 100's handling very simply, by saying that: "It handles as well as it looks". The pleasing manners of the car were enhanced by the manner in which the controls worked too - the gearchange coming in for detailed comment by *The Autocar*:

Top left Jaguar ancestor - the Swallow sidecar in its 1929 form, but still showing the same lines displayed by the original 1922 version. It is attached to a Brough SS80 motorcycle in this picture

Top right A young Lyons portrayed on his 1919 Motor Show pass as a representative of the Metropole Garage

Centre left A Swallow advertisement in the *Blackpool Gazette*. The small print makes very interesting reading

Centre right Not factory sponsored, Swallow sidecars were, however, to be seen in competition. This particular Brooklands drama was photographed in 1928, probably during a 200 mile race *(photo The Motor)*

Bottom William Lyons' first car - the catalogue illustration of the original 1927 Austin Swallow Seven, wearing its hard-top

Top left A *Light Car* advertisement of April 1931 depicting four popular Swallow models, stressing style and colour in the copy

Top right The only non-British chassis to be built upon by Swallow was that of the Tipo 509A FIAT which was graced with a body which was more or less an enlarged version of the Swallow Seven - although the FIAT radiator was not cowled but left as standard

Centre The original Swallow factory in Bloomfield Road, Blackpool photographed in 1950 *(photo Jaguar Cars)*

Bottom left Lyons could not resist this tantalising reference to the forthcoming S.S.1 some three months before it actually arrived, in *The Autocar* July 1931

Bottom right The Swallow Hornet introduced in 1931 sold for £220 and was Lyons' first coachwork based on a 6-cylinder chassis. The car's tail was given very stylish treatment

Top left and right The S.S.1 of 1931, Lyons' first car. Perhaps a little bizarre to modern eyes, it created enormous interest upon introduction despite a slightly doubtful 'speed - looks' ratio *(photo The Autocar)*

Centre left The S.S.1 Four-seater Tourer, in 16hp and 20hp form, was the first car from S.S. to show true sporting potential, while its looks were handsome and bore no trace of the original S.S.1 oddities *(photo The Autocar)*

Centre right With the S.S.1 Tourers came an official interest in competition. Shown here is the 1933 Alpine Trial Team lined up outside the Swallow works at Foleshill *(photo Jaguar Cars)*

Bottom Charles Needham and Ray Munro contesting the 1933 Alpine Trial; their white tourer was the only surviving member of the S.S. Team. The rest of the team were afflicted by the lack of preparation and retired, whilst this car suffered too, but managed to come through *(photo The Autocar)*

Top left Georg Hans Koch, Lyons' Austrian S.S. Distributor entered his own S.S.1 Tourer and finished well ahead of the surviving Team car. (1933 Alpine Trial). With co-driver Karl Reitmeyer he finished 6th in class *(photo The Autocar)*

Top right The S.S. Team emerges from the *parc ferme* at Marano during the 1933 Alpine Trial *(photo The Autocar)*

Centre The Hon. Brian Lewis and his co-driver outside the S.S. factory at Holbrook Lane with their 1934 Monte Carlo S.S.1 Tourer. Note the car's twin front-wing mounted spare wheels, a feature of both the 1933 and 1934 rally Team cars *(photo Jaguar Cars)*

Bottom left The S.S.1 Airline Saloon of 1935 was a concession to the 'fastback' styling craze of the time and was not one of Sir William's favourite cars; its reputed failings included poor bulkhead sealing which led to the interior becoming hot and stuffy. The spats on the car are contemporary but not factory embellishments *(photo The Motor)*

Bottom right An S.S.2 Tourer taking part in driving tests at Brooklands *(photo Robert Danny)*

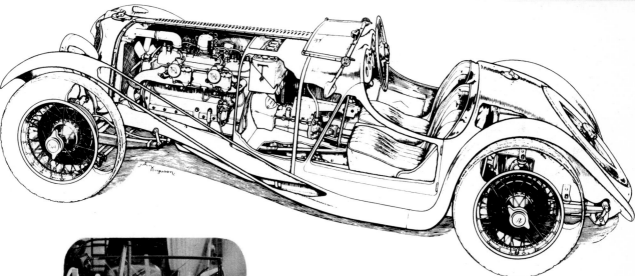

Top left and right The SS Car Club flourished before the war, actively promoted by the factory. Its membership brochure is shown here, depicting the stylish - and now very rare - SS Car Club badge (top) and the club's various activities (bottom)
Centre The prototype S.S.90, Lyons' first sports car, shown in cutaway form. The subsequent 22 cars lacked this car's rounded tail being given the more conventional exposed petrol tank and upright spare wheel (*photo The Autocar*)
Bottom Jaguar Cars' archives turned up this piece of history - a photograph of the S.S.90's production wing line and hood being achieved. Here, the bones of the car have been constructed and on this the wing shape is being tried. Parts of the background have been painted-out to allow the outlines to be seen clearly - note the characteristic inward slope of the wing at its top and the beautiful curve at the bottom. See too how the hood irons are held up by pieces of wood so that the contours of the hood can be determined

Top left The very first competitive appearence of an S.S. or Jaguar sports car off public roads - the Hon. Brian Lewis (now Lord Essendon) conducts the round-tailed prototype S.S.90 up Shelsley Walsh, May 1935. The car was placed 3rd in class with a time of 52 seconds *(photo The Motor)*

Top right William Lyons himself in an S.S.90, probably the first car to follow the round-tail prototype in having the vertical spare wheel arrangement. Note that the radiator bears an S.S.1 Saloon motif; usually the S.S.90 was bereft of such identification. Here Lyons sets up 'Best Performance' during the 1935 S.S. Car Club's Rally at Blackpool

Centre A G Douglas Clease driving the early S.S.90, AVC 477, in the 1936 Scottish Rally. The works SS 100, BWK 77, is following in the distance

Bottom left and right In an age when the horse drawn cart was still a common sight the SS Jaguar 100 represented the last of the traditional, fast British sports cars. Revolution came after the second world war and banished big seperate headlights, upright radiators and sweeping mudguards *(photo The Autocar)*

Top left The SS 100's hood matched the car's lines quite well and could be erected in one minute. Sidescreens were stowed in a locker behind the rear seats when not in use *(photo The Motor)*

Top right SS 100 engine compartment. The absence of air cleaners was normal - probably there was simply no room for such things under the narrow bonnet!

Centre There is a surprising amount of room behind the seats in an SS 100. The hood when folded was extremely compact and neatly covered by an envelope which was matched in colour to the interior carpeting *(photo The Motor)*

Bottom left BWK 77 in 2½-litre form on the Alpine Rally of 1936. Driven by Tommy Wisdom and navigated by Elsie Wisdom, the SS 100 surprised many by making Best Performance irrespective of class and winning a Glacier Cup

Bottom right The 1937 RAC Rally saw the Manufacturer's Team Prize won by the SS 100s of (from left to right) E H Jacob/E W Rankin, Hon. Brian Lewis/G Davis and Mr and Mrs Wisdom. Harrop and Wisdom also won individual awards *(photo The Motor)*

Top left Wisdom and spouse on the 1937 RAC Rally. Note the driver smoking!

Top right The SS 100 was a tough car and was not above entering the London-Edinburg Trial which demanded the fording of streams amongst other things. This is the 1937 event

Centre left Kicking up the dust, an SS 100 completes the Ganaron Sands tests during the Scottish Rally of 1937 *(photo The Motor)*

Centre right Tommy Wisdom at Brooklands in 1937 with 'Old No.8' lapping the outer Circuit while keeping an eye open for faster cars overtaking such as the Talbot *(photo The Motor)*

Bottom BWK 77 in the pits at Brooklands, with Tommy Wisdom at the wheel. Note the rigid tonneau cover enclosing the petrol tank now repositioned directly behind the seats and with a quick-release cap (far left). Again the year is 1937 *(photo The Motor)*

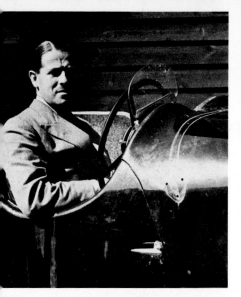

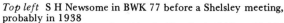

Top left S H Newsome in BWK 77 before a Shelsley meeting, probably in 1938

Top right Near miss at Brooklands. Fleming's 2½ litre SS 100 spins under the *Motor* bridge and gives Wooding a fright during a 16 mile race for British sports cars in June 1938 *(photo The Motor)*

Centre left An interesting overseas victory for the SS 100 was the win by Casimiro d'Oliveira in the 1937 International Villa Real sports car race. The 2½ litre SS 100 is about to overtake a German Adler

Centre right George Matthew's SS 100 in front of a Frazer Nash in a 3 hour race for standard sports cars held over the Campbell Circuit at Brooklands in July 1938 *(photo The Motor)*

Bottom Lyons, Newsome and Heynes on the grid at Donington having tossed up for their SS 100s at this SS Car Club meeting in May 1938. The MD of SS Cars Limited won after several false starts when he jumped the flag!

Top left How the SS 100's shape evolved from that of the tourers is clearly shown in this photograph taken at Donington in 1938. The cars await starter's orders on the grid. Numbers 24 and 12 are SS 100s, and 1 an S.S.1 Open Tourer *(photo The Autocar)*

Top right The 3½ litre SS 100 Fixed-head Coupe of 1938 on display at Earls Court. It is now in the hands of Jaguar collector Robert Danny after being in America for some years

Centre left SS 100s in various stages of dress and undress at the Crystal Palace Stanley Cup relay races of April 1939. George Abecassis' much altered white 100 with faired dumb-irons, Brooklands exhaust and BRITAIN labelled on the side of its bonnet is seen centre, a standard bodied car is seen right, while parked on the left is C E Truett's stripped 2½ litre *(photo The Motor)*

Centre right SS 100 and perennial rival the BMW 328. Crystal Palace never did suit the SS 100 *(photo The Motor)*

Bottom Sammy Newsome losing time at Shelsley Walsh, June 1939. On a tidier run he put up a very fast time of 42.95 seconds to beat an 8 litre Bentley

Top left and right The Newsome SS 100 Drop-head Coupe. Avon, a rival to Swallow, built the rather heavy body. The folding windscreen did, however, have the competition-minded owner in mind

Centre left The SS 100 was well to the fore in early post war events. R M Dryden's 3½ litre at the Hants and Berks Motor Club's West Court Speed Trials of September 1946

Centre right Pycroft's weird special bodied 2½ litre SS 100 winning the first race to be held at Goodwood in 1947

Bottom The Pycroft Jaguar was ingenious and quite fast. The petrol tank was placed forward of the rear axle for better weight distribution. The rigid canopy could be detached in two sections and stored in the car's hinge-up tail. The car has now been rebodied using traditional SS 100 parts by its Dutch owner

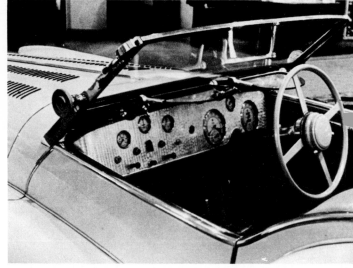

Top left Vanden Plas of Belgium built this streamlined SS 100 shown at the 1947 Brussels show - an interesting blend of old and new, all enveloping body and traditional radiator

Top right Inside the Vanden Plas SS 100 - SS instruments arranged on an engine turned aluminium dashboard. The windscreen still folded, placing the unused aero-screens in a potentially lethal position for the passenger!

Centre left Swiss coachbuilder Willy Bernath produced this body on an SS 100 chassis. It is suggested that durability was not its strong point - the firm ceased to exist around 1948-1949

Centre right This strange caricature of an XK 120 is, believe it or not, an SS 100, chassis no. 39057 to be exact. It was fitted with this drop-head bodywork by the now defunct Czech coachbuilder Uhlik soon after the XK 120 appeared *(photo Milos Skorepa)*

Bottom LNW 100 descending the Falka Pass on the way to its Coupe des Alpes in the July 1948 Alpine Rally

The gears are quiet, especially third and second the use of which is scarcely noticed as regards gear audibility. Also, the gearchange is an excellent one. The synchromesh provided on all gears except first gives a virtual certainty of quiet changes, up or down, and the movements of the short and rigid remote--control lever are smooth and light. Changes can be made quickly. The lever could with advantage be slightly nearer as regards first and third gear positions.

A higher final drive ratio of 3.8:1 was fitted to the 3½ litre SS 100, and the overall ratios of the intermediate gears were 12.04, 7.06, and 4.58:1 for first, second and third. Putting the lever into reverse incidentally, automatically operated the reversing light.

Increased performance had not reduced the margin of reserve held by the brakes which still were considered superb: "They have great power, but are not fierce or sudden, and want only moderate pedal pressure. Also, these brakes are entirely safe at high speed", said *The Autocar,* which also mentioned that the "conveniently placed" handbrake was of the normal type not the fly-off pattern that was fitted to *The Motor's* car. Towards the close of their 1400 mile test, *The Autocar* achieved "an altogether exceptional emergency stopping figure from 30 mph" - actually 27 feet - which indicates that these brakes were up to their usual efficiency. They did not require constant adjustment, and provided that when they were adjusted the job was done correctly, uneven pulling was not - and is not - a feature of the system. A moderate pedal pressure of about 88 lbs was needed for an optimum stop from 30 mph.

When it came for driver comfort to be discussed it was *The Autocar's* turn to complain of not enough room for the left foot, but that was about the only criticism. The seat cushions with their coil spring and Dunlopillo construction were "not notable for softness" but gave firm support to which the curved back-rests also contributed. *The Motor* thought that tall drivers might find the car difficult to enter but had more to say on luggage space than driver

well-being - always an important factor for consideration in a car like the SS 100, with a potential for long-distance touring:

Due to the sensible method of attaching the hood to the outside of the car there is a reasonable amount of luggage space available, and with a little careful planning two persons might comfortably pack in all their necessary gear for a month's holiday.

Storage space is usually a problem where two-seater sports cars are concerned, and although we are not particularly partial to a tool locker which is located under the passenger's seat, it is difficult to see where else the tools could be accommodated'.

For those who can't quite believe that the SS 100 could hold a month's holiday baggage for two, the present day exploits of Mr GEH Godber-Ford and number 39013 can be cited. He and his wife have clocked something like 27,000 miles over the past few years with their 3½ litre, regularly undertaking 3,000 mile continental trips with no tender car. Behind the rear seats goes two holdalls, 35 pounds of spare parts, three quart tins of oil, two collapsible stools, a bag of cleaning materials, spare shoes, anoraks and coats, towels and swim-wear, warning triangle and fire extinguisher. Other tools are distributed around the car and in the side screen locker (the side screens aren't carried). Reliability is almost total, with only a rear spring breakage slowing - but not stopping - progress on one occasion, and this inspite of competitive motoring in rallies and driving tests *en route.* Servicing, such as greasing at 600 miles, is carried out at the roadside on long trips; fuel consumption varies from a steady 21 mpg driven fairly gently, to 11 - 17 mpg during rallies (the PVT variety). Oil is consumed at about one pint to 1000 miles, and the brakes need adjusting only once a year. Although six foot tall and taking size 11 shoes, Mr Godber-Ford finds the car's driving position 'very comfortable' incidentally.

Countries visited by Mr Godber-Ford include France, Austria, Germany, Switzerland, Czechoslovakia, Poland Spain and Portugal, and the activities of this 3½ litre reflects admirably the toughness and longevity of the SS Jaguar product - few cars of its age can, or do, regularly cruise across continents at 70 mph with such reliability.

Contemporary road tests found the 3½ SS 100 an economical car in relation to its performance as well, the figures tieing up quite accurately with Godber-Ford's. *The Autocar* obtained an average of 16 - 18 mpg, while *The Motor* managed no less than 20 mpg overall, or the same as it had recorded for the 2½ litre model.

Notwithstanding the introduction of the 3½ litre version, the 2½ litre SS 100 still continued in production alongside the new addition to the range. Apart of course from the power unit, there were few variations between the two cars, about the only visible difference with the bonnet closed being the 120 mph speedometer fitted to the larger engined variant, as opposed to the 2½ litre's 100 mph instrument. A slightly different bell housing was used on the 3½ litre to accommodate a bigger flywheel and clutch, but generally speaking all parts were interchangeable and engine swops between the two models are quite easy to arrange, providing one has a reasonable knowledge of the subject.

Similarly, production changes to the SS 100 during its years of manufacture were very few. For 1938 the engine was moved back in the chassis about an inch, and the method of mounting the front of the engine altered; there was also a change in the method of connecting the brake rods to the brake pedal. Although the track on the 1938 saloons was slightly widened due to a hub alteration, this modification was not carried over to the SS 100; nor were any of the chassis and damping changes to the saloon range incorporated in the SS 100's specification.

In other words, the SS 100 remained throughout its production much as it had originally been when introduced in 1935; which is surely a mark of the success of its design compared to some other sports cars of around that time, which suffered many changes of power unit and **chassis** detail in attempts to arrive at the right

formula. The SS 100 was reliable and very fast, it stopped efficiently, and by the standards of the day it held the road well. Thus it did what it was designed to do, and until it was made obsolete by the general progress of sports car design, it was not in need of constant alteration.

Private owners did of course try to improve upon the factory's specification. Besides raising the compression ratio and sundry other efforts aimed at increasing the brake horse power, typically period modifications included exchanging the standard rear dampers for the similar but larger items from the post-1937 saloons (the SS 100 was certainly under-damped at the rear), and fitting the larger front brakes of the 2½/3½ litre saloon car range in place of the '100's original equipment. A number of owners fitted cycle-type wings, or even clipped the originals, which were attempts to cut down both weight and wind resistance - not because as so often has been asserted, the SS 100 had aeroplane tendencies at high speed! While it is true that under a very few freak conditions the car did appear to generate lift (ie when breasting a steep hill at over 80 mph in gale conditions), normally at or near maximum speed it gives the driver no feeling of uncontrollability, with only a slight lightening of the steering to indicate that the car is travelling at well over 90 mph.

Other owners strove to 'improve' the appearance of their cars by routing the exhaust manifold down pipes out through the side of the bonnet and down into the wing, usually via plated flexible tubing; or maybe it really was an attempt at free-flow manifolding. Perhaps the most extreme example along these lines was George Abecassis' SS 100, which looked like an SSK Mercedes, 3½-litre Bentley and Marendes Special rolled into one! Many SS 100s gained P 100 headlights (as fitted to the SS Jaguar saloons) which they retain to this day, but this private-owner modification at least had the practical attribute of providing a lot more light.

The 3½ litre Jaguar SS 100 cost £445, and it

is interesting to compare it on a price/performance basis with its contemporaries. For almost the same price, or £5 more to be exact, one could buy the Riley Sprite, certainly a more nimble car than the SS 100 but even though its 1½ litre engine gave an exceptional power output for its size, its acceleration and top speed did not match those of the SS - at least in standard form. The 2-litre AC two-seater with its stubby tail cost £55 more than the SS 100 but was probably slower than the Sprite, and the 2-litre ohc Aston Martin at no less than £775 could only attempt to keep up with the 3½ litre SS 100 by virtue of its extremely good handling qualities. To obtain a better straight-line performance from a British motor car one had to venture into the realms of the really heavy metal, such as the Lagonda Rapide with 4½ litres - it was a Lagonda which won the 1935 Le Mans race, the last British car to do so until the advent of the Jaguar C-type in 1951. The top speed of the Rapide in TT form was around 120 mph, but the standard production version cost £1,330, or getting on for £1,000 more than the SS! The V12 Lagonda was announced at about the same time as the 3½ litre SS 100.

The stiffest competition to the SS 100 undoubtedly came from the continent, particularly in the realms of trials and speed events, the BMW 328 traditionally being the SS 100's arch-rival. Purely as a road car too the BMW, inspite of giving away 1½ litres to the SS, had qualities lacking in the car from Coventry by virtue of its compact, streamlined body and independent front suspension, and its general performance was undoubtedly examined hard by SS Cars before the war. But again, it also cost a lot more than William Lyons' sports car, at £695. Frazer Nash of course marketed the cars in Great Britain, along with their own chain-drive sports cars which were of a totally different character but which in blown form could exceed 100 mph. Such continental exotics as the Bugatti type 57S (practically a road-going version of the Grand Prix chassis and engine), the Delahaye (which like the SS 100 had a push-rod ohv 3.5 litre engine) and more especially the Alfa Romeo two-seater with its classic 2.9 litre eight-cylinder ohc engine, were all rather in the fantasy class so far as price was concerned, the Alfa costing £1,950 in this country. To put the matter simply, there was nothing at anything near the SS 100's price that could equal or exceed its performance, and it was necessary to spend twice or three times as much to ensure leaving it behind under all conditions. Even then one might not automatically ensure the reliability and lack of temperament displayed by the SS 100 as a Mr Percy Silberston pointed out to the Editor of *The Motor* in a rather eulogistic letter written in September 1936:

I have just returned from a Continental tour embracing France, Germany, Austria and Italy ... The car used was an SS Jaguar '100' and for 3,000 miles it gave an absolutely trouble-free run, a thing that I cannot say for many of my 'Going Foreign' cars that I have costing more than double the amount.

A year later Mr Silberston updated us with a further progress report on his SS 100 which by that time had done 25,000 miles and had completed another 3,000 mile continental trip without the owner "bothering to see if the radiator needed any water." It was still giving 2,000 miles to the gallon of oil as well. These letters of course referred to the 2½ litre model, but the 3½ litre SS 100 adhered as we have seen to exactly the same simple formula of a large unstressed engine in a straightforward, good handling chassis and gave similar reliability over high mileages. Although as engine cooling was only marginal on the 3½ litre under some conditions (the larger engine actually had a slightly lower water capacity than the 2½ litre due to its narrower cylinder head and upper part of the block), it would not be wise to intersperse checking the coolant level with such high mileages with that model!

Whilst one can gauge fairly accurately the esteem in which a car was held in its own age and how it performed in comparison to its rivals simply by studying comtemporary opinion, it becomes rather more difficult to describe it objectively in today's terms without appearing unfair, so greatly has the art of automobile design progressed since 1938. Thus the SS 100's hard ride, occasional scuttle shake and confined interior all too obviously betray its unsophisticated beam axles, its 'cart springs', and its narrow and rather flexible chassis, when it is directly compared with today's independently suspended, monocoque construction high-performance car. But the acceleration, particularly the 3½ litre's, remains quite good and is still sensibly better than the average saloon of the 1970s. The car's 0 - 60 mph time of 10.4 seconds *(The Autocar)* compares favourably to the automatic XJ 4.2's 9.6 seconds, and is quicker than either the 3-litre Ford Granada or the Triumph Dolomite (1974 version!). Certainly the top gear acceleration of the SS 100 still borders on the exceptional - out of approximately 150 non-automatic cars listed in *Motor's* road test summary of May 18th 1974, only five bettered the 3½ litre SS 100's time from 30 - 50 mph (7.3 seconds) in top gear. Across that speed increment it was therefore quicker than such cars as the 3-litre Reliant Scimiter GTE, Triumph Stag, BMW 3.0Si, and the Rover 3500S saloon. It was only .3 second slower than the Aston Martin V8!

One must not read too much into these figures however, as the low-compression, low-revving 3½ litre engine has the advantage over its modern counterparts in the speed range under discussion - but they do prove that the SS 100 still possesses a very reasonable road performance and correctly driven will not get left behind in today's traffic conditions, in or out of town.

As a very rough guide, one can compare the 3½ litre SS 100 with the Triumph TR4 so far as performance in a straight line is concerned, while its cornering capabilities (on a smooth road!) are about equal to those of the Austin Healey 3000 - without the roll. But above all, the car remains fun to drive in both 2½ and 3½

litre forms, is vice free, and when properly maintained is extremely reliable. Allied with its superb looks, these virtues go a long way towards justifying the high prices now being asked for SS 100 sports cars.

One other version of the SS 100 was produced by SS Cars before the war, and that was the fixed-head coupe displayed at the 1938 Earls Court Motor Show. Built on a 3½ litre chassis (number 39088), this was a fascinating styling excercise by William Lyons in which is to be seen the genesis of the XK 120 shape - its similarity in profile to the XK 120 Fixed-head Coupe of 1951 is quite startling. Unfortunately it was not terribly practical - "one of Sir William's bad dreams" says Wally Hassan - as entry into the car was difficult and driving it almost impossible, with pedals, seat and steering wheel all in the wrong relative positions. It was listed at £595, and this, the most expensive by far of the pre-war SS Jaguars, was indeed an eye-catching exhibit on the SS stand at Earls Court, with its gunmetal paintwork and red leather and walnut interior. Only the one was made however, so the proper arrangement of the controls was never arrived at; the eventual owner had to have a considerable amount of work done before he could actually drive the car with any degree of comfort. Pleasingly this unique fixed-head survives in reasonably original form, although having acquired XK 120 bumpers over the years, and is back in this country after a number of years in the United States, the property of Robert Danny.

A true drop-head coupe SS 100 was also made before the war, though this was not a factory project but a private enterprise venture by SS 100 driver and dealer, the late S H Newsome. He considered that the standard '100' with its elementary weather protection was rather too spartan for some people who would otherwise have enjoyed its performance, and so obtained permission from William Lyons 'to design and build a special convertible body on the SS 100 chassis, and if satisfactory to market it as the Newsome SS 100 Special in the season 1939-40', as he wrote in a letter printed in the CJA's News and Technical Bulletin of August 1971. The completed prototype turned out very well and arrangements were put in hand to produce 50 of these Specials, which were to retail at £535 in 3½ litre form, and £485 in 2½ litre form. Only two chassis were supplied by SS however, before the outbreak of war in September 1939 halted the project.

The drop-head coupe bodies were built by an erstwhile rival of SS (or Swallow), the Avon Body Company of Warwick. The SS 100's wing line was tamed to an extent by spats over the rear wheels and increased side protection, while the convertible top could be fixed in three different positions - it also had detachable cantrails ("an important feature from the point of view of competition entries") and a fold down rear window section for extra ventilation. This last feature was almost an essential, as with the top erected the car is remembered as being exceptionally hot. The windscreen could still be folded flat, and aero-screens were standard. Inside, the instruments were re-positioned behind the steering wheel which left room for a cubby hole on the passenger's side. Only one of the two cars built seems to survive (no. 39115), owned by James J. Stickley in the United States.

As for the numbers of 'production' SS 100s made, a full breakdown will be found in the Appendix, but 191 2½ litre and 117 3½ litre cars left the factory, making a total of 308. Going purely by chassis numbers, the proportion is 190 and 118 for 2½ and 3½ litre cars, but the matter is complicated by the fact that number 39055, built as a 3½, was actually sold (in November 1938) with a 2½ litre engine. The last 2½ litre SS 100 to be sold in this country was 49061, which went in March 1941, via Henlys; the last 3½ was despatched to Henlys in the December of the same year. One 2½ litre SS 100 was, however, retained by the factory (49010) and this was to become Ian Appleyard's rally car LNW 100, fitted with a 3½ litre engine after the war.

Of the total SS 100 production of 308, well over one third was contained in the Classic Jaguar Association's SS 100 Register of 1974 of which 104 were resident in the United States, 26 in Great Britain, 15 in Australia, and the remainder scattered over another 13 countries. At the close of 1974, the SS Register of Great Britain calculated that by combining the CJA's latest listings with its own unduplicated figures, a possible total of no less than 262 SS 100s were still in existence - an astonishing survival rate which once more underlines the toughness of Lyons' pre-war sports car. As for the S.S. 90, it is thought that 23 were originally built including the round-tailed prototype (which is thought to have been recently discovered after being 'lost' for many years), and of these, the CJA lists at least 11, with a further 3 being known to the SS Register.

Some fifty SS 100s were exported new by the factory (sometimes fitted with a kilometer speedo), but a large number found their way across the Altantic during the Fifties and early Sixties; a trend which is now on the reverse. All cars were, of course rhd - the export market was not taken very seriously before the war.

THE SS 100 IN COMPETITION

The efforts of SS 100 drivers in competitive motoring met with early and most encouraging results. One of the SS 100's first successes, and undoubtedly one of the most underrated, was Tommy and Elsie Wisdom's winning of a Glacier Cup in the 1936 International Alpine Trial - and, as they lost no marks at all on the road in this premier continental event, the equivalent of an overall victory too. As Tommy Wisdom himself recalled years later:-

If ever the international motoring press found itself drinking the wine of astonishment, like whoever it was in Psalm 60, this was it. Pre-Alpine '36 few continentals had ever seen an SS 100, and those who had regarded it as mere crumpet bait, weak to perform and mighty to pretend, more than a serious rally car.

Reluctant as William Lyons was to commit

himself and SS Cars Ltd to any sort of official competition activity, this initial victory probably did a great deal towards persuading him to allow factory participation in selected events. The 2½ litre 1936 Alpine car was in any case owned by the factory, and 'Old Number 8' as it became known (from its chassis number, 18008) was to become the most well known '100' of pre-war years, being the factory's principle development and competition guinea-pig. Completely standard at first, finished in black paintwork and registered BWK 77, it was placed in the hands of SH 'Sammy' Newsome who shared it with driver/journalist Tommy Wisdom. It was to prove a successful arrangement, Newsome usually driving the car in hill climbs, and Wisdom in rallies and in track events. Newsome's first competitive drive of BWK 77 was probably at the September 1936 Shelsley Walsh meeting where he ascended in 51.62 seconds to win the over 3,000 cc unsupercharged class, at least a second quicker than the Hon. Brian Lewis's S.S.90 had managed. By this time the car differed from standard by having a higher compression ratio and probably the optional 3.75:1 final drive; fitted with a higher rear axle ratio the car went to Brooklands in October, where Tommy Wisdom came second to Charles Follett's Lammas-Graham "after lapping at between 103 mph and 105 mph, a great velocity for an unsupercharged sports car" as *The Motor* remarked in its report. It must have been especially gratifying to Lyons and Wisdom that the low pressure supercharged Lammas-Graham, the British relative of the American Graham Paige car, cost almost £100 more in chassis-only form than the SS 100 did complete!

BWK 77 was not the only SS 100 in contention for honours during 1936. In July, Australian driver F J McEvoy had won the 2 - 3 litre class in the Marne sports car GP at Rheims (in chassis no. 18007) to the surprise of many, although admittedly the French were more concerned with the larger engined classes, which they dominated with the 3.3 litre Bugattis. SS

100 appearances at Brooklands during 1936 also included H Bolton's car which ran in an MCC High Speed Trial in September; a standard 2½ litre, it completed a lap at 87.91 mph and much impressed those watching, as indeed did the other SS Jaguars competing.

The following year, 1937, was to see even greater success at home. In the RAC Rally, the official works SS 100 team of Wisdom, Rankin (Lyons' publicity chief) Jacob and Lewis were beaten - but by Jack Harrop in his own privately entered SS 100, who was first in the General Classification and the Open Cars over 15 hp class, and who won the Buxton Starting Control prize. Tommy Wisdom and BWK 77 were runner-up in the General Classification, and the SS Team came away with the important Manufacturer's Team Prize as the other two nominated SS 100s came fourth and fifth (they included CHP 402, the *Autocar* and *Motor* road test car, which is now owned by Bryan Omar Weddell of Whitefield, Manchester). Wisdom also gained the award for the best placed Leamington starter.

The Welsh Rally in July was also something of an SS benefit, with E H Jacob's SS 100 putting up best overall performance, and the works SS 100 team of Jacob, Rankin and Matthews once more pocketed the Manufacturer's Team Prize - and the Club Team award too as they were the nominated SS Car Club entries as well. Newsome made another assault on Shelsley in September 1937, but this time BWK 77 had the prototype 3½ litre engine under the bonnet. This resulted in Newsome storming the famous old hill in "a resounding 45.52 seconds which showed us something of what may be expected of this new and larger SS engine", as *The Motor* put it.

The SS 100 was actually placed second in its class to a 4.2 Hudson engined Minor, but was the fastest unsupercharged car in the 5 litre class - although Paul Heinaman's BMW 328 achieved a time of 45.46 seconds in the class below. Newsome's time was not in fact much quicker than he had previously set with the modified 2½ litre engine in place, as it was found that the final drive ratio of 4:1 was too high. The 3½ litre engine was not standard, having a 13.9:1 cr obtained by using specially made lozenge topped pistons, while a Scintilla magneto was fitted. The car ran with its wings, front tray and spare wheel in position, but without headlamps, battery, starter and dynamo. Front tyres were 5.25 x 17 racing, and rear tyres 6.50 x 16 racing. In exchange for its 3½ litre engine, Old Number 8 lost its registration number and was from thenceforth to become purely a works development and competition car.

The new engine's reaction to sustained high revolutions was tested at Brooklands in October 1937, when it was once more Wisdom's turn behind the wheel. He immediately enlivened proceedings by lapping at 118 mph and averaging 111.85 mph to win the First October Long Handicap, 12 seconds ahead of the nearest challenger - "I don't think Mr Ebblewhite ever quite forgave him!" says Bill Heynes. Those were the days when one quietly pushed the compression ratio up, hoping the handicappers wouldn't notice, until one had won something. In No. 8's case, its 3½ litre engine was running with experimental 10.5:1 pistons and one of the three modified cylinder heads that were to be tried over the next year; a methanol based fuel was used and a good 150 bhp was developed; or well over 25 bhp more than standard. William Heynes was of course directing this work on the 3½ litre engine, in which Dick Oates of OM fame also played an important part - he was a consultant to SS Cars at that time, mainly, it seems, to help evaluate the work that Weslake was doing at the time. At this stage in the proceedings, No. 8's wings and lights were dispensed with.

Tommy Wisdom fortunately left behind reminiscences of his SS 100 drives at Brooklands, and these give a fascinating insight into what it was like to drive No. 8 round that great and still lamented circuit:-

At the point where the Outer Circuit rises on concrete stilts over the River Wey, forming what was familiarly known as the Big Bump, any car, as long as it had enough speed, would take off and aviate for perhaps fifty feet. This was all right if the touchdown was predictable. With the SS 100 it was anything but. On landing, until or unless you learnt how to handle it, it would act like the proverbial pea in a collander, darting to the left or right, but always leaving you guessing until the situation was practically irretrievable. It was Kaye Don, four times breaker of the absolute lap record who gave me the advice that possibly accounts for my surviving to tell the story here. The old wrists of steel thing was OUT. The secret, said Kaye, was to let the steering wheel go limp in your hands at the moment of take-off and leave it limp on landing ... like the lambs in the nursery rhyme: 'Leave them alone, and they'll come home, bringing their tails behind them.'

It worked, though I'm not denying it took all the courage that I could muster.

Nineteen thirty-eight began well for SS Cars, Jack Harrop bringing his new 3½ litre into first position in his class during the RAC Rally in May. The SS 100 scored again in the Welsh Rally two months later, Mrs V E M Hetherington winning her class, but the Scottish Rally saw Newsome and Matthews unplaced with their SS 100s. On the race track, the managing director of SS Cars Ltd took the wheel when in May 1938 the SS Car Club held one of their meetings at Donington. The race, for trade drivers, was thought "highly entertaining" by *The Motor*, whose report went on:

W Lyons, MD of the SS Company, simply could not wait on the starting line and was twice hauled back by the starter. When he did get it right he drove with the most awe-inspiring determination, and despite having tossed up for cars was soon in the lead.

Sammy Newsome in another SS 100 finished a close second, with Bill Heynes in third place - who told me that in actual fact his car had proved fastest in practice, and Lyons had insisted that he swopped with him before the actual race! This was the second SS Car Club Donington meeting held in successive years, and it was duly noted that on no occasion was any mechanical failure experienced by any of the competitors. The SS Car Club was, incidentally, a thriving organisation in those days. It was factory sponsored and administered from Foleshill with Rankin as secretary. Besides its Donington meetings, the Club organised a wide variety of rallies and driving tests, as well as the usual social events which were often attended by Lyons and his fellow directors. It had an unfortunate ending - either just before or during the war, an official of the Club absconded with all the funds! This was not considered at all amusing by anyone, especially Lyons, who more or less had to pay for the loss out of his own pocket. No wonder the instigators of the post-war Jaguar Driver's Club had such a job persuading the factory to give them an official blessing years later!

The spring of 1938 is also notable for the recruitment of Walter Hassan to the engineering staff of SS. While employed by Thompson and Taylor at Brooklands, Hassan had worked on an SS 100 belonging to Edgar Wadsworth who intended racing the car in Ireland; this brought him into contact with Heynes, who helped him with various parts - including high compression pistons similar to those used in Old No. 8. There followed an invitation from SS Cars for Hassan to join them, to work with Heynes on the experimental side. This was accepted, and Lyons had gained another valuable addition to his engineering strength, as Hassan's experience with Bentley Motors and with Captain Wolf Barnato (with whom he had built the Barnato-Hassan Special) was highly applicable to the various projects underway at SS in those years. Part of his time was spent on engine development with Old Number 8, which was still proceeding apace.

Wally Hassan well remembers the SS factory in pre-war days. A hive of activity, every available inch was in use with work carrying on in every corner. The body building side of the company was by far the most important at that time, and in fact there was no machine shop as such at all, most of the hardware being 'made-out'; the woodmill was still one of the most vital sections of the factory, where the wooden jigs were made on which the metal body panels were

shaped. The saloon bodies were in fact made up from quite a large number of small panels spot welded and leaded together - and walking between the rows of counter-balanced spot welding machines with their scattering fall-out of sparks, the 'leaders' with their blowlamps, and the 'dingers' - men with hammers and dollies whose job it was to beat out sections which didn't quite meet - it was, recalls Wally, like a good imitation of hell. The SS 100 of course was being built on more traditional coachbuilding lines, and must have been considerably more civilised to work on.

Mr Heynes' office, where Wally was to spend much of his time, was built over the assembly tracks, and the whole of the engineering development section in 1938 was comprised of an engine test-bed, a welding set, a bench, a car hoist - and very little else. Nevertheless, some exciting projects were under way, and it was here that the final power output from the 3½ litre pushrod engine was developed and measured. For Old Number 8 was still getting faster.

In September 1938, Newsome had reduced his time at Shelsley to 43.6 seconds, the engine running on a mixture of methanol and petrol. The time however was a disappointment, as 41.5 seconds had been put up in practice - the official factory report stated that "slight gearbox seizure on the layshaft took place on the finishing straight" which slowed the car down. Number 8 was now running minus wings, and with various chassis modifications, including shorter rear springs which moved the axle centre forward 4 inches, while the front axle was also moved forward an inch; this was to "get more weight on the rear wheels and increase the stability and roadholding", which it did very successfully. A 5:1 final drive was now used, starts being made in 2nd gear and only 2nd, 3rd and top used during the climb.

The Paris-Nice trial of 1938 attracted a number of British entries, including the SS 100s of Wisdom, Vernon and Pycroft. Wisdom ran with a 2½ litre engine on this occasion to fall in the 3-litre class, but the result was an unspectacular 9th position overall in the rally, just behind Innes' FN-BMW which was the second British entered car to finish. However, some consolation was offered by the performance of the SS 100s in some of the individual tests. At Montlhery, where the competitors had to complete one flying lap of the 'piste de vitesse', Vernon's 3½ litre came third behind a Darracq and Lord Waleran's Lagonda in the big car class, while both Wisdom and Pycroft put up the two fastest times in their class at Montlhery, and at the La Turbie hill-climb test which followed. The month before, Mrs V E M Hetherington had furthered the SS cause with her win of the Open Cars (15 hp) class in the Welsh Rally, her 3½ litre SS 100 also winning her a Lady's Award.

With the political climate rapidly deteriorating, the 1939 season came to a premature end, but not before the SS 100 had once again proved its excellent road performance by a second place in the Open Cars over 15 hp class in the RAC Rally of May, gained by Sammy Newsome (though not with No. 8); the SS 100s of Gordon, Gibson and Mann (with Newsome), also achieved another second place, that for the Club Team Prize. In July, W C N Norton won the Open Cars over 15 hp class in the Welsh Rally, and Miss V Watson, also driving a 3½ litre SS 100, took home the Ladies' Prize (Open Cars).

It was in June 1939 that Old Number 8 had its final pre-war fling at Shelsley. Development of the push-rod engine had continued and a compression ratio of 14:1 was arrived at, from the use of special pistons, and in this form the relevant factory test sheets show that a highest pre-war brake horsepower reading of 169 bhp at 4,250 rpm was obtained from the unit. This enabled Newsome to lop even more time off his very fast previous ascent, covering the winding 1000 yards of Shelsley in 42.95 seconds - a pretty staggering time which netted him a win in the unsupercharged 3-5 litre class. This was actually faster than John Bolster's already famous four engined Special (43.30 seconds), and Forest Lycett's 8-litre Bentley (44.08

seconds), which was reckoned to be one of the fastest 8-litres built; only the supercharged cars of Baron (3.3 Bugatti) and Hans Ruesch (3.8 Alfa Romeo) were quicker than the SS in its class, and then by less than two seconds.

At about the same period, Wisdom entered 18008 at Brooklands again, in this its highest state of tune and with a 3:1 final drive. He recorded the incredible lap speed of 125 mph in practice, but alas - as he was driving the SS 100 to the start area for the beginning of the actual race, the crankshaft at last called enough, and broke. This was to be No. 8's last appearance at the great banked circuit.

As the Newsome/Wisdom car was - and is - the fastest and most highly developed SS 100 ever, it is certainly relevant to examine it a little more closely, and follow its history up to the present day. By the time Wisdom drove it for the last time at Brooklands, the SS had acquired a neat rounded tail - though still remaining a two-seater - and a great deal of work had been carried out on the chassis. All the main frame members had been heavily drilled, the radiator, engine, and firewall repositioned 6 inches further back in the chassis while the rear axle was located by a bracket of drilled steel which was mounted to the differential casing, and which ran back to the centre point of the chassis cross-bracing at the rearward end of the gearbox. For hill climbs, a twin rear wheel set-up was available as well.

World War II brought to a temporary end further experimentation with the push-rod 3½ litre engine, and in any case Lyons and Heynes had set their sights on an altogether new power unit - and it was the 160 bhp plus that was extracted from the old engine before the war began that became the target figure for the new engine. However, while the famous XK engine was being perfected after the war, more work was done on the pre-war push-rod engine to establish its ultimate power output, and 1947 test sheets record a figure of 171 bhp at 4,500 rpm using the last of the three special pre-war heads (no. EXPR3). A mixture of 80% methanol and 20% benzine was burnt by the engine in its high compression form, and ignition was of course by magneto.

After the war, the factory retained 18008 until at least 1948, during which time it was again driven in anger although the only notable result obtained was probably Elsie Wisdom's Ladies' Class win at the 1947 Bouley Bay hill climb, which was also probably the last time the car appeared in competition during its factory ownership. Thereafter George Matthews raced the car occasionally as a private entrant (his mechanic, Phil Weaver, was later to head Jaguar's competition preparation department) until he was involved in a monumental accident at Boreham. Number 8's history then becomes obscure although it was seen during the Fifties at Prescott, fitted with elementary road equipment in the form of cycle wings and lights. In 1968 it was re-discovered in a Liverpool suburb by David Barber, who meticulously restored the car from its rather sorry state to its original pre-war Brooklands trim. It was sold to its present owner Peter Danny but Barber continued to look after it, finally obtaining its original Brooklands head and high compression pistons.

Furthermore, David Barber continued development of the car from where Heynes had left off, and in 1973 succeeded in bettering Newsome's time up Shelsley with a run of 41.67 seconds, albeit aided by modern tyres on the original (single) rear wheels. After a season of engine failures in VSCC racing, Barber finally obtained reliability during 1974 and in April of that year the immaculately prepared SS 100 beat an ERA (Hanuman II) in a straight fight! To date, the car's power output is 160 bhp at 4,000 rpm, and 172 bhp at 4,800 rpm, measured at the rear wheels; allowing for a power loss of 25% in the transmission, this means a gross figure of something like 215 bhp at the flywheel - and Barber is confident that there is more to come.

Returning to the 1930s however, it must not be thought that the Tommy Wisdom 18008 car

was the only SS 100 to be seen at Brooklands. In fact quite a large number of SS 100s in both 2½ and 3½-litre form were extensively campaigned by their private owners at all the major circuits in this country, and sometimes abroad. While the car's exploits were almost exclusively confined to club events, there were some exceptions; McEvoy's Marne GP success has already been mentioned, and a notable victory was also recorded by Casimiro d'Oliveira in the July 1937 Villa Real International Road Race for sports cars in Portugal. The car was a 1936 2½-litre and in an exciting dual lasting almost 100 miles over a very winding course, d'Oliveira vanquished strong BMW and Adler opposition, and broke the sports car lap record with a lap of 98.181 kph as well.

On the home front, SS 100s became a familiar sight at Brooklands, Donington and the Crystal Palace. To list all the regular competitors would take far too much space but these included the exuberant H E Bradley, G E Matthews, F M Wilcock (no. 39026), C E Truett, A Goldman, G E Abecassis, J M S Alexander, C Mann and J D Firth to literally 'name but a few'.

A number of drivers modified their cars quite expensively, and of the 2½-litre cars, C E Truett's was probably amongst the most highly developed.

Chassis number 18105, Truett's 1937 car was originally driven in standard form until it was returned to the factory for various modifications. These included a special engine with a bronze-coated head (thought in those days to assist heat dispersal), stepped pistons giving a compression ratio of 10:1, polished Dural rods, and magneto ignition. The chassis was lightened by drilling too, the car obviously being modelled on 18008.

Thus modified, Truett's SS 100 was quicker than many 3½ litre '100's. Cyril Mann recalled in *The Autocar* of June 11th 1943 that he just beat Truett at Donington Park with his own modified 3½ litre SS 100, but had to work very hard to do it. Restored by David Barber, Truett's car is now owned by Jack Tattersal of Burnley,

Lancs.

Cyril Mann also had some interesting facts about his own car to relate, including some performance figures taken at Brooklands after certain engine modifications had been carried out. The car accelerated from 0 - 50 mph in 6.8 seconds (the standard 3½ took 7.8 seconds), achieved 106 mph in top gear with as much as 93 mph coming up in third gear. A standing lap at Brooklands was completed at 86 mph, and a flying lap at 97 mph.

On the car's general behaviour, Mann considered that the '100' "was a positive delight to handle from both a road holding and performance point of view, a cruising speed of 75-80 mph seeming just about right". So far as racing went, the car was most definitely more suited to Donington than any other circuit - particularly the Crystal Palace where the SS 100 never seemed very much at home. Mann hazarded that its weight distribution might have been a contributory cause there. But his general satisfaction with the car's handling is given further emphasis when one learns that Mann's previous car was no less than a 1936 1½ litre TT Aston Martin - sold because the successes of the official works rally team of SS 100s during 1937 had so impressed him. In fact, Cyril Mann only campaigned in one RAC Rally, where he noted that the SS 100 drivers were at a disadvantage to the shorter and lighter BMW 328s because of the 100's long wheelbase and rather poor lock. Also, both he, Wisdom and Harrop all got their feet stuck between the clutch pedal and steering column trying to get reverse gear quickly in the driving tests. But Mann also recalled getting his own back, when at the JCC's Test Hill Sweepstake at Brooklands in 1939 he made fastest time of day, beating Hugh Hunter's very quick BMW. The only trouble encountered by Cryil Mann during 1939 was the failure of one part, and that incidentally was not manufactured by S.S.

This rivalry between the SS 100 and BMW 328 was fierce during the years leading up to the war, and both *marques* had their various supporters who argued heatedly over the respective merits or otherwise of each make. The SS Jaguar probably did better in rallies than the BMW (especially in the final speed tests, which the 3½ litre '100' usually dominated), while the German car was often superior in circuit racing, particularly at venues where handling was at a premium (not to mention tyre wear - the SS 100's appetite for rubber could be excessive!); although it should be pointed out that one or two BMW 328s were far less standard than their looks might have implied, even down to special lightweight bodies which appeared outwardly to be original. And of course, if one takes price into account, the SS 100 must inevitably come out in front. It should also be said, though, that the factory itself never regarded the SS 100 as true sports car racing material, and with the exception of 18008 - which was a development car as much as anything - left the racing scene entirely alone, restricting official SS entries to rallies where the SS 100 could perform in its designed capacity - as a road car. In this context it is interesting to note that when Lyons heard that A Cuddon-Fletcher and Arthur Dobson had entered a 2½ litre SS 100 in the RAC TT race (to be held that year at Donington), the factory - almost at the last minute - persuaded them to withdraw the SS 100, and even refunded them their entry fee. "We knew its limitations", says Sir Williams, "inspite of its outstanding performance."

This was probably a wise move; the race was won by Gerard's Delage which was actually in the 3-litre class in which the SS 100 would have run. The BMWs did very well too - and if the results of the 3-Hour sports car race held over the Campbell Road Circuit at Brooklands a month or two beforehand was anything to go by, it is very unlikely that the SS would have finished in the first five. The time was yet to come when a Jaguar sports car could take on all comers, and as Sir William says, "it was in fact this limitation which led to the determination to design and produce a new engine which would meet every requirement, and which of course gave birth to the XK." Despite various rumours about a team of three Le Mans cars being built before the war, Sir William stated firmly in reply to my question on this point that "there was quite definitely never any question of entering the SS 100 at Le Mans", and the cancelled TT entry underlines the factory's pre-war policy on racing.

Private owners still put up a good showing in slightly less exotic events however, and a spectacular H E Bradley gained an early 3½-litre success when he won a five-lap handicap race at the MCC Donington meeting in June 1938. At the same circuit in July, Newsome drove his 3½-litre to first place in the last race of the day, Truett's 2½-litre being second and J B Carr's Bentley third. In the 3-Hour Light Car Club event at Brooklands that month, the highest placed SS 100 was admittedly 6th, but had not Matthews' 3½-litre spun when a tyre burst, forcing him to retire because the SS had simply used up all the spares, it is conceivable that he might have got in amongst the BMW 328s (which included most of the regular BMW drivers of the time such as H J Aldington, A F P Fane, and Hugh Hunter - but not Leslie Johnson on this occasion) even if there was no hope of catching the leading trio headed by the Willing/Jarvis 3½-litre Delahaye. At least *Grand Vitesse* commented afterwards in *The Motor* that the "SSs went well and fast".

In September 1938, H Bolton (now in a 3½-litre SS 100) averaged 94.62 mph during an MCC Brooklands One Hour Trial to gain a 2nd Premier Award behind Wooding's Talbot, while A Goldman's 2½-litre example took another Premier Award in the second High Speed Trial of the day, in front of G Wood's 3½-litre SS 100.

Before the war put a stop to such pleasant pastimes SS 100s were still fairing quite well on the track in 1939, at least in minor events. Donington could usually be relied upon to produce favourable results for the *marque*, and the United Hospitals and University of London Motor Clubs meeting there in May did just that. Although Truett's 2½-litre SS 100 was beaten by

a 2.6 Alfa Romeo in one heat of a scratch race, Goldman's SS 100 beat Gerard's Riley in heat two; while Goldman, Dennis and Truett came first, second and third in the over 1,500 class in the four lap handicap race. Goldman also won a five lap handicap race for sports cars; it was a very good day for SS.

Cambridge University's Motor Club held their meeting at Donington the next month, where Truett and Goldman - with Gibson - averaged 67.39 mph to win the relay race; the similar event at the MCC's Donington meeting was also annexed by three SS 100s, and the type also won three handicap races, two of them over 20 laps (N V Terry, G J Gibson and J M S Alexander were the chief stars on this occasion). Brooklands wasn't ignored and SS 100s managed at least one win and a number of 'places' in 1939 - this JCC Members' Day meeting was also the scene of Cyril Mann's vanquishing of the BMW 328s on the Test Hill. At the annual SS Car Club Day at Donington, Truett's car was the most successful '100'. And when the entry lists for the 1939 TT were published in August, it was seen that yet again a private entrant was intending to field a 2½ litre SS 100 - but SS Cars were saved any possible embarrassment by the event's cancellation due to the gathering clouds of war.

So the war came to SS Cars Ltd. Car production continued for a few months into 1940 but soon tailed off as war contract work took over; while many sidecars and something like 100,000 light trailers were made for the Army, much of the work taken on by SS concerned aircraft repair and manufacture, including the rehabilitation of damaged Whitley bombers. These last were to cause some headaches to the company, new to aircraft industry practice. Sir William Lyons:-

I have a vivid recollection of the arrival of the first Whitley bombers at our Foleshill factory, as they went past my office window on a convoy of Queen Mary transporters. I followed them into the factory and was surprised how little they appeared to be damaged. Together with the works manager and chief inspector, I examined them carefully, and I made a remark to them - which I will never forget - 'We'll have these repaired in under a month!' Some of them were still there a year later. I was at the time ignorant of the stringent. Aeronautical Inspection Directorate requirements.

Sir William is still of the opinion that some short cuts should have been made in the repair of these aircraft, in view of the desperate shortages of planes in those fraught years. Towards the end of the war, SS Cars made the first Meteor jet fuselage.

THE SS 100 IN POSTWAR YEARS

When the war ended motor sport gradually re-established itself, firstly in the form of sprints and hill climbs, and then races. The first timed event to be held after hostilities ended was probably in August 1945, when the Bristol Clubs held a hillclimb meeting at Naish House in which an SS 100 became the first sports car to break the minute, "inspite of much swerving and some resounding changes of gear" by the driver, L H Parker - who also fitted snow grips to the rear wheels of his 3½ litre in a search for more traction. He finished second in his class to Baillie-Hill's HRG.

In fact the SS 100 played quite a big part in those slightly unreal early post-war events, in which a weird selection of machinery took part including a good smattering of vintage cars - nothing new was available at all. Thus it was that BMW versus SS battles were once more resumed. In June 1946 Newsome returned to Shelsley and although he didn't beat his pre-war time with 18008, the 46.95 seconds he did record was fast enough to beat Leslie Johnson's BMW by almost two seconds. Cyril Mann also brought out his 3½ litre SS 100 with effect, and when Prescott re-opened, R M Dryden gained a third place in the Unlimited class (unsupercharged cars), behind two Allards, in May 1947 - and headed them at

the June Prescott meeting. In 1948, an SS 100 won the first motor race held at Goodwood, Pycroft's re-bodied 2½-litre taking the flag.

But more significantly, the SS 100 was still a strong contender in such events as the Alpine Trial, and ironically some of its greatest successes in International events were to be in the post-war years, a considerable time after the car was obsolete. The Alpine Rally (as it became known more familiarly) is in Jaguar terms inseparably linked with the name of Ian Appleyard, who entered the 1947 Alpine with his 9-year-old SS 100. At first it seemed as if he would finish unpenalised, but he was rather caught out by the rapid wear of the '100's tyres and ended the rally third in his class - Descollas' Type 43 Bugatti gained the only 'Coupe des Alpes' for a penalty-free run. But undeterred, the young Yorkshireman returned in 1948 with LNW 100, a virtually unique SS 100 - chassis number 49010, it had been stored during the war in Sir William Lyons' garage at Wappenbury Hall and then fitted with a 3½-litre engine in exchange for its original 2½-litre unit, and was first registered in 1947.

It was a dramatic rally for Appleyard and his navigator Dr Dick Weatherhead; in appalling weather which made every corner treacherous, Norman Hiskin's Sunbeam Talbot left the road just before Appleyard's SS 100 came upon the scene, to find an upside down car and a badly injured co-driver. Stopping to give medical assistance to Marsden made it seem that all hope of a victory was gone for Appleyard, but he drove the SS 100 to such effect over the remaining 32 miles of the stage that he averaged a heroic 64 mph, and ended by winning a 'Coupe des Alpes' and finishing first in his class. He gave a dramatic account of his dash in Jaguar's house journal in 1949:

For some miles I drove at a snail's pace - reaction after seeing the crash I suppose. Then gradually the queer feeling wore off and soon we were dicing as never before. But the road gave us no chance to get up speed. Twisting incessantly it wound up and down over scrub-covered hills towards the coast. Not until

Grasse did it begin to straighten out at all but it was almost too late. We had exactly half an hour left for the 32 miles to the finish-that meant averaging 64 m.p.h. all the way into Cannes and along through Juan towards Nice on roads which were seething with Saturday afternoon holiday-makers. It was a terrifying ride. Clocking between 70 and 80 m.p.h. most of the way, and with the horn blowing incessantly, we passed obstructive vehicles on whichever side looked the more promising, whilst cyclists scattered before us like chaff in a hurricane. Cars coming against us were often forced on to the pavement as we swerved in and out of the traffic stream, whilst all around us sounded the horns of dozens of outraged Frenchmen. But as we emerged on to the promenade at Nice there was still a minute to go and with the speedo needle creeping towards the century mark, the Jaguar hurtled towards the final control. Dick was ticking off the seconds now. We'd just do it if nobody got in the way. Those final few yards seemed to take ages as we screeched to a standstill and handed over our route card. It was stamped. We were in on time.

Further evidence of the SS 100's speed and reliability some fourteen years after its inception is given by Ian Appleyard's first place in the over 1500 cc class, and second overall in the General Category, when he campaigned the 1949 Tulip Rally in May of that year. Few cars have been so successful when so thoroughly obsolete! Appleyard shared one of the new Healey Silverstones with Donald Healey in the Alpine that year (the XK 120 not being ready) - and might have won another *'Coupe'* but for a delay at closed crossing gates - but he was, of course, to have an incredibly successful career in International rallying with NUB 120 from 1950 onwards. In fact, the SS 100 remained quite competitive - particularly on the club scene in Great Britain - until the advent of the XK 120, although Sydney Allard was beginning to produce American engined cars which could outperform the SS. Cyril Mann even ran his faithful 3½-litre in the first Production Sports Car race at Silverstone in 1949, rather to the annoyance of Rob Walker whose 3½-litre Delahaye (which

had won the similar race held at Brooklands in 1939 to determine 'the world's fastest production sports car') was not accepted by the organisers. Thereafter, anyone who ran an SS 100 in a competitive event did so purely for fun, rather than with any hope of a 'place', although the unexpected still happened. Rallies still saw the occasional SS 100 contend the larger-engined classes during the early fifties, but the 'classic car' drain to the States gradually began to deplete the ranks of those cars still in active use.

Eventually, the SS 100 became accepted by the VSCC as a post-vintage thoroughbred and appeared at vintage events during the sixties in this class, with reasonable success by such drivers as Michael Wilcox, a Bentley Drivers' Club committee member who won the Montagu Trophy with his 3½ litre car in 1960, and Tony Peters who drove his ex-factory road test 3½ litre (DHP 734, no.39053) in VSCC races - this car was considerably modified with XK 120 brakes, its engine repositioned an inch further back in the chassis and a post-war Jaguar gearbox (certain types of which bolt straight on to the 2½ and 3½ pre-war engines).

Abroad SS 100s were still competing in obscure parts of the world in quite open competition; Alan Lowe drove his cycle-winged 3½ litre in the 1962 Singapore Grand Prix and at many other local events, and the car's racing career was continued by its present owner Ian Boughton who entered it in the 1973 Singapore Grand Prix.

Thus we arrive at the present day, with Barber's driving of the Newsome/Wisdom Brooklands car putting the SS 100 to the forefront in at least one division of Vintage/PVT racing. At the time of writing however, few if any other SS 100s are to be seen on the track although a number take part in old-vehicle rallies - notably the Godber—Fords' ambitious excursions in 39013 already described, while in France Phillip Renault has over the past five or six years entered many similar events with No. 39012 (a 1937 3½ litre); Renault also owns HEW 888, another 3½ litre which competed in 1951 and 1952, and a modified 2½ litre (no 18012) which has been timed at 172 kph.

As for non-competitive appearances, these are not quite so rare and the SS Register here in Great Britain reckons to see some ten or fifteen SS 100s at their annual Rally, and the big Concours d'Elegance meetings in the States - particularly those organised by the Jaguar Clubs of North America - attract at least similar numbers. Very few SS 100s are now in every day use in any country and most surviving cars have been fully restored (for subsequent sunny weekend work only) or are in pieces undergoing renovation. Many of the cars imported into America during the fifties and early sixties were restored upon entry, and some collected XK engines - though probably not more than a dozen - at that time, when originality was not the highly regarded attribute it is now. One or two '100s' were even given V8 engines, though one can expect a gradual return to original specification as the cars' value increase even more.

Chapter Three   The XK 120

Nothing like the XK 120, and at its price, has been previously achieved - a car of tremendous performance yet displaying the flexibility, and even the silkiness and smoothness of a mild-mannered saloon

The Autocar
April 14 1950

A machine in which to challenge all the gods and poets...sometimes...

Dick O'Kane
Road & Track January 1967

XK 120

The XK 120 of 1948 was a revolutionary sports car. This was not because it contained in its specification any spectacularly original advances in technology, or broke any new ground with its coachwork - it was that, quite simply, the XK 120 achieved for the first time ever saloon car standards of ride and comfort in a sports car which had a performance exceeding that of virtually any other production car. And it did it at a price so low that it was incomprehensible to most of Jaguar's rivals.

In its hey-day, the XK 120 was certainly the fastest British car you could buy that was in anything resembling series production, and the impact it made upon its announcement in October 1948, echoes down the years to this day. It spearheaded the penetration of the British sports car into the American market (with MG), it convinced Jaguar themselves that Le Mans could once again be won by a British car, and it provided a valuable starting point in the career of many a famous racing driver; not to mention the enormous fun and sheer driving pleasure it has given to countless owners all over the world, in its intended role as an ultra-fast, untemperamental road sports car.

In consideration of all the foregoing, it is therefore interesting - surprising even - that the XK 120 might rightly be termed an afterthought so far as Jaguar were concerned, and might conceivably never have been made at all - and most definitely not in the numbers it eventually ran to, during its five years of production. Once again it must be emphasised that the company's chief preoccupation was, and is, with the saloon car range. That meant, as the war ended, the Mk VII saloon. A sports car "was not even thought about until the Mk VII was well advanced in design...and was really a by-product in the programme" to use Sir William's own words. Thus the XK120 stemmed directly from saloon car development work that had begun prior to World War Two; its suspension, engine, and even chassis frame were those created for Lyons' first all-new post war saloon, the Mk VII Jaguar.

Research into chassis and suspension developments for a new Jaguar car had commenced in 1938, when Chief Engineer Heynes had tried a number of independent front suspension systems. Not that he was any stranger to the gradual trends towards independent front suspension, for while he was employed by Humber he had designed several experimental ifs configurations for the Hillman Minx. These used either coil or leaf springs, but when Heynes began experimenting with ifs for S.S., torsion bar springing was included in the development programme, an indication of Heynes' liking for the way Citroen used the medium.

Several ifs designs were built and tried out on converted SS Jaguar saloons before the war put a stop to progress. These included a variety of short and long wishbone suspensions including one using coil springs - this being an early exercise by Bob Knight, one day to succeed Heynes as 'engineering overlord'. An interest was even taken in strut-type suspension, using cylinders filled with air or a mixture of air and oil with a shock absorber in between, though in the end it didn't prove itself practical for a production car.

Before peace-time activities ended, Heynes had arrived at the basis of the suspension he was to use after the war. It combined the torsion bar with upper and lower wishbones which projected from the chassis to carry a ball or socket joint at their ends; Heynes was probably the first to use such an arrangement in conjunction with torsion bars, although Maserati had tried something similar in the thirties, and so had Porsche, although they combined it with trailing arms. Likewise, thoughts of a new engine which could power the second generation of Jaguar saloons were already in existence before 1939, and over the long war years these thoughts gradually crystallised during the now-famous fire watching discussions at Foleshill. There, in the modest Development Department office built over the assembly tracks, William Lyons, William Heynes, Claude Baily (who had joined the SS drawing office during the war) and Walter Hassan chewed over the various requirements for the new power unit - sustained high power of at least 160 bhp, reliability and long life, silence in operation, and a strong resistance to obsolescence. Heynes sketched out the basis of a twin over-head camshaft design, and before the war was out, several experimental engines had been built to test various forms of valve gear, and to evaluate cylinder head design.

Four, six and twelve cylinder configurations were all "seriously considered" at this stage, but it was the four and six cylinder versions that were finally adopted. The only reason for the parallel development of the 'four' was that the company completely under- estimated demand for the new range of cars (particularly that eminating from the North American sector of the market), and it was thought that a smaller engine - which could be manufactured on the same major tools as the larger unit - would be needed to amortise production costs; for besides the Mk VII, a smaller saloon was under active consideration in which was to have been installed the 'four', it having been intended to parallel the original pre-war range, ie the S.S.1 and S.S.II. The small Jaguar however "died a natural death when the Mk VII appeared with the six cylinder XK engine with such success... we had an order book so full that we had neither the time nor need for a small car" (Sir William Lyons).

The evolution of the XK engine has been detailed so many times, and the famous Paper read by W M Heynes to the Society of Mechanical Engineers in February 1953 covers the subject so thoroughly, that it is rather unnecessary to go deeply into its development here. But four principle experimental power units were made, code-named XF, XG, XJ '4' and XJ '6'. All featured twin over-head camshafts and the hemispherical head design which Heynes considered essential, except the XG, which was basically the Standard 1,776 cc engine that Jaguar adopted for their 1½ litre saloon, but fitted with a BMW 328 inspired head and valve gear.

The close examination of the BMW 328's engine which provided the inspiration for this particular experiment was made possible through Heynes' friendship with Leslie Johnson, who lent the S.S. factory his highly developed 328 which he had successfully raced before the war. A BMW saloon was also procured during the war, and this was actually fitted with the XG - Hassan used the car as every day personal transport for quite a long time and recalls that it ran well but the opposed push-rod valve gear was noisy. A pre-war 2½ litre SS Jaguar saloon was similarly used for testing out prototype ohc engines but the great majority of development work took place on the test-bed. Not suprisingly, a small Citroen saloon was also on the test fleet, for suspension experiments.

The XF was of 1360 cc and was built purely to prove the type of head and valve gear, while the XJ was the true forerunner of the XK engine. It was built in two forms, four cylinder and six cylinder. The 'six' was of 3,200 cc (83 x 98 mm) and this was to be the single replacement for the 2½ and 3½ push-rod engines previously used, while the 'four' was, as already explained, intended for use in a 'small' Jaguar saloon. The 'six' was found to be slightly deficient in low speed torque, so the stroke was increased to 106 mm; the resultant engine, with a bore and stroke of 83 x 106 mm, was termed the 'XK'.

The XK engine incorporated all Heynes' thoughts on high performance production engines; the cylinder head was the result of much work by Harry Weslake, with its hemispherical combustion chambers and efficient cross-flow design, and it was cast (by William Mills Ltd of Wednesbury) in aluminium - a material chosen by Heynes chiefly because of its light weight, as at 50 lbs 'bare', it was 70 lbs lighter than a similar head of cast iron.

The block (made by Leyland Motors) took advantage of the camshafts being upstairs and consequently was of comparatively light weight with webbing providing a high degree of strength in the right places; it carried a very strong, seven bearing counter-balanced crankshaft with large main bearing diameters of 2¾ inches; lubrication was wet-sump with a normal but carefully developed gear-driven oil pump.

The camshaft drive was eventually by duplex roller chain, but this arrangement was only arrived at after considerable headache by Heynes and his team. Originally a design using a single chain was proceeded with, but after a long time had been spent in trying to overcome a peculiar whine only audible some distance from the engine, it was finally dropped in favour of the two-stage configuration; much on the insistence of Wally Hassan who considered the noise to be most inappropriate to a Jaguar, and that besides,

noise always meant wear and tear somewhere. The valves were placed at an angle of 70 degrees to the vertical and a 5/16 inch lift camshaft was used - the valve size and camshaft lift on the original XK engine were chosen solely to eliminate the possibility of the valves touching if, when the head was being worked on by a mechanic, the camshafts were turned independently of each other. The competence or otherwise of the average garage when turned loose on such a sophisticated piece of machinery as the XK engine was an unknown quantity in the 1940s, and Heynes was taking no chances. In the event, it was found that the engine fared better than expected under outside maintenance, and when the 3/8 inch lift camshaft was introduced in the Special Equipment models within a couple of years of launching the XK 120, bent valves from careless handling were a rare occurrence.

Two individual branch exhaust manifolds were used, the down-pipes converging to join a single exhaust pipe and silencer, and the petrol/air mixture was supplied by two 1¾ inch SU carburettors. The engine was rated at 160 bhp at 5,400 rpm on an 8:1 compression ratio, and 150 bhp with a 7:1 cr. It *looked* efficient too, as Heynes was determined that the appearance of the engine should reflect "some idea of the thought and care which has been expanded on the design and construction of the unseen functional parts". Hence the impressive, polished aluminium camshaft covers (lacking studs at the front on early engines), the chromium plated cylinder head bolts, the polished aluminium finish on the inlet manifold, and the glossy black stove-enamelling of the exhaust manifolds.

While the development of the new engine was proceeding, Lyons himself was also involved in other matters vitally effecting the future of his company, including a change of its name. It was time for the initials 'S.S.' to go, and in March 1945 the company's name was changed to Jaguar Cars Ltd. The reasons for this were probably two-fold; firstly of course, the activities of the German S.S. troops - "a sector of the community which was not highly regarded" as Sir William put it - had considerably tarnished the name and secondly, the adoption of the name 'Jaguar' cut ties with the past that still might have associated the company with a 'special building' image - which was an incongruity now that it was an increasingly self-contained manufacturer of very individual cars which were inspired entirely by Lyons himself.

This progression towards antonomy so far as bought-out components were concerned took a big jump forward when, a few months before the end of the war, John Black of Standard told Lyons that he intended to resume production with only one model, the Vanguard, and would no longer be able to supply engines to him. It was subsequently agreed that all the plant which had been specially installed for the manufacture of the 2½ and 3½ litre ohv engines at Standard would be sold to S.S. (as it then still was), at a bargain price - its written-down value. Lyons leapt at the chance.

Before the war, Black had given me reason for a great deal of anxiety on the question of exclusive continuity of the engine he was making for us. Several other makers had asked him to supply them, and I had not found it easy to prevent him from doing so, even though he accepted that the design of the engine, apart from the cylinder block and crankshaft, was ours. Therefore, I was delighted to learn of his proposals as I felt it was a release from an arrangement which I could not have broken honourably, having regard for the fact that it was his willingness to put down the plant, which we could not afford at the time, that got us off the ground with this new engine. I saw this as a great step towards our becoming the self-contained manufacturing unit at which I aimed. I had a great admiration for John Black in many respects, but I quickly grasped the opportunity to obtain security. Therefore, within a few days, I sent transport to collect the plant and sent our cheque in payment for it. It turned out that I had been right to do so for it was not long before Black proposed that we should revert back to the old arrangement and return the plant to Standards. I said 'No thank you, John, I have now got the ball, and I would rather kick it myself.' He pressed me very hard, even to the extent that we should form a separate company

together, but I was unwilling to accept his proposals, even though I so much appreciated his help in the past. Thus the post-war Jaguar 2½ and 3½ litre engines were all made by Jaguar, and the XK engine naturally followed suit.

It was about the period when Jaguar took over the production of these push-rod engines that there was a possibility that Lyons might have bought the Triumph Company, which had fallen onto hard times and had been in the hands of the receiver since 1939. After a careful consideration of the financial aspects, however, Lyons decided that it would place too great a strain on Jaguar's own resources to make the company viable, though interestingly, the matter re-involved John Black to a certain degree. In fact, it could be said that in a way Lyons was responsible for the acquisition of Triumph by Standard in 1945, for when the chief of Jaguar once again refused to join forces with him, Black threatened to buy Triumph and go into competition with Jaguar if he didn't change his mind. When Lyons still remained adamant, Black did indeed purchase Triumph and forecast that Jaguar wouldn't survive the competition; but although he did revive the company to some extent, it had no measurable effect on Jaguar's sales. If that rather bulbous oddity, the Walter Belgrove designed Bullet (or TRX) of 1950 with its complex electrohydraulically operated windows, hood and headlights, was meant to sound the death-knell of Jaguar, it didn't work - only two or three were ever built. The TR2 of 1953 was infinitely more successful, but hardly in Jaguar's class. The reluctance of Lyons to enter into any sort of pact with Black after the war, and the swiftness with which he implemented the agreement reached over the engine plant, is easily explained when one considers the character of the late Sir John Black himself. As Graham Turner wrote in his book *The Leyland Papers:*

He was subject to violent fluctuations of mood and in the view of one of his closest colleagues had become almost schizophrenic - 'he could be the kindest or the cruellest man in the world, the gayest or the most depressed, a heavy drinker or a total abstainer. He lived on a razor's edge and nobody knew which side he would fall'. The result, according to Alick Dick, was that 'no decisions were being taken except by mood.' Black was not only a dictator, but an unpredictable one as well.

In fact, it was Black's impetuous sacking of Heynes' old boss Ted Grinham that led to a revolt by the Standard board in 1953, which thereupon forced Black's resignation. So finally ended the relationship between S.S. and Standard that went back to the very beginnings of Lyons' car making days - Black died in 1965 and, said Sir William some years later, "inspite of our differences I would like to pay tribute to him for his great energy and the success he made of the Standard Motor Company in the early postwar years."

Lyons was just as astute in his dealings with the Government as the war ended. Steel was heavily rationed and the permits needed for its purchase allowed very little for home market consumption. Although S.S. Cars had not exported very many vehicles before the war, being able to sell all they produced in Great Britain, "we set out to convince the Government that the models we had coming along would command a substantial export market." To do this, Lyons prepared a "very elaborate" brochure listing all the countries to which cars would be sent, how many vehicles could be made, and the amount of steel required, and then delivered it personally to Sir George Turner, the Permanent Secretary to the Ministry of Supply. The result was that within a couple of weeks, Jaguar received a permit for the entire amount of steel they needed · a "tremendous boost" as Sir William said afterwards. It was then a case of establishing retail outlets throughout the world as quickly as possible, and simply making the cars.

To help finance the resumption of production, £100,000 5½% Preference Shares of £1 each were issued by Jaguar in March 1946 - the second and last such issue, which meant that the total outside finance introduced into the company up to its amalgamation with BMC in

1966 was £185,000; these shares, together with bonus shares of par value £2,147,000 which were issued between 1955 and 1964, were worth, by 1966, no less than £16 million to the holders!

Meanwhile, chassis development was continuing apace in parallel with the work on the new XK engine, and the engineering department under Heynes had designed the new Jaguar's chassis together with the final production version of the torsion bar front suspension that had undergone such a lot of experimentation previously. The new chassis frame differed from the old one (which had continued in production more or less in pre-war form as the basis of the post-war 1½, 2½ and 3½ saloons) in a number of ways. It was torsionally stiffer having deep box section side members that remained straight for their entire length, until they swept upwards over the rear axle to provide room for the increased suspension movement given to the car. An 'X' bracing piece added even greater resistance to twisting forces - which were reduced anyway by virtue of the long torsion bars which carried some of the suspension reaction forces nearer to the centre of the car - while across the front of the chassis was a further heavy box-section cross member, which also provided a rigid base for the front suspension itself.

This frame was designed with the Mk VII saloon ultimately in mind, but in the meantime it was decided to market an interim model - the Mk V saloon. This car retained the push-rod engine (in either 2½ or 3½ litre form) and inherited a slightly altered form of the previous Jaguar saloon's bodywork - the new XK engine was not sufficiently tested nor was it then possible to make it in the required quantities for the Mk V; and in any case, it would have been bad policy to place the new power unit in an out-dated body. The testing and experimentation involved with both a new engine *and* a new chassis obviously put quite a strain on the development staff, and "although the Managing Director was very understanding" as Heynes said, he was not above goading the chassis and engine team into even greater efforts. On one occasion, Walter Hassan remembers, "when William Lyons thought that progress was not as fast as he desired it to be, he 'went up to Fred Gardner in the wood mill and said, 'Come on, Gardner, I want to make a car'. And old Fred got a lot of steel tubes, and bits and pieces from other cars, welded it all up, and produced a car within a week. It did manage to drive round the factory, before the wheels fell off". It is unrecorded what eventually happened to this Lyons Special!

Although an announcement from the factory in September 1945 had stated that "the 100 series is temporarily out of production", sports cars were the company's least important concern immediately after the war, even though Lyons had long before realised that the SS 100 was due for replacement at some stage - the 100's "competition successes (had) helped the company to build up a name for performance and things were going in the right direction, but I knew we had a long way to go before we were producing the type of car at which we were aiming".

But while efforts were indeed generally concentrated on the new saloon cars, the building of a sports car was investigated and at least one prototype made. A product of Jaguar thinking immediately post-war, it was smaller than the XK 120 to come as the power unit envisaged for it was smaller too - probably the four cylinder, opposed - pushrod unit inspired by the BMW engine. The bodywork was possibly by an outside coachbuilder. The little car's lines are extremely interesting, anticipating as they do the wing-line of the XK 120, but it was not deemed a suitable replacement for the SS 100 and so never reached production. It was broken up many years ago. Unitary construction was also investigated, and one car was built around a 'backbone'; box-like in shape, it was purely experimental and was powered by a small engine.

However as both the Mk V/Mk VII chassis and the XK engine neared completion in 1948, it became obvious to Lyons that at last a worthy successor to the SS 100 was possible - in fact,

"such a car with the XK engine could not fail (provided of course we made no serious mistake) to become outstanding, as it should easily outperform everything else on the market by a wide margin, irrespective of price". Equally important, a new sports car with the XK engine would be the ideal medium in which to try out the new engine in actual service conditions, before going ahead with the large-scale production necessary for the Mk VII.

The decision to go ahead with a sports car came very shortly before the October 1948 Motor Show, and it was obviously desirable to build a car to display there. A Mk V chassis was commandeered complete with suspension, brakes and steering, one foot six inches was cut from the length of the centre section, and the 'X' bracing was removed and replaced by a single box section cross member; the frame was also narrowed slightly. The result was a chassis having a wheelbase of 8 feet 6 inches, as opposed to the Mk V's 10 feet.

The sports car's suspension was therefore exactly like the Mk V's, the front being the final production version of Heynes' independent wishbone and torsion bar design. The lower wishbone was made up of two components - a strong 'I' section beam which ran out from the chassis at right-angles, and a tubular bar which ran out to join the 'I' beam at its extremity, just before it met the wheel hub. The torsion bar, which ran along the inside face of the chassis from a mounting point near the car's scuttle, acted on the 'I' beam where the latter pivotted on the underside of the chassis frame. The upper wishbone was made of built-up steel forgings, and with the lower wishbone, ran out from the chassis to carry the ball joints. The choice of ball joints here enabled the pivot joint of the wishbones to coincide as closely as possible with the king-pin centre line, and meant that the king-pin bearings themselves required far less frequent rebushing. Material for the ball joints was the object of much experimentation, a tough steel with a hard chrome finish eventually being specified with sintered bronze for the cup itself (changed some considerable time later to a moulded asbestos and resin material). The cup was designed so that it had only angular contact with the ball (at about 70 degrees to the vertical) which gave the ball a tendency to bed into the cup and thus take up wear automatically. An anti-roll bar connected the two lower wishbones, and Newton telescopic-type shock absorbers were mounted on brackets above the top wishbones, and acted on the ends of the lower wishbones.

The torsion bars were of silico manganese spring steel and being of comparatively great length, were very strong; while rear spring breakages were sometimes a sore point with XKs, torsion bar failure on a Jaguar is almost unheard of. The rear mounting of the torsion bar incorporated an adjuster for ride height and tension.

Altogether, this was to be a very hard wearing and reliable front suspension and it was used by Jaguar on all their non-unitary construction cars from 1949 to 1961 - and even then it survived in essence on the E-type long afterwards. Like the new saloon, the sports car had a Burman recirculating ball steering box, and the steering was in fact to be one of the few more fundamental aspects of the chassis to be changed during the XK's long production run. The car's rear suspension was entirely orthodox, employing a hypoid bevel live axle sprung by long half-elliptic leaf springs, with no further location. Damping was by Girling lever-type PV7 shock absorbers.

While the car's suspension was something of a minor revolution, at least in its ride qualities, without doubt it was the 3442 cc XK engine which lifted the XK 120 - so named because of its estimated top speed - into the realms of the exotic so far as 1948 was concerned. The Heynes/Hassan/Baily masterpiece was installed in the new chassis together with a four-speed gearbox and 10 inch single plate Borg and Beck clutch; the last two mentioned were of familiar pattern, having been employed in substantially similar form in the previous Jaguar saloons. While a divided propshaft was used on the Mk V,

the XK 120's was one-piece.

In looks too, the XK 120 'struck a new note' so far as British sports car design went, just as the original S.S.1 had done seventeen years before. The XK 120's body style has remained a classic example of Sir William's art and its sweeping lines and sculptured curves are as beautiful today as they were in 1948 - a rare tribute to a car of that period. The broad outlines of the XK 120 shape were not on the other hand unique, at least to those who were attentive to sports car styling trends in Europe. Even before the war all-enveloping coachwork had clearly been seen as an inevitability, and back in October 1938 when the SS 100 was in full production, *The Motor* sagely remarked that in Italy, "the open two-seater has become a thing of sweeping curves and enclosing metal." Although in Britain in 1948 at least, the appearance of such a modern sports car might still be as *The Motor* remarked in the same article, "a grave shock to those who have been bred to the British tradition of a long bonnet, two small seats and a short stubby tail decorated with a spare wheel" (a remarkably accurate description of the SS 100 as it happens!). In fact, a close examination of the 1938 one-off fixed-head coupe SS 100's profile does reveal the beginnings of the XK 120's shape (even in the latter's initial roadster form), and various efforts at 'streamlining' the SS 100 by coachbuilders also pointed the way ahead occasionally - the Belgian division of Vanden Plas showed a rather heavy design in February 1948 which, if not generally very happy, did have something of the XK 120's wing line about it, if you ignored the upright radiator grille. Likewise, P de F C Pycroft rebodied his 2½ litre '100' during 1947 in a similar all-enveloping style which in a crude way also held a hint of XK lines in its wing. Then AFN Ltd imported one of the two special streamlined open two-seater BMW 328s which had taken part in the 1940 Mille Miglia, gave it a Frazer Nash grille, and put it in their 1947 catalogue as the Frazer Nash 'High Speed Model'; it too had something of the same theme running through it. But when the XK 120 arrived, it displayed such subtlety of line, such elegance, and such superb attention to detail that it made most of these earlier attempts at the streamlined sports car appear distinctly amateurish. There is little we can criticise in the XK 120's shape even today. It has a rare purity of line that remains a joy to behold no matter what has passed since.

The altogether rather amazing story of the XK 120 takes another surprising turn when one learns that this superb body design did not take months or even years to evolve, but was indisputably the most rapid exercise of its type to be carried out by Lyons - and probably the quickest in the history of the series-production motor car. Sir William has a very clear recollection of how the XK 120 body shape was arrived at, "because it was done more quickly than anything before or since, and I could compare weeks, almost days, with years and it was not altered from the first attempt".

From start to finish, the task of designing the body shell took less than two weeks. Sir William worked in his familiar and probably unique way; a skeleton frame was formed to eye under his direction on a cut-down Mk V chassis, and a skilled sheet metal worker shaped panels under his guidance to fit the frame. One point that Sir William remembers as the work progressed and the XK shape emerged, was that the way the bonnet came to be made-up revealed that the obvious thing to do was to leave it in one piece with the radiator grille - hence the 'alligator' method of opening the XK 120's bonnet.

This work was carried out using aluminium as the material (besides being light and easy to work by hand, it was after the war relatively cheap and plentiful, and not subject to rationing) and it was this alloy that was adopted for making the XK 120's 'production' body shell when the prototype car was made, just in time for the Earls Court Show which opened on October 27th 1948 (it has been said that this car, the first XK 120 of all and later registered HKV 455, was constructed in something like six

weeks). For it was initially proposed that a first run of only 200 XK 120s would be made, with further small batches being built if the demand warranted it, the car's chief role being a useful guinea pig for the new XK engine - and, of course, Lyons and Rankin could not have been unaware of the publicity value of a 120 mph sports car! It was not until the 1948 Motor Show had opened and the new two-seater had received an overwhelming reception that Lyons realised, even within the first week of the show, that it would be completely impossible to make the numbers that had already been ordered in the hand-built method intended. Before the Show was over, arrangements were therefore already being made with Pressed Steel of Oxford for them to manufacture steel pressings for the body.

But obviously, it was going to take time for Pressed Steel to tool up for the new body, and so when XK 120s eventually began to leave the factory - in very small numbers during the latter half of 1949 - they carried the originally intended aluminium bodywork. The exterior aluminium panels, made by H H Cooke and Sons of Nottingham, were mounted on a laminated ash frame in a small corner of the Foleshill works, rather in the manner of the SS 100 before the war and probably by the same men. The front wings and scuttle arrived as a complete unit, and the body was assembled on a wooden jig in the shape of the car's chassis before being placed on the actual steel item. The front bulkhead and firewall, the inner wings and part of the boot interior were in steel.

Concurrently with the 3442 cc six cylinder XK 120, the XK 100 was announced. This was identical to the XK 120 with the exception of the power unit, which was to have been the smaller, four cylinder twin over-head camshaft engine that had been developed in parallel with the larger engine, principally for the small Jaguar saloon which as mentioned was originally thought necessary to supplement the forthcoming Mk VII. With a bore and stroke of 80.5 x 98 mm, the 'four' had a capacity of 1,995 cc and produced 95 bhp at 5,000 rpm; valve gear and many other features of its design were identical to those of the six-cylinder XK engine. A neat and efficient little engine, it was never to attain production even in the XK chassis, as the glamour of its 120 mph sister completely overwhelmed the 2-litre car which would probably have had a maximum speed of about 100 mph with its 4.09 final drive ratio. This underestimation of the XK 120's success in the world market was actually quite costly, in one sense, for about 50 units of the smaller engine had already been built prior to the announcement date - they hung around for years in dusty corners of the Development Department before being broken up for scrap, though one was fitted for a while in an XK 120 fixed-head that Lofty England used for a time during the early fifties, and a few more were resurrected from the experimental department at the time of Jaguar's 50th Anniversary, to be used as exhibition pieces. So no XK 100 was ever actually made; if it had been, performance would possibly have been similar to the early Triumph TR2 sports cars, but at only ½ cwt lighter than the 3½ litre XK 120, it is unlikely that the XK 100 would have been competitive for very long either on the road, or in the 2-litre classes on the track - though this last would scarcely have worried the factory.

While the bronze XK 120 two-seater displayed on the Jaguar stand at Earls Court in October 1948 made an impact which perhaps has not been exceeded by a British sports car either before or since, even those sympathetic to Jaguar's aims were a little doubtful of the car's ability to really achieve the maximum speed implied by its name - after all, 120 mph performance had previously been the prerogative of only the most expensive Continental sports or sports racing machines, built in small numbers and usually supercharged; or perhaps the 8-litre Bentley of the vintage era - though this was even less a production car in the true sense of the word than the two-seater Alfa Romeos and Bugattis. Yet here was Lyons offering what

amounted to pre-war racing car performance at an amazing £998 basic, or for the same price as the newly announced Mk V saloon. And if the XK 120 really could attain the speed of two miles a minute on the open road, it was speculated, would it not be an impossible device in town, and at low speeds, with oiling up plugs, 'sudden death' clutch, and a camshaft completely unco-operative under 2,500 rpm - all of which must surely go with such performance?

The motoring world's education in respect of all these points came relatively slowly, but were none the less impressive for that. In May 1949, a Douglas DC3 flew a party of journalists to Belgium, where they witnessed for themselves a production XK 120 exceed not 120 mph, but 130 mph. And motor quietly past them at 5 mph afterwards - in top gear! Needless to say, this demonstration on the Jabbeke-Aeltre autoroute was carefully planned and rehearsed. The site of the runs was not entirely strange to Jaguar either, having been the scene in September 1948 of Major Goldie Gardner's 176.694 mph two-way average in his streamlined MG Special, powered by the experimental XJ 2-litre Jaguar engine - with a 12:1 compression ratio, this engine gave 146 bhp at 6,000 rpm and would happily run up to 6,500 without damage.

Ron 'Soapy' Sutton was the driver of the white XK 120 scheduled to make the runs - registered HKV 500, this car was the second left-hand drive XK 120 built (chassis number 670002). Sutton had previously bolstered both his faith in himself and in the car with some early morning runs near Coventry, and when these went supremely smoothly, it was this that decided Lyons to initiate the Jabbeke demonstration. So Sutton travelled with Jack Lea (mechanic, and who had also ridden with Sutton in the 1930 TT) to Jabbeke for a dress rehearsal. The car behaved perfectly and the only change made for the actual runs in front of the press was the substitution of a higher (3.27:1) ratio in place of the standard 3.64:1 gearing in the ENV axle - although in the event, this made virtually no difference to the car's speed.

A large number of locals turned out to watch, joining Lyons and Heynes who had flown out with the party of journalists. All were kept abreast of developments by the thoughtful provision of a loud-speaker van, and of course the carriageway in use was closed for the official runs - which were timed by the car breaking a thread across the road. Timing was under the auspices of the Belgian RAC.

First, Sutton drove the XK with the hood and sidescreens erected, and recorded no less than 126.448 mph mean. Then a short halt while the windscreen was detached and replaced by a small aluminium cowl, and a metal tonneau cover fitted over the passenger's seat (the car ran with an under-shield attached for all its runs). To be completely sure that maximum rpm was built up, Sutton used a run-in of 2½ miles although in fact the car was up to its maximum within a mile; and this time, the electric timing apparatus clicked out the car's time on the paper tape as 131.916 mph for the north run, and 133.596 mph for the south - which gave the resounding mean speed of 132.596 mph. The standing mile was covered at an average of 86.434 mph mean.

Needless to say everyone was highly delighted, including Sutton who was grateful to Wally Hassan for allowing him the glory of making the runs - it really having been Hassan's prerogative to have taken the wheel as development engineer, but as illness prevented him from carrying out the previous testing and rehearsal runs, he generously told Sutton that as he'd done the spadework, it was only fair that he should have the glory too. But Hassan did drive HKV 500 back to England, embarking on a considerable detour with Tommy Wisdom in order to survey much of the forthcoming Alpine Rally route, and ascending at least one frozen *Col* in the process.

So the XK 120 earned its type designation. These early Jabbeke runs made a deep impression back home, where interest was high in all quarters. The then Minister of Supply telegrammed Lyons with congratulations, and even

The Times carried news of the 'British Car's Speed Record', beautifully sandwiched between paragraphs headed 'The King Not To Attend Derby', and 'Woman Golfer Struck By Lightning'. The 'record' was a Belgian production car one, incidentally.

HKV 500 was much more representative of the 'production' aluminium-bodied XK 120s than was the 1948 Show car. The last mentioned was of course the very first XK 120 built, its chassis number being 66001 ('66' denoted rhd XK 120 open two-seaters, '67' lhd), and it displayed a number of features not seen on succeeding examples. There were no brake-cooling apertures at the front of the car, the small bumpers being mounted where these air holes were to appear on later cars, the front number plate had a plinth mounting, the straight-sided screen bolted directly to the scuttle via three bolts in each side pillar (instead of through the scuttle to an internal mounting point), and the spats covering the rear wheels lacked the external 'T' key hole for their removal. The fuel tank filler could only be reached by lifting up the boot lid, and the prototype carried no rear bumpers at all, having little more than a chrome strip running along the bottom of the boot lid. The rear lights were smaller than on the production versions, and the rear number plate lacked a plinth mounting. But these points really only relate to items of trim, as the body shape itself was to remain unaltered. About the only mechanical changes were the later use of a single SU petrol pump mounted on a chassis member, instead of the twin SU pumps positioned on HKV 455's engine bulkhead (which was also different to that on later cars), and a repositioned starter motor.

The streamlined body of Jaguar's first post-war sports car brought many benefits besides a reduction in wind resistance. The enveloping body was wide by current standards, and the wooden floor of the driving compartment overhung either side of the chassis for quite a distance, thus allowing the use of wide, pleated leather seats and providing rather more elbow room than had been available in the SS 100, where the seats had been mounted within the width of the chassis frame. The hollow doors had use made of their thickness, being given large pockets, and they were trimmed in leather to match the dashboard. The dashboard had the usual array of instruments to be found on a Jaguar, comprising matching speedometer and revolution counter, ammeter, fuel gauge, and combined water temperature and oil pressure gauge. By pressing a button, the fuel gauge could also be made to register the oil level in the sump. All the minor controls were dashboard mounted too, except for the headlight dipswitch (floor mounted) and horn (steering wheel boss activated). A short gear lever protruded from the central transmission hump, and the chromium plated fly-off handbrake was positioned to its left (or right, if a lhd car). The car's 'V' shaped windscreen was detachable in several sections, and the first few cars (18 rhd and 26 lhd according to the parts book) had straight sided pillars with the three-point scuttle mounting as found on 660001. The remainder of the aluminium-bodied XK 120s had curved side pillars, but unlike the later steel-bodied cars, these were fitted with large rubber grommets at their base as opposed to the thin rubber washers of their successors. The first 28 rhd and 68 lhd cars had provision for a starting handle too.

In William Lyons' successful attempt to civilise the sports car, the XK 120 was provided with quite a lot of luggage room. There was storage space behind the forward tipping seats on top of the twin six-volt battery boxes, and a useful amount too in the boot, the spare wheel being segregated from the suitcases in a separate compartment under the boot floor. The hood, which was generally agreed didn't look particularly pretty when erected, at least folded down out of sight behind the seats when not in use and was relatively easy to erect, while the side-screens could be stowed neatly in a slot underneath the rear tonneau panel.

Under the alligator bonnet, the twin-cam 'six' looked highly impressive, though accessibility on the XK 120 was never one of the car's strong points - the distributor lay rather buried under the top water hose, while the bottom water hose has been the subject of much bad language over the years during attempts to replace it. Certainly, the Jaguar mechanics' old saying, 'If I could find it I'd fix it', held some truth here. Fortunately, things didn't go wrong all that often with the XK 120, thanks largely to the long development period of the engine - by the time a car was ready for it, most faults had been ironed out and barring a little initial gasket and timing chain tensioner trouble, and the rather notorious water pump, the engine behaved extremely reliably under service conditions. About its only design fault was a tendency towards poor exhaust valve cooling and although not serious, this too was eventually remedied - albeit many years later.

Deliveries of the XK 120 did not start until the second half of 1949, and prior to that it is highly probable that the factory itself had only three cars - the Jabbeke car HKV 500 (now converted to rhd), the Show car HKV 455, and 670001; these three cars were those used in August 1949 at the Silverstone Production Car Race meeting (see Chapter Four). When XK 120s did begin to leave the works, it was the overseas markets which were of course favoured, and no home price was listed by *The Motor* for the XK 120 until September 1949, when it was seen to cost £1,263..3..11d with purchase tax (by fixing the basic price at just below £1000, Lyons had avoided a doubling of this still new tax). Three months later, *The Motor* also conducted the world's first full road test of the XK 120.

The car lent to the magazine for this first independent appraisal of the XK 120 was HKV 455, which had largely been brought into line with the production XKs although it still retained its luggage compartment petrol filler cap, and the rear number plate was still attached directly to the boot-lid instead of on a raised mounting.

Harold Hastings and his colleagues on *The Motor* fully vindicated the XK 120's promised performance. A trip through France and Belgium, although rather fraught with the currency exchange problems of those early post-war years, enabled the car to be extended on both the Jabbeke motor road and around the banked circuit of Linas-Montlhery. In consequence the car could be given its head, and a genuine 124.6 mph was reached, the best one-way speed being 126.8 mph. This was within 1.8 mph of Sutton's own demonstration run at Jabbeke with HKV 500 in similar trim (hood and sidescreens erected, and with the optional undershield).

When it came for the car's performance through the gears to be described, *The Motor* enthused that "it will provide acceleration such as most drivers have never even imagined." Translated into seconds, this meant a 0 - 60 mph time of 10 seconds, 0 - 80 mph in 15.7 seconds, and 100 in 27.3 seconds, with the standing quarter-mile being covered in 17 seconds dead. The engine's extreme flexibility was shown by a 0 - 100 mph time of 44.6 seconds using top gear only, and by the fact that 10 - 30 mph and 60 - 80 mph were covered in top gear in 6.7 seconds and 8.5 seconds respectively - or within 2 seconds of each other. The standard 3.64:1 final drive was fitted, and the intermediate ratios were 4.98:1 (third), 7.23:1 (second), and 12.3:1 (first and reverse). Maximum speeds in second and third gears were 62 mph and 90 mph.

Few other cars in production could in 1949 approach any of these figures, and none could match or better them all. The Aston Martin DB2 introduced the next year, although a 'sports saloon', was certainly a competitor to the XK 120 but as it took 11.2 seconds to reach 60 mph, and 34.5 seconds to gain 100 mph, it just wasn't in contention when it came to performance - or on price either, as it cost £650 more than the Jaguar! The Cadillac-engined Allard J2 which appeared in 1951 was one of the few road cars that were faster off the mark than the XK, reaching 60 mph in 7.4 seconds and 100 mph in 23.6 seconds, but at 110 mph it was limited to a maximum speed of 6 mph less than the Aston; it

also cost (supposing you managed to get one in this country) a basic £1200 compared to the XK 120's £998, and it hardly had the refinement or looks of the Jaguar.

Not that the XK 120's performance was in any way intimidating. Said *The Motor*:

There is no embarrassing sudden response to the accelerator pedal, but rather a docility of the power unit and a smoothness of the clutch which makes for a delightful willingness to crawl in tightly packed traffic.

This feature, together with the very real degree of comfort provided by the soft suspension and good damping, was a major reason why the XK 120 was so popular in the States. It was easy to drive, even for a woman, and this counted for a lot.

In fast driving, the XK's seats were thought by *The Motor* to provide only "moderate" lateral support (the factory offered a lightweight bucket seat as an optional extra for racing later on), and the steering wheel was thought to be a little too steeply raked for rapid lock-to-lock manoeuvres. The clutch movement was light, yet displayed the typical Jaguar trait of a rather long travel; the gearbox excited no criticism at all, though this was not always to be the case in the future!

When it came to the car's handling, we find that, as in the case of the SS 100, a longer acquaintanceship paid:

The car's precise controllability is not always fully appreciated at first, but once it is realised that only small wheel movements and finger-and-thumb are needed it is instinctive to negotiate winding roads at really high speed, audible protest from the tyres being very, very seldom heard except during violent braking.

The Motor's testers also noted the XK's extreme stability at speed, a feature of the model that was to become almost legendary, and "only a single guiding hand on the steering wheel" was necessary during the maximum speed runs.

Surprisingly, in view of owners' less satisfactory experiences and even the factory's own tacit agreement years later that they were not all they might have been, the XK 120's brakes were rated as "excellent" by the magazine, which went on to say: "...what is especially creditable is the way in which the car can be slowed or brought quickly to rest from speeds above 100 mph without fuss or misbehaviour on smooth or rough surfaces." One wonders if this feat was ever attempted twice or more in succession, as quite serious fade was a genuine problem with the drum braked XKs. Lyons pioneered the all-enveloping body work and small wheels on the fast production sports car, and these two characteristics prevented in the first instance a free flow of cool air to circulate around the brakes, and in the second the fitting of adequate size brake drums (12 inch as opposed to the SS 100's 13 inch effective diameter). These factors conspired to create a heat dispersal crisis which was not fully overcome until the advent of the disc-braked XK 150 in 1957. Although to be fair, severe fade was only encountered in fast driving, and after all, what other sports car could be bought 'off the shelf' at that time which went fast enough to be afflicted by this malady? Lyons paid the price for being an innovator, and it is not as if he left the problem alone - the ultimate result of the XK 120's stopping problems was the Dunlop disc brake.

To turn to other aspects of the car's equipment, the Lucas headlights with their characteristic 'Y' centres were not thought worthy of the car by *The Motor,* with 70 mph only comfortable at night on a good straight road. But the automatic 'choke' was liked (it was in fact an auxiliary starting carburettor, solenoid controlled from a thermostat in the inlet manifold water jacket), and so was the cigarette lighter on the dashboard - "especially useful on an open car." In the final paragraph of this November 16, 1949 road test, the writer concluded that the Jaguar team had evolved a winner, "...a car which is superb even at this early stage in what should be a very long and honourable career."

By the time that *The Motor* had put HKV 455 through its paces, a trickle of aluminium-bodied XK 120s had just about begun to leave the factory. Bryson's of New South Wales, Australia, received the second rhd car to be built (chassis no. 660002, body no. F.1005), the car being despatched on July 21st 1949, but the flow did not begin properly until August or September 1949, and even then it was slow - cars were made at the rate of about 12 a month, and only around 60 XK 120s were completed in 1949, more or less equally divided amongst rhd and lhd. Most of the former type went to Australia, with a few to other countries such as New Zealand and Hong Kong, while Hoffman or Hornburg in the States took the majority of the latter.

The greater number of 'alloy' cars were therefore manufactured in 1950, their production just overlapping that of the steel-bodied cars which were to replace them. The final lhd aluminium XK 120 (670184, F.1240) was despatched from Jaguar on April 12th 1950, while the last rhd car of similar construction was sent to Brinkman's in Australia on May 1st 1950 (660058, F.1218). Thus by body number exactly 240 aluminium bodied XK 120s were made (two chassis in the alloy series were used for the first two steel XK 120s), or rather fewer than the total SS 100 production before the war. Australia, incidentally, also received the first steel-bodied roadster to be sold in rhd form (660059, F.1264), the car leaving the factory on April 20th 1950 having been completed 16 days earlier; the first lhd steel-bodied car sold (670185, F.1244) left the factory a month later, on May 19th 1950.

The changeover to steel bodywork seemed scarcely to be noticed at the time by the general public or motoring press, and indeed remained of only incidental interest to subsequent owners and used-car dealers right up to the late sixties, by which time the rarity value of the earlier type had at last begun to evidence itself in a higher price when an example changed hands. This itself did not happen very often simply because few aluminium-bodied XK 120s existed in this country; when new, all had been exported forthwith - mostly to the States - and the only 'alloy' cars remaining in Great Britain originally were the works development cars and six others which were allocated to selected drivers for competition purposes (see Chapter Four). Virtually all others that are now registered here are export cars which have subsequently been re-imported.

The change of material from aluminium to steel meant delays in production, as the XK 120's entire body construction had to be re-designed. Thus there are very few body parts which are common to both steel and aluminium cars, although of course the chassis, engines, and running gear are identical in almost every respect. The shape and outward dimensions of the car remained virtually the same, although it is possible to detect certain differences in the curvatures of the steel and alloy bodies - the headlight nacelles of the earlier car protrude a little less, the front wings do not slope in towards the radiator grille quite so much as with the steel-bodied car, and the shape of the rear wings differ very slightly. Also, being hand-built, there are occasional small discrepancies in the construction of the aluminium-bodied cars - like the brake cooling apertures in the front wings not being quite level.

Under the skin, the internal structures of the two cars differ markedly. The main sills which run under the doors - and which in the XK have the important function of holding the two halves of the bodywork together - were re-designed, with rather complex, hollow-section mild steel sills replacing the simple wood and single-thickness steel composite item of the aluminium car. Another spot-welded mild steel structure replaced the alloy and wood door-shut faces of the early car, and at the same time the door hinge area was effectively boxed-in with another steel structure, rendering the door hinges difficult to lubricate properly and almost impossible to replace without major surgery -

though this drawback of course was not to manifest itself for some years. The steel-bodied car was given a completely new engine bulkhead too, with different hinge mounting points for the bonnet - which itself was heavier, with more cross-bracing pieces (the early bonnet had been subject to cracking due to flexing). Bonnet, doors and bootlid remained in aluminium, and the early steel-bodied cars also retained the separate, chromium-plated side-light housings (up to chassis no. 661024 rhd and 672926 lhd). Inner wings on both types were in steel, but generally of different design. So far as exterior trim was concerned however, both cars shared the same bumpers, lights, number plates, reversing light and reflectors. Windscreens differed as already noted, but in all cases the side-pillars were a chromium-plated alloy. Inside, the pattern of trim and upholstery remained essentially unchanged, although the transmission hump in the cockpit of the steel car differed in shape to the alloy car's, the raised moulding for the starter motor being absent.

There has been some controversy over the respective weights of the aluminium and steel-bodied XK 120s. Although the originally quoted 'dry' weight of the alloy car was 22 hundred-weight *The Motor's* road test car - admittedly the prototype HKV 455 - weighed in at 25½ cwt ready for the road. When *The Autocar* road tested one of the first steel-bodied XK 120s, they listed its weight as 26 hundredweight - inspite of claiming that in fact the steel-bodied cars were lighter. From this evidence and from my own independent weighings, I conclude that the steel cars were in fact about 1 cwt heavier than the alloy cars. Not really a great enough difference for the early cars to be called light-weights as they are sometimes colloquially termed, but enough to affect the performance of the car (only three XK 120s can - possibly - be referred to as 'lightweight'; see Chapter Four). This difference in weight can be substantiated by examining *The Autocar's* road test figures of JWK 675, the lhd XK 120 tested by the magazine in April 1950; it was the first steel bodied XK 120, chassis no. 670172.

The Autocar ducked out of the expense and time involved in taking the car over to the continent for an accurate recording of the maximum speed, so we can't unfortunately compare the outright top speed of HKV 455 and JWK 675. We can, however, compare their acceleration, and we find that the later car was considerably slower than HKV 455.

In fact, it took some 2 seconds more to achieve 60 mph, and 8 seconds more to reach 100 mph; and while these differences might ordinarily be explained by a less brutal technique on behalf of *The Autocar's* test staff (in those days, *The Motor's* standing start figures were traditionally better), an equally large discrepancy is apparent when the top gear acceleration figures are examined - which don't rely on driver technique. While HKV 455 took 6.7 seconds to reach 40 mph from 20 mph, and 6.6 seconds to reach 50 mph from 30 mph, JWK 675 took 7.5 seconds and 7.8 seconds respectively to cover these same increments. This is rather more than can be explained by the fact that JWK 675 was less well run in than HKV 455, so it must be concluded that the steel-bodied XK 120s were a little slower than their earlier counterparts mainly due to this difference in weight. Both road test cars were fitted with the same (standard) 3.64:1 final drive, and both had 8:1 compression ratio engines; HKV 455's undershield would not influence the top gear figures quoted - indeed, it would at those speeds merely represent extra weight.

But these minor discrepancies apart, JWK 675 was still an exceptionally fast car, and *The Autocar* was as enthusiastic over its performance and behaviour as *The Motor* had been over its road test XK 120. Said the magazine: "there is a temptation to draw from the motoring vocabulary every adjective in the superlative concerning the performance, and to call upon the devices of italics and even the capital letter!" The handling of the car was felt to more than match its speed; the steering being "firm but light...allowing of a quick swerve with complete safety", while the suspension was described as "thoroughly comfortable...yet the XK can be hurled round bends with quickly increasing confidence...extremely fast cornering is achieved with no more than tyre scream and the body leaning over so far and no further."

The Autocar didn't criticise the brakes any more than *The Motor* had done, and in fact it was specifically mentioned that "they did not fade"; likewise the gear change was obviously tolerable by the standards of 1950 (though it was to be progressively less so as time marched on) and while the gear lever was thought to have been positioned a little far back to be ideal, "the movements are quite pleasing."

Of comfort, *The Autocar* thought that the XK 120's elbow room was "adequate", and that the separately adjustable seats gave "suitably upright positions and good support to the shoulders", though short drivers found the steering wheel placed a little high (it was adjustable 'fore-and-aft' but not for rake). Amongst the car's furniture and fittings, the useful attribute of lockable doors was noted (a button type lock like Mk V's was placed near the leather-cord door catch operating strap - as the XK 120 lacked outside door handles altogether, there was of course no key). The headlights may have been improved as the journal rated them good enough for 90 mph driving "on known roads."

Undue thirst for petrol did not come hand in hand with speed in the XK 120 Jaguar. *The Autocar* found that consumption fell between 13 and 17 mpg according to how the car was driven, while *The Motor* recorded an average of 19.8 mpg. If the car had to be driven for economy, the incredibly flexible engine allowed most motoring to be done in top gear, which certainly in the early 1950's still provided a greater degree of acceleration than most family saloons could manage flat out through the gears.

But while the British motoring magazines sampled with delight the new pleasure of XK motoring, few XK 120s found their way onto the home market. True to his promise to the Government, Lyons intended that most XK 120s should be sold abroad; he certainly had no trouble finding buyers - in October 1949 it had been announced that the Hoffman Motor Company, Jaguar's Eastern States distributors, had bought the entire XK 120 production for six months (which meant something over 60% of all the aluminium-bodied cars).

It was in fact the XK 120 which laid the real foundations of Jaguar's export market in the United States, and much time was devoted in those years to signing-up agencies. This was complicated slightly by the fact that no American franchise holder was allowed to sell competitive makes, so most of Jaguar's early American dealerships were very small concerns. But they soon found that Jaguars sold extremely well with the only limiting factor being the number of cars the factory could make, and many expanded to become large and prestigeous organisations. Not only did Jaguar (with MG) open the way into America for British sports cars, but it could also be said that they prepared the ground for all imported cars - and that includes Volkswagen, which in those early years wasn't selling at all well. Sir William recalls the then Jaguar distributor for the East Coast of America insisting that all dealers who ordered a Jaguar took two Volkswagens as well! How to make enough cars has always been a problem at Jaguar, and by 1951 it was once again apparent that to fulfil orders - especially from the States - yet more space would have to be found. So Lyons negotiated for the lease and eventual purchase of the company's present buildings at Browns Lane, Allesley, on the outskirts of Coventry. These were in fact a shadow factory which had been temporarily occupied by Daimler, and Lyons was fortunate in eventually persuading the Government to sell and not lease it as was usually the case. The only condition made was that Jaguar should take up the production of the Rolls Royce Meteor tank engine (a descendant of the Spitfire Merlin engine), which was commenced (well ahead of

schedule) although the contract was actually cancelled after a couple of years - a move which suited Jaguar as it allowed even more energy to be devoted to car production.

Jaguar's attack on the world's markets was spearheaded by their stand at the 1950 New York Show, which was a masterpiece of elegant - not to say opulent - presentation with flowers and small illuminated fountains surrounding a scarlet-draped turntable on which a white XK 120 Roadster revolved, amid a selection of Mk V saloons and dropheads. To emphasise the speed image, HKV 500 had been brought out for the show too.

This type of display was not lost upon the American citizen, Mr and Mrs John R. Ripp at least feeling moved to write to *The Motor* saying that in their humble opinion, "the Jaguar XK 120 is about the most beautiful car we have ever laid eyes on." And in the same year, Englishman Alan Clark writing from America also spelled out exactly how the XK 120 went straight to the average American's heart:

There is, moreover, one English car which stands head and shoulders above the others. Clark Gable has already had three. Another owner once described it to your correspondent as 'the car which rings all the bells'. And so it does...Everything about the Jaguar is just dead right, from the name on. The same price as a Cadillac, it is the ambition of everyone who enjoys Motoring with a capital 'M' to own one. The owner of an XK 120 confided in the writer the opinion that if the company were to cease producing this particular model tomorrow, those that already had been delivered in the States would change hands for as much as 10,000 dollars. Certainly, it is very difficult to see how this car could be improved; except that it would be rather nice to have a long chassis XK put on the market, with wind-up windows and a squab seat behind. It would undoubtedly be oversubscribed at a list price of £2500.

Never complacent, Jaguar were to take full note of comments concerning occasional rear seats, and wind-up windows were just around the corner. By October 1950, more than 2,000 XK 120 Roadsters had been made ('roadster' was the American term for the British designation 'open two seater', and Jaguar themselves adopted it for later Jaguar sports cars); this total was reflected in Jaguar's profit figure when the accounts for 1950 had been completed - it was £311,432, as opposed to £124,577 for 1949.

Road & Track magazine tried an XK 120 roadster for themselves in 1951, obviously eager to see what the magic was. The car's dual character was at once revealed: "The performance alone makes it a man's car in the truest sense, yet its concours design and feminine appeal make it equally attractive to women", while the XK 120's ability to potter around town in top gear was found to be combined with acceleration "far better than will ever be needed in the fiercest stop-light GP." This was of course years before the American horse-power race had culminated in the muscle-cars of the sixties with their 5,6, or 7-litre V8 engines, able to leave virtually any European sports car eating dust in a straight line (doubtful though their ability might sometimes have been to stop for, and get round, the corner at the end!).

Road & Track was especially keen in determining the true top speed of their XK 120, controversy being rife about the actual figure amongst American sports car enthusiasts. Taking pains to point out that their test car was "completely stock, with no engine alterations, under pan or tonneau cover", the magazine reported that a mean maximum speed of 121.6 mph was achieved, with a best one-way run of 123.2 mph. The optional extra aero-screens were used for the high speed runs ("which resulted in both the driver and photographer turning a deep blue in the desert cold"), the decreased wind resistance afforded by the absence of the full windscreen being partly offset by the lack of an undershield, when comparing *Road & Track* figures with *The Motor* (which were 124.6 mph and 126.8 mph for mean and best times respectively).

The American magazine found the XK's suspension "very stiffly sprung" compared to the home saloon car product - as one would expect,

and indeed hope! The testers rated the leather seats comfortable for long journeys, even "luxurious", although the car's luggage accommodation obviously compared poorly with even the smallest American automobile; but then one could order one of the new Mk VII saloons if one wanted to travel with space as well as pace, and the Mk VII had more cubic feet available in its 'trunk' than almost any of the home-brewed colossi.

The acceleration of *Road & Track's* XK 120 was in the main virtually identical to *The Motor's*, with 60 mph coming up in 10.1 seconds, and 100 mph in 27.5 seconds. Fuel consumption varied between 16 and 22 mpg, which tallies fairly well with the British magazine's 19.8 mpg average.

Surprisingly, the XK 120's brake pedal pressures were thought to be "a little too low" by *Road & Track* drivers (one wonders what they would have made then, of the typically over-servoed American car of today!), and although generally behaving well, the brakes did fade slightly "under the most extreme abuse." Significantly too, the engine was inclined to overheat in traffic, a distinct tendency of the XK 120 in hot climates when it wasn't going fast enough to push sufficient air through that stylistically beautiful but rather small radiator grille. On the debit side again, the car's hood was found to be "far from weatherproof." However, *Road & Track* wasn't blinded by these detail deficiencies and summed up by predicting "immediate and lasting success in the US market" for the XK 120, and they weren't wrong of course.

True, the XK 120 - like any car - wasn't perfect, as *Road & Track* found out. A contemporary opinion from another American journal outlines most of the annoyances that were sometimes found:

Its faults, despite being minor, were real and irritating; the factory has remedied some of them, such as overheating (six bladed fan), weak clutch throw-out bearings and timing chain tension springs. Other limitations remain, such as the cramped quarters for tall drivers, awkward steering wheel and horn-button position, ugly makeshift top and visibility-killing side curtains, doors which hit the curb when opened, seats with inadequate thigh supports. Directional indicators are lacking, as is a heating and de-frosting system. For some drivers, the gearshift has an excessively long travel and stiff operation, compared to that of an MG.

Poor dust sealing was another grumble, particularly from owners in hot, dry countries such as Australia, where there was a large market for Jaguars - the original distributor who had handled the cars before the war had been replaced in 1946 by a little firm called Bryson Motors, who had up to that time only represented Morgan and several motorcycle companies but ambitiously offered to contract with Jaguar for 2,000 cars (compared to 100 by the previous firm). They only failed to sell that many because Jaguar could not send them the full contracted amount; a real success story, Bryson soon took over the original distributor's showrooms (described as "the finest in Sydney" by Sir William) and went from strength to strength thereafter.

Naturally, Brysons imported XK 120s, of which some twenty aluminium bodied examples reached Australia and a good many more steel-bodied cars. The former included 660002, the second rhd XK 120 built, which after extensive use by Brysons for advertising purposes was the car offered as an Art Union prize in a competition held early in 1950. It still exists though seemingly semi-derelict, near Nowra, in New South Wales.

However, it was a steel-bodied car that was to achieve by far the greatest fame in the Antipodes - delivered on July 6th 1951, within a month of its purchase it had covered no less than 6,000 miles! Some 965 miles of this total were clocked up during an extraordinary run which took owner Les Taylor and observer Dick Rendle across Australia from Darwin to Alice Springs at the staggering average speed of 91.3 mph. As the 10 hours 32 minutes that this took

included 45 minutes of stops (one of which was to make repairs after hitting a bank), the running average was nearer 98 mph.

The run was carefully planned, and far from being completely straight, the route included almost 1,000 bends and a lot of hill climbing. Fuel consumption for the trip was 11 mpg, and only one quart of oil was used - in fact the level was only checked once, when the car bottomed so heavily that Taylor thought the sump must have been cracked (it wasn't). Both Taylor and ex-RAF pilot Rendle expressed amazement at the way the car stood up to the "terrific buffeting" it received upon hitting the ground, after being airborne for sometimes scores of yards. Three stops were made for petrol, each of about 5 minutes duration and up to 24 gallons of fuel were taken on aboard each time - which means that the car was obviously equipped with the large optional Le Mans petrol tank. The bronze roadster ran with its full windscreen, and the maximum revolutions noted were about 5,300 rpm, and the highest speed shown on the speedometer 135 mph. The last 109 miles were accomplished at no less than 111 mph average, over roads which Taylor had never driven before. The XK 120 drove into Alice Springs in daylight - the first time anyone had left Darwin by road to arrive at Alice during daylight on the same day. It would also seem that Taylor established some sort of unofficial open road world record, the previous best having been put up by Clemente Biondetti with his Ferrari in the course of the 1949 Mille Miglia, when he travelled 971.8 miles at an average speed of 81.53 mph. Not that all this was in any way appreciated by the Justices of the Peace at Alice Springs Police Court - Taylor was charged with dangerous driving, speeding, driving without a Northern Territory licence, and driving a car not registered in the Northern Territory. For this, he was fined a total of £18, with £2 costs!

But there is no doubt that the run made quite an impression at the time, and was a splendid piece of publicity for Jaguar's product. As the *Brisbane Telegraph* pointed out, "No production car of any other country - ie one that can be bought off a showroom floor in the normal way - could approach the XK's speed and stamina over that trying course." And they were of course perfectly right. That was not the last heard of the car either. Almost exactly a month later, on September 2nd, the 35 year old Taylor raced the car at Leyburn and came second to GP winner Whiteford and his Lago Talbot; and after a further racing history in the hands of several other owners, and some fifteen years on an out-back mail run, the car has now been restored by its present owner.

In Great Britain, members of the motoring press were still reporting their experiences with the XK 120 Roadster, William Boddy of *Motor Sport* sampling the car for the first time early in 1951 and devoting two pages in the April edition of that magazine to his impressions. An interesting and valuable appraisal of the car, Boddy's opinion was typical of many who drove the XK 120 in contemporary conditions - initial caution followed by increasing enthusiasm as the at first hidden potential of the car is realised:

First impressions of an unfamiliar fast car are not always the most favourable, and so it was with this XK. The snug hood and side curtains were erect when I took over, and as the reassurances of 'Lofty' England were cut off abruptly as he stood upright I realised that I was alone in the maelstrom of London's rush hour traffic in England's fastest standard car. Naturally no self-respecting motoring journalist wants to loiter in such a vehicle but as I pressed strongly along I was embarrased to discover the great distance my throttle foot had to travel to encounter the brake pedal and a bit put out at the way the Jaguar wallowed and howled its Dun-lops when deflected from the straight ahead - you have to be used to sailing small boats to master this chap, I thought.

At first I felt alarmed at the idea of hurrying along the twisty bits in a car so softly sprung, for the XK 120 is that all right. It gives a most creditably comfortable ride over atrocious roads. The Jaguar also rolls freely and dips its nose if you anchor at all sharply, then 'breasts the waves' as you accelerate. But I realised how well the wheels followed the sur-face contours and later, when I negotiated twisty roads at advanced throttle openings, I was surprised

how correctly geared the Burman-Douglas steering seemed... Indeed the Jaguar 'holds in' splendidly round fast bends and is exceedingly stable on wet roads.

William Boddy became equally enamoured of the XK's engine, its response being "magnifi-cently simulating" and unaffected by long periods of idling in heavy Bayswater traffic. On the open road, it gave the car an almost un-equalled performance:

Even driving the Jaguar as essentially a top-gear car, 90 mph becomes commonplace in between dodging the lorries along any main or secondary road, so great is the accelerative ability. No particular speed can be cited as the cruising speed - rather do you make a series of hawk-like swoops past slower traffic, punctuated by firm applications of the brakes to tuck you safely behind prevailing obstructions. It is all tremendously exhilarating - that is the word! - and accomplished so easily that after hundreds of miles you never even begin to feel blase. The 'quick' steering and this smooth, unending surge of acceleration brings familiar towns and villages quite astonishingly close together...

This suave Jaguar was so enormously quick from one place to another that to plot its true performance seemed somewhat pointless. In any case, it was in absolutely standard trim, with the 7 to 1 compression ratio instead of 8 to 1 and the low 3.64 to 1 axle ratio, and, of course, no undershield. The engine 'pinked' almost inaudibly on 'Pool', started from stone cold instantaneously and ran straight up into 'the red' - well over 5,000 rpm - without the slightest anxiety. It was silk smooth to 4,000 rpm, a bit rough beyond that, vibration travelling up the gear lever at 4,500 rpm and above.

Boddy discovered the failings of the XK 120's drum brakes however - the car tested, KHP 30, had the standard solid steel wheels with spats at the rear, and manifested the usual fade sym-ptoms when pressed:

The 12-inch Lockheed brakes normally do their stuff admirably, too. With only slight pressure and small travel on the pedal (I soon found it wasn't *really* inaccessible) truly powerful, progressive, snag-free retardation is available, without which the XK 120 wouldn't be half the car it is. I write 'normally', because I did come up against rather disconcerting fade. I had braked hard from about 80 mph - one is so seldom *under* 70 or 80 in this car - for a minor crossroads and entered some narrow lanes, which I took at about 50, braking for the incessant corners. All of a sudden I found almost all anchorage had evaporated, just as if I'd wetted the shoes in a water-splash, only I hadn't. The harder I pressed the more negative was the effort, until negotiation of a conjested high-street at 20 mph constituted quite an adventure. By this time you could *smell* how hot the drums and linings were from the cockpit. After I had had lunch, temperatures (and tempers) were normal again and the brakes as good as ever. Now this fading did not occur in really fast main road driving luckily, but I can now sympathise with XK 120 drivers who have slapped the straw during a sports car race or come down an Alp a thought too quickly.

The editor of *Motor Sport* also delved into the XK 120's home comforts, which he found surprisingly civilised for a car of such performance. His views on the efficiency of the hood was not always echoed by owners though:

This is a snug car, too, when hood and side bits are unfurled, absolutely suited to taking the popsie to - well, to the pictures. Open, the big screen gives excellent protection even at 100 mph, at the expense of a bit of a blind spot created by its centre support. Even torrential rain blows clear of the occupants over 40 mph...

Lack of cubby holes is compensated for by excellent flap-covered door pockets, the door 'pulls' and internal locks are nicely done, the doors shut 'expensively', and getting in and out couldn't be easier. The lines of the car are superb, and the hood stows neatly away. Minor grumbles - a draught about my feet, the irritation of speedometer and rev.-counter needles moving in opposite directions and a craving, unsatisfied, for an oil thermometer, direction indicators when the car was enclosed, a fuel range greater than 200 miles (15 gallons - only about five hours running time in an XK), and some means of knowing whether the 'side lamps on' had been selected correctly with the single rotary lamps switch.

A few rattles intruded but the gears are well behaved. Having to unlock a flap before you can refuel has mixed blessings. I was spared a radio and heater, liked very much the fly-off handbrake, and found the headlamps (foot-dipper) penetrating, if a thought 'uppish'. The big luggage locker is useful, too - and in case anyone asks what this has to do with *real* sports cars, let me say that the very rapidity and driving pleasure afforded by such cars make them appropriate for long-distance touring.

The late Laurence Pomeroy also had some sensible comments to make when he wrote in *The Motor* of January 2nd 1952 of his experiences with a borrowed factory car. He considered that it was "pre-eminently an excellent and very high performance touring car", notwithstanding the rather racing-car image which had been built up by that time. He went on to explain why he didn't think the XK 120 was in any way a competition vehicle.

I admit to feeling restrained from flinging this particular car about on ordinary roads by a number of factors not all of which are of a truly technical nature. Even after some long acquaintance one continues to be awed by the length of the bonnet and reminded of the man who said that the worst thing about his dachshund was that when he fed it in the dining room he had to go into the kitchen to see if it was pleased.

Similarly, on the Jaguar I felt that I was placed too far away from the accident and that a moderate change in angle on a bend resulted in very large lateral displacement of the nose of the car. This impression was heightened by the exceedingly low seating position from which one looks along the bonnet instead of looking down on top of it as one used to do on the type 35 Bugatti and, as a further point of criticism, the seats seem unnaturally low in relation to the pedals. For these reasons I found myself taking corners at a much lower speed than was really imposed by the true road-holding powers of the car.

I did not learn how good these really were until I, by accident, arrived on a corner far sharper than it looked and found to my surprise that by turning the wheel fairly sharply the car took me round with little ado. On this occasion, Uhlenhaut was my passenger and said: 'There you are, you see, it really will do it.' Meaning, I suspect, 'why have you been mucking about so long?' Nevertheless I most enjoyed driving this car at between 70 and 90 mph and I needed favourable circumstances to exceed an average of 50 miles in the hour despite acceleration and hill climbing which are truly prodigious.

The luggage accommodation was far greater than I thought at first, but the hood has not been designed to cope with the English climate. If working single-handed, one would get so wet in the time taken to put it up that one might really just as well rely upon natural draught to carry the rain over the top of the screen without stopping the car. With the hood up, backwards visibility is almost nil and this, coupled with the absence of direction indicators, puts London driving into catagory H.

Top left The winning British team including Ian Appleyard's 3½ litre SS 100 after the 1948 Alpine Rally

Top right SS 100s often collected cycle type wings. This is J Forbes Clark's start at the July 1952 Bouley Bay Hill Climb meeting

Centre left 'Old No. 8' turned up once or twice in private hands during the fifties before retirement. The car is shown on familiar ground once more, at Shelsley Walsh in June 1953. Here H A Mecran drives the car equipped with twin rear wheels

Centre right 'Old No. 8' as it is today at an XK Register gathering. The car now has a super-charger for racing

Inset The rear suspension of 'Old No. 9' showing the heavily drilled chassis members and locating arm. The car is shown here under restoration by David Barber in 1970

Bottom Alan Lowe's 3½ litre SS 100 (49034) as it ran in the 1962 Singapore Grand Prix. Its driver states that it was capable of holding E-types on slower circuits

Top left Major Gardner's EX 135 record breaker minus streamlined bodyshell, with the experimental XJ twin oh 1996cc engine installed, prior to its running in Belgium i August 1948. This was the first appearance of the Jaguar twin cam engine. A speed of 176.7mph was recorded ove flying kilometre, from 146 bhp at 6100 rpm - very credi from a 2 litre production-type engine of the period

Top right A close up of the Gardner car's engine, this ti with the body fitted

Centre left and right This well-finished prototype was completed shortly after the war - it points towards the XK 120. The wheelbase was shorter than that of the XK and the engine was probably a 1½ or 2 litre, these being experimented with at the time. The body itself may well have been made outside the works, by a speculative coachbuilder - this happened from time to time although Lyons never actually took-up any designs submitted *(ph Jaguar Cars)*

Bottom The first XK 120 takes shape, its bodywork sections being laid and chocked-up on a chassis for the fi publicity and catalogue pictures *(photo Jaguar Cars)*

Top left and right First showing, October 1948 at Earls Court. This metallic bronze roadster with biscuit upholstery (body number F1001) was the first XK 120 made - note the differences in external trim to later examples. After a re-spray in birch grey and a time as Jaguar's road test demonstrator, the car went to Dunlop for disc brake testing; it was eventually cannabalised by the works for another prototype. Registration number was HKV 455 *(photo The Motor)*

Centre left HKV 455 on road test with *The Motor*. It wasn't particularly elegant with the hood up and early catalogues did not show it in this guise - it did however fold down out of sight! *(photo The Motor)*

Centre right A good study of a new aluminium bodied XK 120 Roadster ready for export. In common with most alloy XKs, the windscreen pillars display big rubber grommets at their base, the only exterior point to distinguish them from a steel bodied car. Note the partially painted wheel trims - later cars had all chrome trims

Bottom XK 120 Roadster interior (HKV 455) showing the simple instrumentation. Note the light coloured steering wheel, fitted to some early cars. A passenger grab handle should be fitted *(photo The Motor)*

Top left An aluminium bodied XK 120 under construction; the alloy panels are being assembled on a wooden 'chassis'. Note the wooden door-shut face and upright engine bulkhead on which the bonnet hinges are fixed - two of the many differences between the alloy and steel bodied XK 120s *(photo The Motor)*

Top right An early supercharger installation on an alloy bodied left hand drive XK 120. This was an impossible installation for right hand drive cars because of the steering column *(photo The Motor)*

Centre Under bonnet view of an early steel bodied XK 120 Roadster. Note the lack of studs at the front of the cam covers *(photo The Autocar)*

Bottom left and inset Unique - this one-off sports car was built on a Standard Flying 12 chassis just before the war by John Black for William Lyons. After the war it was used by John Lyons, disappeared, and then turned up in the United States recently at Preservation Hall, Oklahoma City

Bottom right A steel bodied XK 120 Roadster this time. Photographed whilst on test in 1951 with *The Autocar*, this roadster was apparently later raced by Stirling Moss when converted to right hand drive *(photo The Autocar)*

Top, centre and bottom "Much becoming more"; performance options for the XK 120 became generally available by mid 1951, purchased individually or later as 'Special Equipment' on a new car. They were, left to right, high octane parts kit incorporating higher compression pistons and complimentary ignition and carburettor parts; higher lift camshafts (3/8 inch), with a lightened flywheel and modified damper to meet increased engine speeds; stiffer torsion bars and rear leaf springs; undershield, a less common option that was not standard even on Special Equipment cars; aero screens with aluminium cowl and mirror streamlining cowl

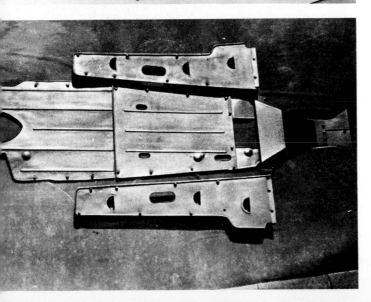

Top left Here is Mr Owen's car with Mlle Janin Vincent who won the *Prix de la plus jolie toilette de jeune fille* (prize for the best teenage frock!) in March 1951 at a Cannes *concours d'elegance*

Top right A period photograph of an early fifties street scene which underlines how great a margin of performance the XK 120 had over most other cars when it first appeared. (MDU 524, driven here by Bob Berry is a mystery car - it could have been the stripped 172 mph roadster which carried the same registration on its journey to Jabbeke. No one is sure) *(photo The Motor)*

Centre The hood stowaway was always neat and out of sight on the XK 120 Roadster. When erected, the space behind the seats allowed more luggage to be carried

Bottom Wire wheels became an option on the XK 120 in 1951 and were an instant success in America, which is where this car was bound

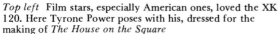

Top left Film stars, especially American ones, loved the XK 120. Here Tyrone Power poses with his, dressed for the making of *The House on the Square*

Top right Special excitement! The result of a Mau Mau sniper's rifle on Sir Anthony Stamer's XK 120 windscreen during the Kenya troubles of 1953/4 *(photo Sir Anthony Stamer)*

Above The XK 120 Fixed-head Coupe, announced in March 1951, was to remain one of the most graceful coupes ever

Centre right Wire wheels became a factory fitted option upon the introduction of the Fixed-head coupe; they greatly improved brake cooling and the car's looks. This is the Special Equipment road test car used by *The Autocar* *(photo The Autocar)*

Bottom Old English quality. The polished walnut interior was after the style of the contemporary Jaguar saloons *(photo The Autocar)*

Top The Jaguar sports car drop-head coupes were extremely civilised cars; this is the XK 120 Drop-head of April 1958. The original classic body lines suffered little in consequence

Centre left The XK 120 Drop-head's hood was smoothly contoured and completely weatherproof. Luggage capacity and spare wheel location remained unaltered from the other models *(photo The Motor)*

Centre right The Belgian coachbuilder Oblin exhibited this successful 'Ferrariesque' coupe on an XK 120 chassis at the 1952 Brussels Motor Show. Unusually for such a car, it had an active rallying career. It still survives today in Belgium *(photo The Motor)*

Bottom Ghia anticipated William Lyon's own Drop-head XK 120 with this rather crude attempt of 1952 *(photo The Motor)*

Top left Carrozzeria Pinin Farina produced this coupe bodywork on an XK 120 chassis *(photo Pinin Farina)*
Top right A Beutler bodied XK 120 Drop-head was displayed at the 1952 Geneva Motor Show - note the familiar windscreen, bumpers, grille and flashers *(photo The Motor)*
Centre Ghia again, this time with a very much happier and more extensive effort. The Paris Show in October 1953 saw this car on display *(photo The Motor)*
Bottom E D Abbott Limited of Farnham built this occasional four-seater on an XK 120 chassis for a New Zealand customer. It was said to have an ash frame panelled in aluminium with a kerb weight of 27cwts 2qrs

Top left Silverstone, August 1949 with the field leaving the start for the XK 120's first race. Sydney Allard makes the best start but the XKs are already after him. Note Cyril Mann's 3½ litre SS 100 just behind them *(photo The Motor)*

Top right A superb study of Leslie Johnson and HKV 500 winning on the occasion of the XK's competition debut *(photo The Autocar)*

Centre left R M V Sutton brings HKV 500 in after its memorable 132mph run at Jabbeke and is surrounded by the assembled Press while a Dunlop engineer has a look at a rear tyre

Centre right Mille Miglia, April 1950; halted at a refuelling station near Rome, JWK 988's steering is closely examined - Wisdom was to retire only a few miles from the finish with a steering fault

Bottom Le Mans 1950 and the three XK 120s begin Jaguar Car's incredibly successful score at Sarthe. Leslie Johnson chats in the foreground while just beyond the furthest XK Duncan Hamilton - future works driver for Jaguar - bends over his Nash-Healey *(photo The Motor)*

Top left The start - Le Mans 1950. JWK 651 is slightly in front of its team mates. The starting area and pit straight look frighteningly narrow to modern eyes *(photo The Autocar)*

Top right Bert Hadley propels JWK 651 through the Esses at Le Mans behind an equally famous British car, intent on keeping up the car's 94mph average *(photo The Motor)*

Centre left The Nick Haines/Peter Clark XK 120 swings through Arnage during the 1950 24 hour Race. It finished 12th after running for many hours without proper braking *(photo The Motor)*

Centre right With no drive left between engine and wheels, JWK 651 coasted to a halt not far short of the pits. Leslie Johnson surveys his stricken car (note the spares carried on the passenger seat - the boot was full of petrol!) *(photo The Motor)*

Bottom Clemente Biondetti, veteran long-distance racing driver, with Sir William Lyons and an early XK 120 (note the straight sided windscreen, a feature of the first few alloy bodied cars); the car is probably his unofficial 'works' car *(photo The Autocar)*

Top left The young Stirling Moss urges JWK 988 round Dundrod's wet and windy road course - only once did he take to an escape road while winning the 1950 TT with ease *(photo The Autocar)*

Top right William Lyons and Tazio Nuvolari, towards the end of the illustrious racing driver's career, pictured on this occasion at the 1950 *Daily Express* meeting at Silverstone. But for illness, Nuvolari would have driven this very early roadster in the Production Car race

Centre left Johnny Claes winning the Production Sports Car race at Spa, Belgium in June 1951. He averaged 81.22 mph. This could possibly be HKV 455 but with Belgian plates

Centre right Liege-Rome-Liege 1951 - HKV 500 re-enters Liege having completed this extremely tough classic event without a loss of marks for the first time in its history; the car was crewed by Johnny Claes and Jacques Ickx. Behind is the 5th place car of Laroche and Radix

Bottom right Herzet and Baudoin achieved second place in the 1951 'Liege' behind HKV 500 in their 'one-off' Oblin bodied XK 120. The XKs also carried off the Team Prize

Pomeroy's thoughts on the XK 120's handling are confirmed to an extent by John Bolster's comment in his track test of Hugh Howorth's car: "The XK 120 will drift a bend in a delightful manner, but it resents being flung about while it is doing so." Not that the XK 120 was, or is, in any way uncontrollable, but it was not as 'chuckable' as some smaller and less powerful sports cars, and some people were rather intimidated by the long bonnet. Its dominant characteristic in road cornering is an initial understeer which can be converted to oversteer on slower corners by the application of the throttle, which results in a progressive tail slide. It has no drastic oversteering properties unless really provoked on the limit.

On the race track, cornering is generally limited by wheelspin unless of course a limited slip differential has been fitted, and although the car doesn't behave badly, a lot of effort is required on the steering wheel to haul the car round long, very fast bends.

For those who wanted their XKs to go faster, Jaguar had by mid-1951 published a Service Bulletin which contained a wide variety of instructions and hints on how to improve the car's performance both in a straight line and round corners. As higher octane fuels were now becoming available, sets of 8:1 and 9:1 pistons were offered, and various distributors could be ordered for varying stages of engine tune, and different jets for the two SU carburettors. More significantly, a new camshaft was catalogued which gave a lift of 3/8 inch lift to both inlet and exhaust valves (compared to the standard cam's 5/16 lift); although this didn't mean that engine timing had to be altered, it was necessary to shorten the valve and tappet guides to provide the extra clearances needed with the new cam.

For the first time too came a dual exhaust system, together with a 'competition' straight-through silencer (made by Burgess) which changed the original, slightly subdued, exhaust note into that beautiful, full-throated Jaguar howl at higher rpm for which the XK 120 is so

nostalgically remembered. The assembly was also worth 8 bhp, and in conjunction with the high-lift camshafts, raised the useful maximum rpm of the engine from 5,400 to 5,800 rpm. With 8:1 pistons as well, the engine was then rated at 181 bhp (standard, the output was 160 bhp on an 8:1 c.r.). A crankshaft damper more suited to higher rpm was recommended, plus a lighter flywheel for a quicker pick-up from low rpm, while the optional 'solid centre' clutch was very definitely a lesson learned from Le Mans 1950! This event also produced the optional 24 gallon fuel tank.

Other recommendations were that the thermostat should be discarded from the cooling system, and that the starting carburetter should be converted to manual operation - this anyway was a common modification amongst owners, who found that the instrument went on supplying a rich mixture rather longer than was necessary after a cold start. It was also advised that the automatic advance/retard vacuum pipe should be blanked off.

As for cornering, the car's inclination to roll a bit and dip its front end near the limit was countered by the introduction of optional stiffer front torsion bars (up in thickness by 1/16 inch) and rear springs (now 7-leaf) which gave a 20% increase in roll stiffness. Little was offered by the factory to improve braking however, except thicker linings and the advice that owners might fit air-scoops to the rear brakes, and remove the rear wheel spats and wheel trims - XKs racing in the early days actually ran with these on! Alternative axle ratios available for the ENV rear axle were 3.27, 3.64 (standard), 3.92 and 4.30:1, which gave theoretical road speeds, in top gear at 5,800 rpm, of 145 mph, 139 mph, 121 mph and 112 mph respectively. Small 'Brooklands' type racing screens, with single screw adjustment for rake and streamlined by aluminium cowls (which were also available for the mirror), lightweight bucket seats (in leather or Bedford cord), undershield and metal tonneau cover were all optional extras - mainly for racing purposes of course.

Wire wheels were at last made an option too in 1951. Already in the United States a Borrani conversion had been available, distributed by Alec Ulmann, but some two years had elapsed before the factory offered them. When they arrived, the rim size and diameter were the same as the original steel disc wheels, at 5 inches and 16 inches respectively, and were of 54-spoke construction. When fitted to cars leaving the factory, the rear spats were omitted as the knock-off hub-spinners would otherwise have fouled them. As for the disc wheeled cars, they were eventually given the same rim width as the Mk VII saloon, at 5½ inches - the wire wheels always remained at 5K. These 5½ inch rim wheels were also stronger than the original steel wheels, racing having disclosed that these could crack around the centres.

No full road test was ever carried out on an XK 120 Roadster equipped with the factory's Special Equipment performance options, but fortunately *Motor Racing* did take figures on one such car which gives us an approximate idea of how the roadster accelerated in that trim. The car in question is in itself a little mysterious, as it carried the registration number MDU 524. *Motor Racing* stated that it was the car used for the 141 mph production sports car run that Jaguar carried out in 1953, and which afterwards was prepared for Tommy Wisdom to use in the 1953 Alpine Rally. Due to illness Wisdom did not in fact run the car, and it was subsequently sold by the factory, although the Dutch driver Gatsonides used an XK 120 so registered in at least one rally. But not only did the 141 mph XK 120 carry the registration MDU 524, but so also did the Roadster that achieved the speed of 172 mph at Jabbeke on a different occasion, in October 1953 (see Chapter Four). Thus *Motor Racing* may have been trying an altogether more famous car than it imagined! When assessing the performance figures, it must be taken into account that MDU 524 was fitted at that time with a C-type head too (optional by 1954), and a 3.77 axle ratio. As

printed, the figures were as follows:

0 – 30 mph	2.8 secs
0 – 50 mph	6.2 secs
0 – 60 mph	7.0 secs
0 – 70 mph	10.3 secs

However, the 0 - 60 mph time should almost certainly be 8 seconds, as the car could hardly take .8 seconds to reach 60 mph from 50 mph, and 3.3 seconds to achieve 70 mph from 60 mph. As for handling, the magazine found that the stiffer springing made the car delightful on twisting roads, even in the wet. In its 'rally' trim, MDU 524 also had twin petrol tanks, a light alloy radiator, and a Mk VII water pump.

Returning to 1951, that year saw the introduction of the XK 120 Fixed-head Coupe. Almost as soon as the XK 120 Open Two-seater was put into serious production suggestions had been made outside the factory that Jaguar ought to build a closed coupe on the XK chassis. In fact, Joe Lowrey's description of the sort of XK he would like to see, written back in June 1949, provides a very accurate description of the XK 120 Fixed-head Coupe as it eventually appeared almost two years later. He had envisaged a car which "would cause the not-so-old executive to sack his chauffeur, sell the limousine and take a new interest in different branches of his business; a car which would carry the driver, his brief case and an occasional passenger around the country at unprintable average speeds. Yes, for once I will mention names, because the Jaguar XK 120 chassis should provide quite enough refinement to carry a well-faired 2-seater fixed-head coupe bodywork." If one were told that William Lyons had taken this paragraph and used it as his brief for the XK 120 Fixed-head, then one would entirely believe it!

Seen for the first time at the Geneva Motor Show in March 1951, the car was immediately recognised as another inspired Lyons design, and indeed the metallic silver example on display with its red leather upholstery was a beautiful sight to behold. Some people in fact believe that the XK 120 Fixed-head was unquestionably the best proportioned Jaguar of the fifties. The coupe top was strongly reminiscent of the Mk VII's roof line, and the car also carried the same curved side windows of the big saloon, all beautifully merged with the XK line to present a perfectly balanced end result.

There had previously been a number of 'private' attempts to produce a fixed-head XK 120, based on the ordinary roadster, particularly in Switzerland where coachbuilders came up with a number of 'one-off' designs. Some of these were quite nicely executed with wind-up windows and so forth but they were mostly rather inelegant when compared with the real thing. These privately commissioned fixed-heads should not be confused with the various proprietary detachable hard tops offered by firms in this country and elsewhere, for fitting to the roadster; they included coachbuilt aluminium examples, one of which came complete with a curved one-piece windscreen, and various glass fibre types such as the rather ugly Universal Laminates one which cost £78 in 1952. The factory itself never catalogued a hard top.

The new fixed-head had a marked resemblance in general line to the 1938 Motor Show Jaguar SS 100 3½ litre Fixed-head Coupe, but unlike its one-off ancestor the XK 120 variant was eminently practical - although coincidentally one of few criticisms offered by *The Autocar* in the course of its October 1952 road test concerned the driving position and pedals, a tall driver (according to the magazine) finding it hard to adopt an "ideal" position whatever that was. But the car avoided the claustrophobic sensation induced by some two seater closed coupes by virtue of its comparatively large window area, the positioning of the dashboard and facia away from the occupants at the base of the windscreen, and the very adequate headroom - inspite of the new roof line being only 1 inch higher than the XK 120 roadster with its hood up.

Wisely, according to *The Motor,* Jaguar "made no attempt to alter the character of the car by either three-abreast seating or occasional rear seats": instead, behind the seat squabs was a ledge on which impedimenta could be placed during a journey (contained on the prototype by a rail that looked as though it had come from a hearse!), and which had a hinged lid covering a fairly shallow locker. When the seat backs were tilted forward, this whole *ensemble* could be swung down for access to the twin six-volt batteries underneath.

Interior trimming followed the Jaguar saloon car pattern closely, with facia and door cappings of figured walnut, and the instruments themselves set into the centre veneered panel were similar in type and layout to the roadster's. A heater was fitted as standard, and both the quarter lights on the doors and the curved rear side windows could be opened - the latter exerting a useful extractor effect. A welcome addition, especially for owners in the hotter parts of the world, were small foot-well ventilators let in to the side of the wings in front of the doors, which could be opened from inside the car. These were also introduced on the roadster from that date (from chassis numbers 660675 and 671097) - though already quite a number of cars had acquired various holes and flaps installed by private owners in attempts to introduce cool air to the footwell, particularly in the United States. The fixed-head was also given wider doors (31½ inch aperture) than the roadster, for ease of access; the main side windows also dropped down at an angle into the doors, giving the XK 120 Fixed-head its characteristic sloping pillar look when viewed from the side.

Neat internal touches included a small cubby hole on the passenger's side of the facia, two sun visors of transparent tinted material (the roadster carried no such protection from the sun), and two interior lights recessed into the rear quarters. All the major controls remained exactly as for the roadster model.

The XK 120 Fixed-head didn't lose out very much on performance compared to the roadster, particularly in Special Equipment form which was soon announced as an alternative to the standard 160 bhp, disc-wheeled car. Incorporating the 3/8 inch lift camshafts, the dual exhaust system, and an 8:1 compression ratio, the 180 bhp developed by its engine propelled *The Autocar's* road test example to 120 mph. The magic 'ton' was reached in 28.2 seconds, and 60 mph in 9.9 seconds from rest. The standing ¼-mile was covered in 17.3 seconds. Weight had gone up though, as was to be expected, and the fixed-head turned the scales at 27 hundredweight kerb.

The Autocar found the fixed-head XK 120 to be a superb long distance tourer - almost a Grand Tourer in the original sense of the term - with a great feeling of lasting reliability:

> The outstanding impression after having driven this car for more than 2,000 miles is the way it goes, and keeps on going. Even after a high-speed Continental journey, and also a complete road test on a Belgian motor road, the car had no feeling of tiredness, nor was there any noticeable falling off in its sprightliness.

The car under test had the latest self-adjusting front brakes; these had appeared for the first time on a Jaguar with the advent of the C-type in June 1951, and were a great improvement on the former manually adjusted 'micram' brakes. A screw-driver was still needed to adjust the rear brakes, but at the front, brake shoe wear and drum expansion was now automatically taken up as wear developed (the working of the system is described in Chapter Five), which meant the end of an inordinately long pedal movement after a few miles of fast motoring. The basic two leading shoe system remained the same in most other respects however, although later cars weren't fitted with the air scoops on the front brake back plates that were a feature of the early micram-adjuster XK 120s - these had been found to be just as efficient at inducting water as cool air, which was inclined to lead to embarrassment if the car had to be stopped quickly after passing through a puddle! The only other change was the adoption of a tandem master cylinder (complete with twin supply tank) which provided a measure of 'fail safe' in its operation, one piston pushing on the other inside the cylinder.

The new self-adjusting brakes, and perhaps even more so the wire wheels, that were fitted to *The Autocar's* fixed-head XK 120, made the magazine's praise of the car's braking equipment sound much more convincing than before. Besides needing no adjustment at all throughout the test, the free pedal travel didn't increase and nor was "noticeable fade" encountered at any stage. Remarking that the "average speed for the journey depends entirely on road conditions and the ability of the driver", the tester also went on to record that Alpine passes did not intimidate the coupe which "is completely at home and responds to every wish of the driver", and that there are "very few cars indeed that can pass an XK coupe that is really in a hurry." Light and positive steering helped to achieve this, together with what was thought to be the right amount of understeer.

On Belgian pave however the car's ride was obviously hard unless the normal low speed tyre pressures were used, and road noise was quite severe on some surfaces - underlining the huge progress which had been made in this sphere since 1951; especially by Jaguar themselves who are leaders in the art of insulating occupants from the road.

For an American opinion on the new car, we can turn to *Auto Sport* magazine who not long after *The Autocar* had finished writing about theirs, tried a similar Special Equipment model - "a conservative little number painted a sort of Gantron red, with white sidewall tyres." Most of *Auto Sport's* testing was carried out in unusually wet weather, but this only served to emphasize the civilised aspects of the new Jaguar, namely "the wind-up windows, adequate heating, panoramic visibility to the rear..." Though one would hardly term the view through the coupe's rear window 'panoramic' today, even if it did happen to be larger than the pillar-box slit in the back of the roadster's hood. There was still complaint about draughts though - from the side ventilators which obviously weren't closing properly, and from the brake and clutch pedal grommets. The clutch itself was described as firm but soft, "though it still has that dreadfully long stroke characteristic of Jaguars."

With its up-rated torsion bars, the coupe was thought to roll less than the earlier XK 120s, and its front wheels hold the road better during high speed cornering, without any sacrifice in ride quality. The straight line performance was rated highly and the total absence of unwanted side effects (no flat spots, spitting back or lumpy tickover) in the 180 bhp 'M' package - the North American designation for Special Equipment - was much appreciated by the magazine's testers. The car's actual acceleration times were slightly down on *The Autocar's* figures, but nonetheless still very good - 0 - 60 mph in 10.4 seconds, standing ¼-mile in 17.5 seconds. The top speed was 120.2 mph. Showery weather which produced a little more wheelspin than was needed probably took the edge off the acceleration figures.

The *Auto Sport* writer certainly liked the new twin-pipe exhaust note - "an utterly distinctive sound - hard, taut, competent; the voice of a really potent high performance sports car" - and it undoubtedly helped to sell the car in the States, even though it was inclined to get the driver tickets from the traffic police.

The car's wire wheels were immediately credited for the notable absence of fade under heavy braking - even "despite some 15 minutes of continuous hard use on a fast-dropping mountain grade." In all, the new fixed-head coupe represented good value at 4460 dollars for the 'M' version, which was 395 dollars more than the standard variety with its 160 bhp engine, disc wheels, and spats. The poor mother country took second place in the queue for the new Jaguar as usual, and at first the fixed-head was only given a basic price (ie without Purchase Tax) of £1,255. By 1953, when it was more generally available, it was listed at £1,775 inclusive of PT, or the same as the roadster;

though both were reduced by some £100 in 1954 with a relaxation of PT by the Government.

The XK 120 Fixed-head quickly became an established favourite and certainly opened the range of Jaguar sports cars to another sector of the market, one which didn't revel in the joys of open-air motoring quite so much as the open car devotee. But in April 1953, Lyons produced something which suited both tastes - the XK 120 Drop-head Coupe.

The announcement of the drop-head came almost exactly two years after the marketing of the fixed-head, and the latest variant on the XK 120 chassis had a similar elegance of line. The convertible soft-top was beautifully executed, and when erected its smoothly contoured shape gave the car an almost saloon car look. From the wing line down, the body shape otherwise remained pure XK 120.

One of the especial delights of the Jaguar two-seater drop-heads, of which the XK 120 was the first factory example, was the ease and simplicity of the hood movements; raising or lowering it was a one man operation that could be carried out in seconds without moving from the driving seat. The head was attached to the (non-detachable) screen rail by three chromium plated 'over centre' toggle catches, and releasing these allowed the top to be swung down in one movement, into its open position behind the driver, the wood-capped cant rails parting and folding themselves neatly and the hood material likewise finding its own folds. Only if one wanted to position the hood envelope over the closed top was it necessary to leave one's seat. Two hooks held the hood down, preventing the wind catching it. Should the skies cloud, then it was an equally swift operation to re-erect the top - in fact, the whole arrangement is one that could well be copied with advantage by latter-day designers of such things.

Inside the car, with the head in its 'up' position, it was difficult to tell that one was indeed sitting in a convertible. The exterior of the head was in mohair, and the interior had a

proper headlining (sandwiching a third layer of padding) which even incorporated a courtesy light. The rear window of the hood, which was of a reasonable size measuring 25 inches by 5 inches, could be unzipped for very effective extractor type ventilation in hot weather. Like the fixed-head coupe the drop-head XK 120 had wide doors (in aluminium) with fully winding down windows, plated metal frames and quarter-lights. Trimming inside was again similar to the fixed-head's, walnut veneer being used on the dashboard, door cappings and cant rails. Instrumentation also followed the fixed-head's, and behind the seats the same arrangements for the battery boxes prevailed.

The XK 120 Drop-head Coupe's chassis was identical to that used hitherto, except that with the coming of the XK 120 Drop-head, the Salisbury axle replaced the previous ENV. Most rhd fixed-heads had already left the factory with Salisbury axles in fact, and the roadsters were to follow suit. The Salisbury ratio fitted as standard was not an exact equivalent of the ENVs, being 3.54:1 as opposed to the former 3.64:1, but there was really little practical difference. Gearing in the intermediates was now 11.95, 7.01, 4.85 and of course 3.54 for the direct top gear. Alternative final drive ratios in the Salisbury range included 4.09, 3.77, 3.31 and 3.27.

The year 1953 also saw the introduction of close ratio gears for the XK 120, an option mainly aimed at racing owners. The alternative constant mesh gears provided closer intermediate ratios - compared to the standard ratios of 3.375, 1.982, and 1.367 (direct), the close ratio set were 2.98, 1.74 and 1.21 (direct). Only the 'JH' or 'JL' gearboxes could be thus modified, having a one-piece input shaft.

As a standard model, Jaguar supplied the XK 120 Drop-head with the 160 bhp engine and 'spatted' disc wheels, but a Special Equipment model was also available for those who wanted the extra urge, noise and the 'wire wheel' look.

John Bolster tried an XK 120 Drop-head in May 1954, for *Autosport,* a basic disc-wheeled example but sporting white-wall tyres - an unusual feature on a non-export car. The performance appeared to be unusually good for a 160 bhp-engined XK, as it out-accelerated the slightly lighter (by about ½ hundredweight) 180 bhp Special Equipment fixed-head tried by *The Autocar* up to 80 mph, and lagged behind after that speed by only a couple of seconds. Its top speed of 119.5 mph was just 1 mph slower than the closed car, although fuel consumption was no better than 14.5 mpg overall, compared with 16.2 mpg recorded by *The Autocar.*

Bolster liked the drop-head:

> A long run in this car is a pleasure that is difficult to put into words. Whether it is its complete indifference to all kinds of road surface, its silence and smoothness, or the feeling of always having more power in reserve, I know not. Suffice it to say that the miles melt away without the slightest effort, and one never makes oneself conspicuous by sounding like a racer.

Cruising was rated as "effortless", 100 mph needing only half-throttle, and even at an indicated 126 mph (120 mph true) the engine remained "quiet and smooth." That the old flexibility was still there was proved by the car's ability to move off from rest in top gear, when Bolster inadvertantly started in top instead of first! Heel and toe manoeuvres were not easy though when it came to sportier driving, and Bolster thought that the steering column was too close to the legs when heavy clothing was being worn.

When he praised the lack of wind noise with the hood erected, Bolster did make the point that the "rear quarters are somewhat blind." This was rather in the manner of a huge understatement, for to emerge from an angled side-turning requires the driver of an XK drop-head to perform all sorts of peculiar contortions in order to look through the passenger's window and see if he's about to be hit by something. But at least the battle against the elements had largely been won, as the hood let in no rain whatsoever during the test, even in the severest conditions.

So far as handling went, John Bolster said in effect that the car rolled too much; or, "corners can be 'drifted', but slightly harder suspension settings would be better for such manoeuvres." And of course, these could be obtained by ordering the Special Equipment version. The brakes were deemed "adequate" for normal use, although Bolster found that they became "very hot when applied hard and repeatedly at three-figure speeds." Generally, however, the car's behaviour remained "utterly controllable on the corners, even when driven to its limit", and that included a thunderstorm racked visit to the Silverstone Club circuit. Even the clap-hands windscreen wipers - inclined to be regarded as a bit of a joke by today's standards - "assured", according to Bolster, "100% visibility"; though one wonders if that '100%' extended to the rather large wedge shaped patch left unwiped at the centre of the divided windscreen. The price of the XK 120 Drop-head Coupe as tested by Bolster was £1,616 2s 6d; and, said Bolster, "how this advanced, twin-overhead camshaft luxury car can undersell smaller push-rod engined machines, only Mr Lyons can say."

Not a great many XK 120 Drop-head Coupes were made and, the last variation to be offered by the factory on the XK 120 chassis, they remain the rarest of the breed. Some 1760 units were built, compared with 2 700 fixed-head and 7600 roadster XK 120s.

Naturally a good proportion of the drop-heads went to North America, where one example was tested by *Popular Mechanics* in January 1955 - or just about the time the model was becoming obsolete, the XK 140 having been announced in October 1954. The Chicago-based *Popular Mechanics* had a unique method of conducting road tests, one half consisting of an appraisal of the car by Floyd Clymer (who incidentally took a particular interest in British automotive machinery and was an overseas member of the Guild of Motoring Writers), and the other a nation-wide survey of owners' opinions, some of which were quoted verbatim but which were in the main used for a statistical analysis of the car's behaviour in service conditions. Thus we have a highly interesting insight into exactly what the average American owner thought of his XK 120 (the survey covered all models).

In the straightforward road test section of the report, Floyd Clymer came to the same conclusions over the XK 120 Drop-head as his European colleagues, with handling, flexibility (except for "a lot of necessary gear shifting in city traffic and on hills"), direct steering and performance all receiving praise. The brakes on this particular wire-wheeled car were thought to be "definitely improved" over earlier models though requiring a pedal pressure "harder than is necessary for braking most American cars." Clymer thought that the 4½ inches through which the foot had to be lifted from throttle pedal to brake pedal "too much."

Another well-known gripe showed through - the inadequacy of the XK 120's bumpers, which did nothing to stave off attacks by the parking efforts of the home product. As for the car's interior furniture, the seats were thought rigid and without much springing by American standards, and the wooden dashboard - even in 1955 - looked "expensive but old fashioned."

As for the owners' portion of the report, the various individual quotations were often apt, and to our ears amusing ("An almost instantaneous response to steering. A fine motor car for the money... *New York Embalmer*"), though it is the statistical survey that is the most useful when trying to define what the American XK owner's real opinion of his car was.

The XK 120's handling, roadholding, steering and acceleration were all rated as 'excellent' by an overwhelming 82% or more of owners, while 87% thought the car's styling 'excellent', and 89% put the engine in the top catagory too. Of roadster owners though, a large proportion - 73% - reported rain leaks ("After the first hot, rainy day with the side curtains up I was ready to sell the car" said one New York executive), and 51% considered that the roadster hood was also difficult to put up. The car's brakes seemed to pass muster, only 6% putting them in the 'poor' catagory, 27% rating them as 'good' and 67% as 'excellent.'

Only 50% thought that the ride was 'excellent', but none actually rated it poor, the 'good' classification capturing the other 50%. In view of the softly sprung nature of the American saloon this was a pleasing result for Jaguar. The gearbox was even put into the 'excellent' slot by 70% of owners, but what is perhaps even more surprising, only 4% would have preferred automatic transmission - which by 1955 had become optional on the Mk VII saloon but not as yet on any of the Jaguar sports cars.

It was Jaguar's dealer service that alas received the largest brickbats - inspite of strenuous efforts by the factory, servicing and spares supplies were a definite weak link in the American dealership chain at that time. The biggest 'poor' rating of all was in fact reserved for the dealer service - 29%. Dissatisfied Jaguar owners expressed themselves with vigor on this point: "I have had trouble with my dealer. It seems to me he has dollar signs in his eyes" said one. But to be fair, 54% thought that the dealer service deserved either an 'excellent' or 'good' rating, which probably compared well with any imported car. Needless to say, such an important facet of overseas business was never neglected by Jaguar, and constant improvement was the theme over the years - resulting in today's vastly more efficient service backed by British Leyland resources.

Besides the thorny question of the dealers, the most frequent complaints about the XK 120 were: water and dust leaks, 14% (this pertaining almost exclusively to the roadster - the drop-head coupe rarely gave trouble in this direction); spark-plug fouling, 9%; brakes pulling when wet, 8%; overheating in traffic, 8%. But 21% of the Jaguar owners quizzed by *Popular Mechanics* said that they had had absolutely no trouble with their XKs, and no less than 81% stated that they would buy another Jaguar, which in the final analysis is what really tells.

The XK 120 was certainly a tough car, and it could be said that some of the trouble afflicting early models in the States were attributable to both unsympathetic drivers and unknowledgeable garage mechanics - the former having bought the car rather as a play-thing, neglected maintainance, and being used to automatic transmission, were also inclined to disregard the gearbox; while the latter were more used to working on the simple American V8s of the period than the comparative complexities of Jaguar's twin cam unit. But both in the States and at home, mileages in excess of 100,000 were quite common from engines untouched except, perhaps, for the odd de-coke or top timing chain replacement - or maybe neither.

Such reliability was an especially valued asset when the car was used in really out of the way places and so was its speed! For example, the aluminium-bodied XK 120 that Ferguson had used in the Johore Grand Prix of Malaya in 1951 was bought by a Col T H Trevor in 1952, who used it during the Malayan war to visit outposts in enemy held territory - it was fast enough to depart before the enemy could react, and low enough to pass under the wire barricade used in those times. A large, non-standard exhaust silencer was fitted to the car, for obvious reasons, but says Col Trevor, "it was also so much admired that no-one had the heart to shoot it up, and at the time it did have two 'extras' - two Thompson sub-machine guns - which may have helped!"

The XK 120 did indeed survive unscathed, and returned to Europe where the Colonel used it while serving as a NATO advisor to the Portuguese Army, during which time "it was much admired and added to British prestige especially when I drove it in full ceremonial uniform on State occasions." Happily 660025 (originally registered JRW 828, now 97 DLA) is now being restored by its present owner Ken Dalziel.

A similar anecdote can be told about another XK 120 on active service. Sir Anthony Stamer also used his XK 120 Roadster in a similarly far-flung corner of the (then) British Empire, Kenya, and on one occasion had a considerably closer shave than obviously had Col Trevor - the XK was actually hit by gunfire! It happened when Sir Anthony and the XK 120 were heading back home to Nairobi on one of the few tarred roads in Kenya; suddenly Stamer received a lapful of powered glass, and the XK a hole in its windscreen. His first thought was that a stone had been thrown up by the wheels but when he saw the size of the hole he realised it had been a bullet, fired from a coffee plantation up on a bank to the right.

"I grabbed my .45 revolver (without which one never moved in those days), but could see nothing moving amongst the coffee bushes in the dark, whereas I was a perfect target in a fully lit XK 120, so I decided it was wisest to push off as rapidly as possible."

Fortunately Stamer had dropped his fiancee off at her flat in Nairobi some ten minutes before, otherwise she might well have been a victim of the Mau Mau terrorist. This XK 120 was, incidentally, first owned by Mrs Mary Wright, who used to race it at the Kenyan circuit Langa Langa near Nakuru.

Sir Anthony's other memories of the car accurately reflect the experiences of XK 120 owners in tropical countries so it's worth quoting the following:

In that wonderful climate it gave me great enjoyment, including several trips down to the coast at Mombasa and Malindi, but the small ground clearance was a limiting factor on the earth-and-rock road surfaces. I knocked the petrol tank adrift on many occasions and became adept at plugging holes temporarily with soap to get me home. The big snag was the dust from the red murram roads. Inspite of sealing the floorboards with adhesive tape, the dust just poured in, while every passing vehicle covered one in it. A cap and usually goggles were very necessary, but one always arrived at one's destination covered with a thick red layer of dust - a bit antisocial at parties where evening dress was normal in those days!

One adventurous soul in another continent discovered the XK 120 Roadster's tendency to accumulate dust an even harder way - he decided, when his new XK 120 arrived from England complete with wire wheels and C-type head, to cross the Andes with it; to, as he put it, "once and for all, debunk the old, very firmly entrenched theory that the Andean chain could be climbed only by American jobs of vast litreage, with substantial modifications to brakes, cooling systems, pumps and the like."

The trip, the worst of which was the 160 miles across the mountains from Mendoza in Argentina to Santiago in Chile, was accomplished almost without incident, the XK 120 surviving hordes of insects, torrential rain, poor petrol and an unnerving tunnel crossing on railway lines, with magnificent disdain. The only item to be attended to afterwards was a loose tie rod- which as the driver Lucio Bollaert said, was "surely a good advertisement for Coventry!" Bollaert was obviously an XK 120 enthusiast, having taken delivery of a very early car a few years before, the 22nd lhd roadster off the line, despatched from Coventry in November 1949.

At home in England, XK 120 owners amused themselves with less adventurous but little less extraordinary exploits - like the crew of an XK 120 who competed in the Cheltenham M C Economy Contest of June 1954. The XK averaged a staggering 58.7 mpg, and covered 578 miles without any intermediate refuelling! The rules of the event were much less strict than the national economy event of today, but even if the car's air filters were removed and a radiator shutter blind installed, the figure still remains an astonishing one.

But in the main, the XK 120 - in all its three forms - provided safe, reliable every-day motoring for thousands of owners, and even towards the end of its production in 1954, was still one of the fastest cars on the roads. A popular and successful choice for concours d'elegance competitions, the XK 120 could still show its teeth in more serious forms of motor sport and often was bought for regular transportation during the week, and for club racing at the weekend. Even when the XK 140, and later the XK 150, replaced the car on Jaguar's production lines, there were still some who preferred the greater agility of the earlier car, or its uncluttered lines, to the heavier and rather more adorned and protected shapes of its successors.

Like most obsolete cars, the XK 120 suffered the usual decline on the second-hand car market and although it always retained a nucleus of enthusiasts, many later owners of the type were not especially careful with their passing acquisition - it was just another old sports car, to be discarded if it looked like going wrong, or if something more 'crumpet-catching' turned up. Prices probably sank to an all-time low around 1965 - 1968, when the later XK 150 and even E-type sports cars were on the second-hand used car lot in relative abundance. It was then quite possible to pick up the very best XK 120 for something like £300 - £400, and sound examples for £150 or so. But prices were on the turn by 1969, and have risen rapidly since as the XK 120 fell prey to the investor's market - it was probably about the first 1950's road car to do so, following the rocketing value of Vintage cars putting them outside the range of most collectors (or even more so, many genuine enthusiasts). A graph published in the May 1974 *XK Bulletin* showed the increase in asking prices for *all* XKs to have risen from an average of approximately £400 in 1968, to £1,500 in December 1973, using *Motor Sport* advertisements as a guide. Individual 'concours' XK 120s during 1974 were being advertised at £2,000 or more.

It is not the purpose of this book to justify such prices for XK 120s, but the car does have much to recommend it for the enthusiast. Even though the XK 120 Roadster is by far the most numerous of all XKs (not just 120s), some 7,600 units having been made, it is in by far the greatest demand - understandably perhaps as it was the first of a unique line of sports cars, and represented a milestone in sports car building altogether; there is also something of the primitive in its lines that still speaks of purposeful speed and power. Of the aluminium-bodied roadsters, the XK Register lists some 20

cars in Great Britain but a considerable number (which may run into three figures) have survived in the States including one example stored virtually from new, and which at the time of writing had covered less than 1,000 miles!; naturally few change hands so it is difficult to estimate their value, except to say that it is maybe 30% to 50% greater than a steel-bodied roadster in similar condition. Obviously their state of preservation depends on where and how they have lived, but the quite thick aluminium outer panels wore well though were susceptible to accident damage of course - it is fairly rare to find one with a completely straight wing line unless it has been properly rebuilt. The wooden frame carrying the rear half of the bodywork was prone to de-lamination under damp storage conditions, but generally the car's very simple construction, with its absence of hollow-thickness steel parts, has stood the test of time well. There were few weak spots in the body-work which were prone to cracking, but corrosion - due mainly to electrolytic action between the aluminium outer and steel inner panels - does occur in the form of bubbles under the paintwork at a few points. Also, if the (steel) inner wings have been removed, stones thrown up by the wheels may have pimpled the aluminium wings.

Naturally a great many more steel-bodied XK 120 Roadsters are extent although they still cannot be called common, and drop-head and fixed-head coupe variants are also to be seen in reasonable numbers. Again, a lot more survive in the States than here, due both to the fact that most went there in the first place, and that the climate in the States has been kinder to them. For rust was an enemy of the steel-bodied cars (in all their forms), much aggravated in Great Britain by local authorities' use of salt for de-icing the roads. The XK's mild-steel box-section sills created an ideal environment for corrosion, and in the manner of the majority of car manufacturers of the fifties, other prestige makes not excepted, Jaguar did very little to protect these internal sections; although it is noted that later

XKs did at least have the spray gun poked into what holes there were, during painting at the factory.

Even quite low mileage cars are usually found to suffer from at least some rusting of the sills, the door-shut areas, and around the side ventilators and leaded-in sidelight housings (where these last two are fitted on later models). It is not always appreciated that the XK's sills, which run under the door, have a very important function - that of literally holding the front and rear halves of the bodywork together, and supporting the floor. Badly corroded sills are a frequent cause of rattling bodywork, although the doors can contribute their quota of noise due to wearing of the hinges - which are almost impossible to lubricate properly, and are a nightmare to replace! The spare wheel well was also subject to rusting, and so was the little box underneath the fuel filler flap, especially if owners neglected to keep the rather small drain hole clear of debris - this could also be a cause of water in the petrol and a resulting mysterious misfire. Chassis corrosion, at least of a serious nature, is fortunately rare although sometimes the members which arch over the rear axle are affected.

On the mechanical side, and this of course includes the aluminium XK 120s (which were virtually identical in this respect), the cars faired rather better with the XK engine usually surviving high mileages and a reasonable amount of abuse. Few early XK 120s still possess their original small-valve cylinder heads however, as corrosion of the water passages took its toll - this could occur on later heads too, over an extended period of time. In any case there is little problem in rebuilding an XK mechanically due to the abundant interchangeability of Jaguar parts which enables spares to be obtained from the saloon car range. Ball joints and certain steering parts are gradually becoming scarce though, and it is likely that Jaguar clubs will eventually have to consider getting such parts especially made.

Similarly, new body parts are virtually un- obtainable from the factory (as one would expect from a car some twenty years out of production) but one or two specialist firms are now manufacturing steel body parts for all XKs, to original specification. It is in the region of the chrome-plated trim that a real scarcity exists at present, with good XK 120 grilles for example fetching something over £50! Bumpers and windscreens are also rather difficult to obtain now, although at least one firm does a good trade in exact-replica bonnet badges.

In recent years, the number of XK 120s seen in every-day use has declined sharply; few if any are now broken up but a great many are under restoration, or are kept for sunny weekends. While an XK 120 in good order is easy to maintain and is still capable of giving perfectly practical use over as many miles as the owner likes to drive it, it is true that by today's standards the car falls down in certain respects - indeed, it would be unfair to expect a car designed in 1948 to behave like today's model! The steering is heavy around town, and the brakes - especially those of the disc-wheeled XK - are still of course prone to fade if the car is driven fast.

The XK 120's driving position is not like any car of the 1970s - the seats are mounted very low in the car and one does, as the late Laurance Pomeroy observed in 1952, tend to look along the bonnet and not over it. A straight-arm driving position is difficult to adopt as although the steering wheel is telescopically adjustable, it is impossible to push it far enough away without modifying the boss - and then one's hands can foul the scuttle surround. The car is not uncomfortable to drive but it is definitely a case of its handling being better than it feels.

So far as the roadster is concerned, wet weather heralds one of the XK 120's draw-backs as the hood was not really up to the job. Here is how Dick O'Kane summed it up in *Road & Track* a few years ago:

When you drove it, you drove it with the top down. If you tried to put it up, you paid penalties. It made the car ugly, you couldn't see, and at anything over 40 you couldn't hear yourself think - the thing roared and clattered and slapped and threatened to blow off. One night it actually did. If the miserable rag had done anything towards keeping the wind, water and cold out, it might have been tolerable, but it didn't, so you left it down.

An XK 120 can still be termed fast, although the performance of an early model which has managed to retain its original mechanical specification can best be described as smooth and persistent rather than kick-in-the-back. Largely because of its higher gearing, the 160 bhp XK 120 was little quicker than the pre-war SS 100 up to 60 mph - about a second faster than an MGB to that speed - but once into its stride there still remains a performance which is above that of most modern family saloon cars - and some of the smaller-engined sports cars of today too.

In cornering, the unmodified XK 120 does feel something of a slightly ungainly understeerer, displaying much roll; although after a few miles, when memories of the taut response of the modern car which you've just left have faded a little, it is still fun. In its handling the car is perhaps best described as being like an enlarged edition of an Austin Healey 3000 (which is a neat little two-seater runabout to the XK owner!), having slightly better road-holding but a little less of the 'chuckability' of the Healey. The Jaguar's scuttle is rather more rigid than the Healey's though, and displays much less shake over bumpy surfaces. The silky smooth response of the engine, and the general effortless feel of the car when cruising at near 100 mph still feel good and make up for other deficiencies.

Of course, many XK 120s left the factory with the more powerful Special Equipment engine rated at 180 bhp, or towards the end of the production run, with the C-type head which was available to special order in the Spring of 1953 and brought the engine rating up another 20 bhp or so. With these options, the car feels considerably more spritely even if the standard 3.64 to 3.54 rear axle ratio is retained, and for those who are not sticking rigidly to an 'as

original' specification for their early XK 120s, the substitution of a later cylinder head (the C-type, or B-type from an XK 150, Mk IX saloon etc) in place of the original 'small valve' head gives a usefully increased performance. A 0-60 mph time of something like 9 seconds can then be anticipated, with 100 mph coming up in about 24 seconds as opposed to *The Motor's* first XK 120 road-test figure of 27.3 seconds.

One feature of the car which is still good is the ride - in fact it's far superior to that of (for instance) the MGB. Stiffening the suspension through the use of thicker torsion bars has little or no effect on ride quality but does cut down the roll. An extra leaf in the rear springs does effect ride to an extent, and in any case some people prefer to leave the rear end of their cars alone, simply making sure that the lever type shock absorbers are doing their job properly - even for racing (though sometimes telescopic dampers are used to replace the lever type for track work, together with such rear axle locating aids as a Panhard rod, Watts linkage, or simply a pair of anti-tramp bars).

The thorny question of originality comes up again when the question of brakes is discussed. It is quite easy to equipe the XK 120 with disc brakes, Mk IX Jaguar saloon units bolting straight onto the XK, and similarly the rear brakes are interchangeable with the saloon; or units from the (rather rare) disc wheeled XK 150 can be used. For wire wheeled cars, XK 150 wire wheel parts again bolt straight on. This is in the nature of a simplification, but these modifications can be done. To the purist, all this is anathema, but is depends how you intend using the car - if it's only to be taken out on sunny Sundays for gentle pottering along country lanes then there is absolutely no point in altering the brakes. If, however, you intend to use the car's performance as it should be used (maybe together with engine modifications) then disc brakes add enormously to driving pleasure - not to mention safety! My own personal philosophy is that bodywork should indeed be entirely 'period', but that engine and suspension modifications which are of a bolt-on, bolt-off nature are admissible, as the car can be returned to standard at any time. It seems a pity to waste the tremendous interchangeability of Jaguar parts when sensible use of this asset can give so much extra pleasure.

The XK owner thus has a whole range of power outputs to choose from, through the fitting of C-type, B—type and straight-port heads to his car - although due to the position of the XK 120's steering column, trying to squeeze in three carburetters is definitely not recommended. With a little modification, saloon or E-type blocks can also be installed in the XK 120 if it is desired, and one day this feature may well contribute to keeping XK 120s running long after all original spares are exhausted.

As for actual engine tuning, this can be carried almost as far as the owner wishes, although if three carburetters are considered essential then the steering will have to be changed to XK 140 or XK 150 rack and pinion type, which lowers the steering column. The use of 9:1 compression ratio pistons, and just two 2 inch (SU HD8) carburettors instead of the standard 1¾ inch instruments, are usually the first steps taken following the fitting of a C- or B-type head however, and produce very worthwhile results. If the owner is willing to incur rather greater costs, then 1 7/8 inch inlet valves can be installed in the head, and D-type cams (or Iskenderian XM2) fitted which give much increased valve overlap, but retain a good degree of low-speed torque. Thus equipped an XK 120 is quite capable of out-accelerating a 3.8 E-type up to 90 mph or 100 mph, and reliability is not effected so long as a reasonable rev. limit is adhered to (a properly assembled XK engine is quite safe to 6,500 rpm and probably a lot more, but in the tune described it is not worth using much more than 5,800 rpm, at which maximum power is developed).

The following acceleration tables may prove of interest as they illustrate the performance to be expected from an XK 120 in various stages of tune. The first column shows *The Motor's* figures on HKV 455 in basic 160 bhp form, the second my own similar aluminium-bodied roadster with much the same final drive (3.54) but fitted with a B-type head, and the third the same car but with a modified engine consisting of a 3.8 block with balanced and polished crankshaft and rods, 9:1 pistons, D-type head (ie C-type casting with 1 7/8 inch inlet valves), D-type cams, two 2 inch HD8 carburetters, and a 3.77 final drive ratio. Wheel size was 16 inch in all cases, and the figures were taken using a 'fifth wheel' and electric speedometer.

Acceleration	XK 120 3.4 Standard	XK 120 3.4 'B' Type head	XK 120 3.8 Modified
mph	sec	sec	sec
0-30	3.2	3.3	2.6
0-40	5.1	4.6	3.9
0-50	7.3	6.5	5.4
0-60	10.0	8.8	6.9
0-70	12.4	11.1	9.3
0-80	15.7	15.6	11.7
0-90	20.1	19.1	14.7
0-100	27.3	23.3	18.4
0-110	--	--	23.3
Standing ¼ mile	17.0	16.5	15.3
In Top mph	sec	sec	sec
30-50	6.6	6.4	5.2
40-60	7.4	6.6	4.7
50-70	8.1	7.0	4.8
60-80	8.5	7.5	5.0
70-90	9.9	8.2	5.7
80-100	11.3	9.6	6.9
90-110	--	--	8.7
In Third mph	sec	sec	sec
20-40	5.0	5.3	4.2
30-50	4.8	5.2	4.0
40-60	5.4	5.3	3.7
50-70	5.9	5.0	4.1
60-80	6.1	6.1	5.5
70-90	--	6.8	5.2

The sort of power now given by LXK 48 (the

author's car) provides a stimulating performance on the road, with which the car's standard suspension coped surprisingly well. However, the extra horses did induce axle tramp more readily on a fast take off from rest, and the car's behaviour in the wet calls for a gentle foot on the throttle - sudden application of which is otherwise likely to cause wheelspin, even in top gear! Needless to say disc brakes are fitted all round, and fade is virtually non-existent. One of the few troubles encountered after the engine modifications were made concerned water cooling - there seems to be little reserve in the XK 120's standard radiator (which was retained) and the extra heat which was a by-product from the conversion caused a rise in temperature commensurate with speed; on the track boiling was encountered after five or six laps and the problem has yet to be fully solved. The larger, sloping, XK 140 or XK 150 radiator can be fitted but this is not easy and entails other changes. But the car's ability to accelerate away from V12 E-types still makes it all worthwhile!

It should not be imagined that LXK 48 represents the ultimate in road modified XK 120s, as the engine specification was drawn up to conform with Historic Sports Car Club racing rules and thus 'period' parts were used where possible. A higher ultimate performance would be given by a big-valve straight-port head (ie modified E-type), or the use of Weber carburetters with this or the E-type head.

More than one XK 120 has even been used on the road with a full dry-sump D-type engine, and the aluminium-bodied roadster used by John Harper in the English Thoroughbred Sports Car races of recent years, which had what was virtually a full race 'mod-sports' E-type engine was often driven to meetings on the road.

At least one XK 120 in the States was fitted with a large V8 engine during the fifties in the search for greater performance, although it is un-

likely that the standard Cadillac unit used produced much more power than a reasonably modified XK engine. Another American enthusiast ordered that his new XK 120 be fitted with a supercharger before delivery, so the car, a birch grey aluminium-bodied roadster, (670150) was sent from Coventry to have an Arnott supercharger affixed. It was mounted a la 4½ litre 'blower' Bentley, in front of the radiator out of which a chunk was taken to allow the drive shaft to run through. The owner obviously approved of the installation and raced the car in SCCA events; the car survives (in this country) but the blower doesn't. A further supercharger installation for the XK 120 was advertised in 1950, using a Wade instrument blowing at 7lbs boost pressure. It was driven from the crankshaft by an enclosed chain in front of the radiator, and four 'Layrub' rubber-bush flexible couplings. The makers, Pat Whittet & Co Ltd of Lightwater, Surrey, claimed that an engine so converted remained "normally flexible and docile."

Few if any of these early attempts at supercharging the XK 120 remain, although it has occasionally been tried in recent years - without notable success. Owners wanting more performance from their XKs are best recommended to use more orthodox methods.

But modified or not, the XK 120 is still capable of giving its owner a good performance even by the standards of the 1970s. It is a reliable car when kept in good order, and maintenance is not expensive or difficult when compared to other cars of roughly the same period which offer the same (or more likely, a lesser) turn of speed. The XK 120 is generally remembered with respect by its past owners, and today has a large following of enthusiasts. It is still one of the most beautiful sports cars ever built.

Chapter Four The XK 120 in competition

The XK 120 was tremendously successful in sports car races in all parts of the world, and it was a result of Leslie Johnson and Bert Hadley's outstanding performance with one of these cars in the 1950 Le Mans race... that we decided that in a car more suitable for the race, the XK engine could win this greatest of all events

Sir William Lyons
1969

XK 120 IN COMPETITION

It was early summer 1949. The XK 120 was not yet in anywhere near full production but was still basking in the glory of its surprise announcement of a few months before, and in its 132 mph runs at Jabbeke. Mk V saloons were now driving away from the despatch area in ever increasing numbers, and behind the scenes the testing programme of the new XK-engined saloon was in full swing. Then it was learnt that the *Daily Express* and the BRDC had decided to include a production car race at their August 20th Silverstone meeting.

This announcement may have been greeted with a little consternation at the factory. The launching of the XK 120 at the previous Earls Court motor show, and the car's subsequent impressive demonstration runs along the Jabbeke/Aeltre highway at over 132 mph, had been given a great deal of publicity in the motoring and daily press and the consequently well-informed motoring public was obviously going to look hard towards Jaguar Cars Ltd to see if the company would venture its new sports car in this novel all-comers contest for standard cars. The XK 120 ran very well in a straight line, they were saying, but how would it fair during an hour long race, against real opposition?

Well, Jaguar themselves didn't really know either, and William Lyons decided that he would only allow his cars to take part if it could be proved that they could win! This resulted in an XK 120 being taken to Silverstone and "flogged round for three hours", as 'Lofty' England put it later, to see if it both lapped sufficiently quickly and hung together. The old club circuit was used, and England, Hassan and Rankin did the driving; Silverstone had only been in use as a motor racing track for a year or so, and none had driven there before. Wally Hassan remembers that he spun off three times, going through the same hole in the straw bales on each occasion! But the funniest incident of the day occurred when Lyons himself turned up - he jumped into the XK 120 where Ernest Rankin was sitting in the passenger seat, slapped his publicity manager on the shoulder and said, "Hey, Rankin, I've left my specs behind, tell me where the corners and braking points are!" and drove off forthwith - to lap nearly as quickly as the others had done. A somewhat shattered Rankin stumbled out of the car when it finally pulled in.

But the point had been proved - the XK 120 was both fast enough and reliable enough to be a potential winner, and so three cars were entered in the *Daily Express* meeting, though under their individual driver's names, not the factory's. So when Saturday August 20th arrived, three XK 120s were drawn up in the paddock creating not a little interest amongst the spectators as the new Jaguar sports car was still an extremely rare beast - indeed, those three cars were probably the only representatives of their type in the country at that time. They were painted red, white and blue. The blue one was HKV 455, the 1948 show car and the first XK 120 built (660001), the white car was HKV 500, still with its left hand drive chassis number (670002) but converted to right hand drive since its Jabbeke demonstration runs, while the red car was almost certainly 670001, another converted lhd car which was never registered for the road in this country. All were fitted with a lower final drive ratio, the drivers being enjoined not to exceed 5,500 rpm , or about 118 mph.

Lyons was taking no chances with his drivers either, all three retained for the race being highly experienced men - Leslie Johnson, Prince Bira, and Peter Walker. Johnson was a personal friend of Jaguar's chief engineer William Heynes, and as related in a previous chapter had already helped the factory out through the loan of his BMW 328, a car which he raced with considerable success before the war. He was not unfamiliar with bigger cars either, witness for example his 7th place in the revived Grand Prix d'Europe in 1947 with a 4-litre Darracq.

Prince Birabongse of Siam should need as little introduction now as he did in 1949, his consistent success at Brooklands and at circuits throughout Europe being well documented. His achievements during the 1949 season had already included two important second places, in the Mar del Plate GP in South America and in the French GP at Rheims, and a 3rd place in the GP held at Zandvoort. Besides the Production Car Race, Bira was also driving his 1496 cc supercharged Maserati in the big event of the day, the International Trophy race for single seaters. The blue XK 120 had been allocated to the Prince, an apposite choice in view of his

usual racing colours, and no doubt the fact that F R W England had acted as racing mechanic to Bira before the war had something to do with that particular choice of driver.

Peter Douglas Conyers Walker was to drive the red car. Walker's main claim to fame had come about through his driving of ERAs, which when in the mood he could take round a circuit as quickly as anyone; an ebullient driver, he liked to put on a good display for the crowd and his cornering techniques were occasionally extravagant as a result.

The hour-long race itself commenced with a Le Mans type start, the cars lined up against the crude scaffolding which composed the pits - which were between Abbey and Woodcote corners at that time. The field of 30 was a cosmopolitan mixture to say the least, although the organisers from the BRDC had done their best to select, from the 90 or so entries they'd received, cars that were in current production; in which task they were only partially successful. Two 4½ litre Lagondas headed the line, appearing to dwarf practically everything else, except possibly the 4375 cc V8 Allards, one of which was being driven by the builder and designer of all three entered, Sydney Allard. With Jaguar, Lagonda and Allard comprised the over 2,500 cc class, the XK 120s being joined by Cyril Mann's 3½ litre SS 100 which had somehow been allowed in.

The strongest competition to the XKs was to materialise from the 1501 cc - 2500 cc class, Norman Culpan's 1971 cc Speed Model Frazer-Nash - a frankly middle aged Halifax wool manufacturer, novice driver Culpan was to have surprising successes with his Frazer Nash, often harrying the XK 120s. The new Healey Silverstones were out in force with an official works team of three cars driven by Louis Chiron, Major A P R Rolt and Tom Wisdom. Various 2½ litre Rileys, J W Rowley's pre-war 2-litre Aston Martin and Rose's Lea Francis Sports Model made up the remainder of the class. The small car division was stocked by HRGs and TC Midgets (three of each), a works

Morgan and two Jowett Javelin saloons.

The programme summed up the forthcoming contest with glee: "Here is an unrivalled opportunity of watching the car of your choice matched in open competition with its rival in engine size, or in price; to compare its acceleration, road-holding, and 'flat-out' speed in this race of one hour's duration round the 3-mile Silverstone circuit. A sort of Mobile Motor Show..." In view of the foregoing, it's no wonder that Lyons was most careful to ensure that the XK 120 was almost certain to win before allowing the cars to enter - failure in front of the vast crowd would have been ignominious to say the least, and possibly a damaging blow against a car already being billed as 'the world's fastest production car'.

As the flag dropped and the first cars pulled away after the sprint across the track, it was Potter's big Allard that headed the melee - but only briefly as the XK 120s soon established themselves in line ahead, displaying both speed and an amount of roll that was decidedly non-vintage.

Bira in HKV 455 took the lead, followed very closely by Johnson with Walker not far behind in the third XK. Norman Culpan was next, and he was soon to be pressing Walker quite hard; this leading group soon began lapping the slower runners, and it was this that provided much of the race's excitement - particularly as some of the competitors weren't paying much attention to their rear view mirrors. In fact Leslie Johnson lost a lot of time when the driver of one of the Jowett Javelins, Wise, "over-estimated the cornering power of his rear tyres" which resulted in a slight collision and the demoting of the white XK to 5th position with a dent in its front wing. But by dint of some really fast motoring, Johnson regained his ground and had actually repassed the scrapping Walker and Culpan when he was almost involved in another drama - on the 17th lap, "Bira swirled into Woodcote Corner fast, bang went a rear tyre and the Jaguar shot backwards into the straw bales", as *The Motor* described it. Johnson was right on

Bira's tail at the time and his avoidance of the spinning car was rated as a "miraculous piece of driving" by the same journal.

There is actually doubt as to whether Bira's flat tyre caused his spin, or was a result of it; anyway, the Prince's efforts to change the wheel were brought to nought by the jack sinking into the soft turf. Perhaps he was lucky that the car didn't turn over, the fate of more than one car launched into the air by the controversial straw bales lining much of the circuit - certainly it was the bales that John Bolster blamed for the consequences of his frightening accident at Silverstone, in which his ERA turned over, breaking his back and putting him out of motor racing for good.

But fortunately, Johnson thereafter conducted HKV 500 round the track without incident and at the end of the sixty minutes, took the chequered flag. Walker crossed the line 5.6 seconds later in the red XK 120 having managed to keep ahead of the determined Norman Culpan, who was only 14.2 seconds down after an hour's racing. Johnson's race average was 82.80 mph with a fastest lap of 84.9 mph, and he had covered 28 laps; the speed of the first three cars was such that they had lapped every other competitor, and that included fourth place man Tony Rolt in his Healey Silverstone, although he could be more than pleased at leading the Healeys to a team victory, handed to them when Bira couldn't regain the circuit. Though at the same time, Donald Healey must have realised that the XK 120 had more or less rendered his sports car obsolete in the first year of its life, at least so far as outright wins were concerned, and in fact no Healey or Austin Healey was to win a major overall victory of any sort until 1960. Cyril Mann's SS 100 came a creditable 15th, after spending some time in the pits, and obviously its inclusion in the race annoyed Rob Walker who had wanted to run his famous pre-war Delahaye but wasn't allowed to.

David Brown was also a little upset that his new car was not allowed to race either, although proper production of the DB series hadn't actually began by then.

So the XK 120 had entered, and won, its first race and after the 1949 Production Car Race no-one could seriously dispute that the car was Britain's fastest production car. As a competition debut, it was not an especially planned one and although Lyons would undoubtedly have embarked upon a limited competition programme in due course, the *Daily Express's* happy idea of reintroducing a type of event seen at Brooklands before the war certainly advanced the XK 120's entry into motor racing. But Lyons had always approached the subject of competition very carefully. He was fully aware of the amount of money and time that could be spent on even a fairly unambitious racing programme with very little return, and as Lofty England expressed it years later, the company in those difficult post-war years "didn't exactly have money rolling out of its ears." A less cool-headed policy had been the downfall of more than one contemporary of SS Cars Ltd before the war, and Lyons could not have been unaware of their various fates.

However, encouraged by the promising performance of the car at Silverstone, the factory lent or sold six aluminium bodied XK 120s to selected drivers during March and April 1950. These were to embark on a limited competition programme, always as private entrants but with more or less full factory support and mainly works preparation, and were:

Leslie Johnson, JWK 651 chassis number	660040
L H 'Nick' Haines	660041
Peter Walker, JWK 977	660042
Clemente Biondetti, JWK 650	660043
Ian Appleyard, NUB 120	660044
T H Wisdom, JWK 988	660057

Although these cars were never officially entered in events by Jaguar, I shall refer to them as 'works' cars for the purposes of this book.

Apart from Biondetti's car which the veteran driver took back to Italy with him, the other 'works' cars stayed in this country - virtually the only aluminium bodied XK 120s to do so as it seems that all the rest of the production went abroad, mostly to the United States.

In January 1950 Leslie Johnson himself had flown to the States, to take part in the Sports Car Club of America's meeting at Palm Beach that month. There, he managed a second-in-class position to a Ford Duesenberg Special, an effort well publicised at the time in the States even though it was not, by later standards, a particularly auspicious result. A rarity in 1949 and early 1950, XK 120s were to become an increasingly common sight in SCCA racing as production at the factory went over to pressed steel, with the corresponding rise in output.

The first sortie by any of the works XK 120s (Johnson did not take delivery of JWK 651 until two months after his Palm Beach expedition) was on April 2nd 1950, when Biondetti entered the Targa Florio with 660043. The Italian driver was a past master of these frightening road races, and had won the previous year's Targa driving a Type 166 Ferrari. In 1950 with his new Jaguar he was not quite so lucky and retired with engine trouble some way before the finish - but not before he had pressed a no doubt surprised Albert o Ascari very hard indeed, actually leading him at one point.

In fact Ascari himself with the V12 2.4 Ferrari was to retire, one of 107 out of a field of 186 to drop by the wayside and it was eventually the 2½ litre Alfa Romeo of Mario and Franco/Borsigia which won, having averaged 53.87 mph over the tortuous 670 mile route around the island of Sicily.

Three weeks later came the 1950 Mille Miglia. That year the event took place in appalling weather and the wet roads took an enormous toll of the 383 starters, including the lives of Peter Monkhouse who was killed when the Healey Silverstone in which he was co-driving left the road near Padua, and Aldo Bassi who crashed his Ferrari. XK 120s contested the race in strength, Biondetti, Haines, Johnson and Wisdom all entering their work cars. The 52-year-old Biondetti had also won the Mille

Miglia the previous year, and in 1948, on both occasions with his Type 166 Ferrari after various up-datings, but this year his chances were ruined when the XK 120 broke a rear spring early on - the myriad hump back bridges, pot holes and hairpins had obviously wrought their worst on the XK's rear suspension, where the leaf springs were never a strong point. After repairs Biondetti restarted and, reported *The Motor*, "his speed over the last few hundred miles was sensational" as he tried to regain the 40 minutes lost.

Nick Haines faired rather less well, crashing within 200 miles of the finish while lying quite well up in the field. But nothing quite matched the ill fortune of poor Tom Wisdom, who had JWK 988 throw in the towel with transmission problems a mere forty miles from the end, after having run for well over 1,000 miles on the streaming wet Italian roads. It was made all the more galling for the driver/journalist as he had won the touring car class in a Healey Silverstone the previous year. It was therefore left to Leslie Johnson and JWK 651 to carry the Jaguar flag to Brescia, and 14 hours and 29 minutes after leaving it, the travel-stained XK 120 Roadster entered the town again in 5th place - a tremendous effort by both car and driver as *The Motor* acknowledged: "Leslie Johnson's drive with the Jaguar XK 120 was an outstanding performance which, with Cortese's 2-litre Frazer Nash, demonstrated the capabilities of British cars matched against the best Italian productions on their own ground. Johnson actually made fifth fastest time irrespective of category..."

Giannino Marzotto won ahead of Serafini, both men in the new 3.3 Ferraris, and that Johnson's place was not easily gained is shown by the retirements - Villoresi's Ferrari retired with engine problems and of the Alfa team only Fangio survived to finish in third place (inspite of hitting a gulley at 112 mph!); Ascari was another non-finisher and joined the 173 retirements, 30 of whom were reckoned to have crashed. In fact said *The Motor*, "the wrecks piled at the roadside reminded some of the drivers of the tales of the Paris - Madrid of long ago. In several smashes, spectators, as usual crowding along the sides of the roads, were bowled over like ninepins by cars hurtling sideways."

In the United States, which XKs were now reaching in increasing numbers, private owners had began to field their XK 120s - mainly against other imported makes as the first true American sports car was a long way off. In May 1950 the first major US airfield circuit meeting took place, at the vast Suffolk County Airport near the tip of Long Island. The course was a three mile one, described as fast and difficult with an enormous appetite for tyres. A E Goldschimdt ran his XK 120 and his main opponents were one-time SS 100 driver Tom Cole with his new 5,420 cc Cadillac-Allard, and Briggs Cunningham with a 2-litre Ferrari. The XK could not out-power the J2 Allard nor out-corner the Ferrari, so in both the races entered by Erwin Goldschimdt the Jaguar was placed 3rd. But at least he managed to hold off Stevenson's Ford-Meyer Special of very similar capacity to the XK's, and Kulok's well-driven Frazer Nash. The meeting was, incidentally, given a generally British flavour by the distinguished presence of both Lt Col Goldie Gardner and Capt G E T Eyston; Gardner was the first man to publicly run a Jaguar twin-cam engine when he used the 2-litre fore-runner of the XK engine to power his record breaking Special in 1948, and Eyston was later to adopt an XK for his personal motoring. Another personage at that meeting soon to become closely associated with Jaguar was of course Briggs Cunningham.

Back in Europe, Tommy Wisdom drove JWK 988 1,200 miles across Europe to compete in the Circuit of Oporto sports car race, and inspite of its trans-continental trip the XK 120 finished an excellent 3rd behind Bonetto's Alfa Romeo and Carini's OSCA, the Jaguar's average speed being 71 mph against 72.3 mph and 71.8 mph for the two leading cars. To *The Motor*, Wisdom's performance in Portugal "would seem to bear out the maker's claim that their XK 'is the touring car with racing car performance!' "

Very shortly after the Circuit of Oporto, a rather more significant race was due to take place - the 1950 Le Mans. Johnson, Walker and Haines were all entered in their XK 120s, a major step by the unofficial Jaguar works team. Tom Wisdom was also to run, but in a Jowett Jupiter.

Lyons knew full well the enormous prestige of the famous 24 hour race, and the vast amount of publicity which surrounded its victors. The entry of the three XK 120s for the 1950 race was however mainly exploratory - Lyons and his engineer Heynes wanted to see exactly how the near-standard XK would fare, with any favourable result being in the nature of a bonus.

Since the 1949 event, the circuit (made up of closed public roads) had been almost entirely resurfaced and many of the corners widened or eased, which as *The Motor* pointed out made it somewhat faster "than in 1949 when Chaboud in a Delahaye lapped at 95.4 mph, or in 1939 when Mazoud's Delahaye went round at 96.71 mph", the latter's speed remaining as the lap record to be aimed at by the 1950 contestants.

The three XK 120s were entered by their drivers who were paired as follows: Leslie Johnson/Bert Hadley in JWK 651 (660040), Nick Haines/Peter Clark (660041), and Peter Whitehead/John Marshall in JWK 977 (660042). Service Manager F R W England acted as team manager, a role he was to adopt officially when the factory itself entered racing - more or less, he said, because there was nobody else around at the time to do it.

The cars themselves remained remarkably true to their catalogued specification, and "were probably the most standard cars that have ever been run in this race". To continue quoting from William Heynes' *Milestones in the life of an Automobile Engineer,* delivered to the Institution of Mechanical Engineers in October 1960 : "The cars were, of course, carefully prepared and the racing programme well organised, but no development work had been done

to give extra power over the unit we supplied to the public, or to reduce the overall weight of the vehicle". Thus the XK 120s retained their 8 : 1 compression ratio, small valves and 5/16 inch lift camshafts "over a particularly moderate timing designed for flexibility necessary for a saloon car".

Of the few departures from standard, one was the installation of a 24 gallon petrol tank in place of the 14 gallon item, and others concerned the brakes. No-one at the factory had any illusions over the doubtful ability of these to stand up to 24 hours' more or less continuous use, particularly as wire wheels with their better cooling properties, were not yet available for the XK 120. But what could be done to the existing stopping apparatus was done.

One apparently obvious aid was not adopted however - Al-Fin drums, made of ribbed aluminium with cast-iron liners, which were a popular choice of competitors then. However, tests by Jaguar proved that they wouldn't take the punishment of long distance racing as well as the standard solid cast iron items. Instead, heat dissipation was aided by a rather weird device in the form of turbine-like fins rivetted to a disc which was then sandwiched between the brake drum and the pressed-steel wheel; the brake drum itself was drilled on its outer face to allow air from the 'fan' to circulate. As each of the three Jaguars weighed over 30 cwt laden (ie with driver, tools and spares), any such aids to braking were worth trying!

Externally, the cars used the catalogued optional speed equipment in the form of bucket seats and aero-screens, but ran without tonneau covers of any sort. Headlights were supplemented by two big Lucas 'Flamethrower' type spot lights fixed to the inner front bumper mounting points (the cars ran without front bumpers). As the big petrol tank effectively filled the boot, spare parts and tools were carried in a box on the passenger's bucket seat. A quick-action filler cap was fitted in place of the standard hinged lockable flap, and bonnet straps were employed.

Le Mans in 1950 was a vastly different race from its counterpart in, say, 1970. The majority of the entries were genuine road cars, and all were road going. In those early post war years, a number of the cars were distinctly venerable too, like the Bentleys of Hay and Hall respectively - the former was driving a 1939 Corniche, the latter a 1934 TT car! There were some oddities too by our standards, like the diesel engined cars, one a 4½-litre supercharged two-stroke MAP., another the Delletrez 4.4 litre car. Briggs Cunningham's entries might justifiably come under that heading as well, one being a huge and outwardly standard Cadillac saloon, (nicknamed 'Petite Patoud') the other a sort of Cadillac Special, an open two-seater clothed in a vast enveloping bodyshell of aerodynamic intent. Both cars were powered by a Cadillac engine of 5.4 litres breathing through twin-choke carburetters. Cunningham, like Lyons, regarded his mission as a reconnaisance rather than an assault, and was to run his cars with commendable restraint.

As the potential winners, the Ferraris of Chinneti (last year's victor) and Sommer could not be ignored, while the Talbot driven by father and son Rosier was also a favourite - it was this car over which there was considerable controversy as to whether or not it was a GP car fitted with road equipment, and if so whether this should be deplored or applauded. The similar Talbot of Mairesse and Meyret, and Sydney Allard's 5,434 cc Cadillac engined two-seater (co-driven by Tom Cole) also constituted potential candidates for the outright distance award. Interesting entries included the Wade supercharged 1½ litre Simcas, one to be driven by Fangio and the other by Trintignant - their stressed-skin construction, one day of course to be almost universal amongst saloon cars, causing much discussion.

The British entries formed an important section of the field. Besides Jaguar and the Allard already mentioned, Aston Martin were represented by three cars (one of which was a substitute for the DB2 team car which had crashed on the way out from England), there were two Frazer Nashes (a make which had finished third in 1949), Donald Healey's re-bodied Healey Silverstone fitted with a 3.8 litre Nash engine, the Jowett Jupiter conducted by Tommy Wisdom, and a 2½ litre Riley roadster driven by Lawrie and Beetson - Lawrie was to enter an XK 120 in the 1951 race.

Race day weather was fine and warm, as the flag fell at 4pm for the familiar Le Mans start. The usual tense silence was disturbed only by the pattering of feet as the drivers dashed across the road to their cars, and then a surging wave of 60 cars accelerated away from the pits and under the Dunlop Bridge - with the three XK 120s quite near the front. At the end of the first lap, Whitehead in JWK 977 was chasing after Meyret's big 4.5 litre Talbot, Sydney Allard, and leader Raymond Sommer in his Mille Miglia 2.3 litre Ferrari saloon which had lapped so quickly in practice (at virtually 100 mph). Trintignant in his very fast little supercharged Simca was not far behind Whitehead, and in front of Johnson and Haines.

However, by the end of the first hour Johnson was driving the leading Jaguar, in fifth position overall. Briggs Cunningham wasn't having a great deal of luck and had to dig himself out of the sandbank at Mulsanne which delayed the Cadillac Special somewhat, and later the American car was to be troubled by its three-speed Cadillac gearbox. On lap 19 Sommer broke the old course record with a lap of 98.3 mph, but this was not to stand for very long as Rosier drove his Talbot round at a very fast 102.84 mph while the Ferrari was in the pits changing a plug. As evening approached, Sommer was soon in grave trouble with dynamo malfunction, and Rosier swept into the lead as the Italian car slowed. Not long afterwards the Ferrari retired with complete electrical failure.

Already the XK's brakes were losing efficiency, though Johnson and Hadley retained fourth place and were promoted to third when in the early morning Rosier pitted to change a broken rocker arm. Rolt's Healey was behind

JWK 651, with Abecassis in his DB2 following him. Allard was now down to 6th, with Reg Parnell and Charlie 'Brack' in the second DB2 saloon separating him from the Clark/Haines XK 120 in 9th spot. The Whitehead/Marshal XK was running steadily around 15th position.

Inspite of his brake troubles, Johnson was speeding up and around 12.30 on the Sunday put in a lap of 96.98 mph, and was averaging almost 94 mph. This was highly significant as JWK 651 was now circulating faster than the leading Talbot, gaining at the rate of a lap and a quarter every hour - a rate of progress which those in the Jaguar pit excitedly realised would bring the XK into the lead if Rosier did not increase his speed; perhaps the Talbot was failing? But the matter was to be resolved in quite a different way, for at 1.05pm the white Jaguar coasted to a halt not far from the start/finish line. Johnson demounted and stood disconsolently beside the roadster, but there was nothing he could do. The XK's clutch centre had pulled out, weakened by hours of hard use through efforts to save the brakes by using the gearbox to slow the car down.

As for the remaining two Jaguars, they survived the entire 24 hours and crossed the line in 12th and 15th positions. Neither were in the fullest of health however, the Clark/Haines car in 12th place suffering from oil on the clutch, though inspite of this had averaged 80.94 mph for over 24 hours, and covered 230 laps of the 8.68 mile circuit compared to the winning Talbot's 256. Johnson's XK 120 and the reserve Aston Martin were in fact the only members of the British contingent to fall by the wayside, causing *The Motor* to headline the results as a "British revival in evidence." Certainly Sydney Allard's 3rd place behind the two Talbots of Rosier and Meyrat was a real achievement, as was Rolt and Hamilton's 4th place in the Nash -engined streamlined Healey (a consistent performance which did not go unnoticed by those in the Jaguar pit). Team managed by John Wyer, the Aston Martins finished 5th and 6th, the Abecassis car tieing for the Index of

Performance with a little Monopole.

It may or may not be over-stating the case for Jaguar to say that the XK 120 of Johnson and Hadley very nearly did win the 1950 Le Mans race, but to Heynes, watching from the pits with William Lyons, the car's performance was quite enough to convince him that to win Le Mans was perfectly within the factory's capacity. The race, he afterwards said, "debunked the tradition of the tuning wizard with a life experience on the track and a special gimmick in his tool box." He realised that it would be possible to build a car for the event using all the main mechanical features of the XK 120 but in a lighter chassis, which would stand an excellent chance of winning. Lyons gave him the go-ahead on the spot while they were still at the track, and the outcome was of course the XK 120C, or C-type Jaguar, which was to win the race in 1951 and 1953. This decision also meant that the XK 120 had been the last genuine *road* car to have stood a good chance of winning the race outright, at least for many years.

Not long after the Le Mans expedition, the XK 120 won its first laurels in the world of rallying, and the soon to be familiar registration number NUB 120 was first seen in the motoring papers. The name of the car's driver, Ian Appleyard, was already well known to those who followed the sport, especially in connection with the Alpine Rally for which Appleyard and 660044 were entered in July 1950. In 1948 Appleyard had won a *Coupe des Alpes* with the semi-works SS 100, LNW 100, and in 1949 had, with Donald Healey, taken the new Healey Silverstone on its competition debut - only a two minute delay at a level crossing had prevented the car and its drivers winning a *Coupe* on that occasion too.

One of the tougher European international rallies, the 1950 Alpine was as hard on cars and crews as it had· been in previous years, although retirements were to be slightly down on the 1949 event. The big engined cars especially had a very tight schedule, allowing little time for maintenance such as brake adjusting - at this stage the XKs still had the manually adjusted front brakes, and this was a significant factor as the time credited to each competitor for crossing a pass was the sum of the ascent and descent.

Appleyard's rally was not made any easier when first gear lock-up occured (one of the very few faults which could afflict the Moss box when it was used hard), and it was when trying to avoid the use of first gear afterwards that he tried to take one particular hairpin on the Forclaz Pass in the French Alps rather faster than he would normally, in an effort to get round in second; the result was a rather dented offside front wing.

The Rally was one of constantly changing fortunes for many of the competitors but Appleyard drove the big white sports car consistently well, with his wife Patricia navigating (the daughter of William Lyons, Appleyard had married her in May of 1950). Poor girl, this sort of motoring was new to her and she suffered considerably from car sickness during the early part of the event, but soon got over it and was in the future to be Appleyard's passenger on all his major continental and home assaults.

Apart from completing the road section without loss of marks, Appleyard also made fastest time on the Col de Vars hill climb, in the driving tests at the conclusion of the rally, and over the flying kilometer measured on an autostrada. Here, the Jaguar's 109.8 mph was far quicker than the second fastest car, a 4½ litre Lago Talbot (a small revenge for Le Mans?); third over the flying kilometer was Gordon Wilkin's Healey Silverstone at a creditable 95.7 mph. The latter led its class for a while but dashed any hopes for a repetition of 1949 when it crashed with a jammed throttle. Appleyard took home with him a *Coupes des Alpes* for a penalty free run, and a class win in the over 3,000 cc section of the rally. To Joe Lowrey writing in *The Motor*, the 1950 Alpine proved that "the XK 120 can go fast in confined quarters and withstand more punishment than

any ordinary driver is likely to be able to mete out to it... To score successes in an Alpine a good power to weight ratio is needed, backed up by good controllability, powerful brakes, and reliability which permits maintenance work to be almost forgotten for 2,000 very hard miles."

To see just how these 2,000 miles had effected NUB 120, *The Autocar* borrowed the XK almost directly on its return to this country. Besides the obvious outward battle scar of its damaged offside wing - part of which had been cut away to prevent it rubbing on the tyre - the XK had suffered little. First gear was of course doubtful and wasn't used, a loose baffle in the silencer added to a noisy exhaust, and a few rattles over bumpy surfaces could be traced to the stricken wing whose stay had broken behind the front wheel, and the left rear wheel spat and the boot lid not being as good a fit as they should have been. On reflection, it is amazing that the spats remained on the car at all after such a strenuous exercise!

The highest speed reached on the try out was around 105 mph, "and the car felt perfect at it, steering, stability and everything included." Predictably, the brakes had suffered to the extent that pedal travel had vastly increased, and although good enough for ordinary road driving the pedal was nearly flat on the floor. When using the car's performance, which was still as impressive as ever, inpromptu warm-air central heating and a smell of hot oil were provided for the car's occupants by faulty sealing of the floor boards, which had apparently been removed at some stage during the rally.

It is interesting to note that NUB 120 displayed little departure from standard - engine, brakes and suspension appeared to have been left alone, although the formerly automatic choke was now operated by a manual switch. Rather unsightly louvres had been let into the bonnet during the event, following a scare about petrol vaporisation - afterwards it was discovered that the blame lay with the petrol used, and they were quickly filled in again. Both headlights were fitted with rather attractive chrome stoneguards, and the bonnet had a precautionary leather strap over it. Inside the cockpit, the speedometer was calibrated in kilometres, and the passenger's facia had mountings for two chronometers. The optional 24-gallon fuel tank was installed, and the car ran on the standard 3.64 : 1 axle ratio.

In August 1950, the *Daily Express* sponsored its second International Trophy meeting at Silverstone, which featured as its main event a race for GP machinery in which such stars as Juan Fangio and Guiseppe Farina in their Alfa Romeos were entered, and the V16 BRM to be driven by Raymond Sommer. Once again a Production Car race was included in the programme. This time the number of entries for the Production Car event was such that two races had to be held, the first for cars up to 2-litres, and the other for cars of 2001 - 3000 cc capacity, and over 3-litres. In the big car race, no less than five XK 120s were originally entered, to be driven by Leslie Johnson, Peter Walker, Tommy Wisdom, Tony Rolt and A J C Schwelm - though the latter's entry was taken over by Peter Whitehead in the end.

Ranged against the Jaguars were four Allards, three Aston Martin DB2s (the famous VMF cars), no less than eight Healey Silverstones, and a variety of slower vehicles.

The first practice session on the Thursday before the race was enlivened by a slight conflict between Duncan Hamilton and the great Italian racing driver Tazio Nuvolari. Hamilton had previously been engaged by Donald Healey to drive a works Silverstone, but on practice day was confronted by Nuvolari who claimed that it was he who had been retained to drive the car. Healey himself was crossing the Atlantic at the time, so until a reply was received from the constructor in answer to a frantic cable asking what the true situation was, things looked awkward - Duncan was not the sort of man to stand down for anybody, Italian ace or not. Anyway, the cabled reply confirmed Hamilton's appointment as Healey works driver for the occasion (Nuvolari had apparently misunderstood

a previous conversation with Donald Healey about the race), and face was saved all round when Jaguar offered Nuvolari an XK 120 - which was appropriately finished in red.

While Nuvolari was reported as being delighted with the car, his practice times were not on the other hand sensational, tieing with Tom Wisdom's 75.91 mph in JWK 988 - compared to Rolt's and Walker's joint fastest lap of 81.24 mph. It is of course a matter for speculation whether or not the Italian driver was trying particularly hard, or whether the spur of competition in the actual race would have brought forth the old fire; for he fell ill before the event itself and didn't even take part in the second practice session.

It was Cuthbert Harrison's Allard which actually posted the fastest practice lap of 85.24 mph, though Walker and Rolt took the lead right from the beginning of the race. They travelled almost nose to tail throughout and were never challenged: "rolling a lot less than in 1949 but still appearing to lift a good deal of weight off the inside front wheel on corners, they had a useful margin of speed and acceleration", commented *The Motor*. But perhaps it was Duncan Hamilton who put up the most meritorious performance, as he beat the entire Aston Martin works team in the works Healey Silverstone to come 3rd overall behind the two leading Jaguars! The fastest DB2 was Summers', losing first place in the up to 3-litre class to Hamilton by only .2 second. Peter Whitehead, who had been lying third in his XK 120 for the first 20 of the 60 minutes, retired with engine failure at Maggotts, dispensing a lot of oil over the track in the process which delayed Johnson for one who was sent onto the grass. Wisdom managed a 6th place overall, and 4th in class after Sydney Allard's J2 but ahead of Johnson.

While Walker's winning average speed of 81.88 mph (under ½ second quicker than Rolt) was somewhat less than Ascari's average in the 'small' car race with the Ferrari, the big cars had to contend with a mainly wet track, having raced later in the day by which time it had rained. It would have been an extremely interesting race. had both marques been pitted directly against each other!

Walker also won at Shelsley Walsh with JWK 977 a few weeks later, coming first in the over 3-litre production car class with a time of 44.61 seconds (or just over 1½ seconds slower than Newsome's best SS 100 time before the war). JWK 977 also distinguished itself by being one of the few XK 120s racing to have wheat growing in the boot - Walker was a farmer and thought nothing of driving the XK across the odd field to get home, and the vegetation was found by Jaguar mechanics when the car was left at the factory for one of the periodic up-dating and maintenance sessions!

An important appointment for the XK 120 works roadsters took place on 16th September 1950 - the date of the first post-war Tourist Trophy race. Held in Ulster for the first time since 1936, the 1950 TT was run over a course at Dundrod not far from Belfast, mapped out over public roads closed for the event. The longest straight was just over half a mile, while the remainder of the route took the cars round 14 right hand bends and 7 left hand, with switchback sections and hills thrown in to make things even more interesting. Weather conditions were poor from the start of practice onwards and deteriorated to the appalling - arguably the worst under which any long distance race had been run in these Islands since the war. On the face of it one could scarcely imagine a more unsuitable course for the XK 120, its size and power appearing to weigh heavily against any possibility of success on those streaming wet, narrow Irish roads. But it was also a course which seemed to suit a big engined car, and there was also the virtuosity of Stirling Moss to be taken into account.

If Tom Wisdom's offer of JWK 988 to the young racing driver was to be a happy one for Jaguar, it was even more so for Moss himself. He had tried unsuccessfully to borrow a car for the previous year's Production Car race at Silverstone but inspite of (or because of) his

spectacular successes in 500 cc racing and his exploits for John Heath's HWM team, no manufacturer had been inclined to lend him one - probably thinking he was going too fast too soon, and they didn't want him writing himself off in one of *their* cars. Wisdom, however, discerned that it was pure talent that was making Moss go so quickly, and propositioned him - the loan of the XK for the race, with the sharing of costs and any winnings. Stirling accepted with alacrity. This didn't mean that Wisdom was without a car for the event as he had already arranged a works drive for Jowett, in one of the Jupiters which had gone so well in Tommy's hands at that year's Le Mans.

Like many of the competitors in the 1950 TT, Moss put in quite a few miles with JWK 988 round the circuit, before the roads were closed to the public. But it must have surprised a few of the old hands when the young man was found to have returned the fastest official practice lap, at 5 min 28 seconds (81.39 mph) - quicker than Leslie Johnson in JWK 651, Peter Whitehead also in an XK 120, the Aston Martins of Parnell, Abecassis and Macklin, Sydney Allard's J2, and Norman Culpan's Frazer Nash. The rest of the field wasn't really in contention for an outright win, and was made up of HRG, Jowett, MG, and Healey cars.

It was however the white roadster of Leslie Johnson which took an initial lead at the start, heading the pack of 31 cars disappearing into the rain after the Le Mans style start.

But JWK 651's lead only lasted for one lap before Moss asserted himself, JWK 988 thereafter steadily pulling away from Johnson. The older man hung on to second place for 17 laps but Moss never faltered, urging the big Jaguar around in relaxed style, head slightly on one side, in a way which was to become so famous in the years ahead. Then JWK 651 slowed with brake trouble (JWK 988 had Al-Fin drums which seemed to be an advantage on that circuit) and the car's place was inherited by Peter Whitehead, and held by him until the end of the three hours - a moment no doubt longed for by most of the drivers, who were soaking wet and lashed by almost hurricane force wind and rain. Sydney Allard had with commendable skill managed to control the big 4,375 cc V8 Allard to hold 3rd position initially, but after only four laps the car had taken charge and left the circuit, and following gearbox problems was never to offer anything of a challenge.

Moss crossed the finishing line an unchallenged leader, and had shown exactly what he had in hand by making his last lap the fastest of the race, at 77.6 mph. No-one exceeded their set handicap time but Moss got nearer to it than anyone else. JWK 988's speed down the straight was in the region of 121 mph, shared within a mile an hour or so by the other Jaguars, compared with the Aston-Martin DB2 team cars' 113 mph, and the Healey Silverstones' 108 mph. Moss, Whitehead and Johnson also collected the team prize for Jaguar, even though Johnson finished an unusual 7th on handicap, amid the Astons. The day after the 1950 TT it was Moss's 21st birthday.

It had been a significant race for Jaguar, as its length of over 225 miles made it the marque's first important long distance success with the new XK engine. The event also brought Moss into the official Jaguar team that was being formed to campaign the planned new competition model - Lyons, who was in Ireland watching the race himself, signed Moss up the very same evening of the race.

Moss is appreciative of Wisdom's gesture in lending him the XK, and does not underrate the importance of the win which JWK 988 brought him, as this Harvey B Jones interview underlines:

I remember this race terribly well because it was really raining like hell and because the Jaguar was to me fairly difficult to drive; it was a very fast and large car. I think it was the big, big turning point in my career, because I went from driving, professionally yes, but HWM which was a small team, to heading up

what was then the world's leading sports car racing team.

On the production front, steel-bodied XK 120s were now leaving the factory in ever increasing numbers, and within a short time would be built at a rate approaching 100 a week. While most were marked for export, a few filtered into British hands and began to appear regularly on the track in this country.

Most XK 120s were still going to the States, and if the *Popular Mechanics* poll of 1955 is anything to go by a comparatively large proportion were used by their owners in speed events of one sort or another - 20% of the owners contacted said that they competed, and the percentage probably wasn't much less in the early fifties. The car's chief opposition was from two other imported makes, namely Ferrari and Frazer Nash - for instance, at the sports car meeting in July 1950 at Linden Airport, New York, Kulok's Le Mans Replica Frazer-Nash led British journalist John Bentley's XK 120 home by a large margin (never mind that the 'Nash cost twice as much as the XK). At the dramatic venue of Mount Equinox, an SCCA meeting the same year saw Bill Spear - a regular XK 120 driver - relegated to 4th place behind Briggs Cunningham's 2-litre Ferrari, the Jaguar's time being 7 min 45.6 seconds against 7 mins 31.2 seconds for the Ferrari (the class was won by a special). Nineteen-fifty also saw Phil Hill, future World Champion, win his first race - with an XK 120 at the 2.3 mile Palm Beach airfield circuit in the Los Angeles desert. Chief of his pit crew was Ritchie Ginther, another driver later to become world famous.

Moving forward to 1951, the first Sports Car Endurance Race, lasting six hours, was run at Sebring, but an XK 120 didn't appear in the results until 18th place, its drivers being Fitch and Whitmore. But the car did win its class despite finishing the event completely brake-less. The next year, with the event lengthened to 12 hours, things were a lot better with Schott and Carroll gaining joint second place on distance with their XK 120. This gradual improvement in the XK's fortunes continued as private owners modified their cars more effectively, and the peak year for XK 120 competition achievements in the States was probably 1952, Phil Hill and Sherwood Johnston being two of the outstanding drivers involved. Johnston in fact was rated champion sports car driver of 1952 by the SCCA, having driven his XK 120 Roadster in 11 out of the 13 national qualifying events and amassing 10,100 points, which was 4,000 ahead of his nearest rival. The same year, the XK 120 itself was voted sports car of the year by the same club. Walter Hansgen and John Fitch were also active with XK 120s during 1952, consolidating what was to be a long association with Jaguar.

The XK 120 was a somewhat rarer sight in other parts of the world, and never failed to be an enormous attraction wherever it went; an even higher proportion were probably raced than in the States too. The first XK 120 to reach New Zealand and race there had left the factory in October 1949 and was imported by motor agent Eric Shorter together with a Mk V saloon. He circumvented a local regulation banning the import of new cars by citing the two Jaguars as the allowed fully-assembled examples in preparation for setting up a local assembly plant for putting together 'knocked-down' Jaguars. In the event, neither were built in this way, but the bronze coloured roadster (aluminium bodied of course, chassis number 660009) was used for over a year by Shorters, appearing in parades and demonstration runs - with the name 'Jaguar' written in bold script across its boot, simply because otherwise no-one knew what it was!

After a fairly sedentary first 12 months, the car was sold to A J Roycroft for his son, a promising racing driver, to use in sports car and other events. Ron Roycroft's first race was in December 1950, but it wasn't an auspicious start and the car retired with tyre problems. It did very much better early the next year and in February 1951 at Mairehau, won both the 100 Mile Centennial Race and the New Zealand

Road Race of Champions, coming away with fastest lap of the day too. The XK 120's third race was in March, and in the 70-mile Ohakea Trophy Race it was placed first on handicap and second on the road. In the prestigeous Wigram 100 Mile race during the same month, Roycroft managed second place to Les Moore's P3 Alfa Romeo GP car, only 3½ minutes in arrears after a hundred miles of racing.

The car ran in almost completely standard trim apart from the addition of air scoops on the brakes, and ram tubes on the carburetters in place of the air filters. Contemporary press reports noted the stability of the car at speed (in contrast to the behaviour of several local specials!) though it displayed the usual tendency of the first, rather softly sprung, XK 120s to dip its front end on corners. Roycroft remembers its major fault being (predictably) the inadequacy of its brakes for racing - after juddering badly for several laps they would fade right out, and he ended most races driving brakeless. Air scoops helped a bit but the heat generated was such that at the end of the season it was discovered that the inner tubes had vulcanised themselves to the tyres!

After completing a number of sprints and a trip round the South Island with his wife ('the touring car with racing car performance' again!), Roycroft reluctantly sold the car in mid 1951, with 9,000 miles on its clock, to a gentleman by the name of Vodanovich who had waylaid him on every possible occasion so keen was he to possess the XK. Roycroft's resistance had finally crumbled when Vodanovich sat on his doorstep with 33 £50 notes pinned to the inside of his coat. This early right hand drive car still remains in New Zealand, owned today by Grant McMillan.

It was on October 24th 1950 that Leslie Johnson and JWK 651 commenced their first marathon at the Autodrome de Linas-Montlhery. Not in any way a record attempt, the objective was to motor for 24 hours at an average of 100 mph. Co-driver for the event was Stirling Moss, having his first semi-official works drive after being recruited at Dundrod.

For the run, which was timed and observed by the Automobile Club de France, JWK 651 was left virtually standard although a higher axle ratio was probably fitted. After a practice run, the white roadster started its serious lapping of the giant concrete banked track at 5.15pm on the 24th in fine weather. The XK went like clockwork, Johnson and Moss taking spells and with one precautionary change of the Dunlop racing tyres; thirteen of the twenty four hours were driven in darkness. Exactly a day later the car had covered 2,579.16 miles at an average speed of 107.46 mph - the goal had been achieved. Inspite of already having some 4,000 miles of competitive motoring under its belt, the XK 120 ran faultlessly and actually averaged 112.4 mph during its final hour. The fastest lap recorded was 126.2 mph.

However, by March 1951 some more urge had obviously been found by Heynes, and Montlhery was revisited once more by JWK 651. Again the XK 120 (now acknowledged as 'famous' by *The Motor* at least) set off round the 3.8 miles of the banked track, this time for just one hour but at a much higher average - 131.83 mph to be exact. This was followed by another hour but from a standing start, the average being 131.2 mph. As before the exercise was an 'officially observed and timed' demonstration run, and no records were obtained. But it certainly served to emphasise the capabilities of the XK engine, and the speed of Jaguar's road sports car; the motoring press were suitably impressed and described the run as "remarkable." JWK 651 ran with a single aero-screen, an undershield, and with the passenger seat covered by a metal tonneau. The percentage increase of the fastest lap in this, the latest attempt, over the previous one - 134.43 mph as opposed to 126.2 mph - was quite considerable and in view of the fact that bhp requirements rise steeply when an increase in speed is needed at those rates of progress, it is not unreasonable to surmise that Heynes might well have been trying one of the new C-type heads on this occasion, as part of the test programme prior to its use on the still-secret competition model.

The year 1951 in fact represented the XK 120's most successful 12 months in competition, and it becomes impossible to chronical all but the major individual victories because of their sheer number. Biondetti had resorted to a Jaguar Special for the Circuit of Sicily in April, where he managed 7th position, so it was Ian and Pat Appleyard who with NUB 120 brought the XK its first international laurels for 1951, coming first in the Tulip Rally on General Classification. Starting from The Hague, the Appleyards lost no points at all over the very difficult road section. Runner-up was the Swiss entered XK 120 (660731) of Habisreutinger and Horning - a combination which brought a good deal of success to the Jaguar name even though their exploits were not always as well publicised as the Appleyards'. The French international Rallye du Soleil in April was completely dominated by XK 120s, which were placed first, second, third, fourth and sixth! Peignaux drove the first car home followed by Taylor and Bray.

In England, Best Performance in the Rallye Automobile Yorkshire was put up by Grantham in his XK 120, and Appleyard returned another Best Performance in the Morecombe Rally towards the end of May - half the unlimited class in that event was made up of XK 120s, indicating the popularity of the car for rallying as it gradually became available on the home market.

The Production Car Race at Silverstone during the International Trophy Meeting brought the expected Jaguar victory. In fact *The Motor* said "rumour has it that an evening paper had 'Moss wins, Jaguar 1,2,3' all printed in advance..." For that was certainly the result, Moss leading Dodson, Hamilton, Wicken Johnson, all in XK 120s, to the chequered flag. After an Aston Martin DB2, Holt and Wisdom made up 8th and 9th places too. A very convincing demonstration. Duncan Hamilton was driving LXF 731, a steel bodied roadster which he was to modify and drive quite extensively as a private entrant.

Scotland was not immune to the tide of XK successes and the' Scottish Rally, scene of pre-war SS 100 victories, was won by Leslie Wood, his XK 120 covering some 726 miles without loosing a mark. Close behind was Alexandra McGlashan and A. Reid-Walter to add further substance to the XK 120's domination of the event. McGlashan's roadster was, into the bargain, judged to have been the finest open car in the coach-work competition forming part of the rally.

Appleyard followed up his Morecombe Rally success with a Best Performance on General Classification in the considerably more important RAC Rally of Great Britain, although hounded by Morgan Plus 4s; Miss M Newton, a regular XK competitor, put up best open car performance by a lady with her XK 120 in the same event. The International Alpine Rally saw the Appleyards win their second *Coupe des Alpes* for another penalty free run in NUB 120, in the face of quite fierce competition from a Cadillac Allard, and Habisreutinger and Horning's similar XK 120 Roadster, right up to the final tests. Soler's XK finished well too, and with NUB 120 and the Swiss XK, won the team prize for Jaguar. Mackenzie, Gatsonides and Sutcliffe also fielded XKs in that Alpine.

By this time, NUB 120 had acquired Special Equipment engine options and its driver a great deal of experience with the braking system! This, shrouded as it was by the disc wheels and spats with which the car ran in 1950, had given Ian Appleyard a certain amount of worry during the 1950 Alpine, the car suffering from "severe brake fade towards the bottom of the longer Passes, and we had a few frightening moments as a result of it. The pedal just went solid and the car did not slow down at all." He had to adjust the 'micram' front brakes at virtually every time control following a long descent, and during the 1951 Alpine the front linings wore out altogether. So he managed to hire a car during a 'rest' day, and drove back along the route to

where he remembered another XK 120 had crashed the previous day. He extracted the front brake shoes from the wreck and fitted them to NUB 120, one side at a time, during time made up on the road afterwards. The next year, spare sets of front shoes were carried and a complete change was made halfway through the event.

An obscure fault which Appleyard remembers cropping up on one occasion resulted in a rapid trip right back to Coventry from near Grenoble, when NUB 120's brakes developed a severe pull to one side for no apparent reason. Despite the whole system being rapidly dismantled at the works, no cause could be discovered and Ian and Pat had to make an equally rapid return journey to arrive in time for the start with the brakes still pulling. For the duration of the event the XK had to be constantly 'aimed off' on the approach to a corner, and not only that, one front tyre began to wear out faster than the other which created another type of problem. After this particular rally the whole braking system was replaced in its entirety which cured the trouble without determining the cause - Appleyard surmises that it might have been a slight constriction in one of the brake pipes caused by a stone being thrown up by the wheels. Apart from this freak occurance however, the trend in braking was towards a gradual improvement - NUB 120 was later fitted with the self-adjusting front brakes, and wire wheels, used from the 1952 Alpine onwards, helped the braking "enormously." Linings were constantly improving too.

On the racing circuits, XK 120s were appearing in ever increasing numbers, and at Boreham in May 1951 a race was organised for the model alone - during a test meeting to see whether the track could be a possible replacement for Silverstone, as at that time it was thought that a renewal of the latter's lease by the RAC might not be negotiable. Hugh Howorth, one of the fastest XK 120 private owners, won the race. Duncan Hamilton had a field day at the same circuit in August with two wins, the competition in one race extending to

Rob Walker's 3½ litre Delahaye, driven by Jack Fairman, an Aston Martin DB2 conducted by Tony Rolt, and Roy Salvadori in another XK 120 who pressed Hamilton close until he spun. Duncan wrote in *Touch Wood:* "although I knew my XK was probably the fastest car in the race, what gave me great pleasure was the fact that I won on a wet track in pouring rain. This was a time when the critics were saying that Jaguars were no good in the wet, that their great power could not be used because their road-holding was suspect. Having always said this was nonsense, I was pleased to back up my opinion with a practical demonstration."

Even more significantly, Johnny Claes and Jacques Ickx put up a magnificent performance with HKV 455 to win the Leige-Rome-Leige rally in August, and to complete the 3,000 mile event without the loss of a single mark for the first time in its history. Herzet and Baudoin had come 5th in the Liege-Rome-Liege in 1950 with an XK 120, but their effort was not really to be compared to the Claes/Ickx achievement. Later in 1951 Claes was awarded the Belgian National Trophy of Merit, the country's highest award for sport, in recognition of his drive with Ickx (the father of the GP driver) in this, one of the toughest of the great European rallies and ranking ahead of the Alpine and Tulip in its severity.

There were no British Jaguar entries at all in the 'Leige', only the Riley/Lamb Healey travelling out from England to contest the event, but the team prize still fell to the company - Herzet and Baudion came second in their XK 120, and Laroche and Radix finished 5th. The former car had been fitted with a quite attractive fixed-head coupe body by Oblin of Brussells, rather in the Ferrari idiom (it still survives, in unrestored form, in Belgium).

Johnny Claes himself had already brought Jaguar success earlier in 1951, when in June he had won the Production Sports Car race at the very fast Spa circuit, using an XK 120 sent over by the factory at the request of the Brussells Jaguar agent. An interesting aside here is that during practice for this event, Paul Frere (then works manager at the same Jaguar agents) was asked by another XK 120 entrant, Baron Jean Dufour, to take his car round the circuit just to see if it was in perfect order. Frere agreed, "and proceeded to do three laps, the last proving to be the fastest of the day", as he recalled in his book *Starting Grid to Chequered Flag.* This occurance made an impression on Jacques Ickx and prompted him to put forward Paul Frere's name for an important Oldsmobile 'works' drive at Spa in the following year's production car races, which was to be a significant step up in the career of this brilliant racing driver and journalist - who of course was to eventually join the Jaguar works team.

Another European racing success was Scherrer's first place in the Production Car class in the Bremgarten Preis event at Berne, the XK being 8 mph down on the overall winner's speed, put up by Daetwyler's 1937 4½ litre V12 Alfa Romeo running with road equipment.

The Tour de France of September 1951 didn't herald such convincing successes for Jaguar as had the 'Liege', a 2.6 Ferrari being the outright winner, but at least Jaguar took the first four places in the over 3-litre class, headed by Hache and Crespin, with Simone/Schlee second, and Descollas (whose Bugatti had often proved faster than the SS tourers in pre-war Alpine Trials) partnering Gignoux for third place. The same month saw the Tourist Trophy race at Dundrod, but the day of the sports racing car had arrived and Moss repeated his 1950 win in a C-type. The highest placed XK 120 was J B Swift's, which was 15th on handicap.

Ian Appleyard and NUB 120 were still scoring at home, winning the London Rally in September although navigation was by Gordon Wilkins on this occasion - not that Pat Appleyard was exactly resting, as she took the Ladies Award in the Northern Rally held the same month. A different combination in the personages of F P Grounds and J B Hay won their class in the 1951 MCC Rally with an XK 120 in November, while the revived Welsh Rally (another pre-war SS 100 preserve) also held in November brought yet another win, C Heath's XK 120 finishing the event with a clean sheet.

XKs were now frequent visitors to hill climb meetings too, as was proved by the July Bouley Bay event on the island of Jersey - the entire over 3-litre class was made up of XKs, R L Sangan driving the winning car with A Owen as runner up.

Although David Murray's Scottish racing team Ecurie Ecosse was not formed until right at the end of 1951, its individual drivers were already becoming known in their XK 120s, Ian Stewart in particular driving his XK with effect. He was placed third at Winfield in July, and borrowed Freddie Mort's XK 120 to win the Formula Libre race at Turnberry in September. The celebrated Louis Chiron drove an XK 120 in the 1951 Ulster Trophy race in Northern Ireland but together with the other big-engined cars was rather handicapped out of a possible 'place', the event being won by a certain Mike Hawthorn in his 1936 TT Riley. Success did not always attend Jaguar efforts in the big international events entered either - two 'unofficial' works XK 120s set off on the 5th Mille Miglia with crews arranged on the basis of driver and 'fixer'. Leslie Johnson drove JWK 651 (of course) with mechanic John Lea (who was later to act as such to Bob Berry during his XK days), and Stirling Moss was behind the wheel of the almost equally well-worn HKV 500, accompanied on the excursion by Frank Rainbow. For this event, JWK 651 was fitted with a low full-width Perspex windscreen, although HKV 500 had the more traditional optional extra aero-screen and cowled mirror.

The 1951 Mille Miglia was run over a shortened course of some 970 miles, and the two Jaguars were among eight British entries out of a field of more than 300 cars. An Aston Martin won its class, and Donald Healey brought the new Nash-Healey production car into 30th position in the general category, but both the XKs retired with braking problems - the frequent heavy rainstorms were obviously not enough to cool the drum brakes! There had been an XK 120 entered in the 1951 Le Mans too, the last of its type to run in the 24 hours race. It was strictly a non-factory effort, though the car was prepared at Jaguar's service department 'at cost'. A very standard, wire-wheeled roadster (AEN 546), there was little extraordinary about the car, one of its few distinguishing features being the holes let into its bonnet to allow the radiator and oil caps to be removed without having to spend the time undoing and lifting the bonnet. On the other hand, quite an interesting story does attend its chief driver, Bob Lawrie.

As with Norman Culpan and his Frazer Nash, the 1949 Le Mans event had been Lawrie's first-ever race, in which he drove an Aston Martin DB1. He had no previous competition experience at all, but had become friendly with the organisers of the race while in France after the war; this friendship with one or two key people in the Automobile Club de l'Ouest led, after he had expressed an interest in the event, to the offer of a place in the first post war race. As they (or indeed Lawrie too) had no idea whether he would be fast enough to keep out of everyone's way, the proviso was made that should he prove too slow in practice beforehand, he was to withdraw - but on the basis of an imaginary mechanical ailment to avoid embarrassment!

However, he was seen to be entirely competent and so not only did he run in 1949, but was given the privilege of an entry in 1950 with the Riley Roadster, in 1951 with AEN 546, and finally in 1952 as a works driver for Morgan (a car which, after the others he'd driven round the circuit, he didn't like so much).

The XK 120 completed the 1951 epic without drama, co-driven by Waller, and finished a very creditable 11th having averaged 82.52 mph for 1,992 miles - which was only five or six miles behind the works DB2 of Mann/Morris Goodall, and ahead of the Lancia Aurelia saloon driven by Count Johnny Lurani and Bracco, two DB2s, the Ferrari 166 of Betty Haig, and both the Frazer Nashes. Quite rightly, it was the winning C-type Jaguar making its fantastic competition debut that received all the glory and acclaim, but is should not be overlooked that the Lawrie/Waller car was the highest placed **XK 120** to feature at Le Mans (after Johnson's retirement the previous year, Clark and Haines had finished 12th) and had to cope with tougher opposition than the team cars met in 1951.

In connection with the 1951 Le Mans race, mention should be made of the three special XK 120s which were built for the event in case the C-type sports racing cars weren't ready. Work on the new C-type was going ahead at a good pace and Heynes himself was confident that three cars would be built in time to take part in the race, but Lyons, who had to leave for an important business tour of North America lasting some four to six weeks, only a few months before Le Mans, gave orders "for three lightweight bodies on more or less standard XK 120 lines to be built and fitted to lightened production chassis", to quote William Heynes.

Three bodyshells were indeed completed before Le Mans, but despite Lyons' worries so were the C-types, with the result that the 'lightweight XK 120s' were redundant even before they turned a wheel.

These special bodies, designated LT 1, 2 and 3, were very different even to the normal aluminium-bodies XK 120s, and resulted in a weight saving of about 3 cwt. Magnesium alloy was used, and the shell was mounted on a metal tubular sub-frame attached to the chassis. There were no internal boot panels or bootlid, the rear half of the body being in one piece, including the rear wings. Standard XK 120 doors were fitted, but cut off at the sill line; front wings were integral with the 'bonnet', access to the engine being via a small centre lift-out panel. It is not clear whether any of these bodies were actually fitted to a chassis upon their first being built, but at anyrate two were saved from the usual fate of factory prototypes when Charles Hornburg, Jaguar's Western United States distributor, spotted them while on a visit to the

factory a short while after the 1951 Le Mans race. He promptly purchased two and had them shipped to the States, mounted on normal XK 120 chassis taken apparently at random from the production line. LT-2 was placed on chassis number 660748, and LT-3 on 660741.

The two cars then began their very active lives, racing for Hornburg as a team (LT-2 green, LT-3 white). Phil Hill drove LT-3, while a number of people had a go in LT-2. The cars' first race of note was at Elkhart Lake, Wisconsin, where Hill finished 3rd in LT-3 behind the big and rather imposing Cunninghams; LT-2 was 4th. Later in 1951, Hill took a 2nd place at Palm Springs, California, while in October both cars went to Reno to do battle with such as Bill Pollack in Tim Carsten's Cadillac-Allard. LT-3 (Hill) sat on Pollack's tail for 30 laps in second place until the oil pressure relief valve blew out, dropping the car to 10th. Meanwhile, Bill Breeze in LT-2 had difficulty keeping on the track and finally spun into some boulders, badly damaging both himself and the car.

LT-3 continued to complete in major races during the next year, 1952, with its last 'National' appearance being at the accident-shortened 1952 Watkins Glen Grand Prix; it was then sold to a big Jaguar dealer in St Louis and campaigned in local events alongside a C-type. Thereafter, it changed hands many times though always remained in the St Louis area, even being used at one time as a 'modified stock car' for oval dirt track racing. Meanwhile, LT-2 had disappeared from view and has only recently surfaced, being brought back to England in 1974. LT-3 finally secured a safe berth also during 1974 in the hands of Tom Hendricks, one of America's foremost XK enthusiasts, who found that the car was in a remarkable state of preservation with little needing doing. It was found to have a C-type head, an early replacement for the original which was discovered to have been warped, causing the engine to boil after a few laps - as Hornburg said, the car would "go like hell" for a few laps and then overheat. A

C-type radiator had also been fitted, along with two 2 inch C-type carburettors, and a vitrous enamelled 'branch' exhaust manifold; wire wheels were fitted, on an ENV axle at the rear of the car. A very large 'Le Mans-type' petrol tank was in place, while the interior of the car was properly trimmed with door side panels and kick panels in grey-blue leather; bucket seats in a similar material featured too. The car is now being restored from the chassis up by Hendricks.

While LT-2 and LT-3 were leading active lives in the States, body number LT-1 was to languish at Jaguar for several years before it too was given a chassis and brought to life - by one Bob Berry, Jaguar employee and an enthusiastic amateur driver. The story of LT-1 is related further on in this Chapter.

At the close of 1951, Jaguar could look back on an incredible list of competition achievements by its road sports car, both in the hands of its 'semi-works' drivers and through the efforts of genuine private owners. Very few single models of sports car can have equalled or excelled in one year the XK 120's 1951 tally of national and international victories and 'places' - the list makes awe-inspiring reading: winning performances in the great trio of Alpine, Tulip and RAC rallies, first and second places in the Marathon de la Route, or Liege-Rome-Liege, a class win in the Tour de France, 11th at Le Mans, the complete overwhelming of the Rallye Soliel, first in the Production Car races at Spa and at the International Trophy meeting at Silverstone, and first at Watkins Glen, USA. Then there were the myriad club successes in Britain and in many other countries, far too many to mention in a book of this nature, plus Leslie Johnson's performance at Montlhery where JWK 651 averaged well over 130 mph for an hour.

It would be unfair to label the XK 120's subsequent competition career as a decline (after all 1952 was probably the model's peak year in the United States), but the car did begin to follow more closely its designed role as a comfortable and very fast road sports car rather than an out-and-out racing machine. Factory support was largely transferred to the new C-type which had been expressly designed for competition work, although help was still given to selected private entrants of XK 120s - Ian Appleyard and Leslie Johnson being the most obvious examples. The factory roadsters, except for NUB 120, no longer ran as semi-works team cars and were gradually dispersed, their drivers now racing the C-type.

Not that XK activity lessened much during 1952. XK 120 Roadsters abounded in club racing and rallying, now joined on occasions by the new fixed-head coupe which had been announced in 1951, and nor were rallies of international status ignored. Here, Ian Appleyard was still very much in contention with NUB 120 both at home and abroad. The RAC Rally of Great Britain in April didn't bring the Yorkshire Jaguar distributor complete success however, as he was placed third behind Jack Broadhead's XK 120, with an Allard winning the event outright and Morgans taking the team prize. Wharton's Ford Zephyr won the Tulip Rally, though Habisreutinger and Horning won the over 1,500 cc sports car class with their XK 120, followed home second and third respectively by Mr & Mrs Grounds and the Lestrange/Bacon XK 120. On this occasion, the Appleyards were in a Mk VII, second on general classification and winning the over 3-litre Touring Car class. Neither did the XKs repeat their Rallye Soliel benefit of the previous year, although Mr and Mrs D O'M Taylor won the over 2,500 cc Sports Car class with Habisreutinger and Horning runners up.

The Scarborough Rally of May saw a Best Performance by W F A Grantham, while the following month XK 120s dominated the over-2,000 cc Open Car class in the Scottish Rally - G P Denham Cooke took first place, J H Cunningham and M H Lawson were second, while Jack Broadhead teamed up with Leslie Wood to come third. The July Eastborne Rally wasn't an XK success though several did well in some of the tests; overall winner was a Dellow, and the Unlimited Open category was won by an SS 100!

However, when it really counted Ian Appleyard could be relied upon to bring home the bacon. The 1952 Rallye des Alpes was yet again the occasion of a penalty-free run by NUB 120, this year the famous white car running with wire wheels. By this achievement, Appleyard became the first man to complete three consecutive Alpine rallies without losing a mark, and thus won the first Alpine Gold Cup ever to be awarded. This feat rather overshadowed the superb performance put up by the Dutch driver Maurice Gatsonides in the same event; using a factory car (MDU 524) he not only won the over 3,000 cc class (Appleyard was second), but also came second on general classification to the winning BMW, gaining 11 cups in the process and returning the quickest time on the timed mountain ascent. An exceptional performance in a very tough rally, which saw only 23 survivors out of 95 starters. The opposition was no easier, and included Hawthorn and Moss in Sunbeam Talbots, and other XK 120s driven by Grant Norton, Herzet in the Oblin-bodied coupe, and K S Richardson in SEV 970. Said *The Motor* of the event, "Jaguars have added lustre to their laurels again".

While the Alpine was in progress, the annual Welsh Rally was under way. In this, Farquharson's XK 120 won the over 1,500 cc Open Cars class chased by a Healey and another XK 120. Appleyard gained a first class award in the Lakeland Rally at the end of October (although another Dellow achieved Best Performance), and in the MCC Rally held during November, Mr. and Mrs D O'MTaylor came first in the over 3,000 cc Open Car class, Stirling Moss managing a similar performance in his fixed-head coupe in the equivalent closed car division, partnered by John Cooper. Of the concours d'elegance section of the MCC Rally, *The Motor* said: "As usual the winning cream Jaguar XK 120 entered by Mrs Snow was resplendent with leopard skin seat covers, the owner herself being suitably dressed in a coat and hat of similar material." Hardly a conservationist attitude, but it was 1952! The car, PPC 120, won many concours awards and still looks as beautiful as ever in the hands of its present owner, Peter Spackman.

Stirling Moss's car was a two-tone fixed-head (LVC 345) which he used quite extensively, not only for rallying but also for towing his Nomad caravan from circuit to circuit on the continent. The most important rally entered by the car was the Lyons-Charbonnieres in 1952, an event rated by experienced rallyists above the Alpine although below the Liege-Rome-Liege in severity. That year, the rally was a little spoilt by many protests, and Heurtaux's XK 120 crashed - Moss stopped to help but inspite of losing some time, still made third best time on that particular climb although he was not highly placed overall. XKs had figured in the 1952 Liege-Rome-Liege as well, and very successfully too as Laroche and Radix brought their XK 120 Roadster into 2nd place on general category, and first in the over 3,000 cc class.

On the 1952 racing front, that season was the occasion of Stirling Moss's last win on the track with an XK 120. The event was the International Trophy meeting of May, and Moss had a good day winning three races, in a Mk VII saloon, C-type, and an XK 120 respectively. The latter car was one of eight identical left-hand drive roadsters provided by Jaguar for a 'Race of Champions', including Claes of Belgium, Bira of Siam, Gaze of Australia, de Graffenried of Switzerland, Pietsch of Germany, and of course, Moss representing Great Britain. Run over five laps, the race was won by Moss quite easily.

A significant happening early in the year was the emergence of Ecurie Ecosse onto the race tracks. This famous Scottish team was formed by David Murray who already had an interest in a mews garage in Edinburgh together with W E Wilkinson, famous since before the war for engine preparation. Murray had retired from racing himself after crashing a Maserati single-seater at the Nurburgring (although he was to drive one of the team's cars on a single occasion afterwards) so had transferred his enthusiasm for the sport to managing an all-Scottish motor racing team. The original drivers, apart from their nationality qualification, all owned Jaguar XK 120 Roadsters; they were Ian Stewart, Bill Dobson and the 20 year-old Sir James Scott-Douglas, Bart., the novice of the team. All three cars were painted in what was to become known as Ecurie Ecosse Blue (actually flag metallic blue), and with £1,000 backing from Esso, began their highly successful career - though in a small way at first, at the local Charterhall circuit and in club meetings generally.

Although first appearing as a team at Charterhall in April (where they were severely handicapped), the first big meeting to be contested by the blue XK 120s was the 1952 British Empire Trophy race, held on the Isle of Man on a 'round the houses' road circuit. Murray himself was behind the wheel of an XK 120, joining Stewart, Dobson and Scott-Douglas, but unfortunately his re-entry into motor racing didn't last long as, due to failing brakes, he first spun off at Parkfield, then missed a turn at Ochan and clipped a house. Sir James Scott-Douglas did somewhat better and finished a good 6th overall on the rather strange handicapping system, also winning the over 3,000 cc class at an average speed of 65.22 mph.

Scott-Douglas followed his Isle of Man performance with a superb 3rd place at Rheims in June, behind the C-type of Stirling Moss which had taken the lead after Manzon's Gordini had crashed. This was the highest placing an Ecurie Ecosse XK 120 achieved in International racing and proved that, while the C-type might actually be doing the winning, Jaguar's road sports car was still capable of being 'placed' in an important racing event.

The team's XK 120s performed another back-up role to the C-type in July, but this time it was to the car of Ian Stewart, which had just been added to Ecurie Ecosse's strength. The event was the Jersey International Road Race and Stewart brought the brand-new C-type to victory, marking up the team's first major win. Bill Dobson and Jamie Scott-Douglas drove their XK 120s and proceeded to come 5th and 6th respectively - in one heat Dobson's roadster actually had the legs of Parnell's works Aston Martin DB3 down the straight, quite leaving it behind on acceleration! Four other XK 120s also ran in this race.

Stewart repeated his Jersey win by another at The Curragh in Northern Ireland, his C-type finishing first in the Wakefield Trophy race organised by the Irish Motor Racing Club in September; Scott-Douglas and LXO 126 netted third place behind the C-type in this event, and acted as runner-up to Stewart in the handicap O'Boyle Trophy race run on the same occasion. In the same month, Bill Dobson won the second September handicap for sports cars at Goodwood, averaging 77.76 mph.

When Ecurie Ecosse's first season had ended, they could look back upon 13 wins in 18 events entered, with 7 second places and 8 third places to their credit as well. An excellent beginning for the team in no small measure due to the hard-worked XK 120s. While these were to be largely pensioned off when Murray acquired C-types for the 1953 season, Sir James Scott-Douglas at least had a final fling in big-time motor racing with his roadster. During practice for the 1953 Nurburgring 1000 km race, he crashed his C-type rather violently though luckily emerging "more startled than hurt". But unabashed, he unloaded his luggage from LXO 126 and completed the race in the XK 120! Stewart and Salvadori came second overall in their C-type, one of Jaguar's best results over that difficult circuit.

Besides the well-known race tracks of Europe and the United States, XK 120s found their way onto the starting grids of some very strange races in various far-flung parts of what had been the British Empire, and in other obscure corners of the globe. Witness for instance the Johore Grand Prix, which sounds and was a rather unlikely sort of event. Like other Grands Prix of the time in similarly out of the way places, it was rarely supported by visiting professionals and it was usually left to the nationals or, quite often, resident British subjects to scrap amongst themselves. Run on a formula libre basis, a weird selection of monoposto and sports car machinery appeared on the grid and the racing was none the worse for that. The XK 120 was closely associated with this Malayan epic, run over a 1.3 mile circuit at Bahru during the early fifties; in 1950 an XK 120 'special' had won (this was little more than an XK running without front wings and other impedimenta) followed by a Cooper JAP and F M Ferguson's XK 120 Roadster, and 1951 had seen a win by a supercharged MG TC to which Hawes and Freddie Ferguson were runners up on their XK 120s. Ferguson's car was an early aluminium bodied roadster (660025) purchased in the UK through Brinkman's who were then Jaguar agents for Singapore. Like the other XK 120s in the country, the car was also campaigned in local events such as the Lornie Mile Sprint at Kuala Lumpar, and at the Malacca hill climb, before being sold to Col. T J Trevor (see Chapter Three).

The 1952 Johore Grand Prix was actually won by an XK 120 - the roadster of Derek Bovet-White. Purchased in June 1950, the car was updated to Special Equipment form (180 bhp) and Al-Fin brake drums fitted - but still ran without the rear wings for extra cooling of the rear brakes! Although it appeared at the 1950 Brighton Speed Trials, most of the car's many successes were in Malaya and included some eight course records over the local sprint venues, and fourth place in the 1951 Johore Grand Prix. A rubber planter like Ferguson, Bovet-White retired to England in later years and now runs the Anchor Inn at Barcombe, near Lewes, in Sussex which is a regular meeting place for Jaguars and Aston Martins; he retains his enthusiasm for XKs through a red XK 150 Drop-head Coupe.

East Africa was another country in which the XK 120 had an important (by local standards) competition role, and it was undoubtedly

C J Manussis, Coca Cola bottler and racing driver, who was the leading Jaguar exponent there in the fifties. His XK 120 Roadster (660886) was quite extensively modified, with certain unusual deviations from standard which were perhaps aimed at combating the local high ambient temperatures - for instance, glycol was used in the cooling system. An advanced move was the installation of a Pye two-way radio in the car for communication with the pits (also used by Jaguar themselves on one occasion). George Pyman was another driver who raced an XK 120 (though was killed while doing so towards the end of 1952), and Viscount Mandeville was well known for his XK 120 drives at the Langa Langa circuit near Nakuru. Manussis himself broke a number of records at that circuit, and finished the 1953 season as East African Champion; he also raced a C-type and was seen behind the wheel of a Jaguar at European tracks too, on occasions.

To return to Great Britain once more, an increasing number of club drivers were turning to the XK 120 for their part time racing, and some ventured their cars in quite important races. Brigadier Michael Head began a successful amateur career behind the XK engine when he purchased GOT 900, a white XK 120 Roadster. This he drove in Scandinavian races during 1952, finishing first in the over 2-litre class of the Finnish Grand Prix for sports cars - Brigadier Head's connection with that part of the world came about because he had been with the Military Attache at the British Embassy at Stockholm. The white XK became a familiar sight on British tracks too, until it was replaced by the ex-Wisdom/Cannell C-type Jaguar, MDU 212 - this too was painted white, as Head felt that this was his 'lucky colour' after his happy experiences with the XK 120. Amongst the many regular XK entrants of the period were included E W Holt, J B Swift (660493), George Wicken (660328) and Hugh Howorth; the latter was one of the most successful in his two-tone roadsters. Howorth's first car was EBN 722 which went extremely

Top left Peter Walker and Stirling Moss in combat during the Production Sports Car Race at the *Daily Express* meeting of 1951. Moss and JWK 977 won, making it a hat trick for XK 120s in this race (*photo The Motor*)

Top right A highly creditable 11th place at an average of 82mph in the 1951 Le Mans race was achieved by this near standard, privately entered XK 120 of Bob Laurie (*photo The Motor*)

Centre The Swiss driver Ruef Habisreutinger and his roadster (660731), seen here on the Cortina 'closed section' during the 1951 Alpine Rally, provided great success for Jaguar. On this occasion a *Coupe des Alpes* was gained (*photo The Motor*)

Centre right Magnificent scenery with which Ian Appleyard and NUB 120 will be forever associated. The most famous of XK 120s crosses the mountains during the 1951 Alpine Rally (*photo The Motor*)

Bottom Ian and Pat Appleyard (nee Lyons) in NUB 120 during final tests at Olivers Mount in an RAC Rally. The scuttle ventilator was added to this alloy car after the production steel cars were so equipped in 1951 (*photo The Motor*)

Top left Probably the most active 'works' XK 120 in its time - Leslie Johnson's faithful JWK 651, veteran of Le Mans, Mille Miglia and TT, to n a few events. The owner stands behind the car with William Heynes (left) shortly after returning to the factory following another run at Montlhery *(photo The Motor)*

Top right Cooper 500 versus Ferguson's XK 120 during the 1951 Johore GP. The XK eventually finished second

Centre left European success; Scherrer winning the Sports Car race held at Berne on the occasion of the Swiss GP in May 1951 *(photo The Motor)*

Centre right An August 1951 Boreham meeting with Hugh Howorth leadi Duncan Hamilton. Note the use of a headlight nacelle as an air intake *(photo The Motor)*

Bottom A type of race common today - a number of identical cars with 'celebrity' drivers. This is the 1951 Silverstone British GP meeting where in a 'Race of Champions' the GP drivers of the day fought it out in XK 120s. Moss won by a long way

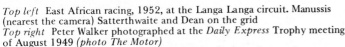

Top left East African racing, 1952, at the Langa Langa circuit. Manussis (nearest the camera) Satterthwaite and Dean on the grid

Top right Peter Walker photographed at the *Daily Express* Trophy meeting of August 1949 *(photo The Motor)*

Centre Roy Salvadori, a successful XK 120 campaigner later to become better known for his driving of Aston Martins *(photo The Motor)*

Bottom left Bill Dobson at Boreham in August 1951 *(photo The Motor)*

Bottom right A superb picture by George Moore of *The Motor* which captures all the atmosphere of a big continental rally - the XK 120 of Escalier passes through the village of Tal during the 1953 Alpine Rally. Note the non-factory but neat side-screens *(photo The Motor)*

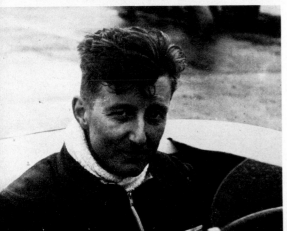

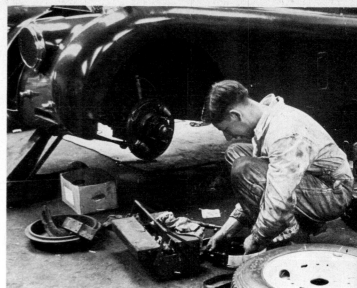

Top left Preparation for the 1952 Empire Trophy Race. In the very immediate foreground is Sir James Scott-Douglas' car, while just behind, David Murray watches Wilkie Wilkinson carry out a last minute adjustment to his roadster; the other cars are those of J B Swift (32), Ian Stewart (36), W Belfrage Block (33) and S J Boshier (31). *(photo The Motor)*

Top right An Ecurie Ecosse mechanic at work on the brakes of Ian Stewart's XK 120 before the 1952 British Empire Trophy Race. The heavily drilled road wheel also has scoops welded onto it in an attempt to provide much-needed brake cooling *(photo The Motor)*

Centre left David Murray's Last Ride: an obviously dejected Murray (hand on hip) watches his car being pushed away after failing to make a turn during the 1952 British Empire Trophy

Centre right John Lyons, son of Sir William, conducts his XK 120 in a driving test at Morecombe during the May 1952 National Jubilee Rally. In 1955 he was to lose his life while driving out to Le Mans - a major personal tragedy for his father, and perhaps an important factor in determining the future of Jaguar Cars Limited *(photo The Motor)*

Bottom Ian Appleyard examines his XK's front suspension as Joe Lowrey of *The Motor* helps by moving the steering wheel. By the time of the Alpine Rally of 1953, when this picture was taken, RUB 120 had replaced NUB 120 *(photo The Motor)*

Top left How RUB 120 ended up - carrying a drop-head coupe body. After its re-bodying by Appleyard and 'Lofty' England, the car was sold to Scott, who with Cunningham drove it in the 1954 Alpine Rally (as seen here) *(photo The Motor)*
Top right Just how popular XK 120s became for rallying is illustrated by this photograph of a control on the May 1953 Morecombe National Rally. Note NUB 120 towards the end of the queue, and the SS 100s too
Centre left Mr and Mrs Reg Mansbridge on the Alpine Rally of July 1953 with their successful XK 120 Fixed-head. They won a *Coupe des Alpes* *(photo The Motor)*
Centre right Stirling Moss brakes his left hand drive XK 120 Fixed-head to a halt during a test on the *Daily Express* Rally - one of a number of national and international rallies Moss entered with his duo-tone car which was also equipped for towing his caravan from circuit to circuit on the continent *(photo The Motor)*
Bottom LWK 707 returns home after its 7 days and 7 nights at Montlhery. From left to right are, William Lyons, the Mayor of Dover, Leslie Johnson, Bert Hadley, 'Lofty' England, Jack Fairman and Ernest Rankin

Top left Preparing the 172mph XK 120 Roadster. Note the sloping XK 140 type radiator, the 2 inch carbs and the C/D-type camshaft breathing arrangements. The number plate was, of course, removed for the runs; the special low-resistance Dunlop tyres can be seen to the left of the car

Top right Bob Berry hurls LT1 round a corner at Snetterton, one wheel clear of the ground, during the August 1954 International Trophy meeting. Note the car's lift-out bonnet panel, 'high' door shut line and one-piece rear quarters *(photo The Motor)*

Centre left How LT2 ended up during its United States racing career, with special bodywork reminiscent of the C-type; photographed at Pebble Beach in 1955. The car was recently brought back to Great Britain

Centre right Phil Hill driving what was probably his last race for Charles Hornburg in LT3, at Pebble Beach, Montlhery, April 1952. In front is the 2.6 Ferrari he'd just bought, but couldn't race in that event because he'd promised Hornburg that he would drive the XK

Bottom An innovation for the Commonwealth, a 24 hour race was set in February 1954 on the short and winding Mount Druitt circuit near Sidney, Australia. It was won by Mrs Anderson's XK 120 Fixed-head, seen here at Dam Bend driven by one of her two male co-drivers; and that was in spite of an hour's stop to replace (from a spectator's car) a carburettor which had fallen off! The XK covered 573 laps, 4 more than the second place Bristol 400, after the leading C-type had retired. Mrs Anderson later imported a D-type

Top Rob Beck in the now 'cut and shut' MXJ 954 temporarily holds off Jackie Stewart in Eric Brown's modified XK 120 Drop-head, 1 ALL; Stewart eventually won this race at the National JDC meeting at Crystal Palace in June 1964 *(photo The Motor)*
Centre Dick Protheroe and the 'Ancient Egyptian' at Oulton Park, clipping the grass at Old Hall during the Gold Cup meeting of September 1959 *(photo The Motor)*
Bottom John N Pearson's racing XK 120 Drop-head, the ultimate of its breed and the fastest Modified Sports Car of its time - Lotus Elans and E-types notwithstanding! *(photo The Motor)*

Top Under the bonnet of the 1951 Le Mans C-type showing part of the car's tubular framework, partly stressed front bulkhead and the power plant. Note the 1¾ inch carburettors, spare coil and absence of studs on the front of the cam covers *(photo The Motor)*

Centre Front suspension of the 1951 C-type. The use of many standard XK 120 parts is apparent though the brakes, still drum, are automatically adjusting. Unlike all but the earliest XK 120s, the C-type had provision for a starting handle *(photo The Motor)*

Bottom The 1951 Le Mans team assembled at the factory. Bedford tender lorry alongside, prior to leaving by road for the race. Note the saloon bodyshells in the background *(photo The Motor)*

Top left On its way to victory, the C-type of Whitehead and Walker circulates in company with the Parnell/Hampshire Aston Martin DB2 which came 7th, Le Mans 1951 *(photo The Autocar)*

Top right A short while before the 1951 Le Mans race, and a young Stirling Moss white-washes a tree for use as a marker or braking point during the hours of darkness *(photo The Autocar)*

Centre Sir William Lyons in a relaxed mood at a continental circuit, with William Heynes (right) and Tommy Wisdom in patterned shirt *(photo William Heynes)*

Bottom An informal group at Le Mans 1951. (l to r) Moss in kidney belt, something he always wore when racing, Whitehead, 'Dunlop Mac' (David John Mc Donald), Heynes and an unknown person *(photo William Heynes)*

Top The 1952 Le Mans C-type with its new, longer front and rear bodywork sections, photographed shortly before the retirement of all three team cars *(photo The Motor)*
Centre How Jaguar's 1952 Le Mans challenge ended; the three team cars in the paddock whilst the race continues without them *(photo The Motor)*
Bottom left Ian Stewart at the wheel of Ecurie Ecosse's first C-type just before the start of its first race, the July 1952 Jersey Road Race, which he won. Stewart now sells Ferraris! *(photo The Motor)*
Bottom right Rare photograph of the 1952 Le Mans C-type's engine compartment. Note the bulkhead mounted header tank *(photo The Autocar)*

Top A superb shot of Tony Rolt and the C-type at Goodwood when he beat Stirling Moss in a similar but disc braked car in September 1952 (*photo The Motor*)

Centre left On the way to the start of the 1952 Mille Miglia. Bob Berry took this picture of the C-type and support car, a white Mk VII saloon. Moss is at the wheel of the C-type and mechanic Frank Rainbow in the centre. The event was the first to be entered by a disc braked C-type

Centre right An interior view of the 1952 production C-type neatly trimmed and painted. Note the 6,500 rpm revolution counter and 160 mph speedometer, and the mounting of the headlight dipswitch below the gear lever (*photo The Motor*)

Bottom Truly a road sports car - *The Motor's* road test production C-type in a pastoral setting (*photo The Motor*)

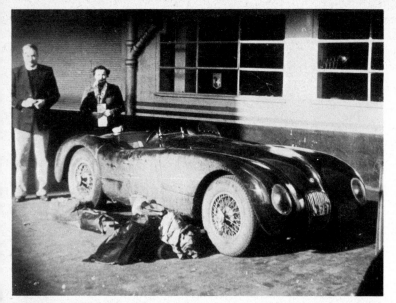

Top left During the course of *The Motor's* 1952 road test of the production C-type, Mr and Mrs Christopher Jennings took the car to Germany. They are seen here during a short halt with the luggage they managed to cram into the cockpit displayed in front of the car *(photo Christopher Jennings)*

Top right British Empire Trophy Race 1952 - Jimmy Stewart has a slight drama with the Ecurie Ecosse C-type on the Isle of Man circuit *(photo The Motor)*

Centre left Hunting in packs! Moss heads Sanderson, J Stewart J B Swift and the Aston Martin of R Dickson during the British Empire Trophy Race of June 1953 *(photo The Motor)*

Centre right Mercedes Benz Competition Manager Alfred Neubauer looks at Jaguar's new disc brakes, probably at Rheims on the occasion of the C-type's win with disc brakes

Bottom Duncan Hamilton chases Tony Rolt around Lodge Corner at Oulton Park during the 1954 Empire Trophy Race. The Weber carburetted OVC 915 eventually beat the Ecurie Ecosse C-types to win the event *(photo The Motor)*

well, and he intended replacing it with a C-type but never quite managed to extract one from the factory. As a sort of consolation though, Lofty England sold him JWK 977, and gave him a complete C-type back axle and rear suspension set-up, and this Howorth grafted onto the ex-Peter Walker roadster. The arrangement worked remarkably well and Howorth was usually up at the front in any scrap involving XKs, and won the William Lyons Trophy in 1952 and 1954.

JWK 977 afterwards passed to Jack Haslam, then Gillie Tyrer, before Gordon Brown bought it in 1956. He exchanged the 3.4 C-type engine for a full dry-sump, 30/40 head, D-type engine and drove the car in sprints for many years. Due to the C-type rear end, Gordon Brown remembers the handling of JWK 977 as being "unbelievably better" than a normal XK 120, though he thinks it could have done with a small diameter anti-roll bar at the back as it was inclined to understeer on slow corners.

A major event of 1952 which captured the imagination at the time, and brought Jaguar a considerable amount of publicity, was the epic sortie to Linas-Montlhery in August by Leslie Johnson and LWK 707, an XK 120 Fixed-head Coupe, chassis number 669002, the second rhd example completed.

After his successful runs at the huge banked concrete track with JWK 651, Johnson had set his heart on averaging 100 mph for a week with a Jaguar, and finally persuaded the factory to back him in the attempt. The bronze-coloured fixed-head coupe used was ostensibly Johnson's own for the purposes of the Montlhery excursion, but it was in actual fact prepared at the works and immediately after the project was over, was retired to a life of publicity appearances.

Surprisingly little was done to the car beforehand, except of course for meticulous preparation; the larger capacity C-type sump was used (holding 2¼ gallons of oil) and a C-type branch exhaust. The Le Mans 24-gallon petrol tank was placed in the boot, an extra windscreen wiper fixed above the driver's windscreen, and a Pye radio transmitter and receiver was fitted inside. The optional wire wheels were used, and a 3.27 axle ratio was employed. The drivers were Johnson, his Le Mans co-driver Bert Hadley, Stirling Moss and Jack Fairman, with Morris-Goodall and Desmond Scannel in attendance on the organising side. Shell, Dunlop and SU all sent along their usual experts too.

The run began quietly as the idea was not to announce the intention of running for seven days and nights at 100 mph until success was actually established. This was probably as well, for the attempt began with a dramatic false start. Behind the wheel for a night-time stint, Fairman was lapping steadily at around 120 mph (in an effort to gain the 48 Hour record, which stood at well over 100 mph) when one of the XK's wheels ran over a lump of dislodged concrete, not an unknown hazard of that circuit, and burst an offside rear tyre. This wasn't all - the shredded rubber not only attacked the wing but also cut the main lead from the battery, so Fairman had to cope with a simultaneous loss of both lights and engine power! To make matters worse, the loose battery cable swung about causing vivid blue sparks as it touched the bodywork every so often. But somehow Fairman managed to coax the XK off the banking and down to a standstill at the bottom without further damage.

After sundry repairs, the run began in earnest at 16.00 hours on August 5th, with the car settling down to lap in around 52 seconds, or about 110 mph. Refuelling and driver changes were made every four hours, when the tyres were checked and replaced as necessary (the least loaded covers lasted some 2,000 miles, the most loaded 1,000 miles). Some delay was caused when oil got onto the clutch, and so the speed was increased in another attempt to capture the elusive 48-Hour International Class record, which had been set by a Delahaye at 109.54 mph. But although the XK managed to average 110.39 mph this didn't give the required 10% margin, and furthermore the higher speed was having a detrimental effect on the dampers.

This was evidenced by a rear spring breaking on the fifth day, and although it was replaced in a fraction over 4 hours 14 minutes, the rest of the run could not stand as an official record as the new spring had not been carried in the car as the regulations demanded. The remainder of the run therefore had to be an officially observed and timed demonstration only.

Despite atrocious weather settling in for the last day or so, the XK easily completed its seven days and seven nights at a far higher average than the existing record even though that still had to stand; the car actually covered 16,851 miles in 168 hours, the average speed being 110.31 mph - surely a supreme effort by a largely standard, luxuriously equipped road-going coupe available 'over the counter'.

On its triumphant return to Dover, the fixed-head was accorded no less than a civic reception by the Mayor of Dover, Councillor Fish, and Lyons himself came to welcome the car and its crew, together with William Heynes and Harry Weslake. The technical editor of *The Motor*, Laurance Pomeroy, was given the honour of driving the car away, and to his surprise he found virtually no signs of deterioration on his journey back to London - "no slack in the steering, no shake in the body and despite the high top gear and a refuel on British Pool petrol one could drive comfortably in top gear through crowded traffic. The brakes appeared to have full efficiency and were in perfect adjustment; all the instruments were working and the rev. counter showed 3,300 rpm on the very high 'high' during the run back to London."

After a period of public demonstration runs and special displays, LWK 707 returned to Browns Lane as a more or less static exhibit although it now usually resides in the Herbert Museum in Coventry. Still in its original trim and bronze paintwork, it does however emerge from time to time under its own power to appear at exhibitions and parades as a reminder of an epic endurance feat.

The car took the following records:

Distance/Time	Record	Average Speed mph
10000 kilometres	International Class C	107.31
3 days	World Record	105.55
3 days	International Class C	105.55
15000 kilometres	World Record	101.95
15000 kilometres	International Class C	101.95
4 days	World Record	101.17
4 days	International Class C	101.17
10000 miles	World Record	100.66
10000 miles	International Class C	100.66

XK 120s still remained highly competitive in rallies during 1953, even if their appearances in international racing events were now rare. For the first time, the Lyon-Charbonniers rally of March featured a Jaguar victory, Peignaux and Jacquin achieving what Moss could not the previous year in this very tough event, their XK 120 heading the general category. Peignaux was Jaguar's Lyon agent, which was rather appropriate.

Appleyard had lost nothing of his touch, and brought the faithful NUB 120 home to a first place in the RAC International Rally during the same month, losing no marks over the 1,600 mile road section and making best aggregate time in the special tests. Jaguars finished 1st, 4th 8th and 10th in the general category and won the Team Prize.

The Appleyards used a Mk VII saloon in the 1953 Tulip Rally (and won their class with it), but were back in the XK to put up another Best Performance in the general category of the Morecambe Rally in May. The same month saw Taylor take the 'Firth of Scotland' prize in his XK 120 - but although seven XK 120s figured in various results, they did not repeat their outright winning performances of previous years in this the Scottish Rally - an Allard won the big sports car class on this occasion.

The entry lists for the 1953 Alpine Rally once more featured the name Appleyard, but at last NUB 120 had been allowed to rest, after clocking up something like 50,000 miles in competition; the Morecambe Rally had been the last in which the car was used in anger. The aluminium-bodied roadster was finally getting a bit tired, as Ian Appleyard put it, and so NUB 120 was retired. It was placed on show at Jaguar's Browns Lane factory for some time before finally being loaned to what is now the National Motor Museum at Beaulieu; and there it remains, apart from the odd journey to and from a special display, still in exactly its 1953 international rally trim.

As a replacement, Appleyard obtained a brand new steel bodied roadster for which he found the registration number RUB 120. A special equipment model in the familiar white paintwork, it incorporated all the performance options then available and was of course delivered with wire wheels.

The new car did its best to live up to the reputation gained by its older sister, and responded sufficiently well to win its class in the 1953 Alpine, and to give the Appleyards their fourth *Coupes des Alpes* in an XK. Behind them in the over 2,600 cc class was the XK 120 Fixed-head of Gendebien/Fraikin, and third another fixed-head driven by Mr and Mrs Reg Mansbridge - both these two cars were presented with an Alpine Cup too for a penalty free run. A good number of other XK 120s finished that rally too, including the cars of Borgeaud/Conte (6th), Henson/Cooper (7th, and mainly running to assist Ferodo with a brake testing programme), and Mattock/Worthington (8th). Horning from Switzerland crashed, though fortunately without injury.

RUB 120 was not, however, to remain in its original form long. Some time after the 1953 Alpine, Appleyard went into the lead for the 1953 European Rally Championship, the nearest he'd ever got to actually winning it, but was being pressed very hard by the German driver Polensky. I will let Ian Appleyard take up the story himself through the medium of a letter published in the XK Bulletin of December 1969:

It therefore became necessary to enter the Norwegian Viking Rally, for which the regulations were somewhat vague. They indicated that the chassis and engine had to be standard, the car had to have four seats of unspecified size, but that special bodies were allowed, as long as they had winding windows.

Lofty England and I therefore dreamed up the idea of removing the white two-seater sports body from RUB 120 and replacing it with a dark green drop-head coupe body of that period. We then modified this body by cutting away as much as possible behind the front seats and we installed two very small rear seats in this space. By pushing the front seats completely forward and sitting with one's knees under one's chin, it was just possible to demonstrate that four people could be carried - in incredible discomfort I might say!

We therefore entered this four-seater XK 120 in the Viking Rally but I was so bothered that it might be rejected by the scrutineers that I also took to Norway the Mk VII in which I had come second in the Monte Carlo Rally earlier in the year. We hid this second car at the docks, and presented ourselves to the Rally scrutineers with the small car. They were horrified as they said that I was bound to win in such a vehicle - which of course was the object of the excercise, as winning the Viking would have given me the European Rally Championship for certain. They read and re-read their regulations but in the end they had to pass the vehicle as complying in every respect with the official text. However the President of the Club took me on one side and said that it had never been intended that such a vehicle should qualify and that no Norwegian national would have a hope against it. Would I therefore, as a sporting Englishman, please withdraw the car, and use the other one which he had heard we had brought with us as a spare. This rather shook me, as I had no idea that the officials knew I had brought two cars.

Being a bit soft, I agreed to do this, and we had to use the very unsuitable Mk VII, which was far too big for the narrow Norwegian roads.

As a result, during the third night, we went through a bridge, and into a river, and that was the end of that, as Polensky collected enough marks to give him the European Rally Championship.

Towards the end of the 1953 season Appleyard ran the re-bodied car once more, securing a second place in the Lisbon Rally in October. Subsequently RUB 120 was sold to rally driver Scott who used it during the 1954 season. The car was finally broken up in the late sixties, when it was described as being in "shocking condition".

Returning to the summer of 1953, the Evian-

Monte Blanc Rally in August gave Air Vice Marshall D C T Bennet and Mrs Bennet a win in the over 3,000 cc class with their XK 120, while Gendebien and Fraikin brought their car home to an excellent second place in the Liege-Rome-Liege marathon. In October, the XK's rallying season came to an end with a win by the fixed-head coupe of Mr and Mrs J Hally in the Modified Production Closed Car class of the MCC Rally.

As for circuit racing in 1953, the XK 120 was still being seriously campaigned and it was that year that the name of Flt. Lt. Elmer Richard Protheroe, DFC, RAF began to become known in racing circles. Dick Protheroe had served in Bomber Command during the war, and after 1949 had returned to the RAF to fly first in the Transport Command and then as a test pilot for three years. The engineering experience gained during this period probably explains why Protheroe became widely acknowledged as a Jaguar engine tuner of repute.

After mixed experiences with MGs, a blown monoposto Austin 7, and a Type 37 Bugatti, Protheroe obtained an early aluminium bodied XK 120 Roadster whilst on service in Egypt. This he drove successfully at local venues such as the Korkrit airfield circuit, and then brought back with him to England in 1953. There it was registered GPN 635, to become famous as the 'Ancient Egyptian', a nickname reputedly coined by David Pritchard of *Autosport*. The 'Ancient Egyptian' was raced intensively for the next two years, particularly at Goodwood, with engine and chassis modifications being carried out all the while; quite a reasonable degree of success was achieved, and as Protheroe estimated that his general racing expenditure over those two years was something like £2,000, it must be regarded as a serious attempt at keeping the XK 120 competitive on the track.

An XK 120 was very nearly entered in the 1953 Carrera Panamericana, Alan Clark's roadster being prepared at the factory for the event which was a round of the new sports car constructor's championship introduced by the FIA. Originally a C-type had been built for the race but the works entry hadn't been proceeded with (Duncan Hamilton bought the car eventually) and so, Alan Clark recalls, "they really went to town on my car". A modified engine was installed complete with 2-inch carburettors, a short-shafted competition gearbox "with wonderfully close ratios", the suspension was uprated all round, and a 40 gallon petrol tank was substituted for the original. Even the bodywork was disassembled, and the mating surfaces scraped and rubberised before being put back together again - obviously to make sure everything would stay in one piece for the duration of that long and arduous road race. Despite the support of *Road & Track* for which he was European Racing Correspondent at the time, Clark decided not to tackle the race in the end, rather regretfully considering all the work that had been put into the car.

But PFC 999 wasn't exactly left idle, being taken to the continent in 1954; and although it doesn't directly refer to a racing topic this reminiscence of Clark bears reprinting (from the June 1969 XK Bulletin):

> The following year I took it to Italy. I recall a visit to Ferrari and a crazy demonstration drive in a 3-litre Monza driven by Sighnolfi (he was later killed doing just that). The XK was tremendously fast now, and I remember leaving the factory at Maranello one evening behind Ascari in a prototype, unpainted 4.4 litre, 6 cylinder, and going up to Abetone. I was trying like mad, he - to start with at least - was relatively leisurely. After about 30 miles he had around half a minute on me; I would be burning the brakes out downhill on to the bridges while the silver Ferrari was climbing up, about fifteen lacets away, into the pine trees of those endless and bleak Alpine valleys. But by half distance to Florence I had lost him completely.

Undoubtedly the most dramatic happening of 1953 so far as XKs are concerned was the fantastic 172.412 mph recorded by a modified XK 120 Roadster at Jabbeke in October. Some publicity was needed by the factory on the eve of a motor show, and the whole project was set up within ten days of the evening on which William

Lyons decided he wanted to do it. The car used was a steel bodied roadster registered as MDU 524, which was apparently the XK 120 used by Gatsonides and Samworth in the 1952 Alpine, and which had been driven along the same motor road by Norman Dewis the previous April. On that occasion it had run in standard Special Equipment form and had recorded 141.846 mph over the flying kilometre, but when it returned to the Belgian autoroute in October, MDU 524 was considerably more modified.

No details were released on the car's mechanical specification, but as its top speed was virtually the same as a production D-type's, and only 13 mph slower than the highest speed ever officially recorded for a D-type (Rutherford, at Bonneville in 1960, recorded a mean of 185.47 mph), one can confidently assume that an experimental D-type head was used (Jaguar's new sports racing car did not appear itself until the spring of 1954). Certainly MDU 524's engine was fitted with similar breather arrangements on the cam covers to the sports racing cars, though two 2 inch SU carburetters were used and not Webers. A sloping radiator similar to that which was to appear on the XK 140 in 1954 was employed, and the much higher than standard rear axle ratio of 2.92 : 1 was used.

Quite a lot of attention had been paid to bodywork detailing, though the car still looked like what it was, unlike some high speed 'specials' with grafted-on snouts and tails. That the XK 120's basic silhouette remained unaltered surely points to a surprisingly efficient shape for a 1948 design. Basically the work done amounted to a 'smoothing out' of the car's features by the company's aerodynamicist Malcolm Sayer; the brake cooling openings in the front wings were blanked off by plates, the radiator aperture was partially masked off, the sidelights were removed, and the headlights were coned for better penetration (the offside nacelle possibly being used as an air intake for the carburetters as well). The cockpit was completely cowled over, the fortunately fairly short Mr Dewis grasping a very small diameter steering wheel under a Perspex glider canopy. Bumpers were removed fore and aft and the rear wheels were left spatted - the car apparently ran with its nave plates in place too! An undershield was fitted of course. Everything possible was done to lessen rolling resistance, the car wearing special Dunlop tyres with a very small contact area and virtually no tread pattern. With the XK 120 (which was driven to Belgium, minus its glyder canopy) came the C/D prototype, though the running of this car was more of an incidental, advantage being taken of the timing gear and observers being assembled on the autoroute. The Jaguar entourage arrived on a Sunday, and on the following Monday the XK was taken up and down the road just to make sure it was firing on all cylinders, and to determine the right amount of radiator masking to give the correct running temperature. The actual timed runs were scheduled for 8 am the next morning, when the road was to be closed.

Mr. England remembers the occasion well. He arose at 4 am on the Tuesday, opened the window of his hotel room, and surveyed the conditions. He knew at once that the going was good. "If you prayed on your knees for ten years you couldn't have found a more suitable day to do a record attempt - there was no wind at all, about 90% humidity, and about one mile visibility, or in other words just enough to do it. And I mean, no wind *at all* - in fact I lit a cigarette and we held it up and the smoke just moved slowly upwards. Well, I thought, we can't miss on this."

Nor did they miss. With instructions to "take it easy", Norman Dewis was sent off in the sleek dark green roadster, watched by England, 'Dunlop Mac', mechanic Len Hayden, John Webb who was observing for the RAC, and the various Royal Automobile Club of Belgium officials.

When, not long afterwards, the XK 120 flashed through the measured mile at something over 170 mph there was frank amazement amongst the Jaguar personnel. This was repeated when Dewis travelled back in the other direction at almost exactly the same speed a few minutes later, to give the mean speed of 172.412 mph. For, although officially unsurprised at the time, Jaguar would have been "quite happy with 155 mph", as Lofty England confessed years later - the freak conditions and the success of the streamlining effort had produced results beyond the wildest expectations. The ideal conditions extant on that day were indicated by the difference between the car's runs in either direction - it was fractional. Also, Jaguar's Antwerp dealer had come along to watch bringing with him his own XK 120 Roadster, a car which he had bought crashed and rebuilt himself, incorporating a little tuning at the same time. He asked whether he could take his XK through the timing traps while they were still in place, and permission granted, proceeded to accomplish a run at no less than 154 mph! It was fortunate that the C/D prototype's presence *was* only incidental, as its speed over the measured mile only exceeded MDU 524's by 6 mph.

So 1953 ended on a high note for Jaguar, its road sports car distinguishing itself in quite a dramatic way only a few months after the C-type had won Le Mans. But the new year of 1954 was, for the XK 120, to witness a gradual descent from heady overall wins in international rallies and races - though there were to be exceptions. With production C-types now reasonably common on the circuits, and with the D-type Jaguar soon to make even those obsolete, the XK's role on the track was more than ever transferred to club level. One of the exceptions occurred though when Mrs Anderson won the newly instigated Australian 24-Hour race early in 1954; with male co-drivers, she averaged 53.8 mph over the duration of the race with her Special Equipment fixed-head coupe, after the C-type of Whitehead and Gaze, brought over for the event, had retired with a broken rear radius arm. In this country, the car still continued to provide great enjoyment for many people in club racing, and joining their ranks for

the 1954 season was Bob Berry, a young Jaguar employee.

Berry approached the project in a businesslike way and ended up with one of the fastest XK 120s racing in the fifties. The basis of his car was a 1952 XK 120 Roadster with already some 35,000 road miles behind it (plus the odd track appearance), and the main angle of attack when the car came to be modified was the reduction of weight - on the premise that this would not only help the power-to-weight ratio, but result in better braking and handling too. Berry was helped enormously in 'adding lightness' to the car by being able to obtain and fit one of the lightweight XK 120 bodyshells which had been built for the 1951 Le Mans race as already noted in this Chapter. This already very light shell was further stripped of unneccessary internal panelling (wing valances, rear wheel arches, boot floor, spare wheel tray and so on), together with anything else not serving a strictly functional purpose. The wooden floorboards were replaced by thin aluminium sheet, not reinforced on the passenger's side until the gradual subsidence of a passenger to nearly road level on a journey back from Snetterton caused Berry to have second thoughts!

The offside headlight nacelle was utilised to supply cold air to the carburetters via an aluminium duct (as was quite fashionable for racing XKs of the time), but the engine was at first left very standard, the 1¾ inch SU carburetters being retained and modifications limited to machining the flywheel from 19 lbs 10 oz to 15 lbs 3 oz, the fitting of a competition clutch, and careful balancing of the major parts. After some four month's work, the car was ready to race; it weighed 20 cwt 2 qrs 5 lbs, about 4 cwt lighter than a standard XK 120 stripped for racing and about the same as a C-type! Weight distribution was 11 cwts on the front wheels and only 9 cwts 2 lbs on the rear, but with driver and fuel a state of near equilibrium obtained. The following notes from an article by Bob Berry which appeared in Jaguar's apprentices' magazine gives a clear outline of what it was like to 'sort' an XK 120 for racing in the 1950s:

On test the car was quite impressive. The performance - especially the acceleration - was vastly improved as was the braking , but the handling was decidedly poor. The reduction in weight had raised the tail of the car to a much higher position than normal and this had been counteracted by fitting spacer blocks between spring and axle to provide an axle position midway between the bump and rebound stops when the car was fully laden. The tests showed that the clearance between the axle and the rebound strap was insufficient - the strap tending to lift the axle on acute corners. In addition there were definite signs of movement between the axle and springs via the spacer blocks - thus allowing the nose of the axle to move quite an appreciable amount in a vertical plane. The elimination of the spacer blocks cured both troubles, and instead the spring cambers were reduced by 2½ inches - thus producing a near flat spring when laden. This also increased the distance between the axle and rebound stop, at the expense of the distance to the bump stop. Further tests were carried out at Oulton Park on rear spring rates and two spring settings were eventually used. The first was the standard spring with the free camber reduced by 2½ inches and with one leaf removed (for short distance racing), the other being the competition spring with the camber reduced by 1½ inches only. This latter was only employed in long distance races where a full load of fuel was required, though it was used once or twice at Goodwood where the smoothness of the circuit made it possible to use these springs with a consequent reduction in the amount of roll. Standard shock absorbers were used with normal XK 120 settings.

After experimenting with 6.00 and 6.50 tyres as sets and pairs, it was found that the 6.00 tyre at 30 lbs sq in front and rear produced the best results. At Goodwood the pressures were increased to 35 lbs sq which seemed to improve the handling slightly on that circuit.

Unfortunately the brakes still proved inadequate. After only a few laps the brake pedal travel became excessive, making it necessary to 'pump' to produce a reasonable travel. As the front brakes were self adjusting the trouble obviously lay with the rear brakes, and we finally decided to convert these to the leading shoe/ self adjusting system as well. This proved none too easy for the welding and alterations required to adapt front brake back plates to rear axle mountings caused not inconsiderable distortion of the plates. However the job was successfully completed

after one or two attempts, and two separate master cylinders operating on a 60/40 ratio front to rear completed the system. In addition air was carefully ducted to both front and rear drums, the latter via a duct drawing air from scoops mounted on the side of the body. Ferodo produced some racing linings, Alford and Alder some line bored drums free from balancing holes and the combined result was most impressive. In fact it was found possible to outbrake practically any other sports car with the exception of the three disc braked C-types and the H.W.M of Abecassis. Admittedly the braking became rough after hard usage and the drum consumption phenomenal, but at least we did have a car that would stop whenever required. Praise must be given to the linings which though emitting a high pitched squeak and some smoke under extreme conditions, never once showed any signs of fade.

Bob Berry went on to have several very successful years with MWK 120, the XK being "faster than the slower C-types" even in its first season. An early win was in the all-Jaguar Lyons Trophy Race in June 1954, when Berry beat Protheroe in GPN 635, and in August 1954 MWK 120 finished 2nd on handicap in the O'Boyle Trophy Race at the Curragh, Northern Island. Much credit must go to John Lea for the success of the car, for it was Lea who helped Berry prepare the XK; MWK 120 eventually wound up with a full D-type engine complete with Webers. Berry sold the XK when he began to drive Jack Broadhead's D-type, and the new owner promptly took out the D-type engine and placed it in his XK 120 Fixed-head Coupe, which he then attempted to enter in saloon car events! When the car passed eventually into David Cottingham's hands in the sixties, it was once more given a wet-sump D-type engine, and raced at club meetings; it also appeared at Santa Pod, a rather anachronistic sight amongst the brightly painted hot-rods, but more than held its own there against V8 Mustangs and such machinery over the standing ¼-mile, its best time over that distance being well under 14 seconds. MWK 120 was sold to a Canadian buyer in 1968 and it is presumably still in that country.

Besides Bob Berry and Dick Protheroe, Gillie

Tyrer joined the fray with an XK 120 Fixed-head, and Mike Salmon drove an XK 120 Roadster with success including at the Bo'ness Speed Trials in June and September 1954. Lord Louth still won at the Bouley Bay hill climb, winning his class there again in his roadster at the July meeting, while Jack Sears is on record as driving an XK 120 to a 3rd place at Snetterton in October. On the rallying front, the International Alpine Rally was still good for a Jaguar class win, Haddon and Vivian's roadster winning the over 2,600 class after Scott and Cunningham were delayed by a broken rear spring in RUB 120 (carrying its drophead-coupe bodywork). Haddon and Vivian's XK 120 roadster also won a similar class for open cars in the MCC Round Britain Rally of November 1954, Mr and Mrs Stoss in their fixed-head coupe heading the equivalent closed car class. The former pair won the road section of the Tulip Rally but were prevented from scoring in the overall results when the XK's throttle linkage broke at the start of the final test, a number of laps round the Zandvoort circuit. Eric Haddon's car, incidentally, solved the ground clearance problem by having its twin pipe exhaust system routed out through two holes in a rear wing! XKs entered the 1954 Tour de France but did not figure high in the results.

An interesting but rather obscure win was recorded by an XK 120 in the Circuit of Tananarive, Madagascar, in May 1954, one Dubois averaging 68 mph to beat a Porsche and an Austin Healey. In America, the car could still be competitive in SCCA racing, as Charles Wallace won the C-Production national Championship in 1954 and 1955.

For the remainder of the decade, one has to rather search for notable performances by the XK 120 in racing and rallying even though the type was in regular use in both fields; the smaller, lighter sports car was coming to the fore, and even Protheroe forsook his XK for one season (1958) for an Austin Healey 100S, a very fast car (aluminium bodied like his XK 120) with which he had a good deal of success,

beating XK 120s such as Peter Sargent's on occasions. But he was back behind the wheel of GPN 635 in 1959, now 3.8 engined, entering and winning his class in most rounds of the 1959 Autosport Championship.

The 1958 Sestriere Rally saw a surprising entry in the form of American Don Delling's 'veteran' 1954 XK 120 Fixed-head. While a Mercedes 300SL finally won the class, the rally's final stage was run on snow-packed roads as a round-the-houses race in Sestriere where, in the Unlimited GT category, Delling "astonished all" by making best performance - the XK 120 could still score in important rallies, even ten years after its inception!

Nineteen-sixty arrived, and XKs were still racing. Protheroe continued to field GPN 635, but that old war-horse was joined by another XK 120 Roadster, MXJ 954, which also featured disc brakes and Weber carburetters. This latter car (an ex-rally car) passed to Rob Beck and in shortened-chassis form was successfully raced by him into the mid-sixties (it eventually found its way to America). Protheroe's final XK 120 was registered CUT 6 and "with every possible modification" it beat all the new E-type Jaguars, much to everyone's surprise, at the inaugural Clubman's Championship meeting in 1961 - one of the few occasions it appeared on a track as Protheroe was shortly to continue his competition activities with a succession of E-types.

One other notable racing XK 120 of the early sixties was Eric Brown's famous '1 ALL', which started life as a standard XK 120 Drop-head Coupe but was gradually modified to become one of the fastest XK 120s to be seen - it was kept in road-going trim and surprised quite a few Ferraris on continental autoroutes too. Its distinctive features included a certain amount of remodelling of the front end, the headlights being set into the wings and different bumpers fitted; mechanically, a full dry-sump D-type engine was featured! 1 ALL has the distinction of being raced on one occasion by Jackie Stewart, who took the XK to victory ahead of Rob Beck's MXJ 954 at the Jaguar Driver's Club national Crystal Palace meeting of 1964.

Others who raced XK 120s in the sixties included Norman Watt, whose fast dark green fixed-head coupe was often seen at Crystal Palace, Graig Hinton whose similar car boasted Webers (it was very quick while it ran but was rather comprehensively crashed by Hinton; the car is believed to have been rebuilt as a glass-fibre bodied modified sports car, driven by champion weight lifter Brian Abbott of Bournemouth for a season or two some time later), David Cottingham in MWK 120, Peter Butt with his familiar metallic blue roadster (MAL 253) and Rhoddy Harvey Bailey, probably the fastest of them all in JWK 650 which also ran with Webers and disc brakes. David Llewellyn (TAL 81) and Howell Smith (XY7) were amongst those who 'mod sported' their XK 120 Roadsters, though TAL 81 was bought by Richard Goode around 1971 and converted back into a rather fast road car - low slung, still with widened wheel arches and now running on Andorra number plates, it became a very distinctive car!

In America, at least one enthusiast soldiered on in sports car racing up until at least the late sixties - Hap Richardson and his immaculate XK 120 Roadster had by then completed more than 200 races, and been the 1960 C-Production Champion on the Pacific Coast. While no overall wins were recorded, some 40 or 50 first-in-Class successes were; and the XK managed an overall third at Willow Springs in 1961 behind Dave McDonald's Corvette, and Bob Bondurant in first place.

In view of the XK 120's gradual and not dishonourable decline from international racing, through club racing, to appearances in historic-type formulae, it was therefore a great surprise to many when in 1969 an XK 120 began consistently to take the chequered flag in a totally up-to-date branch of the sport. The car was John N Pearson's 1954 Drop-head Coupe and it quickly gained fame - or perhaps notoriety - in modified sports car racing, as it soon became apparent that the XK was considerably quicker than any racing E-type.

Although the car won its first race with its original steel bodywork in place (just wider wheels and a Mk 10 engine being installed) it was the object of intensive development by the Birmingham enthusiast over the next few seasons. For 1970, the drop-head appeared with glass fibre replica bodywork of exactly the same shape as the original (from which the moulds were taken), except for the obligatory wheel arches covering the wider wheels. Although a full race E-type engine complete with Webers, giving about 290 bhp at the flywheel, obviously assisted, the XK really scored over the E-types then racing by the vast reduction in weight occasioned by the 'plastic' body - modified sports car rules ensured that the E-type could not follow suit as much of its body shell was stress-bearing and therefore had to be left original. The XK's old fashioned chassis however was its only stress-bearing entity, and so as long as that was kept intact between the axle centres, the car was 'legal'.

Considerable changes were wrought in the suspension department too. While the rear axle had to be retained, springing was free so off came the heavy leaf springs, to be replaced by Lola T142 coil spring/damper units; axle location was provided by radius arms and a Panhard rod. Similar coil spring/damper units eventually replaced the front torsion bars too. E-type disc brakes were fitted all round at an early stage in the proceedings, with twin vacuum boosters - though pedal pressures remained rather high and it was found impossible to lock a wheel; the reason perhaps why Pearson was never bothered by brake fade!

The engine itself, finally fitted with a big-valve straight port head modified by John Pearson himself, was mounted 2½ inches further back and considerably lower in the chassis than standard; the radiator (not a Jaguar item) finally found its way into the boot! The author well remembers his drive of the car during a track test for *Motor* (w/e January 27th 1973), round a rather damp Silverstone GP circuit. Astonishingly fast in a straight line and with a high cornering capability around smooth surfaced (and preferably dry) bends, the car's major disadvantage was probably its old live axle, which was far too heavy in relation to the rest of the car. Despite efforts to move as much weight as possible to the rear of the car, this unfavourable sprung/unsprung weight ratio was to remain a permanent feature of the car. John Pearson, and many others, still retain a soft spot for 'Jessie', and certainly her many titanic battles with such modern machinery as the late Brian Hough's 5-litre Tuscan and Rhoddy Harvey-Bailey's Stingray will long be remembered; while the records books stand witness to her race and Championship wins, and her many class lap records.

Although John Pearson's development of this ultimate racing XK 120 was in a sense 'dead-end', the car remains significant in that it was undoubtedly the fastest Jaguar ever to have raced on a British circuit - only the prototype mid-engined XJ13 was capable of putting up better lap times, and that car of course was never driven in competition. The XK's best times around the Silverstone club circuit were just under the minute and at the time of writing no E-types - and very few other modified sports cars - have bettered it.

While John 'Plastic' Pearson remains effective in the Modified Sports Car field, it is pleasant to record a further renaissance of the XK 120, this time in the area of Thoroughbred sports car racing. This formula was in fact introduced by the XK Register of the Jaguar Driver's Club in an effort to re-create 'marque' and GT racing of the late fifties, in which of course XKs used to figure prominently. Fittingly enough, it is the XK 120 which is currently a leading contender in the Thoroughbred Sports Car championship, John Harper's left hand drive aluminium-bodied roadster winning many of the 1974 rounds of the series; while in 1973 another John Pearson (very confusing this!) drove an XK 120 in similar events to win the Vandervell Novice Driver's award for that year (although this car is

somewhat confusing too, as it is sometimes known as the XK 140 Fixed-head Coupe Prototype!). In Historic racing the author's own aluminium bodied roadster (670144) was, in 1972, the first of its type to re-enter racing under the Historic Sports Car Club's formula for selected pre-1960 sports cars.

Finally, although Ecurie Ecosse may no longer be entering Jaguars, Scotland is by no means left out today as XK 120s are currently fairing extremely well in hill climbs and sprints 'north of the border'. Jamie Gibbon and Tom McCallum head a small band of XK owners who drive XKs with fiercesome determination, Gibbon's roadster actually winning the over 3-litre class of the Scottish Hill Climb Championship during 1973!

When it comes to reviewing the survival rate of the more notable 'racing' XK 120s, it is very pleasant to be able to record that virtually all still exist, and mostly in very original order. For instance, nearly all six of the works XK 120s can be accounted for. The late Leslie Johnson's JWK 651, perhaps the most historic of all in view of its racing history, lasted in entirely original condition complete with 'disc' wheels and kilometre speedometer until the late sixties, when it was "tastelessly mutilated" as Johnson's son-in-law sadly put it, through the addition by a motor trader of various louvres cut into the bodywork, and the substitution of wire wheels for the originals. Very fortunately however it soon passed into the hands of an enthusiast who recognised the car's true historic worth, John Panton of Surrey, whose stable also includes three XK 140 Roadsters.

Biondetti's car, JWK 650, was owned up to recently by Harvey-Bailey who was the last to race it, and retains its additional Protheroe modifications made in the sixties. It is no longer seen on the circuits but does grace the occasional XK Register gathering with its presence. JWK 977 belongs to David Cottingham who has restored this ex-Peter Walker XK 120 to perfect order, although it retains its various modifications such as its C-type rear end and wire wheels, and once more includes a D-type head in its specification. While still in Gordon Brown's hands JWK 977 was raced by Brian Redman and John Cuff, and was bought by D-type owner Nigel Moores for the purpose of removing the dry-sump D-type engine - Cottingham purchased the car minus an engine. After a painstaking rebuild however, the present owner prefers not to use the car in historic racing ("too precious") and instead drives an XK 120 Fixed-head in Thoroughbred events.

The car with which Stirling Moss won the 1950 TT, Tommy Wisdom's JWK 988, is now owned by Jaguar collector Robert Danny, and although extremely sound and original (apart from a conversion to telescopic dampers at the rear), is to be restored and repainted in Wisdom's particular shade of green. NUB 120 is of course still owned by Jaguar Cars though is usually kept at the National Motor Museum at Beaulieu.

Amongst the 'non works' cars, Dick Protheroe's GPN 635 has amazingly enough survived a number of rolls and other alarming incidents, and is currently undergoing a body-off-chassis rebuild by Gordon Brown for its new owner. After leaving Protheroe's hands it was raced by Harvey-Bailey, David Howard, Alan Ensoll, Gray, and the late Chris Summers, before Gordon Brown bought it. Brown also witnessed the final demise of MDU 524, the XK

120 Roadster rallied by Gatsonides and possibly the car which achieved 172 mph at Jabbeke - in convoy with Brown on the way to a sprint meeting, it crashed very heavily into a tree; with such force in fact that the engine parted company with the chassis, though the latter, in mutilated form, is rumoured to still exist somewhere. Eric Brown's Drop-head Coupe '1 All' now belongs to D-type and Lister-Jaguar owner Peter Sargent, albeit lacking its famous registration letters.

The Lawrie/Waller 1951 Le Mans XK 120 exists though is at present in rather poor condition, owned by Bob Kerr whose home on the hillside above Loch Lomond has seen a number of other interesting Jaguars in the past - Bob also hill climbs an XK 120 Fixed-head which rejoices in the registration number JAG 120.

Quite a number of the XK 120s campaigned in international rallies during the fifties are still to be seen including LOE 3, LOE 409, SEV 970, RJH 400, PPC 120 and a number of others, indicating another aspect of the XK 120's character - toughness. We can therefore leave the XK 120 Jaguar in the knowledge that suitably modified it is still holding its own in every class of motor sport for which it can be entered, and that many old veterans survive in good order to remind us of the type's illustrious history in premier events of bygone years.

Chapter Five The C-type

The 1951 Le Mans twenty-four hour race was a classic event even when judged by the standards of its own illustrious history. For Jaguar Cars Ltd, it was the scene of their most important race victory of all time, a victory that came as a profound surprise to many, both at home and abroad. For in those days, the fact of a British car actually winning a major event was something akin to a minor miracle in itself, and that the car should be a Jaguar was even more astonishing - after all, the company had in most people's living memory originated through building special bodies on Standard chassis, and now suddenly the name 'Jaguar' was elevated to a position alongside Bentley and Lagonda, all within the space of twenty-four hours.

The car which made the world's sports car manufacturers re-think their entire approach literally overnight was the Jaguar XK 120C - or the C-type as it became known by common usage. Rarely, if ever, has a car been built for so specific a purpose, for the C-type was not made for sports car racing, not for long distance racing even, but purely to win at Le Mans.

Both Lyons and Heynes had closely watched the 1950 race, and with England and the rest of the small Jaguar team, were more aware than the majority of the spectators of exactly how close the almost entirely standard XK 120 had come

to actually winning the event. They also noted that virtually no-one had a completely modern, streamlined car. Furthermore, Heynes knew that none of the very few maladies which had sunk the hopes of the XK 120 drivers concerned the fundamental components of the car (Johnson in the leading XK 120 had been lapping faster at the end of his 21-hour run than at the beginning, even with sub-standard brakes) and so, although he'd not thought about the possibility before, he realised that it would be quite feasible to construct a special car, using a great many production components, that would be both fast enough and strong enough to stand an excellent chance of winning Le Mans, "given reasonable luck."

By thus incorporating road-car engine, transmission and even suspension parts, not only would there be the security of a proven reliability factor gained by hundreds of thousands of road miles, but also the bonus of time saved in the design office, on the shop floor, and on the test track. There are no spare people at Jaguar so this last point was a vital consideration, and with the Mk VII Jaguar saloon soon to be launched, and the steel-bodied XK 120 just getting into full production, long hours could not easily be expanded on a competition project.

So busy in fact were Heynes and his production engineers, working hard to get the Mk VII built in time for the 1950 motor show and testing saloon car prototypes over high mileages on the road, that the new competition car was only given a thought after October 1950 - the original sanction for building a car to take to Le Mans in 1951 had been given by William Lyons while actually at Le Mans, back in June 1950. Only eight months remained to design, build, and test a completely new car, so the pressure was certainly on as Heynes recounted afterwards:

Three or four of the staff and a little band of stalwarts in the shops worked assiduously on drawings, models and schemes. We built up frames and bodies in wood, and models in paper and even broomsticks were in demand for mock-up tubular frames. Time went on and eventually our schemes crystallised. It was then that the heat was really turned on; everyone in the little band was working every spare moment that he could find, weekends were merged into the normal week and to leave the factory at 8 o'clock was having a half-day.

Although Heynes himself never doubted that the cars - there was to be a team of three - would be completed in time for the 1951 Le Mans race, William Lyons entertained quite serious misgivings about the situation. Off on an important business tour of North America, he therefore left instructions that in his absence three lightweight XK 120 bodies were to be built and mounted on lightened XK 120 chassis, as an insurance against the failure of the engineering division to finish the C-type. This was actually done, although the three 'lightweight' XK 120s which resulted never ran at Le Mans (see Chapter Four). It acted as a spur however, and when Lyons returned from the States, he found that the first C-type had been completed exactly six weeks before the race.

The object had been to produce a car which would show a sufficient superiority in every department over the XK 120 road sports car so that it could lap the 8.37 mile Le Mans circuit at a speed which could not be reliably matched by any likely rival. These improvements were wrought in all the five major parts of the car - engine, chassis, body, suspension and brakes.

To turn to the first mentioned, the C-type's power unit varied little from the standard production unit fitted in the XK 120, and in the Mk VII saloon on its announcement in October 1950. Furthermore, the alterations which were made, as Heynes pointed out in his famous Paper read to the Institute of Mechanical Engineers in 1953, were "none of them of a major character or even beyond the capabilities of a private owner who is experienced in these matters." Many of the developments were in fact to be incorporated in production engines later on.

The standard cylinder head casting was taken and fitted with larger exhaust valves, which went up in diameter by 3/16 inch to 1 5/8 inch. Inlet porting remained the same size but the exhaust porting diameter was enlarged from 1¼ inch to 1 3/8 inch.

The valve springs were given a slightly increased free length which postponed valve bounce to over 6,500 rpm, and more importantly, valve lift was increased. This was achieved through the use of a new camshaft which gave 3/8 inch lift instead of 5/16, by eliminating the dwell and raising the top radius, which Heynes found could be done with little alteration in flank radius.

Compression ratio on the three 1951 Le Mans cars was 9:1, although this was reduced to 8½:1 for the 1952 race as Heynes was suspicious of the true octane rating of the fuel supplied by the race organisers. Changes in compression ratio were affected by using different pistons, which were of the solid skirt variety for the C-type.

Carburetters on the original C-type were the usual 1¾ inch SUs, but following the 1951 Le Mans race these were replaced by two 2 inch items of the same make, with their familiar rough-cast dashpot casings. The inlet manifold was as for the XK 120 but with the entry opened up for the bigger carburetters, which breathed from an open-ended cold air balance-box which gathered air ducted from the front of the car. The exhaust manifold was still cast like the XK 120's, but with the 'branch' effect more pronounced. About the only change made to the engine's bottom end was the substitution of Indium-coated lead bronze bearings for the standard items, as more of a precaution than as a necessity, and the fitting of a high-speed crankshaft damper. The XK 120's big cast aluminium sump was retained, and in the ignition system, a different distributor head was fitted.

This engine gave approximately 204 bhp at 5,500 rpm in its 9:1 compression ratio form, and about 8 - 10 bhp less on an 8:1 compression ratio. There was no loss in reliability over the original XK engine, which itself had very nearly duplicated an entire Le Mans race on the test bed, where it had been run for 24 hours at 5,000 rpm on full load with five minutes at 5,250, 5,500 and 6,000 rpm every two hours - on strip-down afterwards no components showed any ill-effects.

The C-type's transmission differed little from the XK 120's, although it included a lighter flywheel and the Borg and Beck 10 inch diameter clutch had a 'solid' centre section to prevent a re-occurrence of the fault which put Leslie Johnson out of the race in the previous year. The gearbox itself now had a one piece input shaft which meant that ratios could be more easily changed. The C-type also introduced the Salisbury rear axle to the Jaguar range, which was to replace the formerly used ENV axle on all Jaguars after 1951/52. Although the Salisbury axle didn't offer quite the ease of changing the final drive ratio that the ENV did, a wide range of alternative ratios became available which included 2.93, 3.31, 3.54, 3.77, 3.92, 4.09, and 4.27:1. At Le Mans in 1951, the C-type used the 3.31:1 axle.

Quite substantial and much needed improvements were effected on the car's braking system. As with the road cars, the rear brakes remained manually adjustable but at the front a new Lockheed automatic adjustment design was adopted. This used the previous two leading shoe arrangement, but the shoes were now interconnected by two adjuster bars which were pulled over friction pads as the shoes were forced against the drum. Due to the action of the friction pads and a ratchet, when the braking pressure was released, the bars allowed the shoes to return only to the correct lining/drum clearance. Thus after a number of long, hard applications which caused the brake drum to expand and the lining material to wear, the result was not the inordinately long brake pedal movement which was a feature of a quickly driven XK 120. Fortunately, this automatic adjustment of the front brakes was adopted on the XK 120 too shortly after its appearance on the C-type. A similar tandem master cylinder to that used on the road car featured in the C-type's hydraulic system, providing a degree of fail-safe braking should pressure failure occur in either the front or rear circuits. The use of alloy-rimmed wire wheels with their centre-lock fixing not only speeded up wheel changes, but also contributed greatly to a reduction in brake fade by providing a much better flow of cool air around the drums. Diameter of the wheels was 16 inch, and they carried either 600 or 650 x 16 Dunlop racing tyres.

The C-type's aluminium body shell, besides succeeding in its primary purpose of reducing wind resistance, combined elegance with practicality. The front section integrated wings with bonnet, and hinged forward from a detachable framework in front of the engine to provide very easy access to engine, radiator, steering and front suspension. The rear section of the car was also in one piece, and after the undoing of a series of bolts was detachable as a complete unit to display the rear suspension and tail framework. This framework could itself be removed very easily after four nuts had been unbolted to allow even greater access to the axle and rear suspension members. The aluminium 40-gallon fuel tank was carried over the rear axle on a three-point rubber mounting, while the spare wheel was stored underneath the tank and removed through a small rearward facing hinged lid in the bodywork. While frontal area had only been reduced by a small amount, the C-type's shape required only 53 bhp to propel it through still air at 100 mph, compared with the 68 bhp required by the XK 120 with aeroscreen.

Covered by its beautiful enveloping bodyshell, the C-type's chassis construction was a major factor in the big reduction in weight achieved over the XK 120. Heynes used a tubular framework in place of a conventional chassis, and while this was not an innovation in itself, it did include some interesting features. There was, for instance, an element of the monocoque method of construction around the car's front bulkhead, where the welded panelling of the scuttle, facia, dash and bulkhead was stressed to improve rigidity in the vertical plane; while at the rear a similarly welded panel stiffened a rectangle of tubes to form the rear bulkhead where the main frame ended. This last actually stopped short of the rear axle, but extended right forward to converge around the engine. At the front of the car, the frame met a complex of diagonal cross-members which carried the main front suspension units. Heavily drilled channel members running in a diagonal direction between the main frame members contributed stiffness at floor level, while at the centre of the car the triangulated structure of the frame was an impressive 10 inches deep.

Depending on the load to which they were subjected, the welded steel tubing of the C-type was varied in diameter; the main bottom tubes, and the right-angled cross members, were 2 inches in diameter, the upper tubes 1½ inches diameter, and the various connecting struts 1 inch in diameter. For some reason the 1951 Le Mans cars were built from 16-gauge tubing, although the original workshop drawings had specified a lighter 18 gauge. The whole structure was still very light and extremely rigid by the standards of the day however, and this of course contributed to the C-type's good braking and handling qualities even though the major consideration had been that of providing the least amount of weight for the engine to propel.

Much of the C-type's superiority in handling

and roadholding over the XK 120 came from the new car's suspension and steering. Front suspension did resemble the earlier car's though, having wide-based wishbones top and bottom, Newton telescopic dampers mounted on an upright suspension post, and springing by long torsion bars which were anchored back by the scuttle. The lower wishbones were both shorter and wider based than the XK 120's, however.

The C-type's steering was radically different. The recirculating ball system was dropped in favour of a rack and pinion arrangement, used with a steeply raked, universally jointed steering column; besides a small reduction in the number of turns lock to lock (now 2½) the new steering provided greater 'feel' for the driver.

Considerable originality was displayed in the C-type's rear suspension, which although using a production Salisbury rear axle, was suspended and located in quite a novel way. Instead of heavy leaf springs, a single torsion bar was used, mounted transversly across the bottom of the rear bulkhead and secured at its middle - it was actually contained inside the large tubular cross member which formed the bottom of the welded-up bulkhead. To either end of the torsion bar was connected a trailing arm which led to hanger brackets under the axle casing; being anchored at its centre, the single torsion bar acted like two independent bars. The outer ends of the bar, just before they met the trailing arms, were bushed into the tubular cross member, which thus absorbed thrust. Only one other link connected the axle to the car, and its design not only enabled it to locate the axle firmly, but also to combat the tendency of a car's right-hand rear wheel to spin during violent acceleration.

The bracket in question was placed at a predetermined distance inboard of the right hand rear wheel, where it had a two-point rubber bushed mounting, angled to the rear, on top of the axle casing. It extended to a single mounting point on the rear bulkhead, and was thus 'A' shaped. By virtue of the bracket's carefully calculated position on the axle, it used the force exerted upon it by the tendency of the whole axle to rotate through torque reaction from the drive train, to bear down upon the right hand side of the axle and so largely cancel out the forces which were at the same time trying to lift the right-hand wheel. It thus did much the same job as a limited slip device in the differential, which in those days wasn't generally available, by preventing the wheel from spinning and wasting power. The effectiveness of the bracket in this respect could be demonstrated by the tyre marks left after a wheelspin standing start - two black lines would be laid on the road, ending simultaneously. But it was during cornering that the 'limiting slip' action was most beneficial, the C-type being able to accelerate out of a bend without the serious loss of applied power that occured with the XK 120 in similar conditions, due to wheelspin. A further function of the 'A' bracket was, of course, its lateral location of the axle.

Although the C-type's suspension was a compromise in that front and rear systems were not designed together, Heynes had certainly produced a car which could out-handle most other sports cars of its day, and get its power down onto the road better than many big engined cars of the period. Distinctive and responding best to a firm hand, the C-type's handling was generally liked by its drivers in the fifties even though it may not have had the finesse of later designs. One of the very few weaknesses of the original suspension was, funnily enough, the clever 'A' bracket itself - a fabricated item, it was prone to fracture under some circumstances although on the smooth surfaces at Le Mans it was satisfactory. This might have been due to the fact that an alternation in axle ratio effects the strains imposed upon such a bracket, and so perhaps when the car was geared down for short British circuits the increased load was not to its liking. A revised bracket was fitted to the 1953 C-types.

The C-type was an exception to the normal rule for racing cars in that it required very little alteration after its first try-out round a circuit. Unpainted, the first car was taken to Silverstone five or six weeks before the race for secret 'shaking down' test sessions, during which Stirling Moss and Jack Fairman were given the car to try to see if they thought anything needed doing. That they didn't one suspects came as no surprise to Bill Heynes and Lofty England - not that there was much time to rectify a fundamental defect had there been one! About the biggest change was the repositioning of the bonnet straps so that undoing them became a one-man operation. Testing also took place on the Motor Industry Research Association's track at Lindley, near Nuneaton, where the new car was found to be an impressive 12% faster round the same circuit than the XK 120 in its 1950 Le Mans form.

The chassis numbers of the C-type were prefixed with the letters 'XKC', and it was XKC 001, 002 and 003 that set off by road from Coventry to contest the 1951 Le Mans *Coupe Annuelle*. Arrayed against them were the 4½ litre Talbots, similar to the last year's winning car but faster still, Ferrari with both 2.6 and 4.1 litre cars (though none were works entries), Cunningham with three new 5.4 litre Chrysler engined sports cars, Aston Martin with five entries including the three DB2 team cars, and the 3.8 Nash engined Healey fitted that year with an aerodynamic 'saloon' body. In this their first race, the C-types were driven by driver pairings of Stirling Moss and Jack Fairman, Peter Walker and Peter Whitehead, and Leslie Johnson and Clemente Biondetti.

The pre-race practice session was wet, and nearly ensured that the first mentioned drivers didn't get a race at all - Moss arrived at White House to find Mortimer Morris—Goodall's Aston Martin stationary in the road, having been forced to stop when one of the fast little 1100 cc Porsches had overturned. Quite unable to pull the C-type up on the wet surface, Moss collided with the Aston giving it "remarkable acceleration up the road" as *The Autocar* put it! Fortunately damage to the C-type was nothing worse than a crease in the bodywork under the headlights - clearly visible in photographs taken after the start.

Race day weather was similarly dull and showery, but this didn't deter the 20-year old Moss any more than his fright in practice had done. At the end of the first lap he was second by four seconds to Gonzales in his 4½ litre Talbot, and that was from a start position almost halfway down the field. By the third lap he had passed the French car and was pulling away with ease, posting laps with an assurance that belied the speed at which the Jaguar was circulating; on the twentieth *tour* the lap record was broken, Moss averaging 104.1 mph, and it was shattered twice more before by the flying Moss until he left it it at 105.2 mph, or 4 mins 46.8 secs. And, he said afterwards, he could have lapped at 107 mph had the occasion called for it.

Right from the fall of the flag the other two C-types followed the leading car at only a slightly lesser speed, first Biondetti and then Peter Walker, fighting it out with the Talbots of Gonzales/Marimon, Rosier/Fangio, and Chaboud/Vincent. Tom Cole had hung on to an initial third place until a *contretemps* on the fifth lap forced the Allard to make a pit stop and bend a wing away from a rear wheel, spoiling whatever chance it had of keeping up with the leaders. The Ferraris made very little impression and were slower than expected, but the Aston Martins were running with clockwork precision even if their 2½ litre engines never allowed them to be candidates for the lead. The heavy Cunningham sports cars certainly had speed in a straight line but were obviously cumbersome to manage, and eventually two crashed.

But drama was not lacking in the Jaguar camp. After 4½ hours of racing, by which time the C-types had established themselves first, second and third, disaster struck the Biondetti/Johnson car - an oil pipe flange gave way. The oil delivery pipes were of steel, and prolonged vibration had caused crystallization of a flange welded onto the pipe. So one C-type was out of

the race, without Johnson even getting a drive. The consternation in the Jaguar pit can be imagined, as the other two cars had exactly similar flanges and there was absolutely nothing that could be done about it. When indeed the Moss/Fairman car broke a connecting rod through a lack of oil pressure stemming from the same cause, it began to look as if a certain 1-2-3 win was turning into ignominious defeat through a tiny defect totally unconnected with the C-type's basic design.

But the Talbots too were in dire trouble, probably through having over-reached themselves in the early stages of the race trying to keep up with Moss; the Gonzales/Marimon car gave up with a blown head gasket before dawn on the Sunday, while Rosier and Fangio had retired even earlier, ostensibly from a broken oil tank but in actuality from a similar overheating problem. In any case they, like everyone else, had been completely outclassed by the Jaguars, for upon the retirement of Moss the Walker/Whitehead C-type passed into the lead, no less than 90 miles ahead of the nearest competitor - and following strict instructions from Lofty to "take it easy" lest the oil pipe flange break on their car too.

Of the only two Ferraris to have shown any mettle, Chiron had run out of fuel early on, and the Hall/Navone car, another 4.1 litre, had failed to start after a pit stop due to its inadequate battery being flat. It eventually got going after a number of hours wait, in the hope of being classed as a finisher. But no Ferrari had approached the speed of the C-type, and while the Italian cars' reliability might have been adequate for the 900 miles-odd of the Mille Miglia, it obviously wasn't for the 24 hours of Le Mans.

The Whitehead/Walker C-type continued to circulate with remarkable consistency right until the end of the race, its average speed over the second half of the race hardly varying by more than a mile an hour or so between each lap. When the car crossed the line for the last time shortly after 4pm, the little British contingent in the pits, and scattered over the spectators' enclosures, could hardly believe their eyes - for the first time since 1935, a British car had won at Le Mans. Peter Whitehead and Peter Walker received their garlands in a swirling crowd of excited Frenchmen and elated fellow countrymen. They had averaged 93.49 mph.

In England, a country already beginning to have its doubts about the BRM project, the win was hailed as the "best motor racing news for years". Whitehead and Walker had won by a clear 67 miles, Moss had knocked six seconds off the lap record, and at one time Jaguars had been placed one, two and three - which is probably how they would have finished but for the oil pipe failure. The Talbot of Meyrat and Guy Mairesse finally finished in second position, while the British successes in the race were underlined by the Aston Martins, the Macklin/ Thompson DB2 being placed 3rd and all five Astons finishing. The highest placed Ferrari was the 4.1 litre car of Chinetti/Lucas in 8th position, and the Ferrari camp, like that of the Talbot, must have suffered from considerable disappointment in the opening hours of the race as the speed possessed by the new Jaguar became so obviously and uncomfortably apparent. As *The Motor's* eye witness said, "I have an idea that there were several very shaken men in some of the pits and in some of the cockpits." Even Briggs Cunningham, with some 17 tons of equipment, a caravan headquarters in the paddock, and pit organisation bordering on the military in its efficiency, faired no better than he had done last year, inspite of entering three cars with a fourth as reserve.

Thus the C-type Jaguar proved itself to be completely superior to all its competitors both in speed and in reliability. A major victory had been won by Jaguar, both in terms of prestige and in the bountiful harvest of publicity which only Le Mans, with its world-wide coverage and fame, could bestow. Certainly Jaguar received ample column inches in its own country, where the newspapers were only too pleased to headline a British success.

Only two more events after Le Mans were entered by the factory in 1951, the first of which was the RAC Tourist Trophy on the Dundrod circuit. A contrast to the previous year's event, the weather was sunny almost throughout the race; once again it was Moss who completely outshone everyone. He took the lead with his C-type from the beginning, with the team cars of Walker and Johnson following. A challenge might have been offered to the Jaguars by the new DB3 Aston Martin, but Lance Macklin's chances were ruined when the car's exhaust system kept falling off.

Johnson however began to lag behind after about 200 miles of the race had been run - he was far from being well at the time. This was the big chance for A P R Rolt, who had come across to Ireland at his own expense on the strength of a hint from Lofty England that he might be given a drive if the occasion arose; having previously badgered the Jaguar team manager for most of the year for a place in the team. When Johnson finally pulled in at just over half distance, Rolt was sent out in his C-type. He proceeded to set an almighty pace, bringing the car up from 7th to 4th position, and breaking the lap record which he left at 86.40 mph! This last effort was not initially looked upon too kindly by the rest of the team, as the reserve driver isn't the one who is supposed to set lap records; but it gained for Tony Rolt a firm place in the 1952 works team.

Jaguars finished just as they had done in 1951, taking first, second, and fourth places (third spot being gained by Bob Gerard's Frazer-Nash), and a straight one-two-three win in the over 3-litre class.

It was Stirling Moss's success in the TT, preceeded by Jaguar's resounding win at Le Mans, that prompted an exasperated reader of *The Motor*, rankled by the failure of the BRM at Monza, to write and suggest that the future of Britain's GP team should be placed in the hands of "the genii behind the XK 120C", with the thought that "Perhaps an XK 200C 4½ litres unblown could uphold Great Britain's reputation for mechanical ability"! A fascinating idea, but not a practical one in the face of Jaguar's commitments.

The other competitive appearance of the C-type in 1951 was at Goodwood, at the end of September, where Moss won both the Sports Car Race and a 5-lap handicap race with comparative ease. This of course was the first time the C-type had been seen in action by the general public in England.

December 1951 is significant in the Jaguar story as being the month in which Ecurie Ecosse was formed, the private Scottish motor racing team which was to do so much for the name of Jaguar at events where the factory cars were not competing, and in the years after Jaguar officially withdrew from racing. At first XK 120s were the team's first cars, but a C-type was added to the fleet later on in 1952.

It was Stirling Moss who opened the 1952 season for Jaguar, and Goodwood was the circuit again although the C-type was rather handicapped out of its event at this International Easter Meeting, recording only a fourth place. But Moss was as ever good to watch as he strove to catch the Aston Martin DB3 of Geoff Duke; he didn't succeed but did gain an exciting 16 seconds in six laps on the Aston. At least a Jaguar still won the handicap however - Holt's privately entered XK 120.

The C-type Moss drove at Goodwood was on drum brakes, but already Jaguar and Dunlop were deeply involved in developing a reliable and effective disc brake. Moss himself contributed to the project by undertaking a lot of the test driving, in conjunction with Norman Dewis, Jaguar's own experimental department test driver. One exercise largely designed to try the new brakes was Jaguar's single entry in the 1952 Mille Miglia, a disc-braked C-type driven by Moss with Dewis as co-driver embarking on the gruelling road race.

Despite the support of only one tender car - a white Mk VII saloon driven by Bob Berry accompanied by mechanic Frank Rainbow - tyre problems and a leaking petrol tank, Moss

with his usual brilliance took the C-type into third position at one stage. However, a momentary mistake caused the car to leave the road, and with the steering badly effected Moss had to abandon the race at Bologna, only 150 miles from the finish. Bracco's Ferrari won, second place being taken by Karl Kling in one of the new Mercedes-Benz 300SLs.

The event had been an excellent proving ground for the disc brakes, but perhaps the most far-reaching consequences of the expedition were the tales brought home of the 300SL's straight line speed, which were ultimately to have a disastrous effect on Jaguar's 1952 Le Mans aspirations.

The very next weekend following the Mille Miglia, Moss continued Jaguar's traditional monopolisation of the *Daily Express* Production Car race at Silverstone by winning the 1952 event outright, beating all three Aston Martin DB3s. His team mates didn't have such a successful day however as Rolt retired with a broken half-shaft and Walker with brake trouble. Not that the C-type Jaguars were really 'production' cars at this stage - but then the Astons were even less so! Later in the year, the C-type was put into limited production and while most were sold to the States, a few did find their way into the hands of certain drivers in Britain.

It was Duncan Hamilton who managed to obtain a C-type rather before anybody else, and he put the car (MDU 214, XKC 004) to use immediately by entering the British Empire Trophy Race in May 1952. The Isle of Man course was very demanding, with plenty of street corners to negotiate and not really an ideal Jaguar circuit. Nevertheless, and inspite of not having sat in the car before the meeting, Duncan attacked it spiritedly and put up the fastest lap in practice - "which shook everybody up a bit" as he reminisced years later! Although he completed the first two of the 52 laps in the lead, the C-type came to grief over the sharply rising Kavanagh's Bridge, where speed and the weight of a full tank of petrol resulted in a fracturing of the rear axle support brackets. After "waltzing crazily for two hundred yards" the C-type came to a standstill, its race run.

While Hamilton was "waltzing" on the Isle of Man, Stirling Moss was also having fun round street corners, though with the more exotic venue of Monte Carlo as a background. The event was the Monaco GP for Sports Cars, and with remarkable agility for a car designed for the 140 mph plus straights of Le Mans, the works C-type was holding its own against the nimble and quick 2.3 Gordini being driven by Manzon in one of its first events. But during their closely fought combat, with Manzon in the lead, they arrived at the scene of an accident at Ste Devote, to which they added further interest by joining. The Gordini was eliminated forthwith, but Stirling managed to continue in fourth place only to be disqualified for receiving outside assistance while extricating the C-type from the straw bales. Tom Wisdom was placed 6th in this event, with the second privately entered C-type to appear in a race - Wisdom's car, XKC 005 and then registered MDU 212, had succeeded the motoring journalist's XK 120, JWK 988, which had been sold to him on a similar basis; it was also partly owned by Bill Cannel, of Moore's of Brighton.

But these escapades were only in the nature of asides to the factory, which was concentrating its major resources on the 1952 Le Mans race. Here, things did not seem to be as straightforward as they had been in 1951, as Mercedes Benz had re-entered motor racing and furthermore had entered an official team in the coming 24 hours race. Normally Jaguar might not have been too perturbed, and would have had the necessary faith in their own engineering, but Moss's alarming reports of the new 300SLs going past his C-type "like it was standing still" were given credence by the type's overwhelming victory in the International sports car races at Berne, where Mercedes were placed first, second and third - and but for Caracciola's accident might have been fourth too.

Had the cars been Ferraris (for instance), it is possible that Jaguar wouldn't have taken too much notice, but Mercedes Benz had an almost legendary reputation for mechanical reliability, and furthermore, Mercedes saloon cars were most definitely rivals to the Mk VII in the world's markets - and it was, after all, largely to sell the Mk VII that Lyons went racing.

It was only a matter of six weeks or so before the 1952 Le Mans when the decision was made by Jaguar to change the C-type's shape in order to gain extra top speed. The three team cars were given almost completely new front and rear sections, featuring longer and more steeply sloping noses and wedge-section extended tails with deeply recessed rear lights. The name 'Jaguar' was carried on the noses above the radiator grille, on a small badge similar to that used on the D-types some two years later. Mechanically there were few differences from the 1951 Le Mans cars, except for the larger 2 inch SU carburetters which had been in use for some time, and minor modifications to the engine to give a small middle range improvement. The slightly lower compression ratio of 8½:1 was used to ensure against piston damage caused by any variation in petrol octane rating.

The 1952 Le Mans race was a very short one for Jaguar. During the first day of practising, the lack of proper development and testing due to the last minute nature of the changes immediately became obvious, when on the Mulsanne Straight the newly bodied C-types began to run some 20-25 degrees hotter than they should. So severe was the overheating that all three cars had virtually ruined their engines by the time they assembled at the pits for the start of the actual race, and as Heynes has said, "we would probably have been wiser not to start at all". As it was, the entire Jaguar team had retired by the end of the first hour.

The driver pairings were Tony Rolt and Duncan Hamilton, Stirling Moss and Peter Walker, and Peter Whitehead and Ian Stewart. With his usual agility Moss was the first to move from the long line of cars after the sprint across the track, but the C-type was surrounded by a mass of slower cars before there was any chance of it pulling away. It was Walters' enclosed Cunningham that had the distinction of leading past the pits on the first lap, with Moss second, and then Simon and Ascari, in 4.1 and 4.9 litre Ferraris respectively. The Jaguar's high placing was not to last, although it was not Moss but Ian Stewart who first pulled in to report over-heating. His car had been left with the original radiator configuration, which for 1952 had included a separate header tank, whereas the other two cars had with some desperation had the 1951-type radiator installed. This last minute pre-race bodge, which had necessitated hammering a bulge in the C-types' bonnet to accommodate the extra height of the 1951 radiator, postponed the inevitable a little longer for the remaining two cars, of which Hamilton's was the last to succumb. By tucking his C-type in behind one of the little DB Panhards on the Mulsanne Straight, and coasting at 100 mph in its slipstream until the Mulsanne corner, Hamilton managed to complete the obligatory number of laps before the rules allowed water to be added - but to no avail, for as he recalled in his book *Touch Wood*, "unfortunately the damage was done, and as the water was put in steam came out of the exhaust pipe. Sadly we pushed the car away."

As for the 300SLs, they were nowhere near as fast as had been feared, and were certainly not the fastest cars in the race. But nevertheless they won. Ascari's 4.9 Ferrari put in a lap at 107.3 mph before retiring with clutch trouble, Simon's 4.1 litre car also retired after leading, as did Manzon in his Gordini, the latter after being in front for almost 12 hours. A Mercedes only circulated in front when Levegh, who had insisted on driving the entire 24 hours himself, changed into first gear instead of third during the 23rd hour and broke the Talbot's crankshaft. So Mercedes finished a rather fortunate 1st and 2nd with Lang (in 1939, the equivalent of World Champion) and Riess driving the winning car. Leslie Johnson and Tom Wisdom benefitted enormously from the decimation of the field, and their consistent drive in the Nash Healey

(the previous year's coupe, but now converted into an open car) resulted in 3rd place, and first British car home. Ironically, had Wisdom entered his own C-type (MDU 212) with Johnson, he would probably have won!

The argument that had the C-types appeared in 1952 with their original bodies they would have won the race easily is given weight by the fact that in the 1953 event, the privately entered, standard production C-type of Laurent and De Tornaco, which was in almost exactly the same mechanical trim as the 1952 works Le Mans cars but with normal bodywork, covered a distance that exceeded Mercedes' 1952 winning total by 20 miles. It was also some 10 mph faster down the straight than the German cars had been.

It has all too often been assumed that the whole blame for the 1952 cars' overheating problems stemmed from the smaller air intake in the new nose. In fact, plenty of air found its way to the radiator, and as Laurance Pomeroy stated quite clearly in *The Motor* a year after the disastrous race, "It is no secret that the retirement of all three works Jaguars in the 1952 Le Mans race was caused by defects in the water circulation *which were independent of the alteration of the front air intake on the bodies*" (my italics). This is further supported by the fact that efforts to remedy the situation in between practice and race were entirely centered around changes to the cooling system, not to an enlargement of the air intake itself - which would have been an easy matter with a pair of tinsnips, after all.

Thus the new bodywork was only an indirect cause of the trouble, in that a new cooling system had to be designed at short notice to fit underneath the sharply sloping nose. This involved mounting the header tank separately to the actual radiator, and it was positioned *behind* the engine. This needed a considerable length of tubing to plumb it into the cooling system, and too small a diameter was chosen for the interconnecting piping - 5/8 inch instead of 1¼ inch. The rise in water temperature resulting from this constriction of circulation showed up a fault in the shape of the water pump impellor, where cavitation occured followed by the formation of steam at the eye of the pump, after which the water stopped flowing altogether, with all too obvious consequences.

Post-race experiments showed that fitted with larger diameter piping and a revised water pump impellor, the 1952 Le Mans C-type circulated MIRA quite happily for hours on end without overheating. The 'droop snoot' bodies were not used again however as although the improved shape gave four or five mph more top speed, and a decrease in the horse power needed to sustain 100 mph from 53 to 42 compared to the normal C-type body, there was an alarming alteration in weight distribution brought about by wind pressure changing the car's attitude at high speed - its drivers reported that it became unstable along the Mulsanne Straight due to this factor. Expressed in percentages, the car's weight distribution at speed became 65½ front, 34½ rear compared to 51½/48½ stationary; the same figures for the 1951 C-type are 58/42 at speed, with an identical 51½/48½ static weight distribution. Frontal area, incidentally, remained the same at 13.8 sq ft for both cars. The whole exercise brought home very forcibly to Jaguar the folly of making last-minute changes which could not be completely checked out by wind tunnel or other experiments.

With the calamitous 1952 Le Mans over, work was resumed on the 'production' C-type with deliveries beginning in August 1952. Three months later, *The Motor* published its road test of a production C-type, which was similar in specification to the car which had been sold to Tom Wisdom (XKC 005) but without that car's experimental disc brakes. Although acknowledging that the C-type Jaguar was designed purely for competition use, the magazine's road test staff decided that as "Safe and comfortable transportation for two people must form an essential part of any sports car however spartan", the C-type should be put through the normal road test routine adopted for the

evaluation of any fast road car. This meant driving it in both town and country, and on the continent too, in order to determine its prolonged high speed cruising abilities.

Touring with a sports racing car usually calls for some thought, and the first problem encountered by *The Motor's* staffmen was where to put the luggage for a continental trip! The 40-gallon fuel tank didn't leave much space in the boot, and there was no room behind the seats. The dilemma was solved when it was discovered that the driver's door, and the corresponding part of the body on the passenger's side, could accommodate all that was needed for such a journey including the "waterproof clothing rendered necessary by the absence of hood and normal windscreen". Small aero-screens (the driver's adjustable by a single butterfly nut) and a permanently attached tonneau cover provided all the protection that there was from the elements, but as both driver and passenger sat quite low inside the C-type these were quite affective, as "despite pouring rain very little road dirt penetrates even when the car is driven fast". A heater wasn't fitted of course but the engine itself provided a good amount of heat through the bulkhead.

The driver of a C-type on the open road in 1952 was undoubtedly master of about the fastest thing on four wheels. *The Motor* found that 120 mph was an easy cruising speed, and 135 mph was quickly reached. Second and third gears "cope with any situation from walking speed to 100 mph", and the car inspired enough confidence for it to be driven at 120 mph and beyond within a "very few hours" by an experienced driver fresh to the vehicle. This, combined with its ability to "trickle through traffic and proceed along slippery pave and wet tramlines with most of the silence and comfort of the modern touring car", fully justified the magazine's description of the C-type as "flexible and viceless." One cannot really imagine driving an equivalent sports racing Ferrari with such ease on "slippery pave", and indeed it is the generally unstrained manner in which the C-type performed which provided a very strong clue to its success at *Le Mans* - its main components were simply very lightly stressed, and the result was the car's enormous reliability over long distances. Quite often the Jaguar would not put up the fastest practice lap; but much more importantly, it would still be racing 12 or 24 hours later.

There was little discussion of the C-type's roadholding in the magazine's road test, beyond a description of "really excellent" and a reference to its stability in the wet. This might have been due to the fact that no-one outside motor racing knew very much about high speed handling, and therefore hadn't any basis on which to judge such a thing - and even amongst racing car drivers and designers the true science was very little appreciated in those days. The car's ride is not mentioned at all. Steering and directional stability were enlarged upon however: "The highest praise must be given to the steering characteristics of the Jaguar. This rack and pinion mechanism is not only light and responsive but sufficiently high-geared for the driver to change direction more by wrist action rather than arm movement. Additionally the car must be one of the truest 'straight-line runners' the world has seen." The C-type's turning circle was 33ft, with 2½ turns lock to lock of the steering wheel.

That there was still improvement to be gained in terms of high speed aerodynamics was shown by the fact that above 130 mph, the car "tended to feel light... a curious sense of becoming airborne": though pains were taken to emphasise that this was not accompanied by any loss in directional control, "nor is there anything to indicate that much higher speeds would not feel equally safe to the occupants of the car."

The new self-adjusting brakes and the extra cooling of the drums afforded by the centre-lock wire wheels contributed to stopping equipment that was vastly superior to that of the XK 120. Pedal pressure was thought to be high though, but the almost complete freedom from fade

even when use of the brakes was "deliberately rendered excessive" on the down-hill parts of the Nurburgring, round which circuit the car was taken, more than compensated for that.

The general docility of the C-type's engine has already been remarked on, and while supplying its lazy power, it used no appreciable amounts of oil or water over the test's 500 miles, nor did it loose anything of its tune, "despite its severe thrashing." It was quiet too, "apart from a curiously rasping note which could be heard only momentarily at a little above 2,000 rpm", and was a good starter even from cold despite its battery being somewhat smaller than the XK 120's. About the only criticism of the engine was the design of the dipstick guide, which tended to collect road dirt. Accessibility to the engine was of course incomparably better than to the XK 120's power unit, due to the racer's hinge-forward bonnet - which was even given an automatic under-bonnet light. The small chrome side-handles on the bonnet weren't liked though, "because their quick operation will almost certainly remove a large area of skin from the fingers." The air scoops above the side handles had, incidentally, been exchanged for a row of louvres, and the bonnet of the production C-type carried a badge identical to that of the XK 120. The headlights also lacked the aluminium rims given to the first four works cars.

According to *The Motor*, the driver's seat was "exceptionally luxurious" if a little narrow for the hips, and it located the *conducteur* very well. The passenger was not quite so well looked after - he or she had a bucket seat of similar appearance to the driver's but as the large tool-box was located directly under it (as on the SS 100!), the depth of its cushion was not all it might have been. The passenger also sat a little higher than the driver, and so ran into slight problems with the slipstream making goggles obligatory above 50 mph - double that speed could be obtained before the driver had to don such protection.

A good range of instruments confronted the C-type driver, and the easily read, matching speedometer and rev counter were in traditional Jaguar styling with white letters on a black background. The other instruments were an oil pressure gauge, ammeter, fuel gauge, and water temperature indicator. An interesting accessory was the switch which caused the horns to operate continually until cancelled, an auxiliary to the normal horn push which was located for operation by either the driver or passenger. Lights were operated through a row of switches on the passenger's facia, the headlights being dipped by a hand control on the transmission tunnel - which like the rest of the interior was tastefully trimmed to add an air of civilisation to the cockpit.

The rear view mirror was neatly cowled into the scuttle, and other thoughtful touches with the would-be racing driver in mind included drillings in the large flip-top fuel cap and the screw-on oil cap to facilitate the work of the scrutineer, should the car be entered in long distance events where these items had to be sealed.

As for performance, the C-type's acceleration in the lower speed ranges was very good but not unbeatable by a few other low-production thoroughbreds, and even some of the fastest supercharged vintage machinery could match the car's 0 - 60 mph time of 8 seconds, which after all was only 2 seconds faster than Jaguar's own XK 120 Fixed-head Coupe in Special Equipment trim. But an ultra-quick getaway is not the primary consideration at Le Mans, and it was in the higher speed ranges where the C-type, with its slippery shape and high gearing (usually 3.31 for Le Mans but variable to special order), began to excell. Its 0 - 100 mph time was exceptionally good for 1952 at only 20 seconds, and only another 4.4 seconds passed before the car was travelling at 110 mph. Speeds in the gears at the recommended 5,750 rpm limit were 48, 82 and 119 mph. Top speed reached by *The Motor*, under rather wet and unsuitable conditions on the Ostend-Ghent motor road, was 143.7 mph mean, with a best one-way speed of 144.404 mph. These figures were to remain the fastest recorded by the magazine until the E-type

passed through its hands nine years later.

This efficiency was echoed in the C-type's fuel consumption figures. Those who were content to cruise at 50 mph could obtain 28.5 mpg, while at 100 mph petrol was still only being consumed at the rate of 15 mpg. Overall, the car returned 16 mpg. An aerodynamic shape and the low weight of 20 cwt (kerb) contributed to this relative frugality for a racing machine.

On a practical note, the C-type was supplied with Dunlop racing tyres, its engine held 19 pints of SAE 30 oil, the radiator needed 25½ pints of water, and 12 points on the chassis needed greasing every 2,500 miles. And for a car which, exactly as sold, was a potential candidate for the first five places at Le Mans, the price was very low indeed - £1,495 plus £832 purchase tax bringing the total in this country up to £2,327.

The lasting impression left with *The Motor* was that of the car's utmost suitability for normal day-to-day motoring, quite aside from its potential on the track, and one writer summed it up later as follows: "...in ordinary road driving, either at high speed or in city traffic, this is such a comfortable, responsive and well-behaved car as to make me feel that if fitted with a normal windscreen and hood (plus a luggage compartment where some of the 40 gallons of fuel are now carried) this would be quite the nicest possible every day car for the lazy journalist!"

Christopher Jennings and his staff were not the only ones who thought in similar terms about the C-type. Amongst those who bought a production C-type for road use was veteran GP driver Dr Guiseppe Farina, who collected his new car (XKC 032) from Jaguar's Belgian distributors in Brussells in March 1953. It was fitted with a wider than normal windscreen made of Perspex, though it appeared to retain its big petrol tank. There is no record of the car being raced by its distinguished owner, and it soon passed to the USA.

As for Jaguar themselves, far from retiring to Coventry to lick their wounds, they entered Moss at Rheims within weeks of their disastrous Le Mans. He didn't drive a works car but used the Wisdom/Cannell C-type, and the resulting win did something to assuage the company's Le Mans grief. In familiar fashion Moss was first away at the start, and although Robert Manzon's Gordini passed the C-type the French car's fraility showed up again and a front suspension failure caused Manzon to skid off the road in a big way. This left Moss able to drive home as he wished, an easy winner over 50 laps at an average speed of 98.19 mph. The heat on this occasion was immense so in some ways the win wasn't easy. Said Moss afterwards:

Inside the cockpit of the C-type there was no air intake for the driver, and on the last few laps I was putting out my hand and literally scooping the air into my mouth. I won the race by two laps, but then had to prepare at once for the Grand Prix. I asked for a bucket of water. They poured it slowly over my head.

Duncan Hamilton also rejoined battle very shortly after Le Mans, driving his own C-type (MDU 214) direct from Le Mans to Oporto. Poor Duncan, not only did MDU 214 break down leaving Castellotti to win one of his early victories, but he also received a telegramme from his wife Angela at home saying that five summonses had arrived, one for dangerous driving. They related to an incident where Duncan and the C-type had been timed at 120 mph in a 30 mph limit! In the event he managed to get off fairly lightly by explaining that he'd lost his way in bad weather, and hadn't realised he was in a built-up area.

July 1952 saw the debut of Ecurie Ecosse's first C-type (XKC 006). It was a happy one too, for Ian Stewart brought the Scottish team's production C-type to an easy win in the Jersey Road Race, over 60 seconds ahead of the second car home "after an unflurried and faultless drive". XKC 006 had drum brakes and only 900 miles on the clock, but nevertheless it had set fastest practice lap too, at 89.72 mph, and had no trouble keeping well in front of the Aston Martin DB3s, who were more concerned at trying to stay ahead of Bill Dobson's Wilkie-

tuned XK 120! A great performance was put up by Ken Wharton's Frazer-Nash which came second, and Oscar Moore's HWM-Jaguar which finished in third place. Scottish enthusiasts were to be similarly entertained when Stewart returned home and won two races at Charterhall with the C-type, the first time the car had been seen north of the border.

In August 1952, Stirling Moss again borrowed Wisdom's car to win at Boreham, the airfield circuit which is now rented by Fords for private testing but which in those days was an important International venue. Duncan Hamilton with MDU 214 followed Moss home in second place, without much opposition from the rest of the field, which included Reg Parnell's DB3 in third position. Ian Stewart (no relation to Jackie Stewart) had retired on the very first lap of that 100 mile race, a similar misfortune befalling the C-type driver the following weekend at Crimond, although not before he had won the preceding Sports Car race at the same meeting.

If Jaguar's official entry in the BARC Goodwood 9-Hours race in August 1952 was an attempt to regain a little face on their home ground it was doomed to failure. The C-types appeared with their 'proper' bodies but with similar driver pairings as at Le Mans. In the opening stages of the race the situation looked bright, with the cars placed first, second and third. Peter Whitehead was the first to break formation however, by crashing. Then during the seventh hour and while lying second to Moss, the Rolt/Hamilton car shed a wheel when a halfshaft failed. Hopes were still high in the Jaguar pit though as the Moss/Walker C-type was still miles ahead of everybody else and going like a train. Then disaster - the car's 'A' bracket broke, less than two hours from the finish. The C-type hobbled into the pits where it was immediately set upon by the mechanics, who did a tremendous job installing a new bracket in 30 minutes. But all hope of an outright victory had gone when the car finally resumed racing, its five laps credit having turned into a 15 lap deficit. Moss put on a characteristically brave 'last ditch' effort even though he knew the task was hopeless, and finally took the flag in 5th position, and first in the over 3-litre class, behind Peter Collins' winning DB3, two Ferraris and a Frazer-Nash.

While Ecurie Ecosse didn't contest the Nine Hours, Ian Stewart and his compatriots crossed the Irish Sea to contest the Wakefield Trophy at the Curragh in Country Kildare during September. On the handicap system, Stewart in the C-type won from Sir James Scott-Douglas in LXO 126 by 2 seconds, while the O'Boyle Trophy also went to Stewart and JWS 353. Back on the mainland, the Ecurie Ecosse C-type had a runaway win at the pleasant Castle Combe circuit in Wiltshire, before returning to Scotland where on home ground Stewart was able to defeat Moss at Charterhall, no doubt to the delight of his fellow Scots. He did not repeat this at Turnberry however, where at the Ayrshire circuit he was placed 3rd in a C-type 1-2-3 finish - Duncan Hamilton being sandwich man on this occasion.

Nor did hill climbs escape the C-type's attention. Peter Walker drove to a sports car record at Shelsley Walsh in August, recording 41.14 seconds, and accomplished a similar feat at Prescott a month afterwards, with a time of 47.53 seconds.

It was in September 1952 that Tony Rolt also managed that rare feat of vanquishing Stirling Moss in fair combat, though there was a certain amount of guile involved! The event was the BARC Goodwood meeting of that month, and the race a short five lapper for sports cars. Rolt had managed to persuade Lofty to lend him a C-type for the occasion, a drum-braked car unlike Moss's disc braked machine. The significance of this was that the drum brakes began working at more or less peak efficiency from the very start of an event, and gave away little or nothing to disc brakes on short distance racing where fade and wear problems did not have time to arise. Moss therefore had to contend with brakes that were slightly 'dead' until they

became properly warmed up, which took a lap or two of hard driving at Goodwood. So when Rolt made a very good start and headed the field off the line, he was able to gain those few extra yards which enabled him to keep ahead of Moss until the chequered flag was waved. There was only .6 second in it by then, but victory it was for Rolt nevertheless; and he recalls that beating the works' star driver in equal machinery caused something of an uproar at the time!

With production C-types now reaching the States in a steady trickle, the car was beginning to make its impact on the American racing scene too. The first outright win to be recorded by a C-type there was probably gained by Phil Hill at Elkhart Lake in early September 1952; a couple of weeks later John Fitch won the Seneca Cup race at Watkins Glen. Sherwood Johnston, a renowned campaigner and sports car championship winner in an XK 120, was also coming to the fore driving a C-type.

In England, the last appearance of a works car in 1952 was the demonstration runs which Lofty England and Stirling Moss gave at Goodwood on the occasion of the Guild of Motoring Writers' Test Day. The season closed with an announcement by Jaguar that Mortimer Morris-Goodall was to hold the position of Competitions Manager for the works team. This was to allow Lofty the time he needed in his role as Service Manager for both home and overseas territories.

'Mort' already had an enormous experience of the type of races Jaguar were entering, particularly Le Mans itself where he had competed 13 times and had won the Biennial Cup driving an Aston Martin in partnership with Robert Hichens in 1937. This, combined with a wide range of other racing and rallying experiences (including with an XK), made the well-known driver a good choice for the job, although he was to hold it only for a year. But Jaguar took pains to point out that the appointment did not portend an expansion of their competition activities.

For the official Jaguar team, the 1953 season

opened with the Mille Miglia in April. Three cars were entered, driven by Moss, Rolt and Johnson, but none of them were to reach the finish and it was Marzotto's 4.1 Ferrari that won, after all but one of the new 3,576 cc 'Disco Volante' Alfa Romeos retired (only Fangio's 'Flying Saucer' Alfa survived, and that only just after the *maestro* had driven much of the distance with only one wheel connected to the steering!). Leslie Johnson was the first to retire, his C-type suffering from a split petrol tank; as an experiment, this car had been fitted with an overdrive in an attempt to provide the correct range of ratios for the event's long straights and multitude of tight bends on the mounting passes. Moss, who was paired with works test driver Norman Dewis, lasted a little longer but was finally put out by rear axle trouble; two years later, he was of course to be the second non-Italian to win the Mille Miglia, driving with Denis Jenkinson in a Mercedes 300SLR.

It was Rolt who survived the longest, inspite of being the last car to leave the starting area in Brescia. He was driving Tom Wisdom's well-used but immaculate works-prepared car, accompanied by Jaguar mechanic Len Hayden - for whom such speeds as the C-type reached (Rolt cruised it at 140 mph) were entirely new, as the fastest he'd gone previously was to "touch 70 in the old Vanguard once"! The disc brakes fitted to MDU 212 were still being evaluated and thermo-couples had been attached to them for Hayden to read - the idea being for him to nudge Rolt whenever the temperature reached danger point, to indicate that he no longer had any brakes. But in the event, this wasn't necessary very often.

The car was put out of the race by oil surge, brought on by the numerous hump back bridges along the Adriatic coast over which the C-type would often take off. As Rolt recalled in an interview with Philip Turner in 1972:

We found out afterwards that when this happened, all the oil was rushing to the top of the engine as the C still had a wet sump lubrication system. However, we did get down to Ravenna where we turned west again. We had averaged 100 mph for the first 400 miles when we came in to refuel there, where John Wyer was expecting his Aston team. The Aston boys had been out for months practicing, but we had beaten all the Astons and were up in the first 10. But as we pulled in, the engine started to rattle, rattle, rattle. The bearings had gone as a result of oil starvation over those bridges and that was that.

Le Mans 1953 was however a considerably happier occasion for Jaguar, and resulted in an overwhelming victory for the C-type against worthy and extremely fast opposition - even if it didn't include Mercedes Benz who pretended that their 1952 victory had been conclusive, and maintained that a further demonstration of their prowess was not necessary.

For the race, the C-type had undergone a quite substantial revision, and carried similar but slightly lighter bodywork to the 1951 cars (the 1951/52 cars, XKC 001, 002 and 003 were presumably broken up; they were never sold or registered for the road, carrying only temporary 'trade' registration numbers). From the changes which were made, one can deduce the influence of Mille Miglia and previous Le Mans experience, particularly in the revamped rear suspension arrangement. The lessons learnt by the factory might sometimes have been hard, but they were learnt well!

A consistent weight-reduction policy had been carried out right the way through the car, commencing with its basic tubular frame. For the 1953 C-types, this was made up of 18 gauge tubing as opposed to the previous cars' 16 gauge material, although the diameter and geometry of the structure remained the same. The welded aluminium petrol tank, which had caused at least two retirements in long distance races through leaking, was exchanged for a flexible aircraft-type bag tank made by ICI; this, by virtue of its multi-point attachment to the car's frame and its inherent resilience, was almost totally immune to leaks, and its weight of 11 lbs made it considerably lighter than the metal tank it replaced. Its capacity was 50 gallons, although in service at Le Mans the most it usually carried was some 10 gallons less than this total.

Although not at first sight a particularly rewarding area, the electrical side of the C-type had undergone close scrutiny, and a weight saving of some 53 lbs was made over the 1951 cars. A big proportion of this total was contributed by the use of a much lighter battery, a single 12 volt item being substituted for the two six volt batteries used before. The reduction in capacity from 64 amp hours to 37 didn't matter as there was still plenty in reserve. The battery was placed under the driver's door on the right hand side of the car. A similar examination was made of the dynamo and starter, in view of the special conditions in which they were operating. As the rate of charge for the dynamo at low engine rpm was unimportant, while its reliability at high speed was vital, it was run at 0.9 engine speed by using a smaller pulley than before; the dynamo was made lighter too. And as the C-type's engine would only be started from warm during the race, a smaller starter motor was employed for the 1953 cars with aluminium covers contributing to more weight saving. Even the electrical cable was changed from tinned copper core to light alloy, saving an ounce a foot - and there's a surprising length of wiring in any car.

Changes under the bonnet were considerable and immediately visible. Gone were the familiar twin SU carburetters, and in their place were three twin-choke Webers. The chief virtue of these were not so much their adding of some 10 bhp to the maximum output of the engine, but the endowment of around 25 bhp at 4,000 rpm and the general fattening of the torque curve up to 5,200 rpm. Heynes was fully aware of the surprising amount of time even a racing car spends at comparatively low rpm, and that bhp applied exactly where it was needed, to pull the car out of a corner, was far more important than an impressive gross increase at the top end. It also meant that the engine did not have to be revved so high to obtain the same power, which thus reduced the stress on virtually every moving component in the engine; and of course,

acceleration in top gear above 100 mph was usefully improved too. Maximum power was in fact about 220 bhp at 5,200 rpm.

The 40 mm Weber carburetters breathed from a cold air box under the bonnet, each one being fed individually from a separate channel which ducted air from the single air scoop on the top of the bonnet. John Heath was probably one of the first to mate the XK engine with these Italian carburetters, incidentally, in the HWM-Jaguar which George Abecassis had run in a number of events before the 1953 Le Mans, although it is known that the factory too had been experimenting in secret for some time previously.

Even though the constant use of high rpm was not envisaged at Le Mans, several changes of a minor nature were made to the engine to ensure reliability should peak revs be used in the gears. The crankshaft damper was made in steel to prevent any possibility of it bursting, a reasonable precaution as the engine could and occasionally was run up to 8,000 rpm in error (or during testing at Coventry), an incredibly high figure for such a long stroke engine! But both the crankshaft and even the valve gear usually survived such momentary speeds without ill effect.

Wet sump lubrication was still used for the 1953 C-type, and to cut down the passage of gasses past the piston rings and into the crankcase (pressurisation of which could force oil out of the engine breather and down past the valves into the bores) special top piston rings were used. Known as 'Dykes' rings after their inventor, they were developed at MIRA and had great tensile strength and elasticity, and excellent wear characteristics, besides accomplishing their main function of preventing blow-by.

The cooling system was as for the normal C-type, the separate header tank being quietly forgotten, at least for the time being! Following the 1952 Le Mans, much experimentation had been carried out to discover the most efficient shape for the water pump impellor, and the improved design which resulted was effective in stopping cavitation at 5,000 rpm and above, which otherwise meant a sudden and drastic reduction in the pump's throughput. Marston Radiators had also put a lot of work into developing the radiator core itself, which was now in light alloy and combined a useful saving in weight with an improvement of 30% in water flow at a given pumping rate. An oil cooler was still not thought to be necessary though.

The biggest change in the transmission was the adoption of a new Borg and Beck triple-plate clutch which had its origins in the unit developed for the G-type ERA. Its diameter of 7¼ inches was considerably less than the previous single plate's, which at 10 inches had proved too near the limit as regards centrifugal loadings to be safe. Drive take-up was a little abrupt with the new clutch, but it rarely broke.

Experience gained in the previous two years of racing the C-type were thoughtfully applied to the car's rear suspension. The fabricated 'A' bracket was replaced by a single cast torque arm, and a Panhard rod was added to resist transverse movements of the axle; while to prevent the axle tubes turning as had occured in the Mille Miglia, these were located by both pegs and welds where they entered the differential housing.

The biggest advance over the previous car, and indeed over every sports car then racing, was the inclusion of the Dunlop disc brakes in the C-type's specification. These new brakes were the outcome of long and often painful research carried out by Dunlop, Jaguar and Girling, and amongst the drivers employed by Jaguar to test them were Moss, Hamilton and Rolt.The problems experienced in the early days included hub-flexing during cornering, which pushed the brake pads away from the disc resulting in an alarming increase in pedal travel on the next application, and boiling brake fluid. This last would manifest itself when, after the car had been braked hard for a slow corner, heat would soak through the pads to the wheel cylinders while the car covered the next straight, and create vapour in the system, so that at the next corner the driver would find he didn't have any brakes!

But by the time the cars took to the road for the journey to Le Mans in 1953, most of the fundamental faults had been ironed out. To overcome the problem of long pedal travel and high pedal pressures associated with disc brakes, assistance was provided by a Girling hydraulic servo motor driven from the back of the propellor shaft - an arrangement which, incidentally, antedated Citroen's similar power assistance by twelve months. It maintained a pressure of 30 lbs sq in, and when the brake pedal was depressed by the driver, this pressure was released to supplement driver effort. The design of the dual master cylinder was such that a failure of the pressure system didn't deprive the driver of his own direct action on the brakes.

Heat soak from the disc (a risk during pit stops too), was largely prevented by steel spacers which cut the heat path between the pads and the fluid contained in the wheel cylinders. The disc itself was chromium plated steel and was gripped by a multi-pad caliper of rather more complex design than the later versions which were fitted to the XK 150 in 1957.

If the 1951 Le Mans had been a classic, then the 1953 event was an even greater one. Almost every major sports car manufacturer in Europe sent a works team, with drivers whose names read like a major Grand Prix entry list. Ferrari's principle pairing was Hawthorn and Villoresi, Alfa Romeo was running a revised version of their fearsome Disco Volantes driven by Sanesi, Fangio, Marimon, Kling and Riess, Cunningham was trying once again with Walters and Fitch expected to make the running, and Aston Martin, Allard, Frazer-Nash, Talbot, Porsche and Gordini all fielded works teams. After the previous year's fiasco, Jaguar's chances were not rated highly by most, the more so as the C-types had been well beaten on their home ground at Silverstone not long before the 1953 Le Mans, Hawthorn and his 4.1 litre Ferrari winning at the International Trophy meeting and Aston Martin taking 2nd and 3rd places. Add to this the breaking down of the entire works team in the Goodwood 9-Hours race, and the failures during the Mille Miglia the previous April, it is no wonder that many of those watching as the C-types were wheeled into position for the start did not expect Jaguar to repeat their triumph of 1951.

It was therefore something of a shock to Ferrari, Aston Martin and Alfa Romeo to name but three when, after the hour of four o'clock came and the race began, Moss promptly took the lead in his C-type having passed Villoresi in the big red 4.5 litre Ferrari after only four laps, to head the field of sixty cars.

But within the first hour, the old Moss jinx struck again, and XKC 052 pulled into the pits with fuel feed problems. Tony Rolt saw Moss in the pits and closed on the Ferrari, regaining the lead for Jaguar with XKC 051. There ensued an exciting battle between Jaguar and Ferrari - Rolt and Hamilton versus Ascari and Villoresi. Moss dropped back still further, to 21st position, with another stop to clear the fuel lines; then gradually worked his way back again and reached 14th place before handing over to Walker after the first 3½ hours of racing. Rolt too came in to refuel, Hamilton taking over the C-type to rejoin battle with Ascari in the big Ferrari. The Jaguar's disc brakes helped compensate for the Italian machine's superior power, though Hamilton's task was made more difficult when a bird hit the C-type's screen at almost maximum speed on the Mulsanne Straight - apart from Hamilton's damaged nose, half the aero-screen was broken off and thereafter he had to lean to the left in order to miss the slipstream.

The battle continued into the night and apart from a short time when the leading C-type, no. 18, pulled in to refuel, Jaguar were always leading. Soon only the Ascari/Villoresi Ferrari and the Kling/Riess Alfa Romeo were even on the same lap as Hamilton and Rolt, the Fangio/ Marimon Alfa having retired with a broken piston at 6pm. Two laps down, the Carini/Sanesi Alfa was fourth, followed by the Walters/Fitch

Cunningham and the two other C-types of Whitehead/Stewart and Moss/Walker; the latter having pulled back enough to gain 7th position. Nineteen of the original field had already dropped out or crashed.

It wasn't long before the retirements were added to by both the surviving Alfa Romeos, Sanesi with a collapsed rear suspension and Kling with clutch trouble. At half distance, Hamilton and Rolt had put two laps between their C-type and the fastest Ferrari, taking full advantage of their superior brakes in the difficult dawn light, as Hamilton remembered in *Touch Wood*: "First light coincided with the arrival of the usual mist and our disc brakes really paid dividends; I was never in danger of overshooting at Mulsanne whereas poor Ascari was obliged to brake early just to make sure".

A sad note was struck when at 6.30am it was announced that the American driver Tom Cole was missing; his Ferrari had crashed at White House, killing its driver.

At 8.30 in the morning the pit stops of Ascari and Rolt coincided; the Jaguar pit crew under the eye of Lofty England and Morris-Goodall performed their tasks in their usual efficient manner - it took them only 4½ minutes to refuel the C-type, replenish its oil and change all four wheels - and it was Hamilton who accelerated away from the pits first. When Villoresi started off after him, it was apparent to all those listening in the pits that the Ferrari's clutch was slipping, and that retirement was only a matter of time. Two hours later, the Ferrari lay abandoned out on the circuit. Moss was now lying second, the Cunningham third, and the car of Whitehead and Stewart fourth, and these became their finishing positions when the flag was dropped at 4pm, coinciding with Hamilton crossing the line. Jaguar had achieved its second Le Mans win and Duncan Hamilton had achieved his "dearest sporting ambition" in partnership with Rolt. The winning C-type's average was a record 105.85 mph, a big increase over the 1952 average and the first time Le Mans had been won at over 100 mph.

While the C-type's disc brakes were certainly an important factor in Jaguar's 1953 Le Mans win, they should not be given blanket credit for the result, and a quote from Tony Rolt himself will underline John Wyer's remarks at the head of this chapter: "The disc brakes did play a tremendous part, but it was no tortoise and hare affair. It was not that everything passed us on the straights and then we overtook again on the approach to the corners. In fact very few cars indeed passed us anywhere in the circuit."

Neither did Jaguar's success end with the three works cars. The single Ecurie Francorchamps C-type, XKC 047, driven by Belgians Roger Laurent and Charles de Tornaco finished in a highly creditable 9th position. The car, in its bright yellow Belgian national colours, had only been collected from the Jaguar distributors in Belgium about a fortnight before the event, and was a standard production model. The 'standard' nature of the car was emphasised by its progress over one of the fastest stretches of the Mulsanne Straight - its timed speed of 143.59 mph compared exactly with *The Motor's* road test production C-type, an exactly similar drum braked, 2 inch SU car which achieved a mean maximum of 143.71 mph. The works team cars achieved 146.16 mph (Whitehead/ Stewart), 147.46 mph (Moss/Walker), and 148.83 mph (Rolt/Hamilton).

Interestingly, the two faster cars had higher, 2.9:1, gearing than the Whitehead/Stewart car which retained the previous 3.31:1 axle. A very accurate indication of the 1953 works C-type's top speed capabilities had in fact been given a little while before, when in another expedition to Jabbeke Norman Dewis had driven the latest Weber-carburetted car at 148.435 mph.

Not that the C-types were the fastest cars on the circuit in a straight line - the Disco Volante Alfa Romeo of Sanesi had clocked an average of 150.88 mph, the 5.4 litre Cunningham 150.37 mph, and Ascari's 4.5 litre Ferrari 149.87 mph.

It being Coronation year, Jaguar had the happy idea of informing the new Queen personally of the victory, and they sent the following very 'British' telegramme from the circuit to Buckingham Palace:

"The Jaguar team humbly present their loyal duty to Her Majesty and wish to advise her that in her coronation year they have won for Britain the World's greatest international car race at Le Mans, France, yesterday."

The 1953 Le Mans race was the last event to see an official works team of C-types compete though certainly not the last C-type to appear on the Sarthe Circuit. However, the works drivers did enter a couple more events in 1953 of which the Rheims 12-hour race in July was the most successful for Jaguar. The principle contestants were Moss's C-type, Rosier's Talbot, Behra's new 3-litre Gordini, John Fitch's Chrysler-engined Cunningham (which had finished 3rd at Le Mans), Abecassis' HWM-Jaguar and the 12 cylinder 4.5 litre Ferrari coupe of Maglioli and Carini. The Ferrari was the centre of an enormous row when it was rather harshly disqualified for turning its lights on too early and for receiving a push start, while it was well established in the lead. The matter so upset Ferrari himself that he threatened to withdraw all his single seater cars from the French Grand Prix! When the Ferrari eventually had to withdraw, Moss and Whitehead had an easy win especially after Fitch crashed spectacularly at 125 mph in the beam-axled Cunningham. His pioneering use of a seat belt probably saved his life.

The Goodwood 9-Hours race of 1953 turned out no better for Jaguar than it had done in 1952, for although the works cars of either Moss/Walker or Rolt/Hamilton were in the lead for eight hours, both C-types retired almost within minutes of each other with severe bearing trouble. It was another instance of the C-type's wet sump manifesting itself again; oil surge on Goodwood's succession of right-handed corners plus an under-estimated rate of oil consumption proved the cars' undoing. The race was won by the Aston Martin DB3S of Parnell and Thompson, well ahead of the surviving works Jaguar in 3rd place, driven by Whitehead and Stewart, and which had been plagued by overheating brakes - the disc glowing bright red through the night. The Ecurie Ecosse C-types weren't far behind, their drivers being Jimmy Stewart/Dickson, and Lawrence/Curtis, in 4th and 5th positions respectively.

Neither did the Ulster Tourist Trophy bear fruit, Aston Martin again taking the flag. All the three works C-types retired with similar gearbox failures, an unusual fault in a Jaguar and apparently due to over hardening of the gears. Moss managed a 4th place on handicap (3rd on distance) but only by creeping along on the downhill stretch near the finish, and waiting for the winner to be flagged home before struggling across with the stricken machine. But at least his partner Walker came away with the lap record, at 87.53 mph, and until their retirement the Jaguars were always ahead of the Aston Martins which eventually finished in first and second places. The race was also notable for the ruinous effect it had on tyres, the Moss/Walker C-type undergoing at least five changes during the nine hours of the event, due to a new and abrasive surface.

There was a possibility that an official Jaguar team, or at least a car, might have contested the epic Carrera Panamericana, and Lofty England and Stirling Moss followed the 1953 event as an assessment exercise. They had quite an exciting time, including one diverting moment caused by what looked like a Mexican bandit ordering them off the road at gunpoint. The character turned out to be a course marshal, Mexico style!

A C-type was in fact specially built for this 1,900 mile race (which counted in the new Constructor' Championship), having a suitably reinforced frame and given the usual works extras in the form of disc brakes and Weber carburetters. This car was apparently intended for Masten Gregory, but when the 1952 entry was not preceeded with the car, which had been used as the 1953 Le Mans practice car, was sold to Duncan Hamilton early in 1954. Chassis number XKC 038, it became registered as OVC 915.

Had a C-type been successful in either the Panamericana or the Ulster TT, then Jaguar would have ended 1953 with the sports car manufacturers' Championship which had been introduced by the FIA that year. But Jaguar were simply not interested in winning it, for the very good reason that the great majority of their potential customers wouldn't know what it was - unlike Le Mans of course.

So there were no works Jaguars at Spa or the Nurburgring either. Ecurie Ecosse however entered both, and surprised both Ferrari and Alfa Romeo by the speed and reliability of their C-types during the 24 hour race at Spa, although it was the Ferrari of Hawthorn and Farina which won. The C-type driven by Sir James Scott-Douglas and Guy Gale came second, and while Laurent's Belgian-entered C-type retired, third place was taken by the similar car of Roosdorp and Ulmen (XKC 019). The first 1000 km race at the Nurburgring witnessed an equally impressive performance by the Scottish team, Ian Stewart and Roy Salvadori netting second place. They finished only 15 minutes behind the Ascari/Farina Ferrari after 44 laps of racing, an especially good effort in view of the circuit's general unsuitability for the Jaguars of that era, and was one of Jaguar's best-ever results there, apart from later saloon car racing successes.

Ecurie Ecosse had an excellent season in fact, another quite meritorious second place being taken by Ian Stewart at Wicklow on the occasion of the Leinster Trophy race in July 1953. Baird's 4.1 Ferrari won, but Scott-Douglas backed up Stewart in third place. A variety of successes were chalked up at many lesser events by the team, which now had four production C-types in action - XKC 006 (JWS 353), usually driven by Ian Stewart, XKC 041 (KSF 181), XKC 042 (KSF 182), and XKC 046 (MVC 630) usually the mount of Sir James Scott-Douglas. Ninian Sanderson was a further name which came into prominence during 1953 driving for Ecurie Ecosse.

One other long distance event came the way of Jaguar in 1953, and that too was won by a private C-type entry. This was the Hyeres

12-hour race, and it was in partnering Peter Whitehead to victory that Tom Cole drove one of his last races in a Jaguar, before his tragic death in the 1953 Le Mans. Second place on that occasion also fell to a C-type, brought home by Frenchmen Armand Roboly and John Simone (XKC 025).

Other production C-types were also continuing to make an impact on the racing scene, Sherwood Johnston taking third place at Sebring early in 1953, with co-driver Robert Wilder, and followed by the C-type of Harry Gray and Bob Gegan. A Cunningham won with Aston Martin second. In Sweden Oscar Swahn was having a good measure of success with his car, and while it was still America that absorbed the greatest number of C-types (17 or 18) the cars did reach other countries too.

Perhaps the most active 'privateer' in Great Britain with a C-type was Duncan Hamilton, who directly after the 1953 Le Mans race took MDU 214 out to Oporto, driving to Portugal with his wife Angela and mechanic Len Hayden in his Mk V drophead while the C-type travelled by boat. It was fortunate that they did bring the Mk V as Duncan crashed the C-type very comprehensively into a pylon during the early stages of the race, after making fastest practice time.

Suffering from nine broken ribs, a broken jaw and a fractured collarbone from the foregoing incident, it was sometime before Duncan could begin to drive again. He then entered the Pescara 12 hour race in Italy with Peter Whitehead in the latter's C-type (XKC 039), but mechanical failure ended their run while they were lying fourth. His drive for the ill-fated works team in the Goodwood 9-Hours race followed, and he ended his season by entering his rebuilt C-type at the final 1953 Goodwood meeting, against the background of Mike Hawthorn's rousing drives in the Thinwall Special. In the C-type's handicap race Hamilton recorded fastest lap at 81.82 mph, which was as he said, "not bad for a car that had been a total write off after the Portuguese GP."

As the 1954 motor racing season got under-

way, it became quite clear that the C-type had made its last entry as a works car at Le Mans, as in May its yet-unnamed successor had been taken to Le Mans where it had put up a lap that was seconds quicker than any which had been accomplished by any other car, the C-type included. Then the 1953 works 'lightweight' C-types (XKC 051, 052 and 053) were sold to Ecurie Ecosse, and it was realised that the factory had indeed raced its last C-type.

David Murray then took up the car's banner, and campaigned the team's 'new' C-types far afield during 1954. The 1000 km race at Buenos Aires was contested, Ninian Sanderson and Sir James Scott-Douglas finishing in 4th place, while in Europe the team visited Zandvoort where Sanderson won, and Barcelona where Salvadori was second and Sanderson third.

At home, Desmond Titterington gained fourth place at an early Snetterton meeting, the press remarking of him that "...a new Ecosse driver, Titterington was prominent and looks like being a worthy member of the Equipe". So he proved to be, although it was actually Salvadori who won that race in another Ecurie Ecosse C-type, beating Tony Crook's Cooper Bristol. At Goodwood Jimmy Stewart and Ninian Sanderson were first and second in the June 21-lap sports car race, repeating their Easter Monday success, and further wins were chalked up by the team at Ibsley, Oulton Park (where Titterington won the Unlimited sports car race at 71.65 mph), Charterhall and elsewhere. But not yet the glory of Le Mans.

Amongst the individual private entrants, Duncan Hamilton was now driving OVC 915 (XKC 038), the 'Mexico' C-type which had been sold to him by Jaguar at the end of the 1953 season. He was joined by the late Brigadier Michael Head who had bought the Wisdom/Cannel car, MDU 212 (XKC 005). Head's programme included an epic trip through Scandinavia, driving the C-type (complete with wife and tools - there was no tender car) over roads that were in the main muddy and atrociously surfaced to compete in a series of races in Finland and Sweden. Now resplendent in Head's racing colour of white the car won every race it entered, at Helsinki, Lapeenranta, Hedemora and Stockholm. In all, the car travelled 1140 miles in the two trips involved, completing four races and six practice sessions, with the C-type performing "as if it had been leading the most sheltered life...perhaps the last of the sports cars which could be driven all over the continent and... yet able to give its driver a good chance of success", as Michael Head recalled in 1959. Moreover, MDU 212 was raced virtually every weekend while it was in England during 1954.

Duncan himself had a similarly successful season with OVC 915, the car being prepared by Fred Boelens, a Dutchman whose five brothers were all priests, and who was a "remarkably fine mechanic". The first 1954 outing for the car was the British Empire Trophy race, transferred from the Isle of Man to Oulton Park. There, Duncan beat all three ex-1953 Le Mans C-types entered by Ecurie Ecosse in his 'scratch' heat, though he was relegated to fourth place in the final on handicap. The following weekend two second places came the way of the C-type and Hamilton, Jimmy Stewart keeping ahead for Ecurie Ecosse on both occasions. Then, with Fred in the passenger seat, Duncan drove to Montlhery for the Coupe de Paris - "I have always believed that sports racing cars should be driven to the track whenever possible," he said. "If they cannot be driven on the road it is a reflection on their design. Apart from fitting softer plugs my C-type was in racing trim. All Fred had to do was to fit hard plugs, check water and oil levels, ensure the tyre pressures were correct and that the car was carrying the right quantity of fuel. The only spares we carried were the sort of spares any keen motorist would take with him on a motoring holiday."

Later owners of OVC 915 have agreed with this philosophy; as late as 1973, the car was driven to Le Mans once more for the 50th Anniversary celebratory historic race held on the famous circuit, and achieved 10th position in the

45 minute event!

Duncan won the Coupe "very easily" at an average of 93 mph, and reckoned that he was getting 155 mph along the straight, and 135 - 140 mph on the banking.

Continuing a pattern of success, OVC 915 won the first sports car race on the circuit at Aintree, overtaking Jimmy Stewart's Ecurie Ecosse C-type on a streaming wet track. "The track was new, wet and very treacherous, yet I drove with tremendous confidence, and indeed almost ignored the adverse conditions. A retrospective view of this race causes me to shudder when I think of the abandonment with which I went into the corners."

Although he managed to finish the 1954 Oporto sports car race, the Ferraris proved too fast for Hamilton and the C-type, while at Zandvoort a bearing went leaving Ecurie Ecosse to win the International Sports Car race, an event which had been put on in place of the Dutch GP which didn't take place that year. OVC 915 was leading the field before retiring, finding the sand dune surrounded circuit exactly to its liking - "so much so that it was difficult to believe that IRS or de Dion back axle would have allowed me to lap any faster".

Duncan Hamilton's last continental sortie with a C-type was at Montlhery, where the result was a third place in the Coupe du Salon; the event was won by Jean Behra's straight-eight 3-litre Gordini, closely followed by Masten Gregory's 4.5 litre Ferrari. Hamilton pointed out that he and the C-type averaged 73 mph from Claridges in Paris to Dieppe on the way home!

However, by the end of 1954 Hamilton was negotiating for the purchase of OKV 1, the short-nose D-type he had driven in the 1954 Le Mans race and at Rheims in partnership with Tony Rolt. The C-type in turn was sold to Danny Margulies, and in December 1954, OVC 915 had the distinction of being the first of its kind to race at Brands Hatch. It finished in 3rd position driven by Margulies, who continued to field the car regularly in club races here, and abroad too on occasions, with Graham Hill as riding mechanic!

The car passed to its present owner, Rupert Glydon, in 1967, via Frank Sowden.

Of the C-types raced by owners on the continent, it is probably XKC 047 that has the most active history to its credit. This was the production C-type extensively raced by Roger Laurent for Ecurie Francochamps, and in 1954 he and Jacques Swaters took the car to Le Mans. Unfortunately, the car crashed while being driven there - as it was overtaking a little 4 CV Renault on a wet road, the French car swerved out causing the C-type to slide and hit a concrete pylon. The occupants were thrown out and the C-type rolled over. Fortunately the scrutineers accepted the wreck, brought to Le Mans on a lorry, in lieu of the spare C-type being flown over from the factory. But the substitute machine faired extremely well being the epitomy of reliability and finishing in 4th place overall. Either this car or the rebuilt XKC 047 also gained 3rd position shortly afterwards in the Rheims 12-Hour race, behind the works D-types.

Further afield, Curt Lincoln raced XKC 044 in Finland with success, while XKC 045 commenced its active life in Italy but then travelled to Switzerland, where it counted Silvio Moser amongst its drivers, and Hans Maag who ran the car up until the sixties. Several cars went to France, Jaguar's Lyons agent Peinaux writing off XKC 016 in an accident, which was the fate met by XKC 035, its driver Heurtaux being killed - after making FTD at Planfoy, Heurtaux inverted the car after the finish line! Roboly (025) and Simone (027) regularly campaigned their C-types, and they partnered each other to achieve a second place in the Hyeres 12 hour race of 1953 as mentioned previously. One C-type went to Holland (043), being eventually brought back to this country a few years ago after surviving as a children's plaything in a field for a number of years!

C-types also went to rather obscure parts of the globe - XKC 029 went to Mexico, and XKC 036 to Morocco. The Antipodes were the eventual destination of XKC 037, where it was raced in Australia by Boorman, Gardner and Matich amongst others, having arrived via East Africa where its driver had been Manussis. Peter Whitehead took XKC 039 to New Zealand, where he sold the car after racing it.

As with nearly all Jaguars, however, it was North America that had the largest share of the C-types. XKC 015 was amongst the first half dozen to reach the American shore, and it certainly had an interesting life being first owned by Jim Hall, who sold it to Masten Gregory. It suffered a disastrous fire in the latter's hands after it had enabled the up-and-coming young driver to make a good start in SCCA racing, and after a brief spell in Sherwood Johnston's hands (during which time the car was rebuilt and, running without bodywork, made FTD at a Mount Washington Hill Climb) was relegated mainly to street work. It was lovingly rebuilt by Mark Daniels who bought it in 1964, and a further point of interest is that XKC 015 was tested by *Road & Track* in 1953. Achieving 60 mph in 6.6 seconds, and 100 mph in 16.8 seconds with its 3.92:1 gearing, it was the quickest car to have passed through the magazine's hands up until that time.

In Great Britain, by 1954/55 the D-type Jaguar had become the *sin qua non* for the serious Jaguar competitor, though the C-type continued to be raced for a number of years by a variety of amateur drivers. After passing through the hands of Berwyn Baxter, Max Trimble bought MVC 630 (XKC 046), Sir James Scott-Douglas's old car, and raced it extensively, while other regularly successful drivers included Joe Kelly in Ireland with XKC 050, Peter Blond and Alan Ensoll in the ex-Ecosse XKC 052, Gillie Tyrer (053, also ex-Ecosse), W.T. Smith (who was tragically killed in XKC 051 while beginning what appeared to be a brilliant motor racing career), John Bekaert who raced XKC 008 (MHP 825, Leslie Johnson's car) for Ecurie Anglo-Belge, Mike Salmon (011, ex-works, Dunlop), and many others who counted the C-type amongst their early track experiences.

Altogether 54 C-types were made, including

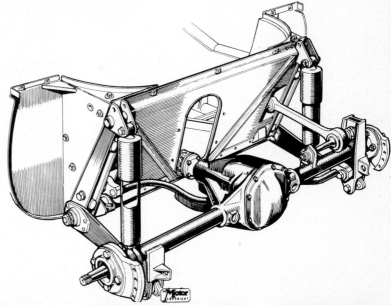

Top The 1953 C-type with bonnet open showing the cold air box for the Weber carburettors *(photo The Motor)*

Centre left Guiseppe Farina taking delivery of his C-type from the Brussel's Jaguar agency in March 1953; the car was apparently bought for road use. It soon found its way to the United States *(photo The Motor)*

Centre right The revised axle location of the 1953 C-type with the A-bracket replaced by a one-piece torque arm and Panhard rod which were more effective in controlling axle wind-up and less prone to fracture *(photo The Motor)*

Bottom Not long before the start of the 1953 Mille Miglia while Tony Rolt (in suit) and mechanic Len Haydon wait by their works C-type. They did not finish *(photo The Motor)*

Top left The 1953 winning C-type of Duncan Hamilton and Tony
Rolt takes the Esses with the Ferrari 375 of Ascari/Villoresi
temporarily in front, having lapped the DB3S of Salvadori/
Abeccassis (photo The Autocar)

Top right Definitely a Lyons Special - the 'Brontosaurus' resulted
from a collaboration between Fred Gardner and Lyons around
1952; body was aluminium on a wooden frame and originally was
purely a design exercise, until 'the boss' wanted to see it running.
The experimental shop then took over from Lyons' personal little
workshop and strengthened the shell to accept C-type suspension
and engine. It never ran outside the factory and died within a few
months - the same fate befell the Jaguar 'Grand Prix' car, another
Lyons idea, which consisted in essence of the front halves of two
C-types fitted together to form an all-torsion bar independently
sprung single seater with a space frame. This was never bodied and
was cut up in probably the year it was made, 1953. No photographs
seem to have been taken of this though

Centre Duncan Hamilton leaps into the 1953 Le Mans winning C-
type after a night refuelling stop, while the scrutineer seals the
petrol filler cap and the mechanics strap the bonnet down (photo
The Motor)

Bottom The victorious C-types return to the factory after the 1953
Le Mans race, in their order of finishing, watched by the workforce
and civic dignitaries. The mixed suburban and country surroundings
to the Browns Lane works are substantially unchanged today

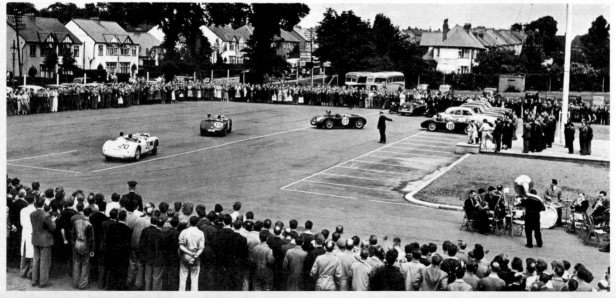

Top The C-type competed successfully in America too - here two private entrants at Sebring in 1954
Centre Tony Gaze shields his eyes during the 1954 Australian 24 hour race on the Mt Druitt circuit near Sydney. The car was brought out for the race by Peter Whitehead but shortly after midnight a rear axle bracket broke and, unsteerable, the car was retired
Bottom left Curt Lincoln of Finland competed locally with success in 1955
Bottom right Successful private entrant Michael Head in the ex Wisdom/Cannell C-type at a March Goodwood 1955 meeting. He is followed through the Chicane by Peter Blond in the ex Ecurie Ecosse car and J Hogg in MHP 825 *(photo The Motor)*

Top It was this car with which Sir William Lyons originally intended to replace the XK 120, and not the XK 140 that we know today; it would have stayed in production right up until the E-type of 1961
Centre The intended XK 120 replacement, shown alongside an XK 140 Roadster, the car which took its place
Bottom The fixed-head version of the Jaguar sports car that never was, again in mock-up form only. Note that it is simply the roadster illustrated previously but with made-up hard top placed over the cockpit, complete with 'painted in' rear window

Top This two door, drop-head prototype makes an interesting comparison with the experimental XK 120 replacement. It would appear to be based on the 2.4 Mk 1 saloon platform and would therefore have been of unitary construction

Centre The XK 140 Roadster retained most of the 'primitive' aspects of its predecessor, having no wind-up windows and a detachable screen which allowed aero-screens still to be an option. It was the most numerous of the XK 140s.

Bottom This *Autocar* cutaway drawing is of the prototype XK 140 Fixed-head, and shows non-standard items such as the steeply raked side window pillar, and repositioned seat cushion for transverse seating in the back *(photo The Autocar)*

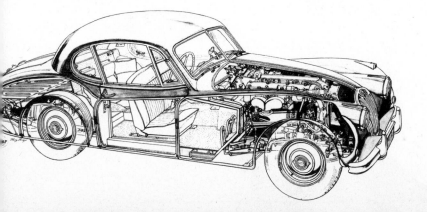

Top left The XK 140 Drop-head Coupe had the same exemplary hood arrangements as its XK 120 forebear, but with the added advantage of occasional rear seats

Top right Works driver Hawthorn was a customer for the new XK 140 Drop-head. He is pictured here at the factory, accepting delivery from Mr England

Centre The Bolton/Walshaw XK 140 arrives for scrutineering prior to the 1956 Le Mans race. Extra cooling was provided by the additional inlets either side of the radiator grille, the slats of which had also been laboriously filed down to let in more air! Bonnet louvres and strap are other visible departures from standard *(photo The Motor)*

Bottom Mike Hawthorn in the works D-type overtakes the near standard XK 140 of Bolton and Walshaw during the 1956 Le Mans race; it will be seen that the bumper iron holes in the front wings have been enlarged to provide better brake cooling, in between practice and race

Top left An XK 140 Roadster on test, displaying extra cooling vents similar to those let into the front wings of the Le Mans fixed-head. Note the wool tufts which show the airflow, and the louvre in the bonnet

Top right Ian Appleyard continued his rallying career, though less actively, with an XK 140 Fixed-head. VUB 140 is seen here completing a test during the March 1956 RAC Rally *(photo The Motor)*

Centre left Trouble on the Tulip. A J Burton's XK 140 comes to an involuntary stop against a boulder during the May 1956 event *(photo The Motor)*

Centre right Guyot's XK 140 Roadster about to embark on the 1956 Mille Miglia race; the car ran well and won its class

Bottom Ivor Bueb beats Tony Brooks driving Rob Walker's 300SL Mercedes-Benz at Oulton Park, driving the ex-Le Mans XK 140 to win this race during the *Daily Herald* Gold Cup meeting of September 1956

Top left David Hobbs had a successful innings with his XK 140 Drop-head Coupe until he rolled it at Oulton Park as this dramatic sequence shows! *(photos The Motor)*
Top right G H F 'Bobby' Parkes was an active and successful campaigner with his XK 140 Fixed-head KFR 712, and was a winner of the BTRDA Silver Star. The car is seen here departing for a Monte Carlo Rally, having started at Glasgow *(photo The Motor)*
Bottom During the early sixties, the ex-David Hobbs drop-head was re-bodied for Dick Tindell by Freddie Owen, the car being given quite a pleasing shape reminiscent of an E-type. It subsequently made regular appearances at sprint meetings and is still in circulation today

Top Designed by Raymond Loewy for his own use, this somewhat futuristic car was built round a Special Equipment XK 140 chassis; bodywork was by Boano of Turin, the year 1955

Centre Ghia bodied XK 140, as shown at the Geneva Show of March 1956. It is now owned by Jaguar collector Phillip Renault of Paris *(photo The Motor)*

Bottom With overdrive fitted, the XK 140 was endowed with very relaxed cruising - in fact maximum permitted revolutions simply could not be exceeded in that ratio, even down hill. This picture was taken during *Autocar's* road test of a Special Equipment XK 140 Fixed-head, with the instruments showing an indicated 135mph at only 4,800rpm *(photo The Autocar)*

Top The original D-type emerges from the workshop, and those who worked on building the car gather round for a sort of 'handing over' ceremony. They are (from left to right): Malcolm Sayer, Phil Weaver, Bob Knight, Norman Dewis, Joe Sutton, Keith Cambage, Gordon Gardner, Arthur Ramsey, 'Lofty' England and Len Hayden

Bottom left At the Le Mans circuit, May 1954, closed for a local rally, Tony Rolt takes the D-type out for two or three fast laps, the new sports car's first serious trial. The tubular framed C/D prototype was also tried out on the same occasion, seen in the foreground. Mr England watches from extreme right *(photo The Motor)*

Bottom right En route to the circuit for a brief but successful practice session, Jaguar experimental engineer Phil Weaver conducts the first D-type through the streets of Le Mans; following is Norman Dewis in the C/D prototype *(photo The Motor)*

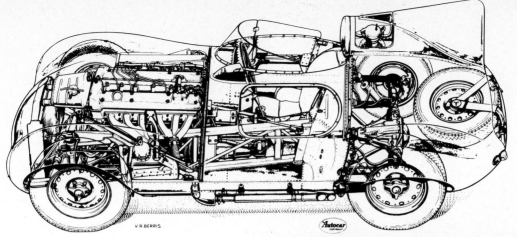

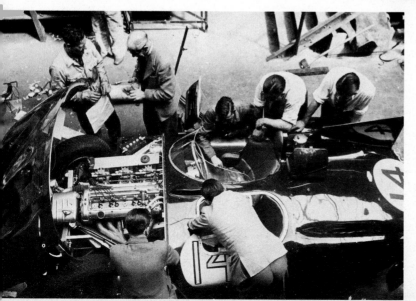

Top D-type anatomy; cutaway drawing of the 1954 works D-type by Vic Berris of *The Autocar*. The car's centre monocoque/tubular frame construction can be clearly seen *(photo The Autocar)*

Centre The prototype D-type being worked on in the competition section of Jaguar's experimental department - now with its correct registration number showing, OVC 501 (not OKV 501) *(photo The Motor)*

Bottom On the eve of the 1954 Le Mans race, the D-type of Hamilton and Rolt has its final check over at the Garage Rue de Sarthe. From left to right, top row, are Jaguar mechanic Frank Rainbow, Jack Emerson (one of Jaguar's leading engine and carburettor experts), Jack Thompson of Jaguar, pointing out something in the D-type's cockpit to William Heynes, and John Turner of Alford and Alder. Nearest the camera, Norman Dewis, Jaguar test driver and Bob Knight, Jaguar engineer, also watch the proceedings *(photo The Motor)*

Top Le Mans 1954, and the D-types line up for their first race
(*photo The Autocar*)
Centre Duncan Hamilton takes OKV 1 through the rain as he
pursues the Ferrari of Froilan Gonzales in a dramatic bid for
victory (*photo The Autocar*)
Bottom Anxious examination of the Hamilton/Rolt D-type during
the early stages of the 1954 Rheims 12 Hour race, after Behra's
Gordini had run into the back of it. Although not serious at first
glance, the damage eventually caused the back axle to run dry
losing the car a sure first place - it just managed to finish second
(*photo The Motor*)

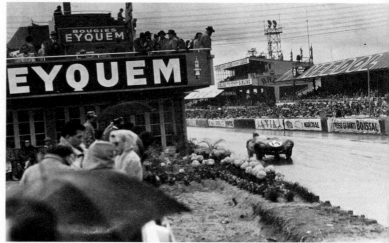

the 1951/2 and 1953 works team cars, and the survival rate is quite good - even now 'lost' cars still come to light occasionally in various parts of the world. It is not the purpose of this book to list all the existing cars and their present owners, but it is pleasant to record that some of the most famous C-types have survived to this day. Amongst these, the only Le Mans winning C-type in existence, XKC 053 and originally registered LFS 671, resides in Briggs Cunningham's museum in the States (both its sister cars, 051 and 052 which also passed through the hands of Ecurie Ecosse are still in this country), while Duncan Hamilton's OVC 915 (038) now belongs to Warwickshire dentist and Historic driver Rupert Glydon, and the Tom Wisdom and Michael Head XKC 005 (now registered RRW 3) has been in the ownership of Tony Woods in Northamptonshire for many years now. XKC 046 is the current property of Tom May who has also restored Sir James Scott-Douglas's other Jaguar, the ex-Ecosse XK 120 LXO 126. In all, about 15 C-types can be accounted for in Great Britain, while probably a lot more still live in America where of course they are highly prized possessions.

In attempting to assess the C-type by today's standards, one must bear in mind as a first principle that the car was built to win Le Mans, and that it was successful in its designed purpose. More than any other car which Jaguar have since made - and one may include the D-type in this - the C-type brought the company into the eyes of the world. Lofty England is quite unequivocal about this: *The race that did the most for Jaguar was the 1951 Le Mans... It put us on the map.*

This must be taken into account when examining the car by the engineering yardstick of the 1970s. The acceleration of the C-type, particularly in its twin-SU production form, can be improved upon by quite a number of mass production saloons and coupes of today, a time of 8.8 seconds to 60 mph no longer being inordinately quick (about the same as a 3-litre Ford Capri); while a top speed of 143 mph is now considered normal for a present day Jaguar road sports car, and indeed the XJ5.3 saloon can actually exceed this figure under good conditions, with its five seats and air conditioning!

To sit in a C-type now one feels distinctly short of room, although this was also apparent when the car was new; to quote Rolt, "I could never get into it with any comfort because it was very cramped - they always seemed to be built for short-legged people".

On the road, the car's handling is open to question in some respects, there being controversy about its rear suspension even when the C-type was in current production. "I used to argue a lot in those days about whether it needed independent rear suspension, but in fact the rear suspension was very crafty with its offset arm which did cancel out torque reaction. It suffered from wheelspin in the wet and we were at a disadvantage compared with the Aston Martins which had the full treatment, with their de Dion rear suspension", remembers Tony Rolt.

There is a feeling of 'rear end steering' with the C-type too, and the car has been described by those who have driven it quickly as cornering "in a series of arcs, no one of which quite matches the radius of the curve", which is how *Road & Track* put it when trying the rebuilt XKC 015 some 20 years after it left the factory. On the same theme, the magazine goes on to say:

"The C-type must be forced beyond this, by entering each turn at maximum velocity and loading both ends of the car to their extremes. Then the car can be steered with power and it all works well."

One finds in practice that the C-type in normal road driving handles as well as many high performance road sports cars of today, and it still remains a practical form of transport for those who wish to use it as such, which is more than can be said for a lot of its contemporaries. But perhaps one can leave the final few words on the C-type Jaguar to Le Mans winner Major

Tony Rolt, who succinctly summed up Jaguar's first competition vehicle by saying: "the car as a whole was very simple, very light and very effective." And no-one can deny that.

If the XK 140 is an extremely fast car, it is also a very docile one. It has absolutely perfect traffic manners, and entry and exit is easy, even for a lady in evening dress

John Bolster
Autosport November 4 1955

Purists will undoubtedly take offence at the more massive, and substantial, bumpers, but all should agree that the larger luggage compartment is an improvement

Road & Track 1955

THE SPORTS CAR THAT NEVER WAS

With the coming of the XK 140, there was a gentle shift of emphasis in the make-up of Jaguar sports cars. For while true performance was still offered by the XK 120's successor, most of the advances which came with the new model were in the direction of greater creature comfort rather than in the cause of out and out speed. Thus a 2-plus-2 configuration made its first appearance, establishing a 'grand touring' image which the XK would begin to adopt.

Unlike the XK 150, the XK 140 had basically the pure lines of its immediate predecessor the XK 120 Jaguar, and in common with all the XK series it used the same chassis. But the beautiful 'flow' of the XK 120's styling was partially killed by the necessary imposition of heavy, Mk VII type bumpers and more chromium plate.

What has not been revealed before however is that the XK 140 as we know it was never intended to follow the XK 120 as it did. William Lyons had, in fact, prepared an entirely new body design with which to follow up his post-war styling masterpiece, and it was this completely different shape that was to have superceded the XK 120 at the end of 1954.

The reason why this did not occur is closely bound up with Jaguar's position in the early 1950s. With the largely unsuspected success of the sports car, and with the Mk VII saloon also selling supremely well, the factory found that when the time came to consider replacing the XK 120, there was simply not the spare capacity or time to tool-up and put into production an entirely new body shell for its successor - every employee and every machine was already working at full capacity in a vain attempt to meet the insatiable demand for Jaguars that already existed. In other words, it would have been pleasant to have announced with a flourish an utterly different looking new sports car, but Lyons realised that this would have been a luxury that could not be enjoyed in the face of many more practical considerations. The outcome was therefore a 'compromise XK 120', namely the XK 140, which retained the earlier car's body pressings but with various necessary up-dating features - like the heavier bumpers - hung upon them rather than being 'designed-in' to the overall shape as would have been the case with the Jaguar sports car that never was.

This previously undisclosed prototype was styled on a totally different theme to that of the XK 120, or to any Jaguar sports car which has appeared since. It was given a far smoother shape than any of the XK series, its front wing line being continued almost horizontally at scuttle level right to the rear of the car, only beginning to slope gently down after the cockpit to form the rear wing line. The cockpit sides did not have cut-away doors like the XK 120 Roadster but formed a continuous line with the front and rear portions of the bodywork.

No head-on photographs of the front of the car seem to have survived (maybe none were taken), but from the curve of the front wing it can be conjectured that it might have borne a family resemblance to the 'Mk 1' Jaguar saloon. The rear half of the prototype displayed a striking similarity to that of the Mk 10 Jaguar saloon when it appeared seven years later - ignoring of course the rear wheel spats worn by the prototype. The sports car also wore a chrome side strip running from front to rear, a flush door handle, and a chrome centre strip on bonnet and bootlid; although such items of minor trim may or may not have been intended for the final production car.

A one piece, full width curved windscreen was fitted, anticipating the XK 150 by some four years, and the car was obviously destined to have wind-up side windows. Strong wrap-round bumpers were another feature of the car, these being carefully incorporated into the overall shape of the vehicle especially at the rear.

The 'XK 130' (as I suppose it is bound to be nicknamed, although so far as I am aware the very few people who knew about the prototype at the factory never gave it such a designation) was very much lower than any XK, being about six inches lower at both scuttle and windscreen height than the XK 140 Roadster. Its shape was extremely simple to be sure, but it was none the less effective for that and it would undoubtedly have been a beautiful car indeed, had it reached production.

The prototype as pictured in this book was only a body design mock-up mounted on a wooden frame, and the car almost certainly never got much beyond this stage. Had it carried out its intended function as the XK 120 replacement, then it would probably have been

mounted on the revised 1954 XK chassis which was adopted for the actual XK 140. As the cockpit was longer than the XK 140 Roadster's, it can probably be assumed that occasional rear seats would have featured in succeeding examples - and there would have been a fixed-head version eventually too. It can definitely be stated that had this car entered production, it would have meant that the XK 150 would never have been made either - the 'XK 130' being intended to remain as Jaguar's sports car up until the advent of the E-type in 1961.

Besides just being a fascinating story for its own sake, the fact of this prototype's one-time existence has a genuine significance in the history of the Jaguar sports car, as it indicates that William Lyons did not regard his XK 120 design - beautiful though it was - with complacency but was busily working behind the scenes on a successor that would have embodied a much more up to date shape. It also enables us to look a little more kindly on the XK 140 itself, now that it is realised that the large bumpers and other impositions on the car's XK 120 shape was not something that Lyons had particularly planned, nor was necessarily overjoyed about. The XK 140 has always been something of a slight enigma, and the prototype XK 120 replacement explains a lot.

But to return to what actually did take place at the end of 1954, rather than what might have been, the XK 140 was first shown to the public on the occasion of the Motor Show at Earls Court in October. From the commencement of its production, all three types of body work were available - open two seater, fixed-head coupe, and drop-head coupe - and although the revised exterior trim was at once evident, the more interesting changes has taken place beneath the skin.

The 190bhp engine of the Special Equipment XK 120 was adopted as the XK 140's standard unit, together with the 3/8 inch lift camshafts, but with a single exhaust system. Further power for those who required it came in the form of the 'C-type' head, which was an optional extra on Special Equipment XK 140s. This cylinder head, which had also been offered on the XK 120 towards the end of its production, was that developed for the C-type Jaguar sports racing car. While the inlet valve sizes remained at 1¾ inches (as in the 190bhp engine), the inlet and exhaust porting was increased in diameter, and so were the exhaust valves, which went up from 1 7/16 inches to 1 5/8 inches. The same XK 120 Special Equipment 3/8 inch lift camshafts were employed, and when fitted with this head the car's engine was rated at 210 bhp at 5750 rpm. An easy identification of this head was provided by the letter 'C' cast into its plug well.

A more fundamental change was the re-positioning of the engine in the chassis frame, the unit being moved forward three inches. There were two reasons for this - it meant that the car's bulkhead could also be moved forward to provide more room inside, and it introduced more understeer into the XK's handling characteristics. Although the latter made the XK 140 an extremely controllable car and one that was much more difficult to 'lose' than the XK 120 when pressing on, it is probable that the former aspect of the change was the chief reason for moving the power unit - lack of leg room, a small adjustment range for the seats, and rather cramped quarters generally for the driver had for some time been a criticism of the XK 120 in all its forms. In any case, extra space was required inside the car for the two 'occasional' rear seats which were from now on to be a feature of fixed-head and drop-head XKs.

The engine itself was little changed in essence, still being fed through two side-draught 1¾ inch SU carburettors in either standard or C-type trim (with which came a dual exhaust system, using two separate silencers and pipes which ran through the chassis cross-member and emerged under each over-rider at the rear of the car). Cooling was improved though by a new and more efficient radiator, inclined at an angle, and by a new 8-bladed fan operating in a cowl. Gone, however, was the XK 120's big cast aluminium sump, replaced by a smaller capacity pressed-steel one.

The second major change to the car's layout was the substitution of Alford and Alder rack and pinion steering for the XK 120's Burman re-circulating ball arrangement. This too was a 'productionised' version of a piece of equipment used on the C-type Jaguar, and it provided more accurate and responsive steering for Jaguar's road sports cars. Although the number of turns from lock to lock of the steering wheel remained the same at 2¾, the turning circle of the car was increased by two feet to 33 feet by this change. Kick-back from the road (which could in this system be transmitted to the steering wheel) was minimised by a rubber-bonded rack mounting on the chassis frame. A useful by-product of the rack-and-pinion steering was the cranked, universally-jointed steering column now used, allowing the steering wheel to adopt a more comfortable angle in the car.

Then for the first time, an overdrive was offered as an optional extra on an XK, in the form of the Laycock-de-Normanville unit which had been a very successful extra on the Mk VII Jaguar. This meant a slight alteration to the centre transverse chassis crossmember, to allow for the extra length of the car's transmission when the overdrive unit was bolted on to the end of the gearbox.

So far as the XK 140's suspension was concerned, this was essentially unchanged in principle compared to the XK 120's; the latter's Special Equipment torsion bars (which had been up-rated from 128 lbs/in to 154 lbs/in over the original XK 120's by an increase in diameter of 1/16 inch) were adopted as standard on all XK 140s, while at the rear the XK 120's lever-type shock absorbers had given way to Girling tele-scopic units. These were mounted at their upper ends on a gusset which triangulated each corner of the chassis crossmember which ran across the car just aft of the rear axle, and they ran down to meet a bracket extending backwards from the axle casing. Their main virtue was that they lasted considerably longer than the lever dampers, although their location on the axle was not quite so ideal as with the earlier type, being a little further from the outer end of the axle.

The XK 140's braking system remained similar in specification to the XK 120's, with self-adjusting front brakes and bevel-wheel rear brake adjustment, but there was a reversion back to the single master cylinder of the earliest XK 120s. Fifty-four spoke wire wheels were an option from the outset, and like the wire wheeled XK 120s, the front brake drum was dished and not interchangeable with the rear. These wire wheels were (as always) of 16 inch diameter and 5 inch rim width while disc-wheeled cars had the 5½ inch rim width which had been adopted on the 1952 fixed-head XK 120, and used subsequently on all disc-wheeled XKs.

The external changes to the car which, as we have discussed, may have detracted somewhat from the basic design of the body shell, had largely been dictated by the requirements of the North American market. The XK 120's tiny bumpers, complimentary though they might have been to the car's lines, were purely ornamental - particularly in view of the way in which they were mounted at the front, being bolted solidly through the front wings with a spring steel bar *behind!* They were completely ineffective in warding off car park assaults, so they were replaced on all the XK 140 models by bumpers of a similar section to the Mk Vll's. These were mounted at the front on very strong bumper irons which passed through the large openings in the front wings (which had originated in the brake cooling apertures on the XK 120) and bolted directly to the chassis. The mountings were covered by a valance which ran between bumper and bodywork. At the rear of the car, quarter bumpers were used, mounted equally strongly but almost flush with the rear bodywork so that a valance wasn't needed here; equally tough over-riders were fitted front and rear too. It was the new bumpers which were responsible for the XK 140's extra inches in length - it measured 14 feet 8 inches from stem to stern which was 3 inches more than the XK

120. Wheelbase and track were not of course affected.

Also changed was the radiator grille - gone was the XK 120's neat, multi-slatted decoration, to be replaced on the XK 140 by a die-case alloy item, with thicker and less numerous slats cast integrally with the outer rim. An enamelled badge was also set into the grille, in place of the bonnet-mounted brass and 'ivory' badge of the XK 120. Improved headlights (incorporating a 'J' monogram at their centres) and separate wing-mounted flashing indicators further influenced the XK 140's looks from a frontal viewpoint. Valance mounted matching spot and foglamps came with the Special Equipment specification and a chrome strip decorated the centre line of the bonnet on all variants.

The rear view of the car had changed too, quite apart from the big bumpers. The rear light units were larger and included stop lights and flashing indicators, and a chrome strip matching that on the bonnet ran down the centre of the bootlid, abutting a medallion set in a chromium plated surround proclaiming Jaguar's Le Mans wins, while a new push-button bootlid handle was fitted. The number plate had been moved down to between the new quarter bumpers, as instead of the spare wheel being withdrawn horizontally from the back of the car, it was now lifted up vertically from a well in the boot floor, via a hinged lid. Access to the boot was now also possible from inside the car, through the provision of a hinged bulkhead. Similarly to the XK 120, bonnet and bootlid were in aluminium.

THE XK 140 FIXED-HEAD

All the foregoing applies to each of the three XK 140 body styles, and the alteration in engine positioning especially had a big effect on internal dimensions. The XK 140 Fixed-head Coupe was in fact a very practical car with a marked increase in roominess over its XK 120 predecessor. Not only was advantage taken of the power unit being moved forward, but the front bulkhead was also swept round the engine on either side, enabling the seats to be brought forward a total of almost one foot. Much of the extra space thus created was used for the two occasional seats, which were ideal for children and quite tolerable for one adult sitting cross-ways. The two six volt batteries which in the case of the XK 120 had occupied some of this space had been transferred into the car's front wings.

The saloon top of the XK 140 Fixed-head extended back another 6¾ inches compared to that of the equivalent XK 120 model, in order to clear the rear seats, and at the same time the windscreen was brought forward. It also gave a further 1½ inches of headroom to the occupants, so that in all the greater space and larger window areas made the car pleasantly light and 'airy' to ride in.

The doors of the fixed-head were wider too, at 38 inches instead of the previous 32½ inches and although the prototype car illustrated in Jaguar's first announcement of the new range had a lever door handle, the production XK 140 Fixed-heads had a push-button type. This 'first off' fixed-head also varied in other respects to following cars - most noticeable was probably its steeply sloping side window pillar, changed to a design which followed the more upright line of the door in all later examples. It may also have had the aluminium doors which according to published factory service data were used on the first 100 or so fixed-heads, although it seems that this was not the case in practice, steel doors being fitted to all cars. Inside, the prototype displayed occasional - seat back rests which extended up to the rear parcel shelf - later cushions were much shorter.

The interior trim of the XK 140 Fixed-head was the usual tasteful blend of leather and carpets, with burred walnut for the dashboard and door cappings. The woodwork where fitted on all XKs, incidentally, was supplied in sets of matched grain and colouring, and when ordering spares it had to be specified whether a light or dark shade was required. Instrumentation followed the pattern set by previous XKs; the new flashing indicators were operated from a centrally placed switch on the dashboard which cancelled itself by a clockwork time mechanism. Overdrive, when fitted, was controlled by a switch of mock cut-glass which was internally illuminated when 'on', and which was positioned on the facia to the right of the steering column (on rhd cars).

THE XK 140 DROP-HEAD

The XK 140 Drop-head Coupe, like the closed car, followed its XK 120 forebear in overall conception, but with a considerable increase in room internally - although this was not quite so marked as in the XK 140 Fixed-head, as the bulkhead was not projected either side of the engine, but just moved forward the 3 inches allowed by the repositioned engine. This gave an increase in adjustment of the front seats of three inches too (from 4 inches to 7 inches); also, the bottom of the facia was raised an inch. The drop-head XK 140 was given two occasional rear seats like its closed sister and these were likewise quite adequate for conveying the owner's offspring. The drop-head now had a single twelve-volt battery, carried in the near-side front wing - a practice followed by the XK 140 Roadster too.

Fortunately, the car's 'drop head' was of almost exactly similar pattern to that of the XK 120's before it, being simplicity itself to erect, completely weatherproof, and with headlining and central courtesey light. Erected, it followed the curves of the body perfectly, and folded it could be covered with the hood envelope supplied.

Evident in both the new versions of the XK was the type's trend away from the uncompromising sports car image of the original XK 120 Roadster, and towards an appeal based on that of an ultra-fast touring car. And very successful too was this gentle transition, combining as it did comfort, luxurious appointments, and complete protection from the elements with a performance on the road that was nearly as good, and in some respects better, than the much lighter, strictly two-seater XK 120 announced in 1948.

THE XK 140 ROADSTER

The XK 140 Roadster on the other hand retained many of the essentially 'primitive' features of the first XK - no wind-up windows, no occasional seats, and a detachable windscreen. That was what the majority of Jaguar's American customers wanted, and that is what they got!

Contrary to what appears to be popular belief in this country, the XK 140 Roadster is by far the most numerous of all XK 140s, some 3,354 units having left Coventry during the car's production run, compared with approximately 2,800 each of the fixed-head and drop-head body styles. The one qualification here is that only a very few rhd XK 140 Roadsters were built, about 73 in fact, and not all of those remained in this country.

The XK 140 version of Jaguar's roadster did incorporate some advances over the earlier type however, when it came to creature comforts. As it shared the same forward bulkhead position of the fixed-head and drop-head XK 140s, the roadster too was roomier inside with an increased seat movement of 3 inches. The car's scuttle line had been lifted by an inch and this allowed the steering column to be raised, which gave a welcome increase in clearance between the rim of the steering wheel and the driver's thighs; it also had the effect of providing greater headroom when the hood was up.

Behind the seats, the space left by the batteries being moved forward of the front bulkhead was now available for extra luggage. The car's interior trim was left much as it had been on the XK 120 Roadster, a wood finish on the dashboard and facia still being eschewed for the more practical leather covering. But the angled mounting of the dashboard had been

changed for a vertical one. Alone amongst the XK 140s, the roadster had aluminium doors.

The roadster owner could still order from the factory nearly all the competition options that had been made available for the XK 120, including the bucket seats and aero-screens. In addition a competition ('solid centre') clutch, and the lead-bronze main and big-end bearings which were one day to become standard on all Jaguars, could be ordered by the owner of any XK 140, along with 9:1 compression ratio pistons - and even the big H8 2 inch SU carburettors used on the C-type Jaguar.

THE XK 140 ON ROAD TEST

Not that the XK 140 Roadster was slow in standard form - particularly when it was ordered with the C-type head and overdrive transmission. No British journal road-tested an XK 140 Roadster, in any trim, export being the cry as always, but the American *Sports Illustrated* magazine tried an XK 140MC Roadster in April 1955, John Bentley reporting on his findings with enthusiasm (on the North American market, 'M' designated wire wheels, dual exhaust, and auxiliary lights, and 'C' the further option of the C-type). Mind you, even he had to borrow one from a willing owner, the dealers not being able to keep a demonstrator in stock long enough for it to be run-in sufficiently for a road test!

The car was the quickest XK off the mark yet tested, at 8.4 seconds knocking 1½ seconds off *The Autocar's* time to 60mph recorded with the Special Equipment XK 120 Fixed-head in October 1952. Eighty miles an hour was reached by the XK 140 in a very fast 13.9 seconds. "On a half-mile test strip I easily hit 110mph," said Bentley, "at which point - had their been room enough - the Laycock-de-Normanville overdrive (an optional extra) would really have come into its own. Flick a dashboard switch and instantly the high-gear ratio goes up 28% while the engine revs drop accordingly."

Bentley liked other aspects of the XK 140's new character, the "light, positive and accurate steering...(and) what's more the decreased angle of the universal joint on the column provides better vision over the top of the wheel. It also affords two inches more space between the bottom of the rim and the seat." The new cooling arrangements were also working well - "Gone is the annoying tendency to overheat in traffic which once plagued XK owners."

There was a debit side though, and *Sports Illustrated* went into the particular on two points. By far the most significant was John Bentley's comments on the brakes - more 'go' hadn't been matched with more 'whoa' and while the XK 140's brakes were safe for "occasional panic stops from moderate speeds", energetic use of the car's performance could cause problems: "Repeated hard applications at 80 or 100mph, however, induced brake fade. On the car tested, the linings gave forth an objectionable burning smell".

Bentley thought that enthusiasts would gladly pay to have Al-Fin brake drums fitted as a factory option (these were a popular choice for racing in those days, and were available for a wide range of cars; cast-iron linered, their finned aluminium construction dissipated heat much more rapidly than did the usual solid cast iron drum. They were made by Wellworthy).

The other, considerably more minor, complaint made by Bentley was the "gooking-up of the hood and trunk lid with fancy medallions and chrome strips. These trimmings rob the car of its former arrogant sleekness and spoil the patrician simplicity that was the very essence of its good looks. As one American enthusiast put it: 'The British unfortunately don't have the right kind of bad taste for styling.' " Although so embroidered ostensibly for the US market, it seems that Americans were often the least appreciative of these efforts on their behalf! These criticisms did not mean that Bentley came down against the XK 140 Roadster - far from it, as he closed his test by saying:

But the debits against the XK 140MC are insignificant besides its credits. It is a wondrous machine - docile, fast, quiet, flexible, comfortable and easy to drive. It has almost everything the enthusiast could wish for and it has it at a price that makes the Jaguar one of the best sports car dollar values on the market.

Road & Track magazine also ran a test on an XK 140MC Roadster, but this was a non-overdrive car and instead of the 4.09 rear axle fitted to *Sports Illustrated's* roadster, it had the 3.54 ratio. Inspite of the higher gearing it equalled *Sports Illustrated's* time to 60mph at 8.4 seconds, but was appreciably slower to 80mph, at 15.7 seconds. The 'ton' came up in 26.5 seconds and the mean maximum speed was 121.1mph - the other journal didn't try a maximum speed run nor did it record a 100mph acceleration time, so there is no comparison to be made here.

The XK 140 Roadster was very much liked by *Road & Track* drivers, although they were a bit doubtful about the gearbox and (of course) it was hinted that the aesthetics of the new bumpers were not all that they might have been. The most missed feature from the XK 120 Roadster though was its magnificent war-cry, the latest (twin box) silencers being rather too effective - "This may be something of a disappointment to those enthusiasts who took pride in the rap and crackle of the earlier mufflers."

The test staff were surprised to find that far from making the XK 140's ride harsher, the adoption of the stiffer torsion bars still left the car's ride "excellent". Some roll was still apparent though, but this was thought to be a "reliable indication of safe cornering speed", a remark followed up by this pronouncement on the car's handling: "we feel that the Jaguar is one of the easiest and safest automobiles on the road today"; which must have pleased everybody at Browns Lane. That the car was only partially civilised however is shown by the fact that *Road & Track* had to bend the side curtain frames to cure some of the drafts with the hood up, which when erected left visibility to the rear still pretty poor.

Road & Track found that the car's petrol consumption averaged out at around 16 - 18mpg, which contrasts strongly with *Sports Illustrated's* 12.7mpg! This last figure was said to have included "all tests", and indeed it is so high that it seems likely that John Bentley did no general motoring at all on the open road, as with over-drive, one could reasonably expect something around 18 - 20mpg from the XK 140 Roadster even driven quite hard. There is also a dis-crepancy between the weights quoted by the two magazines, but this time it is probably *Sports Illustrated* that is the more correct, put-ting it at 27 cwt kerb - or about 1 cwt lighter than the XK 140 Fixed-head Coupe. In the States, the roadster was good value at 3745 dol-lars, which included 295 dollars for the MC options. Specifying the overdrive unit cost the purchaser another 160 dollars. It was probably a bit theoretical as to whether you could buy one in Great Britain, but it was initially listed at £1,692 in basic form, inclusive of purchase tax.

The fixed-head and drop-head coupes were on the other hand to become a relatively common sight in this country. *The Autocar* tested a fixed-head coupe, RHP 576, at the end of 1955; it was a Special Equipment model complete with C-type head and overdrive - no standard 190bhp car, with its disc wheels and spats, was apparently released by the factory for testing. Jaguar obviously preferring to submit the more impressive 210bhp version for expert analysis, its wire wheels also helping to minimise the car's tendency towards brake fade.

The Autocar found the new XK to be much more civilised than its old XK 120 counterpart, although actually slower on acceleration in all speed ranges - this includes top gear acceleration where it would seem that the XK 140's considerably lower overdrive rear axle ratio of 4.09, and an extra 20bhp, were still not enough to compensate for the increase in weight of 1cwt over the earlier car (which seems in retrospect to have been rather fast). For instance, the XK 140 took 7.4 seconds to accelerate from 30-50mph

in direct top, and 9.4 seconds to reach 80 mph from 60mph; the XK 120 Special Equipment with its 3.77 final drive took 7.3 seconds and 8.1 seconds respectively to cover the same increments.

Standing start figures showed about the same result; the XK 140 took 11 seconds exactly to reach 60mph, and 29.5 seconds to get to 100mph - the XK 120 took 1.1 and 1.3 seconds respectively less to gain those speeds from a standstill. Not that the later car's figures were in any way a disgrace, few cars of the day being able to match them, and as for maximum speed there was simply no contest - the magazine recorded a highly impressive 129.5mph!

This overdrive top figure was of course achieved after a suitably long run-in on a continental autoroute and under ideal conditions (the best one way speed was only .25mph faster than the mean quoted), but as *The Autocar* said, "the readiness with which 100mph can be reached, rather than the absolute maximum, is the car's outstanding attribute". In fact, 100mph "can be held in overdrive to become a comfortable cruising speed with very low throttle openings and to record a petrol consumption of near enough 22mph", with the engine turning over at a modest 3,800rpm. Even the maximum velocity of the car was finally governed by wind resistance rather than gearing, as at 130mph, the engine was pulling no more than 4,900rpm.

Thus cruising speed could very nearly be said to have been any figure you'd like to mention in the range embraced by the overdrive gearing - *The Autocar* found no rise in water temperature and no drop in oil pressure on a very fast return run abroad, following the maximum speed runs in Belgium, inspite of using all the revs. in the gears and engaging overdrive at 5,500rpm in direct top (110mph).

The magazine also approved of the changes in handling wrought by moving the XK 140's engine forward - the car's weight distribution expressed in percentages was now 50.3 front, 49.7 rear, compared with the XK 120 fixed-head's 47.5 front and 52.5 rear. "The extra weight on the front wheels is the most decisive factor in the improved cornering capability. It results in a controlled degree of drift such as was achieved on racing cars of the past, when small section tyres were fitted to the front wheels to achieve the same purpose by sliding, without the science of the action being fully understood."

This increase in understeer was not accompanied by any change in the quality of the car's ride, which remained good:

...there is comfort at low speeds with none of the teeth-chattering effect which in the past was associated with a sports car, even over cobbled roads, and with the tyres inflated to the pressures recommended for high speeds, the ride is still comfortable. Indeed it is possible to write a legible hand at 110mph.

A note of caution was sounded about the car's behaviour in the wet, the rear wheels being easy enough as it was to spin in the dry. The new rack and pinion steering was liked, being light yet positive, although it was found that some road shocks were transmitted to the driver - *The Autocar* suggested a steering technique of "allowing the wheel to 'float' in the driver's hands" to minimise this tendency.

The XK 140's gearchange got away with a "satisfactory" from the magazine's staff though the long movement of the gear lever from 1st to 2nd was commented on, and the magazine would have preferred the ratios of these two gears to be closer together too. While the clutch transmitted its large amount of brake horse power without slip or judder, the typical Jaguar feature of a long travel was noticed, together with the necessity of using it all if a noiseless gear change was to be achieved.

Those owners who opted for wire wheels on their XKs did more than just enhance the looks of the car - the increase in air circulation around the brake drums brought about a very useful increase in heat dissipation and *The Autocar* asserted that the brakes on their car were "entirely adequate for the high speeds involved. Under extreme conditions they did not fade or grab, but each application was accompanied by a rather annoying squeal from the front drums."

It was thought that some servo-assistance might be appreciated by some drivers though, as the pedal pressure was heavier than average, a stop of 88% efficiency needing a push of 100lbs. The Mk Vll saloon with a basically similar (though all trailing shoe) braking system had a vacuum servo, but no such apparatus was to be fitted to an XK by the factory until the disc brakes were adopted on the XK 150 in 1957. While few owners would have argued with *The Autocar* about a servo, there were no doubt quite a number who didn't see eye to eye with that magazine when it came to discussing 'fade or grab!'

The Autocar recorded a very moderate fuel consumption figure of 22mph for its XK 140 Fixed-head, rather better than the 17½mpg John Bolster managed when he had borrowed the same car for *Autosport* a month before. But at the same time, he had made the car go a little faster in terms of acceleration, his 0-60mph time probably being more representative of the type at 10 seconds - or exactly the same as that of *The Motor's* road test XK 120 of 1949. Bolster's time to 80mph (16.8 seconds) and 100mph (26.2 seconds) were also better than *The Autocar's* although top speed was down at 121.6mph - largely due to a lack of room in which to get the car really wound up, as 'snap' speedometer readings of 135 mph were obtained on the slightly optimistic instrument on occasions, without them being held long enough to be accurately measured over a set distance.

Bolster liked the car's handling, and in fact wrote very enthusiastically about its attributes in that respect:

"There is a wonderful feeling of complete control, and this is one of those very rare cars that seems to help the over-impetuous driver out of his difficulties. The rack and pinion steering gives beautifully precise control, and one can fling the 26cwt car around like a 1½ litre." (The weight quoted by Bolster here is 'dry').

But it was the car's brakes which Bolster rated as the most improved feature of the XK, it apparently being possible to really drive the car hard without running into stopping problems - only a "choice scent of hot linings" resulting from their repeated use at 120 mph.

Bolster also had some interesting things to say about the XK's conventional live rear axle, when comparing it to the independent systems which by 1955 were beginning to gain in popularity on the continent. While the XK still spun its wheels more easily than was the case with more sophisticated suspensions on some European sports cars, and the heavy old axle was noticeable on bumpy corners, nevertheless he thought that "the Jaguar is far easier to drive than some continental cars with independent rear ends, and in general the chassis design represents a most effective compromise."

The powerful 8:1 compression ratio engine (9:1 was optional) with its C-type head was thought by Bolster to be slightly more audible than the original low compression XK 120 power plant, but still docile in the extreme. Here the low 4.09:1 rear axle helped, making top gear acceleration "really brilliant" and notably improving flexibility.

Inside, "it is at once obvious that the driving position is far better than that of the previous model. The accelerator and brake are arranged for 'heel and toe', and the clutch pedal has a space to its left to permit the foot to be rested. The steering column is adjustable, and there is more leg room than before for a tall driver."

As well as Bolster, *The Autocar* had also acclaimed the increased amount of room in the new body, and said that "a tall driver does not find he has to peer under the top rail of the windscreen, and one very quickly becomes accustomed to the divided windscreen glass." Although the magazine felt that more room for the driver's right elbow would not have gone amiss, most owners overcame this deficiency (if they noticed it at all) by using the conveniently low window sill as a ledge on which to lean their elbow - comfortable if not necessarily good

driving technique!

The XK 140 Drop-head Coupe was never subjected to a full road test by any motoring journal so that it isn't possible to analyse its behaviour as it has been with the other two body styles. But in virtually every respect its character was identical to that of the XK 140 Fixed-head Coupe, with the added attraction of fresh-air motoring when desired by the driver. There wasn't quite as much room for the carrying of rear passengers but the occasional seats were still tolerable for one adult over reasonable distances.

The heaviest of the XK 140s at 29cwt, the drop-head's acceleration was probably very slightly down on that of the XK 140 Fixed-head, although the top speed was at least as good especially as it was an inch lower in height - certainly my own completely standard, Special Equipment XK 140 Drop-head Coupe (JTK 826), with C-type head and overdrive would quite happily wind itself up to an uncorrected speed of 138mph under favourable conditions with the hood up. This was accomplished with a singular lack of drama too - in fact it was almost disappointing! Neither did the hood flap or billow at that speed although wind noise was quite high (but I have driven many cars which at 70mph were much worse in that respect). Running with the hood down reduced its maximum speed quite considerably, and if the hood envelope was not secured tightly over the folded top, at high speeds the material could be pulled out of its folds and attempt to act like a drogue-parachute, or a rudimentary air-brake. Unfortunately it would then also effectively block one's rear view which could make the following stop to re-furl it a slightly hazardous manoeuvre at times.

Not that this spoilt what was an otherwise quite ideal touring car, combining the civilised comforts of the hard-top cars with the open-air freshness of the roadster at will - although loosing out somewhat to the latter car on nimbleness, due to the extra couple of hundredweights it has to carry. This carried a penalty so far as the brakes were concerned too, and they were more susceptible to fade than in the roadster - though not by much as all the XK 140s suffered almost as badly as the XK 120 on this score. My experiences with the car certainly match John Bentley's with the *Sports Illustrated* XK 140 Roadster, rather than those of the British journals - which perhaps kept half an eye on their advertising revenue while writing their tests in the early days. Fast driving did effect the drum brakes' efficiency, and very fast driving could induce almost complete fade. David Wright, whose experiences extended over some 110,000 miles with his Special Equipment, C-type head wire-wheeled XK 140 Fixed-head, wrote graphically of this in *Motor* only a few years ago:

> The problems were so bad that I used to wake up at nights in a cold sweat. There was fade, when you pushed till you thought the seat must break loose and the Jaguar just kept going. But you could avoid that by intelligent driving or, in an emergency, getting the wheels locked before the brakes could fade. Far worse was delayed fade. I have read all sorts of descriptions of delayed fade, usually concerning improbable Alpine situations. In fact it was a daily problem. If you are doing 110mph and see a lorry on the horizon, it is only prudent to ease back to 70 or so. Fine, the brakes handle that without a trace of fade. You trickle up behind the lorry until you finally have to knock off the last few mph, but the brakes have vanished. They have faded after the first application.
>
> Other problems were severe judder, and pulling to one side. Then the brake which pulled would fade first, leaving the other one to pull you the other way. After weaving around like a madman, you hoped you were lined up for the corner.

The 'delayed fade' sympton was of course caused by heat stored up by the heavy cast-iron brake drums, and while the wire wheels did make a much better job of cooling them than was the case with the original disc wheels, it still was not enough to disperse the energy created by dragging down the 210bhp, 31cwt (laden) coupe from three-figure speeds.

The juddering and pulling on the other hand demands a slightly more complex explanation,

involving as it does the principle of the two leading shoe braking system used on the front wheels of all XKs up to the XK 150. This had a self-servo effect (the brake shoes being pulled onto the drum by the turning motion of the wheel when they were applied) which worked well and reduced pedal pressures at moderate speeds. However, when the brakes were used hard and repeatedly at high speeds, and heat built up in the drum and the brake shoes themselves, resin would be released from the friction material which sharply reduced the co-efficient of friction. This also meant that the self-servo effect was lessened, creating what was very much a vicious circle - the harder you pushed the brake pedal, the hotter would become the shoes, and the hotter they became the less they would be pulled onto the drum to stop the car! Furthermore, it didn't always occur equally from shoe to shoe in the same drum (which caused juddering) or from wheel to wheel (which caused pulling), the changes being rung a number of times during any one particularly hard application, resulting in the effect which David Wright described.

To be fair, only a small proportion of XK owners drove fast enough or hard enough to come up against these problems during their ownership of the car, though the few that did often tried to remedy the situation. The XK 140 had gauze-covered cooling vents in its backplates, and a favourite modification was to install scoops to direct the air into the holes - rather in the manner of the original micram-adjuster XK 120s - with the scoop held on by the nut which secured the track-rod ball joint. The unfortunate tendency of these scoops to be as efficient at directing water into the brakes as cool air was solved by David Wright at least by drilling six small holes in each drum at their outer circumference, through which the water centrifuged out over about 30mph. The Aston Martin DB2 had similar holes drilled in its cast-iron brake drums, but this was to allow the heated resin from the friction material to escape rather than water.

The greatest improvements to Jaguar's drum brakes came not so much from any changes in the actual system itself, but from a gradual rise in effectiveness of the brake linings. Ferodo finally arrived at the VG95 material which probably offered about the best resistance to fade on the road. One indication of Jaguar's problems with the drum brakes is given by the XK 120 parts book where it can be seen that a wide variety of brake shoes were tried. Heat-cracking and distortion of the brake drums themselves were another malady which beset the fast-driving XK owner.

The XK 140's rear springs could be a cause of trouble too, and this applied to the XK 120 and XK 150 as well. Already quite highly stressed on the XK 120, the extra hundredweight or two of the XK 140 only made matters worse especially if vigorous motoring was indulged in on poorly surfaced roads with the car heavily laden. That occasionally a leaf broke in these circumstances is not altogether surprising, particularly in view of the fact that they ran at a load of something like 75 tons/sq in, which is very high indeed for a fatigue-type loading. So-called 'Alpine' springs could be ordered from the factory, these having an extra leaf, but the works did not alway advise their fitment on a road car as the handling could be upset thereby, the increased roll stiffness at the rear promoting oversteer. There were ways round this, by either fitting an anti-roll bar of twice the thickness of the original to the front suspension, or mounting an additional standard anti-roll bar over the top of the first. The resultant handling was then great fun for the enthusiast - David Wright again: "Man, it was fabulous. No roll, no wallow, but tons of understeer - until you opened the throttle. You primed the steering wheel, and steered with the accelerator. What I would call total control."

Surprisingly, ride quality didn't suffer too much from this modification (although on the lighter roadster the Alpine rear springs did cause a deterioration in ride) and the stronger rear springs also helped to tame the axle tramp which was all too evident if a fierce take-off from rest was made - the banging of the prop-shaft against its tunnel was quite a familiar sound to XK 140 owners indulging in such antics! The fitting of Koni dampers in place of the originals was another period 'mod', these helping to prevent wallow while also lasting two or three times as long as the original Girlings.

The factory did not consider it necessary to introduce any modification to the XK 140's suspension however, obviously regarding it as satisfactory for the designed use of the car. In fact there were few production changes to the car during its life, which is chiefly why it and all other Jaguars remain such good value for money. On the mechanical side, the timing chain spring tensioner was replaced in the engine by a Reynolds hydraulic type, and at the same time (fairly early on in production) a Hoburn Eaton eccentric rotor type oil pump replaced the gear-driven pump. With the later type of pump, the pressure relief valve was brought back to the filter housing head whereas previous XK 140s had the valve bolted into the oil pump itself.

The only really major change (or rather addition) which was therefore made to the XK 140's specification was the introduction in October 1956 of automatic transmission as an alternative to the manual gear box on the fixed-head and drop-head coupes. It was basically the Borg Warner mechanism which had been used in the Mk VII, with its three-element torque converter and a hydraulically controlled three speed and reverse epicyclic gear train. Only a very few XK 140s were sold with this gearbox, and anyway obsolescence for the XK 140 was only a few months away - the XK 150, with its disc brakes and completely revised bodywork, was announced in May 1957.

THE XK 140 IN COMPETITION

Although it was the very real competition successes of the XK 120 that helped make its name, the rest of the XK line rather basked in reflected glory from the XK 120 so far as speed events were concerned, and contributed little of significance in racing or rallying. But then, even more so than the XK 120, the XK 140's designed function was to provide high speed, effortless motoring for two persons in comfortable surroundings - not to win races or international rallies. Acknowledging its limitations for speed work though the XK 140 still has a record which it needn't be ashamed of.

To ignore a chronological narration of the XK 140's exploits, the car's most important venture - and its greatest misfortune - was probably the 1956 Le Mans race. While John Heath's entry of an XK 140 in the previous year's race hadn't materialised, Peter Bolton and Bob Walshaw didn't fail to arrive in their fixed-head coupe in 1956, and the story of their run makes interesting reading.

The XK 140's role in that year's 24-hour race was played out against a dramatic background, and how the lone Ecurie Ecosse D-type won after the decimation of the Jaguar works team is related in Chapter Seven. The Bolton/Walshaw car was a very standard Special Equipment fixed-head coupe with already quite a high road mileage behind it. Mechanical changes didn't go much further than a couple of larger (2inch) SU carburettors for its C-type head, and apart from two air intakes cut into the front wings either side of the grille, bodywork alterations were also minimal. The bumpers were of course removed, a racing flip-up petrol filler cap was used, and bonnet straps were fitted. The boot was almost completely filled by a 36-gallon fuel tank but the cockpit of the car retained most of its trim - walnut dashboard and all! The XK had the standard drum brakes although much-needed extra air was allowed to circulate by a hasty enlargement of the front wing air vents in between practice and race. It looked incredibly 'touring' amongst all the sports racers.

When the flag fell at four o'clock, the XK 140 made an excellent start and followed Stirling Moss's Aston Martin DB3S, Ron Flockhart's Scottish D-type, and one of the factory's D-types under the Dunlop Bridge. Of course this high placing was only held momentarily, faster cars streaming past down the hill into the treacherously slippery Esses. But even so, as evening approached the fixed-head was motoring superbly well and after two hours had overtaken and left well behind an equally standard Mercedes Benz 300SL (which in any case retired within 7 hours of the start).

After a wet night and a total of twelve hours racing, *The Motor* reported that "to our surprise the Jaguar XK 140 Coupe was not only still in the race, but running 14th in the General Category." After a further five hours the same magazine commented that "the surviving stock car, the hardtop Jaguar, was going really well in 12th place, and the drivers could really claim a Prix de Confort if one were offered."

Not long before 12am on Sunday morning, Bob Walshaw took over from Bolton in a routine driver change - little realising that the car's run was soon to be at an end. *The Motor* takes up the story again:

It was at mid-day that overwhelming misfortune befell the very standard Jaguar XK 140 Fixed-head Coupe, for the driver was brought in and informed by the officials that 4 hours previously the car had been refuelled too soon. This tardy decision was hotly disputed, and the car was allowed to continue while officials discussed the matter, but at 1.10pm it was again called into its pit and thereafter was driven slowly away into the paddock. This very standard looking car whose initial appearance had caused a certain amount of derision, had during the 21 hours during which it was raced covered 212 laps, or a distance of 1,749 miles at an average speed of 83 mph. It was driven by a crew with comparatively little experience of serious racing, and had received only a week's preparation at the Jaguar works.

Autosport commiserated too:

This was the worst of luck. Here was a hack car with 25,000 miles on the clock, keeping its end up with the very latest sports racing cars, brought to a standstill by a slight miscalculation - but that is motor racing.

So after a valiant effort, the car had been eliminated by a premature refuelling stop, after a 33 lap period instead of the regulation 34. But a hint of why this mistake occured is also given in *Autosport*:

It was very hard lines that the privately owned Jaguar XK 140 was excluded for infraction of fuel regulations. Nevertheless, how can one expect to come to Le Mans without any plans for pit organisation whatsoever, or even the provision of a timekeeper-cum-lap scorer. Things would have been completely chaotic had David Murray not given assistance.

Thus ended the XK 140's only real chance to cover itself in international glory; and while the venture came to nought, it was hardly the car's fault - for a near standard, luxuriously equipped road-going coupe, with no factory support, to have held 12th place in the world's most famous and gruelling race, and to have averaged well over 80mph for 21 hours, says a very great deal for Jaguar's road sports cars of the period. Certainly, as the last XK to have run in the 24 hour race, PWT 846 did not disgrace its type. Happily the 'Le Mans' XK 140 survives today, as part of the Robert Danny collection.

Reverting back to the beginning of 1955, it would appear that had the XK 140 been works supported it might still have been capable of winning performances in International rallying, even if racing was 'out'. Eric Haddon, who with Charles Vivian his Austrian-born navigator, had successively campaigned two XK 120 Roadsters in a number of major rallies up to that time, relates how he was lined up for a works-supported drive in the spring of 1955. But Jaguar's rallying plans for that year was interrupted by the disastrous Le Mans crash, and by the more personal tragedy of John Lyons' death on the way to that race. Because of this, Ian Appleyard withdrew from the works supported team of XK 140 Roadsters (as a mark of family respect - he had married Patricia Lyons, William Lyons' elder daughter), and Haddon was invited to take his place. He and the other selected drivers had got as far as being measured for the tailor-made bucket seats, and

the cars themselves had been fitted out, when it became clear that because of the Le Mans crash, motor sport was being curtailed all over Europe. In consequence Jaguar's plans to support these three XK 140 Roadsters in International rallying were shelved for good. Eric Haddon thereafter drove his own privately-owned XK 140 Roadster, but Ian Appleyard never returned to anything like the same scale of activity which he had enjoyed with NUB 120 and RUB 120 - he did run an XK 140 Special Equipment Fixed-head (VUB 140) but this was mainly a normal road car and was only entered in the occasional local rally.

Had a 'semi-works' team actually run in 1955, they would have found that the opposition had become considerably more competitive, with increasingly organised Triumph and Austin Healey works teams to overcome - and an increase in both weight and in under-steering tendencies were not characteristics which would have furthered the XK 140's efforts in the world of rallying. However, a number of private entrants tried their luck and so the XK 140 by no means disappeared from the entry lists of the big International events, and was quite often to be seen competing in big and small rallies in this country.

In 1955, the Scottish Rally (that old hunting ground of the SS 100 before the war) favoured the efforts of W L Sleigh who brought his XK 140 into first place in the big GT cars class - even though a TR2 was quicker up Rest & Be Thankful! Stoss and Pointing entered their drop-head coupe in the Leige-Rome-Leige rally that same year and while they finished behind a TR2 in their class, to make the second best British performance in the event - particularly difficult that year - was not bad going. Together with A90 and A50 Austins, the Jaguar helped win a team prize too. But the days were gone when an XK might be a front runner in such a rally - the winning Mercedes Benz 300SL of Gendebien and Stasse effectively saw to that!

Stoss, with his wife navigating, gained at least one other place during 1955, this time giving best to another Jaguar in the GT and Modified class of the MCC National Rally back home, but beating Patsy Burt's Aston Martin DB2/4 into third spot.

Ian Appleyard had retired from serious rallying after disposing of RUB 120, his second white XK 120 Roadster, but as mentioned was still occasionally to be seen with a white fixed-head Special Equipment XK 140 in home events. Understandably the car was not to emulate the widespread successes of his two famous roadsters, but in the 1956 RAC Rally the XK 140 was placed second overall in the General Classification - and gave Appleyard an "awful fright" while doing so. The XK was being driven down a very switchback road over the Yorkshire moors when there was suddenly a very violent explosion right behind the driving seat and the car filled with fumes. Needless to say a very rapid emergency stop was made followed by the double quick evacuation of the crew, who were relieved to discover that it was only a fire extinguisher that had sprung out of its mounting on the floor and fired itself off. Although retrospectively funny, as Appleyard says "in the dark, and unexpectedly, it was rather unpleasant!" VUB 140 was afterwards sold by Appleyard and is thought to no longer exist, though its registration number was last seen decorating another XK 140 Fixed-head.

Quite a few of the 'classics' were in fact assayed by XK 140s during 1956, including the 23rd Mille Miglia - this fantastic road race was, unbeknown to its entrants, to be the second to last in its great history. Castellotti won in a 3.5 Ferrari, but the XK 140 Roadster of Guyot, helped by the usual Jaguar value-for money factor and an adept choice of class by the entrants, won the Open Cars Under £1,100 class in the over 2-litre section, just in front of Tommy Wisdom's Austin Healey. Guyot led the class from the start and finished at an average of 70.12 mph.

The 1956 Tulip Rally saw sweeping British successes, but the Jaguar cause wasn't advanced very much and in fact the quite elderly

Grounds/Johnson XK 120 did rather better than any of the XK 140s entered. It was noticed during the 6th Eliminating Test at the Col Bayard that the XK 140s seemed "wrongly geared" for the ascent, and *The Motor* commented that "several of them clonked quite loudly during the initial acceleration from the sharper corners." Obviously the old rear axle was tramping merrily away. None of the XK 140s ended well placed, though Stoss in his well-campaigned drop-head was noted for his "very neat and quite quick" progress. Others didn't finish at all - on the climb up to Chamrouss, A J Burton misjudged one of the deceptive bends and entered it rather too fast, with the result that his XK 140 slid off the road and met the legendary immovable object in the form of a large boulder, which bent even the XK's tough front suspension.

The 14th Scottish Rally held in May 1956 was once more the scene of (minor) XK triumph, Hally, Parkes and F D Kerr dominating the Modified and GT cars (over 2,600cc) class with 1st, 2nd and 3rd places. Parkes was the fastest XK 140 up Rest & Be Thankful, his time of 83.4 seconds being 3.6 quicker than Haddow's XK 120, and .8 second faster than Sleigh's XK 140 time of the previous year. To round off another successful Scottish, Miss C V Woodburne won the Ladies' Touring Award with her XK 140 Fixed-head.

No less than seven 2.9 Ferraris were listed in the entries for the 1956 Tour de France, and Moss was there in a Mercedes 300SL, but there was a noted scarcity of British cars; the veteran Jacques Herzet, and Michael Parsy, supported the Jaguar cause by fielding XK 140s but neither were reported in the results as achieving resounding success.

In November 1956 the F I A published its new Appendix J regulations, and the XK 140 in both closed and open forms was firmly categorised as a 'Grand Touring Car' rather than under the 'Sports Car' heading - a term which by now in the competition world had almost universally been taken to mean two-seater machines built expressly for competition, but with body-work and accessories conforming to sports car regulations (indeed Jaguar could be said to have initiated this specialised type of car after the war, with the C-type in 1951). This ruling might have helped the XK 140 if its career in international rallies has been works-backed, but as it was the type's competitive days in big-time rallying was virtually over by the close of 1956 - although as late as 1958 one was entered for the Acropolis Rally.

One bright spot, for Jaguar's publicity men in America at least, were the results of the 1956 great American Mountain Rally, the United State's only International rally, which began and ended in New York. An XK 140 gained a first in class award, and won its class in the hill climb competition incorporated in the event; while one of the new 2.4 saloons also managed a class win even if Saab and Renault took the first two places overall.

But as the decade approached its end, XK 140s were mainly to be seen in 'club' rallies only in this country and few major events were to show spectacular results. Amongst regular XK 140 competitors in the later fifties was included G H 'Bobby' Parkes in KFR 712, who was a consistently good driver in national and club rallies.

On the race track, the XK 140 could be said to have been considerably less competitive than it was in rallying. Weight again, a lack of suitable classes, and the usual braking problems all conspired against any outstanding successes by this very 'road' sports car. A few devotees did persevere with the XK 140 though, and the cars were to be seen in club races from time to time. Occasionally they entered the limelight - Ivor Bueb drove one in a supporting race for a mixture of saloon and GT cars at the Gold Cup Oulton Park meeting in September 1956, finishing second to Rob Walker's 300SL which romped away to win driven by one C A S Brooks; but at least the Cooper works driver managed to keep the Jaguar ahead of Aston Martin opposition in the form of Patsy Burt's

DB2/4!

David Hobbs' drives in his XK 140 Drop-head Coupe are well remembered, the car with its Hobbs Mechamatic gearbox and disc brakes being one of the few XK 140s to be seriously raced in the sixties - Hobbs had an extremely successful 1960 season in GT racing. Jonathan Sieff of Marks & Spencer connections was another who raced an XK 140, as well as faster Jaguar machinery.

In the United States, the XK 140 - particularly in roadster form - was quite a familiar sight in SCCA racing, and on occasions did very well too. Surprisingly, it became the last Jaguar to win an SCCA National Championship, the car being driven by Ron McConkey of Cedar Falls, Iowa, who was also the Central Division's National Champion. This was in 1965, and as late as 1966 Paul Hammer of Richmond, California finished in second place at Riverside, in the first American Road Race of Champions to be held at that circuit.

THE XK 140 TODAY

Viewed as a hobby or collector's car the XK 140 has somehow lacked the glamour of the XK 120 and XK 150, inspite of combining some of the best features of both to render it a very pleasant road car indeed. In the mid - to late-sixties an XK 140 Fixed-head Coupe was undoubtedly about the cheapest XK one could buy, few fetching more than two or three hundred pounds and quite sound examples obtainable for a hundred pounds or even less. It was also rather trampled on in the rush for XK 120 Roadsters when the 'fly boys' realised that being an increasingly saleable prospect as an appreciating 'classic', the earlier car was worth searching out.

While it is still true to say that an XK 140 in a given condition is probably worth a little less than an XK 120 or XK 150 in similar order, the gap has undoubtedly narrowed over the past few years and a pristine XK 140 is now a valuable car. The roadster XK 140 though has always enjoyed a special status in this country - or at least it has since the 'dark ages' of the early sixties - as the very rarest of XKs in right-hand drive form, and so it follows naturally that the roadster is the most sought after of the XK 140s today.

While the XK 140's bodywork suffered the usual depredations of the English weather and salted winter roads, quite a large number survive today, and, traditionally being the cheapest XK to buy second hand have provided many people with their first taste of XK motoring - the XK Register for example was founded almost entirely by XK 140 owners, although there are more of the other two types on its books today.

Like the XK 120 before it, the XK 140 can quite easily be modified to give an even more up to date performance in a straight line, and much of what has been said on this topic in Chapter Three applies to the XK 140 as well - with the added advantage of its engine compartment being able to accommodate three carburettors by courtesy of the car's cranked steering column. Similarly, disc brakes can be fitted, and in fact this was a modification occasionally carried out on nearly-new XK 140s when the XK 150 with its disc brakes appeared in 1957 - by Dunlops or private owners, not the factory, who never officially gave their blessing to such interferences with the car's specification. One car so updated in the fifties was the XK 140 Fixed-head Coupe belonging to the mother of Richard Starley (Sales Manager of Champions) - this Special Equipment car was also specially trimmed in white hide by Connellys. RKV 465 is now in the hands of architect Francesco Scianna, who is one of a small but highly enthusiastic group of XK owners in Italy, and who delights in the XK's ability to equal the performance of contemporary products from Modena - or at least the Ferrari 212 - "on the Futa, the classic and horribly dangerous Mille Miglia road" while on the way home from winning cups in concours d'elegance events!

The enthusiasm shown today by owners such as Scianna, and many others in countries far away from the factory and from sources of easily obtainable new and second hand spares, illustrates very well the particular affection and respect in which the XK 140 is held by its devotees. The XK Jaguar sports car is not to everyone's liking, but acquire a taste for its smooth, long-legged stride, its unique looks, and its dependable good performance, and it can be hard to live without one.

Chapter Seven The D-type

This is the best performing automobile we have ever tested, and we've tested some very potent machinery. An acceleration time from a standstill to 60 mph in under 5 seconds, or to 100 mph in just over 12 seconds is startling enough, but this is combined with a genuine timed top speed of 162 mph!

Road & Track
May 1956

Like the C-type before it, the D-type Jaguar was built to win Le Mans. This it did three times, largely dominating the race for a span of four years, and casting its shadow over the event for maybe a couple of years after that - for although the D-type was first seen on the Sarthe circuit in 1954, a D-type victory was still possible as late as 1958 or even 1959.

It is therefore doubly ironic that Jaguar's own official team in this most famous of long distance races was dogged with consistent misfortune, and without the timely assistance of privately-entered Jaguars, the D-type's record at Le Mans would be far less impressive than it is. In 1954 the factory (and only) D-types were afflicted with fuel-feed problems and lost to Ferrari, and in 1956 two of the works cars crashed and the third was entirely put out of contention by a fault in its fuel injection system. Only in 1955 did a factory D-type win at Le Mans, and that victory was clouded by the disastrous Mercedes Benz accident in which about 85 people were killed. Ecurie Ecosse saved the day in 1956, and when Jaguar retired from racing, won again in 1957, a year in which the D-type utterly smashed the opposition to finish in the first four places.

The D-type's fortunes were even more mixed at other circuits, though it can be said that for a

car designed purely to win Le Mans and for no other purpose whatsoever, the D-type Jaguar's record is extraordinary. Today it has an aura about it which few other cars possess, and it is remembered with respect - almost reverence - by those who drove it or saw it defeat all comers at Le Mans. Ecurie Ecosse ran their last D-type right up until 1960, long after it was fully competitive and for almost no other reason than nostalgia! Such was the character and magic of this greatest of British post-war sports racing cars.

The D-type had its origins in the experimental car which was first demonstrated to the world when the C-type was still representing Jaguar on the track. This car achieved a speed of 178.3 mph, but the biggest share of the publicity stemming from these October 1953 runs at Jabbeke quite rightly fell to the XK 120 Roadster which managed a surprising 172.4 mph on the same occasion. The prototype was a half-way stage between C- and D-types, the first example of Jaguar's new Le Mans contender being completed about March 1954.

Tony Rolt, winner of the Le Mans race with Duncan Hamilton in 1953 driving the C-type, was one of several drivers invited to try out the unpainted and unnamed new sports racing car at RAF Gaydon after it had secretly emerged from the experimental shop at Browns Lane. At the aerodrome, the car was put through an assortment of elementary braking and handling tests around barrels layed out on the super-long runways. There followed more serious testing at the Motor Industry Research Association's testing ground near Nuneaton, and at Silverstone, before a practice session was arranged on the actual Le Mans circuit, not very many weeks before the race itself.

This test session was not without drama - the D-type's clutch had to be changed after the journey out from England on the road, Peter Walker was late because he'd forgotten his passport, and by the time the car was actually on the circuit (closed for a rally), the period which had been allotted to Jaguar for practice had nearly expired. Disobeying the French officials' instructions Rolt took it upon himself to do three laps, not one, but the wrath so incurred was worthwhile enduring as the flying lap had been covered in 4 minutes 22.3 seconds, which was 5 seconds faster than Ascari's lap record! Rolt's impressions after that brief try-out was of a car greatly advanced over the C-type, with all trace of the latter's lightness at speed gone, and with much improved handling, braking and top speed - which was now nearer 180 mph than 150 mph.

There were many reasons for the new car's superiority over its predecessor, the C-type Jaguar, which had been the company's first attempt at building a sports racing car. The D-type was built on fundamentally different lines and had very little in common with the C-type, save that it too incorporated a surprising number of production parts in its make-up.

While the earlier car's construction did include a very small area of stressed panelling, it was basically built around a space frame. The D-type's main centre section was on the other hand almost entirely monocoque except for the intrusion of the frame members from the front tubular part of the car which carried the engine and front suspension. The central 'tub' of rivetted aluminium panelling was strengthened by internal sills which ran from front to rear, and by bulkheads fore and aft - the rear bulkhead being completly double-skinned, with its inner wall following the contours of the driver's and passenger's seat backs; a transverse box--section member gave the front bulkhead its strength. The car's tail section was unstressed and just bolted on to the rear bulkhead.

Front suspension of the D-type was similar in principle to the road XK sports cars, having wide based wishbones top and bottom and being sprung by two longitudinal torsion bars, which were attached to the front of the lower wishbones but via an extension past the fulcrum point on the D-type. The car's ride height was altered by the use of a vernier scale adjuster at the torsion bars' rearward mounting points. Steering too was similar to the production cars, the rack and pinion design being essentially that used on the XK 140 when it was announced three or four months after the 1954 Le Mans, it first having been seen on the C-type of 1951.

Rear suspension owed a little to the C-type as well, springing being by a bottom transverse torsion bar anchored at its centre onto the rear bulkhead, and connected to the axle by a ¼ inch thick steel-plate arm extending from each end to a bracket under the Salisbury axle. These two axle brackets extended an equidistance above the axle casing to meet two similar, but unsprung arms with which they formed a true parallelogram. Rubber bushes were used on both inner and outer links, but the bottom arms were located in metal bearings fitted with grease nipples. Two telescopic shock absorbers (which also incorporated bump and rebound stops) provided the system's damping, one acting on each lower arm, and were angled sharply forwards and inwards to their mounting points on two upright box section members affixed to the bulkhead - which also took the suspension arms themselves. The axle was located transversely by an 'A' bracket pivoting near the bottom of these box section members, its nose attached to the axle tubes via a bearing and bracket. This arrangement also served to determine the height of the rear roll centre.

The D-type's brakes were the Dunlop system as developed on the C-type, largely purged of the various bugs which had afflicted them in the early days, thanks to Jaguar's racing and testing programme over the previous few years. It was still quite complex though, with three pairs of wheel cylinders and pads being used on each front disc, "in order to obtain what we thought was the necessary volume of lining to last 24 hours at racing speed" said Heynes. But it was eventually discovered that the third pad was wearing at least twice the rate of the first, because of the higher temperature it was running at, and later on a large single rectangular pad was used which had the advantage of being able to be replaced in almost seconds - or in not much longer than it took for the car to undergo a wheel change during a pit stop. Two pairs of wheel cylinders acted on the rear discs, plus independent calipers controlled by the single-cable handbrake. The discs themselves were 12¾ inches in diameter, and of chromium-plated (to reduce wear) mild steel. Airscoops were fitted to the front brake assembly for surer cooling.

A similar hydraulic servo system to that used on the C-type assisted driver braking effort, using pressure supplied by a Plessy pump driven from the propeller shaft at the back of the gearbox. A non-return valve prevented the entry of air into the system when the car was reversed, by short-circuiting the pump action.

Wear of the friction material and heat soak were only two of the problems encountered during the development of the brake, and another but less well known snag which had to be overcome was weight transfer, which had a great effect on the front to rear braking ratio needed. For instance, the static D-type had 1000 lbs of its weight on its front wheels, and 930 lbs on its rear. Under maximum acceleration with a full tank this became 720 lbs front and 1467 lbs rear, and under maximum braking with an empty tank it was changed to 1270 lbs front and 660 lbs rear! Braking ratios were altered by the size of the individual wheel slave cylinders.

Gone were the C-type's very traditional wire wheels. The D-type used Dunlop wheels made of a light alloy with a steel centre section, of either 16 inch or 17inch rim diameter and with a rim width in both cases of 5½ inches. Although secured by familiar-looking three eared knock-on hub caps, these wheels were not mounted on splined hubs as before but were located by five domed pegs, which fitted into corresponding holes drilled in the back flange of the hub. Lighter than the wire wheels they replaced, these alloy wheels were also stronger and more durable, lessening the risk of wheel collapse.

While the D type's engine was still remarkably close to the production unit, there had been some marked advances. Dry-sump lubrication was introduced which had the effect of reducing the depth of the sump, which meant that the car's bonnet line and its centre of gravity could both be lowered; the engine was in fact some 2¾ inches lower in the chassis than was the case with the C-type. The designation 'dry sump' is of course something of a misnomer - oil still fell back into the sump after lubricating the bearings, but instead of the sump being used as a reservoir, the oil was immediately sucked up by a scavenge pump and delivered to a separate oil tank, where it 'de-frothed' and was pumped to the engine oilways by a pressure pump. Both pumps were driven via transverse shafts from a worm drive at the front of the crankshaft, and an oil cooler was inserted into the pressure circuit between pressure pump and block. Oil capacity was 28 pints, and another subsidiary advantage of the dry sump method was the elimination of oil surge during changes of acceleration, or on corners.

The D-type's cylinder head was based on the C-type casting which was now a common option on the XK 140 and Mk VII saloon in the road car range. To this was fitted larger inlet valves, of 1 7/8 inch diameter, although the exhaust valves were left the same size at 1 5/8 inch, as were the valve angles. A different camshaft was fitted having the same 3/8 inch lift as that on the production cars but giving a pronounced overlap, although the new camshaft sacrificed little at the lower end of the rev. range and virtually nothing on flexibility. The camshaft covers incorporated quite a complex system of breathers to make quite sure that any pressures built up could escape very easily.

The car's DCO3 45 mm Weber carburetters took their air from an intake duct which ran from the radiator grille to an open ended box around the carburetters' ram-tubes.

The exhaust manifolds were cast, each of the two sections taking the exhaust gases individually from every exhaust port in the usual Jaguar pattern, although the 'branch' effect was more marked than on the C-type engine. The two down-pipes ran through a side-mounted expansion box and ended in front of the inside front wheel. With a 9:1 compression ratio, approximately 245 bhp at 5750 rpm was produced from this engine.

The car's hydraulically operated 7½ inch Borg & Beck triple plate clutch and the starter motor ring acted as a flywheel, helped by a substantial crankshaft damper mounted externally at the front of the engine. The gearbox was a completely new Jaguar-designed unit with the perhaps surprising addition of synchromesh on first gear, bottom being intended as a useful ratio for employing on very slow corners. On the Le Mans axle a 2.79:1 ratio was used with the intermediate gearing of 5.98 first, 4.58 second, and 3.57 third - top gear was direct as always. Reverse was 6.1:1. On top of the gearbox was mounted the starter motor, in front of the gear lever.

Cooling was by a Marston Excelsior light alloy radiator, the same firm making the upright oil cooler mounted along side; as on the ill-fated 1952 C-types, a separate alloy header tank was used to lower the overall height of the system. Moulded radiator hose was used, and the coolant capacity was 29 pints.

Jaguar continued to use the flexible bag tanks that they had introduced on the C-type; two were mounted in the car's tail, inside aluminium containers and supported by the usual multiple attachment points. The capacity was given as 36½ gallons, and the filler cap was under a hinged section of the head-fairing. Twin electric petrol pumps mounted on the rear bulkhead supplied the carburetters, through a common delivery pipe.

The D-type's body design was the work of Malcolm Sayer, Jaguar's aerodynamicist, and was extremely effective. Its functional shape was distinctive and beautiful in an assertive manner, and the D-type has always looked as fast as it is. As with all Jaguar's sports racing cars, great attention was paid to streamlining, the bodies being very carefully developed using 1/10th scale models in a wind tunnel - a reduction in drag was not the overriding consideration either, as the effects of side winds and the alteration of the car's attitude through wind pressure were investigated too. "It is surprising how close the results obtained in the wind tunnel are reproduced when tests are carried out on the road," said Heynes in 1960; "in fact we now find it possible to predict, within 3-4%, the speed a sports car will achieve before it is built."

Needless to say, the D-type was extremely advanced aerodynamically when it appeared, and while it was rarely the most powerful car starting a Le Mans race, it was usually the quickest along the Mulsanne Straight. Like the monocoque centre section which itself formed the middle of the body, the detachable bonnet was made up of welded and rivetted alloy sections, and hinged forward. The similarly built detachable rear section which housed the fuel tanks featured a head-fairing only on the original prototype, a stabilising fin being rivetted onto the team cars a comparatively short while before the 1954 Le Mans race. A semi wrap round windshield protected the driver, who was probably a little more comfortable than he had been in the C-type, installed behind the adjustable steering column and confronted with only three instruments - or about as many as a racing driver can be relied upon to read accurately during a race. These were a revolution counter with a 'tell-tale' needle, an oil pressure gauge, and a water temperature gauge. The steering wheel itself had light alloy spokes (Hawthorn liked four) and a laminated wood rim.

A compact car, the D-type's wheelbase was 7 feet 6 inches, track 4 feet 2 inches front and 4 feet rear, and its overall length 12 feet 10 inches. Dry weight was a little over 18 cwt, or about 150 lbs lighter than the 1953 C-type, and frontal area was down from 13.8 sq.ft to 12.5 sq.ft.

This then was Jaguar's challenger for the 1954 Le Mans race, and as the three cars were pushed to their places abutting the pit counters in readiness for the famous start procedure, they were already noted as favourites for an overall win - the deep impression made by the victorious C-type of the previous year had not been forgotten.

The race began under an overcast sky, and as the cars settled down to serious lappery, it began to rain. This didn't deter the D-type drivers - Stirling Moss/Peter Walker (OKV 2), Duncan Hamilton/Tony Rolt, (OKV 1) and Peter Whitehead/Ken Wharton (OKV 3) - as it probably hindered their chief rivals, the 4.9 litre Ferraris. Fast though they might be, the other big-engined runners were hardly to be in contention for the lead - Aston Martin, Talbot, Cunningham, Gordini and the new V12 Lagonda. Gonzales lead with his 4.9 Ferrari early in the race, hotly pursued by Moss who overhauled the Argentinian as the track became wetter, on the 21st lap.

Then came a cruel blow - Rolt brought OKV 1 into the pits and complained of misfiring particularly along the Mulsanne Straight, and shortly afterwards the Jaguar mechanics had to listen to a similar report from the drivers of the other two D-types. Plugs were changed but that didn't effect a cure. After a number of stops fuel starvation was disgnosed, and traced to blocked filter elements which were found to be packed by a fine grey dust - too fine to have been stopped by the gauze filtering in the gravity refuelling tanks behind the pits.

The clogged filters were taken out of the system altogether - they were the paper element type usually used as oil filters, and had simply proved too efficient; to add a touch of irony to the situation, the D-type's actual lubrication system had no filters at all! After their removal, no more trouble was experienced - until Moss found he had inoperative brakes at the end of the Mulsanne Straight. A resort to the escape road and some frantic changing down avoided a catastrophe; but he and Walker were out of the race. Then Ken Wharton and Peter Whitehead lost most of their gears, and prolonged pulling at low revs in the D-type's very high top gear brought on cylinder head trouble which put them out too. The Jaguar offensive looked like collapsing. Only Hamilton and Rolt soldiered on through atrocious conditions, whittling down the lead built up by Gonzales and Trintignant in the big red Ferrari with bitter determination. At 10.15 am the D-type was delayed yet again, when a Talbot forced Rolt partially off the road and he had to pit for minor repairs.

Then well past mid-day, Trintignant drew in for a routine stop; Gonzales, who took over, tried to restart the Ferrari - but the engine wouldn't fire. Huge panic in the Italian pit, great excitement in the Jaguar camp. Perhaps someone else was having the bad luck now. The rain was coming down again and Rolt pulled in, only a lap behind now, indicating that he wanted to exchange his goggles for a visor, not realising the great drama that was being enacted in the Ferrari pit. Desperately he was waved on; he spotted the red car silent in the pits at the same instant and needed no second telling. The D-type hurtled off into the swirling rain, and still the Ferrari wouldn't start, even under the attentions of about twice the number of mechanics allowed by the regulations. It really began to seem that the Italian car had shot its bolt when suddenly the engine fired, picked up, and

Gonzales was away, wheels spinning. Ninety seven seconds later Rolt came by. Almost blinded by spray but lapping incredibly quickly, he finally came in again for a visor. To save precious time the suitably equipped Hamilton was despatched to take up the chase as soon as Rolt vacated the driving seat. Duncan cast all caution to the winds as he tried to gain on the bigger engined car:

"How I tried... The gearing of our D type was such that we could pull 5,600 rpm in top gear on the straight. This corresponded to something just over 170 mph. I saw suddenly that the rev counter was reading 5,900 and realised that I was getting wheelspin at 170 mph in top gear. I eased my foot immediately for wheelspin can take charge when you cannot control it."

But Gonzales was "impossibly good" in the only Ferrari left running, and when the rain stopped and the track began to dry, he once again began to pull away from the Jaguar. Hamilton relaxed slightly and concentrated on finishing - which he did, just 105 seconds after the winning Ferrari, and with an unintentional flourish, slicing at around 150 mph between the three Bristols which had lined up across the track to finish in formation! A long way back was the 5.4 litre Cunningham of Johnston and Spear in third place, in front of the Belgian-entered C-type of Laurent and Swaters.

But although the D-type had not won on its first race appearance, the 1954 expedition mounted by Coventry had been no disaster. Stirling Moss had set a new fastest speed down the Mulsanne Straight, the Omega recorders having clocked OKV 2 at 172.97 mph, and furthermore, if one adds up the amount of time spent in the pits by the Rolt/Hamilton Jaguar, it will be found that the D-type was stationary in the pits for at least five minutes longer than the Ferrari - including the latter's 7½ minutes when it wouldn't start. So but for the fuel filter blockage, or Rolt's enforced pit stop after the minor shunt, who knows? A defeat perhaps, but an honourable one.

Revenge was certainly taken at the Rheims 12 Hour race held the next month, where the D-type recorded its first win. The three Le Mans cars were paired with their drivers exactly as for the 24 hour race in June, and after a brief lead by a Cunningham, it was Moss who circulated in front after the floodlit midnight start. Tony Rolt suffered an attack from Jean Behra's 3-litre Gordini which had tried desperately to keep up, finally ramming the D-type's tail at the Thillios hairpin. This effectively put the French car out of action but apart from a dent and a broken rear light it seemed that the Jaguar was not very much damaged. Rolt and Hamilton therefore took the lead when Moss dropped out with a broken prop-shaft, ahead of Whitehead and Wharton, and it looked like an easy run home until 30 minutes from the end of the race the back axle ran dry - a hole had been chafed in the casing by a piece of frame bent in the Gordini incident. After a hasty repair with chewing gum, Hamilton took the car around for one more lap at 50 mph, listening to broken teeth grinding up the crownwheel and pinion, and then waited at the line for the 12 hours to come up, hobbling over to be classed as a finisher. Such had been OKV 1's lead that the only car to complete more laps was the Whitehead/Wharton D-type - and Whitehead had been the first to win a race with the C-type too.

These three cars, which with OVC 501 as reserve had made up the factory's Le Mans team, actually had 'XKC' chassis numbers, the D-type designation not having been applied until after the 24 hour race (XKC 402, 403 and 404 for OKV 1, 2 and 3 respectively - OVC 501 was the first D-type built, chassis number XKC 401). Although the new competition car was colloquially referred to as the 'D-type' during its secret building and development, the fact is that pre-race press releases on the car, even those made during its public testing on the Le Mans circuit, never referred to it as such. So maybe Harold Hastings of *The Motor* is quite right when he claims to have coined the name while writing his Le Mans report - frustrated at having to keep calling it the "new competition Jaguar" as everybody else was doing.

The 1954 Tourist Trophy meeting in Ireland was the only other event entered by Jaguar that year, and it began badly and didn't finish very much better for the factory. Someone dropped a crate on William Lyon's Mk VII, the team's stop watches were stolen, and the new 'soft' Dunlop Stabilia tyres which were being tried were inadvertently muddled up, which meant a pressure check on every single one to see which were for front and which were for rear fitment. Then the Ulster Automobile Club's handicap system didn't seem to favour the big-engined cars, so while Rolt and Hamilton in XKC 402 had the normal 3442 cc engine, Whitehead and Wharton in XKC 403 (which was the car Moss drove at Le Mans), and Moss and Walker in their new car XKD 406, had a smaller 2482 cc unit. This had a bore and stroke of 83 x 76.5, and produced 193 bhp gross at 6,000 rpm.

Aston Martin, Ferrari, Maserati and Lancia all sent works teams but it was the little 750DB Panhard of Loreau and Armagnac who won - limit men on handicap, they had 27 credit laps! Hawthorn who was driving a 3-litre Ferrari with Trintignant had 6. The Rolt/Hamilton Jaguar retired with a broken scavenge pump, Moss had terrible trouble with his engine and had to do the waiting on the line act again, which he did underneath a huge umbrella before hobbling across for 18th place, while the other 2½ litre car of Whitehead and Wharton was the sole surviving Jaguar and gained 5th place on handicap overall, and 2nd on handicap in its 2-3 litre class.

But Jaguar were already planning for the 1955 Le Mans, and a new batch of cars incorporating a number of improvements were soon to be built, replacing the six 1954 cars. Duncan Hamilton therefore negotiated with the factory for the purchase of OKV 1, the car in which he and Tony Rolt had driven to second place at both Le Mans and Rheims. This meant the sad departure of OVC 915, his C-type, to Dan Margulies, and Hamilton collected XKC 402 in February 1955, driving it back to Surrey in heavy snow, "without incident thanks to the tractability of the engine"!

Shortly afterwards, John Bolster drove OKV 1 away from Byfleet to add a D-type to his already impressive list of sports racing car tests. Bolster rated the car as an all-round improvement on the C-type, as it felt smaller, lighter, easier to drive, "and can be used for shopping without any thought of its potential performance". The steering was light and responsive, the "ultra close ratio gearbox could not be easier to handle", while the brakes were responsive and took anything handed out to them. Low speed ride was obviously a little bumpy, but it all smoothed out at higher rates of progress. Bolster didn't have time to assemble performance statistics, but he did say this:

What no figures show, however, is the indefinable feeling of quality that this machine imparts. I am in the lucky position to sample many successful competition cars. Although such vehicles always show high performance, it is frequently accompanied by roughness and intractability, plus some odd rattles and the drumming of body panels. The Jaguar, on the other hand, gives that same air of breeding which the XK coupe possesses. It is indeed, a new conception in sports racing cars... I feel this is one of the easiest of the real flyers to handle. Unlike some of the latest speed models, it does allow some margin for error, and there is nothing tricky about it.

Much of this had indeed already been discovered by other gentlemen of the press, when with what seems incredible optimism Lofty England brought a D-type to the Guild of Motoring Writers' Test Day at Goodwood, and let people loose in it - explaining that he thought those not used to very fast cars would not be inclined to drive it too fast, and that those who were capable of driving the D-type fast were capable of driving fast cars anyway, and wouldn't find the D-type difficult. It didn't sound terribly convincing at the time either, but at any rate the car survived the afternoon and left great memories behind for a number of people.

This car had been left with its Le Mans axle ratio and was showing around 100 mph in second gear, so most drivers that day found using top gear out of the question. It was not an intimidating car at all however, though it was certainly a "driver's car", *Motor Racing* likening it to "riding a very fast motorcycle, in that you feel completely part of it in all its high speed movements." Exhaust noise disappeared at 80 mph and the speed was altogether deceptive - hence the "rather disturbing sight of about 8 saloon motor cars, approaching Woodcote all with their brake lights flashing and apparently all in reverse..."

Having taken delivery of his D-type, the generous Duncan was not content with letting Bolster test the car, but moreover lent it to Michael Head to race in Finland, where he won the sports car race held in the 'Hyde Park' equivalent of Helsinki - the same race that he had won the previous year in MDU 212, his C-type. Encouragement arrived in the form of a telegramme from Duncan saying "Remember it's the small pedal you must press"! This win in the Djurgardsloppet was the first by a D-type in the hands of a private entrant.

Duncan's first win in his own car didn't come until July 1955, when he won two races at the Whitsun Goodwood meeting (Bob Berry was second in both instances with OKV 2) - he had driven in the sports car race held during the Silverstone International Trophy Meeting earlier but having rolled one of Amedee Gordini's little Formula One cars in practice when its back axle locked up, he was understandably a bit shaken and only managed 5th place with XKD 406; afterwards he was sent to bed for a fortnight with concussion!

The occasion of the International Trophy meeting was Hawthorn's first Jaguar drive on British soil, leading the sports car race in OKV 3 until the top radiator hose blew off; he'd already set the lap record but after that he had to be content with a gentle 4th place behind Rolt in OKV 2, and the works Aston Martins. The enthusiastic Northerner Jack Broadhead bought OKV 2 almost on the spot, for Jaguar employee Bob Berry to drive in a private capacity - Berry

had been sufficiently impressive in MWK 120, his lightweight XK 120, to be described as "one of the most formidable club drivers" by at least one motoring journal.

Ecurie Ecosse had also received their first D-types, in May 1955, actually the first two 'production' D-types, XKD 501 and 502. These had run at Silverstone too, Jimmy Stewart crashing 501 in practice but Ulsterman Desmond Titterington gaining a careful 6th place while running in. He was to win a week later though, carrying off the Ulster Trophy in the repaired XKD 501. However, both new Ecurie Ecosse D-types were to suffer accidents very shortly after, when both Titterington and Stewart left the road while practicing for the *Eifelrennen* at the Nurburgring; even more unfortunately, the two drivers were injured to an extent that lost them their promised 'works' places in Jaguar's 1955 Le Mans team.

Duncan Hamilton meanwhile made his usual entry in the sports car GP at Oporto, driving his own D-type OKV 1 into third position - quite relieved at having finished there without personal injury or mechanical failure after five years of trying. Bob Berry managed 5th place, after having to drive OKV 2 980 miles across France, Spain and Portugal when the transporter broke down. Loaded with spares, the D-type also averaged 50 mph and 30 mpg while doing so!

In the meantime, the 1955 'works' cars had been built. These looked noticeably different from the 1954 cars, and there were even more changes under the skin although the essential design remained exactly the same. Experience had merely resulted in cars which were more aerodynamic, lighter, and simpler to build and repair. The most radical alteration was made by giving the car's forward framework its independence from the central monocoque. While the 1954 frames had been largely welded on, the new structure was purely a 'bolt on' fixture, and additionally, it was made from nickel-steel not magnesium alloy tubing (the main members being of 18 swg, the lesser tubes 20 swg). The radiator, oil cooler and bonnet pivot were now carried by a separate tubular framework out-rigged from the front of the main frame, which could be detached by undoing four bolts. This made repair after a minor frontal accident cheaper and easier.

Aft of the front bulkhead, only the two lower frame members now penetrated the monocoque, the upper two being replaced by considerably smaller, circular section, tubes which sloped down to meet the bottom main members at the rear bulkhead, giving the driver somewhat more elbow room. All that was now necessary if the centre section and frame had to be parted was the unbolting of a series of nuts, and the dismantling of the battery and oil tank compartments by drilling out the rivets in that area; the entire front section of the car, which held the engine, front suspension and radiators, could then be withdrawn as a unit. By virtue of its greater simplicity, and from the use of lighter gauge tubing which the stronger metal made possible, the new steel frame was actually lighter than the alloy one it replaced, at 56 lbs. The new D-type's tail section, although looking much the same from the outside, was now of entirely stressed-skin construction like the centre monocoque, the internal framework being discarded and integral strength being given by aluminium buttressing. The new arrangement both 'added lightness' and gave more wheel clearance.

Initially, eight of the new D-types were constructed, over the first four or five months of 1955; these were specifically destined for the factory's own use, and for two major private entrants - Ecurie Ecosse who received their two cars in May as already mentioned, and Ecurie National Belge who were sent XKD 503. The remaining five cars (up to XKD 508) were retained as the works team, reserve, and experimental cars, and were outwardly distinguishable from both the 1954 cars and the 1955 private entrant D-types by their longer noses - the snouts had been extended by 7½

inches to give an improved air penetration, and they now incorporated two air ducts for additional brake cooling. Also, the long-nose cars had a much more comprehensive wrap-round windscreen which was intended to protect the driver from cross-wind buffeting which had been a nuisance the year before at Le Mans, especially down the Mulsanne Straight. It was faired into the headrest, which itself was all part of a new integral fin which now ended at the extreme rear of the body.

Malcolm Sayer was responsible for most of these exterior bodywork changes, which were about as many that could usefully be made, his original 1954 shape being difficult to improve on - even the technical personnel at RAE Farnborough who were glad to carry out various tests with Sayer could find little to improve on; all that they could suggest was that air-tight rivetting be used, the body joints filled with wax before a race, and the importance of a good paint finish on the nose of the car, all factors which have to be taken into account at the sort of speeds that the D-type was reaching.

Mechanically, the biggest change that came to the 1955 'works' D-types involved the cylinder heads. Heynes had a reasonable suspicion that Mercedes were planning to enter the 1955 Le Mans race, and also knew that the 4.9 litre Ferrari of 1954 had been considerably quicker on acceleration (though not top speed) than the Jaguar the previous year. More power was obviously needed, and if low speed torque was not to be sacrificed by 'wild' timing, then a further increase in valve sizes was the obvious alternative. Thus the inlet valve diameter went up from 1 7/8 inches to 2 inches, and the exhaust valve from 1 5/8 inches to 1 11/16 inches. To prevent the valves from touching it was then necessary to re-design the cylinder head to enable the inclination of the exhaust valve to be changed from 35 deg to 40 deg - hence the name '35/40' for this wide-angle D-type head. At the same time, camshaft lift was increased for the first time since 1951, from 1 3/8 inches to 1 7/16 inches lift, and the timing was widened too. The same 45 mm Weber carburetters were used but on a slightly modified manifold, while the car's exhaust pipes no longer ended in front of the rear wheel but were continued right the way along underneath the body to emerge at the rear, with the idea of increasing the extractor effect. All these changes brought about an increase in power of some 30 bhp, 270 bhp now being produced at between 5,500 rpm and 6,000 rpm.

Brakes, apart from a slight lessening of the servo action to give a more progressive feel, steering (35 feet turning circle), and suspension remained basically as for the 1954 cars although the three cars (plus spare) destined for Le Mans 1955 had ZF differentials. Wheelbase and track were not of course affected, but the overall length of the long-nose car was 13 feet 5½ inches.

Meanwhile, the short nosed version of the 1955 D-type was actually being put into limited but quite genuine production, its new features like the bolt-on front 'A' frame being now much easier to fabricate and assemble. Whereas previously a team of specialist Argon-arc welders had to be brought in to weld the magnesium alloy sub-frames of the original 1954 cars, the 1955 steel frames could easily be brazed up by Jaguar's own fitters.

Production of the cars was soon put on a more rationalized basis too - at first the experimental/racing department assembled the production D-types alongside the factory's own team cars, but there was very little room so most of the work was transferred to the road-car production and engineering department, where a true D-type assembly line was laid down in the main hall at Allesley, surrounded by Mk VII saloons and XK 140 sports cars.

The production D-type might have been made on something similar to a normal assembly line, but it was still very much a racing car and preparation was appropriately meticulous. Before the fully-assembled engine was installed in the frame, its main components were crack tested, dynamically and statically balanced, its

pistons carefully balanced and graded, and valve clearances checked and rechecked by clock gauge. Tab washers on nuts were avoided in favour of drilling and wiring. When finally put together, the engine would be bench-tested on one of the three or four 'brakes' in the experimental department, and individual power outputs noted.

The engine didn't meet the chassis until the completed central tub had been equipped with its sub-frame, suspension and wheels. Then with bonnet and rear end in place (these were made by Abbey Panels), the car passed to the experimental department where it underwent an exhaustive checking procedure before eventually arriving at MIRA for further comprehensive mobile testing.

Andrew J A Whyte ('John Appleton'), in his authoritative *Profile* of the D-type Jaguar, supplies us with a number of interesting facts from the factory archives relating to the testing and distribution of the production D-type. The first car to go through the full production system was XKD 509, which completed some 60 laps of the banked outer circuit at MIRA in July 1955. The first line built D-type to be sold to a private customer was XKD 514, which went to Sir Robert Ropner in County Durham in August 1955 - and which was, and is, used as a road car by its original owner. Sixty-seven D-types were constructed and tested in the years 1955 and 1956, over 20,000 test miles being covered in the process. Although every car was tested at least twice, factory records show that XKD 525 completed the most miles in this way, before finally being passed as OK and despatched to the States - it clocked up some 650 miles in eight test sessions.

It was in fact the United States which received the largest single share of these 67 D-types, 18 reaching its shores. Britain was next with 10, Australia had 3, France 2, and one each went to Cuba, Finland, New Zealand, Spain, San Salvador, East Africa, Mexico, Belgium and Canada. These totals account for the 42 cars sold and of the remainder, 9 chassis were destroyed in Jaguar's February 1957 fire or used as parts, and 16 were used as the basis of the XKSS. At a price of £3,878 the production D-type probably represented even greater value than Jaguar's road cars, and the new owner of each even received an informative 57-page service handbook.

The new long nose 'works' cars first saw action in the 1955 Le Mans race, one of the most dramatic and certainly the most tragic in the event's long history. The scene was set for a Homeric battle between Jaguar and Mercedes, who had returned to motor-racing and finally to Le Mans itself with their advanced 300SLR open sports racing cars, one of which had already won the Mille Miglia that year. Ferrari too looked like being well in contention, with a team of 4½ litre six cylinder cars, while the threat from Maserati and Aston Martin could never be discounted. Ranged against this awe-inspiring opposition were the factory's three dark green D-types, with driver pairings of Mike Hawthorn/Ivor Bueb, Tony Rolt/Duncan Hamilton, and Norman Dewis/Don Beauman; backed up by two privately entered short-nosed cars, Johnny Claes and Jacques Swaters in the Belgian car, and Phil Walters and Bill Spear driving Briggs Cunningham's first Jaguar entry at Le Mans.

It was Castellotti with his Ferrari who set the Grand Prix-like pace at the start of the race, leading Hawthorn in his works D-type and Fangio in the air-braked Mercedes for the first hour, all three cars being breathtakingly close for much of the time. In this company, Hawthorn was delighted to find he could pass the German and Italian cars with ease down the Mulsanne Straight, the D-type pulling some 5,800 rpm on its 2.69:1 axle (or around 180 mph), compared to the 7,200 rpm being held by Fangio in the 3-litre fuel-injected Mercedes in his vain attempt to keep up.

The British and German cars engaged in the struggle makes an interesting comparison.

The D-type relied strongly on well-proven and highly developed production parts in a com-paratively simple - though novel - 'chassis', with relatively unsophisticated suspension, while Mercedes Benz put their faith in the engineering ingenuity of their desmodromic valve, petrol injected straight eight engine, and all round independent suspension (although the compli-cated down-draught inlet M196 engine was to be slated by Harry Mundy years later as "an example of poor performance" inspite of its complexity and huge 1.968 inch inlet valves, as with "the advantage of a well developed reliable desmod-romic valve gear, roller bearings throughout, it developed barely 300 bhp at 7,450 rpm and a maximum bmep of 185 lbs sq in").

As an overall package, the D-type was the more successful 'Le Mans' car with its disc brakes and superior streamlining - the 300SLR, inspite of carrying a smaller engine, had an excessive frontal area and was actually larger than the Jaguar. Although so far as the 3-litre engine was concerned, Uhlenhaut was quoted as saying that had not expediency demanded the use of what was basically their Formula 1 engine, Mercedes would have preferred to have used a larger unit in their sports car. And besides its mediocre power output, L J K Setright once described its torque curve as being like "a drunkard's design for a scenic railway" which didn't make the car any easier to drive! In braking, Mercedes replied to Jaguar's Dunlop disc brake with their controversial air brake supplementing the car's inboard drums; it was first tried out on the early racing 300SLs although not at Le Mans. Driver controlled, the air brake certainly cut down the car's speed dramatically at high speed, and even at low speed the drivers found its use worthwhile. As another indication of Mercedes' lack of faith in their drum brakes, the driver of the 300SLR had an array of four syringes to press, by which means oil could be delivered to any drum should grabbing occur - provided he could guess which drum was giving the trouble!

The Mercedes-Jaguar battle continued for some 2½ hours, the Ferrari gradually dropping behind. Hawthorn found that on fast corners the Mercedes suspension scored, Fangio gaining quite considerably at places like White House, but on slow corners the difference between the two cars was not marked. Out of the very tight Mulsanne corner the D-type held the 300SLR on acceleration in first and second gears, but Fangio's five-speed box allowed the German car to pull away until fourth gear on the Jaguar was engaged. Of Castellotti's Ferrari, Hawthorn had this to say in his autobiography *Challenge Me The Race:*

> The Ferrari's brakes were not as good as ours and their behaviour on corners was not all it might have been; but on acceleration Castellotti just left us both standing, laying incredible long black streaks of molten rubber on the road as he roared away.

But notwithstanding its fiercesome acceleration, the Ferrari inexorably fell behind as Hawthorn and Fangio repeated, or even excelled, their memorable Rheims single seater encounter. At one point in the race Fangio forced the Mercedes in front, and but for Hawthorn's courage and determination that might have been it. But as he retold afterwards:

> I suppose at this stage I was momentarily mes-merised by the legend of Mercedes superiority. Here was this squat silver projectile, handled by the world's best driver, with its fuel injection and desmodromic valve gear, its complicated suspension and its out-of-this-world air brake. Then I came to my senses and thought: 'Damn it, why should a German car beat a British car?' As there was no-one in sight but me to stop it, I got down to it and caught up with him again.

This Hawthorn did to such effect that he set a new lap record, at an unprecedented 122.39 mph. By this time, all but four cars out of the entire field had been lapped by the leaders - and then came the terrifying accident in which up-wards of 85 people were killed, and many more injured. There are still varying accounts of how exactly it occured, but all that can really be said

is that as Hawthorn pulled into the pits for the D-type's first scheduled fuel stop, Lance Macklin's Austin Healey came into the path of Pierre Levegh's works Mercedes, which, travelling at somewhere around 150 mph, suddenly had no-where to go. In the freak accident that followed, the silver car flew over the safety barrier and disintegrated amongst the crowd in front of the grandstand opposite the pits.

Hawthorn, only dimly aware of what had happened, rolled past the Jaguar pit in the confusion, and as reversing wasn't allowed, ran back to Lofty England and asked if he could complete another lap. He did so, then in a state of near collapse left the D-type at the pits. Ivor Bueb stepped into the cockpit, having had to stand on the pit counter for a solid five minutes watching the carnage while Hawthorn completed his extra lap. It was his first race in the D-type, and his first Le Mans. But nevertheless, he took the car out of the pits and drove - although admitting later that for the first six laps at least, passing the flames each time round, he fought against the urge to come in and hand over to Bob Berry, the reserve driver.

The shocked Hawthorn was in a similar - though worse - state of mind, and had to be persuaded to continue by Lofty England. Of this moment, Hawthorn recalled in his book:

> During those terrible hours he was a tower of strength. While people went back and forth con-sulting precedents and debating about what should be done, Lofty saw the situation quite clearly and simply. Nothing that he could say or do would alter the consequences of the accident in the slightest degree. He had come to Le Mans to win a motor race and so long as the race kept going, it was his job to win it.

Win it Jaguar did too, at the record average speed of 106.99 mph, after the entire Mercedes team had withdrawn on orders from Stuttgart with their leading car ahead of the Hawthorn/ Bueb D-type by some two laps. The latter (XKD 505) was the only 'works' Jaguar to finish - Don Beauman, something of a Hawthorn protege, had been paired with works test driver Norman Dewis in XKD 508, but had run the car into the sandbank at Arnage; he had just dug it out when the sudden arrival of Colin Chapman's Lotus-Climax effectively made it a non-runner. Rolt and Hamilton meanwhile had retired with loss of oil from the gearbox, which had left them with only third and top gears after running in second place for a while following the Mercedes retirement.

The only finisher of the two private Jaguar entrants was the D-type of Claes and Swaters, which came in a good third behind the Aston Martin of Peter Collins and Paul Frere. Americans Walters and Spear retired on the evening of the first day with engine failure, probably on account of the car's air box breaking up and destroying a valve.

It will always be a matter for speculation whether Mercedes would have won the 1955 Grand Prix d'Endurance but for their withdrawal after the accident. But that being said, it can be argued that the odds were in fact in favour of the Jaguar, inspite of the fact that the Hawthorn/Bueb car was about two laps down on the German leader when the latter retired. Not only had the D-type already put up the fastest lap, and therefore proved itself the quickest car around the circuit(Fangio admitted afterwards that he could have gone no faster), but it also proved that it was capable of finishing the whole 24 hours after the flat-out motoring in the initial stages of the race; it was rumoured that the Fangio/Moss 300SLR had been suffering clutch problems towards the end of its run.

Furthermore, the Rolt/Hamilton D-type had covered 14 laps in its last hour of the race, compared to the Mercedes' 13, indicating some additional reserve on behalf of the British cars.

The occasion of the 1955 race was also a personal tragedy for William Lyons. His son, Michael John Lyons, was killed in a collision between his car and an American forces' lorry over a blind brow, about ten miles from Cherbourg, shortly after he had disembarked from the air ferry on his way to Le Mans.

Amongst the many repercussions of the Le Mans accident was the cancellation of the Rheims 12-Hour race that year, and the next appearance of a works D-type was the sole entry of Hawthorn at the British GP meeting at Aintree. He led initially but was overwhelmed by the nimbler Aston Martins and finished 5th; in common with opinions expressed by other D-type drivers, Hawthorn decided he didn't like Aintree, its slower corners not suiting the Jaguar's rigid rear axle, losing the car a lot of time through wheelspin. Discussing the respective merits of the D-type and the DB3S Aston Martin, Hawthorn and Peter Collins came to the conclusion that the Aston, with its de Dion rear end, liked either very fast corners or very slow ones, which is why it often excelled at the Nurburgring (or Aintree) to the detriment of the Jaguar, but didn't suit medium speed bends; this would explain why the Jaguar could be hard to beat at Silverstone where these latter type of corner predominate. Of Le Mans, Hawthorn had expressed the opinion that the only place where the Jaguar lost out to its independent or de Dion rivals was White House.

Ecurie Ecosse had been considerably more active with XKD 501 and 502 however, Desmond Titterington and Ninian Sanderson together driving to an excellent 2nd place in the Goodwood 9-Hours race in August 1955, in between the works Astons. Bob Berry and Norman Dewis managed 5th place in Jack Broadhead's car but might have finished even higher had they not underestimated the pace of the event.

The Tourist Trophy of 1955 at Dundrod was notable for the resumption of the Hawthorn/Fangio battle so sadly broken off at Le Mans, and for the fact that this was to be the last such race held over that marvellous circuit of closed public roads. Again only one works car was entered, driven by Hawthorn and local man Titterington. It was originally meant to run a de Dion axle car, this type of rear suspension having already been tried in the works development car XKC 401; however, the Metalastic joints proved troublesome and it was the normally suspended XKD 506 that appeared on the grid.

Moss almost immediately took the lead for Mercedes as the race began, although a good start by Bob Berry in his Broadhead-entered D-type saw him temporarily head the German car. Alas for Berry and co-driver Sanderson who never got a drive, a nudge of a bank on the second lap resulted in a deflating tyre which put OKV 2 into a field shortly afterwards. On this same lap at a different spot, two drivers lost their lives in a multiple accident which contributed to the closure of the circuit so far as the TT was concerned.

With Moss always ahead, Hawthorn and Fangio indulged in an awe-inspiring display of competitive driving which on occasions brought the crowd to its feet as the two cars flashed past the pits almost level. Fangio managed to slip past the Jaguar on the descent of the Deers Leap, but Hawthorn re-took the Mercedes two laps later and soon a new lap record was posted - Hawthorn had circulated the D-type in 4 mins 42 seconds, or 94.67 mph, to set a four-wheel record for Dundrod that was to stand in perpetuity. It was actually faster than the record Farina had set driving the supercharged 158 Alfa Romeo.

While the D-type didn't have the five speed gearbox of the Mercedes, the Jaguar team had the tyre situation well in hand and the Dunlop Stabilia tyres provided excellent dry weather grip and withstood the abrasive surface of the roads excellently. Seventeen inch wheels were used to further minimise tyre wear, and with an axle ratio of 3.31:1 the car was well geared for the hilly circuit, whose many medium speed bends seemed to suit the Jaguar's primitive (by Mercedes' standards) rear suspension. A rear anti-roll bar which was being tried on Hawthorn's car for the first time in a race obviously assisted in overcoming the D-type's understeering qualities which were a handicap in some instances. Hawthorn also set the highest maximum speed recorded over the timed

kilometer at Dundrod, at 148.5 mph. The German team, on the other hand, lacked Jaguar's experience of the circuit and were particularly afflicted by tyre problems, Moss's offside rear wing being almost completely ripped away by a flailing tread when a rear tyre shredded.

Hawthorn, backed up valiantly by Titterington, made a soul-stirring attempt to stave off the Mercedes attack which had now been taken up by Moss, but it could not be done, typical Ulster rain cancelling out the Jaguar's tyre advantage; and although fuel stops by the German car put the Jaguar ahead, Moss again overtook Hawthorn and went on to win. Even what seemed to be a safe second place was denied the Jaguar, as the D-type's crankshaft broke when Hawthorn was in sight of the pits. So Mercedes were first and second (though even Fangio had been lapped) and although by the number of laps covered, Jaguar would have been 3rd, the rule book didn't acknowledge it and the Mercedes of von Trips and Simon took that place. Ferrari had made a surprisingly poor showing, the highest placed being Castellotti and Taruffi in 6th position, while the Aston Martin of Walker and Poore were 4th, and the Maserati of Musso and Musy 5th.

Meanwhile Duncan Hamilton had bought a second ex-works car, XKD 406, which he loaned to Michael Head and George Abecassis who scored 2nd places at Goodwood and Snetterton respectively. Duncan himself previously won the 50 mile 'Unlimited' sports car race at Silverstone in September (with OKV 1), and while beating Abecassis at the Snetterton meeting, spun backwards across the finishing line when a tyre burst. It was, he said, the only race he could remember winning while pointing the wrong way.

The 1956 Le Mans race was the last the factory were to enter officially, and six new cars were built specifically for the event. With long-nose bodywork, they resembled the 1955 works cars except that for the 24 hours race they wore the regulation 8 inches deep full-width windscreen, demanded for Constructors' Championship events with a view to keeping speeds down. The best was made of the new regulations by positioning a Vyback transparent cover over the passenger compartment, effectively streamlining the area as much as possible; previously the passenger seat had been covered by a removable aluminium lid. Other concessions to the regulations included a door for the theoretical passenger, and wider seats (at 20 inches). The new cars were however some 50 - 60 lbs lighter than before, weight being saved by the use of lighter gauge alloy where possible, and the use of yet lighter brackets. The inside of the tail was slightly altered to accommodate the smaller, 28 gallon, fuel tank which the regulations also demanded.

Handling was improved by increasing the roll stiffness of the car, this being achieved by bringing the diameter of the front anti-roll bar up from 9/16 inch to 11/16 inch, and by incorporating the ¾ inch rear anti-roll bar which had been tried out at Dundrod. This connected the top two suspension links together.

An important mechanical innovation was the Lucas petrol injection system which was fitted to Hawthorn's D-type for Le Mans 1956, and which received extensive testing in the months beforehand both on the original 'injection' car XKD 504, and on XKD 605 itself at Rheims, held before Le Mans that year.

By the time Le Mans came around, a minor modification had been made to the gearbox; this was a lock-out mechanism which ensured that bottom gear could only be selected by fully depressing the clutch, an alteration prompted by Tony Dennis's fatal crash at Goodwood earlier that year.

Driving Hamilton's car, XKD 510, he inadvertently changed from top to first gear at about 110 mph which of course caused the rear wheels to lock up and throw the D-type off the road. Lyons had all possible D-types recalled to the factory to have this safety device fitted following this incident.

The new works cars first appeared at Silverstone in May 1956, where Titterington wrote

off XKD 604 in an opening lap crash. This was the D-type equipped with a de Dion rear end, and so the only appearance of the Jaguar de Dion rear end in a race was very brief! Titterington had however got below 1 min 50 seconds in practice, only Hawthorn in XKD 603 and Salvadori's Aston Martin also getting under that time. Not a good day for Jaguar, Hawthorn retired too after setting a record fastest lap at 1 min 47 seconds.

Hawthorn did try the de Dion car round Silverstone before the race, and found that it did indeed cut out a lot of the wheelspin which occurred on corners even with the ZF limited slip differential. While the de Dion arrangement weighed more than the standard D-type rear end, on balance Hawthorn decided he preferred it and only drove the other car because Titterington said that he couldn't manage so well with the rigid rear axle car.

The Nurburgring was the second factory visit of the season, and it was soon obvious to those who hadn't driven a D-type around that incredible circuit before that it was no place for a Jaguar. Paul Frere, who had joined the works team a month or so beforehand, wrote afterwards:

"In many places our speed was limited not so much by the convolutions of the circuit as our desire to keep the car in one piece. Along the whole stretch from Breitscheid to the Karrusel the back wheels were more in the air than on the ground, and with a full tank the suspension was bottoming frequently."

Frere was in fact to leave the track rather dramatically during practice, though he was gracious enough not to blame XKD 603! Norman Dewis drove out a replacement from Coventry in nearly record time, but that failed too when the gearbox broke. Hawthorn was lying 4th in the other works D-type (XKD 601, injection) when with only five laps to go a supplementary 2-gallon metal petrol tank mounted in the passenger's seat sprung a leak, necessitating a pit stop to effect a repair as the fumes were making Hawthorn ill. Titterington took over but the car's run came to an end when a half-shaft failed half a lap from the chequered flag. Hamilton, paired with Frere, didn't get a drive at all.

The re-instituted 12-hour race at Rheims was, however, a much happier affair for the team, even though it caused some internal conflict. Two cars had already put in considerable private practice during the previous May, the results of which indicated that they should do well, especially as the circuit had always suited Jaguars. In fact, the team's only worries were those of finding worthy opposition as neither Aston Martin, Ferrari or Maserati were represented by works teams. Fortunately the late entries of a new 3½-litre Maserati driven by Villoresi and Piotti, a Monza Ferrari, and the HWM-Jaguar of Leston and Cunningham-Reid made things appear a little more worthwhile.

The works Jaguars immediately established themselves in the first three places when the race began, backed up by the Ecurie Ecosse D-type driven by Sanderson, who had won the 100-mile Belgian Production Sports Car race at Spa two months earlier. The only real drama of the race occurred when, after the whole Jaguar team was under orders to slow down, Hamilton in XKD 605 overtook Frere. To his consternation the Belgian driver/journalist found that the carburetted engine in his XKD 601 was rather less powerful than Hamilton's fuel injected unit - contrary to the results of tests held the previous May on the circuit. So the finishing order was thus Hamilton/Bueb, Hawthorn/Frere, Titterington/Fairman, and Sanderson/Flockhart for Ecurie Ecosse. Poor Duncan got his marching orders from Lofty after the speeding up episode - he always swore that he *did* slow down, but that it enabled him to take a better line through a corner which had the side-effect of reducing his lap times!

So the Jaguar team was in good spirits when Le Mans came round in July. The cars were equipped with their full-width windscreens and the other Le Mans regulation items, and the cylinder heads had been modified with economy in mind - the cars would need to average around 11 - 12 mpg now that the tankage had been reduced. Importantly, the cars' disc brakes had quick-change pads for the first time, so that the friction material could be changed at the same time as a wheel change with virtually no penalty incurred in terms of extra time lost.

The capacity limit for prototypes was now 2½ litres, but Jaguar were able to run in the production class due to the number of D-types which had been, or were intending to be, made - in fact it was the biggest engined car running. Quite how the two Aston Martin DB3S cars came to be accepted is a mystery!

The works driver pairings were Hawthorn and Bueb again in XKD 605 (injection), Frere/Titterington XKD 606 (Webers), and Fairman/Wharton XKD 602 (injection). Ecurie Ecosse were running XKD 501 as an exploratory excursion for a team entry next year, while Equipe National Belge had entered a new production D-type, XKD 573, prepared by the factory and driven by Laurent/Rousselle.

In practice (which was still just before the race in those days, not weeks beforehand as now) the works Jaguars were a comfortable six or seven seconds faster than any other make, with little difference in either speed or fuel consumption between the injected or carburetted cars. Titterington ran off the road in XKD 606 and although it didn't appear to be damaged, it was replaced by the spare car, XKD 603. Hawthorn's car had to be fitted with a new engine because of an insistent misfire, and he also suffered a thrown tread at 140 mph - this prompted Lofty to investigate the remaining tyres which were tested on the track, mostly by Bueb. Sure enough, several more 'rogue' covers were discovered. But still Hawthorn expressed a feeling of pessimism, as although the Jaguar drivers had the fastest cars in the race, with only Aston Martin likely to even be within striking distance, the number one driver felt that it was all too good to be true. His fears began to be justified on the second lap of the race.

Top Victory handshake. Lyons congratulates Peter Whitehead just after the D-type's first win, at Rheims in July 1954; Whitehead's co-driver was Ken Wharton, the car OKV 3 (XKC 404). Right to left in background: Norman Dewis, Len Hayden (white overalls), Stirling Moss and Phil Weaver (*photo The Motor*)

Centre The 1955 D-type. This view shows the petrol filler cap housed under the headfairing (common to all D-types), the oil tank for the dry sump system with pipe running to the engine between the exhaust manifolds, and in the centre section of the car, the passenger seat aperture normally covered by a lift-out panel (*photo The Autocar*)

Bottom The 1955 Le Mans D-types under construction at Browns Lane, with a completed 'short-nosed' car second from the far wall. The monocoque in the foreground clearly shows how the D-type 'ends' at the rear bulkhead (*photo The Autocar*)

Top D-type engine on test at the factory, perhaps having its power output measured, a figure which was then documented in the 'case book' for that particular unit *(photo The Autocar)*
Centre Rear suspension of the 1955 D-type. The axle was primarily located by four trailing links, the bottom two on either side connected to the springing medium, a transverse torsion bar; the links themselves were in torsion during cornering *(photo The Autocar)*
Bottom The Jaguar team cars are pushed onto the grid for the start of the 1955 Le Mans race, led by Hawthorn's car no. 6, which is just drawing level with the Cooper-Jaguar of brothers Peter and Graham Whitehead *(photo The Motor)*

Top Hawthorn versus Fangio, Le Mans 1955, during one of the greatest battles ever witnessed over that famous circuit *(photo The Motor)*
Centre The contest between Jaguar and Mercedes-Benz was renewed at the 1955 Tourist Trophy, when Hawthorn drove one of the outstanding races of his sports car career to keep ahead of Moss and Fangio for many laps, assisted by Desmond Titterington. Here at the start, Bob Berry in Jack Broadhead's car takes a brief lead, glancing back at Hawthorn; Moss's 300SLR is coming up on the right *(photo The Motor)*
Bottom left Sir William chats to Briggs Cunningham, who sits in one of his D-types which is on display at a New York show. Standing on the left is Joe Eerdmans, president of Jaguar North America
Bottom right The main hall at Allesley, showing the line of 1955 'production' D-types under assembly alongside the XK 140 and Mk VII trim lines

Top left Duncan Hamilton having fun at Oulton Park, during the British Empire Trophy race of April 1956; pursuing is the HWM-Jaguar driven by Noel Cunningham-Reid *(photo The Motor)*

Top right Paddock scene; Ecurie Ecosse's D-types at Silverstone on the occasion of the 1956 Daily Express meeting, with the team's original transporter displaying large numbers of advertisements *(photo The Motor)*

Centre Jaguar pit signals during the Rheims 12 Hour race of 1956 - this was the occasion which got Hamilton (partnering Bueb), the sack, as he ran against team orders to win the event, followed by Hawthorn/Frere and Titterington/Fairman *(photo The Motor)*

Bottom Factory representation at the 1956 Le Mans race - six D-types lined up in Le Mans before the race, the four works cars (one practice), Ecurie Ecosse's single entry (no. 4) and the Belgian-entered car, far right *(photo The Motor)*

Top The fuel injection equipment of the Hawthorn/Bueb D-type, Le Mans 1956. A minute crack in the fuel lines led to miss-firing which dropped the car right down to 20th place before the fault was corrected. It finished 6th *(photo The Motor)*

Centre Disaster at Le Mans! On the second lap of the 1956 race Paul Frere spun on the approach to the Esses and smote the bank backwards. Jack Fairman, following, also lost control but stopped without hitting anything - only to be struck by de Portago's Ferrari. Here the two D-types are seen limping off, de Portage still across the track *(photo The Motor)*

Bottom Le Mans 1957, and Paul Frere rounds Terte Rouge in the gathering dusk, on the way to a 4th place with 'Freddy' Rouselle and the Écurie Belge D-type *(photo The Motor)*

Top left Runner up in Ecurie Ecosse's domination of the 1957 Le Mans race, the Weber carburetted D-type of Ninian Sanderson and John Lawrence rounds Mulsanne corner *(photo The Motor)*

Top right The winners - a happy Flockhart and Bueb after their 1957 Le Mans victory, joined by 'Wilky' Wilkinson (right) *(photo The Motor)*

Centre Contrast in styles: Jack Fairman's Ecurie Ecosse D-type high up on the Monza banking with A Linden's Indianapolis single seater special passing below. The Scottish team's D-types finished 4th, 5th, and 6th in that rather unusual 500 mile race of 1957 *(photo The Motor)*

Bottom left Mille Miglia 1957, and Ron Flockhart's D-type leaves the start - it was not to finish *(photo The Motor)*

Bottom right Ecurie Ecosse in South America; Mieres in the D-type temporarily leads Behra's 3-litre Maserati during the Buenos Aires sports car race. XKD 603 was partnered by Ninian Sanderson and finished 4th

Top left Motor racing in Rhodesia - Malcolm Gardner driving the ex-Lord Louth D-type on the Belvedere race track in 1957, while it was in a Mr Watson's ownership. Back in England it is now regularly raced by Longbacon Engineering in Historic events *(photo Malcolm Gardner)*
Top right 'Lofty' England and Mike Hawthorn, with the pit counters of Le Mans as a familiar back-drop. Not surprisingly, England rates Hawthorn as one of the greatest drivers of his day *(photo The Motor)*
Centre left Jack Fairman and Desmond Titterington pictured at Rheims with their works D-type *(photo The Motor)*
Centre right Ivor Bueb and Duncan Hamilton *(photo The Motor)*
Bottom A rather pensive-looking William Lyons, with Stirling Moss, before the start of the 1954 Le Mans race

Top Peter Blond in OKV 2 being chased by Duncan Hamilton, at Oulton Park, April 1958 *(photo The Motor)*
Centre The Nurburgring, June 1958, and M. Gregory takes the Ecurie Ecosse D-type round the Karousel during the 1,000km race of that year *(photo The Motor)*
Bottom Just after the start of the 1959 Le Mans race, and the single Ecurie Ecosse D-type accelerates away from the pits followed by its Tojeiro-Jaguar team mate. The D-type occupied 2nd place for some hours before dropping out with engine trouble, the fate of the Tojeiro too; driver pairings were Ireland/Gregory and Flockhart/Lawrence respectively

Top The last D-type to run at Le Mans was the 1960 Ecurie Ecosse entry, which alas was not to finish. Note the high, full-width windscreen topped with a racing mirror to see over the compulsory 'boot' on the car's tail. Following is a Chevrolet Corvette *(photo The Motor)*

Centre Ecurie Ecosse's famous custom built transporter, finished in the same metallic blue as the team's cars. This picture, taken at a 1960 Silverstone meeting, shows the last two Ecurie Ecosse D-types, no. 32 sporting its rather ugly 'Le Mans' luggage compartment. The transporter is now owned and used by Historic racing driver Neil Corner *(photo The Motor)*

Bottom Jaguar D-type with Michelotti coupe body. This car used the chassis of XKD 513, which had been crashed by Jean-Marie Brussin at Le Mans 1958, killing the driver. It was first displayed at the March 1963 Geneva Salon, but has recently been bought by a British collector and is now in the UK *(photo The Motor)*

Top D-type in America; Hawthorn driving at Sebring, 1955, when he and Phil Walters won the 12 Hour race at a record average speed
Centre Phil Walters in the works D-type, sent out primarily for the 1955 Sebring 12 Hour race, crossing the line at 164.136mph average at the Daytona Speed Trials of that year. This was the first appearance of the D-type in the States
Bottom Bonneville, 1960, and the young Tom Rutherford with his ex-Walt Hansgen D-type which achieved a 185.47mph two-way average with the help of wheel discs, 3.8-litre engine and rear mounted exhaust pipes. This is the highest officially recorded speed for a D-type or any other Jaguar

Top left The first, and unofficial, road version of a D-type was the conversion of John Goddard's OKV 1 by previous owner Duncan Hamilton in 1956. It is seen here outside the factory, with makeshift hood frame and Austin Healey windscreen in evidence *(photo Jaguar Cars)*

Top right Twelve of the sixteen original XK SS cars went to the United States, where this one is pictured

Bottom One of the few to be seen in England, this XK SS was hill climbed by its owner, J Browning. This car is shown at a June 1960 Prescott meeting *(photo The Motor)*

Top Slightly more restrained and much more civilised than the XK 120 or XK 140, the XK 150 displayed very similar lines to the coming Mk 2 saloon range. Note the high scuttle and door line

Bottom Still basically XK 120, the XK 150's chassis retained all the modifications made for the XK 140, including telescopic rear dampers and the altered central cross-member which accommodated the overdrive unit and twin exhaust system when these were fitted *(photo The Autocar)*

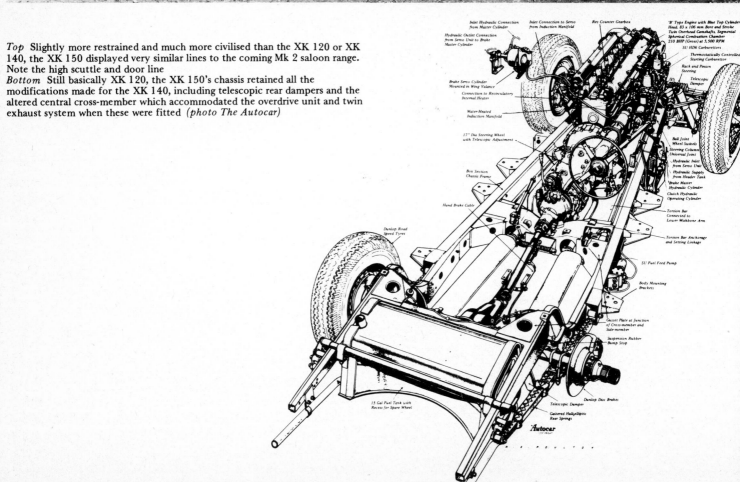

A light drizzle had started just before 4 pm, and as the field left the new pits area and accelerated under the Dunlop Bridge for the first time, the track was undoubtedly in a treacherous state. Hawthorn at this time "felt a shock as though another car had hit me... The tyres were alternately gripping and slipping on the slippery road surface" Then on the second lap, Paul Frere braked gently and in plenty of time - as he thought - for the Esses, but he had already left it too late. Although he took the widest line possible in the hope of finding a drier patch on the inside of the road, the D-type spun round on the wet surface (made even more deadly by the fine Le Mans sand which had blown onto the track before the rain had come) and hit the wattle fence lining the earth banking on the outside of the bend. Jack Fairman, following, spun XKD 602 in a successful attempt to avoid his team mate, but was promptly struck by de Portago's Ferrari which had also 'lost it'. Hence, the race had hardly begun and two thirds of the Jaguar team were already wiped out!

Fairman managed to hobble back to the pits but the mortified Frere could only manage to get clear of the Esses and pull onto the verge. And to make matters appear totally disastrous for the factory, the remaining unscathed D-type of Hawthorn began a series of pit stops suffering from an elusive misfire. It taxed the wits of the Jaguar mechanics and Lucas fuel injection specialists alike, and eventually the trouble was traced to a hair line crack in a fuel line (faulty brazing on an injector nipple according to Hawthorn) - the only thing that hadn't been changed when the new engine was installed just before the race. By that time, any chance of victory for the works team had vanished, and all that remained was the fastest lap to go for; this Hawthorn dutifully accomplished shortly after midnight and before handing over to Bueb, although due to the new windscreen the speed, at 115.8 mph, was a long way down on the previous year's Jaguar record. By dint of some

exceptionally rapid motoring the car was brought up from its 20th position to 6th - but it was Ecurie Ecosse that saved the day for Jaguar.

All the while, Flockhart and Sanderson had been engaged in a furious battle with the DB3S Aston Martins, particularly the car of Moss and Collins, but as daylight came the Jaguar drew ahead, and by the end of the morning had established itself a safe lap ahead of the Aston.

The Scottish Jaguar incorporated the various chassis refinements of the factory cars (such as the rear anti-roll bar), but did not have the big-valve 35/40 head or petrol injection. Its progress was aided though by the new quick-change pads, which could be replaced in 40 seconds merely by withdrawing a split pin and pulling them out. The new quick-change braking system was further simplified by the use of a single pair of wheel cylinders instead of three on each of the front calipers.

Watching the leading Jaguar from the touchline, Paul Frere was keeping all his fingers crossed. "Never in all my life had I hoped so fervently that a car would win a race as I did then". One can well understand why! But faultlessly, calmly, the Ecurie Ecosse Jaguar tucked away the laps, and finally crossed the line as the 24 hours of motor racing were completed, sounding as healthy as when it had begun the afternoon before.

So ended the last race in which Jaguar Cars competed as an official team. The company's exploits in the French classic had had an amazing impact on their sales figures all over the world, and had helped make the name 'Jaguar' universally known - which it certainly wasn't in the early post-war years. This probably needs emphasizing today, when it is hard to believe that many people had never heard of the small concern building fast cars in Coventry; that however is the reason why Jaguar went to Le Mans. Mr England:

By winning Le Mans we established a reputation worth having. I know this from personal experience. When I first started to go to the States in 1948 when we were just starting to get into the market, people didn't even know what a Jaguar car was. If you were in one people would pull up beside you and say, 'What is it?', but as soon as we won Le Mans, people who were interested in cars immediately knew what a Jaguar was, and the name went forward very quickly.

After the 1956 24-Hour race, Heynes and his small group of engineers considered that so far as they were concerned, the D-type was an obsolete motor car. A new car was needed, and there simply weren't the available personnel to develop and build it, as the production side of Jaguar urgently demanded the skills and knowledge of the men who had built the racing cars to improve the current road cars. They also had to prepare for the next generation of road Jaguars - even in 1956 the E-type replacement for the XK 150 (which itself hadn't even been announced then!) was beginning to take shape on the drawing board, and would be running in prototype form by early 1957.

However, the factory's withdrawal was, at the time, only meant to be temporary. To quote Lofty England again, "When we pulled out in 1956 it was with the intention of staying out for a year and coming back, subject to our having a car which we felt was right."

But once out of racing, it becomes increasingly difficult to re-enter and what probably killed any possibility of it actually happening was the fire at the factory in February 1957. It destroyed what had been the D-type 'production line', together with a number of vital jigs and tools needed by the competition department. The effort needed to re-establish this competition-orientated section of the factory was just too much at a time when all energies were being directed into getting normal production under way in the quickest possible time after the ravages of the fire. As Mr. England says:

   All things relating to competition were forgotten - had to be. The main object was to get the factory going again with all possible speed, back into profitability, which was done very quickly. The demand for

cars had lifted up like *that*, and therefore everybody's main interest was to make sure we were doing our job properly production wise, and also take care of our future model range, which meant that there wasn't any great necessity to rush back into motor racing. We didn't have to motor race to make sure we were getting enough orders, neither did we want to take up our people's time on motor racing projects when we really needed them on our production lines.

Thus ended Jaguar's own competition career, and although support lingered in America and the company was to remain in touch with the racing scene right up until 1966 when the XJ13 prototype was secretly finished, Jaguar were never again to enter the sport officially themselves.

THE XKSS

Production of the XKSS came to an abrupt halt too after the fire. This exciting car had originally been created towards the end of 1956 both to use up unsold D-type monocoques, and for private owners to compete with in 'Class C Production' racing in the USA, simply being a D-type road equipped to conform to the Sports Car Club of America's regulations; it was catalogued at the beginning of 1957, but due to production being cut short by fire, not enough were made for it to qualify for this type of racing. Anyway, it wasn't selling well. Including the two D-types converted by the factory for their owners into XKSSs in 1958 (Pierre Chemin, XKD 533, and Phil Scragg, XKD 540), only 18 of the cars were made.

No structural alterations were carried out during the making of an XKSS - the completed 'production' D-type, minus headrest, had its division between passenger and driver removed, the passenger compartment itself enlarged at the top, a door introduced into its nearside, and a wrap-round windscreen fitted. The chromium-plated surround of the last mentioned was integrated, after a fashion, into the car's shape by an extra body panel that sloped up from the scuttle. The windscreen glass itself was rumoured to have come from the rear window of a Buick or Chrysler! There were no winding windows of course, sidescreens supplementing the folding hood; the interior was trimmed in hide. Nor was there a luggage compartment, suitcases being carried on the rack mounted behind the cockpit on the tail. Neat quarter-bumpers, resembling to an extent those appearing on the E-type some four years later, were mounted front and rear. One XKSS appears to have been made using a D-type front sub-frame and a glass fibre centre section and panels, but this was more likely to have been an apprentices' exercise rather than a serious investigation into possible production using glass fibre as a medium. The car still exists, having run around for some time with an Austin Healey 3000 engine - without dry sump equipment a normal Jaguar engine wouldn't fit.

Under the skin, the XKSS was identical to the 'production' D-type with a performance that was only slightly impaired by its extra frontal area and weight. *Road & Track* magazine sampled an XKSS on behalf of their readers a couple of months after the type's first racing success, at Mansfield, Louisiana, in the spring of 1957 (driven by C Gordon Bennet, the car was XKSS 701, built in 1956 from XKD 563 and shipped to America as the company's New York demonstrator).

While the magazine didn't rate the XKSS as a genuine dual-purpose racing/road machine, they were highly impressed by it. Practical shortcomings included too loud an exhaust note, uncomfortable localised heating of the passenger's floor by the side exhaust system, and too much wheelspin due to the lack of a limited slip device in the differential. This made good acceleration times difficult to obtain, but with practice 60 mph was reached in 5.2 seconds, 80 mph in 8.8 seconds, and 100 mph in 13.6 seconds. The standing quarter mile took 14.1 seconds. Fast enough for a genuine road car! The battery was liable to discharge rather quickly as the dynamo wasn't geared to cut in below 2,000 rpm, though the car's equipment did include a larger pulley for use at low speeds, at the cost of having to keep the revs down to avoid disintegrating the dynamo windings.

The windshield was found to give very adequate protection and the goggles required on the standard D-type weren't an obligation, while the car's ride was "rather soft in comparison with the spine-jarring ride of Italian road-racing machinery". The steering was direct at 2.3 turns lock to lock, though even moderate bumps were signalled to the driver at lower speeds.

Interestingly, the same journal had performance-tested a largely standard production D-type a year before, which had been "the best performing automobile we have ever tested". With a non-standard (American Spicer) rear axle ratio of 3.73:1. the car was a little lower geared than the XKSS with its standard 3.54:1 ratio, and the owners of the car did not feel bound to comply with Jaguar's strict rev. limit of 5,800 rpm - 6,200 rpm was used through the gears, and for the D-type's maximum speed run, 6,600 rpm was held. *Road & Track's* fastest previous road test had been of a 2.9 litre Ferrari in May 1954, and they set out the comparative figures. As can be seen, the D-type was definitely faster than both the Ferrari and the XKSS:

	D-type	2.9 Ferrari
0-60	4.7	5.1
0-80	8.0	8.5
0-100	12.1	13.7
SS ¼	13.7	14.4
bhp	250	240
torque	242 ft lbs	178 ft lbs
axle ratio	3.73	4.25
top speed	162.2mph	135 mph
Drag at 60	80 lbs	123 lbs
Test weight	2460 lbs	2350 lbs

While *Road & Track* had been playing with their XKSS, the rival magazine *Sports Cars Illustrated* (now *Car & Driver*) was engaged in quite a prolonged track testing of a production D-type, and the different evaluation of the car for the road and for the American race track makes an interesting comparison too.

While *Road & Track* found that the D-type's low speed characteristics were, in the XKSS, about what was wanted for a road car - "a light poke will readily put the rear end out and into oversteer when using any of the indirect gears" - *Sports Cars Illustrated* found that the machine's tendency to travel straight on when a high speed corner was approached a disadvantage on a typical American circuit. Generally, the D-type puzzled the drivers but in the final analysis all that the magazine really found out was that the D-type had been designed for Le Mans, which it had known all along. Modifications to introduce oversteering characteristics, such as the fitting of a rear anti-roll bar (which of course the works had done on the later team cars), were speculated upon, but one must look askance on their conclusions to some extent - after all, the D-type was designed for Dunlop racing tyres, not road Michelins! An acceleration check showed that the car - XKD 527, belonging to Jerry Austin - reached 100 mph in "just over 12 seconds". It too had a 3.73:1 axle ratio, and a Hi-Tork limited slip device whose fitment Jaguar had approved.

As usual, there was praise for the tractability of the Jaguar engine even in tuned form. Having quoted the owner as saying "it's almost unbelievable that this car can be bought 'over the counter'", *Sports Cars Illustrated* went on to say:

The delivery of horsepower without temperament at low rpm is astonishing, especially today when with some cars you can find yourself in a corner at 4000 rpm with a spitting recalcitrant engine and at 4200 rpm something happens all over you and you discover you're looking at where you've been for no better reason than a hundred horsepower came in all at once. This amazing engine combined with all the other design goodies incorporated into this car, ie disc brakes, triple-plate clutch, dry sump lubrication and other things too numerous to mention, should make the D top dog in this country.

The Jaguar D-type did of course have a long and on the whole honourable racing career in the United States, whatever its handling problems might have been on American circuits. Briggs Cunningham, more or less on the principle of 'if you can't beat 'em join 'em', concentrated less on trying to win Le Mans with his own, US-built cars, and more on pursuing victory with the D-type. He first became truly involved with the cars when XKD 406 entered the country, the first of its type to do so. Under the care of Cunningham, the D-type first showed its paces to American followers of the sport when it took 2nd FTD at the Daytona Speed Trials in February 1955 - its time through the measured mile was 164.136 mph, a good 10 mph faster than a 4.9 litre Ferrari of the type which had beaten Jaguar at Le Mans in 1954. Only an old Formula One 4½ litre GP Ferrari was quicker than the D-type and its driver Phil Walters, and the 300SLs were completely out of contention, the fastest being 30 mph slower.

Then Cunningham entered the D-type in the famous 12-hour race at Sebring, with Hawthorn and Phil Walters driving, and Len Hayden from the factory attending to the mechanics. It was rather a chaotic race - at one time Hawthorn, who was having his first race for Jaguar and his first in America, "heard a frightful clanging noise and looked round to see a fire engine racing me. It was a great monster festooned with ladders and things, with characters in long-tailed helmets clinging on all over the place, just like a scene from an old-time film comedy" - and it ended in even greater disruption when Ugolini disputed the official results after the Hawthorn/Walters Jaguar had won from the Hill/Shelby 3-litre Ferrari. The protest was not upheld however and the D-type was declared the winner a week later; it had been a near thing in any case, XKD 506 having suffered from a warped cylinder head, and distorted discs necessitating several extra pit stops. The 5.2 mile airfield circuit had "a lot of sharp corners which are absolutely murder for the brakes", as Hawthorn commented afterwards.

The car then returned to Europe and a D-type was not seen again in the States until Cunningham acquired the car he had entered in the 1955 Le Mans race. Driven by Sherwood Johnston, this car - XKD 507 - finished a close second to Phil Hill's Ferrari at the opening meeting at the 'Road America' circuit, won the Watkins Glen Grand Prix, and defeated Phil Hill by a narrow margin once more at the aerodrome circuit of Hagerstown, Maryland. These successes helped Johnston win another SCCA Championship in a Jaguar.

Hawthorn again drove at Sebring the following year, 1956, partnering Titterington in XKD 601 which was making its first appearance as the long-nose injected car that Hawthorn was to drive in the 1956 Le Mans race. Two other works Jaguars were entered, driven by Hamilton/Bueb (XKD 508) and Johnston/Spear (XKD 506). Although at first the fuel injected car led the Moss/Collins Aston Martin, brake trouble again cropped up after the pads had worn to such a degree that leaking fluid caused the car's retirement. The race was won by Fangio and Castellotti in their 3½ litre Ferrari, and the only Jaguars to finish were XKD 538, driven by Ensley/Sweikert to third place, and XKD 521 which finished in 8th spot, driven by Mena/Santiago Gonzales. Briggs Cunningham himself drove XKD 507 but was yet another retirement.

The gifted driver Walt Hansgen was brought into the Cunningham team very soon afterwards, when he beat Briggs' own cars with a privately owned D-type (XKD 529) at Cumberland, Maryland; thereafter his talents were to be exploited to the full within the Cunningham equipe with its four D-types. The team's successes are too numerous to mention, but Hansgen won the Class C Modified Championship in 1956, and was awarded the 'Driver of the Year' citation in 1957.

Hansgen's fortunes were helped during part of 1957 by the use of a works petrol injection car, XKD 605; this was the car driven by Hawthorn and Bueb in the 1957 Sebring 12-Hour race, and it used a 3.8 litre engine. Although from as early as June 1952 Oscar Moore had been using a bored 3.4 engine in his HWM-Jaguar, taking it out to 3814cc, it was apparently the experiments of the expatriot Italian Alfred Momo, who was working closely with Cunningham, which had finally encouraged Jaguar to produce their own 3.8 litre engine. Unlike early attempts to enlarge the XK engine by private owners however, Jaguar used wet liners to overcome the cylinder wall cracking which could otherwise occur, and modified the block's water passages at the same time.

At Sebring, it was the D-type's brakes again that were nearly the cause of XKD 605's retirement, though it managed to hang on and finish behind Fangio and Moss - the drivers of the D-type were perhaps over confident of the Jaguar's disc brakes which had stood them in such good stead at Le Mans. But then John Wyer has been quoted as saying that the French circuit was the easiest on brakes of any he visited during his management of the Aston Martin team - and after Sebring, Hawthorn certainly stated that he thought the American circuit to be the toughest test in the world for brakes.

In fact, the same trouble of leaking hydraulic fluid caused the distress again, and during the race the rather desperate measure was resorted to, of cutting the D-type's rear hydraulic circuit off and running on the front only. This did nothing to improve steering feel coming into the corners (ironically, Hawthorn previously had rated this 3.8 D-type as steering "better than any other Jaguar I have ever driven"), and two laps from the end of the race the car's rear axle ran dry, the pinion bearing seal having gone - probably another manifestation of the heat, which during the daytime was giving a road temperature of 95 deg. F.

The remarkable Chevrolet Corvette SS sports racing car prototype, itself inspired by the D-type's design, was present at the 1957 Sebring race, and Moss, Fangio and Hawthorn all tried it round the circuit. This 300 bhp car, with its tubular chassis and de Dion rear end, makes an interesting comparison to the D-type Jaguar. In their private try out, both Moss and

179

Fangio equalled Hawthorn's D-type lap times, and Hawthorn himself thought that it cornered better than the Jaguar, had better acceleration in the lower two ratios, and probably possessed an equal top speed. It was Fitch who actually drove the Corvette SS in the race, and it went well until dropping out with trouble from (amongst other things) its fuel injection equipment. Three *production* Corvettes finished the race although troubled with brake problems, but these should not be confused with Zora Duntov's prototype.

Hawthorn was also to try the small C6R Cunningham which had run at, but not finished, Le Mans 1955 with an Offenhauser engine. It had been fitted for Sebring with one of Briggs' own bored-out D-type engines, but alas the car succumbed to the dreaded cracked cylinder walls while Cunningham himself was warming it up!

While the Cunningham team undoubtedly headed Jaguar successes in the United States, quite a large number of private entrants did well in their own production D-types - assisted where possible by Jaguar Cars of North America who thoughtfully provided a factory trained mechanic, free help, and a whole truckful of spares at some east coast events.

The D-type's last major win in the States was the victory of Carlyle Blackwell and Ken Miles in the 6-hour race at Pomona in 1958. Funnily enough, the same British-born Miles had acquired minor notoriety for a while in England by writing a rather ill-considered letter to *Autosport* casting considerable doubt as to whether the production D-type bore any relationship to the factory cars. As we have seen, the two types differed very little, and Miles was suitably and thoroughly squashed by an erudite Gregor Grant in a subsequent issue!

As Lister-Jaguars, and later still the 'birdcage' Maseratis, began to dominate the American sports car racing scene, some D-type owners resorted to fairly desperate measures to up-rate their cars, some by boring their engines out, others by fitting V8 Ford or Chevrolet units (a fate met by at least one XKSS too). Though

not generally successful, Bill Krause with XKD 519 was one who made such a marriage work, and notched up a few 'places' with his D-type so converted - this car has recently returned to this country, incidentally, where it is to be returned to its original specification; a 're-conversion' that is overtaking most such D-type hybrids as their value escalates.

To return to the European scene following the 1956 Le Mans race and Jaguar's withdrawal from sports car racing there, the D-type was still enjoying great popularity and a good measure of success on its home circuits in the hands of private owners; although ever stiffer opposition was now being provided by Aston Martin. Ecurie Ecosse were very active with their three D-types, while other private entrants included Duncan Hamilton of course, Peter Blond, and Henry Taylor who was to put up some fine performances with the Murkett brothers' car, XKD 517.

By December 1956 however, Ecurie Ecosse were accepting delivery of the 1956 long nose works D-types, which they had bought to replace their 1955 series cars. David Murray then undertook to contend events counting towards the Constructors' World Championship, using the new cars (XKD 504, 603 and 606) and one of the older, short nose D-types (XKD 501). The season commenced with a long - and expensive - haul out to Buenos Aires in January 1957, where Sanderson and Mieres drove 'steadily' to 4th place in XKD 603, although Flockhart unfortunately crashed one of the cars in practice. The race was won by the Gregory/Castellotti/Musso 3½ litre Ferrari.

The Scottish team didn't enter Sebring, and in May Lawrence's car only managed 6th place in the Spa GP for sports cars, with Hamilton and Rousselle, driving for Equipe National Belge, ahead of him. This event was notable for Henry Taylor's impressive drive through the rain in the Murkett-entered D-type - he passed the Aston Martin works cars, including Salvadori, and was within 1½ seconds of Tony Broooks' DBR1/300 when the sun came through; he finished an excellent third.

Neither did the Nurburgring give Murray much cause for rejoicing. The D-types were at their usual disadvantage and were never anywhere in contention, Flockhart and Fairman picking up 8th place, Bueb and Lawrence 11th, while poor Sanderson went off the track near the end of the race and had to use his shirt and passenger seat to coax the D-type off marshy ground back on to the track! After missing a lap he managed to regain his 12th position. Things were a little happier for the Ascension Day races near St Etienne, where the Scottish Jaguars found the 3.5 mile circuit to their liking and filled the first two places - although this was not a championship event.

But it was Le Mans 1957 that overshadows all else in the story of Ecurie Ecosse's exploits. Flockhart/Bueb (XKD 606, injection) and Sanderson/Lawrence (XKD 603, Webers) were the team's drivers, and it was the former pair who took their 3.8 engined car to victory in this completely Jaguar-dominated event. Ninian Sanderson and Ron Flockhart backed them up in second place, although at one stage Paul Frere and Freddy Rousselle were running in that position, until their yellow Equipe National Belge D-type (XKD 573) was delayed an hour by a broken point in the distributor. They climbed back to 4th place however, where they remained in front of the Lewis-Evans/Severi 3.8 Ferrari - the slowest of the Ferraris but the most reliable!

Duncan Hamilton and Masten Gregory had a fraught time too, Duncan's latest car (XKD 601, fitted with a 3.8 litre engine) threatening to fry its drivers through a hole in its exhaust pipe. However, aided by a lot of familiar faces in the form of Jaguar personnel (which included Lofty himself, mechanic Len Hayden, and Bob Berry) who had come out to give a little unofficial help, the flames were quelled and the hole which had been burnt in the car's floor patched up with sheet metal. But ¼-hour had been lost and the D-type was in virtually last place when it rejoined the race. It began a dramatic climb up through the field which ended in 6th place, and as its running average proved it to be the fastest of any car left in the race, it may well be that a second Le Mans victory escaped Duncan Hamilton.

As for the opposition to Jaguar in the 1957 race, it literally fell apart. The very strong Italian challenge faded completely, the 4.5 litre Maserati of Stirling Moss retiring after less than two hours with engine trouble, and the second 4½ litre Maserati of Behra following it not long afterwards. The Aston Martins, despite lying as high as 2nd place during the early hours of the event, also began to expire quite soon, the Whitehead brothers' 3.7 litre car dropping out with engine problems, while the 3-litre of Salvadori and Leston was afflicted with serious gearbox problems. The Brooks/Cunningham-Reid Aston spun and crashed during the night.

Once again, the innate reliability of the Jaguar had triumphed. It has often been said that racing experience enables manufacturers to improve their road cars, but Jaguar also turned it the other way about, incorporating into their racing cars major components which had benefitted from many hundreds of thousands of road miles over a number of years in all conditions. The Italian sports racing car builders on the other hand, often failed to allow one design to become even halfway developed before turning to another; and while Ferrari or Maserati frequently fielded the fastest car at Le Mans during Jaguar's racing years, their reliability up to 1957 was never to be compared with the D-type's.

Not long after their triumphant 1957 Le Mans, David Murray and his team ran in the controversial 'Two Worlds 500 Race', or 'Monzanopolis' as it came to be called, held around the great banked track at Monza. The only European entrant to take part due to boycotting of the event by certain drivers and manufacturers (who feared tyre problems, and various more political reasons), the organisers were very appreciative of the Scottish team's gesture. Jack

Fairman and Wilkie Wilkinson had previously taken one D-type over to Monza for testing, and discovered that as expected, the limiting factor was overheating of the tyres. But as the D-type's bodywork did not allow anything other than the normal Dunlop tyres to be fitted, albeit on 17 inch wheels, nothing could be done except buff the treads down to half thickness to reduce centrifugal force to a minimum. Even then, the Jaguar threw a tread at 165 mph, as predicted by Don Barlow of Dunlop who was with them!

Originally it had been intended to run the race on the 6-mile road circuit at Monza, but in view of the design of the Indianapolis cars which were supposed to challenge Europe's best, it was decided to use the 2.64 mile banked track - simply two heavily banked corners connected by two straights. The D-types with their streamlined, full-width bodywork made a strange contrast to the offset single seater 'Indy' cars, nearly all of which were powered by the legendary 4.2 litre, 4-cylinder twin-ohc Offenhauser engine, and which were about half the weight of the Jaguars. There was a contrast in reliability too - the bumpy surface took its toll of the American cars and but for the race being divided up into three sessions of 166 miles each, which left time for substantial rebuilds in between, the D-types might well have been placed even higher than they were. The New World competitors were enormously impressed, almost awed, by the manner in which the Jaguars had circulated, running strictly to team orders and as regular as clockwork.

But probably the most memorable incident of the day took place at the beginning of the first heat, when Fairman in the fastest Jaguar used the car's four speed gearbox to its full advantage (the Indianapolis cars only had two gears) and accelerated right through the field from the back, and led past the pits at the end of the first lap. As Fairman said as he savoured the moment afterwards:

However, my mild surprise at leading the field was, according to eye witnesses, nothing to compare with

the utter incredulity of the Italians in the stands and the Americans in the pits. Apparently quite a few were speechless as they had been laying bets on whether Jimmy Bryan in the Dean Van Lines Special would be leading Troy Ruttman on the John Zinc Special, or Tony Bettenhausen on the Nova Special. The last thing they expected to see was a shiny blue Jaguar, with no advertisements on its sides, come sweeping into view at the very top of the banking, all on its own, about 150 yards ahead of the next car and going like a dingbat.

A track surface of 128 degrees prevented Fairman keeping up this pace, and the car's lap speeds had to be reduced to a regular 153 - 155 mph to preserve the tyres. Fairman, with John Lawrence and Ninian Sanderson who drove the other two D-types, were feted as much, if not more, than the actual winners when they finished in 4th, 5th and 6th positions. Fairman's average speed had been about 150 mph, which for 500 miles over that bumpy track was no mean feat, especially as two of the cars had already completed at least one Le Mans 24 hour race.

So great had been the impression created amongst the Americans that an invitation to David Murray to actually run at Indianapolis was a distinct possibility, and Briggs Cunningham himself superintended some tests around the famous 'brickyard' towards the end of 1957. Pat O'Conner lapped at 131.965 mph in a D-type, which was only 7 mph down on the 1957 qualifying times. An experienced Indy driver, O'Conner thought that limited chassis changes, bigger tyres and a longer stroke engine (running on alcohol fuel perhaps), could give the D-type "a real good chance". Whether it was with Indianapolis in the back of his mind that David Murray devised, with Brian Lister, the single--seater D-type engined car that Ecurie Ecosse ran in the 1958 'Monzanopolis' it is not possible to know. When built, this car turned out to be slower than a normal D-type however, and Ecurie Ecosse didn't do so well in the 1958 event.

Another Monza exploit took place during 1957, when Captain Ian Baillie of the Life

Guards took his 1955 production D-type (XKD 511, registered TNG 99) there for an attempt on International Class 'C' records. April 12th was selected as the date, "as Queen's Birthday troop drills had not then started", and on a wet and windy morning the run began. Despite the weather conditions all went well, the D-type (standard except for the optional tail fin and a higher rear axle ratio) circulating at a steady 140-142 mph for about an hour and a half, with one stop for checking the tyres. The fastest lap took 1 minute 05.6 seconds, an average of 144.92 mph, and the following records were secured:

50 km	at 140.76 mph
100 km	at 140.95
100 miles	at 140.73
200 km	at 140.82
200 miles	at 137.42
1 hour	140.67 miles covered

For 1958, the Sports Car Constructors' Championship carried a maximum capacity limit of three litres, and this ruling was to effectively ensure that the D-type would never again win a major international motor race; not necessarily because the 3-litre engined D-type wasn't fast enough for long distance racing, but because the car lost one of its greatest attributes - reliability. Two versions of the XK engine were built to meet the new regulations, Jaguar's own 2986 cc unit, and Ecurie Ecosse's bored and stroked 2.4 which displaced 2954 cc.

Neither of these 3-litre engines were successful, which was largely the reason why a D-type Jaguar wasn't even to finish a Le Mans race after the type's final win in 1957. Ninian Sanderson's Ecurie Ecosse car was in the pits by the third lap of the 1958 event, with the piston trouble it had already suffered in practice; he and Lawrence were soon out of the race entirely, to be joined by the car of Fairman and Gregory, damaged pistons being its cause of retirement too. Maurice Charles' ex-Ecosse D-type crashed (XKD 502), and so did Jean—Marie Brussin ('Mary') - the latter fatally after loosing

control of his D-type (XKD 513) under the Dunlop Bridge, where a lot of mud had been washed down across the track.

The rain in fact had come down shortly after 5pm, which was about the time that Duncan Hamilton began a tremendous drive with XKD 610, backed up by Ivor Bueb and attempting a sixth Le Mans win for Jaguar. The car soon lay second behind the leading Testa Rossa Ferrari of Phil Hill and Olivier Gendebien, either a lap or two laps in arrears according to the weather and fuel stops. Hamilton was hoping that the Ferrari's drum brakes would begin to loose their efficiency but in this he was to be disappointed as the rain was helping to cool them. All hopes of even a second place were lost however just after mid-day, when in a blinding rainstorm Hamilton swerved to avoid a Panhard which had stopped in the middle of the road near Arnage. The D-type put a wheel on the grass, spun, and ended upside down across a ditch. Duncan was lucky to escape with his life, though he was in hospital for a week afterwards with severe bruising and a damaged leg.

This accident made even that courageous character realise that one's luck doesn't necessarily last for ever. Up until that time Hamilton had still been achieving a very great measure of success both at home and abroad with his two D-types, but it was obvious that the car was no longer an outright winner in an international event - barring a great stroke of luck at Le Mans. His last big race was the Tourist Trophy at Goodwood, where he shared his D-type with Peter Blond, finishing in 6th position. He had bought XKD 505 which up until then had been retained by the factory as a test car, and it was this that he drove at Goodwood.

It was at the Goodwood meeting that Reg Parnell offered Duncan a few laps during practice in the Aston Martin DBR 1 - a very different car to the D-type as the Jaguar driver recounted in *Touch Wood*:-

The car handled quite differently from a D-type

and I could appreciate why it had performed so well on circuits such as the Nurburgring. The traction was good, and very little steering effort was needed on a corner compared with the D-type. The engine was rough; it lacked the turbine-like sweetness of the Jaguar engine. The brakes were good, but required much more pedal pressure than the 'assisted' discs on the D-type. The five-speed gearbox was pleasant in use. All in all a very good and interestingly designed sports racing car. I do not think it could have been driven on the road as one could drive a D-type, but on the Nurburgring, in a race, it was superb.

The D-type was increasingly meeting its match in cars like the DBR/1, and the Lister-Jaguars were finding no difficulty in vanquishing the Coventry product almost wherever they met. The only factor which might have persuaded Duncan Hamilton not to retire when he did would have been the release of the 'E-type', or rather one of its racing cousins which was under development behind the scenes. But this was not to be.

David Murray too had realised that the D-type's long career was almost at an end, and reluctantly sold all but one of the team's cars, replacing them with Tojeiro and Lister - Jaguars, but it is true to say that the team never aspired to the dizzy heights it attained in 1956 and 1957. Ecurie Ecosse entered their remaining D-type in both the 1959 and 1960 Le Mans races - in 1959 it lay second for a long period and survived until 3 am before retiring, not crankshaft or piston trouble but a warped cylinder head removing it from the list of finishers this time. Equipped with its Appendix C 'boot' the car also retired in the 1960 event with a broken crankshaft, while lying in fifth position after eight hours of racing.

The 1960 Le Mans race also saw the last factory D-type 'variant' appear, an interesting sports racing car which used the essentials of both the D-type and the forthcoming road E-type. Code named E2A, the car was lent by Jaguar to Briggs Cunningham who raced it in the event, driven by Hansgen and Gurney.

With the usual centre monocoque combined with a framework carrying the engine and front suspension, the car featured independent rear suspension of a similar nature to the E-type's, with inboard rear disc brakes too. Race regulations still demanded a 3-litre engine, and an alloy-block, 85 x 88 mm, 2997 cc fuel-injected engine was used, giving the very high output of 293 bhp at 6750 rpm - or rather more brake horsepower than any 3.4 or 3.8 D-type had given at Le Mans in the past. This unit ran with a 10:1 compression ratio and used the 35/40 head, fitted with massive 2 3/32nd inch inlet valves. See Chapter Ten.

Although the car put up the fastest lap in the practice session before the race (at 124.11 mph), in the event itself it suffered a series of misfortunes, and retired. Cunningham took it back to America with him, where it ran equipped with a 3.8 engine and won at Bridgehampton in August 1960, driven by Hansgen, beating a Lister-Jaguar and a 'birdcage' Maserati. It eventually returned to this country and now resides with Guy Griffiths in Gloucestershire.

In Great Britain the D-type was to be a useful contender in club meetings throughout the late fifties, and foremost amongst those who cut their racing teeth on that particular Jaguar was the young, unassuming Jim Clark. The Border Reivers had bought XKD 517, the car prepared by the Murkett brothers for Henry Taylor, and in it they placed the protesting Clark - "I told them it was far too quick for me but they persuaded me to go along to Charterhall one day and try it out. All I did was take it up and down the straight, for the track wasn't even open, and it scared me to death. It was extremely fast and had a beautiful engine."

Clark's first meeting with the D-type was at Yorkshire's Full Sutton, a very fast 3.2 mile airfield circuit, in April 1958. In the first race on the programme for the car, Clark put up a standing lap of 97.4 mph, realised he was far in the lead, and backed off to an extent that all the following laps were slower than the first! The D-type averaged 103.8 mph over its fastest lap in the second race however, which it also won, and gave Clark the distinction of being the first person to lap a British circuit at over 100 mph in a sports car.

XKD 517 (or TKF 9 as it was registered) also travelled to Spa that same year, and Clark, having been taken round the circuit in a Volkswagen by Jack Fairman who "very kindly pointed out all the places where people had been killed", drove the car to 8th place, just behind the said Jack Fairman in his D-type. This of course was the race in which Archie Scott Brown was tragically killed during a titanic battle between his Lister-Jaguar and that of Masten Gregory.

Clark gradually came to have more faith in his capabilities and was soon dicing on more or less even terms with Ron Flockhart and Masten Gregory at Charterhall, where he realised "that I could at least race with people of that stature, driving the D-type on its limit, and still keep up." He also considered that for him, driving the D-type taught him more than an equivalent period spent in Formula Junior racing; and he was a little later to continue Jaguar-powered motoring in HCH 736, the Lister-Jaguar bought by 'the Reivers' to replace the faithful TKF 9 (which now belongs to Bryan Corser).

The Border Reivers team sold its D-type simply because it was no longer fully competitive. Other owners followed suit and as a new decade approached, D-types became a less frequent sight at race meetings, even in 'big car' classes. As even the Lister-Jaguars were being quite outclassed by the much smaller engined Lotuses and suchlike by 1960, the D-type soon afterwards almost completely retired from the active racing scene along with most other big front-engined cars of its generation, and was not to emerge from semi-obscurity until Historic racing ushered in its return to the track.

There had been attempts to keep it competitive however, such as Maurice Charles' experiment in the early sixties with MWS 302, an ex-Ecurie Ecosse car (XKD 502). This he fitted with an independent rear suspension using

parts left over from Jaguar's own E2A competition prototype, but the resultant machine still wasn't particularly fast (it retains this suspension today and is now owned by David Clifford). The D-type did hit the headlines occasionally though - the daily papers took up the story of Mrs Pat Coundley's attempt on a women driver's speed record at the Belgian records week in May 1964, when she drove 2 CPG (the ex-Hamilton, Sargent car, XKD 505) out to Belgium and achieved 161.278 mph. Unfortunately this proved to be .021 mph slower than that claimed by an American woman driving a Studebaker Avanti the previous year! Mrs Coundley (wife of John Coundley) won her class at Brighton the following September however, vanquishing a Ferrari which might have proved a small consolation.

The D-type truly returned to the competition scene when in 1966 the 'Griffiths Formula' came into being, and separate races for sports racing cars of the fifties were organised. Thereafter nurtured by the Historic Sports Car Club, the Historic racing movement flourished and the D-type with it, four or five often being seen on a grid - until history repeated itself and once more Lister-Jaguars and Tipo 61 Maseratis began to take the chief honours.

A big impetus was given to Historic racing by JCB, the giant excavator firm, Anthony Bamford being instrumental in organising the JCB Championship which featured a mixed grid of sports cars and racing cars of a similar era. At first rather in the nature of a supporting event at various race meetings, such was the popularity of these races that the JCB Championship round rapidly became one of the leading attractions on any organiser's programme; JCB rounds have also featured at the British GP and other meetings of the highest importance.

Anthony Bamford himself has a large collection of historic cars, not the least of which being XKD 603, the car in which Ninian Sanderson and John Lawrence came second to the 3.8 litre petrol-injected D-type of Flockhart and Bueb at Le Mans in that great year of 1957. This car ran once again at Le Mans, in 1973; still in its original Ecurie Ecosse flag metallic blue paintwork, it won the magnificent 45 minute historic race which celebrated 50 years of Le Mans that year, driven by Willie Green to a great victory over Ferrari, Aston Martin and Lister-Jaguar opposition. Its speed over the course would, incidentally, have qualified it for the 1973 Le Mans 24-hour race which took place the following weekend!

So the story of the D-type closes - but without a true ending, for although the value of an individual car may now be counted in thousands of pounds (if not tens of thousands), the D-type can still be seen on our circuits in all its glory; and very often it will have been driven to the event by its owner, in the true tradition of a sports racing car that could win Le Mans, but still fulfil its function as ultra-fast transport on the open road.

Chapter Eight   The XK 150

The combination of high speed, very vivid acceleration and safe handling qualities, of which the disc braking is especially praiseworthy, renders the Jaguar a superb super sports car...

W. Boddy
Motor Sport October 1958

...it is true to say of the XK 150S that it is one of those very rare cars in which even fast drivers find a margin of performance at their disposal under almost any conditions

The Motor
August 19 1959

The Jaguar XK 150 was the final expression of the XK sports car. It represents either the pinnacle of development of the XK series, or the spoiling of a near-ideal concept of a sports car which had been born in 1948, according to your view point.

Similarly, there is often a difference of opinion amongst enthusiasts as to whether the XK 150's lines are the ultimate and most beautiful formulation of the XK shape, or its partial ruin by over-bulky modelling of the front wings. Maybe the truth lies somewhere between these two extremes of thought, and while the XK 150's body design is certainly heavier in appearance than that of either the XK 120 or the XK 140, no-one can say that it doesn't carry the 'Lyons Line' in all its elegance - even if some of the XK 120's primitive sleekness was replaced by a dignified rotundity more befitting of middle age. There is no doubt at all however that culminating in the 3.8, triple-carburettor engined 'S' version of 1959, the XK 150 was the fastest production XK ever to leave the factory.

THE XK 150 FIXED-HEAD AND DROP-HEAD COUPES

On its announcement in May 1957, the XK 150 was immediately recognised as being the logical progression from the XK 140 that it was,

rather than a radically new sports car. It incorporated many refinements but underneath its new skin it was essentially the same car. The chassis frame was basically still that of the original XK 120 of 1948 - and like that car's relationship with the Mk V, it was still being shared with a Jaguar saloon, by this time the Mk VIII which had superceeded the Mk VII during 1956. Similar body styles were offered on the XK 150 chassis to those which had been available on the XK 120 and XK 140 ranges, although only the fixed-head and drop-head coupe versions were initially catalogued. The roadster was not announced until March 1958, and then was to remain for export only for a number of months.

Almost too important an advance to be described as a mere 'refinement' was the adoption of disc brakes on the XK 150; at last Jaguars had transferred the fruits of their years of experience with these ultra-efficient brakes on to a road car. Experiments by Jaguar with disc brakes had begun in 1951, when work had commenced with Dunlop to develop a system for the C-type sports racing Jaguar, based on Dunlop's aircraft disc brake. The C-type successfully used its disc brakes at Rheims in 1952, and of course won Le Mans in 1953 similarly equipped. The system was gradually improved during its use on D-type, although it was somewhat simplified before its adoption on road vehicles.

Ironically, it was not Jaguar who first offered the disc brake to the general public in the fifties, three other manufacturers getting into production beforehand with cars which offered this great advance in stopping - Austin Healey with the 100S of 1954/55, Triumph with the TR3 announced in October 1956, and Jensen, whose de luxe version of the 541 equipped with the Dunlop disc brake all round also became available in 1956. When the XK 150 was finally announced, its disc brakes were even then a theoretical optional extra, a basic car having been catalogued with Lockheed two leading shoe drum brakes very similar to the XK 140's; but almost certainly no cars to this specification were made.

Unlike the disc brakes used on the competition C- and D-types, the XK 150's system used a single pair of calipers instead of three to grip the disc, which was of chrome iron and 12 inches in diameter. For a considerable time circular friction pads were to be used which required the dismantling of the individual wheel cylinders whenever the friction material had to be replaced. Front to rear braking bias was governed by the size of the wheel cylinders.

Not having the self-servo effect inherent in the two leading shoe drum brakes, vacuum servo assistance was added to the XK 150's disc brake system; of Lockheed manufacture, it used inlet manifold pressure to produce the vacuum, which gave assistance in proportion to the effort exerted on the brake pedal by the driver - up to a certain point, beyond which all additional effort was provided solely by the driver. A reservoir was included in the vacuum circuit and this allowed two or three assisted applications of the brakes to be made with the engine stopped; in any case, should the vacuum have failed for any reason, the brakes still retained their direct unassisted response to the brake pedal.

The XK 150's handbrake used a separate caliper acting on the rear disc - without servo assistance of course. It was rather notoriously ineffective during the production run of the car although its weakness was aggravated to an extent by the inability of some mechanics and/or owners to hit upon the correct way to adjust it - the linkage needed knowing before it would give its maximum potential efficiency (which was just about 25%!). A fly-off lever inside the car was used to work it.

While the XK 150's brakes may have been drastically different, the new car's suspension was much as the XK 140's, there being no changes in the half-elliptic rear springing or in the torsion bars up at the front. About the biggest change to the XK's suspension was in fact to be the use of Nylon interleaving between the main and second leaves in the road springs, which was adopted throughout the range upon the introduction of the XK 150 Roadster later on.

The XK 140's rack and pinion steering was also retained, with its divided steering column joined by a rubber-bonded universal joint. In an attempt to lessen the amount of kick-back at the wheel over rough surfaces (which had been complained of by some XK 140 owners), not only was the rack mounted via a bonded rubber sandwich to the chassis, but further damping of unwanted feed-back was also given by a section of rubber cushioning at the top of the steering column.

The XK 150's engine was substantially the same unit that had emerged into the limelight in 1948, but incorporating the experience gained through its use in the XK 120, XK 140 and the various saloon cars which had since been marketed - in fact by early 1957, over 65,000 XK engines had already been made. Not to mention lessons hard won on the race track with the C- and D-types. The mounting of the engine in the XK 150 was the same as that of the XK 140, ie further forward in the frame than the XK 120, and initially two power options were available. The standard car was rated at 190bhp, this output coming from the standard XK 140 head (which was the uprated version of the original head used on the 160bhp engine of the XK 120), while a more powerful unit giving 210bhp could be (and usually was) specified as an alternative in the Special Equipment models.

The 210bhp engine used a 'new' cylinder head developed with the aim of producing a similar power output to that given by the C-type head (which had been an option on the later XK 120s, the XK 140 and Mk VII Jaguars), but with the emphasis on an improved performance lower down in the rev. range. This was achieved by using the larger exhaust valves of the C-type head, but retaining the smaller diameter inlet port throat of the standard head.

The smaller diameter of the inlet porting kept the speed of the mixture up at lower rpm, with a consequent improvement in both bmep and torque in the lower speed ranges. As another aid to a more efficient gas flow, the angles of the inlet valves were changed from 30° to 45°, and their faces were made in convex form rather than completely flat as previously.

The result of all this was a cylinder head (commonly referred to as the 'B-type') which gave much the same maximum power as the C-type head, but at the lower rpm of 5,500 instead of 5,750. Even more important, the maximum torque of 216 ft lbs was developed at 3,000rpm, a full 1,000rpm less than with the 'C' head; similarly, the maximum bemp of 155 psi was developed 1,000rpm lower too.

Designed mainly with the Jaguar saloon cars in mind, the new head was intended to give an improved pick-up in top gear and thus provide a more restful performance; about the same acceleration overall was given but it was not necessary to rev. the engine so hard to get it. When driving a car equipped with a B-type head there was little point in taking the revolution counter needle much past the 5,000 rpm mark on the road, whereas for the maximum performance from a 'C' headed car anything up to - and maybe a little beyond - the 5,750rpm mark at the beginning of the rev. counter's red sector could

be used profitably.

No change was made to the camshafts, which remained the same 3/8 inch lift items that were introduced with the 180bhp XK 120 engine; they were in fact to be used in all XK engines from the XK 140 right up to and including the 4.2 engined E types and saloons.

The option of the B-type head on the XK 150 was the biggest change made to the familiar 3442cc XK engine, which otherwise looked much the same under the bonnet; although the inlet manifold was modified, having a separate water gallery running along its top, instead of this being cast integrally as before. Two SU HD6 1¾ inch carburettor were still employed, and a single electric SU petrol pump (apt to play up at times) still brought the petrol from the 14 gallon tank. Sump capacity incidentally was 15 pints, and an interesting 'extra' was a sump guard; this was fitted as standard to cars destined for certain foreign markets where road surfaces were suspect.

The transmission followed the pattern set by the XK 140, with a similar short-shafted Moss gearbox, Borg & Beck 10 inch diameter single plate clutch, and the option of either overdrive or an automatic Borg Warner gearbox of similar pattern to that fitted on the Mk VIII. The standard rear axle ratio when the car was equipped with the Laycock overdrive was, as before, 4.09:1 which gave an overall gearing with overdrive engaged of 3.18:1. The direct top gear was of course 4.09, third 4.95, second 7.16, and first 12.18. When either the non-overdrive or automatic box was fitted, a 3.54 rear axle ratio was supplied. With the manual box this gave the usual direct top, 4.28 in third, 6.20 in second and 10.55 in first gear. The Borg Warner box gave the equivalent gearing of 5.08 to 10.9 in 'intermediate', 8.16 to 17.5 in 'low', and a similar direct gearing to the manual box of 3.54:1. Other final drive ratios in the Salisbury range were occasionally supplied to special order.

Road wheel options were as for the XK 140 -

either steel disc wheels, 16 inches diameter by 5½ inches rim width, (in which case spats were fitted over the rear wheels), or the far more common 54- or 60-spoke wire wheels, 16 inches in diameter but only 5 inches rim width, fitted on splined hubs with knock-off eared hub caps. The 60-spoke wheels were standardised in June 1958 on wire-wheeled cars. Dunlop Road Speed 6.00 x 16 tyres were standard equipment, often supplied with white walls for the North American market in the fashion of the two previous models. Further adornments for the disc-wheeled car were available in the form of Rimbellishers, which were offered by the factory as an 'extra'.

Dimensionally, the XK 150 was almost exactly the same as the XK 140 in its external measurements, and the basic method of construction was also similar, two box section steel sills running between the two halves of the body beneath the doors, and steel being used for all the bodywork except for the bonnet and bootlid, which remained in aluminium.

Viewed directly from the front or from the rear, the new sports car very much resembled the 'Mk 1' Jaguar saloon, and, when it appeared at the end of the decade, the Mk 11 saloon even more so - to the extent that it is often hard to tell which is approaching beyond a certain distance. This was partially due to the fact that the XK 150's grille had reverted to the thin slats of the XK 120 design, although it was considerably wider than the XK 120's 'mouth' in order to alleviate any possibility of overheating in equatorial climes. The width of the new grille was carried over in the bonnet shape which still opened in alligator fashion but allowed a better access to the machinery underneath.

While the XK 150 carried the purposeful bumpers of the XK 140, the straight line of the XK 140's front parking defence was relieved under the XK 150's grille by a semi-circular depression, which was a definite aesthetic improvement. A chrome strip ran down the centre of the bonnet, and a Jaguar mascot became

available for the first time on an XK - when specified it came with a chrome moulding for the top of the bonnet which matched the similar moulding on the bootlid.

The rear of the car was tidied-up by the use of a completely 'wrap-round' bumper (in place of the quarter-bumpers of the XK 140) a la Mk 1 saloon, and the chromework on the boot was somewhat increased in area. The XK 150's rear light units were of a larger size than previously too.

Finally, gone was the XK's distinctive divided windscreen, replaced by a modern curved screen of toughened glass. It was mounted on a rather higher scuttle than that of the XK 140, and it is this combined with the car's high waist line - the front wing line was continued to the rear of the car as before but at almost the same level as the top of the rear wing which it met - that is the chief reason for the heavier appearance of the XK 150. But the greater amount of room inside made this slight sacrifice in looks more than worthwhile for most.

This extra space was provided where it was most wanted - at shoulder level, where the extra four inches made the car feel a lot bigger inside and made a genuine contribution to comfort. However, the raised scuttle line didn't exactly further forward visibility, and sitting back in the large and comfortable leather seats, one is inclined to get a feeling of consciously peering over a ledge.

As in the XK 140, two occasional seats were provided in the rear of the car which were ideal for smaller children, one adult sitting across, or as extra luggage space. A hinged lid again allowed access to the boot from the interior of the car, or for carrying such lengthy items as golf clubs. There was a revolution inside so far as the trim was concerned - for the first time on fixed-head or drop-head XK, a wooden facia and door cappings were absent. In place of figured walnut was leather - the instrument panel was set into a panel of padded leather, and the same material covered the entire facia and doors. A contrasting colour was used for the instrument panel - sometimes a light shade was chosen and this was inclined to get very grubby after a while. The instruments themselves, and the layout of the minor controls, were much as on previous models, with the starter button still separated from the ignition switch. The top of the facia was covered by a sponge-padded roll of leather, and the interior driving mirror was now roof mounted - taking advantage of the XK 150's larger rear window.

Heating and ventilation followed that of the XK 140, and so gradually began to fall behind the times, these aspects of creature comfort having been the subject of much research on the continent and in America by the time the XK 150 was announced. The scuttle ventilators and 'extractor' rear side windows were the chief suppliers of fresh air, but by the end of the XK 150's production run, face-level ventilation was being offered in other advanced grand touring cars.

The XK 150 had the short, stubby gearlever of its predecessors, and the overdrive on cars so equipped was cut in and out through a switch mounted on the right hand side of the facia (on rhd cars); indicators on earlier XK 150s were operated from the top centre of the dashboard but later were controlled by a stalk to the right of the steering column, which was a little more in keeping with the times, although unfortunately the stalk didn't move with the adjustable steering column and so was not always within easy finger tip reach from the big four-spoke 17 inch diameter steering wheel. The quadrant control of the automatic transmission cars was positioned on the facia, its lever having a horizontal movement.

The usual pleated leather upholstery covered the seats, which still didn't have back tilt adjustment. Wider than the XK 140's by about ½ inch they were still poor from the point of view of lateral support and inhibited fast cornering to a certain extent. They hinged forward to allow entry into the rear occasional seats. Interestingly, competition bucket seats were still offered as an alternative by the factory although

they were rarely to be seen. Some owners did however opt for various proprietry seats such as the expensive and fully adjustable Reutter seats - which were a factory optional extra for the Mk VIII but not for the XK 150. Generous map-pockets for both driver and passenger were included in the trim panel on each door, plus pull-out ashtrays, and arm rests/door pulls. In common with the XK 140, the doors themselves had no check straps.

Similar in capacity to the XK 140's, the XK 150's boot area was shallow but quite long with the spare wheel and tools being stored under the lift-out floor section. In early cars the boot lid prop took valuable room, but later cars had a strutless sprung bootlid. The catches operated by the bootlid handle could occasionally play up, resulting in a corner not closing properly. The XK 150 also had the locking petrol filler flap (which used the glove compartment key) of the earlier cars, with most of the attendant minor irritations too; it was also criticised because of the slow rate of filling, and an occasional smell of petrol inside the car when the tank was full.

The aforegoing description applies broadly to both the fixed-head and the drop-head models; the latter's folding top had the same smooth look of the XK 140's when erected, and its operation was similarly an easy one-man operation. Like Jaguar's previous drop-head models, it was also fully headlined inside, with the outer material being mohair. A hood envelope enhanced the neat appearance of the hood when it was down. One of the few distinguishing features of the XK 150 Drop-head inside was its anodised aluminium dash panel in place of the fixed-head's leather finish.

Notwithstanding the many improvements embodied in his new sports car, Sir William Lyons had endeavoured to keep any increase in price over the superceded XK 140 to a minimum. The Special Equipment versions rose by only £46, and the standard cars by £35 - thus the Special Equipment fixed-head coupe was £1,969 (inclusive of PT), and the standard version £1,793 upon introduction. Needless to say, it was the typical Jaguar policy of long production runs that enabled the company to offer so much for so little - few, if any, other sports cars dating from 1948 were still in production in 1957. Automatic transmission added £192 to the price of any car, overdrive £67, and a radio about £35.

Weight had risen somewhat however, for both bodywork versions. The fixed-head coupe weighed fractionally under 29cwt ready for the road, and the drop-head coupe - the heaviest XK to be made - was 29½cwt. This represented an increase of just on one hundredweight over the equivalent XK 140 models. Frontal area had also gone up from 17.5 sq ft to 18.2 sq ft. This had the effect of slightly reducing the XK 150's maximum speed compared to that of the XK 140, but on the other hand the acceleration of the new car was generally better due probably to the B-type head.

THE XK 150 ON ROAD TEST

There was no independent road test of the 190bhp car from which it is possible to quote (in any case very few were made), but *The Autocar* tried an XK 150 Special Equipment 210bhp Fixed-head Coupe in February 1958. The top speed of VDU 882 (as it was registered) was found to be 123mph in overdrive top, some 6mph slower than the Special Equipment XK 140 tested by the same magazine at the end of 1955. On the other hand, acceleration from a standing start to 60mph was, at 8.5 seconds, a big improvement over the XK 140's 11 seconds. Top gear acceleration also benefitted from the B-type head's beefy low speed torque, and the XK 150 reached 50mph from 30mph in 6.3 seconds, 1.1 seconds faster than its predecessor. The new sports car also passed the now traditional test which the motoring press delighted in setting the XK, that of starting from rest in top gear. In this manner it reached 100mph in 36.4 seconds, or 8.2 seconds quicker than when

The Motor tried the same feat with its original XK 120 Roadster.

Speeds in the gears at the permitted maximum rpm of 5,500 were 91, 62 and 33mph; first gear was obviously thought to be a little low but the speed range in second usefully extended to 58mph, there being little benefit in holding on to it past that figure. While there was a noticeable gap between 1st and 2nd gears, 3rd was so close to top that it was quite possible to cruise happily along at about 70mph and think that the car was in top! The gear change itself came in for the usual criticism: "The movement between the ratios is sweet, but the synchromesh mechanism on the car tested was scarcely adequate. In order to engage a gear silently with the car stationary it was necessary fully to depress the clutch pedal, which has a long travel."

The overdrive with which the test car was fitted was thought to be "worth every penny of its cost". A slight lag was sometimes noted before it cut in (not an unusual feature this), but the unit on VDU 882 engaged very smoothly - although this varied slightly from car to car. The extra gear also brought superlatively easy high speed cruising to the XK 150, and *The Autocar* found a comfortable gait on suitable roads to be 110-115 mph. As with the XK 140, it was impossible to achieve maximum engine revolutions in overdrive top - its mph per thousand rpm in that ratio was 25.1. At a leisurely 4,500rpm the car would settle down at an easy 112mph or so.

The Autocar approved of the new one-piece curved windscreen which provided "excellent visibility with little interference from the side pillars", and although no distortion was noticed where the glass was curved, reflections from the dashboard were a distraction; there was also the annoyance of the wiper blades lifting off the screen at speed - and in any case they didn't sweep the curved area.

Heating and ventilation marginally passed muster and it was noted that the car was surprisingly free from wind noise when motoring with the window open, a pleasant feature on a hot day which certainly helps make the XK 150 more habitable.

Other minor drawbacks concerned the doors. A consistent source of complaint by users of all types of XK at home and abroad, they had a tendency to foul the kerb when they were opened, and *The Autocar* noted that clearance at the tip on level ground was only some 9 inches with car unladen. This was decreased to as little as 3 inches when the camber of the road was combined with the weight of the crew.

Needless to say the new disc brakes came in for high praise. "Their behaviour is superb, and the fade free retardation always available permits an experienced driver to travel very quickly with confidence" was the magazine's verdict. The progressive action of the brakes and the light pedal pressures needed to operate them were all much appreciated, and the only criticism of the system concerned the handbrake with its auxiliary pads:

"Their power was not up to the high standard of the footbrakes, (and) even when applied hard, they would not hold the car on a steep gradient."

The Autocar was not all that explicit when it came to discussing the XK 150's handling though one learns that it did not suffer from roll or pitch (the former point is maybe arguable), that the wet road grip was good, and that too much right foot would break the tail away "but the driver senses that the car, correctly handled, will take care of him." The driving position found favour, with the adjustable steering column, upright seat squab and generous amount of seat adjustment travel tailoring the car to suit the needs of almost every driver. Some feed-back from the road was felt through the steering wheel but the various layers of rubber were obviously fulfilling their function as it was not thought to be disturbing. "First class", "positive", and "reasonably light" were the words and phrases used to describe the action of the steering's rack and pinion, with an "immediate response to the driver's move-

ments". Self centering action was slight at low speeds, and at high velocities "the directional stability adds to the crew's confidence." No detailed comment was offered on the chassis engineering, which by European standards was becoming a little dated for a fast and luxurious GT car, beyond the statement that Continental pave caused no discomfort even with the tyres inflated at high speed pressures.

Competition to the XK 150 in Europe was in fact scattered and much more expensive. Only the exotica could equal or better its straight line performance - the Mercedes Benz 300SL at £4,651, the BMW 507 at £4,201, and of course the products stemming from Modena - while none could consistently out-brake it. In great Britain, the lingering Allard Palm Beach (with its optional XK engine, the only road going non-Jaguar allowed by Lyons to use his engine), the fabulous expensive Frazer-Nash 'Continental' model (at £3,751), and the Aston Martin DB2/4 Mk 11 (at £2,889) were among the few vehicles which could possibly be labelled as rivals to the XK.

In the United States, the horse-power race was in full swing with the big American manufacturers producing bigger, faster and even more under-braked expressions of what they thought the sportier section of the US car buying public wanted. From a standing start acceleration point of view a number of these monsters could see off an XK 150 with ease in 1957 - the Studebaker Golden Hawk saloon in supercharged form were credited with 275bhp and a 0-60mph time of 7.4 seconds, which was probably quicker than either of the only two home-produced automobiles which might be vaguely described as 'sports cars' - the Corvette and the Thunderbird.

But inspite of the cheapness of these cars on their home market (they were often priced at several hundred pounds less than the Jaguar sports car), the old maxim that to the American the only sports car is an imported sports car held good; and anyway, straight line acceleration figures are a poor guide when it comes to assessing a motor car. The XK 150 could probably out-handle most American cars and could unquestionably out-brake the best of them in 1957; and in any case there would have been little difficulty in selling every XK that could be made and shipped across on sheer looks alone. Jaguar, MG and Triumph had already carved out a very substantial niche in the North American market, and the XK 150 more than kept up the momentum set in motion by the XK 140, and the XK 120 before that. The American economic recession of early 1958 had little or no effect on Jaguar's sales in the States.

THE XK 150 S AND ROADSTER

But Heynes and Jaguar's small engineering team had no intention of allowing the XK 150's edge over its competitors in the realm of performance to be eroded, and at the beginning of 1958, the 'S' engine became available, at first only in the XK 150 Roadster which had finally been released.

It is possible that the announcement of the roadster version of the XK 150 had been delayed by the great fire at the Jaguar works in February 1957, which certainly had a far reaching effect on the company's racing programme (see Chapter 7), and production generally for a while. Damage estimated at some £3½ million pounds was done, but fortunately the machine shops and engine assembly line had been spared - it was mainly the service, trimming and testing areas that had been gutted so at least nothing was destroyed that was not almost immediately replaceable. Everyone rallied round to help with the rebuilding, which was started within 48 hours of the fire-brigade leaving. Limited production was under way within nine days, and six weeks after the fire it was back to normal, a tribute to the workforce and Jaguar's component suppliers alike.

But when the 'S' specification became an option of the XK 150, customers could obtain an extremely useful increase in performance over the standard versions of the car. The extra brake horsepower came largely from a new cylinder head, engineered - naturally - by Harry Weslake. It was developed using his favourite methods of working which included the extensive use of flow tests, whereby wooden or aluminium mock-ups of the head under development were made and the air flow through their porting and valve arrangements carefully measured, before and after alterations to the porting and manifolding. Highly accurate 'male' cores were then taken from the final model, and given to the pattern maker who prepared his core boxes from which the production castings were made. All this had to be done to the highest standards of accuracy of course.

The new Jaguar head was to become known as the "straight port head", a slight misnomer but indicating the biggest change which had been made - the partial straightening of the ports, which was found to produce a better flow of mixture at high rpm.

In order to take advantage of this, the 'S' engine was given an extra carburettor, and in fact all three SU carburettors that were now fitted to the XK 150S went up in size from 1¾ inch to 2inch. They were mounted on an entirely new manifold built up in three sections, each carburettor feeding two tracts which separated and led direct to one inlet port; the design was such that all tracts were of equal length, thus ensuring the same ram effect at each inlet valve. This science was continued in the three carburettors' intakes, where air trumpets of optimum length breathed in a steel-mesh air silencer.

The standard compression ratio of the 'S' engine was 9:1, and complimentary modifications to the rest of the engine included lead-bronze bearings in the main and big-ends, a stronger clutch assembly, and a lighter flywheel.

It was intended that the new cylinder head would appear with the 3.8 litre version of the XK engine that was under development, but as this larger version wasn't ready, the XK 150S first appeared with the normal 3442 cc capacity. The new engine was rated at 250 bhp at 5,500 rpm, with a torque figure of 240 lb ft at 4,500 rpm - compared to the standard XK 150's 210 bhp at the same rpm and 216 lb ft at 3,000 rpm. Twin SU petrol pumps now supplied the carburettors.

An important improvement that was announced simultaneously with the new roadster model concerned the XK 150's brakes. These were now given the square, quick-change brake pads which had been developed on the D-type. Changing of the friction material now became a job of minutes and there was no need to bleed the brakes afterwards because the hydraulic system was not interfered with at all; it was simply a case of extracting the old pads and pushing new ones in.

There was no surprise when it was known that the new 'S' engine and the latest body style, the roadster, was to be available only overseas. In the States, the XK 150 Roadster cost 5,020 dollars with the 'S' engine, although it could also be ordered with either of the previous two optional power outputs of 190bhp or 210bhp. Borg Warner automatic transmission could be fitted to the roadster if one of the two less powerful engines were specified, but on the XK 150S Roadster (and on the other 'S' models that were to follow) the transmission was strictly manual gearbox with overdrive - the lever for which was placed near the gearlever, operating the unit manually (this arrangement also became optional on the other XK 150s).

The XK 150 Roadster followed the concept of its XK 120 ancestor as closely as it could. Inside, there were no occasional seats and the rear tonneau panel was brought forward to end just short of the driver's and passenger's seat backs, allowing enough room for the much improved (both in looks and in function) single-thickness mohair hood to fold down neatly out of sight. Stowed thus, there were special straps to stop it rattling, and the aperture between the tonneau panel and the seat backs was hidden by a neat cover which snapped in

place over the top.

The more sporty type of driver looked askance at the car's wind-up windows, which disappeared into the doors and which some thought rather inappropriate on a roadster. There was even a chrome plated ledge along the top of the doors - supplemented by the chrome 'S' motif when the straight-port head was fitted - and of course the car wore the single piece, non-detachable windscreen of the other XK 150 variants.

Road & Track magazine tried an XK 150S Roadster soon after the type had become available in the United States during 1958. The car was certainly the quickest XK they had ever tested, as it reached 60mph in 7.3 seconds, 100mph in 21.4 seconds, and had a top speed of 136mph. Bearing in mind the growing number of very powerful American cars that were being made during the escalation of the horse-power race in that country, *Road & Track's* comments on the car's speed are interesting!

Upper limit speed runs in high performance automobiles are always memorable in one way or another, some good, some bad - some downright dangerous. At high speeds however, the XK 150S was superb - one felt that it had been designed expressly for this purpose, and was performing easily and under perfect control.

The steering of the roadster was rated "superb" too though kick-back on rough surfaces was still making itself felt; "hard cornering produced very little roll' but in common with many keen XK 150 owners, *Road & Track* immediately put the XK's tyre pressures up to the recommended high speed setting of 30lbs front, 35lbs rear, which cut out the squeal associated with the softer 23/26 setting.

The increasingly civilised nature of the latest XK was looked upon with mixed feelings by the magazine. While not lamenting "the passing of the former drafty and leaky side curtains...the wind up windows do seem a little incongruous in a roadster." Also, "The 4 inch gain in width at shoulder height adds considerably to riding comfort, but it is all too evident from outside the car, and causes the rakish front and rear fender line that distinguished the previous XK models to be all but lost." Interior comforts were commented on as follows: "The leather seats are individually adjustable over a considerable range and are very comfortable, though a little deeper shaping in the backs would have given us better lateral support. Inside appointments include a tiny, and all but useless, open glove box in front o f the driver, and another, with a locking lid but equally tiny, at the other end of the instrument panel."

The trusty old gearbox was thought to have an easier and smoother action than previous XK Jaguars tested, but this might very well have been a matter of chance, as the box could vary from car to car for no apparent reason.

The separate body/chassis construction was a long way from becoming dated in America, but scuttle shake on the XK 150 was noticed by *Road & Track* on very rough roads. Though as the magazine said, this appeared to be "one of the penalties of open body construction - every American convertible we have driven has displayed the same fault."

Naturally the roadster's brakes received full marks, being described as "powerful, light and sensitive, and seem entirely immune to fade." Fuel consumption did not seem much worse than previous XK 150s, ranging from 14-19mph. The car generally was rated by *Road & Track* as still the best all-round value in its branch of the sports car field, despite its "certain minor faults."

In Great Britain meanwhile, motoring journalists were still sampling the 210bhp XK 150 Coupe, William Boddy in particular penning a very objective report in *Motor Sport* dated October 1958, in which the vices and virtues of the XK 150 were well set out.

"There is no question," said Mr Boddy of the overdrive fixed-head coupe which he tried, "but that the Jaguar provides very real high speed performance, not only in respect of a maximum speed exceeding 125mph, but because roadholding, steering and braking are in keeping." Clubroom accounts of creditable journey times being no excuse for exaggeration where the driver of an XK 150 is concerned."

The editor of *Motor Sport* was of the opinion that the XK 150's engine could almost be said to make the car, and he was as ever deeply impressed by its flexibility, depths of reserve, and "lazy power" which put the Jaguar "amongst the very fastest cars in the land." However, there were areas where he felt that the XK 150 did not quite reach the heights of perfection for a top GT car:

Indeed, in matters of detail the Jaguar disappoints, because there are items which seem to lack the touch of experienced drivers in the planning of this fast coupe. The seats, for example, are deep and luxuriously upholstered but the driver would appreciate more support from cushion and squab, and on the test car the seat was insecure in its slides. The pedals are biased to the right, so that the driving position is not entirely natural, while so low is the seat that the driver of average height can only just see both front wings.

The steering wheel rim is conveniently thin but not sweat-proof. Below it on the right extends a stalk for operating the self-cancelling direction flashers; this might be placed slightly higher up the column, a shade nearer the wheel.

The doors tended to bounce open unless slammed shut and, open, foul high kerbs. Curiously, they lack 'keeps'. The luggage boot is roomy if shallow and there is access to it from within the car, although small objects stowed thus soon slide inaccessibly to the back of the boot. The boot lid locks and has a self-propping strut, but it tended not to shut, one corner sticking open. The spare wheel lives below the luggage, under the floor.

Behind the seats, which possess folding squabs, are two (very) occasional seats, useful only for very abbreviated children. Occasionally petrol fumes made the interior of the car objectionable, usually after a spit back from a cold engine. The accelerator action tended towards jerky running when opening up from low speeds. The doors have quarter windows. When fully open, that on the driver's side tended to remove skin from the knuckles of the right hand as the steering wheel was turned, while dazzle from the sun on the plated beading along the base of the instrument panel occured under certain conditions - minor criticisms, but ones which bear out our statement that as a connoisseur's fast car the Jaguar can be disappointing. The main windows require just over four turns, fully up to fully down. Additional ventilation is provided by toggles enabling the back windows to be slightly opened, and two scuttle ventilators, operated by levers in front of the door openings, are also provided. All this ventilation is a good thing, because the gearbox gets quite hot and blows warm air up its gaited lever.

Of the XK 150's steering, Boddy found that inspite of the factory's efforts to damp it out, some kick-back was still present. That he also found the steering "spongy" must have meant that the various layers of rubber had at the same time placed a little too much insulation between the driver and the road. Accurate at speed, the steering was found to be heavy during parking manoeuvres and never really light even at speed, this also being apportioned to the strong castor action "which spins the wheel through the fingers after a corner." The car's turning circle was a small 33 feet, with a lock to lock movement of the wheel of 2¾ turns.

While the XK 150's suspension "effectively kills road shocks" the age of the car's basic design was at last becoming apparent: "..there is a sense of vintage style flexibility about the chassis and although not normally noticeable, over really rough or ripply surfaces the back axle makes it presence felt, reminder that the action of the rear wheels is not independent... The hypercritical may perhaps feel that the Jaguar chassis is not so advanced as the splendid power unit."

With this last sentiment Jaguar would have undoubtedly agreed if obvious commercial reasons had not prevented them from official comment, as already the completely independently sprung successor to the XK 150 had been built in prototype form and was undergoing secret testing on the open road. On balance William Boddy liked the XK 150's behaviour: "In general, however, the XK 150 handles splendidly, especially in the hands of big-boned, bowler-hatted Britishers. The Dunlop RS4 Road Speed tyres do not protest audibly under rapid cornering, and the car feels safe up to its very high maximum speed."

Full marks were awarded to the disc brakes, and they were compared with the best drum brakes for feel - "until the user gets back into a drum-braked vehicle, when he immediately awards the Jaguar very high marks." They were prone to a "horrid squeal" under light pedal pressures though on *Motor Sport's* car. The much-maligned handbrake must have been properly adjusted on this occasion, because although heavy to use it was found to be "absolutely effective."

In October 1958, sterling prices were quoted by Jaguar for the XK 150 Roadster, the car becoming available on the home market for the first time. The standard car cost £1,292 basic (£1,457 with all extras), or with purchase tax, £1,939 (£2,186 with extras). At the 1958 Motor Show however, it was an XK 150 Special Equipment Fixed-head Coupe that took its place on the Jaguar stand, next to the newly announced Mk lX saloon - which featured the 3.8 XK engine for the first time in a production Jaguar. For the company, 1958 had been a successful year especially on the export market, where 54% of production had gone during the 12 month period. Also, a 42% increase in Continental sales were recorded over the previous best in 1957, and no less than 22 million dollars worth of business had been done in North America. These statistics represented a doubling of Jaguar's profits for the year ending July 1958 - the actual total was £1,665,039.

During the first few months of 1959, it was announced by the factory that the 'S' engine option was now to be available on the drop-head and fixed-head coupes as well as on the open two seater; and that the Dunlop disc brakes were now a standard fitment throughout the range - as they had been in practice ever since the production of the XK 150 began in 1957. Prices for the 'S' versions of the fixed-head coupe and roadster were £2,187, and the most expensive of the Jaguar sports car range, the XK 150S Drop-head Coupe, cost £2,217 (all figures include purchase tax).

So far as the 250bhp 'S' version of the XK 150 was concerned, *The Motor* was one of the first British journals to test one, after it was made available in the home country from March 1959. Again, it was a fixed-head coupe (XDU 984), seemingly the only body style Jaguar released for a full scale road-test in Britain.

The XK 150S's performance was immediately compared to that of the C-type Jaguar which the magazine had tested in 1952. To the astonishment of *The Motor's* staff, "this everyday motorcar...with complete closed-car comfort and amenities" was very nearly as fast as the stark, open, aero-screened sports racing car of seven years ago. In fact, the acceleration figures of the two cars up to 100mph were virtually identical, the XK 150S reaching the 'ton' in 20.3 seconds, the C-type in 20.1 seconds; while to 60mph, the fixed-head coupe was actually quicker, if only by .3 of a second. Both cars returned the identical standing quarter mile time of 16.2 seconds, and when respective flexibility was examined, it was found that thanks to the overdrive XK 150's 4.09 axle and increased low speed torque, the road car was much quicker in top gear acceleration runs than the racer - 30 - 50mph took the XK 150 6.1 seconds, and the C-type 7.2 seconds, while the XK 150S knocked even more off the C-type's time over the 80 - 100mph increment, which it covered in 7.4 seconds as opposed to other's 9.2 seconds. As a further indication of the big boost in mid-range torque given by the new cylinder head, the standard XK 150 took 6.2 and 10.2 seconds respectively to bridge those same speeds in top gear.

The 132mph (mean) top speed of the XK 150S was also thought to be outstanding by *The Motor,* approaching as it did within 11mph or so of the C-type's maximum, despite such wind-catching encumbrances as bumpers, spotlights and full width windscreen. "If the truth of the time-worn tag about the racing car of today being the touring car of tomorrow ever needed proving, these two tests supply all the evidence

necessary" declared the writer.

In view of the prolonged high speed motoring which the test would involve, Jaguar offered to fit the optional R3 racing tyres to the XK 150S; but *The Motor* staffmen elected to run on the normal Dunlop RS4 tyres being of the opinion that "the car should be driven in the condition in which it is normally sold." Pressures were put right up to 40 lbs front, 45 lbs rear however for the duration of the performance testing on the continent, which was a good 10 lbs higher than the normal high speed touring pressure but was recommended by both tyre and car manufacturer.

While this extra inflation of the tyres was primarily to prevent overheating of the covers by undue flexing at near the maximum speed of the car, surprisingly perhaps the ride remained comfortable, even over cobblestones, and also helped keep the car "beautifully steady" on high speed bends - confirming the experience of most people who drove the XK 150 far and fast. As the test team remarked, "this car is remarkably well sprung for comfort, and low tyre pressures tended to both reduce the responsiveness of the steering and increase the effort required. At 'fast driving' pressures, both handling and comfort reached a very high standard. Corners can be taken fast without appreciable roll and whilst the 150S is not, perhaps, so 'tidy' as one or two quite exceptional sports cars we have tried, when cornered near the limit, it nevertheless displays cornering qualities which are very much above average and has no unexpected vices to catch the unwary." Although the car would have had little excuse if it had given a poor ride, in view of the fact that its kerb weight was now 29cwt, or 'as tested' with two up, 32½cwt - figures which were virtually identical to the full four seater, automatic 3.4 saloon of the period!

But the heavy, cart sprung rear axle was beginning to feel the effects of engine development, and *The Motor* noticed that axle patter could be induced both on hard acceleration from rest, or out of slow corners. As for wet road cornering, it was remarked that "the vast power naturally needs to be used with some discretion." There *The Motor* left the subject, but although the XK 150S was pretty well as controllable as its less powerful sister in the wet, with a sliding tail being amenable to correction - or even to holding at an angle if the driver was brave enough and clever enough to arrive at the correct balance between throttle and steering - the limited slip differential which was an option (at £45) did make things slightly more difficult - although initially providing extra grip on a wet corner, it was now possible to get *both* rear wheels to spin if too much throttle was applied on the exit, with a consequent reduction in the grip available for lateral location of the rear wheels on the road surface, the 'safety valve' of the spinning inside wheel no longer being operative.

Apart from the very high power output, there was otherwise little indication of the XK 150S's relatively high state of tune. It was found that 100 octane fuel was essential if the plugs were not to be 'cooked', but otherwise, the engine started easily on its automatic cold starting device (which cut out at about a water temperature of 30° C), and remained "beautifully smooth, flexible and quiet (with only a pleasantly restrained exhaust note when working really hard)".

Like its forebears, the XK 150S produced its performance on what was relatively very little petrol, considering the engine size and the car's weight. *The Motor* recorded an overall fuel consumption of 18.6 mpg for its 2,632 mile test, and this included the performance testing programme and much high speed continental cruising. The computed "touring" consumption was a fairer indication of the car's thirst under average conditions of use, at 22mpg. Many owners consistently bettered 20mpg, and really gentle driving using the overdrive whenever practical could produce 24 or 25mpg - with the XK still keeping ahead of most traffic. Even at a constant 100mph in overdrive top, 18.5 miles were obtained from each gallon of petrol by the 'S' model. These consumption figures were not much worse than the standard 210bhp XK 150, which could better them only by about 2mpg.

It is however, even more startling to compare XK 150S petrol consumption with that of the very first XK, the aluminium bodied roadster which the same journal tried at the end of 1949. Witness the petrol consumption at a steady 100mph for that car - HKV 455 could only manage 13mpg! In fact the earlier XK had to reduce speed to 70mph before it could achieve 18.5mpg, and at that speed, the XK 150S in overdrive was returning an easy 25.5mpg. "Moderate" driving over a distance brought an overall fuel consumption of 19.8mpg to the original XK 120 driver, but a similar mode of driving behind the wheel of an XK 150S produced around 22mpg - and with quite an increase in average speed. Considering the great increase in weight which the XK 150 had to carry (29cwt kerb, as opposed to the XK 120's 25½cwt), and the 1959 car's greater frontal area, this was an achievement indeed by Heynes and Weslake.

Predictably, the XK 150's gearbox was "the least pleasing feature of the car and cannot be regarded as reaching the very high standard of the car", all the usual old faults being there. Some of the pleasure of driving the XK 150S was also nullified by the unprogressive and jerky operation of the throttle - the extra carburettor had complicated the linkage somewhat and it was now difficult to get the XK off the mark smoothly.

A further re-occuring criticism of the XK that appeared in *The Motor's* road test too was that of driver location on the wide, almost bench-type seats. But then, this was a feature of many cars of that period, although maybe it wasn't quite so forgiveable in a vehicle with the cornering potential of the XK 150. While visibility was generally rated by the magazine as excellent, support was given to Bill Boddy's observations on the subject by the fact that it was reckoned that the driver had to be average to tall in order to see both front wing tips; the length of the "long high bonnet" took some getting used to as well by newcomers to the car.

The servo-assisted 12 inch disc brakes easily coped with the extra power given by the straight-port engine. "Not only are they powerful, light and sensitive, but they remain so after repeated applications from high speeds so that a driver in a hurry on winding or congested roads can use the car's performance without fear of brake fade."

Gone were the delayed-fade traumas experienced by XK 120 and XK 140 drivers under similar circumstances - no more did large lorries or sharp corners loom menacingly, with brakes under the XK driver's foot that appeared to have been injected with grease! But nothing had been done about the handbrake with the coming of the XK 150S, which was still "scarcely as powerful as one could desire."

One small touch that was appreciated by *The Motor* was the car's comprehensive tool kit, stowed with the spare wheel under the boot floor. It had remained much the same since the days of the XK 120, and in actual fact the quantity and quality of its contents were very similar to that supplied with the big pre-war SS Jaguar saloon, a remarkable hangover from a different era that Jaguar were to adhere to for some considerable time yet. The kit consisted of: adjustable spanner, 6 box spanners, sparking plug box spanner, 2 tommy bars, 4 open-ended spanners, jack and lever, wheelbrace, pliers, copper and rawhide mallet (supplied with wire wheel cars, for the knock-off wheel spinners), screwdriver, grease gun, tyre gauge, feeler gauge, distributor screwdriver, valve timing gauge, brake bleeder and container, and a valve extractor. Quite an impressive collection!

The Autocar tried the same XK 150S (XDU 984) some few months after it had been through *The Motor's* hands, and its report generally substantiated all the latter's enthusiastic observations on the car. Although top gear acceleration times proved that XDU 984 had lost nothing in the way of tune, *The Autocar* didn't get it off the line quite so quickly which resulted in a gain of 1 second in the time the car took to reach 60mph, and 2 seconds to 100mph. The performance was still revelled in though. At 5,500rpm, the beginning of the red section on the tachometer, the speeds obtainable in the gears were 33mph in first, 59mph in second, 86mph in third, and 111mph in direct top; with overdrive switched in the car's maximum speed was 134mph mean, which was 13.5mph faster than the standard 210bhp XK 150 tested by the magazine. Those were some of the statistics - here is the way *The Autocar* described how it actually felt: "This is a driver's car in all respects, yet the engine's exceptional flexibility makes it also a splendid ladies' town carriage. Regard the performance data, which, in stark printing ink, fail miserably to convey the sheer thrill of the real thing. When 136mph was achieved, even the Continental autoroute seemed to have exchanged its curves for corners. Indeed, at one stage the observer ensconced himself in the rear compartment and happily photographed the speedometer needle at its exciting limit: 140 mph (136 true speed). Even then the engine was turning at a modest 5,100 rpm - well within its 6,000 rpm limit."

The Autocar did detect occasional signs of an ageing design however - not only in the gearbox, but in the chassis too. While the magazine was of the opinion that the limited slip differential fitted helped to limit axle hop, this unwanted oscillation of the rear axle did occur when the car was accelerated hard out of a slow corner in second gear. "In this respect alone does the increased power output appear to be getting ahead of the basically unchanged chassis design" said the writer. But by and large, the original XK 120 suspension was still providing an acceptable standard of ride and handling judged by the yardstick of the late 1950s.

John Bolster, the first British journalist to test an XK 150S, had expressed similar findings when he had road tested VDU 984 for *Autosport* in June 1959:

If the XK 150S is regarded as an ultra-high speed touring car, it can be said to approach perfection. If it is handled fiercely, as a sports car, however, it is perhaps open to some slight criticism. There is no synchromesh on bottom gear, and if the up changes are hurried at all, the synchromesh on the other three speeds may very easily be beaten.... The acceleration figures are, of course, stupendous, and were no doubt aided by the optional limited slip differential. Even so, rear axle tramp can be induced if the full power is applied on bottom gear, and on second and third speeds too if the road is wet. The entirely conventional chassis may not have the extreme cornering power of some more radical designs, but it scores by giving the driver plenty of warning that the limit is being approached. For this reason, the XK 150S is a particularly safe sports car, and one that may be handled with confidence by any competent fast driver.

Bolster also underlined the fact that variations in tyre pressures had a distinct effect on the car's behaviour. At first disappointed by the steering which he thought heavy and unresponsive, Bolster changed his mind when he inflated the tyres to a higher pressure - the whole "feel" of the car was improved by this action.

The top speed of the car obtained by Bolster was 132.3mph, compared with *The Autocar's* 134mph and *The Motor's* 132mph dead - all easily within the tolerances imposed by wind and road surface conditions. Bolster's acceleration times resembled *The Motor's* figures rather than *The Autocar's,* with 60mph coming up in 7.4 seconds, and 100mph in 20 seconds. "Being a Jaguar", Bolster concluded, "it is hardly necessary to remark that it represents outstanding value for money." The XK 150S cost £2,065 with the normal axle, and £2,110 with the Powr Lok differential.

That the XK had remained incredibly cheap can be shown when contemporary sporting machinery is examined alongside it. The basic price of the standard XK 150 Fixed-head Coupe in 1958 was £1,175. The 1971 cc AC Ace was £13 more, the Lotus Elite £125 more, the Jensen 541 £260 more (and much thirstier than the XK as well), and the Aston Martin DB4, announced in September 1958, was all of £475 more - and which despite a claimed weight

of only 26 cwt, and an output of 263 bhp gross from its shorter stroke twin ohc six cylinder engine, could not reach 60 mph any quicker than the 210 bhp XK 150 Fixed-head. Though to be fair, once it was wound up it went better, and managed to equal the XK 150S to 100 mph.

Perhaps one of the most successful attempts to equal the XK 150's price/performance ratio was in fact the new MGA Twin Cam, which had a basic price of £854. With a 0-60 mph time of 9.1 seconds (quicker than the DB4) and a maximum speed of 113mph, it was one of a new generation of good-handling sports cars that were beginning to prove that cheaper cars were getting faster - or, maybe that faster cars were getting cheaper!

All this did not mean that it was impossible to find a car that could out-perform the XK 150S; there were a number from Italy and at least one from Germany that could do so reasonably comfortably - if you were prepared to pay for the privilege. Laurance Pomeroy sampled some of the Jaguar's continental rivals and wrote of his experiences in *The Motor* of June 4th 1958.

In a ride with Enzo Ferrari in a 250GT road car, Pomeroy found that Ferrari's 12 cylinder engine was very flexible in top gear from 1,000rpm, although the traditional Ferrari "whirr and whizz" from the engine compartment was something that the XK 150 driver did not have to tolerate (or enjoy). Like the XK 150, one sat very low in the 250GT, behind a very long bonnet. Pomeroy compared the Ferrari with the Mercedes Benz 300SL which he also drove; the Italian car felt "very vintage" after the advanced Mercedes, "which is much more like an aircraft (or.. a railway engine!) in that it is absolutely rigid and whatever the road surface just rolls it out into something which is quite smooth. When on a corner you just turn the wheel and with a kind of computing machine accuracy the apparently large car sweeps round..." The 250GT, like the XK 150, was a "powerful understeerer" on first entering a bend, but Pomeroy thought that an experienced driver on say, the Tour de France, could use the car's 240bhp "to provoke a true drift with no loss of inherent stability." The XK 150 could be 'drifted' too, but it is unlikely to have been as neat as the Ferrari in this condition.

Although the 250GT didn't have disc brakes, Italian manufacturers had by steady development brought the drum brake up to its peak of efficiency, and with its light alloy heavily finned drums and wire wheels, the lighter Ferrari would probably have lost little to the XK 150 in this respect; though a rather higher pedal pressure was required compared to the servo assisted disc brake system of the Jaguar. Of course, the Ferrari's 5-speed gearbox with its Porsche 'magic ring' synchromesh was infinitely superior to the Jaguar's transmission, although the latter's overdrive probably allowed more relaxed cruising.

Pomeroy also tried a Maserati 3500GT and he thought this genuine 2 plus 2 had marginally superior handling to the Ferrari's. It shared one feature with the XK 150 - kick back through the steering wheel over rough roads. The Maserati's maximum speed a claimed 140mph, about 3mph slower than the Ferrari's but of course still some 6mph faster than the 3.4 litre XK 150S. As for prices, the 250GT cost £3,350, and the Maserati £2,750 - presumably in Italy. The basic 3.4 XK150S cost £1,457.

A few months before the Technical Editor of *The Motor* had been sampling the best that Modena could produce, the Institute of Mechanical Engineers in Great Britain had honoured Heynes for (amongst other achievements) designing the fastest British sports car, by awarding Jaguar's Chief Engineer the James Clayton prize (jointly with the distinguished electrical engineer, Sir Ewert Smith). The citation was "...for his outstanding contribution to the design and development of the modern automobile."

Motor Sport borrowed the factory XK 150S press car to cover the RAC Rally in the closing months of 1959, and put up some epic average speeds while doing so. On the newly built M1 motorway, the XK averaged 114½mph over its length, with the "slightly optimistic" speedometer reading 120mph for much of the time, spending some periods at 128mph at which the engine was turning over at less than 5,000rmp. While this sustained gait did not effect either oil pressure or water temperature (which remained constant at 40lbs and 70 degrees respectively), the usually faithful XDU 984 did suffer from a blown exhaust flange gasket, and worn splines on a rear wheel hub. However, one can make the same allowance for these minor defects that William Boddy did, in view of the fact that the car had undergone two Continental road tests, many miles at maximum speed, and numerous standing start acceleration tests in the hands of a variety of motoring journalists - or in short, XDU 984 had been through much more in the first year or so of its existence than most of its type suffered in a lifetime.

While *Motor Sport's* trip to Scotland and back during the course of covering the rally was accomplished at a petrol consumption of "a commendable 17.05mpg over 1,000 of the faster miles", the XK's oil consumption brought a frown - no less than 14 pints had been added over that mileage. This indicated something like an oil consumption of 900 miles to the gallon, which was not untypical of the XK engine when run at a comparatively high sustained rpm, or when maximum use is made of the gears. Later on in the unit's life various modifications gradually brought this consumption down to a negligible amount, through the use of different piston rings, and the introduction of sealed valve guide inserts which prevented oil finding its way down the valve stems into the bores.

THE 3.8 XK 150

The ultimate XK 150 came with Jaguar's showing of their 1960 range of cars. The Mk lX saloon (still on its Mk Vll chassis but now with disc brakes all round) had pioneered the use of the 3.8 capacity XK engine in a road Jaguar since October 1958, and now the unit was to be offered in the XK 150. The 3.8 engine could be specified in any of the three XK 150 variants, either in straight-port head 'S' type form, or with the two carburettor B-type head. So the choice of power ratings for the XK 150 was becoming quite complex - to assist identification, engine numbers were prefixed with a letter indicating the state of tune and the range was now V, VS, VA and VAS. 'V' alone indicated a standard 3.4 B-type head, two carburettor unit; 'VS' a 3.4 straight-port head, triple carburettor 'S' engine. 'VA' stood for a 3.8 B-type head unit, while 'VAS' indicated a 3.8 straight port head 'S' engine. There were also three compression ratios that could be chosen - 7:1, 8:1 and 9:1.

The new 3.8 engine was rated at 265bhp in its straight-port head, triple 2 inch SU 'S' form, and 220bhp with the B-type head and two 1¾ inch SU carburettors. To arrive at the capacity of 3,781cc the bore was increased from 83mm to 87mm, and while it had been possible for some private owners to bore their 3.4 engines out to at least that degree, it didn't leave much margin for safety so far as cracking between the individual bores were concerned, so Jaguar used dry liners. Other revisions were made to the cylinder block at the same time, partly to counteract some cooling deficiencies in the original block. The front three and the rear three cylinders were given a full water passage between them, and part length water passages were also milled between the upper parts of the bores where the cylinders were interconnected.

Another 1960 arrival was the new Mk 2 Jaguar saloon, and the 3.8 overdrive version had a turn of speed that was better than the XK 140's and with a 0 - 60mph time of 8½ seconds, it also ran the 210bhp XK 150 pretty close - at last, unitary construction was beginning to catch up with the XK and its heavy chassis. But fast though it was, the 3.8 Mk 2's performance was no match for the 3.8 XK 150S, an example of which John Bolster tested for *Autosport* in June

1960.

This car, a fixed-head coupe, was a clear 4mph faster than the 3.4 XK 150S tested by *The Motor*, its maximum speed being 136.3mph. That the standing start acceleration figures showed only a minimal improvement over the 3.4 'S' in the lower speed ranges was mostly due to the limited ability of the car's rear end to put the power down on the road efficiently - Bolster was of the opinion that independent rear suspension would have reduced acceleration times by a very useful amount, just as the "cleaning up" as he put it, of the front end of the car (ie the removal of such items as bumpers, fog lamps and so on) would have resulted in 140mph being reached in both directions. Also, it seemed to Bolster that the limited slip differential (standard on the 3.8 'S' models) wasn't working properly as there appeared to be an excessive amount of wheelspin from the right hand rear wheel. Unusual though it might be for a worn unit to be found in a 'factory' car, it is not unknown for the Powr Lok to wear out its friction plates quite quickly if given a lot of work to do - such as a great deal of hard second or third gear acceleration out of corners where weight transfer puts a big load on the unit as it tries to prevent the inside wheel spinning.

Anyway, the results of Bolster's acceleration runs showed that the bigger engined car actually took .4 second longer to reach 30mph than the 3.4S which he had tried previously. The extra power of the latest engine still hadn't compensated for the time wasted on take off when 60mph was achieved, the figure being 7.6 seconds against 7.4. By 100mph though the 3.8S was exactly one second ahead, at 19 seconds to the 'ton', and by the time 110mph had come up, the gap had widened to 3.4 seconds, at 22.2 seconds (transferring our comparison to *The Motor's* road test of the 3.4S as Bolster's figures hadn't run to more than 100mph with that car).

But the lower speed standing start figures don't really do justice to the car as the extra .4 of a litre made a very definite difference to its performance on the road, once under way. Said John Bolster: "Let's face it, the 3.4 is a tremendous car but the 3.8 litre has that extra torque just where it matters most. For example, acceleration from 100mph to 120mph is not noticeably less brisk than that from 80mph to 100mph, and the car continues to surge forward even after the overdrive has been engaged at 115mph."

Fast though it was, Bolster was fully aware of the XK 150's development from its sports car origins to a luxurious Grand Tourer, noting its "extremely solid construction and no attempt at weight reduction", which warranted its description as a "very fast touring car rather than a tamed-down racing car" - and adding that treated accordingly, "extremely safe motoring will result." Bolster also thought that the car's high speed stability greatly excelled the earlier XK models, a slightly odd remark in that the straight line stability of all XKs, from the first XK 120 onwards, was so good that it is hard to see how it could have been improved upon.

With the 4.09 axle ratio fitted to overdrive XKs, maximum speeds in the gears were inevitably lower than with the cars supplied with a 3.54 axle and even the 3.8 XK 150S could not attain a true 100mph in third gear. Bolster recorded maxima of 32, 60, 92 and 115mph for 1st, 2nd, 3rd, and direct top gears.

That the XK 150S worked hard for its living in Bolster's hands is indicated by the overall "driven hard" petrol consumption figure he recorded. At 13mpg, it was to be the highest for any production Jaguar independently road tested by a British magazine until the advent of the 5.3 litre V12 cars.

THE XK 150 IN COMPETITION

While increasing numbers of XK 150s gave their owners fast and reliable service on the road, in competition the car was a little like a duck out of water - circuit racing and the like were just not its *forte*. So far as the race track is concerned, the matter can be very simply

summed up by saying that anything the XK 150 could do, an XK 120 or XK 140 in similar tune could do better, and faster - disc brakes notwithstanding.

Weight was the chief factor against the XK 150's success in competition, particularly weight in the wrong places. The forward engine position was inclined to make it too much of an understeerer, while the high scuttle and wing line raised the centre of gravity which made the car much more prone to roll than the XK 120. In rallies it faired slightly better than on the track, though by now these increasingly professional road races were becoming the preserve of the highly organised 'works' teams, and no XK was ever entered by Jaguar in a rally. But even more than its XK 120 and XK 140 predecessors, the XK 150 was never intended for any form of motor sport, so any successes which did come its way in private hands must be looked upon purely as a bonus.

The XK 150 did have its occasional moments of glory though, and certainly one or two owners had a great deal of fun rallying, racing and sprinting their every-day car in club events - or in the case of rallies, sometimes at International level too. A year after the car's introduction, the FIA listed the XK 150 Drophead and Fixed-head Coupes as 'GT Cars' (not enough roadsters had been made to include those), along with such cars as the Aston Martin DB2 and DB2/4, and the Austin Healey 100-6 This gave the XK 150 at least a sporting chance in rallies, with Haddon and Vivian re-forming their XK partnership to score the XK 150's best results in this field. The car's most prominent achievement was probably their winning of the GT class in the 1960 Tulip Rally, ahead of the Burton/Cuff Jensen. The roadster also came a good 10th overall in the General Classification, just in front of the Boardman/Whitworth 3.8 saloon, beating at least one 300SL Mercedes, the Morley brothers, and several Porsches; the rally was won by a battered DS19 Citroen driven by Verrier and Trautman. The XK 150's biggest success in this rally though was probably its ascent of the six mile Mount Ventaux hill climb, where Haddon and Vivian picked up maximum bonus points and were delighted to have beaten the Swann/Sager Aston Martin DB4. Conversely, in the same climb, another XK 150 driven by Whatton broke *both* its rear springs on a pothole!

Earlier, the 1957 Tour de France had been contested by the Whitehead brothers, but they retired with brake trouble (of all things) quite early on in the proceedings, keeping 14th place as far as the ten laps of the Pau circuit, but dropping out by the time the Tour had reached Le Mans. A few years later, revenge would be wrought by the 3.8 Mk 2 Jaguar!

XK 150s were also to be seen in rallies at home, though the big events saw no important successes by the type. In 1959 McCracken put up Best Performance on the Charterhall circuit stage of the RAC Rally, but didn't finish in the first 20 when the final results were published - and that was about typical of what could be expected of the XK 150 in such events without full factory backing.

The car did appear "on the hills" quite regularly - often after fullfilling the role of tow-car on the way to the venue, and again after the event was over! There were occasionally bright moments too - like Phil Scragg's successful Whit Monday Prescott in June 1960, when after winning the over 3-litre sports car class in his 3.8 Lister-Jaguar, he made fastest time with his XK 150S in the Grand Touring car class - beating a Lotus Elite, and AT Norton's standard XK 150.

On the track, a regular competitor was Jack Lambert who campaigned his XK 150 from late 1958 right up until 1961, when he bought one of the first E-types. Don Parker also drove an XK 150 from time to time, and even won a race with it - finishing in front of Sir Gawaine Baillie's Elite at Oulton Park in May 1960. In America, Walt Hansgen brought the type one of its rare successes when he drove a stock XK 150S to third place at Bridgehampton in June

1958, behind an MG special and a 250 GT Ferrari.

XK 150s continued to appear spasmodically in club hill climbs and races throughout the sixties, but were of course completely outclassed by the E-type and by any of the faster XK 120s. Rosemary Massey (later Protheroe) drove an XK 150 (UDU 591) with some success, and Warren Pearce raced an alloy-panelled XK 150 at the beginning of his Jaguar career, but it was probably Peter Vernon-Kell who went the furthest in modifying an XK 150 for the track - his car featured a one-piece, hinge-forward bonnet and front wings assembly in aluminium, faired-in headlights, much stripping of unnecessary weight internally, and a modified 3.8S engine. This car was used quite regularly in 'marque' (later 'modified') sports car racing, until written off in 1971 at Thruxton, during a new owner's first race.

Several XK 150s were tempted out onto the track again in the 1970s by the XK Register's successful attempt to re-create the 'marque' sports car racing of the late fifties, with the introduction of 'thoroughbred' racing. Mrs Sylvia Rouse was the leading exponent of the type in this form of competition, usually beating her husband in his XK 120 Fixed-head!

JAGUAR'S CONTINUING EXPANSION

To return to 1960, with the XK 150 still in full production Jaguar had taken the step of buying the Daimler company. This was made necessary by the space that would be required for the volume production of the new Mk II Jaguar, and the forthcoming Mk 10 saloon (not to mention the new sports car around the corner), as an extension of the Browns Lane factory was contrary to local government policy at that time.

Only two miles from the main works, the fine Radford factory meant a doubling of the floor space available to Jaguar. Sir William Lyons was also pleased to acquire a stake in the bus division of the vehicle market, and under the influence of the vital Jaguar concern this side of Daimler's business soon flowered, the 'Fleetline' series of double-decker buses becoming an extremely successful line. Daimler's car division was in a sorry state however, and the existing models were quietly faded out by Jaguar. This of course meant the demise of the Daimler SP 250 - quite fast, its very flexible chassis and bouncy suspension had never really allowed it to be a serious rival to the XK 150 even though it had a heart of gold - the excellent Daimler 2½ litre V8 engine, which Jaguar placed in their Mk 2 bodyshell to create the very popular Daimler 2½ litre saloon. Jaguar toyed with the idea of re-bodying the SP250 but costings showed that the re-vamped car would have to be priced at virtually the same as the new and vastly superior E-type, so the project was dropped.

The cost of assimilating Daimler, and of establishing production lines for the new cars imminently to be announced, did seem to have an effect on Jaguar's profit figures, which were announced about a month before the XK 150 became obsolete. The year 1960 had brought the company £1,022,043, as opposed to the previous year's £1,385,059 - despite an increased turnover in the US market.

So as 1960 drew to a close, the XK 150 - and virtually every other big sports car - was shortly to be eclipsed by an entirely new Jaguar, which was to have an impact on its announcement reminiscent of that surrounding the debut of the original XK 120 back in October 1948. The 'E-type' was unleashed in March 1961, and the XK series went into the history books.

At least, it did after a further few months. The XK 150 did not immediately disappear from the catalogues and Jaguar's last 'chassis and cart springs' sports car continued to be listed in *The Motor's* new car price guide right up until October 11th 1961 - just before the Mk 10 saloon's announcement at Earls Court. The last XK 150 had actually left the production line some eight months previously, in January 1961,

but the fact is that Jaguar were not *always* in the happy position of being able to sell everything they produced instantly, as was popularly supposed. There have been exceptions, and apparently the last few XK 150s were amongst them. In the XK 150's case this was possibly due to people holding back in the hope of buying a new E-type, more than anything else.

THE XK 150 IN THE SEVENTIES

How does the XK 150 rate today? The great leap in standards of ride, roadholding and handling that came with the E-type has been the cause of disappointment in more than one newcomer to the XK 150, who happens to have made the mistake of buying one *after* owning an E-type for a while. One must admit that the car does initially feel a bit of a lump after the responsive nimbleness of the E-type, but this criticism is in one sense a little harsh because of the strong contrast and close proximity in time between the two cars - the E-type being so good that almost everything paled before it. Taken on its own, or at least in comparison to other cars of the late fifties and early sixties, the XK 150 still has great merits. Not that the XK 150 lost out on every single count to its usurper, as Laurance Pomeroy pointed out in *The Motor* of February 13 1963. Beginning by talking of the E-type, he said:

It is ludicrously low priced, but by being an *absolute* two seater its appeal of necessity is limited, especially as the convertible suffers from very meagre luggage capacity. In this respect it is inferior to the XK 150 Series, and one of the most pleasurable mornings of 1962 was driving Cecil Clutton's 3.4 example. The XK 150 has never made much impression in the competition world, and I doubt if this particular car, with the lower-powered engine, will exceed 125mph. This notwithstanding, it is a rapid cross-country vehicle and scores in relation to the E-type by having Laycock-de-Normanville overdrive so that one may sweep along at 100mph with the engine doing only 3,800rpm and with the pistons swishing up and down at a mere 2,760 ft/min. With fine braking and a most comfortable driving position, this car took my fancy in a big way and if I were in the market for an all-round two seater which could take additional persons in modest comfort for short distances I should comb the small ads. for a good example of the fixed-head; or, could I avoid the temptation to anticipate the summer with a drop-head? Both could be had for the price of one E-type and the loss of 20mph in top speed. .

Much of what Pomeroy wrote in 1963 applies today - the XK 150 still makes an attractive and practical long-distance touring car in the 1970s, capable of high speed cruising at a relaxed gait and in relative silence. The car's greater spaciousness, better ride, and even its one-piece screen, can be said to make the XK 150 a better proposition for regular use than either the XK 120 or the XK 140, even if it doesn't have quite the historic appeal of the early cars.

The XK 150's straight-line performance remains largely undated too, particularly in 'S' form. As *The Autocar* wrote in 1959 of the 3.4S: "Even the traffic queues on a sunny summer Sunday lose much of their significance. A group of half a dozen vehicles or so can be overtaken on next to nothing of a straight, again in complete safety. When the traffic is at its worst, when most cars even in expert hands are fumbling their way along our main roads, the Jaguar still manages to achieve altogether exceptional average speeds."

Such is the performance of the XK 150S - or even to a slightly lesser degree the 210 bhp versions of it or its predecessors - that this happy state of affairs still exists today, despite the rise in average speeds of inter-town traffic over the intervening years. It is perfectly possible to accomplish a long cross-country journey over main roads without using anything but top and overdrive top gears while on the move, the great low and mid range torque of the six cylinder engine being sufficient to push the car with relaxed ease past most other cars on the road.

While an increasing number of modern-day saloons with their 'GT' options can approach the standing start acceleration figures of the XK 150 (there are still very few which can equal XK

150S times), virtually none have quite the punch of the big XK engine when it comes to applying the power in a given situation - ie overtaking a line of cars on the open road. A glance at the third and top gear acceleration figures of our typical modern high performance saloon (or even sports car) compared with those of the XK will immediately reveal why. Standing start figures can sometimes be misleading when estimating a car's performance on the road, and the XK has always been a faster car than even its very creditable acceleration-from-rest times would appear to indicate.

Conversely, it should also be said that virtually every modern saloon - even those with no sporting potential - can out-corner any of the XK variants with ease; but this pre-supposes that they are being driven near their maximum potential, which is rare due to a diversity of driver skills, visibility round bends, and road conditions in general. In practise therefore, the competent driver of an XK 150 which is in top condition (or indeed of the higher powered versions of the earlier cars) will not often find himself left far behind even on twisty roads. Here again it is the excellent middle-speed power of the XK engine which comes to the rescue and compensates for an elderly chassis design, for while an XK's progress into, and round, a given corner may not be as great as a modern car, the torque available for pulling it *out* of the corner, and propelling it along the intervening straight to the next one, is usually sufficient to keep it ahead of all but the fastest cars of today.

Thus the XK 150, and if one is willing to put up with a little less civilisation, the XK 120 and XK 140 too, need only be a museum piece if the owner wishes it to be. The cars have certainly appreciated in value from their all-time 'low' in around 1968, when an excellent XK 150 could be bought for about £400, but inflation has ensured that it is still possible to buy two *concours* examples for the price of one current Jaguar sports car - except that today the latter is V-12 engined and not the six cylinder edition of

Laurance Pomeroy's memory.

It is reasonably easy to find a good XK 150, the fixed-head version being by far the most numerous in this country - anyway, more of the closed cars were built than any other type. the figure being 4,462 units approximately as opposed to 2,671 for the drop-head coupe, and 2,265 for the roadster. Most of these cars went abroad, and the roadster particularly in rhd form is an extremely rare bird in these Isles (only about 90 were made). Being of a slightly more practical nature than the XK 140, and certainly the XK 120, the XK 150 is in moderately widespread use as an 'only' or every-day car, though this is unlikely to be the case in the 1980s - or even sooner, unfortunately, to judge from the ever increasing value of the car. Corrosion certainly took its toll of the cars and although few are broken up today, the XK 150 suffered at least as badly as the earlier models from this unfortunate malady (in this country at least), and generally in the same places - the sills, boot area, sidelight and headlight nacelles, scuttle ventilators and door-shut faces. Mechanical longevity was as great as ever though, and the XK 150 has the similarly helpful attribute of being able to utilize quite a wide range of mechanical (particularly engine) components from contemporary and later Jaguar saloon cars to help keep it running efficiently and effectively.

In its ultimate expression as the XK 150, the XK Jaguar sports car concluded a long and honourable term of office. Few cars in series production could outrun it, even after its basic concept was some thirteen years old, and today the XK 150 is prized as both a collector's 'classic', and as an extremely fast, practical, and reliable Grand Tourer. In this context, perhaps the best epitaph I could choose for ending the XK story is that penned unknowingly by an enthusiastic owner, who placed the following handwritten notice in the back window of his XK 150 when it took its place amongst the ranks of XKs at an International XK Day not so long ago. It read:

July 1973

'Hook of Holland, Vienna, Budapest, Belgrade, Greece, Italy via Adriatic ferry to Brindisi, autostrada to Milan, Berne, Aachen, Antwerp, Ostend. 4,500 trouble-free XK miles in three weeks.'

That is what XK motoring is all about!

Chapter Nine   Jaguar Specials

The Jaguar engine is really one of the marvels of the century. With its twin overhead camshafts, seven main bearings, and ultra-rigid construction, it has all the basic features of a successful competition power unit. It deserves to be put into a small, light car...

John Bolster
Autosport April 1 1955

There have been Jaguar specials ever since there was a Jaguar engine of reasonable horse power to be put into a 'better' chassis by the hopeful enthusiast. The 1950s spawned by far the greatest number of these variants, their builders encouraged by the power and reliability of the XK engine (not to mention its relative availability and cheapness). The majority were designed for racing or hill climbing and they can be broadly divided into two groups - one-off 'specials', and those which showed a more professional approach and which in some instances went into what may be termed limited production. HWM, Cooper, Lister and Tojeiro can be listed in the second category.

THE JAGUETTE, JAGUARA AND HK JAGUAR

But to begin near the beginning, one of the earliest post-war Jaguar specials was conceived and built in 1946, and yet was still winning in 1961. This was the Jaguette, a successful marriage of a 1939 SS Jaguar 2½ litre ohv engine with an MG Magnette chassis; it was the first of a notable line of sprint cars constructed by Gordon Parker.

The push-rod engine (similar to that used in the Mk V saloon right up until 1951) was found to fit in the N-type chassis - purchased for £85 -

quite easily; drive was through an SS 1 gearbox to a Standard 20 rear axle modified to accept the MG hubs and brakes. The *ensemble* handled surprisingly well although initial trouble was experienced with wheelspin, whereupon 16 inch wheels were substituted for the 18 inch originals at the rear, together with a wider section of tyre. The Jaguette's inaugural run was at a speed event at Windmill Hill, where it was beaten by Sydney Allard largely because of the car's lack of traction. Once this was sorted out, the 20cwt car with its completely standard engine beat both George Matthew's and Don Parker's SS 100s at a Brighton and Hove MC hill climb, and went on to further successes while still being used by its owner as a practical every-day car.

The search for more power brought about the application of a supercharger, and weight was reduced to something nearer 16cwt by the use of yet-thinner gauge aluminium for the car's bodywork; a Ford 3.55:1 rear axle eventually took the place of the Standard item.

Ironically, the car's more notable achievements occured during W Coleman's ownership, Coleman buying the car when in 1951 or 1952 it was sold to make way for Parker's second Jaguar-engined creation. In September 1952 Coleman set FTD for sports cars and won the Unlimited sports car class at the Brighton Speed

Trials with the Jaguette, and was still competing with the car up to at least 1961 at Brighton, winning the Unlimited supercharged car classes both in 1960 and 1961. A third in class was also achieved at Prescott in 1960, and the Jaguette is still to be seen today at hill climb meetings.

The Jaguara with which Gordon Parker replaced the Jaguette was a much more specialised car, using as its basis a Buckler multi-tubular frame and a 3.4 XK engine, and having a wheelbase of 8 feet. Front suspension was independent and taken from a Vauxhall Velox, and a Morris Minor rack and pinion steering arrangement was used - this last was a common feature of Jaguar and other specials. A standard XK 120 axle was used at the rear, well located by two pairs of radius arms and 'A.R.M.' link. Coil springs and dampers were fitted, and XK 120 Lockheed brakes but with the wise addition of Al-Fin drums. The XK engine was supercharged at about 9 lbs sq in, and with a two-seater aluminium body and cycle wings, the Jaguara still only weighed about 17cwt.

Although Parker's main target was always FTD at the Brighton Speed Trials, the Jaguara was also campaigned at Prescott where for two years running (1956 and 1957) it won the over 3,000cc sports car class (though in 1957 Frank Le Gallais' XK engined special was rather quicker running in the Formula Libre class); the car had narrowly missed a similar class win at Prescott in 1955, when it had been beaten by Phil Scragg's HWM Jaguar into second place - but itself was faster than Sydney Allard's 5020cc Allard.

Over the standing kilometer on Brighton sea front, Parker gained FTD for sports cars in 1953 with a time of 26.88 seconds, and won the Unlimited supercharged sports car class - a division which also fell to the Jaguara in both 1954 and 1955. Cyril Wick's Cooper-Jaguar running in the unsupercharged class in 1955 was faster that year at 25.30 seconds however, Parker's special putting up 28.28 seconds.

Gordon Parker's final attempt to produce the fastest car at Brighton resulted in the HK Jaguar, a frightening single-seater device with twin Arnott vane-type superchargers, each one feeding three cylinders of a 3.4 XK engine equipped with a C-type head. Compression ratio was 7.6:1 and boost pressure was a maximum of 10 lbs sq in. Petrol was supplied (at the rate of around 3 mpg!) from a hand-pump pressurised fuel tank via two 2½ inch SU carburettors. A Lucas racing magneto was used, and the radiator was an expensive Marston light alloy item.

The engine was carried in a two-channel tubular single-seater chassis clad in a light alloy body shell; front suspension was by unequal length wishbones, coil springs and telescopic dampers, plus a double anti-roll bar, while at the rear was a de Dion tube, trailing arms, and coil springs and telescopic dampers again. The power was transmitted through a Wilson pre-selector gearbox.

Although the car was finally completed in 1958, substantial success did not come Parker's way until September 1961, when at Brighton the HK Jaguar hurtled down the Madeira Drive to become the fastest car of the day, recording 24.63 seconds to win the over 2,001cc racing car class (a Norton JAP motorcycle made overall FTD). Gordon Parker had achieved his ambition.

The car was afterwards sold to Anthony Charnock, who up until 1965 used it in sprints and hill climbs; it was still capable of out-running much younger and potentially faster machinery when on song - and on a dry surface, as its past owners speak of the car's almost complete unmanageability in the wet! Charnock slightly remodelled the bodywork during his ownership to include a small passenger seat. This was retained when Peter Quayle rebuilt the HK Jaguar to something approaching its original superbly turned out condition, and the car subsequently passed into the hands of French Jaguar collector Dr Philip Renault around 1972.

THE LGS SPECIAL FROM JERSEY

An early post-war special from Jersey which

Top The XK 150 Drop-head Coupe; a very English car displayed against a very English background. Whitewall tyres were still an essential for the American market, however

Centre Last of the XK 150 body styles to be announced was the roadster version - wind-up windows now, but no rear seats

Bottom With the XK 150 came a revised dashboard and facia which banished the traditional walnut finish even on the fixed-head and drop-head models *(photo The Motor)*

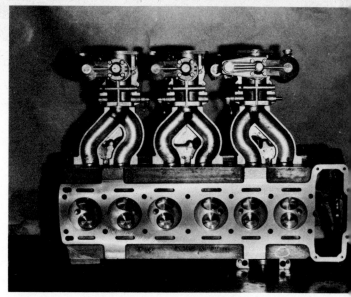

Top left Engine compartment of the XK 150S, showing the unit's three 2 inch SU carburettors; it was used in almost exactly the same form in the first E-type *(photo The Motor)*

Top right The XK 150S 'straight port' head and a sectioned inlet manifold, with its equal length inlet tracts

Centre En route to Monte Carlo, the XK 150 of Merrick and Bevan pictured during the 1959 Rally. The 3.4 saloons were more successful on this occasion, however *(photo The Motor)*

Bottom Perhaps the most meritorious performance put up by an XK 150 in international competition was Haddon's and Vivian's victory in the GT class of the 1960 Tulip Rally, their 150S finished 10th in the General Classification, thereby beating the Morley brothers, a Mercedes-Benz 300SL and a number of Porsches *(photo The Motor)*

Top Jack Lambert was a familiar entrant with his XK 150, both on the track and at hill climbs; his fixed-head is seen here at the National meeting at Shelsley of August 1960. Note the plainly visible anti-tramp bars, a common rear axle 'mod' by competition-minded owners *(photo The Motor)*

Centre Before embarking on a successful club racing career with an E-type, Warren Pearce first campaigned a lightened and modified XK 150 Fixed-head. The car is seen here at Brands Hatch, October 1963, pursuing an XK 120 *(photo The Motor)*

Bottom Peter Vernon-Kell's XK 150 Drop-head, with its composite forward-hinging bonnet and wings, at Thruxton during the 1971 JDC meeting

Top The 1958 Geneva Salon saw this coachbuilt XK 150 displayed on the Zagato stand *(photo The Motor)*

Centre This quite pleasing shape resulted from rebodying an XK 150. It was the work of Bertone in 1957 *(photo Bertone)*

Bottom This slightly disreputable looking XK 150 Drop-head won an Indian Grand Prix in the 'sixties', driven by The Maharajhumar of Gondal... one wonders what the other competitors drove!

Top left A successful attempt at supercharging an XK 150 was made by a Mr du Toit of Denver, Transvaal, South Africa in 1963. The car's radiator has been removed to show the pulley arrangements; after the installation had been sorted out, the XK proved to be completely reliable and capable of a very high performance

Top right Mrs Sylvia Rouse and her XK 150 achieved a moderate amount of fame in British club racing circles during the 1970's, appearing regularly in Thoroughbred sports car racing; the author's XK 120 is in the background

Bottom Roy Richard's XK 150S, well known in the West Country for its speedy performances in sprints and hill climbs, is undoubtedly the fastest XK 150 in Great Britain, with its much modified engine

Top Gordon Parker's first Jaguar special, the Jaguette, in its original 1946 form. Powered by its 1939 SS Jaguar 2½-litre engine, it sometimes proved faster than even the quicker SS 100s

Centre left Gordon Parker's first Jaguar engined special again. This picture was taken in 1960 at Prescott, with W Coleman at the wheel *(photo The Motor)*

Centre right The Jaguara at Great Auclum speed hill climb, with Gordon Parker at the wheel of his second Jaguar special

Bottom The rather fearsome twin-supercharged HK Jaguar, in its original single-seater form competing at a September 1962 Prescott meeting, Gordon Parker driving *(photo The Motor)*

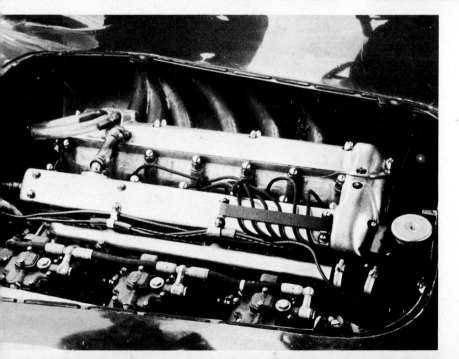

Top An early fifties American Jaguar special, based on the XK 120, built by Fitch Enterprises for Corby Whitmore, a magazine illustrator

Centre left Sand racing special; this push-rod 3½-litre Jaguar engined special won the 1952 Jersey Sand Racing Championship, driven by its builder W Knight. Named the LTS Jaguar, it was one of several Jaguar engined cars used for this type of sport

Centre right Freddy Pope's XK 120 special during the 1951 Johore Grand Prix. The car was simply an XK 120 chassis with an aluminium panelled body but was fast enough to win the event

Bottom D-type engine installation in the Connaught, as campaigned in New Zealand during 1957; the exhaust pipes exited alongside the cockpit at shoulder level to the driver, which was usually Leslie Marr

Top The Hansgen Jaguar Special rather over-doing it at Thompson Raceway, Connecticut, driven by its then-owner, Paul Timmins. Walt Hansgen, later to be killed in a Ford GT 40 while practicing for Le Mans many years later, passes the scene in a C-type
Centre Cooper-Jaguar Mk 1; Peter Whitehead at the International Trophy meeting at Snetterton, August 1954 *(photo The Motor)*
Bottom The Mille Miglia 1957 - Cooper-Jaguar crew Steed and Hall do not appear to be on speaking terms!

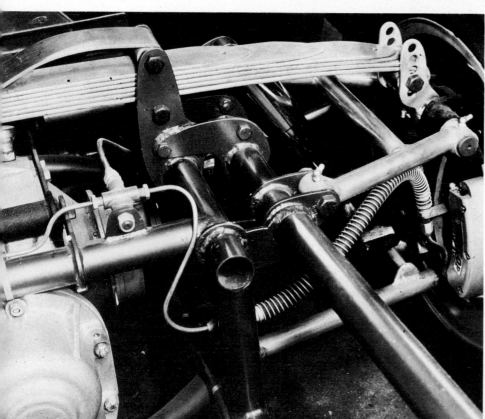

Top A mass of rounded tubes, this Cooper-Jaguar chassis was prepared for display at the Brussels Show of 1955; appearing as the Mk 2 Cooper-Jaguar, it was given rather more orthodox bodywork than its predecessor
Bottom Rear suspension detail of the Mk 2 Cooper-Jaguar, with John Cooper's familiar transverse spring prominent (*photo The Autocar*)

Top left Engine compartment of Oscar Moore's HWM; the combination of Jaguar power and HWM chassis proved to be very successful (photo The Motor)

Top right Oscar Moore at Castle Combe, 1952, with XMC 34, the first Jaguar engined HWM. Moore was also about the first person to bore the XK engine out to 3.8-litres, which he did at about the same time (photo The Motor)

Bottom left George Abecassis takes the original HWM 1 up Shelsley Walsh, August 1953; its second appearance on that hill, HWM 1 climbed in 45.01 seconds to win its class (photo The Motor)

Bottom right Rheims, July 1956; XPE 2 displays the HWM-Jaguar's revised bodywork on the new chassis which were built in 1955 (photo The Motor)

Top The caption on this cutaway drawing of HWM 1 when it first appeared in *Autosport* was 'No Space Wasted'. Note the massive finned brake drums *(photo Autosport)*

Centre left Interior of the HWM GT; doors boast electric window winders. The author drove the car when it was in David Cottingham's hands in 1975, and found it offered a surprisingly modern performance, even if the controls were a little heavy. Overall on-the-road weight was quoted as just over 26cwt

Centre right George Abecassis stands by his unique GT; the HWM chassis used big Al-Fin brakes, and a wet-sump C-type engine fitted with a head to D-type specifications by Weslake. The normal HWM de Dion rear end carried a 3.54:1 final drive

Bottom After John Heath's death in 1956, one remaining HWM-Jaguar chassis was fitted with this GT body for George Abecassis, to a design by Frank Feeley who was responsible for the Aston Martin DB2 and DB3S shapes

Top Phil Scragg taking the term 'hill climbing' a little too seriously! SPC 982, specially commissioned by Scragg and the last HWM-Jaguar to be built, indulges in an unofficial excursion at the August 1958 Shelsley meeting *(photo The Motor)*

Centre The LGS Special, one of the most rapid hill climb and sprint specials to be Jaguar powered. It is shown here at its 'home' venue, Bouley Bay hill climb, when the power unit was a 3½-litre push-rod engine

Bottom Frank Le Gallais, builder of the astonishingly successful LGS hill climb and sprint car. The Jersey man is pictured here at the wheel of his XK 120, not the special, just before the start of the 1952 Jersey Road Race *(photo The Motor)*

had an exceptionally long and active life was Frank Le Gallais' LGS. This was built by the Jerseyman over the 2½ years from 1946 to 1949, after he had driven stripped down saloons and a Wolseley Hornet (later straight eight 1½ litre OM) powered GN with great success at Bouley Bay. Mid-engined, the car's chassis was built up from twin 2½ inch diameter, 19 swg tubes on either side with a 6 inch diameter cross member front and rear. Two further 16 swg cross members braced the chassis in the middle. Wheelbase was 7 feet 10 inches, front track 4 feet 6 inches and rear track 4 feet 5 inches. Interestingly, Citroen front suspension was used, retaining the torsion bars but without the drive shafts of course, while the steering was rack and pinion. The rear suspension incorporated advice from no less a person than Alex Issigonis and featured the swing axles favoured by Le Gallais, suspended by rubber bands as suggested by Issigonis.

The LGS was originally designed with the ideal of using the OM engine which Le Gallais had used before the war in his GN chassis, and which had been buried during the German occupation of the island. Then rumours of Jaguar's new twin ohc engine reached Jersey so that unit was decided upon. But when by 1949 an XK engine still hadn't been extracted from the works, a 3½ litre Mk V engine was placed in the new chassis as a temporary measure.

Thus powered the car was quick enough to come third in the over 2,000cc class at the August Bouley Bay hill climb, with a time of 58.2 seconds, but this was some way off the 55.8 seconds put up by a blown 1½ litre ERA which held the course record. The XK engine finally arrived late in 1950, in Special Equipment form with high lift cams, stronger valve springs and the competition crankshaft damper. With this engine the LGS soon got down to the ERA times and by 1953 had recorded 55.2 seconds, putting up 3rd FTD in the process. An excursion to the mainland in September of that year netted a win in the over

2,500cc unsupercharged racing car class at Prescott, and an interesting comparison can be made here with Peter Walker's C-type. Frank Le Gallais was much quicker at 46.44 seconds, Walker being 3.25 seconds slower - but then the C-type *was* built to win Le Mans, an event of slightly longer duration than a run up that famous hill near Cheltenham!

The LGS was by now regularly winning its class at Bouley Bay, and by 1956 covered the flying quarter mile in 6.8 seconds (or 132 mph average) and ascended the hill in 54.0 seconds. The following year the car travelled to Shelsley Walsh and Prescott, actually being driven there on the road! Flexible tubing from the six stub exhausts ran into two motorcycle silencers, and cycle type wings were fixed over the wheels. At Shelsley, the LGS broke the Shelsley Specials record and won the over 2,500cc racing cars class with a time of 38.2 seconds, beating Scragg's HWM Jaguar by 1.09 seconds. Prescott saw the car win the Formula Libre class, climbing in 45.63 seconds, and back home Le Gallais made FTD at Bouley Bay in September with a run of 53 seconds. This record was later broken by David Boshier-Jones in his 1,098cc Cooper, who ascended a full second quicker.

By this time the LGS had acquired a triple SU induction set up, the carburettors being mounted inwards giving a reverse flow, a method being experimented with by SU themselves around that time. Twin rear wheels (Citroen) were worn at the rear, fitted with tyres "slotted with a circular saw to give better adhesion" to quote from a near-contemporary description of the car. Weight was about 13cwt with the XK engine.

Le Gallais' final achievement with the car was probably in 1958, when the LGS covered the standing ½ mile in 21 seconds - on that occasion George Brown with his Vincent put up 20.5 seconds, and the speeds reached by the two machines were thought to be approaching 160mph. Soon afterwards the LGS was sold, and travelled to Kenya where it crashed for the first time; it is not known whether it survived this accident, but one certainly hopes that this highly successful Jaguar powered single-seater still exists somewhere.

THE HWM-JAGUAR

The HWM-Jaguars were probably the first of the Jaguar variants to be seriously built for circuit racing rather than for sprints and hill climbs alone, although the first car was not constructed by HWM themselves but by a private enthusiast - much as was to be the case with the first Lister-Jaguar.

H W Motors of Walton on Thames was managed by John Heath and ex-SS 100 driver George Abecassis, and had been racing dual purpose Formula 2/sports racing cars under the HWM banner. It was decided that for 1951 however, proper single seater HWMs would be built for Formula 2 racing and so the 1950 works cars were sold. One of these '1½' seaters went to Oscar Moore (who had often driven against the SS 100 in pre-war days with his modified BMW 328), who hit on the idea of removing the Alta engine and inserting an XK engine in its place. Further interest is added to this successful transplant by the fact that Oscar Moore was, it seems, also the first to enlarge the XK engine's capacity by over boring; he thus brought the displacement up from 3442cc to 3814cc, anticipating American experiments in this direction by some years as the car raced with this capacity from at least June 1952. Moore's first success with the car came earlier however, when in May 1952 he won the over 3,000cc unsupercharged sports car class at Prescott with a time of 49.11 seconds.

Oscar Moore's car should really be referred to as an HWM-Alta-Jaguar, to distinguish it from the works built HWM-Jaguars; it carried cycle-type wings and not the all-enveloping bodywork of the works cars, and was registered XMC 34 (it still exists today, in very original order). John Heath's own cars initially sprang from a rebuilt

Alta, and it appears that (just to complicate matters) one Alta chassis was fitted with an HWM cycle-wing body and then with a Jaguar engine (later registered ND 4040).

Phil Scragg drove an HWM-Jaguar at the commencement of his very notable career 'on the hills' with Jaguar engined machinery. He bought an offset two seater cycle winged HWM without an engine, and fitted a new XK engine into it; the registration number of this, Scragg's first HWM, was RPG 418. An early success with this car came to Scragg in September 1952 at the Brighton Speed Trials, on which occasion he won the over 2,500cc sports car class with a time of 29.13 seconds - a little more than a second behind the supercharged Jaguette in another class. RPG 418 continued in action driven by Phil Scragg through 1953 and 1954 and while his string of record-breaking runs were yet to come, he did record a number of class wins at Prescott and elsewhere during that period.

Oscar Moore too, campaigned his HWM-Alta-Jaguar for the next year or so, with success in circuit racing as well as over shorter distances, Castle Combe especially bringing favourable results. But his efforts were eventually overshadowed by HWM's own Jaguar-engined cars, when Heath and Abecassis elected to follow his example, and turned to the XK engine with which to replace the obsolete Alta power unit.

The HWM team had, from 1951 to 1954, bravely fought the cream of European constructors with their rather heavy and underpowered Formula 2 single-seaters, even chalking up some wins thanks to the determination of the works drivers which included Moss, Lance Macklin, Tony Rolt and Paul Frere at various times; but the writing was on the wall and 1954 was the last year to see HWM in 'Formula' racing, as the single-seaters, even with their enlarged Alta engines, were if anything less competitive than before - the previous Formula 2 had now become Formula 1 and the full weight of the major constructors was now concentrated against them. From 1955 onwards, John Heath turned to sports car racing using the chassis and spares left over from the single seaters.

The first works HWM-Jaguar had in fact been built in the early summer of 1953, a two-seater sports racing car with a streamlined bodyshell based on the Formula 2 HWM chassis. This was a parallel twin-tube affair, rather narrow for a two-seater of course and of only 7 feet 8 inches wheelbase, and carried independent front suspension and de Dion rear suspension. The former utilised a transverse leaf spring and a top wishbone, with damping by both a lever type shock absorber, and an auxiliary Andre Hartford friction type; rack and pinion steering was used. The rear end featured torsion bar springing, a quick-change differential, telescopic dampers, and trailing arms. The car was stopped by a dual master cylinder, drum brake arrangement, with large finned brake drums. Engine was basically C-type, with Weber carburettors and additional modifications by John Heath. Two cars to this pattern were built, the works car registered HWM 1, and one other usually raced by Peter Collins (XPA 748).

The first appearance of HWM 1 was in June 1953 at Shelsley Walsh. George Abecassis was its driver, and he continued behind the wheel of the car for the rest of the 1953 season, including in his itinerary the Goodwood 9-Hours race. Until it retired with a broken timing chain (an unusual fault for a Jaguar) the car showed a surprising turn of speed, actually setting fastest lap in practice, and at one stage heading the works Aston Martins while lying in third position overall; though tyre problems had reduced this initial high placing before the mechanical trouble finally forced the car out. At the August 1953 Shelsley meeting, the HWM-Jaguar ascended the hill in 45.01 seconds to win the over 3,000cc sports car class, and in September a Goodwood meeting brought Abecassis a win in an over 1,500cc sports car race.

HWM's sports car competition programme for 1954 was considerably more ambitious, and after a 3rd place at Castle Combe for Abecassis in April, HWM 1 was entered for the Mille Miglia. But the car lasted nowhere near as long as the XK 120s and C-types had earlier in the decade, a broken shock absorber causing retirement after only 200 miles. However, HWM 1 obviously held the road well and was capable of putting its power down, as back home at a very wet Silverstone, Abecassis got the better of the Aston Martins in the International Trophy race, finishing in second place 46 seconds behind Gonzales' 4.9 litre Ferrari - and the HWM driver beat the Ecurie Ecosse C-types as well. Another second place resulted from a trip to Hedemora in Sweden, Abecassis finishing behind another ex-SS 100 driver, Casimero d'Oliveira of Portugal who was driving a 4½ litre Ferrari on this occasion. Duncan Hamilton came third in his C-type.

The Rheims long distance race in 1954 was contested by a revised HWM-Jaguar, driven by Graham Whitehead and Tony Gaze. The de Dion rear had come in for modification, and the front suspension now used coil springs of a similar type to those used on the single seater HWMs. Against Jaguar and Cunningham works opposition, the HWM-Jaguar finished 7th. Gaze (XPA 748) won at Crystal Palace in August after a dice with Anthony Crook's Cooper-Bristol, but retired during the Tourist Trophy meeting held again on the Dundrod circuit - though Abecassis and Mayers with the works HWM-Jaguar finished, in 14th position on handicap and a creditable 4th on scratch.

HWM continued their sports car racing activities in 1955, and thanks to John Bolster, who was to try all the major Jaguar engined sports racing variants, we have some valuable impressions of what HWM 1 was like to drive. So far as performance figures are concerned, Bolster cheated a little during the test as he took advantage of the quick-change final drive and ran on a 4.11:1 ratio for the acceleration runs and a lot of the road work, and on a 3.48:1 ratio for the maximum speed trial. He thus recorded the high maximum speed of 145.1 mph, and the very quick acceleration figures of 0 - 60 mph in 6.5 seconds, 0 - 80 mph in 10.6 seconds, and 0 - 100 mph in 17 seconds. The standing ¼-mile time was 15 seconds.

The car was found to be very manageable whatever ratio was fitted, Bolster discovering that it could be driven with one hand on the wheel at speeds approaching 150mph, and was easily controlled on a corner:

> If a curve is entered on a trailing throttle the degree of understeer is fairly pronounced. There is ample engine power to counteract this, however, and the car corners best with plenty of use of the loud pedal. It fairly flings itself out of faster bends, the absence of wheelspin permitting the very great urge to be fully employed. Altogether, the roadholding and suspension represent a very effective compromise.

The steering Bolster found "odd" at first, before he got used to the strong castor action which made it rather heavy; severe bumps were transmitted to the wheel, but "once accustomed to it, however, I found I could make the car do almost anything". The brakes didn't fade and could be applied hard at maximum speed without pulling, though the pedal pressure was fairly high. The driving position was ideal, the bucket seat holding the driver firmly and the cockpit affording excellent protection for both driver and passenger - who was also provided with perfectly practical accommodation inspite of the narrowness of the car's frame. The HWM-Jaguar's ride passed muster too, even when judged as for a road car, being "fairly firm at low speeds, but is at all times level, and there is no appreciable roll." Needless to say the Jaguar engine received high praise for its smoothness at high revolutions, and its flexibility which allowed the car to be driven normally on the road. Bolster recorded a fuel consumption of around 15mpg.

HWM 1 still had its original chassis when tested by John Bolster in February 1955, but by May of that year three new chassis were built.

One of these was eventually used for a rather desirable GT coupe road car built for George Abecassis (and which still exists today), but the other two were destined for the track. They were given revised body shells and ran with the registration numbers XPE 2 and HWM 1 (it is not clear whether the original HWM 1 was updated, or whether the registration number was transferred to the new chassis). XPE 2 retired in its first race in May 1955, then crashed during the 100 mile race at Snetterton - this meeting was definitely not a good one for HWM, as Michael Keen had HWM 1 catch fire under him! But in the 1955 Goodwood 9-Hours race XPE 2 took 4th place overall with Lance Macklin and Bill Smith driving. At the close of the season, Abecassis won at Castle Combe, finishing ahead of Rosier's Ferrari.

While Tony Gaze was making hay in New Zealand driving his HWM-Jaguar (finishing 3rd at Ardmore and 1st at Christchurch), the works HWMs were updated for the 1956 season by the fitting of full D-type engines; this enabled Abecassis to finish second to Stirling Moss's Aston Martin DB3S at Silverstone. But John Heath was still keen to run in the Mille Miglia and entered an HWM-Jaguar (using the car known as HWM 1). Tragically, the attempt was fatal as the car crashed near Ravenna, and Heath died later in hospital.

In hill climbing, Ray Fielding had a good run of success with his HWM-Jaguar, the ex-Oscar Moore car, recording a number of class wins at Shelsley Walsh, Prescott and Rest-and-be-Thankful. His wife sometimes drove the car too.

The works HWM-Jaguars continued racing officially until the end of 1956, but with the death of John Heath, interest had understandably declined and during 1957 the cars were sold to private owners. In any case, the HWM-Jaguars were soon having to contend with increasing opposition from the ultimately faster Lister-Jaguars.

The last HWM-Jaguar was built up by Phil Scragg to replace his earlier car. He specially commissioned an HWM sports car chassis which he equipped with a cycle-winged body and a full wide-angle, dry sump D-type engine. This car had a very successful career in Scragg's hands and won the Hill Climb Championship in 1959. Scragg's first car incidentally went to East Africa, where it was eventually rescued by Chris Ball. Apparently it was purchased in 1959 by Frank Brown and taken out to Uganda during 1960, after which it was sprinted and raced at various Kenyan venues. It changed hands rather frequently in the sixties but was always one of the fastest cars at the Nairobi and Nakuru race tracks in Kenya, until a piston disintegrated and ruined the C-type head. A D-type head was purchased from Gordon Lee (actually the original head from HCH 736, the ex-Clark, Halford/Naylor Le Mans Lister-Jaguar) but never fitted, and Ball bought the car in mechanically disassembled condition in 1972. Since then he has restored and raced the car both in Kenya and in Historic events here, after bringing the car back to Great Britain in 1973.

One HWM-Jaguar remains as a single seater. This car was originally a works Formula 2 racing car which was fitted with a Jaguar engine in 1954 for Formula Libre racing. It was very badly crashed at Goodwood the same year however by Tony Gaze, and when it was rebuilt the XK engine was taken out and a supercharged prototype HWM/Alta 2½ litre unit put in for hill climbing. But Tony Gaze didn't particularly take to this type of competition, and eventually packed in motor sport altogether and took up gliding! Through George Abecassis the car was then sold to A F Rivers Fletcher who removed the Alta engine and supercharger (the engine itself being sold to John Norris as a spare for his GP Alta) and inserted a 3.4 XK engine once more - quite an easy operation as not only had the car already been fitted with such a unit before, but also from 1953, John Heath had used the C-type gearbox to which the engine of course mated up very nicely. The installation was carried out by Leslie Bellamy, and the bodywork was attended to by Freddie Owen. This Jaguar-engined single seater was then

driven by Rivers Fletcher for three or four years on the hills, both car and driver just surviving a "mammoth shunt" at Prescott in 1960. After two further seasons the car was sold to the 'racing Majors' Lambton and Chichester, whose Wiscombe Park makes one of the most beautiful hill climb courses in the country. They fitted it with a 3.8 litre engine and drive this immaculately turned out car to this day.

As for other HWM-Jaguar survivors, HWM 1 in its final form exists in good order, being raced in HSCC events occasionally by Richard Bond during 1974, and is now owned by Kirk Rylands. The two Phil Scragg cars still exist in excellent order, but XPE 2 however has disappeared. ND 4040, the HWM-Alta-Jaguar, has been nicely restored and is occasionally hill climbed by its present owner Nick Jerrome; XPA 748 belongs to Paul Craigen.

THE COOPER-JAGUAR

The Cooper-Jaguar was both the largest and the final front engined sports car to emerge from John Cooper's Surbiton workshops, and owes its existence to the prompting of Peter Whitehead who realised the potential which lay behind the combination of the powerful Jaguar engine and a Cooper chassis. It was an individual and even slightly eccentric car in some ways, if only because its multi-tubular frame contained not one straight length of steel tubing. This characteristic was a well known fetish of the frame's designer and it at least had the advantage of dispensing with the need for any separate structure on which to hang the aluminium bodywork, which merely followed the oval contours of the main frame.

As one would expect from John Cooper, the car's springing was by transverse leaf both front and rear, though the all independent suspension was a departure for Cooper as it incorporated tubular double wishbones; the leaf springs additionally acted as anti-roll bars, after the fashion of Cooper's later 500 Formula 3 cars. Damping was by telescopic Armstrongs.

The three-point mounted differential with its ENV nose piece had a cast alloy casing designed by Cooper, and took the drive through a short propshaft and passed it to the Dunlop magnesium alloy wheels via two short universally jointed half shafts. The engine in the first Cooper-Jaguars, which were built in 1954, was wet-sump C-type with a C-type gearbox, but these Mk 1 Cooper-Jaguars did have the multi-pad disc brakes with the attendant Plessey pump providing the servo assistance. At 7 feet 7 inches the wheelbase was almost identical to the 1954 D-type's, but the Cooper-Jaguar had a wider track at 4 feet 4 inches and was lighter at just under 17cwt in its original form. The Mk 1 bodywork was rather unusual in appearance, and the first car had a headfairing behind the driver, very low mounted headlights in the nose, and exhaust pipes which emerged high up on the nearside of the car.

The Cooper-Jaguar's first track appearance was at the Daily Express Trophy race in May 1954, but the sorting process that was still going on is evidenced by the car's placing of 9th in the hands of Peter Whitehead, a long way behind the HWM-Jaguar of Abecassis. In June Whitehead invited Duncan Hamilton to share the car with him in the Rheims 12-Hour race, but the ambitious venture came to an end when Duncan experienced complete brake failure approaching the hairpin in practice, spinning to a halt just in front of a flimsy barricade lined with children. A phone call to the ever-helpful Lofty England resulted in the necessary spares being flown out, but the plane was delayed so arrived too late for the car to start. Duncan liked the car, which had undergone modification since Silverstone, its all independent suspension obviously providing better road holding than the C- and D-types he was used to.

The first Cooper-Jaguar did have some real successes however. Later in June at Oporto, Whitehead finished 3rd behind the 3.3 litre Lancias of Villoresi and Castellotti and while these two cars lapped him twice, at least the Cooper-Jaguar proved more reliable than either Hamilton's C-type and Abecassis' HWM-Jaguar. The International Snetterton meeting of August 1954 saw a win by Whitehead ahead of Michael Head's C-type and Bob Berry's very fast XK 120, while another win was recorded by the Cooper-Jaguar in the Wakefield Trophy race at The Curragh, Northern Ireland where Whitehead again beat C-type opposition in the form of Joe Kelly's and Duncan Hamilton's cars.

At the Brussels Show of January 1955 there were a number of Jaguars displayed - the XK 140 and the D-type on Jaguar's own stand, and a new Cooper-Jaguar on its own with bodywork removed to display its new features. The foremost of these was the full dry sump D-type engine that now supplied the horsepower, rated at its normal 'production' 250bhp with the usual three Weber carburettors. The big 4-gallon catch tank for the dry sump lubrication system was mounted on the left alongside the engine, which was positioned quite well back in the frame and inclined at 8 deg to the vertical. The frame itself was an improved and simplified version of the Mk 1 car's and was made up of 1½ inch 14 and 16 swg round steel tubing, still of curved section but with less triangulation. The body was rather more conventional looking too.

Although the driver and passenger seats were still widely separated by the gearbox and its embracing framework which formed the backbone of the car, the driver's seat was not mounted so far outboard as in the earlier cars - of which three had been built altogether. The rearward position of the gearbox did make the gearchange decidedly awkward however, the driver having almost to reach behind him to change ratios.

It would seem that four Mk 11 Cooper-Jaguars were constructed, and they were originally sold to Peter Whitehead, Michael Head (HOT 95), Tommy Sopwith (YPK 400) and Bernard Ecclestone. Probably the most consistently successful of these was Michael

Head's car, which the driver modified to improve both its performance and its ability to drive to race meetings both in Great Britain and abroad. Peter Whitehead and Tommy Sopwith had a measure of success too, Whitehead gaining 4th place in the 1955 Oporto sports car race behind Duncan Hamilton's D-type.

Although the Cooper-Jaguar's independent suspension gave it considerably better road holding than the D-type, particularly on bumpy surfaces, the car did have strong understeering tendencies which put it at a disadvantage, and it never looked like rivalling the Lister-Jaguars when they arrived on the motor racing scene.

We are indebted once again to John Bolster for a contemporary opinion of the Cooper-Jaguar, specifically Michael Head's HOT 95 which as mentioned was probably the most developed of the Mk 11 cars. The test took place in the summer of 1957 shortly after the car had won impressively at the Goodwood Whit Monday meeting, beating Maurice Charles' D-type; in Bolster's eyes it was a very successful machine. Its main assets were its suspension and D-type brakes, while a lot of thought had been devoted to the suspension which "improved the handling out of all recognition" when compared to the original versions. As usual Bolster drove the car extensively on the road, where it was entirely practical:

> What a touring car this is! The acceleration bears little relationship to any normal experience, and a touch of third speed caused the seat back to give one a real kick in the spine as one rockets past the 100mph mark. Once underway, the independent suspension permits the full power to be used without a trace of wheelspin.

Bolster found the Cooper-Jaguar difficult to get off the mark cleanly, because the limited slip device usual in this type of car by 1957 was not present, which meant that care had to be taken in avoiding either too much wheelspin from one wheel, or not enough revs which prevented the engine picking up cleanly. The standing ¼-mile time of 14.8 seconds would otherwise have been better, according to Bolster. Maximum speed was limited to 136.3mph at about 6,100rpm with the car's British circuit gearing.

A fair number of Cooper-Jaguars are still in existence today although they are rarely seen in action even in historic racing. Peter Whitehead's original car, UBH 292, was sold to Cyril Wick who drove it successfully in the Brighton Speed Trials and elsewhere, and is now owned by Martin Noel-Johnson. The car is believed to be still unrepaired following John Harper's bad crash with it at Castle Combe in 1966 during an early historic sports car race.

The Tommy Sopwith, Peter Mould car (YPK 400) is the only Cooper-Jaguar to have reappeared in historic racing, driven first by John McCartney-Filgate, and then by Anthony Hutton and John Harper. Michael Sargent, brother of Peter Sargent, past Le Mans driver in Lister-Jaguars and E-types, now has YPK 400 amongst his small collection of Jaguar engined sports racing cars. Michael Head's car (HOT 95) was rebuilt from a "heap of scrap" in 1967 by Gordon Chapman and has since been sold to Philip Renault of Paris.

THE LISTER-JAGUAR

Like the first Jaguar engined HWM, the first Lister-Jaguar was built by a private owner and not the parent company. A new Lister-Bristol chassis (no. BHL 12) was obtained by Norman Hillwood who fitted it with a wet sump, SU carburetted XK engine, C-type gearbox and Al-Fin drums, for use in hill climbs during 1956/7. The first works Lister-Jaguar did not appear until some months later.

Undoubtedly the most important of the Jaguar engined variant builders, Brian Lister first began making cars in 1954, when after obtaining permission from his parents the first Lister frame was laid down in the family light-engineering factory at Abbey Road, Cambridge. The concern was well equipped for such a project, dealing then as now with a variety of light engineering work including one-off experimental jobs in metal.

The frame of the first car was to set the basic design for almost all subsequent Lister chassis, with two large 3 inch tubes forming the two main frame members, braced by three cross members of similar diameter. This frame was unusual for its era in being very wide within the wheelbase, thus allowing the driver to be seated in between, not on top of, the propellor shaft and main frame side-member, which helped achieve the very low scuttle line which was a feature of Lister's cars. Fabricated uprights held the front suspension and rear axle attachments. The car's aluminium bodywork was supported by a simple frame work of much lighter, unstressed, steel tubes and was completely detachable. Brian Lister's previous motor racing experience had been with a Tojeiro-JAP and a Cooper-MG, both of which had taught him something of chassis engineering, and it was an MG engine that went into his first car.

Lister was determined that Archie Scott Brown was going to be his driver, and in fact he had already driven Lister's Tojeiro-JAP towards the beginning of his motor racing career. It was largely Brian Lister's efforts that overcame the RAC's reluctance to give Scott Brown a motor racing licence, together with *Autosport* and The Earl Howe who both felt that his disability (an unformed right hand) was no reason to ban him from competitions.

The Lister-MG was not very successful, suffering from a lack of power, so the Bristol 2-litre power unit was chosen as a substitute. The Lister-Bristol was raced from mid-1954 onwards and was an immediate success; by the end of the 1955 season, Scott Brown had won 13 races, including the 1955 British Empire Trophy at Oulton Park. For 1956, a Maserati engine of about the same capacity was tried, but it proved to be unreliable in the extreme and never brought Scott Brown the successes of his previous season. Then in 1956, almost coincidentally with Normal Hillwood's experiment, Brian Turle of Shellmex-BP persuaded Brian Lister to build a Jaguar-powered car for circuit racing, as he considered that it couldn't fail to do well.

The 1957 season saw the debut of the works Lister-Jaguar. The car may have been the original Lister-Bristol, MVE 303, with its chassis suitably adapted for the dry sump 3.4 litre D-type engine that was inserted into it. Like the chassis, the suspension remained much as before: equal length wishbones and coil spring/damper units at the front, and at the rear, a de Dion axle located by four trailing arms and sprung by similar coil spring/damper units. Brakes were Girling single caliper 11 inch discs at the front, and inboard 10 inch disc at the rear. The ubiquitous Morris Minor rack and pinion steering provided directional control. The 18 gallon fuel tank and the dry sump oil tank were both carried on an outrigged frame behind the rear axle - all could be attended to in just three minutes by the removal of the rear bodywork. Such was the Lister-Jaguar's accessibility that it was said that the engine itself could be removed "by two skilled men" in 30 minutes! Wheelbase was 7 feet 5 inches, track 4 feet 2½ inches front and 4 feet 4 inches rear, and the car measured 13 feet from stem to stern; height to the scuttle was 2 feet 5 inches. The D-type engine was tuned by Don Moore after being purchased new from Jaguar, and probably gave more power than the factory's rated output of 250 bhp. It was in fact to be the only power unit actually purchased from Jaguar by Listers, all subsequent engines being gladly supplied on a 'permanent loan' basis by the works for the team cars.

A D-type gearbox with its synchromesh first gear transmitted the power to the rear axle, which was of Salisbury manufacture but incorporated a ZF differential. The car ran on 16 inch Dunlop alloy wheels although these were bolt-on unlike the D-type's knock-off variety. Dunlop 600 section tyres were used on the front wheels, and 700 section on the rears. The completed car weighed under 16 cwt dry, rather less than either the Cooper-Jaguar, or the D-type which of course Jaguar had already given up racing themselves; in fact it was very much the Lister-Jaguar that was to take up the Jaguar torch on British and most continental circuits from 1957 onwards.

The new car first appeared in March 1957, at Snetterton and would undoubtedly have won on its first time out but for the clutch failing to return after the first corner. Rejoining the race seven laps down, Scott Brown made fastest lap but had no hope of catching the winner, Dick Protheroe in a Tojeiro-Jaguar. However, at Oulton Park in April, no such silly fault let Scott Brown and the Lister-Jaguar down, and they led the works Aston Martins home by ten seconds to win Archie his second British Empire Trophy race; Salvadori's 2.5 DBR1 was next home. The Lister driver had also made fastest lap, equalling the lap record set up by the Swiss driver Musy the previous year in a 3-litre Maserati.

This race set the pattern for the remainder of the season. A couple of weeks later at the International Goodwood meeting, Scott Brown again headed the works Astons, with Salvadori second once more, Tony Brooks (DB3S) third and Duncan Hamilton fourth. This time, Scott Brown's fastest lap was an outright class record. Nor was a fast circuit a necessary requisite for victory, as in early June Archie won at Crystal Palace, in front of Whitehead's DB3S and Les Leston's HWM-Jaguar. At Aintree in July, in the 'Unlimited' sports car race held during the GP meeting, Scott Brown continued his domination of sports car racing by defeating the Aston Martins yet again. In fact only once during the 1957 season did the works Astons beat the flying Lister-Jaguar, and that was at the Daily Express International Trophy meeting at Silverstone. Once the preserve of Jaguar, the sports car race included in the programme of that meeting each year had recently seen a run of Aston Martin victories, and these Salvadori continued by finishing in front of Scott Brown with his new 3.7 litre engined car; by this time, the Lister too had been up-graded in engine capacity, now being fitted with the 3.8 litre D-type unit. When the 1957 season concluded,

Scott Brown could look back upon 12 wins out of 14 races entered, one second place, and one retirement (at Snetterton, the car's first race). Moreover, on every circuit at which he had raced the Lister-Jaguar, he had broken or equalled the 'Unlimited' sports car lap record either in race or practice.

John Bolster spent a weekend with Archie's car at the end of the 1957 season, driving it away from Goodwood almost as soon as Scott-Brown stepped from the cockpit having won the Goodwood Trophy for large capacity sports cars, ahead of Jack Brabham. The acceleration figures recorded by the motoring journalist were better than those of any other sports racing car he had tested, the Lister-Jaguar reaching 60 mph in 4.6 seconds, 80 mph in 8 seconds, 100 mph in 11.2 seconds, and 120 mph in 15.2 seconds. In fact Bolster found the car's acceleration to 140 mph "breathtaking", and he estimated that 190 mph might well be possible with suitable gearing (as tested it ran with a short circuit gearing of 3.73:1). Certainly the Lister-Jaguar had a very low frontal area compared with even 2-litre sports racing cars of its era.

Of the handling Bolster said: "There is no roll, the car simply remaining level and answering perfectly to its light and accurate steering. Rear end breakaway does not occur unless it is provoked deliberately with that immense horsepower". The car was driven through several large towns "with no difficulty"- the engine, while at its happiest on the open road of course, "by sympathetic handling...can be made to behave in quite a docile manner". Quite a lot of heat was felt to come through the bulkhead but the warmth in the cool autumn mornings was "most comforting". This factor, combined with the bodywork extending up to shoulder level, made it perfectly possible for Bolster to travel without wearing an overcoat (though no doubt still with his deerstalker!) for the hundreds of miles he drove the Lister. Likewise, the full-width Perspex screen protected both driver and passenger to the extent that goggles weren't necessary.

One comment concerning road driving was that more silencing would have been desirable "for continuous use", but this was the only argument offered against using the car regularly on the road - a contrast to today's sports racing machinery! Touring petrol consumption was about 15mpg, rising to 10mpg when racing.

During the early weeks of 1958, Scott Brown and MVE 303 went to New Zealand to continue their racing; they took on the fastest of the locals and won the Lady Wigram Trophy race at the record speed of 83.93 mph, beating a 250F Maserati, and were in third place while contesting the New Zealand Grand Prix itself when a front suspension fault forced a retirement. Scott Brown won again at Invercargill, but at Dunedin the Lister had differential trouble.

After returning home, MVE 303 was given many detailed improvements, and a small but steady number of cars to a similar specification began to leave the Lister workshops (which were managed by George Palmer) to be sold to a variety of private clients. The main changes were 12 inch diameter quick-change Girling brakes all round (the rear pads could be renewed by taking off two removable panels without detaching the main rear bodyshell itself), the fuel tank (enlarged to 38 gallons) was now carried over the rear axle not behind it, and the oil tank was moved to a position in the nearside quarter of the tail - it too was bigger, of 8 gallons capacity to allow ample room for oil - frothing due to the dry sump lubrication system. Only five gallons of oil were actually in circulation though.

The Dunlop alloy wheels were still 16 inch in diameter and of 5 inch rim width, but were now knock-off. The car's rear track was increased by 3 inches and at the front, a new anti-roll bar of thicker section was added. The 1958 cars were given specially designed bodies conforming to Appendix 'C' requirements for International racing; the effect of the depth of screen regulations was cleverly minimised by cutting short the 'bonnet' just in front of the scuttle, which was lower than the engine. The tail of the car was on a level with the wrap-around Perspex windscreen; the bodies were made by Williams and Pritchard. The cockpit layout was improved with a combined starter/ignition switch as an aid to Le Mans-type starts.

The 3.4 litre dry sump 250bhp engine remained the standard fitment, but in view of the new international regulations a 3-litre 83mm x 92mm version was offered as well - this was Jaguar's own conversion of 2986cc and with the 35/40 head gave 254bhp at 6,300rpm, or slightly more power than that given by a standard 3.4 litre D-type engine. The wide angle head could also be supplied, at extra cost, on the 3.4 engine normally supplied with the Lister-Jaguar. The gearbox was still D-type, and the rear axle came with a Salisbury Powr Lok differential, although a ZF limited slip device could be specified as an alternative by the customer, again at extra cost.

Length had increased over MVE 303's original 13 feet, another 6 inches having been added; turning circle was 40 feet, obtained by two turns of the Derrington light-alloy leather-covered steering wheel. Weight was given as 15½cwt, distributed 48% front, 52% rear. The cost of a complete Lister-Jaguar was £2,750 without purchase tax.

This sort of specification, backed by Scott Brown's brilliant record of the previous season, attracted a number of private entrants keen to run Lister-Jaguars. The first Lister-Jaguar actually built for sale had been completed in 1957, and featured different bodywork (by Gomm of Woking) from the true 'production' cars that were to follow. Registered HCH 736, formerly a Lister Bristol the car was sold to Dick Walsh and was to have a most interesting life, originally being driven by Bruce Halford. Besides individual enquiries, such distinguished private racing teams as Ecurie Ecosse and Equipe Nationale Belge sought to run Lister-Jaguars, finding their D-type Jaguars increasingly outclassed. True production began in 1958, and besides the European teams mentioned, Briggs Cunningham of America also became a customer. He ordered three chassis, two of which came with D-type engines while the third was shipped engineless to have a Chevrolet unit installed in the States. Although it was at first reported that Cunningham found the cars heavier than he had expected, his entries did very well both in 1958 and 1959, Walt Hansgen winning the 'modified' class of the SCCA Championship both years driving Cunningham-entered Lister-Jaguars. In fact Listers became quite fashionable for racing in the States, and as many as 20 or 30 were exported there, through a small network of three distributors - Carroll Shelby, Kjell Qvale, and the Momo Corporation (which prepared Cunningham's cars). When a Jaguar engine was specified as the power unit it was installed in the chassis at the Cambridge works, but if the customer wished to use another type of engine (usually Chevrolet because of the good parts availability) then the chassis was sent engineless. Listers did fit one Chevrolet engine themselves, to work out engine mountings, but it seems that only a couple of Chevrolet-powered cars were raced in Britain, and they weren't terribly successful.

Cunningham entered his Listers in the 1958 Sebring 12-hour race, Scott Brown travelling out to drive one of them - a rare excursion abroad for him, as Continental race organisers still refused him permission to race inspite of his brilliant record on British race tracks. At Sebring however, all the Lister entries retired.

The works Lister-Jaguars ran with 3.8 engines, still prepared by Don Moore. MVE 303 had been joined by VPP 9 of almost identical appearance, though it was to have a particularly unhappy life. The season began well however, Scott Brown winning two races at the March 1958 Snetterton meeting although at Goodwood on Easter Monday while driving VPP 9, he had to retire while chasing Moss due to the car's steering tightening up. At this same meeting, Peter Whitehead was racing his new Lister-Jaguar, and Bruce Halford fielded HCH 736; unfortunately they both retired too.

Scott Brown did not manage to repeat his previous year's winning performance in the British Empire Trophy race of April, MVE 303 breaking the drop-arm in its steering during the qualifying heat. Very sportingly Bruce Halford lent Scott Brown HCH 736 but it proved to be some four seconds a lap slower than the works car, and things weren't made any easier by Archie's small size - despite a number of cushions he still couldn't reach the pedals properly. In view of this, his third place behind Aston Martin opposition was highly creditable. Revenge was wrought by the Lister camp the same month at Aintree however, where Scott-Brown kept ahead of Salvadori's DBR2 to win the '200' event. Masten Gregory was third in the Lister-Jaguar bought by David Murray to supplement Ecurie Ecosse's ageing D-types. At the May *Daily Express* Silverstone meeting, Lister-Jaguars were placed one and two, this time Masten Gregory finishing in front of Scott-Brown, at an average of only .5mph under 100mph; the Lister organisation took great satisfaction in beating Hawthorn's Ferrari and Moss's Aston Martin DBR3 on this occasion.

The rivalry between Gregory and Scott Brown was continued at the Belgian sports car GP at Spa in May 1958. Both were entered in their Lister-Jaguars, Scott Brown in VPP 9. The young Jim Clark was there too, having his first continental race, driving the Border Reivers D-type. He gave a graphic description of the epic struggle between the two Lister-Jaguars in his book *Jim Clark at the Wheel*, as they lapped him near the end of the race:

Suddenly there was an almighty howl of sound, a blast of wind, the whole car shook, and Masten went steaming past like a bat out of hell. He was well out in the lead with the Lister-Jaguar all sideways, his arms crossed up and fighting the steering. I remember having a sudden twinge of shock and thinking 'To heck with this, if this is motor racing I'm going to give it up now'. It really put me off. I didn't think anyone could drive a car as quickly as that...

Then came tragedy. Archie Scott Brown lost

control on a corner and crashed off the track into a field, where the car caught fire. Although a gendarme managed to drag him from the wreckage, he was too badly burned to live and died later in hospital. Almost undoubtedly, the basic cause of the crash was an unlucky shower of rain which dampened that one corner (near the clubhouse) on the circuit and nowhere else. "I honestly think that Archie was caught in that shower of rain", Clark wrote. "He had slid wide, not much, but enough to put him slightly off the road and the car hit a marker and bounced off the road". And so, as Clark also said, "that day racing lost a courageous and colourful character". Masten Gregory went on to win, but it gave no-one great pleasure even though he beat the 3.7 litre DBR Aston Martin.

Brian Lister was all for giving up motor racing on the spot; he had lost far more than a works driver who had helped him evolve the Lister-Jaguar into a car of international importance, he had lost a close friend too. Eventually he decided to continue, perhaps mindful of the fact that the Lister-Jaguar was now the leading hope in British sports car racing.

The 1958 Le Mans race was the scene of two private Lister-Jaguar entries, but the Equipe Nationale Belge entered car failed early on and only HCH 736 driven by Bruce Halford and Brian Naylor finished, in fifteenth place. At one time it had been circulating as high as 6th but was delayed during the night when a camshaft had to be replaced; later on gearbox problems ensured that it would never be in real contention and it even failed to cover the official minimum qualifying distance.

Immediately after the 1958 Le Mans race there was repeated the 'Monzanapolis' event at Monza, in which the Ecurie Ecosse D-types had done so well the year before on sheer reliability as much as anything. It was an attempt to combine extra speed with the same reliability that David Murray asked Brian Lister to build them what amounted to a British version of an Indianapolis car. The single seater which resulted

was based on a normal Lister frame, but had heavy duty suspension to cope with the extra loads imposed by running on the banking at high speed, 17 inch diameter front wheels and 18 inch rear wheels to reduce centrifugal force on the tyres; it had no servo on the brakes and weighed 15cwt dry - or not really a lot less than a production type Lister-Jaguar. A D-type engine powered it of course.

Unfortunately, when tried at Monza it proved to be slower than the D-types - no doubt any reduction in frontal area was more than cancelled out by an increased drag factor over the D-type's efficient enclosed bodywork. Even worse, it ended by comprehensively ruining its engine as it finished the second of the three heats while being driven by Jack Fairman (a camshaft broke up). It was seen no more in Ecurie Ecosse's hands (one wonders whether, had the single seater proved a success at Monza, Murray would have tried for an Indianapolis entry) but was later converted into a road going two-seater and used with excellent results by Phil Scragg as a hill climb car, registered as 254 KTU. Owned today by Gordon Chapman, it is being rebuilt to its original Monzanapolis single seater specification, in which form it will be one of the very few Jaguar engined cars eligible for use in the VSCC's post-war single seater historic racing formula.

Meanwhile, VPP 9 had apparently been rebuilt after the fatal Spa crash, it and MVE 303 appearing at the British GP meeting at Silverstone in May 1958. Stirling Moss was the nominated driver for MVE 303, and American driver Walt Hansgen was to pilot VPP 9. Practice showed that MVE 303 was overheating badly, a problem never encountered before with the car but brought on by a couple of modifications Don Moore had made to its engine, and the very high ambient temperature that day. So when MVE 303 appeared on the grid for the actual race, it sported an extra air intake hurriedly cut into the bodywork between the registration number and roundel on the front. The dodge

Top left Archie Scott Brown, probably the greatest of all regular sports car drivers of his day, sitting in the green and yellow Lister-Jaguar which he made so famous *(photo The Motor)*

Top right The American driver Masten Gregory in a cheerful mood at the *Daily Express* meeting of May 1958; he won the sports car race in the Lister-Jaguar, averaging 99.54 mph

Centre Masten Gregory tries the 'single seater' Lister-Jaguar on the Monza banking, prior to the 1958 'Race of Two Worlds'. Unfortunately it proved no faster than the Ecurie Ecosse D-types *(photo The Motor)*

Bottom The 'Monzanapolis' Lister-Jaguar, in the Ecurie Ecosse pits. Note the 17 inch wheels, Dunlop disc on front, wire on back *(photo The Motor)*

Top Archie Scott Brown leads the pack off the grid on a wet Aintree circuit. This picture shows MVE 303 with its earlier bodywork; behind in the Aston Martin is Roy Salvadori, while the D-type (no. 1) is that of Duncan Hamilton *(photo The Motor)*

Centre Typically exuberant cornering by Scott Brown, this time in New Zealand where the Lister-Jaguar chased the single-seaters, rather to their astonishment! Here, Stewart Lewis-Evans is pursued by Ron Roycroft in a 4½-litre Ferrari with Archie trying to get round on the outside

Bottom left Scott Brown and Brian Lister in the Cambridge workshops, examining the building of the 1958 car *(photo Brian Lister)*

Bottom right Lister-Jaguar rear suspension, showing the inboard disc brakes and coil spring/damper units. The upper mountings for these also incorporated a roll-over bar *(photo The Motor)*

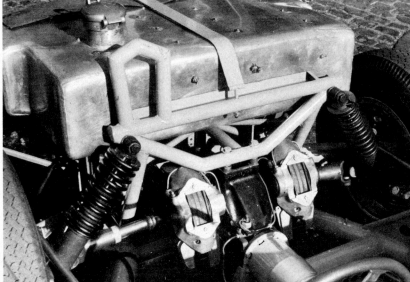

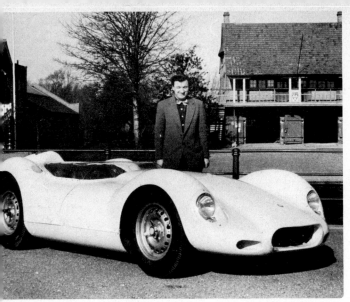

Top left Brian Lister stands by his new Lister-Jaguar
for 1958, on the occasion of its press launch. About
two dozen of these 'knobbly' bodied Listers were
made, most with D-type engines but some with
Chevrolet units *(photo The Motor)*
Top right The 1958 Lister-Jaguar, showing the high
mounted fuel tank, and the oil tank for the dry-sump
D-type engine *(photo The Motor)*
Centre Sebring, 1958, a few seconds after the Le
Mans start. Crawford's Lister-Jaguar temporarily
heads the Ferraris of Phil Hill and Mike Hawthorn
Bottom The Halford/Naylor Lister-Jaguar rounds
Terte Rouge, Le Mans 1958. Although 6th at one
stage, HCH 736 was lying down in fifteenth place
when the race ended *(photo The Motor)*

Top Masten Gregory in the metallic-blue Ecurie Ecosse Lister-Jaguar at the *Daily Express* Trophy meeting at Silverstone, May 1958, when he beat Scott Brown *(photo The Motor)*

Centre British GP meeting, Silverstone in July 1958, and Moss drives the works Lister-Jaguar MVE 303 to victory in the sports car race *(photo The Motor)*

Bottom John Bekeart, one of the most successful private entrants of Lister-Jaguars towards the end of the fifties and early sixties *(photo The Motor)*

Top The Costin-bodied Lister-Jaguar as announced for the 1959 season, photographed outside Lister's Abbey Road premises (note the display and awards in the window) *(photo The Motor)*

Centre Stirling Moss in the Cunningham-entered Lister-Jaguar during the 1959 Sebring 12 Hour race; co-driven by Bueb, he was disqualified after running out of fuel having miscalculated the car's consumption

Bottom left Le Mans 1959, and the Costin-bodied Lister-Jaguar of Bueb/Halford. It did not finish *(photo The Motor)*

Bottom right Ivor Bueb in the works 'Costin' car during the Aintree 200 race of April 1959, followed by the Tojeiro-Jaguar of Ecurie Ecosse and Jim Clark in the Border Reivers' Lister, HCH 736

Top left Phil Scragg and his Lister-Jaguar often proved unbeatable in its class on the hills - this is the Bugatti Owners Club meeting at Prescott, June 1960 *(photo The Motor)*
Top right 'Trouble at mill'. The 3-litre engine of the Ecurie Ecosse Lister-Jaguar dangles from its hoist, giving a good view of the dry-sump equipment, but despite the attention of the mechanics the car failed to last the distance in the 1959 Le Mans race *(photo The Motor)*
Bottom The Lister-Jaguar with space frame and coupe body entered by Messrs Lumsden and Sargent at Le Mans 1963. The last Lister to run at Le Mans, the car did not finish *(photo The Motor)*

Top The RAC TT of September 1959, and the scene in the Ecurie Ecosse pit. As the Tojeiro-Jaguar is refuelled, Jim Clark hands over to Masten Gregory who straps on his helmet; David Murrey watches, just behind Clark *(photo The Motor)*
Centre How the 1959 TT ended for Ecurie Ecosse - the very thoroughly crashed Tojeiro-Jaguar of Masten Gregory and Jim Clark, stuffed in to the bank at Goodwood by the former *(photo The Motor)*
Bottom left Dick Shattock and the re-bodied RGS-Atalanta; note the unusual twin fins at the rear of the car. The occasion is the Daily Express Trophy meeting of 1955 *(photo The Motor)*
Bottom right Larry Humphries and his XK-powered Special at the Mount Druitt circuit, Sydney, Australia; this car evolved into the Dalro-Jaguar *(photo Wheels Magazine)*

Top left Ken Flint's E-type ERA, fitted with a Jaguar XK
engine and campaigned during the mid-fifties. The car now has
a rather more original power unit fitted!
Top right A F Rivers Fletcher with his XK 120-based single-
seater Jaguar, often seen at Prescott. The car is now in Holland
Centre A remarkably good-looking Jaguar-engined single-seater
racing car - the Dalro-Jaguar from Australia
Bottom Ancient and modern - the Panther J72, six cylinder
version, alongside its inspiration, the SS Jaguar 100 (right)
A similar project in the States, the Squire, uses a native
V8 engine

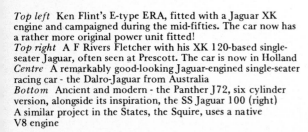

Top An early wind-tunnel model of the open E-type
Centre left The first E-type prototype, E1A, in Christopher Jennings' courtyard - the year, 1958. Note the lack of headlights and windscreen wipers *(photo Christopher Jennings)*
Centre right A rear view of E1A on test in Wales, Mrs Jennings at the wheel. The car's registration number was later transferred to the racing prototype E2A. *(photo Christopher Jennings)*
Bottom E1A's cockpit - note the abundance of rivet heads in the aluminium panels and generally functional appearance. The doors lacked wind-up windows and there was no hood, side screens only being fitted *(photo Christopher Jennings)*

Top The first full-sized E-type prototype, a steel bodied car, photographed in 1959. It displays all the main features of the production E-type except for internal trim, sidelights and indicators, and headlight surrounds and other small items
Centre E2A in sectional drawing. Compare this car's independent rear suspension with that of the E-type's. The car is shown in 1960 Le Mans trim, with passenger compartment covered by the stream-lined 'tonneau cover' *(photo The Autocar)*
Bottom left and right E2A, the sports racing prototype which would have been the D-type's successor. In Cunningham racing colours, it was lent to the American to run in the 1960 Le Mans race, where it is seen during scrutineering. In both looks and rear suspension it forecast the E-type to come *(photos The Motor)*

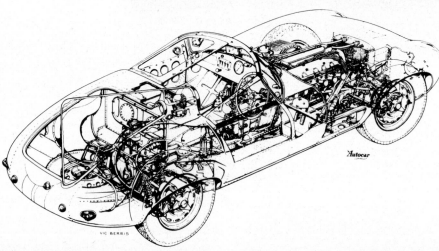

Top left The aluminium monocoque centre section of the E2A under construction. Note the extensive use of rivets, and the weights of individual panels marked on each

Top right Night refuelling stop for E2A at Le Mans; although amongst the fastest cars in practice, it did not finish the race *(photo The Motor)*

Centre After its unsuccessful Le Mans debut, E2A went to the States; but despite the 3.8 engine and more streamlined windscreen which can be seen in this 1972 photograph, the car's fortunes did not improve for very long

Bottom Jaguar prototype based on the Daimler SP 250 chassis. After taking over Daimler, Jaguar investigated the production of a revised SP 250, retaining the V8 engine (albeit moved further back in the chassis) but restyling the bodywork and interior; the similarity of the car's front end to the MGB, which appeared almost a year after this body was built, is probably coincidental *(photo Jaguar Cars)*

Top Debut at the March 1961 Geneva Motor Show for the E-type; although the fixed-head version was almost an afterthought, it was the first variety to be publicly shown *(photo The Motor)*

Bottom left E-type Open Two Seater - this is the 1961 *Motor* road test car, one of the first off the line. Clearly seen is the 'T' key slot for opening the bonnet, a feature of early examples *(photo The Motor)*

Bottom right The Motor's road test E-type photographed against the backdrop of the French Alps *(photo The Motor)* worked, Moss winning the race at 97.92mph, although any threat from Hansgen evaporated when VPP 9 dropped a valve while in second place; Masten Gregory had crashed the Ecurie Ecosse Lister-Jaguar in practise so a challenge from that quarter had been eliminated too.

Hansgen raced for Lister again while visiting Great Britain, his fortune improving at Snetterton when also in July he won the over 2,700cc class in the sports car event at an average of 92.37mph, capturing the class record as well (he was similarly successful in a 3.4 saloon on the same occasion, though at the rather lower speed of 83.92mph!). In the States of course, Walt Hansgen was almost invincible in his Cunningham entered Lister-Jaguar.

Ivor Bueb had now joined the permanent Lister team, and began well by winning the big sports car race at the Bank Holiday Brands Hatch meeting in August, heading the Lister-Jaguars driven by Ross Jensen and Bruce Halford. One of Bueb's last 1958 Lister-Jaguar drives came at Snetterton in September, where very appropriately he won the newly instigated Scott Brown Memorial Trophy race. The Tourist Trophy was another September date for the works Listers, but both cars retired. The weekend afterwards Bueb and Halford finished second and third at Oulton to end their season.

While Brian Lister remained entirely faithful to his original conception so far as the chassis and running gear of his 1959 cars was concerned, the new Lister-Jaguars were of totally different appearance to all the earlier Listers due to their Frank Costin designed bodywork.

One of the leading aerodynamicists of the time in the racing car field, Costin had already produced very effective bodies for Lotus and Vanwall, and typical Costin features were apparent in his Lister designs - particularly the high tail section and the curved windscreen. In general, the car's line was now more penetrating, smoother and a little longer, with a bulge in the bonnet to accommodate the height of the engine without it being canted on one side; air intakes for front and rear brake cooling were incorporated at key points. Although it looked bigger and bulkier than the previous shape (which had been inherited from the Lister-Bristol), the new design was probably more efficient at speed. Mechanical changes were few, the biggest being the adoption of Dunlop disc brakes in place of the Girlings.

Briggs Cunningham ordered two of the Costin bodied cars for the 1959 season, one with a Jaguar engine - the other he fitted with a V8 Chevrolet unit; this made a total of at least five Listers which Cunningham had imported, as he already possessed three 'knobbly' bodied 1958 cars. This was out of a total production of 35-40 Lister-Jaguar and Lister-Chevrolet chassis.

Once again though, the Listers failed at Sebring inspite of what seemed to be a very strong entry in the 1959 event. Three cars were entered, driven by Moss/Bueb, Hansgen/Thompson, and Cunningham/Underwood. All had the 2986cc variation on the XK engine theme, and one had water cooled drum brakes of a type seen on the last Cunningham car to have run at Le Mans. The opposition was fierce however, Ferrari now having both disc brakes and an estimated 320bhp - or about 60bhp more than the 3-litre Lister-Jaguars.

The biggest blow came when Stirling Moss ran out of fuel and was then disqualified for accepting a lift back to the pits. He eventually continued in Briggs' own car and finished 15th, while Hansgen and Thompson drove the other surviving Lister-Jaguar into 12th place. But Walt Hansgan did at least manage to win the Watkins Glen Grand Prix for Cunningham, driving one of the older 'knobbly' bodied Lister-Jaguars; this was one of five races in a row won by that American driver.

In England, Lister fortunes were similarly mixed. Ron Flockhart drove the Ecurie Ecosse Lister-Jaguar to second place in the Formula Libre race at Snetterton in March 1959, John Bekaert in a 'knobbly' bodied car coming third

(NBL 660); both these cars had 3.8 engines. Works driver Bueb had a win at Goodwood during the same month and won the very wet Easter Monday Goodwood sports car race from Peter Blond's Lister-Jaguar and a DBR1. Masten Gregory managed a number of 'places', while Peter Sutcliffe, Bill Moss and Peter Mould all drove their privately owned Lister-Jaguars with reasonable success. The Border Reivers had also bought a Lister-Jaguar, to replace the faithful TKF 9, and so Jim Clark commenced driving HCH 736 - "the best Lister ever made", according to him. Clark travelled down to Luton to pick up the car from Bruce Halford and drove it back to Scotland on the road; the journey included such amusements as passing an unaware Ford Thunderbird cruising at 120mph at full chat in the Lister, at around 150mph! Jim Clark's comments on this car are well worth **repeating**, and again I quote from his autobiography:

The Lister taught me a great deal about racing, and I had fun with that car. It was a beast of a thing, mind you, really vicious, but it was more fun than any except maybe the Aston Martins I drove later. When we got back to Berwick we started to modify the Lister for I honestly don't know how Bruce managed to drive it. It was so cramped in the cockpit. We managed to carve a bit out of the bulkhead behind the seats to push the driver's seat further back and my first race with the car was at Mallory Park where I had a real field day winning three races in the Lister...

I began to learn a lot after those first races for I found that it was a lively car. You could drive it round the corners on the throttle whereas the D-type was all stop or all go. The Lister was very much more progressive. It taught me quite a bit about brakes in that I couldn't rely on them. I had to nurse them and make them work, without overheating them. I remember at Aintree once going to have the tyres checked just before the race. I got up there and put my foot on the brakes and the pedal went straight to the board. I pumped it and the pressure came back and that's how we set off for the race! That was a great day for me for it was the sports car race before the British Grand Prix in 1959 which Stirling won in the Vanwall. In that race it poured with rain and I finished second to Graham Hill in a 2½ litre Lotus,

managing to beat all the works Listers.

...the handling of the car was fabulous. For example, at Gerard's Bend at Mallory you could set the car up going into the bend hard, and get round the corner without touching the steering again. If you wanted to come out tight you just put your boot in it, the tail came round and it was a matter of driving it round on the throttle the whole way. That really taught me quite a bit about racing, particularly about controlling a car by the throttle.

The Whitsun Goodwood meeting in May 1959 was a disappointment for Jim Clark, for after a great struggle and a lot of opposite lock motoring he took the lead in front of Ron Flockhart's Ecurie Ecosse Tojeiro-Jaguar (there being great rivalry between the two Scottish motor racing teams), only to coast to a halt a few laps from the end of the race with an empty petrol tank. Bekaert put up fastest lap in NBL 660 and came second to Flockhart, with Peter Blond's Lister-Jaguar finishing in third place.

At the *Daily Express* Trophy meeting at Silverstone in April, Bueb had managed a third place behind Salvadori and Moss, although it was Graham Hill who had been leading for most of the race before retiring his Cooper Monaco. But generally, it was becoming clear during the 1959 season that the smaller rear engined Lotuses and Coopers were commencing their domination of sports car racing. Bueb's fastest lap at Crystal Palace in April was, for instance, a second quicker than his record of the year before set in the 'knobbly' bodied Lister, but in 1959 it was only good enough to secure him fourth position behind Cooper Maserati, Cooper Climax and Lotus Climax cars. In the British Empire Trophy race six Lister-Jaguars ran but the highest was Bueb in fourth place again (Clark came 8th), while at the Aintree 200 meeting in April Masten Gregory finished third behind Salvadori's 2½ litre Cooper Maserati and Graham Hill's 2-litre Cooper-Climax; Ron Flockhart was fourth in the Tojeiro-Jaguar, Jim Clark sixth.

Nothing came of Ecurie Ecosse's entry in the Nurburgring 1000km, nor did Peter Blond's Lister-Jaguar finish, co-driver Michael Taylor crashing the car. At Le Mans, four Lister-Jaguars ran in 1959 but none lasted the 24 hours, let down by their 3-litre engines. Two of the cars were works entries, driven by Bueb/Halford (a Costin bodied car) and Hansgen/Crawford (VPP 9, now with Costin bodywork). The Bueb/Halford car went extremely well while it was going, and by 2am it was lying in 5th place, a fuel-stop ahead of the leading Aston Martin. Then a connecting rod went, and that was that. The single Ecurie Ecosse Lister-Jaguar entered had Wilkie Wilkinson's 2954cc, 83mm x 91mm XK engine giving about 230bhp (as opposed to Jaguar's own 2986cc unit which put out around 250bhp). It too failed, and likewise the Belgian entered Lister-Jaguar driven by Bianchi and Craisier.

Then came the sad death of Ivor Bueb in August, another blow to Brian Lister even though he wasn't killed in one of his cars. The sole works Lister entry for the Tourist Trophy at Goodwood in September was therefore driven by Peter Blond and Jonathan Sieff, but the header tank sprung a leak and so Brian Lister's last official effort on the race track ended in retirement.

In September 1959 Bill Moss again won the Scott Brown Memorial Trophy in his Costin-bodied car, and Gordon Lee won the sports car class in his race at Boxing Day Brands with HCH 736, purchased when the Border Reivers decided to buy a DBR1 Aston. When the 1959 season closed, Lister had announced his withdrawal from racing, and although this was originally stated to be 'temporary', it so happened that never again was a Lister-Jaguar to be officially entered from Cambridge.

For Lister to have remained ahead of the opposition a completely new car would have been required, and probably an engine with a better power-to-weight ratio than the faithful old straight six Jaguar unit possessed. There was talk of a 5.7 litre Maserati engined Lister, but only Carroll Shelby tried this combination inserting a 450S V8 unit into a Lister frame in the States. It still exists, but apparently was not very successful.

The Lister concern could no longer compete with the specialists such as Lotus and Cooper, and only one other car left the factory after 1959. This was a true space-frame Lister-Jaguar, and it was bought by Jim Diggory who entered Bruce Halford in it during 1960. Its principle success that year was at Brands Hatch, where at the Lewis-Evans Trophy meeting Halford drove the car to victory in the over 1,500cc sports car race ahead of John Bekaert, setting up a class record for the Club circuit as he did so. This car had a Costin body very similar to the 1959 cars.

Lister-Jaguars did not fade away from the circuits with the retirement of Lister as an official force however, John Bekaert having a very successful 1960 season in NBL 660, while Gordon Lee continued to drive HCH 736 with very worthwhile results for a number of years after that, holding the Silverstone club circuit class record for several seasons.

The name Lister didn't disappear entirely from big-time motor racing either, as in 1963 Peter Sargent and Peter Lumsden bought the space-frame Lister-Jaguar and entered it for Le Mans. The car was substantially modified for the event, Frank Costin being called in again to re-design much of the bodywork to make room for bigger brakes at the front, and to convert the car into a closed coupe. This had doors which extended into the shape of the roof, and were to provide a striking instance of the effect of wind pressure at speed down the Mulsanne Straight - at around 170mph, the tops of the doors would be drawn open wide enough for the driver to put his whole hand and wrist through the gap created. Besides the larger brakes and re-worked front suspension, an alloy engine was installed, and the car was just completed in time for the Le Mans test days although it was too new to put in any spectacular times.

The race didn't go at all well for the two Peters. Taking first spell at the wheel, Sargent was confronted with a small French car rolling near the Esses, and although he stood on the brakes he could not stop the Lister just touching the crashed vehicle. In any case, the car was handling "worse than a wet bath sponge" as the suspension was too soft (after the race the spring thicknesses were just about doubled throughout), and clutch failure finally halted progress after only three hours. This was the result of a particular piece of ill luck - the clutch had been one of a batch rebuilt by Borg and Beck with the wrong bolts, and they promptly sheared as the Lister drew away from the pits after its first refuelling stop. The space-frame coupe was the last Lister-Jaguar to run at Le Mans.

Lister-Jaguars continued to race at smaller meetings and at club events well into the sixties, John Coundley winning the 100 Mile Martini Trophy race at AMOC Silverstone as late as July 1962 (this 'knobbly' bodied car was later bought by Mike Wright, and met its end in a road accident - following which it is believed to have been decently buried in a pit!). Gradually however, the new E-type became the car to drive if you wanted to win in Jaguar-propelled machinery.

Whilst there are some notable exceptions, quite a large number of Lister chassis survived long enough to be saved by the historic racing fraternity, and there are now more Listers than ever in this country due to a substantial number having been bought by British dealers operating in the States, and shipped back to this country. In British historic racing the Lister-Jaguar is a leading contender, with few of its contemporaries able to beat it - just as was the case in 1957 and 1958.

The very original Jaguar engined Lister, 673 LMK, is still hale and hearty, and after being campaigned by its builder Norman Hillwood, then Gerry Ashmore, Brian Windmarsh, George Tatham, the Harris brothers and Anthony Hutton, is now the property of Philip Renault. At the time of writing it is still kept in this country, and is driven by John Harper with great effect in historic and JCB events. The author

drove this car to Le Mans in 1973 for the 50th anniversary of Le Mans celebrations, and in the commemorative 45 minute historic race over the famous circuit it finished in 8th position, driven by its new owner Renault. (It behaved impeccably on the journey there and back incidentally, performance from its D-type headed wet sump engine being in excess of most fast cars of today, with controllable handling and roadholding of a very high order even when judged by today's standards for a road car. It did not appreciate some of the rather disastrous French road surfaces however, which limited its cruising speed to 30mph in places and necessitated the tightening of quite a few bolts after the exercise was over!).

Of the two works cars, VPP 9 ended up with Costin bodywork for the 1959 Le Mans race in which it blew up its 3-litre engine, and was then fitted with a wet sump 3.4 litre D-type unit. After an undistinguished period in the hands of various drivers (one of whom is on record as stating that "either the car is a complete cow...or at least, that it was not a car for the amateur") it was sold to a film company who used it for making 'The Green Helmet' in 1960. It finally ended its rather sorry history (it or a car registered VPP 9 was the vehicle in which Scott Brown himself died) by crashing at Goodwood, killing its driver Roy Bloxham; the 3.8 engine that had been fitted by Bloxham went into Richardson's Aceca Special, and thence to Guy Griffiths. The chassis is presumed broken up.

HCH 736 was bought back by Gordon Lee in the late sixties, restored, and was raced by him in historic events before he sold it to Robert Cooper; it still appears regularly in similar events with either Cooper or Richard Bond behind the wheel. Gordon Lee also obtained NBL 660 and rebuilt that too with a new 'knobbly' type body during 1973 - this ex-John Bekaert car then went to Bert Young, a prominent member of the AMOC! David Beckett owned RB 25 for many years, and in his hands became the first Lister-Jaguar to re-enter racing as a historic sports car (in the days of the Griffiths Formula); a Costin bodied car carrying the chassis number BHL 21, this car was originally a Lister-Chevrolet, and is now owned by Chris Drake who drove it in historic events during the early seventies (it also ran at the 50th anniversary Le Mans historic race). Another Lister-Jaguar now seen occasionally in historic events is the Dick Tindell/Freddy Owen car, YCD 422; this also started life as a Lister-Chevrolet, built for Mike Anthony.

The space frame Lister-Jaguar used by Lumsden and Sargent at Le Mans was sprinted by David Harvey in the mid-sixties, owned briefly by J. A. Pearce and then Neil Corner before passing to Hexagon of Highgate. With its coupe top removed it was actively campaigned in the JCB Excavator-sponsored historic series by Hexagon in the early seventies, mainly driven by Nick Faure although Gerry Marshall won a race with it at the last ever Crystal Palace meeting in 1972. This car proved to be one of the fastest Lister-Jaguars running, although John Harper driving a re-imported Lister-Jaguar sometimes beat it. Painted in the original Lister colours of green with a yellow stripe, this latter car has put up some superb performances in historic racing and other events including a double hat-trick of winning three races two weekends running in 1972 (mainly driven by Harper but also on occasions by its then owner Anthony Hutton).

Lister chassis are still returning from the States, and a recent import has been what is stated to be the Cunningham car which Walt Hansgen drove in his SCCA Championship winning year of 1958; in full Cunningham colours of blue and white, this car was restored by John Clark and is now raced by Chris Drake. David Ham is another regular - and fast - contender with a Lister-Jaguar, with an ex-George Tatham car that was formerly Chevrolet powered and built for Phil Scragg. In fact, it can be hazarded that there are more Lister-Jaguars running today than ever left Brian Lister's Cambridge workshops! Another fairly recent import from the States has been a Lister-Jaguar which is thought to have been used by John Fitch for record breaking, possibly purchased by him from Ecurie Ecosse. This car has now been given a new body by Peter Sargent. While the Lister-Jaguar run by Equipe National Belge in the 1958 Le Mans race has not been seen for a number of years, it is thought to have survived in very original order in London. And assuredly, there are yet more to be found both in this country and abroad.

THE TOJEIRO-JAGUAR

John Tojeiro's Jaguar engined cars sprang from a Bristol engined design much in the same way that Brian Lister's car were to do. The Tojeiro-Jaguar had a very light, multi-tubular space frame, with front suspension by unequal length tubular wishbones and coil spring/damper units, and rear suspension by de Dion tube and similar coil spring/dampers. The de Dion tube was cunningly located laterally by a central bronze sliding block arrangement, and longitudinally by two parallel trailing arms. Braking was by disc all round, mounted inboard at the rear. The car's aluminium body was reminiscent of a stretched D-type's with a small integral head fairing. The wheelbase was short at 7 feet 3 inches, and the car was one of the lighter Jaguar engined specials at 15½cwt curb. The original power unit was a wet sump D-type engine, and the first Tojeiro-Jaguar was tested in this form by John Bolster for *Autosport* towards the end of 1956.

Fast the Tojeiro-Jaguar certainly was, but it appeared to lack the controllability of either the Lister or HWM-Jaguar. John Tojeiro in fact warned Bolster that the back end of the car was not all it should have been, and this Bolster found to be true:

The machine holds well on the straight I found,

but the cornering power is not up to the rest of the performance. It is almost impossible to maintain a genuine four wheel drift through a corner, because the back end is always breaking free. My guess is that there is insufficient rear axle movement, and that the de Dion tube is coming up against the bump stops... At present one has to get the car fully straightened up before giving it full throttle.

This deficiency, which was righted to some extent in later cars, was a pity for otherwise the Tojeiro-Jaguar put its power down on the road very well, with very little wheelspin, the concentration of weight over the rear axle and a ZF limited slip differential contributing to this useful characteristic. Bolster's stop-watch recorded a 0-60mph figure of 5.4 seconds, 80mph in 8.2 seconds, 100mph in 12.6 seconds, and a standing quarter mile of 13.6 seconds. Maximum speed (rev limited) was 152.5mph at 6,200rpm on the 3.54:1 axle ratio fitted for circuit racing. A close ratio third gear gave a clear 122mph, and second 84mph. But despite this performance, the Tojeiro-Jaguar (in common with most Jaguar engined racers) was perfectly tractable for motoring around town, and in fact Bolster collected the Tojeiro after lunching at the Steering Wheel Club in the middle of London!

There was one other snag on the early car John Bolster tried and that was the brakes. The discs were smaller than was normal for a car of that size (10 inch front, 9 inch rear) and were devoid of servo assistance. Understandably, Bolster was forced to comment that "they do not possess the reserve of power which one appreciates on a very fast car." Overall however, Bolster felt the car had a great deal of potential.

John Ogier was foremost of those who tried to realise this potential, carrying out much sorting of 7 GNO, the car tested by Bolster. Dick Protheroe shared the car with him, winning at Crystal Palace in August 1956, while Ogier himself put up the fastest time for unsupercharged sports cars at the Brighton Speed Trials in September of the same year with a run of 25.36 seconds. Abecassis in the works HWM-Jaguar was second fastest at Brighton. In 1957

Protheroe again had a measure of success, winning from Peter Blond's D-type at Snetterton in March after favourite Scott Brown had clutch trouble after being fastest in practice. The 1957 British Empire Trophy at Oulton Park was entered, where 7 GNO circulated quite quickly although running with a new crank following big end trouble during practice; in the race evidence of the Tojeiro-Jaguar's rather doubtful brakes and handling at that stage is given by Protheroe's dice with an "excited" Duncan Hamilton, who was driving Cunningham-Reid's HWM-Jaguar - the Tojeiro was faster on acceleration than the HWM, but its brakes let it down badly at Lodge, where Hamilton closed up each lap. However, "by positioning the car in a most gentlemanly manner" according to one eye-witness, Protheroe prevented Hamilton getting past every time. In the end Duncan lost patience and booted the Tojeiro in the tail, shortening it by some 18 inches! An incident that cost him a large number of drinks in the bar afterwards.

By this time the car had been considerably developed. It now ran with a full dry-sump D-type engine and had been further lightened, weighing only 14cwt ready to race. Protheroe followed Scott-Brown's Lister-Jaguar home in second place at Snetterton in May, and at the same circuit in July Peter Gammon repeated the performance with another 3.8 engined Tojeiro. Graham Hill tried a Tojeiro-Jaguar at Brands Hatch, but he too had to give best to Scott Brown and MVE 303. The continuing process of finishing second to the flying green and yellow Lister-Jaguar was Jack Brabham's lot when he drove the works Tojeiro-Jaguar in the Goodwood national meeting of September 1957, during the Unlimited Goodwood Trophy race.

Tojeiro-Jaguars continued to appear at important meetings in 1958, though at the British GP meeting at Silverstone in July the highest placed was Bueb's 3.8 litre car in fourth place behind Allison's 1,475cc Lotus! Moss won this race with MVE 303 of course. In August

1958, David Murray announced that Ecurie Ecosse would be running a Tojeiro-Jaguar, to be driven by Masten Gregory; it was originally to have been entered in the 1958 Tourist Trophy, but was withdrawn in favour of a Lister-Jaguar. It eventually appeared at the rainy Easter Monday Goodwood meeting in March 1959, John Lawrence taking it to 5th place some way behind the winning Lister-Jaguars. An even lower position resulted from the car's entry in the British Empire Trophy of April, Lawrence finishing in 13th spot, but the car at last showed some promise when during the Aintree '200' Flockhart managed to bring the Tojeiro into fourth place ahead of Whitehead's DBR1 and Jim Clark's Border Reivers Lister Jaguar. Probably the car's first important win came in May 1959, where at the BARC Goodwood Whit Monday meeting Flockhart won a 21 lap scratch race - if a little by default, Jim Clark's Lister-Jaguar running out of fuel after half distance when in the lead as already recounted.

The Ecurie Ecosse Tojeiro-Jaguar was entered for the 1959 Le Mans race, and ran with a 'square' 86mm x 86mm XK engine with a 9.6:1 compression ratio, plus a Watts linkage to help tame the rear end. Its weight was quoted as 17cwt dry, with a wheelbase of 7 feet 5½ inches, and overall length 14 feet, and a front track of 4 feet 2½ inches (its rear track was slightly wider). In the race, the car retired with a warped cylinder head at 3 am.

Ecurie Ecosse had also run their Tojeiro-Jaguar in the Nurburgring 1000km race in June, when Flockhart and Gregory were 8th fastest in practice and went off the road with Masten Gregory driving on the fifth lap - anyway the RSK Porsches were rather quicker!

The Scottish team's Tojeiro was finally written off at Goodwood, where the TT was held in September 1959. Jim Clark shared the car with Masten Gregory, as the Border Reivers were not contesting the event (inspite of Clark's inhibitions about driving for the 'opposition'!), and being a World Championship round for

sports cars, the 'Toj' was running in 3-litre form. That year, Ferrari, Aston Martin and Porsche were involved in a great battle for supremacy in the Championship, and all the top line cars and drivers were at Goodwood.

Considering this opposition, the Ecurie Ecosse Tojeiro did not fair badly to begin with, lying around seventh position. It was an easy car to drive however as Clark soon found out:

The Tojeiro we drove was a long ugly-looking car and it didn't handle nearly as well as our own Reivers car. Somehow, it seemed to get up on tip toe going through Madgewick and it was decidedly light to handle in places. It was quite twitchy through the chicane too and both Masten and I were having a great time sliding round the chicane on opposite lock.

But then Gregory entered Woodcote corner at around 90mph and couldn't get round, experiencing trouble with the steering. "He hit the bank so hard that the car jacknifed and folded". The result was a broken shoulder for Masten and he was lucky to get away with that. Aston Martin won the race, to assure their first World Sports Car championship victory; an idea of the pace at which the race was run can be judged from the speed of the Flockhart/Bekaert Ecurie Ecosse D-type which finished seventh - its race average was faster than that of the previous year's winner!

Little was seen of the surviving Tojeiro-Jaguars during 1960, although in 1961 the car came into the news in a small way when Mrs V Lewis won the Ladies Sports Car class at the Brighton Speed Trials with a 3.4 engined car. There is a tragic sequel to this success however - Mrs Lewis was later killed at Brighton while attempting to repeat her 1961 run, the Tojeiro leaving the narrow roadway at high speed and ending up in a fortunately deserted childrens' playground. One theory which might explain this accident is that Mrs Lewis may have lifted off too suddenly near the end of her run, the torque reversal sending the car off the road - not an unknown hazard at Brighton, particularly in the wet. The wrecked car was obtained by Paul

Emery and lay at the back of his garage for years, eventually being sold in 1974.

If this car is rebuilt and appears on the historic racing scene, it will be the first of its type to do so for Tojeiro-Jaguars are now an extremely rare breed. Apart from the car mentioned, only two other Tojeiro chassis are known to exist in Great Britain, one owned by John Ogier, in company with his aluminium bodied XK 120 which he has owned since new. One of the few other surviving Tojeiro–Jaguars is the car raced by Frank Cantwell in New Zealand, which has been restored and still remains in that country. As for Tojeiro Automotive Developments, they went on to design rear engined cars powered by Buick and Ford engines which were raced in prototype form by Ecurie Ecosse; but by that time the Jaguar engine was no longer competitive in sports racing circles, and we have to wait until 1965 before a modern rear engined Jaguar arrived, in the form of Jaguar's own secret XJ13.

OTHER 'ONE OFF' COMPETITION SPECIALS

Having covered the four major Jaguar-engined sports racing cars, we can now return to the efforts of the (mainly) individual enthusiast who decided to build a competition car powered by the Jaguar engine. An interesting sprint car which appeared in 1958 was Paul Emery's 2.4 engined device, a single seater hill climb car which was distinguished by its home-built fuel injection system. This was adapted from a CAV bus injection apparatus but seemed to work very well. The Emeryson-Jaguar won its class at Shelsley in June 1958 with a respectable time of 45.97 seconds (about 3 seconds slower than Phil Scragg's fastest sports car time with the HWM-Jaguar), and appeared at the Brighton Speed Trials. The car started life as an Emeryson powered by a 2-litre Alta engine, the 2.4 XK unit being fitted later; in appearance the car is not unlike a 4CLT Maserati racing car. It is now owned by Martin Noel-Johnson, complete with its original fuel injection system.

The RRA-Jaguar no longer exists, at least in its Jaguar engined form, and anyway it did not begin life with that make of power unit. It was originally built as a single-seater Aston Martin for Reg Parnell to enter in the Tasman series around 1953, but was later obtained by Geoff Richardson who made it into a two-seater and fitted a Jaguar unit in place of the Aston Martin engine. The car's most recent owner decided he wanted an Aston Martin however, so re-installed an Aston Martin engine and converted it into a DB3S, in which form it now remains.

RGS ATALANTA JAGUAR

The RGS Atalanta Jaguar could hardly be called a 'make' in its own right, and its relationship with the pre-war Atalanta car is somewhat tenuous to say the least, but it did enjoy a certain success in the hands of its builder, Dick Shattock.

Shattock had, in the years just after the war, campaigned an Atalanta Special and around 1949 acquired the remaining Atalanta parts from Atalanta Motors, who had ceased making cars before the war. During the early fifties he progressed from supplying Atalanta owners with parts to designing the RGS Atalanta, which was to be marketed in kit form. Although the kit featured the rather novel rear suspension designed by Alfred Gough for the original pre-war Atalanta, it did not in fact incorporate any pre-war parts as such, all components being specially made or adapted. It is almost impossible to say how many RGS Atalantas there were, as both front and rear suspension units were offered separately for the purchaser to fit onto his own chassis, although a complete rolling chassis could be bought in 1952 for £500. The nearest estimate has been a dozen, but it would appear that only one of these had a Jaguar engine fitted, and that was installed by Dick Shattock himself.

The car in question was Shattock's own prototype, HBL 845; tubular framed using 2 inch by 17 gauge frame members, it carried the Atalanta inspired suspension which was the most unusual aspect of Shattock's cars. At the front, Porsche-type trailing arms were used with springing by a cross-wise laminated torsion bar made by Salter - this ran through the front transverse chassis crossmember and was anchored at the centre, very much in the manner of the C-type Jaguar's rear torsion bar.

The independent rear suspension used coil springs which were mounted horizontally in parallel with the chassis frame side members on each side of the car; they were compressed by a rod which projected from a handsome cast-alloy single cranked trailing arm, the other end of the arm carrying the wheel hub. The solidly mounted differential casing was also an alloy casting, and either side of it were the inboard Al-Fin drum brakes. The differential internals were ENV, while the universally jointed half-shafts were of Hardy Spicer manufacture.

This car was first fitted with a Lea Francis engine and a Cotal gearbox, both from Shattock's original Atalanta Special, and a one-off aluminium body shell with separate mudguards was fitted (this was done with the help of friend John Griffiths, who had created the JAG Special in 1950 - though the JAG never ran with any Jaguar components!). In this form it was reasonably successful but in order to "demonstrate satisfactorily the roadworthiness of the chassis" (which was the object of racing the car), Shattock fitted a 3.4 XK engine towards the end of 1953, equipped with a Weslake-modified C-type head and two 2 inch SU carburettors.

A year later, John Bolster tested the car for *Autosport;* at first he found the driving position rather odd, but "once I had taught my feet to find the curiously located pedals I began to indulge in some pretty memorable motoring... The acceleration was literally tremendous and quite the best feature of the car was the astounding traction." This resulted in a 0 - 60 time of 8.2 seconds, and a standing ¼-mile of 15.2 seconds, the best ever recorded by *Autosport* up until that time.

While Bolster was disappointed in the 120 mph top speed of the RGS Atalanta, due to the 'vintage' body shape, he was most impressed by its handling. "The rear suspension gives the sort of roadholding that I normally associate with a de Dion axle, and none of the failings of the swing axle system is apparent. The rear end behaviour in general must certainly be awarded very high marks." The brakes were good, and the car was also tractable in town, "apart from once demanding a new sparking plug in Park Lane".

The car's poor aerodynamics were soon cured by the fitting of a new glass fibre shell which faired in the wheels - with no mechanical alternations, top speed immediately went up to 138 mph (Shattock was possibly the first person to offer the British public an off-the-shelf glass fibre body incidentally; it was based on an HWM sports car body from which the moulds were taken. About 100 of these bodies were sold and fitted to a variety of specials by enthusiasts). This made the car a better proposition on the track, and Shattock's most meritorious showing was undoubtedly during the final of the Oulton Park British Empire Trophy race - which Scott Brown won on handicap thus putting himself and Brian Lister on the map. Despite a fire on the way to Oulton, caused by the severing of the rubber petrol filler when the car bottomed unexpectedly at around 125 mph, Shattock came fifth 'on the road' (the smaller cars had been given a start) and actually succeeded in overtaking and finishing ahead of Duncan Hamilton is his D-type OKV 1 - helped by wet conditions and the use of Michelin X tyres!

But Shattock was finding it increasingly difficult to both maintain and race the car, and its competition career in his hands ended later that year, 1955. The whereabouts of the glass fibre bodied HBL 845 with its distinctive rear fins (they didn't contribute much to stability but, said Shattock, "You've got to be able to tell which way it's going") isn't known, though one does hope that this interesting and effective Jaguar special still survives.

The Alton-Jaguar was up until quite recently proving perfectly competitive at sprint meetings, against much more modern sporting machinery. Completely home built by its driver Mike Barker, construction of the Alton-Jaguar commenced as far back as 1954, and it first took to the road with a supercharged 2-litre Alta engine.

The chassis was welded up from 16 swg steel tubing, and was of 'ladder' configuration with four cross members of similar thickness to the two side members. Front suspension was double wishbone with Lotus coil springs and Aston Martin stub-axles; at the rear was an Aston Martin axle located by an 'A' frame and sprung by coil springs. Girling drum brakes were fitted all round originally. When the Alta unit gave up, a Jaguar engine (basically to C-type specification) took its place, the installation adding 1½cwt to the original 16cwt ready--to-race weight of the car. The bodyshell was a slightly modified 'Mistral' glass fibre item, a little reminiscent of the works HWM-Jaguars. Wheelbase was 7 feet 9 inches, front track 4 feet 4 inches, and rear track 4 feet 6 inches.

Although it occasionally ventured onto the race track (in fact its competition debut in Jaguar-engined form had been at Goodwood, where it would have won a 5-lap handicap race had it not run off the road at Woodcote), the main forte of this Surrey based special was sprints and hill climbs, in which it was capable of going very fast. In the April Prescott meeting of 1960, Mike Barker was placed second only to Phil Scragg himself, whose Lister-Jaguar had broken the class record, and ahead of Coleman's supercharged Jaguette. Thereafter the Alton-Jaguar brought Mike Barker many FTDs and class wins in local sprint meetings, before it was partially retired around 1972 still in the hands of its original builder.

One little-known Jaguar engined variant to appear was the Connaught-Jaguar, driven by Leslie Marr during part of the 1956 New Zealand motor racing season. This car was appar-ently a final attempt by Rodney Clarke and Paul Weldon to make the Formula One single seater Connaught, with its enclosed streamlined body-work, more competitive. The 1955 car exchanged its 2,470 cc four-cylinder Alta engine for a D-type unit, which drove through the original Armstrong Siddeley preselector gearbox. The arrangement in fact worked very well, the car handling better than it had ever done inspite of the greater weight at the nose. In January 1956, Marr was placed third in the Lady Wigram Trophy race at Christchurch, and fourth at Ardmore. The Connaught-Jaguar's history after its New Zealand exploits is not clear, and it may very well still be in that country.

Few single-seater Jaguar specials have been built in Britain although one or two individual-ists did have a go. A F Rivers Fletcher hill climbed such a car during the sixties - it was based on a 1953 XK 120 Roadster chassis, the conversion to single-seater form mainly being accomplished by Bill Moss. The body was rather a pleasing one, on 2½ litre BRM lines and built by Freddie Owen; suspension was still basically XK 120, but with modifications such as upright telescopic dampers at the rear. Of no special significance, the car was however nicely turned out and obviously fun to drive. It was sold in 1968 to Dutch Jaguar enthusiast Mr. Van der Lof by Rivers Fletcher.

Jaguar special building was not confined to the British Isles. Walt Hansgen produced a Jaguar-engined sports racing car with which he had some success, before becoming Briggs Cunningham's star driver. The Hansgen Jaguar's most important victory was its overall win in the 1953 Watkins Glen Grand Prix - although this was not quite so notable as it might have been, as 1953 was a non-sanction year, the SCCA withdrawing their approval of the event at the last minute resulting in rather less competition for Hansgen.

Somewhat earlier, in 1950, Clemente Biondetti had built himself a Jaguar special, not being content with the works XK 120 Roadster which he was using at the same time. It was usually entered in events as a Jaguar-Ferrari but was rather more complex than that. The chassis, of tubular construction, was actually Maserati in origin and was fitted with an XK 120 engine. The gearbox, transmission, front suspension and brakes were also XK 120, but the whole was clothed in a Ferrari Type 166 body and radiator frontage (possibly from Biondetti's own Type 166) - as *Grand Vitesse* said in *The Motor* at the time, "all very confusing!" The car does not appear to have survived.

Australia was the home of quite a number of one-off Jaguar specials, faster 'off-the-peg' machinery being difficult to come by as in other countries away from Europe or the States. Some were entirely XK 120 based, such as Jack Robinson's car which in its hey-day won a good deal of prize money for its driver.

Other home constructors were more ambitious, and one of the fastest Australian-built specials was the Dalro-Jaguar, originally known as the Austral-Union. This emerged from its beginnings as a fairly ordinary XK 120 special in the early fifties to become quite a sophisticated single seater racing car, mainly when under the attentions of Alwyn Rose and his mechanic Les Wigget. Its frame was made up of four straight 1½ inch 16 swg steel tubes, cross braced and carrying double wishbone front suspension (using Vanguard uprights), with light alloy rear support housings taking the double wishbone independent rear suspension. Herald coil spring/damper units were used front and rear, and steering was by Morris Minor rack and pinion in the approved Jaguar special tradition.

The XK 120 engine was left fairly standard, though three SU carburettors were used, and locally made pistons gave a compression ratio of 10:1. Fuel was brought from the petrol tank by air pressure supplied by an AC mechanical fuel pump driven from the right hand camshaft - this rather unusual system proved to be completely reliable and maintained a pressure of around 2½ - 3lbs sq in within the tank. Wire wheels had

replaced the original solid steel XK 120 items, but these in turn were eventually superseded by locally cast alloy ones.

Whilst it was never an important race winner, the car did finish 5th in the 1962 Bathurst 100-mile race, proving more reliable than a number of 'factory' cars, and towards the end of its competitive life in 1963 was returning times very close to the unofficial Australian record for front engined racing cars, set by the 250F Maseratis in the Australian GP of 1958. It is important to remember that the car ran without assistance from D-type or other high-performance engine parts, speed being achieved by a very low weight (13½cwt) and good handling by the standards of its day. The car is now owned by Doug Alton who uses it in the occasional historic events held in Australia.

In America, the famous name of Unser was associated with a Jaguar special, at the equally famous venue of Pikes Peak on the eastern edge of the Rockies. This dramatic hill climb up the side of the 14,110 feet mountain was dominated around 1958 by a Jaguar XK powered car built from a 'Championship' chassis; it was constructed by Unser senior for his son Bobby to drive, continuing the almost traditional string of victories by the family at 'The Peak'.

Finally, returning to Great Britain, one hybrid car which warrants at least a mention is C A Winder's 1929 Lea Francis. This was very successfully fitted with a 1938 3,485cc SS-Jaguar engine which has made the 'Leaf' a fast competition car, gaining its driver a number of awards in PVT events, in which it is still driven.

ROAD JAGUAR SPECIALS

The fact that Jaguar retained a full old fashioned chassis for their sports cars up until 1960 encouraged a number of special builders to exercise their art on that make. Probably the most famous, and certainly the most well thought out, is the car built by Col. Rixon Bucknall MBE. This great Sussex Jaguar enthusiast of many years standing (he bought one of Lyons' first side-cars) decided to build what to him was the perfect touring car, but in the idiom of the thirties.

Its basis was a new XK 140 chassis, fitted with disc brakes and a highly modified XK 150S engine with magneto ignition reputed to give some 270bhp. A competition close ratio gearbox and overdrive featured in the transmission, Armstrong Selectaride shock absorbers provided the damping, while the wheels were purpose-built Borrani alloy rim items. The bodywork itself was of magnesium alloy constructed on a light steel frame, with no running boards and separate front wings painted in black to contrast with the guardsman's red main colour scheme. A 'V' shaped hinged windscreen, a traditional Jaguar-type radiator shell and large chromed headlights specially made by Marchal were other distinguishing features.

Inside the car every conceivable 'touring' extra is fitted, from a large umbrella to a spare half-shaft, all in rattle-proof mountings or lockers, and the car did in fact travel some 22,000 miles in Col. Bucknall's hands, mostly on the continent - which was its designed purpose. The Colonel regretfully had to sell 'The Red Car' during 1971 as he admitted that it was becoming rather a handful to him in his advancing years; it went to a London enthusiast.

No other road-going special can really match up to the specification of Col Bucknall's car, but Panther West Winds of Byfleet, Surrey, have come very close to it in terms of performance and quality. Robert Jankel, founder of the company, used to build a car a year as a part time hobby, and then decided to go into production with the last of the line, which happened to be a 1930's style sports car very much after the theme of the SS Jaguar 100 - he was much encouraged in this venture by the then Technical Editor of *Autocar* Geoffrey Howard. By 1972 the Panther J.72 was well into production and selling mainly to customers abroad, particularly in the United States. The car used a very simple box section chassis, a Jaguar Mk 2 axle at the rear, and a beam axle at the front located in a similar manner (complete with Panhard rod) with springing by Armstrong coil spring/damper units front and rear. The original power unit was a 3.8 XK engine (with a Jaguar gearbox) although later on the 4.2 XK engine or the new V12 Jaguar engine was adopted. One of the early J.72 cars with a 3.8 B-type head engine was tested by *Autocar* in June 1972, and it recorded a 0-60mph time in a very rapid 6.4 seconds, 80mph in 11.7 seconds, and 100mph in 21.3 seconds. Wind resistance limited top speed to around 114mph but the gearing was less than ideal at 3.54:1, which with the overdrive cut in made the car far too high geared. This was sorted out in later models however. Price was £4,380 as tested.

Motor tried a V12 engined version in June 1974, and with 5.3 litres to propel only about 23cwt, performance was quite breathtaking even though the very non-aerodynamic shape of the Panther took its toll in the higher speed ranges. Sixty miles an hour came up in 5.7 seconds, 80mph in 9.2 seconds, and 100mph in 13.8 seconds, and the car's standing quarter mile time of 14.3 seconds was exactly one second quicker than its six-cylinder sister (which continued in production). A full maximum speed run wasn't attempted but it was thought probable that the car would have been capable of pulling 6,500rpm in top gear - or about 140mph.

It is interesting to compare the Panther's dimensions with those of the original 3½ litre SS 100. They are, with *The Autocar's* 1938 SS 100 figures in brackets: overall length 13 feet 4 inches (12 feet 6 inches), width 5 feet 5½ inches (5 feet 2 inches), wheelbase 9 feet 1 inch (8 feet 8 inches), track 4 feet 6½ inches (4 feet 6 inches), and height with hood erected, 4 feet 5 inches (4 feet 7 inches). The Panther was an important 8 inches wider across the cockpit, although the '100' had more luggage space. The pre-war car also weighed at least a hundred-weight more than the Panther, probably due to its wooden frame.

Those who liked very powerful, hairy sports cars enthused over the Panther V12; others were not so sure. Its road-holding was well up to its power unit however, and on smooth surfaced corners could equal most other modern high performance cars with its 205 x 15 radial tyres on V12 E-type chrome wire wheels. Over bumpy surfaces one was certainly given a choppy ride although the car was never deflected from bump to bump like some of its pre-war equivalents. Handling was really quite nuetral though a heavy right foot could induce the tail to come round quite controllably; V12 E-type ventilated discs had no trouble in dragging the car down from the three-figure speeds which it reached very easily. The car was much more pleasurable to drive with its hood down, the weather equipment being the cause of too much noise at speed.

The Panther's main attribute besides its looks, performance and character is the quality of its construction, which is entirely carried out at West Winds' premises in Canada Road, Byfleet. Whether one approves of such a vehicle or not, the standard of the coachbuilding has to be admired and this is one reason why Jankel's order books are full.

At the time of writing almost 200 of the XK engined Panthers had been built; and construction of the V12 engined version, even at £9,925, was building up to a similar level - engines are obtained new, direct from Jaguar.

Just about within the scope of this book, as it is both Jaguar powered and with two (or rather three, abreast) seats, is West Wind's latest project, the Lazar. This is a futuristic wedge-shaped open car built around a derivative of the J72's chassis, powered by a six cylinder XK engine in the prototype although further cars have the V12 unit earmarked for them - around which engine Jankel intends all his cars to be centred eventually. Very much a 'fun' car, one Lazar is scheduled to appear in a James Bond-type adventure film fitted with such extras as a laser gun, and sundry guided missiles. Other projects include a magnificent touring saloon based on XJ12 sub-frames and engine, rather in the Bugatti Royale tradition - but that is definitely not within the compass of this work!

At the beginning of 1975, at the London Speed Show at Olympia, two more replica builders displayed their wares, coincidentally based on the same car - the long-nose Jaguar D-type. This would appear to be a small 'first' in that no other car of the fifties had up until then had bestowed upon it the possibly doubtful honour of being copied as a commercial venture. Both used aluminium monocoque centre sections made by Williams and Pritchard of Edmonton (who had previous experience in this field through building 'real' monocoques for owners of actual D-types) and mainly E-type running gear and engines. In both cases though the centre section was not a direct copy of the D-type's, as it was not penetrated by the engine-carrying framework (an E-type frame was used, simply bolted to the front bulkhead) and thus had to be completely re-stressed. Also, the D-type arrangement of effectively ending the car at the rear bulkhead was not adhered to, as neither replicas had true D-type suspension, so therefore the centre section had to be extended backwards to hold the rear suspension.

The Lynx Engineering car did, as a matter of policy, stick to E-type mechanics far more than the other replica, the brain-child of Brian Wingfield, Alistair Walker, Robert Lamplough and Sidney Marcos Ltd (a London Jaguar dealer), the Lynx philosophy being that using over the counter parts would bring greater reliability and ease of maintenance. The full E-type rear suspension was thus adopted and a completely standard 4.2 XK engine, although Webers were added. The other D-type replica used a live axle at the rear, though suspended by coil springs not a torsion bar like the rear thing, and a. slightly modified version of the 4.2 engine which was given a 'branch' exhaust manifold similar to the D-type's; a dummy oil catch tank was fitted to this car too, which thus scored on accuracy of detail. Both cars were to retail at about £10,000, and at the time of writing there was even talk of a Le Mans entry - which if it materialises, means that the wheel has indeed turned the full circle for Jaguar, who themselves commenced by borrowing someone else's engine and suspension!

Chapter Ten The E-type, XJ13 and XJ-S

If a new car ever created greater excitement around our office than the new Jaguar XKE, we can't remember it

Road & Track
September 1961

The E-type used to be a classic sports car, but as the mid-engined sports racer has developed and certain specialist production cars have followed suit, the appeal of the E-type has changed; its character has softened

The Motor
November 24 1972

It is difficult to decide which made the greatest impact upon their individual announcements, the XK 120 in October 1948, or the E-type twelve years and four months later. What can be said with complete certainty however is that the impression made by the E-type Jaguar on the general public has been so great that the very word 'E-type' has become synonymous with speed and glamour, even to the veriest non-motoring members of the population.

The E-type made its inaugural bow at the Geneva Motor Show in March 1961, and although it didn't seem to have been noticed at the time, Jaguar's new sports car was not what one would have been led to expect had one been guided by the evolution of the XK series before it. Far from being a continuation from where the XK 150 left off in terms of internal space and general character, the E-type went right back to basics. In concept it was much more allied to the original XK 120 Roadster of 1948 than the XK 150 of 1961, for instead of producing a 2-plus-2 from the outset in the manner of the XK 150, Sir William had gone straight back to the XK 120; so there emerged into the limelight at Geneva a true, two-seater sports car with no compromises at all in the form of occasional seats or unnecessary weight.

And like the XK 120 at the end of the forties, the E-type Jaguar at the beginning of the sixties was about the fastest car you could buy from the showroom floor, with handling and (this time!) brakes to match.

The E-type can be cited as the supreme example of competition experience applied to a road vehicle. Many of its major features were derived directly from the racing D-type Jaguar which had dominated Le Mans during the middle fifties. The E-type was not however a development of the D-type itself, in the manner of the XKSS which quite simply *was* a D-type with road equipment hung on it, but was a completely new car designed from the very outset as a road car, the replacement for the XK series. Thus such qualities as ride, comfort and insulation were built into the design at quite an early stage, mated to a superb performance and a standard of road holding and handling which few other cars of its time could approach. It was no less than a triumph of engineering skill for William Heynes and his small team.

The new sports car's affinity to the D-type could clearly be seen in its outward shape; no headfairing of course but still the D-type's curves, softened a little but very definitely there. The fixed-head model was as sleek, if not sleeker, than its open sister, the top blending

237

perfectly with the car's lines. If Heynes can be praised for the chassis design, then Malcolm Sayer - and Sir William himself - should take no less credit for the E-type's outward appearance. While a very few die-hards mourned the passing of the XK shape (which after all was still carried on in vestigal form in the Mk 2 saloon), it was apparent to nearly everyone that here was another classic; a new and totally different Jaguar, but as has so often been said, one that could never be mistaken for another make.

EARLY DEVELOPMENT

The E-type had its real beginnings in two prototypes. Both of them were open two seaters, as the fixed-head only came along near the end of the car's development, and the first was a fascinating and delightful little car constructed almost entirely out of aluminium alloy.'Little', because it was scaled-down compared to the final production E-type, having a narrower track, shorter overall length, and a lower build altogether. It was code-named E1A within the factory, the 'A' standing for aluminium - a metal chosen for the prototype because it was easier to work with, on a one-off basis. Construction began in November 1957, and it was running seven months later. The method of building E1A followed that of the D-type very closely, the centre monocoque with its deep sills and box-section front and rear bulkheads being of rivetted aluminium; unlike both the later D-types and the production 'E' however, the forward framework carrying engine and front suspension was permanently fixed to the monocoque. The framework itself was of a magnesium alloy, of rectangular section and with all welded joints. Heynes recalls that it "never gave the slightest trouble during its very hard life". The outer panelling, stressed at the rear but in the form of a non-stressed, hinge-forward, detachable bonnet at the front, was also in aluminium, but there was no provision for headlights - all the prototype carried was two little side-lamps at the base of the windscreen. Inside the cockpit the car looked more like a racing car than a road car, with unpainted aluminium and rivet heads abounding.

Due to its smaller size, E1A was powered by a 2.4 litre XK engine, its shorter block being the only one which would fit under the bonnet - which at that stage didn't sport the 'power bulge' of the production car. The chief purpose of this car was to evaluate on the road the main features of the new sports car to come, and it therefore carried Heynes' independent rear suspension. This was not carried on a detachable sub-frame at this stage but was attached directly to the monocoque, which was strengthened at strategic points by mild steel sheets. This meant that to remove the suspension entirely, the differential unit had to be unbolted from the boot floor. Much experimentation took place on this suspension and many details ironed out - for instance, twin swinging links were at first used and only later did the suspension acquire its distinctive characteristic of the fixed-length drive shaft forming the top link of the system. Rose-joints were used on the prototype, but the original ones proved to be too small and their size had to be increased. A major realisation was that in order to reach the required standards of silence and road noise insulation, and for easier servicing, the entire rear suspension would have to be mounted in a steel 'cradle', which could then be attached to the monocoque through rubber mounting points. In fact there was very little compliance anywhere in E1A, either in suspension or steering, a marked difference to the production E-type.

E1A had a busy and varied life, putting in many miles at MIRA and on the road. Although possessing only the 2½ litre engine, its light weight and tremendous manoeuverability made it a very quick car, a revelation indeed compared to the cars of its day. We are extraordinarily lucky to be able to refer to road impressions of E1A while it was still very secret, noted down by the then editor of *The Motor,* Christopher Jennings. He and his wife Margaret (who as Miss

Margaret Allen had driven for SS Cars Ltd before the war) maintained a very close relationship with the factory, and were probably the only people outside the works to drive the prototype. The car was delivered to their weekend home in South Wales, and they proceeded to make good use of it. In order to fully convey the feeling of excitement engendered by E1A, I print here for the first time the complete Memorandum on the subject of the car sent by Christopher Jennings to the Managing Director of Temple Press, Richard Dangerfield:

SECRET AND CONFIDENTIAL

NOTE TO: Mr. R.E. Dangerfield

FROM: Mr. C. Jennings   14th May 1958

I spent the past weekend in a car of such sensational potential that I feel that you might wish to know about it. The car is a Jaguar, known at the moment as the E-type. This car has been developed from the Le Mans-winning D-type but incorporates numerous improvements. The rear suspension is independent and the disc brakes inboard. Aerodynamically it is superior to the D-type and therefore faster.

Sir William Lyons asked me last year about my test run course between Brecon and Carmarthen. This route combines a few fast straights with numerous extremely fast bends and some very slow ones. It is seldom flat for more than a mile at a time and for comparative purposes I would mention that a good Ford Zephyr driven flat out can cover the 48½ miles between St. Peter's Church, Carmarthen and the River Bridge at Brecon in 57 minutes. The fastest run until last Sunday was in David Brown's Aston Martin with Le Mans engine and experimental disc brakes. This car covered the distance in 50 minutes. I would explain that on these runs reasonable respect is paid to the several built up areas encountered and cars are never driven in a manner which would hazard the public, but the time of day for fast cars is chosen with care to avoid lorries.

Knowing this, Sir William said he had a proposition to make. It was that he would lend my wife and myself a prototype of an entirely new model and, having acclimatized ourselves to it, we should then make the run with a view to comparing it with the Aston Martin and other fast vehicles driven on that route. Six months later Mr Heynes advised me that the car was ready and we first set eyes on it a few days ago. It is a very beautiful machine and although ours was minus hood and headlamps these are most gracefully incorporated on the production prototype which I also inspected. Production is expected to begin in the autumn and the target is 100 of these formidable sports cars per week. With a 3-litre engine it will develop 286 bhp and I visualise a road test speed not very far short of 150 mph which is going to make us think.

On Sunday morning soon after 7 am in perfect conditions we made a 20-mile warming-up run and then 'had a go'. The result was almost fantastic. The first 20 miles from Camarthen to Llandovery was covered at an average of just over 70 mph and Brecon was reached in 43 minutes, giving an overall average for the 48½ miles of 67.7 mph. The return journey was made at a fast touring speed by my wife but nevertheless equalled the Aston Martin record of 50 minutes. At no time did we exceed 120 mph. Subsequent test runs were equally astonishing, thus a 50-mile section between Carmarthen and Devil's Bridge showed an average of 50 mph despite considerable heavy traffic, and consistently winding roads.

It will be seen therefore that the new Jaguar is a potential world beater and in a separate envelope I enclose a selection of pictures taken this weekend mostly outside my stables because we maintained maximum security and did not let the car come to rest in populated places.

Some of these photographs are reproduced in this book, with kind permission from Mr Jennings himself. The car is remembered as being very practical, with the side-screens being surprisingly effective against the elements. The lack of headlamps meant an inforced curfew soon after dusk but in most other respects the car was fully roadworthy; although Phil Weaver of Jaguar's experimental department remembers a journey he made to Wales in E1A with his son, during which there was a distinct tendency for the car to ground - in fact the sump was cracked rather often over the car's complete test life.

The second E-type prototype was made of steel, and with similar dimensions to the final production car. The steel prototype was familiarly known within the works as the 'Pop

Rivet Special', as that was how it was assembled - the formed steel sheets being pop-rivetted together to produce what was first of all just a mock-up. Then, recalls Phil Weaver, Heynes rang up one day and asked how long it'd take to make the mock-up a runner! So the experimental department set to, removed the pop rivets, brazed and welded the car up, and produced the first mobile all-steel E-type prototype. This car served to perfect the myriad details concerning engine installation, exhaust and suspension mountings, and ran for quite a long time on the test fleet. Many thousands of miles were also put up on the road by a Mk II saloon equipped with a similar 'independent rear' as the E-type to come. Generally, the E-type's development is remembered as being centred around a mass of small problems rather than just a few big ones, but the amount of time required to sort them all out - about four years in all - contrasts with the very quick gestation period of the XK 120, and underlines how much more complex an advanced sports car had become, by 1961.

THE E2A SPORTS RACING PROTOTYPE

The third car concerned in the development of the E-type was the sports racing car intended as a replacement for the D-type Jaguar; code-named E2A, it was purely a racing car but did serve to evaluate various aspects of the road E-type's specification, notably the rear suspension.

E2A was a natural progression from the D-type, and was designed as its successor during the late fifties. Had Jaguar resumed racing at Le Mans in 1958 or 1959 as they had originally intended when they withdrew in 1956, it would have been a team of cars like E2A which would have represented them. Front engined of course, its lines were very much those of the older car except that the longer bonnet carried no power bulge and the front wing line was carried straight back to the rear of the cockpit, where it met a bulky tail which incorporated

space for the required amount of 'luggage' demanded by race regulations. The built-in full width windscreen was also the result of regulations then in force, which were designed to cut down maximum speeds - an after effect still lingering from the disastrous 1955 Le Mans race.

Viewed from the front, E2A looked very similar to the road E-type which was to come, with its long nose and 'proper' windscreen; its wheelbase was indeed the same as the E-type's, at 8 feet, which was some 5 inches longer than the D-type's. At 4 feet, track was actually narrower than the D-type's by 2 inches. Overall length was 14 feet 2 inches, width 5 feet 3¾ inches, and height to top of fin was 4 feet 5¼ inches - which extended 6¾ inches above the screen.

There were some features of E2A's construction which also could have given a hint at the forthcoming road car's specification; although basically D-type, having a centre monocoque of rivetted light alloy sheet with its main strength in two deep sills, and a forward projecting tubular framework carrying engine and front suspension, at the rear E2A's monocoque extended back from the rear bulkhead (where it ended on the D-type) and together with the rear stressed outer bodywork panels, supported the car's new rear suspension. It was in this department particularly that E2A was an E-type prototype, as the suspension was fully independent on very similar lines to that which appeared in 1961 on the E-type itself.

Like the E-type's, the rear suspension featured a rigidly mounted differential unit flanked by inboard disc brakes. Running out from underneath the differential on either side were large wide-based fabricated steel wishbones, which carried cast light alloy hubs at their outer ends. Fixed-length drive shafts, with double universal joints, formed what was in effect the upper wishbone of a double wishbone system; the lower links were joined by an anti-roll bar. Twin coil spring/damper units acted on each lower wishbone as on the E-type, but the suspension lacked the two trailing radius arms of the production car. Also, with noise and vibration suppression not a priority, E2A's suspension did not have the rubber-mounted bridge frame, or cradle, in which the E-type's rear suspension was to be carried.

Significantly, in view of the problems of a similar nature which remained with the Salisbury differential and inboard disc brake unit for many years afterwards with Jaguars, quite a lot of trouble was caused by the "rapid destruction" of the differential oil seals brought about by heat soak from the discs - this was first noticed during experiments with de Dion suspension on the D-type in 1955. During tests on E2A, it was found that three successive stops from 140mph to 30mph brought the temperature of the disc brake units up to over 1,000 deg C, and the oil seals themselves to 330 deg C. Cooling ducts on both the underside of the car (a little like those employed on the last V12 E-types) and from ducting from just aft of the cockpit, reduced the disc temperatures to about 800 deg C, and this combined with the cutting of as many heat paths as was practical between discs and differential, brought the oil seal maximum temperatures down to around 140 deg C. But this still meant that the oil within the differential was getting too hot, to the point of carbonization even, so an unorthodox but entirely satisfactory method of cooling the transmission oil was devised. A small oil cooler was installed in the path of cool air issuing from a rear brake cooling duct, and the differential oil was circulated through it by means of a standard SU electric petrol pump, switched on by the driver if the oil temperature began to rise.

The car's front suspension was substantially D/E-type, with slender forged wishbones and longitudinal torsion bars; an anti-roll bar joined the lower wishbones. Its steering was rack and pinion, and at one stage in development, a rubber mounted rack of the type used on the XK 150 was tried but was found to spoil the handling, obviously through too much compliance. Two and a half turns of the steering wheel gave a turning circle of 38 feet. Outboard disc brakes were of course used at the front, and apparently the braking system had no servo. Dunlop light alloy centre-lock wheels were fitted, shod with Dunlop 6.50 x 15 Stabilia tyres.

E2A's engine was a 2997cc version of the dry sump six cylinder XK unit, and featured publicly for the first time in a Jaguar, an aluminium block. Saving some 80 lbs weight, the alloy block featured pressed-in liners, threaded into heli-coil inserts in the casting. Bore and stroke was 85mm x 88mm, compression ratio was 10:1, and the 35/40 cylinder head carried 7/16ths inch lift camshafts and big 2 3/32nd inch inlet valves. Lucas petrol injection was used, the slide throttles being operated by a rack and pinion system from the accelerator pedal as in the PI D-types. A maximum of 293bhp gross at 6,750rpm was given by this engine, which produced over 230 ft lbs of torque of 6,000rpm. It was mated to an all-synchromesh four-speed gearbox via a triple plate 7¼ inch diameter clutch. The final drive ratio was 3.31:1.

It was Briggs Cunningham who brought the car to Le Mans - apparently he'd seen E2A sitting forlornly in Jaguar's development department while on a visit to the factory to view the proto-type road E-type, and persuaded Jaguar to let him enter it at the next Le Mans, 1960. The car itself had been completed some time previously as the D-type's unblooded successor.

Despite the cast aluminium block however, E2A was by virtue of its greater bulk a heavier car than the equivalent D-type, weighing 70 lbs more than Ecurie Ecosse's D-type which was also entered for the 1960 Le Mans race. Aerodynamically, E2A was probably more efficient than the D-type in its 1960 trim, and during the April 1960 Le Mans test days it was "visibly faster" down the Mulsanne straight than Phil Hill's Ferrari which put up the fastest practice lap of 124.76mph average. E2A was second fastest, Hansgen lapping at 121.42mph, and he might even have improved on this time had the car not coasted to a halt quite early on in the proceedings at Les Hunaudieres, having lost a quantity of oil down the straight.

As for the race itself in June, the car appeared in the Cunningham colours of blue and white, and "upheld Jaguar's reputation for being beautifully prepared" even though it was a day late for scrutineering. But E2A's run of bad luck, which had commenced with the premature ending of its practice weekend in April, was continued in the first pre-race practice session when it collided with a GT Ferrari and damaged its nose; but not before it had put up fastest time (although this made no difference to grid positions). In the second and final pre-race practise sessions, Hill in the Ferrari was still 0.2 seconds slower. In the race proper, nominated drivers Walt Hansgen and Dan Gurney took E2A into an initial third place behind the leading Ferraris, but the Jaguar was soon in the pits where it stayed for a long time, due to trouble with the injection system. When it rejoined, E2A worked up to 18th after two hours, and 10th after three hours - then gradually slid down again as further problems were encountered, brought on by a faulty fuel injection pipe running to the pump - this caused a weak mixture which damaged the pistons. Finally, at 1.40am, E2A was pushed away, defeated at last by a blown cylinder head gasket while in 20th position. As *The Motor* said, "an effort perhaps more sporting than judicious".

The factory then fitted E2A with a 3.8 litre Weber carburetted engine (the bonnet acquiring the now-familiar 'power bulge') and sent it to America, where it was raced by the Cunningham team. The prototype entered and won its first race in the States, driven by Walter Hansgen, ahead of Bob Grossman's Lister-Jaguar and Bill Kimberley's Type 60 Birdcage Maserati at Bridgehampton, Long Island. This was to be the car's sole victory however, although a good third place was achieved by Hansgen in the Elkhart Lake 500 mile event, E2A following a Type 61 Maserati and a Testa Rossa Ferrari home on a wet track. Jack Brabham took the wheel once but without notable result, and eventually the car was returned to Jaguar - it is now kept amongst Guy Griffiths' small but select collection of racing Jaguars at Chipping Campden.

As for the two road car prototypes, when E1A was thought to have lived out its useful life it was forthwith cut up, a morning's work with a torch, and the all-steel prototype met a similar fate. Retrospectively, it would have been nice if they could have been spared and eventually found a place in the works or Coventry museum, but if a motor manufacturer kept all his prototypes, where would the space be found to store them, and where would the spare manpower be obtained to prepare them for exhibition? There is little room for sentimentality in these matters, for it is always the next new car which must head the list of priorities in a company such as Jaguar.

THE PRODUCTION E-TYPES

When they finally arrived, the production open two-seater and fixed-head coupe E-types shared the same basic design under the skin, and their construction followed the prototypes' quite closely in all important points. Basically the car could be separated into two main sections, literally as well as figuratively; the larger formed the passenger compartment and rear quarters and was built up of welded steel panels (mostly in 20 gauge steel), while the second consisted of a framework constructed from Reynolds 541 square section steel tubing which projected forward from the monocoque and carried the front suspension and engine. Onto the front of this was bolted a yet smaller framework of tubular section members whose purpose it was to carry the cross-flow radiator and bonnet pivot. The lessons taught by the expensive repair of the first D-types had been learnt well, and unlike the 1954 works D-types the main framework was not welded but bolted to the monocoque, at six attachment points each with four-bolt flanges. Repair of the structure was further cheapened in that the larger, square section frame could itself be separated into two halves, by undoing more bolts.

The non-stressed nose piece which covered the engine was also made in detachable parts, a middle section with two 'wings' on either side; the joins were concealed by a chromium plated moulding. The centre section of the bonnet had a set of louvres on either side of the power bulge which accommodated the camshaft covers of the engine (the bulge itself ended in a vent beneath the windscreen); on very early cars these louvres were formed in separate sheets of metal let-in to the bonnet, but later were pressed directly into the centre section itself. The whole bonnet assembly hinged forward from pivots on the round section tubular outrigging at the front of the main frame.

Returning to the monocoque, its construction was quite complex. The scuttle was a horse-shoe shaped hollow section which ran across the car at bonnet level and down either side to meet large hollow sills; these projected forward as far as the front wheels, and back under the doors until they met a rear transverse hollow section member just before the rear suspension. The transmission hump, prop shaft tunnel, and the welded steel flooring also contributed strength, assisted by a further square section transverse member running across the floor under the seats. Two more longitudinal floor members of smaller section ran under the floor from the front bulkhead back to the rear cross member. At the rear, the luggage compartment floor, with its two longitudinal box sections along either side, joined up with the rear cross member and the tail section, and the resultant construction took the rear suspension sub-frame. Although the roof section of the fixed-head coupe contributed its share of stiffening, the basic monocoque as described was quite rigid enough not to need any further bracing for the open model.

Abbey Panels supplied the beautifully shaped nose section and the outer curved body panels, while Pressed Steel Fisher made the internal steel sections. The bodyshell was welded up and the joins were leaded-in at Jaguar's Browns Lane factory - this situation extended up until the V12 E-type and it was quite an unexpected sight to see individual craftsmen with blow-lamps and lead strips engaged in this hand work amidst the automation of a modern production line.

The E-type's front suspension owed far more to the D-type than to the XK 150, although longitudinal torsion bars were still the springing medium. Forged wishbones top and bottom were employed, with an inner extension of the lower wishbone being used as the attachment point for the torsion bar, instead of the bar being fixed to the actual wishbone pivot as on the XK series. This arrangement meant that not only was the bar twisted under suspension movement, but it was also bent slightly as well; furthermore it enabled removal and refitting of the torsion bars possible without disturbing the rest of the suspension. The bars' rear anchorages were at the scuttle. Ball joints were again used in the suspension, and inclined telescopic dampers, while an anti-roll bar was also fitted. The steering rack was mounted forward of the front suspension and ran across the car behind the radiator; the steering column was universally jointed.

The rear suspension was something entirely new for a road Jaguar and had been the subject of much experimentation, both on E1A and on the racing prototype, E2A. But now that a monocoque section was to be incorporated into a Jaguar road-going sports car it was imperative that the new suspension be well isolated from the car itself, and this Heynes achieved by mounting the entire suspension assembly, together with the differential, inboard disc brakes and hub carriers, in a pressed steel bridge-type sub-frame, which was attached to the body by four angled rubber bonded mountings (rather similar to engine mounting blocks), two on each side. The only suspension members not directly attached to the sub-frame were the two 'U' section trailing radius arms which located the suspension longitudinally, and these too were fixed to the body through rubber mounts. The anti-roll bar attached to the lower links followed suit, so in the entire assembly there was no direct metal-to-metal contact through which road, suspension and transmission noise could be transmitted to the body shell. Needless to say, it was ensured that whatever compliance existed in this arrangement, it did not affect the suspension geometry in a detectable manner; although intentionally the axle casing was allowed to rotate up to a maximum of 5 degrees under driving torque, and 3 degrees under braking, so that transmission judder could be alleviated by a cushioning movement.

The Salisbury hypoid-bevel final drive unit was essentially similar to the unit used in most previous Jaguars. It was rigidly mounted in the bridge (or sub-frame) member, with the universally jointed halfshafts travelling outwards to the wheel hubs in their light alloy castings; these castings extended downwards to pivots, on which were attached the lower suspension links in parallel to the halfshafts. This link had forked ends, one fork attached to the wheel hub casting and the other to mounting points at the bottom of the bridge piece. The inner mountings had double needle roller bearings about 11 inches apart, and the taper roller bearings on the outer mountings were approximately 5 inches apart; taper roller bearings were also used at both ends of the half shafts, which had to take the transverse loads.

Two coil spring/damper units were used on each side of the differential, mounted on projecting lugs on the lower suspension links, and located at the top on the sub-frame bridge. The reasoning behind the use of four separate units was two fold; firstly the two individual units either side could be made smaller than a single large one, and so would allow more room in the luggage compartment, and secondly, by the springing/damping force acting equally on both sides of the suspension link, there were no additional forces to be taken into consideration

within the suspension geometry. It can be seen that the large diameter half shafts played an active part in the suspension by forming the top link of the system; the lower parallel links were longer, and so the minimum possible variation in either camber or track occured. Thus there was no suggestion of the extreme camber changes or rear wheel steering affects present in most swing axle layouts. Obviously axle tramp and wheel hop did not occur, and the system's ability to put the power down on the road was further enhanced by a Powr Lok limited slip device in the final drive unit.

The inboard disc brakes were unsprung and acted directly on the output shafts of the differential. Ventilation holes were left in the sub-frame bridge, and as the differential unit itself was subject to more heat than was usual due to the close proximity of the brakes, it was given special silicon rubber oil seals which had a far greater resistance to high temperatures. The front discs were outboard, and the disc diameters were 11 inches front and 10 inches rear; each caliper (one per wheel) contained two pistons which activated square-type quick change pads. The handbrake operated on an extra caliper on one rear disc.

The brake pedal was connected by a balance bar to two master cylinders, each with their own fluid reservoirs, and by the same bar to a Dunlop made Kelsey Hayes bellows type vacuum booster. Depressing the brake pedal began to operate the master cylinders, and simultaneously closed an air valve and opened a vacuum valve in the servo unit. The bellows then began to contract, with the result that a load was applied through the balance bar to the master cylinders. The vacuum was obtained from the engine's induction system in the normal way, with a reservoir in the vacuum circuit which allowed a number of powered operations with the engine not running. Should the vacuum servo have failed in any way, full manual control was still present directly through the same balance bar. The Kelsey Hayes unit, originating in the United States and made by

Dunlop under licence, differed from most vacuum assisted servos in that mechanical pressure was applied to the master cylinders, rather than a line pressure in the hydraulic system itself. One advantage of the device was that the dismantling of the servo system did not affect the hydraulic circuits, which therefore did not have to be bled afterwards. The twin master cylinders enabled full braking to take place on either front or rear discs should one circuit fail.

As for the E-type's engine, it was simply the 3.8 XK 150S unit more or less dropped straight into the E-type's frame. It thus had the straight-port head and three 2 inch HD8 SU carburetters. In fact about the biggest change was the substitution of a manually controlled enriching device for the previous automatic, solenoid operated auxiliary starting carburetter. Power rating was the same as quoted for the 3.8 XK 150S - 265 bhp, and 206 lb ft torque at 4,000 rpm on a 9:1 compression ratio.

The engine looked visually much the same as the XK 150's too, except that alongside was a giant circular drum which contained the very thorough air cleaner. Cool air was ducted to this from the nose. There were some novelties in the cooling system however - the header tank was mounted separately between the radiator and the engine, as in the D-type and with the same objective, to reduce height. A thermostatically controlled, electrically driven fan replaced the engine driven fan always used before by Jaguar. It cut in at around 80 deg C from a signal sent by the thermostat in the header tank, and out again at about 73 deg C. The fan was placed behind the radiator, and was heavily cowled to increase its efficiency. The cooling system held 11 pints of coolant.

The car's transmission was familiar - perhaps too familiar, as the gearbox was very much an inheritance from the XK series and although Jaguar themselves eventually took over its manufacture and improved production tolerances, it was never worthy of the E-type. A normal single plate Borg and Beck clutch was fitted, the internals of which were inter-changeable with those of the XK.

For the first time, a road wheel diameter of less than 16 inches was used on a Jaguar road sports car, the E-type's 72-spoke wire wheels being of 15 inches diameter with a rim width of 5 inches. Dunlop RS5 6.40 x 15 tyres were the standard fitment, though the prospective owner could request the optional Dunlop R5 racing tyres; these were usually of 6.00 section front and 6.50 section rear, and came on painted 'competition' wire wheels, the rear pair being ½ inch wider on rim size.

The petrol tank was carried behind the rear wheels and to the left of the spare wheel under the boot floor. It was kidney shaped, and carried 14 gallons of fuel which was brought to the carburetters by a submerged Lucas electric pump; this was the continuous running type and supplied the carburetters at a controlled pressure, surplus fuel being returned to the tank by another line. The idea of this arrangement was to minimise vapour lock problems.

Surprisingly perhaps, the E-type was a shorter car than the XK 150 at 14 feet 7½ inches, and slightly wider at 5 feet 5¼ inches; both wheelbase and track were less than the older car's, at 8 feet and 4 feet 2 inches respectively. Good use was made of the interior space provided by these dimensions, and for most people the E-type was a more comfortable car than the XK 150. The inside still had a familiar air about it though, with the large black faced speedometer and rev counter - a clear and competent style carried over from before the war, and used on the row of smaller instruments comprising an ammeter, fuel gauge, oil pressure gauge and water temperature indicator, all of which were neatly calibrated.

Unlike the XK series, and following the pattern set by the previously announced Mk 2 saloon, the speedometer and rev counter were set square in front of the driver, above the steering column. The smaller instruments were set in a separate central panel above the transmission hump and console. This panel also carried the rather notorious row of flick switches, which if not supremely ergonomic did look neat - and after a period of familiarisation, one did manage to overcome a tendency towards flicking the wrong one. Their sequence was basically logical too; nearest to the driver were the wiper and washer switches, the map light and (after the separate starter button, cigar lighter and ignition key all grouped together in the middle), the two-speed heater fan switch, panel light switch (with two brightnesses), and interior light switch. At the base of the panel, labels denoted the function of each switch, the lettering being illuminated at night. Between the small instruments was set the main light switch with head, side and off markings - another inheritance from XK and older Jaguars and looking a little quaint on the otherwise up to date panel. A vertical quadrant lever to the right of the panel controlled the carburetter enriching device, and a matching control on the left altered the heater output. A red warning light indicated when the 'choke' was in use, and a similar light told the driver that the handbrake was on, or that the brake fluid level had fallen dangerously low. A stalk control to the right of the steering column worked the indicators and headlamp flasher, and the headlights were dipped by a facia mounted switch on the right, which most people found a bit short for hurried use.

Beneath the central instrument panel was a console which could contain the optional Radio-mobile radio set and its two speakers, and which sloped down between the seats. The nicely placed gear lever and fly-off handbrake protruded from the console. Leather was employed for trim, except for the carpeted areas and the headlining, which was foam rubber backed. The facia however was in a crackle black finish, with the centre panel in bright aluminium. The passenger was provided with a small open glove compartment in his (or her) side of the facia. The bucket seats were leather upholstered.

The open E-type's boot space was not generous, the petrol tank and spare wheel (set into a well in the floor) taking up most of the spare room. Smaller items of luggage could be stowed behind the seats inside the car, even with the hood folded down, but the XK 150 certainly had a greater luggage capacity. The fixed-head coupe faired better with quite a large area conveniently available through the side-hinged rear door and of course directly accessible from inside too. The fixed-head's spare wheel was reached by removing a floor panel, and the rear door was opened from inside by a knob situated behind the driver's seat (on the open two seater, this knob operated the boot catch). Toggle handles under the facia opened the bonnet, except on very early cars where this was done by inserting a 'T' key into exterior slots on either side of the bonnet itself.

The open two seater's hood was neat in appearance and a good deal more aesthetic than the XK 120's. It was also given an adequately large rear window, and generally speaking it was waterproof although early cars could be suspect. The hoods were made in Jaguar's own trim shop and each one was individually tailored; when folded down it could be neatly covered by its hood envelope. Similar care was exercised in the making of the attractive optional glass fibre hard top - even cars not ordered with one were temporarily fitted with a 'master' at the factory to ensure that, if a hard top was ordered subsequently, it would fit perfectly.

THE E-TYPE ON THE ROAD

The E-type was as exciting to drive as it was to look at. The first examples of both open and closed types were not ideal in respect of seating comfort however, especially for tall drivers - they had a flat floor on either side of the transmission tunnel which restricted leg room, and the rearward movement of the seat was limited to three inches. Also, pre-1962 cars irritated some people through an unfortunately placed beading across the seat back which could become an annoyance on long journeys. Heel and toe operation of the brake and accelerator was difficult if not impossible, and this feature was to remain, with little space around or between the pedals. The position of the steering wheel was good, if a little low for some drivers; naturally it possessed telescopic adjustment. Headroom in the closed car was not generous, although it was quite adequate for all but the tallest occupants.

Almost always however, minor criticisms of creature comfort - even in the early cars - were completely overwhelmed by praise for the car's handling and performance. Even today there are not many production cars which can equal the original 3.8 E-type's acceleration and top speed, and in 1961 the ability of the car to reach 60mph in under seven seconds, and achieve a maximum speed of 150mph, made an enormous impact - especially on those who were lucky enough to sample one of the cars themselves.

The E-type's rack and pinion steering was reasonably light at low speeds, and was superb at high speeds being direct and responsive and transmitting kickback only from bad surfaces. Hands-off steering was quite feasible for demonstration purposes at three figure speeds! There was concurrently a very definite return action. Although only 2.6 turns of the wheel were needed to go from lock to lock, the turning circle at 38.4 feet was not particularly small so the steering wasn't as highly geared as one might be led to expect.

The excellence of the car's general handling more than matched its steering. A 150mph motor car destined to become the property of many thousands of drivers, all with widely differing skills behind the wheel, sets a certain responsibility on a manufacturer, and this Heynes was perfectly well aware of. The E-type was, and is, a superlatively safe car, with perhaps only one fault in this direction - so smooth, relaxed and quiet was it at high speed that the inexperienced driver sometimes tended to arrive at corners rather faster than he meant to. But even on its original skinny 6.40 x 15 RS5 crossply tyres the E-type was a difficult car to

unstick, a conscious effort having to be made in the lower ratios to provoke the tail of the car into a slide. When driven thus it was still completely controllable and with practice, the car could be steered on the throttle around second gear corners. Initial behaviour on entering a bend was a slight understeer, quickly becoming neutral as the power was applied - in fact, the correct way to drive an E-type was to power it round a corner, as best results weren't obtained with a trailing throttle. Lifting off halfway round caused quite marked oversteer though this could be used to advantage by a reasonably adept driver to tighten his line, if he discovered that he had entered a bend a little too fast. Obviously, a little more circumspection had to be employed in the wet especially in the lower ratios, though the E-type was certainly not left helpless in very wet conditions like some powerful cars.

To summarise, the E-type set new standards in handling and roadholding for the big sports car, and perhaps the biggest tribute paid to the E-type in 1961 was the comparison of its characteristics in these two respects with Colin Chapman's Lotus Elite. This little glass fibre sports car was the only other which road testers and other informed opinion of the day could readily think of which equalled or bettered the new Coventry product. Not a coincidence perhaps that both cars were race bred.

Little less remarkable was the quality of the E-type's ride. Having had to endure fairly constant criticism of the old live axle which had under some conditions, hopped and tramped about under the solid chassis of the XK range for well over a decade, Heynes was at last able to show his critics that Jaguar was quite capable of designing an independent rear suspension that was the equal of anything made anywhere else in the world. Not only did the design enable the car to handle in the manner already described, but it also endowed the E-type with a smoothness of progress over even the worst surfaces which would not have disgraced a two-ton limousine. The E-type Jaguar was one of the first sports cars by which the ride of *saloon* cars was to be judged, and it was to take ten years of progress by other leading car makers before professional critics would begin to suggest that better things could be expected from a Jaguar sports car. About the only concession to a traditional sports car ride was a slight choppiness at very low speeds, where at around 40mph the whole car seemed to ride over a small bump rather than use up any wheel movement. Although this only served to contribute to the rigid, taut sensation experienced with the car.

Another big advance over the XK 150 was the suppression of noise. The E-type was born into an age which was just beginning to appreciate the finer arts of insulating a car's occupants from both road and mechanical noise when using the still fairly new monocoque or semi-monocoque methods of construction, which was more prone to vibration and noise periods than the simpler but much heavier body and chassis method used almost since the beginning of the mass produced motor car. Heynes was amongst the leaders in the use of these new techniques, and his use of sub-frames and insulating rubber worked well. Back axle noise in particular was usually completely absent, though the twin-cam engine could still be heard happily working away in front, but not to an unpleasant extent; in fact combined with what little exhaust noise there was and the distinct whine of the gearbox (perhaps the most prominent of the audible vibrations) the resultant sound was eager and almost inspiring.

Nearly everyone was disappointed to find that the new car still used the trusty but hopelessly outdated gearbox used by Jaguar since before the war. Together with a clutch movement that was overlong, the weak synchromesh and occasional stiff operation of the gearbox made the changing of ratios one of the least satisfactory aspects of the early E-type. Despite its long travel, and the necessity to use it all, the clutch was at least very smooth in operation, and long lasting in view of the power it had to transmit.

For the first time since the XK 120 left the scene in 1954, overdrive was not offered on Jaguar's sports car - there simply wasn't room for it in the drive train. In this respect the E-type lost something to the XK 150, whose overdrive had added greatly to that car's ability to cruise almost flat out at a low rpm and piston speed. Admittedly the E-type was given a higher final drive than the XK 150, but to many people the attraction of a fifth gear was still great. Nor was automatic transmission an option on the E-type, despite the fact that most of the production was aimed at the United States - this was not to become available on the E-type until the advent of the plus-two version, with its elongated centre section, in 1966.

The E-type's performance was well disciplined by its disc brakes, which were very similar to the XK 150's although assisted by the Kelsey Hayes Dunlop-manufactured booster which was a slightly controversial substitution for the more normal type used in the earlier car. Well up to coping with most forms of fast road work, and almost certainly a lot better than that possessed by most other road cars of a similar performance in 1961, the original E-type's braking system could be said to have been working at its upper limits in some conditions, and overheating could be induced on, for instance, a rapid descent of an Alpine pass - it has not been unknown for the discs to glow a brilliant red under these conditions! Racing disclosed the narrowness of the margin too, the inboard rear brakes especially being in need of ducting to effect proper cooling. The braking system was in fact the subject of steady improvement throughout the car's history.

The above should not be taken to mean that the E-type was under braked, but merely that the car was fast enough to occasionally use its designed braking capacity to the full. Road Tests were always loud with praise, as we shall see. Initially the handbrake was not self-adjusting which meant that it rapidly became ineffectual in the familiar manner of the XK 150's device, but very shortly after full production began, a much more sensible fully self-adjusting mechanism was adopted. In fact, an almost fortunate hold-up caused by a delay at the body works enabled Jaguar to rectify a number of obvious faults noticeable in the prototype production cars (which the motoring press sampled and whose comments perhaps helped Jaguar in this respect) before many cars had left the factory. Besides the interior bonnet release catches and the self-adjusting handbrake already mentioned, water deflector shields were quickly fitted to the rear brakes, and a heated rear window was made a (rather necessary) option on the fixed-head model.

THE FIRST E-TYPE ROAD TESTS

Both *The Motor* and *The Autocar* tried early production models at the time of announcement and were able to get full road tests into print by the end of March 1961. *The Motor,* in the person of Joe Lowrey, even waited while the very first open car was assembled and tested by Jaguar's night shift "in considerable haste". This excused some of the car's minor failings which were subsequently experienced in a hectic 3,000 mile test accomplished in seven or eight days - these were mainly body faults to do with such items as door and bonnet locks. But these teething and development problems in no way blinded the magazine from the "landmark in sports car progress" that the E-type obviously was.

When it comes to discussing the original E-type's performance one is bound to add a small question mark, as the road test cars did seem to return acceleration and top speed figures which were a little too good. The XK 150S may have been a heavier car, but so far as acceleration was concerned it had a very much lower final drive (4.09) to compensate for this, thanks to its overdrive. But not only was the E-type almost 20mph faster in top speed, but it also took large chunks off the XK's acceleration times in all speed ranges despite its high 3.31 axle ratio. Few if any private owners seemed to

have achieved the car's road test mean maximum of almost exactly 150mph, and of those who tried, about 143 - 145mph was the limit, even one way. Then there is the story which circulated at *Motor* concerning a proud owner of a new 3.8 E-type who had £200 - £300 worth of tuning carried out on his car at the works, and afterwards brought the car along for testing. It was taken to MIRA, whereupon it returned exactly the same figures as the magazine's road-test car had done!

The Motor's open two-seater became the fastest car that the journal had up to then tested. With the hood up it achieved a mean maximum speed of 149.1mph, and it was commented that the higher optional 3.07 final drive ratio would probably have made the car even faster, as at 150mph (reached one way) the rev counter was showing 6,000rpm which was well over peak power. The standard axle ratio fitted at that time was 3.31:1, the intermediate ratios being 11.18 (1st and reverse), 6.16 (second), and 4.25 (third); top was direct as usual. Optional ratios listed for the Salisbury final drive were the normal 2.9, 3.07 and 3.54.

The magazine elected to carry out its test of the E-type using the Dunlop R5 racing tyres throughout, in view of the considerable time that would be spent at or near maximum speed, and these had the effect of gearing up the car slightly so that acceleration was marginally improved when RS5 tyres were fitted. But even so the standing start, top and third gear acceleration times were quite startling. Thirty miles an hour arrived in 2.6 seconds (both rear wheels spinning a little, but no axle tramp!) 60mph in 7.1 seconds, 80mph in 11.1 seconds, and 100mph in 15.9 seconds. To add 20mph to this took only another 9.1 seconds, and the standing ¼-mile time was 15 seconds exactly (it was reduced to 14.7 seconds when a trial run was made with RS5s). What was almost as impressive was an overall fuel consumption of 19.7mpg, and moderately quick touring would return well over 20mpg. At a constant 70mph a figure of 26½mpg was returned, while at 100mph the

E-type was still giving 21mpg!

Despite its high gearing, great flexibility was still apparent even at very low speeds in third and top gears. For instance, 20mph to 40mph was accomplished in a mere 5.6 seconds in top, while no 20mph increment in that gear from 10mph to 100mph took more than 6 seconds.

The new car's brakes were rated as "exceptional" although pedal loads were felt to be a little high despite the booster; also, an apparent lack of bite was noticed on the initial depression of the pedal though this observation was not born out by the braking figures themselves. A fault of that particular car alone was an air leak which resulted in a spongy pedal, although when given hard sustained use an increase in pedal travel was a feature of the earlier braking systems anyway.

The new rear suspension was rated "a major step forward" providing a high speed ride that very few touring cars could compete with, especially when a particularly rough section of roadway was suddenly struck - then, a "tremendous feeling of security and stability" was experienced by the driver. Of the E-type's handling, *The Motor* had this to say:

> It is basically very near to being a neutral steering car, but, the driver is constantly astonished by the amount of power he can pile on in a corner without starting to bring the tail round; as with front wheel drive, hard acceleration through a bend is the right technique, and lifting off gives a marked oversteering change. Naturally, the power technique can be overdone in the lower gears, but this merely increases the nose-in drift angle in a most controllable way. It is possible to go on increasing the sideways 'g' value to quite a surprising level, because the E-type retains its balance far beyond the point at which most sports cars have lost one end. The very low build (we only realised how low when we saw a small foreign GT coupe towering over it) and anti-roll bars at both ends keep the roll angles right down, and it seems natural to throw the car about in a manner usually reserved for smaller and lighter sports cars.

Examining the E-type Roadster as a 'grand tourer' it was felt to have some short comings; luggage accommodation was far from generous and wind noise from the hood was an intrusion at higher speeds. The seats were frankly "unsatisfactory" not being well shaped or providing much padding in the cushions, and were limited in rearward travel. Cool air ventilation in warm weather was not really sufficient either, and this particular deficiency was to live with the E-type in all its forms for a long time. Lowering the hood was one solution and it was found that this could be done quickly and easily, with reasonably draft free motoring with windows either up or down. The tensioning rod running from the top of the screen to the scuttle tended to vibrate however when the hood was down, which meant that the rear view mirror did likewise as it was mounted on it. Light scatter from the Perspex covered headlights was an annoyance both to other road users and the driver, for whom the lights "were not really adequate for the performance."

The magazine's general summing up could hardly have been more flattering though. Acknowledging that production 'sorting' was far from complete (and in fact within a comparatively short time many of the faults noted by Charles Bulmer and his colleagues were attended to by Jaguar), the closing sentence of the road test was as follows:

> The sheer elegance of line which Jaguar seem able to produce by total disregard for fashion trends is allied to a combination of performance, handling and refinement that has never been equalled at the price, and we would think, very seldom surpassed at any price.

And what did the E-type cost? A quite amazing basic of £1,480 for the open two seater, and £1,550 for the fixed-head coupe. Purchase tax brought these March 1961 figures up to £2,097 and £2,196 respectively. The optional hard top for the roadster cost a total of £76.

Meanwhile *The Autocar* had completed its test on a fixed-head version, a left hand drive example which they ran on trade plates. The writers on that journal expressed similar enthusiasm. The E-type, they stated, "offers what drivers have so long asked for, namely, sports racing car performance and handling combined with the docility gentle suspension and appointments of a town car".

The performance of the fixed-head E-type was found to be as spectacular as the roadster's. Sixty miles an hour was reached in 6.9 seconds, 100mph in 16.2 seconds, and 120mph in 25.9 seconds. The standing ¼-mile was covered in 14.7 seconds, which was exactly the same as *The Motor's* time with the open car when tried with the RS5s - on which all *The Autocar's* testing was done. A genuine two-way 150mph maximum was achieved, although only after the front trade plate had fallen off! The stick-on number plates normally used on E-types had specifically been checked by Jaguar with the authorities, incidentally, and had been declared 'legal'.

Enthusiastic comments on the car's ride and handling followed the pattern of *The Motor* staff's opinion, with the cautionary advice that greasy surfaces needed a light foot. Space inside the fixed-head was however considered "marginal", although most drivers who drove the car for long distances managed to get comfortable. Leg and arm room seemed to be the chief problems, but here again the car was an early one and efforts were made within the year to alleviate the situation. One particular improvement suggested - that a small recess in the floor would give more room - was one of the points specifically attended to by the factory within a short time. The three-bladed wipers (working in unison) were successful however, being efficient in steady rain up to around 110mph, although refraction again caused problems with the headlights in mist or fog - but in good weather their range was thought to be adequate for 100mph motoring at night. *The Autocar's* fixed-head coupe weighed 24.1cwt ready for the road, compared with *The Motor's* open two seater at 24cwt (distributed 51/49); this was over 1cwt lighter than the aluminium bodied XK 120 Roadster tested by the latter magazine in November 1949.

The North American automotive journals were not long to follow with their own road tests of Jaguar's new baby - and in view of the importance of the American market to Jaguar, their opinions were no doubt even more avidly read in Coventry than were their British counterpart's. Not that the factory need have been worried - the E-type's reception was rapturous in the States, and at the New York Show of April 1961, the XK-E (as it was termed for that market) was a star attraction; even at a price of 6,000 dollars it drew the crowds "unaided by gold plate or golden girls".

Road & Track was the first to get into print with figures and a full test. While the magazine did not try for a maximum speed run because of a restricted amount of time with the car, acceleration figures taken on a roadster with the 3.31 axle showed a 60mph time of 7.4 seconds, and 100mph time of 16.7 seconds; the standing ¼-mile was covered in 15.2 seconds. "The car", said *Road & Track,* "comes up to, and exceeds, all our great expectations." The "uncanny adhesive characteristics" and "superb riding qualities" reflected British opinion, and the E-type's delightful handling also came in for praise, second gear especially "providing magnificent cornering over and around twisting mountain roads". The car's steering was rated very close to the best ever experienced by the magazine.

The slight lack of interior space was also detected though, six footers being at a definite disadvantage. Of ventilation, *Road & Track* said: "The heater includes a fresh air vent, but this appears to let in warm air only and ventilation might be a bit of a problem in a summer rainstorm. When the side windows are lowered, a wind-beat noise is very noticeable..." A reason for the warm air problem was undoubtedly because of the close proximity of the cool air trunking from the nose of the car passing rather close to the engine, where an unfortunate degree of heat exchanging took place. Owners who realised what was happening took to lagging the pipe which effected a reasonable cure.

While acknowledging that it was the E-type's

overall appearance which attracted most people initially, *Road & Track* were quick to see the vulnerability of the delightful slim bumpers whose vestigal shapes offered no protection whatsoever against American parking techniques; this was another interesting throw-back to the XK 120 which had similarly elegant but ineffectual bumpers - perhaps we should be grateful though from an aesthetic point of view that Sir William didn't commence with the E-type where the XK 150 had left off in this respect.

Car & Driver also devoted a large number of pages to a very full examination of the new car. in its December 1961 issue. A true 150mph wasn't reached but 145mph was - and that was with the hood down. Handling, ride and steering all received similar praise to that which had been bestowed upon them by *Road & Track* and the British motoring magazines, although it was thought that the steering effort needed at low speeds was a little high - but then *Car & Driver* was probably rather less European orientated than *Road & Track,* and therefore more attuned to the rather over-assisted power steering of many American automobiles. Room inside the car for anyone over 5 feet 10 inches was felt by the magazine to be restricted though it was acknowledged that improvements were on the way for subsequent examples. Oil consumption caused a frown, as indeed it did to many owners of early E-types. *Car & Driver* found a consumption of something like 112 miles to the quart which apparently was considered normal by the distributors. A concomitant effect was sooting of the plugs especially in town, and they usually needed cleaning at 2,500 mile intervals. In late 1963 new oil control rings almost completely cured the problem, and considerably later on Jaguar introduced rubber insert valve guide seals which alleviated it altogether - but not before some clued-up private owners in the States had modified proprietory inserts from one of the big American manufacturers and fitted them into the Jaguar cylinder head.

The magazine appreciated the E-type engine's "marvellous flexibility", not least because it postponed the use of the gearbox - "the kindest thing we can say about it is that we didn't like it" was the comment. The test staff in fact failed to understand "why the development of a new transmission with Porsche-type synchromesh on all forward speeds, which reportedly has been going on for some time in Coventry, is not yeilding results. It's even more difficult to see why the racing D-type gearbox, which had synchromesh even on first, could not be adapted to the new car as an interim solution until a really satisfactory transmission is available". A lot of people in Europe wondered that too, but it was wishful thinking - Jaguar's new all-synchromesh gearbox was as yet three or four years away.

The hinge-forward bonnet brought forth praise from the journal: "Accessibility to the engine and its accessories is excellent and that old Jaguar mechanic's bugaboo 'I'd fix it if I knew where it was' should be forever buried." Anyone with practical experience of the XK 120 will know what they were talking about! It was noted too that the engine compartment kept remarkably clean inspite of motoring being undertaken in wet and muddy conditions. But on *Car & Driver's* particular roadster, the 12th lhd model off the line, the water wasn't kept out of the cockpit with the hood up: "we found rain leakage to be considerable over the top of the windshield, under the cowl and at the edge of the doors. The trunk also was afflicted with leaks which filtered down into the spare wheel well (an apt term) from which it could not escape due to the lack of drain holes". Jaguar seemed afterwards to have tackled most of the hood leakage problems, but the potentially more serious defect of insufficient drain holes was not attended to, and largely accounts for the severely rusted condition of most well-used early and middle-aged E-types surviving today (at least in Great Britain). What drain holes were provided at various points were usually too small, and easily blocked by the small debris which inevitably collected in gutterings and cavities during everyday motoring. No real attempt at providing any sort of internal protection for the box members was made at the factory either, on earlier cars.

However, such long term speculation was not the job of contemporary road testers, and once again the E-type emerged from an appraisal with flying colours. The American sports car buying public fell for the car in a big way, and virtually the only worry at Coventry was how to keep up with demand. Sir William, by unveiling in front of an astonished world a sports car of supreme beauty, ultra high performance and mechanical ingenuity had once more stolen the lime light, and of course, assured even greater profitability for his company. As he himself said at the time of the 1961 Geneva Show, the firm's sales picture had never been brighter. Sir William also took the opportunity to announce a number of new appointments at the factory - familiar names, but now with new jobs nearer the top in their various fields. Arthur Whittaker became Deputy Chairman; William Heynes, Vice-Chairman (engineering); F R W England, Assistant Managing Director; R W Grice, Works Director; and John Silver, Production Director. Two months later Bob Berry became Jaguar's public relations officer - an ex-Jaguar apprentice and a keen sporting motorist, Berry had retired from serious racing although still young, and in his day had been rated one of the best British club drivers. His exploits in MWK 120 and Jack Broadhead's D-type are mentioned in other chapters.

Although it had captured the imagination of the public in a way few cars had ever done, the E-type was a very rare sight on the roads of Britain in the first year of its life. When eventually cars began to come off the assembly tracks in reasonable quantities, export was the main concern and the cars released onto the home market amounted to only a trickle. The first 20 or so of each type in rhd form went to rather selected customers, and Col. Ronnie Hoare of Maranello Concessionaires, the English Ferrari importers, remembers going to the fac-

tory where a small reception took place with Lofty England as host, in honour of the new owners of the first few closed E-types. This was towards the end of 1961.

EARLY RACING ADVENTURES

Racing car it was not, but inevitably the E-type found its way onto the track very quickly. Although Graham Hill and Roy Salvadori had been entered in E-types for the Fordwater Trophy race at Goodwood on April 3rd, the car first appeared on the track a couple of weeks later at Oulton Park, in the 25-lap GT Trophy race. The result was partly reminiscent of the XK 120's debut at Silverstone, in that the car won first time out; two open two seaters were entered, one driven by Graham Hill for Equipe Endeavour (ECD 400), and the other by Roy Salvadori for John Coombs (BUY 1). Hill won, in front of Innes Ireland's Aston Martin DB4GT, with Salvadori in third place ahead of the 250 GT Ferraris of Graham Whitehead and Jack Sears. Hill's average speed was 83.22mph, and the victory gave the 3-litre V12 Ferraris in particular something to think about - the highly successful short wheelbase berlinettas had rarely been seriously challenged up until then.

The second Jaguar E-type/Ferrari 250 GT clash also resulted in a win for the British car, Salvadori leading from start to finish in the GT race at Crystal Palace on May 21st. He was followed by Jack Sears in a second E-type who also kept ahead of the Ferraris of Whitehead and Parkes, the latter eventually retiring. It was a good day for Salvadori who had four wins at that meeting, one in a 3.8 saloon. But the Ferraris asserted themselves at Brands Hatch the first week in June, when in the Peco Trophy GT race Mike Parkes in Equipe Endeavour's 250 GT took the chequered flag; it wasn't a runaway win however, as Salvadori and Hill in E-types were originally leading until overhauled by Parkes.

It was Parkes who took over the dark blue Equipe Endeavour E-type Roadster for the Scott

Brown Memorial Trophy race at Snetterton in July, which he won, ECD 400 being followed but not challenged by Salvadori in Coombs' factory-prepared BUY 1; no Ferraris were present however. A comparison of fastest lap times, incidentally, shows that the as-yet undeveloped E-type was slower than a Lister-Jaguar, John Coundly's example circulating in 1 min 45 secs during another race, in comparison to Parkes' 1 min 47 secs.

Also in July, Jack Sears gained a second place in the GT race run at the British GP meeting at Aintree, while during the British Empire Trophy meeting at Silverstone, Moss and the swb berlinetta Ferrari showed their superiority by winning the GT race from Bruce McLaren (2nd) and Roy Salvadori (5th); the E-types were separated by Davidson's DB4GT and Whitehead's 250 GT, while Graham Hill had also been in contention with his E-type until retiring from engine failure. On a slightly lower level, Jack Lambert drove his E-type Roadster to an easy win in a Silverstone 15-lap 'clubbie', ahead of DJ Smith's XK 150 - a type of car he himself had only recently exchanged for the E-type. An E-type was included in the Jaguar Drivers' Club Team for the famous 6-hour relay event run by the 750 Motor Club, also at Silverstone, on August 12th; but the handicappers have rarely favoured the bigger cars and the Jaguar team was placed third behind Sprites and MGs.

The first event entered abroad by an E-type was at Spa, where Parkes was placed second behind the swb berlinetta Ferrari of Mairesse. Then came the 1961 European GP at the Nurburgring, where the organisers ran a preliminary 6-lap race for GT cars. Here, Peter Sargent in the car he was to share with Peter Lumsden managed 7th place. This car, the first of the two Lumsden/Sargent E-types, was one of the earliest roadsters released by the factory to private owners - Peter Sargent having established quite good relations with Jaguar through a successful club racing career driving XK 120, C- and D-type cars. The Nurburgring excursion occured almost directly after delivery of the car

had been accepted and it ran in standard form except for the stripping out of trim. The 7th place was no mean effort by Sargent, who remembers that the E-type "understeered madly" and finished the first lap with virtually no brakes! Needless to say a big development programme followed.

The RAC TT, also run in August 1961, saw a win by Moss in a 250 GT Ferrari - George Wicken had entered his E-type but didn't actually race. Sturgess however won an Autosport championship round at Snetterton that month, Dickie Stoop coming second in a Porsche Carrera. The weekend afterwards, Sturgess was placed third in the over 3,000cc sports car class at Shelsley.

No less than seven roadster E-types raced at Snetterton at the end of September, in the 25 lap GT race. But it was Mike Parkes in the Ferrari 250 GT who led throughout, Salvadori in the highest place E-type (entered by Coombs) taking second place from Innes Ireland's Zagato bodied Aston Martin. In the *Autosport* 3-Hour race, which ran in darkness for part of its duration, Peter Sargent came third to Mike Salmon's D-type and a DBR1 Aston. Parkes reverted to the E-type again for the BRSCC Brands Hatch meeting and was rewarded by another win in the GT race, the Equipe Endeavour car putting up fastest lap in the front of the Lotus Elites driven by Leston and Whitmore; a Ferrari challenge ended on the grass.

E-TYPE VERSUS CORVETTE

Meanwhile, enthusiasts in the States had been speculating all the year on how the E-type would fare against the Chevrolet Corvette on the track. The Corvette, 'America's only sports car', had come into being towards the end of 1953; its chassis was seen by some as rather a copy of the XK 120's, and its most novel feature was its glass fibre bodywork. Power unit was originally a modified 3.8 litre Chevrolet engine giving 150bhp at 4,200rpm, and this gave the car a top speed of around 109mph: with a remarkable lack of appreciation of the market aimed at, Chervolet gave the car a three-speed automatic transmission. Handling was said to have compared favourably with the XK 120 though. It didn't sell at first, but development continued and by 1961 the Corvette was a fast car by anybody's standards, particularly with the 327 cu inch fuel injected V8 engine and the four speed manual gearbox fitted to the fastest versions. On paper the Chevrolet was marginally quicker than an equally standard E-type, reaching 60mph in 6.9 seconds, although a poorer shape stopped it attaining 100mph in less than 16.6 seconds; while on its 3.70:1 rear axle ratio, top speed was very much down on the Jaguar's. But of course an E-type fitted with the optional 3.70:1 final drive instead of its standard 3.31 would no doubt have been the equal of the Corvette on acceleration, with still a margin in its favour on top speed. In any case, the E-type was capable of walking away from the Corvette on suitably twisty roads, its all-independent suspension being much superior to the American car's live rear axle (even though some location was provided over and above its semi-elliptic springs by radius arms). A lot cheaper at 3,887 dollars (1,718 dollars less than an E-type Roadster), the Corvette might well have been a potential rival to the Jaguar on the sales side, but such was not the case - no home product was considered a real sports car by many American enthusiasts, which by definition had to be of European origin. The pioneering work carried out by Jaguar and MG after the war had certainly paid off!

The eagerly awaited E-type versus Corvette contest came on September 2nd and 3rd 1961, at Santa Barbara, California.

Bill Krause drove the sole Jaguar, and at the start of the first race out-dragged the opposition into the first corner, followed by Bob Bondurant's fuel injected Corvette and Paul Reinhart's similar car (but fitted with two four-barrel carburettors); but the two American cars forced their way past the E-type and Bondurant won by 13 seconds. The next day Krause was again left in third place, headed by Reinhart and Don Wester's Porsche Carrera. Not that this confrontation was regarded as being conclusive - as the United States' own motoring correspondents pointed out, the Corvettes had had a long time to get 'sorted' and the E-type was still a very new car with as yet no factory expertise (official or unofficial) behind it. The hope was for better things from Coventry, and in time their hopes were partially realised, largely through the efforts of Briggs Cunningham. Speculation, both in the States and at home, was rife about an all-aluminium competition E-type!

But there had been gloom amongst Jaguar enthusiasts at Le Mans a little earlier in the year - by a strange stroke of irony, the year of the E-type, 1961, saw no Jaguar or Jaguar engined car whatsoever contesting for the honours over the Sarthe circuit, where hitherto Jaguar had been represented every year since 1950.

As 1962 began, the outlook for the E-type in motor racing did not look particularly bright. This was the period during which the 250 GT Ferrari reigned very nearly supreme in GT racing, at least on the international front, while the Zagato bodied Aston Martins were also very quick. Private entrants were all too aware of the simple truth - the E-type was a series production road car, and was just too heavy to compete favourably with specialised and extremely expensive opposition. Besides being built with competition in mind from the outset, the GT Ferrari weighed only around 18cwt, compared with 24cwt for the Jaguar, and although it would have been an easy matter to equal or exceed the Italian car's 300bhp, this would not have been anywhere near enough to have cancelled out the enormous weight differential which stood in the Ferrari's favour.

However, although still shunning direct participation in the sport, Jaguar had continued to take an active interest in GT racing through the medium of John Coomb's E-type, which had been in effect a 'works' car ever since it left the factory on 27th April 1961, registered BUY 1 in Coombs' name. An early roadster (chassis number 850006), it was driven during 1961 mainly by Graham Hill as already noted, but on the 4th December 1961 it emerged with a new registration number, 4 WPD, and with rather a special specification although looking outwardly near standard. A considerable effort had been made to reduce weight; the monocoque centre section remained in steel but a thinner gauge sheet was used in its construction which resulted in the very useful saving of around 230 lbs over the standard monocoque. The bonnet was in aluminium, and approximately 83 lbs lighter than standard, while the same metal was also used for the hardtop (as opposed to the heavier glass fibre item of the production roadster). The side windows were in Perspex while a competition bucket seat, similar to that of the GP Ferrari, was installed. The steel petrol tank was increased from 14 to 26 gallons in capacity, and now occupied the spare wheel bay as well.

Mechanically, the XK engine had the 35/40 cylinder head with 7/16 inch lift camshafts, a 9.8:1 compression ratio, and Weber DC03 45mm carburettors. Exhaust pipes of 2 inch outside diameter took the exhaust gasses to two circular silencers at the rear of the car. A 10 inch diameter Borg And Beck competition clutch was fitted, which worked in conjunction with a normal close-ratio E-type gearbox. A production-type Powr Lok limited slip differential was used in the rear axle, crown wheel and pinion ratios being varied of course according to the circuit.

The car's suspension was at this stage reasonably standard, although as time went by more and more special parts were to be incorporated to alter camber, toe in or out and other variables. However, both front and rear suspensions were stiffened up by the use of different torsion bars, springs, dampers and mounting rubbers. Tyres and wheels were Dunlop 650 x 15 R5s on 5K x 15 wire wheels on the front, with similar tyres but on the catalogued 'competition' wire wheels of 5½ inch rim width at the rear. Brakes were beefed up using thicker discs at the front, with both thicker discs and larger wheel cylinders at the rear. A single, larger, master cylinder replaced the standard E-type's twin, while the Kelsey-Hayes booster was replaced by a more conventional Lockheed one.

This then, was how 4 WPD appeared at the beginning of the 1962 season to do battle in GT racing, to be entered under Coombs' name but prepared at the factory. At Oulton Park early in April, Hill took the car to second place in the BARC National Meeting - almost exactly a year after the E-type's race-winning debut on the same circuit - but although he beat Tony Maggs' Aston Martin Zagato into third position and Innes Ireland's 250 GT into fourth, he still couldn't touch Mike Parkes in the winning 250 GT Ferrari, which went into the lead from the first lap. David Hobbs in a Peter Berry entered steel bodied E-type finished fifth in this race, just ahead of Dick Protheroe's car.

Protheroe had of course made a name for himself driving XK 120 Jaguars since the early fifties, but in September 1961 had taken delivery of an opalescent grey fixed-head E-type - the fourth one off the production line. This car was ordered with a 'production' D-type cylinder head, triple 45 DCOE Weber carburettors and a close ratio gearbox. Further modifications included an up-rated braking system similar in specification to the Coombs E-type, plus the fitting of mechanical XK instruments and a D-type rev. counter reading up to 8,000 rpm, (these being a substitution for the less sensitive electronically activated standard instruments). Registered CUT 6, this car was to have a considerable amount of success in British club racing over the 1962 season, ending up winning the over 3-litre class of the *Autosport* GT Championship. It also did well in more important international events too.

The International Trophy race at Silverstone in May resulted in another 'place' for Graham Hill and 4 WPD, this time third behind the new 250 GTOs of Parkes and Gregory - he had held second place for a time but couldn't stave off the UDT/Laystall entered Ferrari. In fact the 250 GTO was embarking on a dominating run of GT race successes that was to continue until the end of 1964. This Ferrari was in its time a controversial car, although the reason for this really lay in the wording of the regulations governing the homologation of GT cars. To obtain homologation, a manufacturer was required to produce 100 identical cars within twelve consecutive months - but the term 'identical' applied only to the engine, chassis and running gear, as the bodywork could be varied. Enzo Ferrari certainly had no intention of making 100 GTOs (the 'O' stood for 'Omologato') but was able to qualify the car by including in the count all the 250 GT berlinettas which he had made since 1958, which were virtually identical to the GTO so far as chassis and mechanics were concerned. The GTO itself was even better and faster than its cousins because it was given lighter and aerodynamically more efficient aluminium bodywork, inspired by a Pininfarina design (the Superfast 2) first shown in 1960. It was powered by the familar Testa Rossa type 3-litre V12 engine which gave a claimed 300 bhp at 7500 rpm, and the whole specification added up to a machine that was seldom to be seriously challenged in important GT events over a two year period.

Meanwhile, Jaguar persevered with the development of 4 WPD with the majority of the testing being undertaken by Hill, who was consistent in his demands that the car should be set up harder; this was carried out by using stiffer springs front and rear, while in a further effort to increase the car's cornering power, new light alloy wheels on peg-drive hubs were put into service, using 6 inch rims front and rear. Hill drove the E-type in this condition during the Formula One International meeting at Mallory at the beginning of June 1962, when in both heat and final of the GT race a second place resulted behind Mike Parkes' 250 GTO, though the Jaguar did finish ahead of John Surtees' GTO in third position which must have been encouraging.

The 'works' car was not entered in any overseas events however, and it was left to Peter Lumsden and Peter Sargent to represent the name of Jaguar at the 1962 Nurburgring 1000km race held towards the end of May. Now with Weber carburettors, their car was faster than last year but was very much outclassed by Ferrari, DBR1 Aston Martin, Porsche and Lotus opposition; its run came to an unfortunate end when a wheel broke.

When it came to Le Mans, Jaguar's name once again figured on the entry lists, three privately entered cars being scheduled to run. Of these, the car to be driven by Briggs Cunningham and Roy Salvadori was a factory-prepared fixed-head coupe, running with an aluminium bonnet and Weber carburettors; it was painted in Cunningham's American racing colours of blue and white (Cunningham had already been active with an E-type that year, winning his class at Sebring with a factory-modified roadster). The second fixed-head coupe Jaguar was that of Maurice Charles and John Coundly - though on inspection by the Jaguar mechanics who were rendering support to Cunningham, this was found to be badly prepared, and in fact a spare 'works' engine had to be fitted over-night in between one of the practice sessions and the race itself. The third E-type was 898 BYR, the Lumsden/Sargent car now fitted with a fast-back aluminium top and a bonnet made of the same material, hand beaten by Peels of Kingston; much of the rear end had also been aluminium panelled too. A full dry sump, D-type engine and gearbox with a wide-angle head had been installed, and the car's braking system was uprated using thicker discs and extra air ducting.

In the race, the Charles/Coundley E-type (503 BBO) was soon out of the running, retiring at 8pm through lack of oil, but the Lumsden/Sargent car was going very strongly in 12th position ahead of the Aston Martin Project 212 car, and well clear of the factory-backed fixed-head of Cunningham/Salvadori in 18th place. A steady run brought the two E-types up to fourth and fifth places, with the British entered car gaining on the GTO Ferrari of "Elde"/"Beurlys" immediately ahead of it at the rate of 10 seconds a lap. In fact, Lumsden seemed set to overtake the Ferrari before the afternoon was out but, only an hour before the finish, he pulled in to report that the gearbox was failing. Sargent drove away from the pits only to have the box seize on him, but mindful of the decision taken before the race to finish at all costs, he managed to jam the gear lever into top, in which gear the car was driven for the remaining 55 minutes.

This piece of misfortune meant that the Cunningham/Salvadori car, previously almost two laps in arrears, was suddenly able to gain seconds a lap on its failing counterpart, and in a dramatic ending to the 24 hours, passed its rival only seven minutes before the finish of the race, snatching fourth place much to the chagrin of the British pair.

When 898 BYR's transmission was stripped down, the reason for the trouble was immediately clear - the D-type gearbox had one gasket that was reversible, except that if it was fitted upside down, it blocked off the oilway through which came the lubricant for the forced-feed oil supply. This mistake had unfortunately been made, with the result that the gearbox finally cried enough after 23 hours of racing on splash lubrication only (on this occasion, the engine and gearbox had been assembled at Jaguar; otherwise the car was prepared at Brian and John Playford's garage at West Croydon). However, 5th place out of 55 starters was no mean effort and the two drivers were consoled by the presentation to them of *The Motor* Trophy for being the highest placed Britishers to finish. The actual race winners were Phil Hill and Oliver Gendebien, far ahead in their 4-litre 330LM Ferrari from the GTOs in 2nd and 3rd positions.

After the 1962 Le Mans race, Philip Turner writing in *The Motor* noted that "it would have been possible to run a highly developed E-type in the Experimental and Prototype class for the production of a team of competition versions for next year, for by a recent CSI desision, experimental and prototype cars will in 1963 be restricted to a maximum of three litres". This and other hints to Jaguar about a true competition version of the E-type were not to fall upon totally deaf ears at Browns Lane, and 1963 was indeed to see the unveiling of a 'lightweight' E-type as we shall see.

Back in England, Graham Hill and 4 WPD appeared at Brands Hatch on August 6th for a 25-lap BRSCC GT race over the long circuit having spent some time the previous week testing at Brands for the event; the car ran with a 4.09 rear axle ratio and a full tank of petrol (14 gallons). Fourth fastest in official practice, Hill out accelerated Parkes' GTO Ferrari at the start of the race only to drop back as the cars swept round Paddock bend, but climbed from 6th place to 4th by the end of the event to finish beind Parkes, Salvadori and Ireland all in GTO Ferraris. The race was run in wet conditions, and Hill's fastest lap was 2.3 seconds down on the quickest GTO time, put up by Parkes.

Immediately afterwards, the Coombs car was prepared for an important date indeed - the 1962 Tourist Trophy at Goodwood; there was no time for extra 'sorting' but stiffer rear dampers were obtained from Girling and the axle ratio changed from 4.09 to 3.77 : 1. In view of the distance to be covered at Goodwood, some 240 miles, a 25 gallon tank took the place of the 14 gallon one. In this race, Graham Hill had Ferrari commitments so Roy Salvadori took over the wheel of 4 WPD; practice resulted in him gaining fifth fastest time, behind the 250 GTOs of Ireland, Surtees, Parkes, and G Hill, in that order - with about 1½ seconds covering all five cars! One second slower than Salvadori was David Piper's GTO, with Jim Clark's Aston Martin Zagato next quickest. The other two E-types, those of Dick Protheroe and Peter Lumsden, were 10th and 11th fastest respectively. Alas there was no Stirling Moss present, as he was still in hospital following his terrible Easter weekend crash at the same circuit;

Top Cutaway drawing of the 1961 E-type Fixed-head Coupe. Note the 'bridge' containing the rear suspension, the large cast rear hub carriers and the two pairs of coil-spring/damper units also at the rear. Clearly shown too are the massive sills and the method of strengthening the floor (*photo The Autocar*)

Centre left Sir William Lyons at the Geneva launch of the E-type

Centre right Front suspension and disc brake of the 'Series 1' E-type. Visible is the torsion bar mounting of the lower wishbone, on an extension beyond the fulcrum of the latter (*photo The Motor*)

Bottom The E-type's rear suspension assembly, showing clearly how it was contained within a 'bridge' type sub-frame which had engine bearer type mountings through which it was bolted to the monocoque

Top Victory first time out - the E-types of Hill and Salvadori at Oulton Park, April 1961. Graham Hill in ECD 400, the Equipe Endeavour car, won with Salvadori in the Coombs car third, behind Innes Ireland's DB4GT Aston Martin *(photo The Motor)*
Centre The E-types of Jack Sears and Roy Salvadori sandwich the Equipe Endeavour Ferrari 250GT at the start of a race at Crystal Palace, in May 1961 - one of the early appearances of the E-type racing *(photo The Motor)*
Bottom Sears, Sargent and McLaren fight it out at Snetterton, September 1961. Both ECD 400 and 898 BYR survive today, and are under restoration *(photo The Motor)*

Top The Lumsden/Sargent car in its later form, as prepared for the 1962 Le Mans race, with alloy bonnet which Sargent admits "didn't look quite right", but Jaguar would not sell them the real thing. The roadster was also given a 'non-detachable hard top' _(photo The Motor)_

Centre 898 BYR at the May 1962 Nürburgring 1,000km race; note the special 'fast back', incorporating air cooling slot for the rear brakes _(photo The Motor)_

Bottom Just to show that sideways motoring is not the perogative of today's Group One machinery! David Hobbs (3 BXV) and Innes Ireland enjoying themselves at Oulton Park, April 1962 _(photo The Motor)_

Top Dick Protheroe signals to pull into the pits at Goodwood during the 1962 RAC TT - captioned at the time "Please may I come in now?"!

Centre Early examples entered in rallies caused a lot of attention - this small crowd gathered round R and M Merrick's roadster while it halted for a while during the 1962 Monte Carlo Rally *(photo The Motor)*

Bottom The E-type never had the backing it required to become a real success in International rallying, although a number of private entrants drove the car in a number of important events, such as the 1963 Monte Carlo Rally shown here *(photo The Motor)*

Top left Peter Nocker (left) and Peter Lindner at the factory with their Lightweight E-type, probably at a time when the car was to be fitted with its 'Sayer' nose and tail *(photo Andrew Whyte)*
Top right The brilliantly effective Peter Lindner with his Lightweight E-type, photographed prior to the 1963 1,000km at Nurburgring *(photo The Motor)*
Bottom A moment to remember - Peter Lindner leads the entire field on the first lap of the 1963 Nurburgring 1,000km with the Lightweight E-type *(photo The Motor)*

Top left Sebring, 1963, and the start of the 12 Hour race with all four E-types entered visible amongst a very mixed field

Top right Pit stop and wheel change for the Leslie/Morrill Competition E-type entered by Kjell Qvale; it finished 7th, the highest placed E-type

Centre E-types in unexpected places - the start of the May 1963 Japanese Grand Prix on the newly built Suzuka circuit. Winner of the sports car race was T Yokoyama in no. 41 and Mr Arthur Owen drove no. 48 alongside, an 'invitation' entry

Bottom Cunningham entry at the 1963 Le Mans race - the Richards/Grossman Lightweight E-type cornering hard *(photo The Motor)*

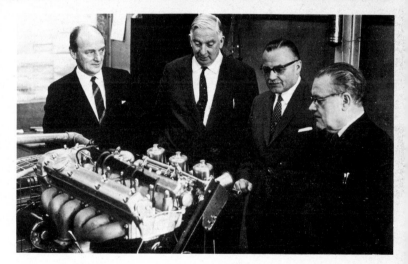

Top The Cunningham/Salvadori Lightweight E-type staves off an attack by a Ferrari GTO, Le Mans 1963 *(photo The Motor)*
Centre left Sir William Lyons chats with Harry Weslake, an instrumental factor behind the success of the Jaguar XK engine, at the 1958 Earls Court Motor Show *(photo The Motor)*
Centre right The basic ingredients of Jaguar's brilliant engineering team, with one of its achievements, the XK engine in E-type form, on the test-bed at Browns Lane. From left to right; Harry Mundy, Walter Hassan, William Heynes and Claude Baily
Bottom A rather worried-looking Briggs Cunningham at the Le Mans practice weekend, 1962. Cunningham undoubtedly did more for Jaguar's racing image in the States than any other person *(photo The Motor)*

Top Salvadori two-wheels the Lightweight E-type round Goodwood in pursuit of Innes Ireland's Aston Martin during the 1963 RAC TT *(photo The Motor)*
Centre left A fine picture of Roy Salvadori and the Lightweight E-type at Goodwood during the 1963 TT *(photo The Motor)*
Centre right Dick Protheroe and CUT 7 lead the Ferraris at Rheims during the 12 Hour race; the car, with its special 'Sayer' body, came to Protheroe via Jaguar's experimental Department and this event was undoubtedly its most successful *(photo The Motor)*
Bottom Lumsden and Sargent's second E-type ended up looking like this, with a Sayer-inspired shape much like CUT 7's. It is pictured here during the Nurburgring 1,000km race of 1964 *(photo The Motor)*

Top An early 'Series 1' 4.2-litre E-type Fixed-head, virtually indistinguishable from the 3.8 version and retaining the slim bumpers and covered headlamps of the original cars *(photo The Motor)*

Centre left Dashboard and facia of the 4.2 'Series 1' E-type, showing only minor differences from the first cars. Note the traditional style headlight switch, separate starter button and the clear black dials. Triple wipers are still fitted *(photo The Motor)*

Centre right Interior of an early 'Series 1' 2-plus-2 E-type. Ideal for children, the rear seats were not very comfortable for an adult over a long distance *(photo The Motor)*

Bottom left First of the 2-plus-2 E-types, and something of the original E-type's lines have been lost by a higher roofline and a more upright screen angle *(photo The Motor)*

Bottom right Drawing of a 'Series 1' 2-plus-2 E-type. With the longer wheelbase came the option of an automatic gearbox - note the quadrant between the front seats *(photo The Autocar)*

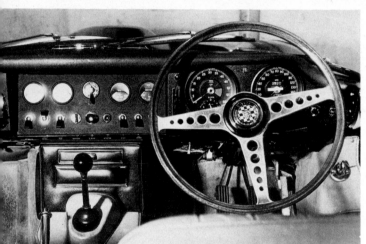

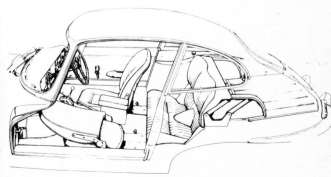

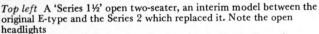

Top left A 'Series 1½' open two-seater, an interim model between the original E-type and the Series 2 which replaced it. Note the open headlights

Top right This mobile cutaway shows quite clearly the E-type's construction, and how the main stresses are born by the big sills which run between the wheels, the cross-braced floor and transmission hump, and the boxed rear quarters. The engine and front suspension is carried by a tubular frame work running from the front bulkhead

Centre left The Series 2 E-types incorporated many changes, including repositioned side and flasher units (beneath the front bumper as can be seen) and headlights (brought forward two inches), a much larger air intake and many under-the-skin alterations. The open two-seater shown here is the American export version

Centre right Commissioned by the *Weekend Telegraph*, Bertone produced this 'ideal' car on 2-plus-2 E-type basics for the 1967 London Motor Show. Many of the car's separate parts and accessories were supplied by British manufacturers; the wheels have a pleasant affinity to the drilled D-type and Lightweight E-type wheels (*photo The Motor*)

Bottom Modified front and rear by Frua, this E-type was exhibited on the Italsuisse stand at the 1966 Geneva Show. It was originally a standard red 1965 Fixed-head Coupe ordered by Coombs of Guildford, who had minor modifications made to engine, suspension, axle ratio and wheels while it was still at the factory. It was then sent to Turin where Frua restyled the nose and tail, shortening the overall length by 5 inches. The present owner bought the car in 1966 and still uses it regularly although the car had covered only about 50,000 miles by 1974 (*photo The Motor*)

Top Bob Vincent in the Red Rose Motors' Competition E-type at Lodge Corner, Oulton Park, during the International Gold Cup meeting in September 1966. One of the last of the Lightweight E-types to be campaigned in contemporary racing, the Red Rose car was also one of the fastest. Note the widened wheels *(photo The Motor)*

Centre left Unexpected victory for the E-type; Dr. Jorge Burgoa's win in the Gran Premo de Automobilismo of 1966, a tough trans-Bolivian road race covering 1200 miles

Centre right The supercharging arrangements on Alan Leeson's 'Modsports' E-type; although possessed of a great turn of speed down the straight, the car was never a race winner

Bottom The Jaguar Egal, as conducted by Barry Williams. He lost this particular battle with the 7-litre beast, while pursuing a GT40 and a Porsche Carrera at a 1967 Silverstone meeting, the car ending up against the bank at Copse corner *(photo The Motor)*

Top John Burbidge has been a regular and successful E-type driver for a number of years now. Here, his well known E-type strives to keep ahead of Rhoddy Harvey Bailey's Chevrolet Sting Ray during a Castle Combe meeting of 1972
Centre left Successful hill climb car; Nigel Pow's immaculate roadster at Loton Park. This car was originally built up by David Harris of Bournemouth
Centre right One of the last race-winning E-types in Modified Sports Car racing in this country; John Harper takes the Forward Enterprises' ex-Ken Baker roadster to another victory at Silverstone in 1972
Bottom Guy Bedington's Series 3 V12 E-type at Brands Hatch, one of the few V12 cars modified for competition in this country

although it was not known at the time, Moss would never race again.

It was the usual Le Mans start for the TT, and Salvadori was down in 9th place before the first corner as he'd chosen to start fitting his safety harness before moving off, and because the low--built E-type was a bit difficult to get into quickly. But thereafter his lap times were both consistent and fast, and when the leading Ferrari of Surtees crashed he was up to fourth position. A tyre changing and fuel stop was required after 55 laps, 16 gallons of petrol and the two rear wheels being changed in 1 min 16 seconds - though unfortunately the car's departure was delayed another half minute because one of the new wheels had its tyre valve damaged by the wheel hub hammer as it was being put on and had to be changed again. Salvadori then held on to his 4th place until the finish, having been lapped once by the leader. He remarked afterwards that the E-type was faster than the Ferraris on the Lavent Straight, but that due to its inferior power/weight ratio it lost on acceleration out of the corners. Derek White, the chassis engineer in charge of the E-type's development, noted that "for a car of this weight and power considerably larger section tyres are required on correspondingly wider rims".

As for the other two E-types, Peter Lumsden spun at the chicane and went backwards into the wall, thus putting himself out of the race, but Protheroe in CUT 6 secured an excellent 6th position overall, a good result for this privately prepared fixed-head coupe. Although he didn't take part in the TT, another private E-type entrant who should be mentioned as racing at that time is Ken Baker, who with his 1961 roadster 7 CXW won club races at Brands Hatch, Castle Combe and elsewhere; these and other successes enabled him to become runner-up to Shaw's Lotus Elite in the 1962 Peco GT Championship, the contest finally being decided at the Boxing Day Brands meeting.

THE 1962 E-TYPE

Meanwhile, production of the normal E-type was well under way, with cars leaving the factory at a rate of something like 150 a day; all the 1962 E-types incorporated footwells in both driver's and passenger's side of the cockpit, and an indentation made in the rear bulkhead on both models also allowed more rearward travel for the seats. The seat cushions themselves were improved too - those of the 1961 cars had, amongst other disadvantages, rather thin padding which allowed the steel floor of the seat to be felt in certain positions. The positions of the pedals had been changed, and the combined result of these alterations was an altogether more driveable car. Few mechanical changes were introduced, although efforts were being made to overcome heat soak from the rear discs which sometimes affected the final drive unit inspite of its special oil seals.

William Boddy of *Motor Sport* took one of the improved 1962 cars to Monaco, on his way to see the Grand Prix, and was generally delighted with the roadster's performance over the 2,000 mile round trip - despite a deviation onto an unmade-up road which ended nowhere, but whose boulders suceeded in flattening both exhaust pipes and cracking the sump. All were repaired by the agents at Monte Carlo, where Boddy found Bruce McLaren fitting a new universal joint to his personal E-type (after which he won the GP in his V8 Cooper Climax).

Mr. Boddy's main criticisms of the car concerned not its performance, handling or ride all of which were upheld as being exemplary - but in the roadster's deficiencies as a true Grand Tourismo. The 14 gallon tank was not reckoned big enough, too many stops for petrol cutting down average speeds, and its capacity was compared with those of the Aston Martin DB4GT at 30 gallons, and the 22 gallons each of the 250 GT Ferrari berlinetta and the Maserati 3500 GT. Luggage space was another problem for the long distance motorist according to Boddy, although he recognised that the fixed-head coupe was far better off in this respect. On his particular car, petrol fumes were obtrusive, and a stop had to be made to "shut the bootlid, which had sprung open, either because the catch rattles free or due to chassis distortion over bad surfaces". Seating and general comfort were passed without criticism, and the soft top came in for real praise - it was easy to erect with its three toggle catches, free from drumming, and fully weather resistant, so progress had been made. "Indeed, let us here and now offer the highest praise for a sports car into which not a drop of water penetrated, or so much as dripped from under the dash, even in thunder storms of tropical intensity - no mean achievement at the customary high cruising speeds of the E-type!"

On its return to England, the car was taken to a Mallory Park race meeting and cruised happily up the motorway at 4,800rpm (117mph), "and held 6,000rpm (153mph) for a mile, although taking a considerable distance to attain this impressive maximum speed". An average of 104mph was achieved on the return journey down the motorway. This sort of motoring only made itself felt by an oil consumption of 920mpg, the car behaving as well at the end of the test as it had at the beginning; although the tyres, after some 2,800 miles in *Motor Sport's* hands, were "pretty well due for replacement". The magazine's Continental Correspondent Denis Jenkinson tried the car while it was in Monte Carlo, and opined that it was "large, noisy and heavy as to steering and gear-change after a Porsche"; but he too must ultimately have agreed with Bill Boddy in saying "we would dearly like one, not only for getting effortlessly and very quickly about Europe, but for shopping and going to the post, especially when only a few minutes remain before the last collection" - because, not too long afterwards, an E-type was bought by *Motor Sport* for Jenkinson's personal transport!

The Jaguar stand at the 1962 Earls Court Motor Show had as its star attraction the new Mk 10 Jaguar saloon, with its rear suspension (similar to the E-type's) making it the first all independently sprung Jaguar saloon. A fixed-head coupe E-type was shown as well,

which displayed a number of fairly minor changes which were to be incorporated in the 1963 E-types; for continued development of the sports car had taken place and this, together with the experience of more than a full year of production, meant that several improvements were carried out for 1963.

The rear drive shafts were given shields to protect their universal joints, and the thickness of the rear discs went up by ½ inch; brake pad material was changed all round from Mintex M33 to M59, and the exhaust system was improved in minor respects. Otherwise the car remained much the same, production increasing to meet the demand which continued unabated in the States, and almost everywhere else. Jaguar's export figure had been up by 12% for the year ending July 1962, and it was still climbing.

THE E—TYPE IN COMPETITION, 1963 - 65

So far as the factory were concerned, the 1962 season had amply demonstrated that the Ferrari GTO was indisputably superior to the E-type in the GT racing, and that included the relatively highly modified 4 WPD; while the latter had indeed been the only other make of GT car capable of keeping the GTO in sight, the fact still remained that the E-type had not won a single important event in the face of Ferrari opposition, and that was without even venturing beyond these shores (apart from Le Mans, and the genuinely private entry of Lumsden and Sargent at the Nurburgring). On the other hand, the issue had often been close enough for the tempting thought to arise that if the E-type's greatest disadvantage vis a vis the GTO Ferrari, excess weight, could be eliminated, then Jaguar might once again have a true race winner - and Jaguar have only ever been interested in race, not class, winners. And if Le Mans itself was unsuitable at the moment for the sort of car that Jaguar wanted to build, then GT racing might be a good substitute, particularly as this increasingly popular division of the sport was, for the

1963 season, to be given the Manufacturers' Championship and would thus attract considerably more attention to itself. Not that Jaguar could aim for the actual Championship itself though, as it was limited to cars of 3-litres or below, but then again the company had been traditionally uninterested in the title which they could probably have won with the D-type back in the fifties had they really set out to do so.

THE COMPETITION E–TYPE

No doubt finally persuaded by the pleas of private entrants, the project of building a true competition version of the E-type was put into hand by Jaguar towards the end of 1962. The factory had accumulated a lot of useful knowledge over the two preceding seasons racing 4 WPD and an outline specification of the car that was needed was soon drawn up. To quote from an early factory memo on the subject, some of the main points were:

The engine in the Coombs E-type could be modified to produce more than its present 290 bhp.

The weight of the Coombs E-type be reduced by approximately 150 lbs to bring it in line with the weight of the present Ferrari (alum. crankcase, axle, tank etc).

The E-type close ratio gearbox be replaced by a 5 speed gearbox as used by Ferrari, either the ZF box or Jaguar's 5-speed box.

However, it is difficult if not impossible to draw up an accurate specification sheet for a 'proper' competition E-type, as virtually no two were the same and some differed in fundamentals. For the same reasons it is hard to say exactly how many were built, as it rather depends on your definition of the term 'competition E-type'. But nearly all began life as right-hand drive open two seaters with hard tops.

Naturally, the greatest efforts were made during the cars' construction to reduce weight and light alloys were employed extensively throughout. The centre monocoque, and all inner and outer body panels including the bonnet, were fashioned from aluminium sheet; only the front tubular frame work embracing the engine remained in steel, for the same reasons that justified its retention on the later D-types - the greater strength of steel meant that a smaller diameter of tubing could be used which resulted in a lighter structure than a magnesium alloy equivalent, and steel had the additional attraction of being easy to fabricate at the works by Jaguar's own fitters. The car's hard top was in aluminium instead of glass fibre, and actually contributed quite usefully to the stiffness of the centre section.

There had been much experimentation on 4 WPD to determine the best arrangement of the E-type's suspension for racing, and advantage was taken of a comparatively 'clean sheet' to include many special parts in the competition E-type's set up, although at first glance everything looked much as it did on the normal production E-types. In fact, the front suspension retained only the upper and lower wishbones of the standard car, all other parts being special including the upper and lower fulcrum housings (both top and bottom) for the wishbones. Torsion bars and the anti-roll bar were stiffer, and the dampers were similarly uprated and had a shorter travel and integral bump stops.

At the rear, the independent suspension was still carried in the steel sub-frame of the production E-type, though the bottom plate from the Mk X saloon was used as it was stronger. From Jaguar's big saloon also came the hub carriers, suitably modified and lightened, and the lower wishbones and their mountings. A standard E-type half-shaft was used, in conjunction with spacers. All four springs and dampers were different, the dampers again having integral bump stops with a rebound movement of 2 inches. The anti-roll bar varied in diameter as development proceeded, while the suspension mounting rubbers, through which the suspension housing was attached to the monocoque, were 25% stiffer than the production E-type's; also the radius rod bushes were turned so that their holes were at right-angles to the car's centreline, again to minimise unwanted movement of the rear suspension assembly. The differential housing was the normal Salisbury cast-iron production item, usually fitted with the Powr-Lok limited slip differential although ZF or Thornton internals were an alternative.

The front brakes were improved along similar lines to those on 4 WPD during the 1962 season, with larger (11¼ inch diameter, ½ inch thick) discs and light alloy wheel cylinders. The calipers were modified Mk 1X Jaguar. At the rear, production E-type discs were employed with 1 5/8 inch wheel cylinders, and air scoops were fitted under the car's bodyshell to supply extra cooling. The familiar DS 11 pads were used all round, and the approximate front to rear braking distribution was 64.5/35.5. The original equipment Kelsey Hayes brake booster was retained initially though was later to be exchanged for a non-bellows, line-pressure booster.

Wheels were similar in appearance to the D-type's, being made by Dunlop in light alloy, but they differed in construction and were of 15 inch diameter with (originally) a 6 inch rim; they fitted onto peg-drive hubs and were secured by 'knock-off' spinners.

The competition E-type was given the most powerful Jaguar engine yet to be seen up until that time outside the factory, the XK engine being brought up to its most sophisticated level. Like the 3-litre unit which powered the Cunningham-entered Le Mans prototype E2A of 1960, the 3781cc engine in the 'lightweight' E-type boasted an aluminium block and fuel injection. The latter was the latest Lucas mechanical injection using a very short, 3 inch, inlet manifold with the throttle butterflies being contained in six small separate alloy castings; the injection nozzles themselves were in the actual manifold. Dry sump lubrication featured as with the D-type, but its workings were peculiar to the competition E-type; a combined scavenge and pressure pump was driven via a cog on the front of the engine's main bearing cap from the crank, while another scavange (or suction) pump was situated by number four main bearing, shaft driven from the front of the engine. All pumps were made from cast aluminium parts.

The crankshaft differed from that of the D-type too, being slightly longer and having a thicker nose. Connecting rods were similar to the sports racer's though, while similar 'wide-angle' Brico squish-crown pistons were used, some sandcast, others forged.

The cylinder head was that developed for the D-type at Le Mans, with valve angles of 35/40 and nicknamed the 'wide angle' head (as explained in Chapter Six). Valve diameter sizes were 2 3/32nd inch inlet, and 1 11/16th inch exhaust; camshaft lift started at 7/16th inch, and was later increased to 15/32nd inch. Compression ratio varied between 9½ and 10:1 and the engine commenced by giving between 290 and 320 bhp gross, though eventually this was increased to as much as 344 gross in certain cars.

Although the original specification sheets for the first competition E-types cites Jaguar's own four-speed close-ratio gearbox as being fitted, the German ZF five-speed box became the cars' standard equipment. This had the effect of giving the cars an improved acceleration in the higher speed ranges, but there were some disadvantages - it added some 80 lbs to the weight of the car, thereby almost negating the 84 lbs saved by the use of an aluminium crankcase, and absorbed rather more power than the production gearbox - as much as 55 bhp compared to about 25 bhp.

Similarly, all was not smooth going with the aluminium crankcase - the engine had not been designed with an alloy block in mind so the new crankcase was something of a compromise, and from this stemmed a number of vexations, including trouble with the cylinder head not sealing properly, cracking, and even the crankshaft bearings running out of true. The stiffness of the heavy ZF gearbox casing added to the problems as it was more rigid than the block itself, and sometimes caused the latter to flex and crack. The engine was also run fairly cool to minimise distortion problems, i.e. between 65°C - 70°C, though this was achieved with production

E-type radiator and parts.

However, the main objective of a big reduction in overall weight had been achieved, and the new car was considerably lighter than its production cousin. Its homologated weight was in fact an impressively low 2028 lbs, or about 100 lbs lighter than the GTO Ferrari in Le Mans trim, and some 500 lbs lighter than the standard steel roadster E-type. On the subject of homologation, it might well be wondered how the competition E-type was able to meet the 100-a-year qualification, seeing that only about 12 cars with aluminium monocoques were ever built by the factory. Well, this was achieved in an even more ingenious manner than Ferrari had managed with the GTO - it seems that the 100 units count was met by the normal run of production steel open two seater E-types, while the aluminium bodywork, special engine and cylinder head, fuel injection and so on was 'legalised' by then citing the *competition* model E-type as the normal production car, and the *standard* model as the 'special' version. This appeared to satisfy the CSI and the competition E-type was homologated as a GT car in January 1963, quietly and without publicity - in fact a Jaguar spokesman was denying the car's existence two months later! The first cars were delivered in March 1963.

These had chassis numbers in the normal sequence of right-hand drive open two seater E-types, but prefixed with an 'S'. The first took over the identity of 4 WPD complete with registration number and chassis number, the car undergoing another metamorphosis and being 'returned' to Coombs as a fully fledged lightweight complete with an alloy centre section. It then continued in its role of unofficial factory development car. The second competition E-type was despatched to Briggs Cunningham in America; the Cunningham team had already accumulated E-type racing experience through the running of an open E-type at Sebring and a fixed-head coupe at Le Mans the previous year, both of which had incorporated factory aluminium panels without being actual 'lightweights'.

At the same time, the third car was sold to Kjell Qvale, another British car importer in the States.

C T ('Tommy') Atkins and Roy Salvadori took delivery of the second home market car, while No. 5 went to Germany where in May 1963 Jaguar distributor Peter Lindner was the recipient. The same month Peter Lumsden and Peter Sargent were sold their car. The next two went again to Briggs Cunningham, being taken direct to Le Mans for the 24 hour race in June. Peter Sutcliffe in Great Britain bought No. 9 while the tenth competition E-type was sent out to Australia, where Bob Jane took delivery through Brysons Ltd. Dick Wilkins and Phil Scragg received numbers 11 and 12, in December 1963 and January 1964 respectively. This completes the list of cars having aluminium monocoques and engine blocks, but several more cars were completed having many competition parts in their make-up but not alloy centre sections. Sir Hugh Ropner bought one such roadster, complete with an alloy bonnet, five-speed ZF gearbox and a wide-angle cylinder head but lacking the special monocoque and fuel injection; it was intended for use purely as a road car. Then M Bardinau purchased one of the few fixed-head coupes to be sold by Jaguar with competition equipment, this car too having a ZF box, alloy block engine and aluminium body parts (this and Cunningham's Le Mans car are the only known examples).

The competition E-type made its debut at Sebring in March 1963, when both Cunningham and Qvale entered their brand new lightweights in the 12-hour race, the cars being crewed by Walt Hansgen/Bruce McLaren and Ed Leslie/Frank Morrill respectively. It was an interesting race, not the least because the new AC Cobras led the Ferrari GTOs at first! But although Phil Hill was lying second in his AC by the end of the first hour, the Cobras proved to be unreliable and Hill's car only finished by "continual patching". As for the new E-types, they were more than a match for the Chevrolet Corvettes and although not as fast as the initially quicker Cobras, held together better. The Hansgen/-

McLaren car might well have spoilt Ferrari's domination of the first six places had it not been delayed for several laps through a broken pipeline to the brakes - this allowed Leslie and Morrill to inherit 7th position, Hansgen and McLaren eventually finishing a lap down in 8th place. Surtees' mid-engined Ferrari prototype won, with Ferrari GT prototypes also taking 2nd and 3rd places; GTOs were 4th, 5th and 6th.

This was not Cunningham's first E-type race of 1963 though, as Walt Hansgen and Augie Pabst had been entered in the Daytona 300 held the month before Sebring, using the modified but basically steel-bodied open two seater car obtained more than a year previously. On that occasion, Hansgen failed to keep what seemed a sure third place behind the leading GTO Ferraris of Rodriguez and Penske when he ran out of fuel on the banking, just a few minutes before the chequered flag was due to be hung out. He wasn't even classified as a finisher, being disqualified for receiving a helping push across the line by team mate Pabst.

The first appearance of the competition E-type in Great Britain came when Graham Hill drove the Coombs-entered works development car 4 WPD at the Lombank Trophy meeting towards the end of March 1963. The combined Sports and GT Prototype race was held in pouring rain but Hill still managed to keep the E-type ahead of Salvadori's Cooper-Monaco to win, after Innes Ireland's Lotus 19 had pitted. Dick Protheroe was lying third until he rolled his E-type on the 17th lap at the end of the Norwich straight.

To digress briefly from the competition E-type story, the car Protheroe crashed at Snetterton was a replacement for his first fixed--head E-type (which was sold at the end of the 1962 season after being re-registered, and at the time of writing is now owned by the Registrar of the XK Register, Ted Walker). Although not a lightweight in the official sense, Protheroe's second E-type had been built in rather a novel way - from the Jaguar parts book, beginning "bodyshell-one, wheels - four" and so on, until

from the resultant heap of bits the lightest car possible was assembled. The accident so soon afterwards was an annoyance to say the least, but the car was rebuilt in time to continue racing a little later on in the season.

Graham Hill and the 'new' E-type were also victorious at the Easter Goodwood meeting held in April, 4 WPD leading from the start from Mike Parkes' GTO Ferrari; the red car was also hounded by Roy Salvadori in 86 PJ, the Tommy Atkins lightweight which had just been delivered - as The Motor described it, "Hill as impassive as ever, Parkes winding on great handfuls of lock on and off at the chicane, and Salvadori exiting from the chicane with the Jaguar's left front wheel clear of the ground." Protheroe was there too, having rebuilt his car just in time to be lapped by the three leaders! Hill also managed a fastest lap which was 0.2 sec quicker than the previous best GTO time, put up by John Surtees - had Jaguar really produced a car to make Ferrari sit up and take notice?

As the season continued it certainly seemed as if the new E-type would have to be reckoned with in GT racing; at the Daily Express Silverstone meeting in May it was once again Graham Hill and 4 WPD first, completing 25 laps ahead of Salvadori and 84 PJ, after pole position holder Parkes spun off in his GTO. Dick Protheroe made it a Jaguar 1-2-3 at Silverstone once more with his own roadster, which helped persuade Jaguar to sell him an experimental E-type closed coupe.

This interesting vehicle had been built by the experimental department during 1962 using a steel-bodied roadster as a basis, but with special bodywork developed by aerodynamiscist Malcolm Sayer to give an even more favourable drag factor than either the standard E-type or the GTO Ferrari, which had been closely examined by Sayer. The car had a longer and more penetrating nose, a more gently shelving windscreen, and a new coupe top. Protheroe was to have a good deal of success with this 'low drag coupe' over the two seasons he was to drive it.

However, although the competition E-type had certainly collected a number of wins in its first few months of active life, they were not in top-level international racing and sterner tests for the car lay ahead. The first of these was the Nurburgring 1000 km race the weekend after Silverstone, where on the grid were two light-weights - the cars of Peter Lindner and Peter Nocker, and Peter Sargent and Peter Lumsden (no doubt the commentators were relieved that the Jaguar drivers at least had different surnames!).

The opening stages of the race were heady indeed for Jaguar enthusiasts in the vast crowd, for in the words of *Motor's* report, "Lindner's silver car leapt away at the start and led as the cars burst out of the south curve... rushed back behind the pits in a glorious howl of sound and disappeared beyond the north curve on the first of 44 laps of the long, winding and wearing 14.1 mile circuit". To the delight of the spectators, many of whom were rooting for their fellow countryman in the Jaguar, the Lindner E-type was still in the lead at the end of the first lap as the cars streamed onto the pits straight once more, ahead of rear-engined Ferrari prototypes, GTOs and all! It was not to last of course and as the pack headed towards the south curve for the second time, two Ferraris - Scarfiotti, and Surtees in the rear-engined 250P prototype - slipped past the silver car.

Twenty-three laps later, and Peter Lindner was holding onto 4th place just behind the Jo Bonnier/Phil Hill Porsche - it was obvious to all that for the first time in international racing the GTO Ferrari had met up with a car that had both the road-holding, handling and sheer speed necessary to leave it behind, and on one of the most demanding courses in the world. Alas, the point was not destined to be rammed home. Shortly afterwards engine trouble on the Jaguar intervened, followed by the car's retirement; and to make matters worse, the Lumsden/Sargent car which had been nearly as quick and which had taken over the Germans' 4th place, left the road on its 33rd lap. Some, but not much, con-

solation was offered to the Jaguar camp by three considerably more standard E-types being placed first, second and third in the over 3-litre GT class, driven by Pherstappen/Ruthardt, Werner/Olsen, and Gaillet/Siebenthal respectively; though they were somewhat slower than the fastest Elites and Porsches of half their engine capacity.

Le Mans 1963 saw three competition E-types in contention, all entered by sportsman Briggs Cunningham; one of these was the car he had run at Sebring in March, while the other two had been driven out from the factory direct to Le Mans, already painted in Cunningham's American racing colours of white with double blue central stripes. The Peters Lumsden and Sargent had forsaken their E-type for a space--framed Lister-Jaguar which was not to last the distance.

Driver pairings for the Cunningham cars were Hansgen/Pabst, Richards/Grossman and Cunningham himself sharing the third car with Roy Salvadori. This was the year of the Rover-BRM gas-turbine car, but unfortunately the Jaguars did not emulate that innovatory machine's smooth and consistent performance. For a start, it seems that there had been disappointments during practice: "One of the Jaguars had covered 150 miles in the hour while under test at Lindley but the Jaguar drivers were, on the whole, disappointed in the straight line performance of their cars; this was possibly because the addition of fog lamps and additional ventilators had resulted in some increase of head resistance" *(Motor)*. Then, just 30 minutes after the race had began, Hansgen pitted to report that he was having trouble with the synchromesh which was making neutral hard to find. Later, the Cunningham/Salvadori car was in similar trouble, though its eventual retirement was not actually mechanical - with Salvadori driving, the E-type left the road on the Mulsanne straight having hit a stream of oil left by an unknown car - others went off at the same place, one Alpine driver being killed; Salvadori escaped with bruised legs.

This left only the Richards/Grossman car running, in 10th position at 2am after the last of three Aston Martins had retired, then 8th at dawn behind six Ferraris and a Porsche. But it too had an off circuit excursion while being driven by Grossman, the damage to the car's nose necessitating a long pit stop while what amounted to a new bonnet was made up and fitted before racing could be resumed. It finally finished 9th overall, behind four other GT cars which included a Cobra and a Porsche among their number, winning the 3001-4000cc GT class at an average speed of 98.90mph. Overall winner of the race was the Ferrari 250P of Bandini and Scarfiotti.

Not long after Le Mans, a 25-lap sports car race was held over the Rheims circuit as a supporting event to the French GP; while no lightweight E-types as such were entered, Dick Protheroe ran his latest acquisition, the ex-experimental department low-drag coupe, now registered CUT 7. He had a magnificent race, finishing second to a Ferrari 3-litre prototype and beating all the GTOs after the Aston Martin Project 215 car had retired after initially leading. On June 30th, Peter Nocker drove the Lindner lightweight to victory on the very fast Avus circuit at Berlin, hotly pursued by a GTO Ferrari and a Porsche Carrera. In keeping ahead of the opposition, Nocker established a new GT lap record of 136.26mph; the E-type ran on a 2.93:1 rear axle ratio.

Back in England, Peter Sutcliffe had accepted delivery of his new competition E-type and proceeded to win the GT event at the Snetterton National meeting of July 1963, beating Ken Baker's steel roadster. The marque had little luck at Bank Holiday Brands the next month, where during the 50-lap Guards Trophy race Sutcliffe crashed, Peter Sargent retired with ignition trouble on lap 10, and Protheroe's car stopped after 32 laps with fuel pump trouble.

However, preceding the Guards Trophy failures had come a more important competition E-type assignment, at Silverstone. On this occasion Mike Salmon was driving 4 WPD, and with Protheroe and Sutcliffe were contesting a 25-lap combined GT and Appendix C sports cars race. David Piper's GTO won the GT section of the field, followed by Jack Sears in a similar car, then Protheroe, Salmon and Sutcliffe. None of the GT cars approached the lap record set up by Roy Salvadori and 86 PJ at the May Silverstone meeting however, which stood at 1 min 42.2 seconds, or 102.9mph.

The next Ferrari/Jaguar clash was the RAC Tourist Trophy race at Goodwood, towards the end of August. Before racing began the scrutineers had a field day, making the Aston Martins run on narrow, but homologated wheel rims (Innes Ireland had equalled GTO times in practice, using Aston's Le Mans wheels), and excluding the AC Cobras altogether! In the actual race however, the GTO Ferrari once more asserted itself and finished in front of the competition E-types of Salvadori and Sears (who drove the Coombs car), which took third and fourth places - the two front running GTOs were piloted by Graham Hill and Mike Parkes. Protheroe ended up a creditable 6th, and Peter Lumsden 9th. The cars of Salvadori and Sears were pulling something like 6,200rpm, or 150mph, along the Lavent straight, helped by a tail wind; the axle ratio on this occasion was 4.55:1, with the ZF's 'overdrive' 5th gear ratio of .834.

At the beginning of 1964, efforts were still being made by the factory to reduce the now undoubted gulf between the competition E-type and its Italian counterpart, while in America the Momo Corporation persevered too, entering Walt Hansgen and Bruce McLaren in the Sebring 12-hour race. This car was beaten by another lightweight E-type prepared by Huffaker Engineering, drivers Ed Leslie and Frank Morrill taking second place in the GT catagory.

In February 1964, 4WPD was taken to Silverstone where Graham Hill tried new 7 inch rim wheels in a comparative test with the original 6 inch wheels, and to evaluate the lowering of the body, the gain of an extra 17 bhp through the fitting of 15/32nd inch lift camshafts and an 81 inch side exhaust, and the reduction of body roll through the use of stronger anti-roll bars fore and aft. The E-type's cornering performance was also compared to that of the Formula 1 BRM which was also on test at the same time, using an 'electric eye' timing apparatus.

The wider wheels did help decrease lap times, by the order of 1¼%, and Hill commented that the car felt less "jelly like" on the wider rims. However, the fastest lap achieved by the E-type that day was still slower than Salvadori's record set nine months previously, though this was thought to be due to gusty conditions and no competition for the driver. Chassis engineer Derek White recorded Hill's comments on the E-type's handling as follows:

Hill's chief complaint of the E-type was that its response to the controls (particularly steering) was not quick enough. He attributed this to the rubber mounting of the rack housing and of the rear suspension and to the rear dampers being too soft. The response of the GTO Ferrari was much quicker and more predictable than that of the Competition E-type.

Hill reported that the car was understeering as he accelerated through Abbey Corner. This could be due to a number of causes, among which is the fact that when Hill repeats or improves on the 1/42.4 lap he will presumably be using more power at Abbey which would tend to increase oversteer; or alternatively, a larger rear anti-roll bar could be fitted.

The cornering comparison with the single seater BRM was also interesting:

The BRM went through Stowe Corner at an average speed of 91.1mph whilst the E-type could only achieve 82.5mph-10% slower. At the same time the BRM's lap time was 1 min 37secs compared to 1 min 43.7secs for the E-type under identical track conditions and with the same driver. However, the E-type reached 148mph before braking for Stowe where the BRM reached 145mph.

The inference is that if the E-type's average cornering speed could be raised to that of the BRM, then the E-type lap times would be up to that of the BRM instead of being 7% slower as at present. In order to achieve this higher cornering speed it will be necessary to increase the size of the tyres (and wheel rim widths) until slip angles of the tyres on the two cars are the same at the same speed and at the same inflation pressure, taking into consideration the in-creased weight transfer when cornering the E-type, due to its unfavourable C of G height/track ratio, and the comparative weights of the cars (E = 2500lbs mid-laden, BRM = 1270lbs mid-laden).

The era of ever-wider tyres had come, and Jaguar were aware of it. More testing followed, including at Goodwood where Hill got his way and the steering rack was mounted solidly to the car; in fact the whole car was stiffened so far as anti-roll bars and dampers were concerned. Hill rated handling as "vastly improved", though the brakes were thought poor and he found it impossible to lock the wheels. The net result of this session was a best lap time of 1min 26.8secs, which was under the lap record of 1min 27.4secs set by Hill's GTO Ferrari during the 1963 season.

A most interesting private practice session occured in June 1964, when the Coombs E-type was taken to Silverstone once more on its new 7 inch rim wheels. The driver reported that the brakes were a little spongy and the pedal had rather a long travel, but generally was "very happy" with the E-type although he felt that a little less understeer would be desirable, and that also a lock to prevent engagement of first and second gear would be a decided advantage, on circuits where these gears weren't used after the start. After ten warming-up laps using 6,100rpm had been completed, the car went out again with the driver using 6,300rpm, and on the fourth lap a time of 1min 41.9secs was achieved, the best of that or any other session. Mr FRW England made the following comment in his report to Sir William Lyons, William Heynes and others at Jaguar:

It is interesting to note that this driver, who had not previously driven a lightweight E-type, put up a better time on a not completely dry circuit than that previously achieved by anyone else with this type of car.

The driver? Jackie Stewart. In fact **Stewart** was to drive the competition E-type on several occasions during 1964, the first time in anger probably being at the Jaguar Driver's Club national meeting at Crystal Palace later on in June.

As for the international 'classics', the Nurburgring 1000km race brought no joy to the Jaguar camp, Sutcliffe's competition E-type retiring after a brush with a Cobra, and Protheroe crashing in practice after lapping very rapidly. At Le Mans though, the Jaguar entries were quite impressive with all four Peters entered - Lindner and Nocker, Lumsden and Sargent. The former's E-type was now in low-drag coupe form, with a Sayer nose and tail on its aluminium centre section; it also boasted the most powerful version of the XK engine ever seen in an E-type, the alloy 3.8 unit developing 344bhp gross, and the car pulled 5,600rpm in fifth gear along the Mulsanne straight, or about 170mph.

In the race, the E-types were not in contention for the lead and nor were they expected to be in the face of rear-engined GT prototype opposition such as the Ferrari 275 P and Ford GT 40. But any hopes of a high finishing position through reliability were doomed when first the Lindner/Nocker E-type slowed with engine trouble, eventually making an unscheduled stop to change its head gasket, and then the Lumsden/Sargent car retired after seven hours with gearbox failure, a bearing having gone in the ZF box.

This car, 49 FXN, now had a steel monocoque having been rebuilt by Playfords after a previous shunt, though it retained all its competition E-type mechanical parts including the full dry-sump, fuel injected alloy engine. At the time of the rebuild, the opportunity had been taken to equipe the car with a more efficient body shape, inspired by Protheroe's ex-factory low-drag coupe and drawings given to Lumsden and Sargent by Malcolm Sayer. An extra long nose featured, this having come about after discussions with Frank Costin. The rake of the windscreen was made less acute by taking the bottom line of the glass out to where the bonnet began, the top of the windscreen being left where it was. Lacking a wind tunnel, tufts of wool had been stuck all over the body and the car driven up and down the M1, an enter-

prisingly practical approach to the science of streamlining which worked remarkably well! While Sutcliffe spoke of pronounced rear-end lift at over 170 mph with his standard bodied lightweight, Lumsden and Sargent only remember their car as being very well mannered at such speeds. Some extra mechanical refinements had also been incorporated into the car's make up, such as an extra fuel pump 'pressure bomb' for the injection system which could be switched into operation should the primary one fail.

In the pits having its new head gasket fitted, the unfortunate German-entered E-type received a further blow in more senses than one when it was struck by the differential nose-piece from Ed Hugus' Ferrari, whose transmission chose to break up just as it was passing the pits. The silver E-type did rejoin the race but, still losing water, was forced to give up during Sunday morning in a lowly 29th position. It had never managed to get anywhere near the GTO Ferraris which finished 5th and 6th, so the run of the last Jaguar to compete at Le Mans ended rather ignominiously.

Things were a little happier at another scene of past Jaguar triumphs however, as both Protheroe and Sutcliffe successfully completed the 12-hour race at Rheims not long after that disappointing Le Mans. They gained first and second positions in the over 3-litre GT category of the event, though Sutcliffe, co-driven by Bill Bradley, had trouble with his battery failing to charge properly and so was forced to run with reduced lighting; otherwise the two E-types (Protheroe's low-drag coupe was co-driven by John Coundly) were evenly matched and reliable, circulating only seconds apart for much of the time. In a report to the factory afterwards, Protheroe noted that he had completed 2,234 kilometers on the same set of tyres (725L x 15 Dunlops), and in 5th gear at 6000rpm was pulling about 168mph. He finished 8th overall.

Jackie Stewart had another drive of 4 WPD on the occasion of the British GP meeting in July, where at Brands Hatch a GT race was included in the programme. Bob Olthoff's Cobra set fastest time in practice, beating Parkes' previous GTO lap record, but shunted before the race leaving Salvadori in a similar car in pole position; Stewart was alongside with Sears in another Cobra. The competition E-type was first off the mark and beat the American engined machinery into Paddock Bend, though it was Jack Sears who finally took the chequered flag, storming through the field after being brought in by the stewards because of starting in the wrong grid position. But Stewart still managed an excellent second place overall, ahead of the Salvadori Cobra and Mike Parkes' GTO Ferrari in fourth position. The Scotsman also drove the Coombs E-type in the Guards Trophy race of August 1964, driving a "fast, steady race" until a puncture ruined his chances.

The 1964 RAC Tourist Trophy once more brought competition E-type and GTO Ferrari into direct conflict, only neither type was expected to produce the outright winner as Appendix C and GT Prototypes over 1600cc were also due to run. Four E-types were entered but the Lindner low-drag coupe lightweight, to be driven by Nocker, was crashed in practice by Sutcliffe (who himself was entered in his own car); this was because Nocker complained of "bad oversteer and inconsistent brakes" and wanted someone else to try the car. Sutcliffe largely confirmed his findings, but although improving on the German's lap times, spun at Woodcote and hit the bank. This left Lumsden, Sutcliffe and Roger Mac (in the ex-Salvadori /Atkins car) occupying the last two rows of the grid, the former two cars having posted practice laps of 1min 30.6secs compared with the best GT time of 1min 27.2 put up by Dan Gurney's 385bhp Cobra coupe; quickest Ferrari GTO was John Surtees, at 1min 28.4secs, while Mike Salmon's Aston Martin had managed a good 1min 28.6secs.

The race was won by Graham Hill's 4-litre 330P Ferrari after Jim Clark's 4.7-litre Lotus 30 had lost time in the pits; Peter Sutcliffe retired with CW & P failure after the rear axle lost its oil (though classified as a finisher on distance).

Roger Mac also retired after what might have been a promising run (blocked fuel pump filter - shades of Le Mans 1954!), but Peter Lumsden soldiered on to fifth place in the GT category ahead of Salmon's DB4GT, two Ferrari GTOs and Phil Hill's Cobra. He was also eighth overall, the only GTO finishing ahead of the E-type being Innes Ireland's. The same weekend, incidentally, Phil Scragg beat his own previous best time at Shelsley to establish another class record with his competition E-type, at 37.35 seconds; a contrast in distance to Lumsden's 124 laps of Goodwood, but a success none the less.

Nineteen sixty-four ended on a sad note, as Peter Lindner met his death driving the silver lightweight at Montlhery during the 1000km race, colliding with a Simca-Abarth; curiously, it is believed that the crashed E-type still remains locked up in Germany having been impounded by the authorities after the accident . Protheroe was also entered in this race, and finished 7th overall and first in the over 3-litre GT class.

The end of the season saw a decline in Jaguar's interest in competition matters, and the company did not pursue its policy of covertly entering a car under the auspices of John Coombs, or through Briggs Cunningham. The competition E-type was now almost completely outclassed and would be even more so as mid--engined GT cars obtained homologation; the role of the E-type on the track was now clearly seen as being that of a competitive club machine rather than a viable entrant in international races. The faithful 4 WPD was sold to Red Rose Motors of Chester at the close of the 1964 season, Brian Redman driving it very successfully in British events on a national level; it was completely rebuilt by Jaguar in early 1966, and at the end of the year passed to its present owner Gordon Brown. He sprinted the car with excellent results up until 1970, when it was retired from active use after a long and honourable competition career.

Peter Sutcliffe however persevered for another year following the work's 'retirement', prolonging the competitive life of his car by taking it to South Africa for the 1965 season. There, he competed in eight GT races, never finishing less than third, and being placed first in class and third overall in the Rand 9-hours race at Kylami, near Johannesburg. This car now belongs to Bryan Corser who keeps it in 'concours' order, besides modifying it for practical road use. In fact most of the competition E-types survive with their whereabouts known today and so do such cars as Protheroe's special coupe and the Lumsden/Sargent 'hybrid'. Perhaps the best known lightweights at the present time, in Great Britain at least, are the two sister ex-Cunningham E-types, which compete regularly in 'post-historic' racing all over the country; the car driven by Willy Green and belonging to Anthony Bamford of JCB fame proved very hard to beat during the 1975 *Classic Car* Championship, for instance.

While the competition E-type is now a treasured 'classic', the original car still provokes discussion. Some, including at least one of the original purchasers back in 1963, contend that it was out-dated from the start and doomed to be an also-ran. Others argue that it could have been a much more consistent race winner if its development had not been such a 'part time' project at Jaguar. This latter point of view is more likely the correct one - Jaguar did not have the time or manpower to spare from production activities to carry out a fully professional development programme with the E-type and its record on the track suffered accordingly. However, perhaps the biggest pity is that the car in its full competition guise could not have been built for the beginning of the 1962 season or even before, when it would have been infinitely more competitive against the contemporary Ferraris.

THE E-TYPE AND RALLIES

As for the E-type in rallying, the car never really had determined enough backing to make its mark - Jaguar did not continue its habit of the early 1950s in unofficially sponsoring a car. The first appearance of an E-type in a big international event was probably R. Merrick's entry of a fixed-head coupe in the 1962 Monte Carlo Rally. In the International Tulip Rally of May 1962, won on a handicap system by the Mini Cooper of Pat Moss and Ann Riley, the Austin Healey 3000s were the quickest cars in the event but were beaten twice in the special tests by the E-type of Cuff and Anderson; the E-type was also second quickest to the Morleys at the Nurburgring, and had the rally been decided on a scratch basis, the Jaguar would have been placed third overall behind the two big Healeys. As it was, Cuff and Anderson had to be content with a third in class placing in the over 2½ litre category. A properly backed and efficiently organised team of E-types might well have achieved widespread success in International rallying, at least up until special stages on unmade-up roads came to dominate this branch of the sport. Limited successes were gained in British events by amateur E-type drivers however, including R T Haddow who brought his car into third place overall in the 1962 Scottish Rally (International Section), "creditable in view of the unsuitability of his car to the rough going" as *The Motor* commented.

Private E-type entries in the 1963 Targa Florio and Tour de France came to nought, although in the latter event the first British car in the 2-hour race held over the Le Mans circuit was the E-type of Klukaszenwski which was 7th overall; but it didn't figure in the final results, even though the 3.8 Mk ll saloons dominated the Touring Car class. Four months later, in the Monte Carlo Rally of January 1964, the E-type fixed-head coupe of Pinder and Pollard finished third in its class behind Ford Falcons, last of the best British finishers in an event which had acknowledged the ascendency of the Mini Cooper.

THE 4.2 E-TYPE

The new year of 1964 was to see some most important revisions in the E-type road car range, and similarly interesting reorganisation within

Jaguar's engineering division. It was announced in January that a Power Units Development Department had been formed at Browns Lane, combining Jaguar and Coventry Climax research and development departments. This move stemmed from Jaguar's acquisition of the Coventry Climax engine concern, famous for its car, fire-pump and GP racing engines, in March 1963, a move which had coincidentally brought Wally Hassan back into the fold. Already a new Jaguar engine was being worked on, and Hassan was to be involved in the final production version when, after Coventry Climax finished racing in 1965, he returned to Browns Lane to work with Heynes, Mundy, Baily and Knight. Ever since he left Jaguar, Hassan had kept in fairly close touch with the factory, to the extent of borrowing the latest products, and so was abreast of major developments when the take-over came.

It was not until the end of 1964 that the great amount of behind the scenes development work was revealed, in the form of the 4.2 litre E-type. The familiar six-cylinder XK engine remained substantially the same, but a new cylinder block was introduced. The extra capacity of 4,235cc was accommodated by re-spacing some of the cylinders, and increasing the bore by 5.07mm. The middle two cylinders, numbers 3 and 4, were moved closer together, numbers 2 and 5 remained unchanged, and numbers 1 and 6 were moved outwards slightly. (Incidentally, although it makes no difference to the sense of the above, it should be remembered that Jaguar have always numbered their cylinders from the *rear* of the engine, ie; number one is nearest the bulkhead). This rearrangement not only allowed the overall length of the block casting to remain the same, but also enabled the same cylinder head as used on the 3.8 cars to be fitted; the overlapping of the hemispherical combustion chambers with the bores that now occured was not found to produce harmful effects. A new crankshaft came with the 4.2 block, endowed with thicker webs to take the extra torque, and its four balance weights were repositioned to reduce main bearing loads. A

new torsional vibration damper was fitted too. While the 'new' engine had apparently lost some of the original balance of the 3.4 and 3.8 engines due to the asymetric spacing of the bores, in practice the 4.2 engine was found to rev as willingly and as safely as the older versions, as is instanced by today's use of the 4.2 engine in racing both in this country and in the States.

The 4.2 block retained the pressed-in chrome-iron liners of the 3.8 unit, but the water jacketing was modified to give a better flow around the bores. New pistons were fitted which with their chrome-plated top and oil control rings did much to reduce the engine's level of oil consumption. The aluminium induction manifold was now cast in one piece, including an integral water heating and balance pipe. The exhaust system was revised after it left the manifolds, and the silencers aluminiumised to give longer life.

The 4.2 engine was still rated at 265bhp, although probably did give a little more power in practice. The main aim had been to increase the torque figure, which rose from the 3.8 engine's figure of 240 lb ft to 283 lb ft, with the object of increasing low down urge, and generally furthering mid-range flexibility.

The most important change to take place after the engine's increase in capacity, and perhaps even more worthwhile, was the adoption (at last) of an all-synchromesh gearbox. It came in a new cast-iron casing and with positive lubrication from an oil pump at the rear of the box. The synchromesh design included inertia-lock baulk rings which positively prevented engagement of the gears until synchronisation was complete, and although absorbing a little more power than the old box, was rather more pleasant to use with the synchromesh first gear finding favour in the States especially. The gearbox was supplemented by a new Laycock diaphragm-spring clutch.

Many more improvements of a detail nature featured on the 4.2 E-type. The Kelsey-Hayes brake servo was discontinued and in its place appeared a new Lockheed vacuum booster

271

which gave a quicker and more powerful response. Larger than the bellows type which it replaced, the servo was now remotely mounted, though still operated through a tandem master cylinder and of course 'failed safe' as before. The front discs were given dirt shields. A pre-engaged starter was fitted to the engine, and so was a Lucas AC alternator which could give a full charge at only 920rpm engine speed; the radiator was now made of copper instead of light alloy, but the separate steel header tank, with its proneness to rusting over an extended period of time, remained. Servicing intervals for the steering and front suspension ball joints were extended from 2,500 miles to 12,000 miles through the use of polyurathene seals - this improvement was especially pertinent to the North American market where sealed for life components were becoming increasingly common, and a servicing interval of only 2,500 miles was considered positively archaic.

Outwardly, the car looked much the same; the headlights retained their Perspex fairings but now had sealed beam assymetric dip light units which gave more light. Inside, the seats were much improved with more support being provided for the small of the back, and the seat squab given adjustment for rake through a small angle. This served to help very tall drivers a little, but those over six foot still found the E-type a little cramped. Most people regarded the interior trim changes favourably - gone was the bright aluminium finish on the transmission tunnel and facia, and in its place was a leather covering which matched the remainder of the trim. A glove box appeared between the seats, and the rear quarters of the fixed-head coupe were trimmed a little more luxuriously even if a little practicality was lost in the process. Covers now disguised the rear door hinges, and the roadster was given a means of locking the boot.

One inevitable effect of all these various refinements was an increase in both weight and price; the latter was small, and the former was not excessive either, though it meant a small alteration to the rear suspension geometry to avoid recourse to the bump stops which had sometimes been experienced by E-type drivers previously. The 4.2 open two seater now cost £1,896 as opposed to the 3.8 equivalent of £1,830, while the 4.2 engined closed car retailed at £2,032, or £78 more than the earlier version. Although it was originally stated that the 4.2 supplemented the 3.8 E-type, production of the latter soon tailed off in favour of the bigger engined car, after some 30,000 3.8 E-types had been made. Incidentally a few of the last 3.8 cars received the new all-synchro gearbox.

ROAD TESTING THE 4.2 E-TYPE

Motoring News tried one of the first 4.2 Fixed-heads in November 1964. Fortunately it came with RS5 tyres and a 3.07 rear axle ratio and so rendered possible a direct comparison to the similarly geared 1963 model 3.8 E-type which they had tested previously. Increased torque had cancelled out the slightly higher weight of the 4.2, and 60mph was reached in 7.3 seconds, which was ½ second quicker than their 3.8 car; by 80mph a whole second had been gained. The 'ton' came up in 17 seconds dead with the new car, as opposed to 17.4 seconds for the 3.8; at 15 seconds for the ¼-mile, the new car was quicker by another ½ second.

In general behaviour, the weekly paper found that the usual E-type virtues of easy three-figure cruising were present in the 4.2 car, together with flexibility and lack of temperament. Piston slap was more noticeable when the engine was cold however, and oil consumption was still fairly high at around 500 miles to the pint - though this was hardly excessive compared to that of the early E-types. The car was still surprisingly economical, returning a petrol consumption (including a lot of high speed motoring) of 19.1mpg - 1.6mpg less than the 3.8 car. The new gearbox was rated "undoubtedly one of the best on the market" with first gear available at any speed within its rev range without double de-clutching. Movement of the lever was considered a little spongy though, with still quite a long travel between the gears. The silence of the new box was much appreciated. The 4.2's handling was again "the mixture as before", and the new seats were acknowledged as being better, although cockpit room was still considered marginal. The now-familiar bugbear of cockpit heat was apparent, and despite the heater fan blowing cool air it still became rather warm inside the car even on mild days; open windows were the rule in really hot weather. A major cause of this discomfort was thought to be insufficient insulation of the transmission tunnel. It was noted that air conditioning was offered as an extra, at the cost of £100. The headlights were thought to be only useful up to 80mph. But generally speaking all the old E-type magic was still very much there - Mike Twite closed his report by urging the reader to "mortgage your house, sell your wife, put your children out to work and indulge yourself in one."!

Early in 1965, *Car & Driver* tried an export 4.2 Roadster fitted with, interestingly, the low 3.54 final drive. The American magazine substantiated most of what *Motoring News* had to say, and had some quite revealing things to say on why Americans bought E-types. As it gives a clear insight into the strange (or perhaps not so strange) hold over the North American sports car buyer that all Jaguars, but particularly the sports models, exert, it is worth quoting the journal in reasonable depth:

No Jaguar was ever perfect, and yet no other make has ever fired the enthusiast's imagination to the same degree, or over such a sustained period of years. The XK-120 overheated regularly but it electrified the keen-types of the late Forties and earliest Fifties. The XK-120M was too fast for its brakes, but nobody cared - it was beautiful and it made the most purely-sexual noise ever emitted by an automobile. The XK-140 and XK-150 were fat, overdecorated versions of the lithe, taut XK-120, but they were Jaguars, by God, and that was enough for the men that bought them.

Then came the XK-E. It had been predicted by the "experts" even since the waning days of the XK-120 series. Everybody *knew* that Jaguar was going to produce a street machine based on the fabulous D-Type racing car. And finally, after more than one false start, it came. Who cared if it still had the old Moss transmission? Who cared if there wasn't any room inside and the seats weren't comfortable? Who cared if it didn't have proper fresh air ventilation? Nobody, that's who.

It was a new Jaguar!

The automobile magazines mewed lamely about the flaws mentioned above, but even those criticisms were washed away in the euphoric flood of exultant prose that accompanied the announcement of the new XK-E.

A man six-foot-six could wedge himself into the driver's seat, acknowledge the fact that he could not possibly drive the car, and still want one worse than he'd ever wanted anything in his life. An old hand, an ex-Jaguar owner, could say that he'd never own another one, only to rush pell-mell to the Jaguar showroom the first time an XK-E droned past.

There's something so sensual, so elemental in the appeal of that car that few men can resist its siren song. It's like that woman you used to love, the one you'd never waste another minute on. You can avoid her for months, but one night she calls and you'd crawl naked across three-hundred yards of flaming gasoline and broken bottles to get to her. Obviously, a car that can excite such primitive urges is bigger than a non-synchro first gear or bad oil-consumption.

So let's suppose that you want a quiet, powerful two-seater that will hold its own in any company and look absolutely stunning from any angle... *Voila!* You discover that the Jaguar XK-E you loved so well has taken a whole new lease on life. It has a revised 4.2 litre version of the tried-and-true dohc six-cylinder engine, a completely new all-synchro transmission, a new clutch, a new exhaust, and more comfortable seats. While you're digesting all that you'd better stop by the bank, because you may be about to buy another Jaguar.

The test weight of *Car & Driver's* 4.2 Roadster was 2,800lbs, kerb weight being 2,515lbs. The low axle ratio limited top speed to around 130mph but provided the best acceleration time to 60mph yet recorded for a standard E-type - 6.5 seconds. Eighty miles an hour arrived in 11.1 seconds, and 100mph in rather a slow 17.4 seconds. The standing ¼-mile was the usual 15 seconds dead. So on balance, greater torque had made up for greater weight and the E-type's straight line performance (taking into consideration varying axle ratios) remained much the same. In round figures, the United States price of the 4.2 Roadster and fixed-head were 5,500 and 5,700 dollars respectively, which was more than the Chevrolet Corvette Stingray but not enough, thought *Car & Driver* to take it out of GM's class. "As competitors, the two cars are admirably suited to one another - similar, yet different enough to give the prospective buyer a choice". But as we may have guessed from the long passage quoted beforehand, the magazine confessed that "...we must be completely honest and admit that the things that really get to us are the looks and the noise. It's a Jaguar. It reeks of purest automotive erotica, and that ain't bad, Jim."

The Motor confirmed the general verdict of its American opposite number, if with a more British approach. The top speed of that magazine's 4.2 Fixed-head Coupe was just 1mph higher than its original 3.8 road test car, and that was attributed to the higher 3.07 axle ratio rather than the increase in capacity. This 150mph maximum produced a reading of 6,100 on the rev counter. Sixty miles an hour from a standing start was attained in 7.0 seconds, 100mph in 17.2 seconds, and the standing ¼-mile was .1 under the 15 second mark.

The various refinements of the 4.2 made it in *The Motor's* opinion a considerably better car, although the E-type characteristics and glamour were still present; it certainly remained the yardstick by which other fast cars were judged: "Preconceived ideas about speed and safety are apt to be shattered by E-type performance. True, very few owners will ever see 150mph on the speedometer but, as on any other car, cruising speed and acceleration are closely related to the maximum and to the ease with which it can lop not just seconds, but half hours and more, off journey times. Our drivers invariably arrived early in the E-type and the absurd ease with which 100mph can be exceeded on a ¼ mile straight never failed to astonish them; nor did the tremendous punch in second gear which would fling the car past

slower vehicles using gaps that would be prohibitively small for other traffic".

Even the traditional start in top gear could be made, no matter that the 3.07 axle gave 24.4 mph for every 1,000rpm. At the other extreme, 100mph cruising on the autostrada was entirely relaxed, the car's speed being mainly governed by traffic conditions rather than by any mechanical limitations on the part of the E-type. Naturally the new gearbox was liked too: "A good box by any standards and excellent for one that must transmit so much power". The new bucket seats added further to driver comfort, although the adjustment for rake only gave two positions and most of the magazine's drivers would have appreciated a greater angle of recline. It was all good enough though for one of their number to complete a one-day solo drive back from Italy "without aches or discomfort". However, it was very necessary to open the windows to get sufficient cool air into the car on hot days, and "some form of cold air ventilation that by-passes the heater would still be a welcome refinement".

The front-hinged rear extractor side windows helped a bit in this respect, "at the expense of some wind whistle". The inside rear door release, like the outside door handles and petrol filler release, was thought to be "irritatingly small for man-sized hands".

On test, the new brake servo proved to cut brake pedal pressures from 100lbs to 60lbs for the same 96/97g stop, although Roger Bell described how a "severe Alpine test descent made the discs glow bright red". But there had still remained braking power in reserve and heat soak did not cause the fluid to boil, although it was hinted that this might occur if the fluid was not the right type or in unsound condition. *Motor's* fade test - 20 ½-g stops from 90mph at one minute intervals - caused only a 10lb rise in pedal pressures; not altogether surprising this, as it was mentioned that Jaguar's own acceptance test was even tougher, involving 30 stops from 100mph, again at one minute intervals.

Road holding and ride of the 4.2 engined car

was found to be very similar to that of the 3.8 E-type - still extremely good. "There is none of the harsh, vertical bouncing that was once part of high performance cars..." RS5 cross ply tyres were still fitted, and *Motor's* fixed-head weighed 25.1 cwt kerb, with a front rear distribution of 49½/50½. This was exactly 1 cwt heavier than the 1961 fixed-head coupe, which had the same weight distribution. Fuel consumption was very much the same too, at 18.5mpg overall and a computed touring consumption of 21.5mpg.

E-TYPE REFINEMENT

Nineteen sixty-five did not see any marked changes in the E-type's specification, merely small refinements being added such as an improved windscreen washer and better water proofing on the slightly vunerable distributor. Significantly though, Dunlop SP41 radial tyres received Jaguar's blessing as replacements for the RS5s although cars leaving the factory still wore the cross ply covers for a while longer. The *Motoring News* staff 4.2 Fixed-head E-type had been fitted with one of the first sets to be issued by Dunlop, and reported on the E-type's behaviour with these radial tyres fitted in October 1965. The paper highly recommended them; wet weather grip was "absolutely fabulous" although surprisingly they were not thought to equal the RS5's performance in the dry, and they did squeal. The greatest advantage of the radials was of course their infinitely longer life - whereas around 8,000 miles was about average for a briskly driven E-type on cross-plies, this mileage could often be trebled on the SP41 covers. On the subject of wear generally, Mike Twite also commented that the paper's 4.2 got through brake pads pretty quickly too, front replacements being required at 7,000 miles, and rear at 9,000 miles. Whilst changing the front pads was an easy job, "those on the inboard rear brakes are very hard to fit". Oil consumption on this car was, incidentally, reduced through the use of Duckham's motor oil, a lubricant favoured by a number of Jaguar

owners of that period for the same reason.

The E-type's interior cooling problems were also discussed by *Motoring News;* Twite insulated the air trunk which ducted cool air from the car's nose to the heater with asbestos and aluminium foil which helped keep the temperature down, and he also mentioned that he planned to do something similar with the transmission tunnel which became "unbearably hot in warm weather". With this particular E-type, directional stability at speed over bumpy roads was suspect, a large amount of kick-back at the steering wheel tending to steer the car, and some 'bump-thump' was noticed from the suspension. Though so far as the latter was concerned, Mike Twite suggested that all that Jaguar needed to do was to fit a noisier exhaust, which would drown out all the other noises! As always the E-type's virtues far outweighed its vices, and the editor of *Motoring News* ended his interim report on the staff 4.2 by saying: "Although the E-type has been in production for 4½ years, I have yet to find a car I would prefer to drive everyday, and although I drive numerous other cars during the course of the year, I still find much pleasure coming back to the E-type."

On the sporting side, the RAC Tourist Trophy race was held at Oulton Park in 1965; David Wansborough drove Protheroe's fast-back coupe - in fact, he drove it into the lake at the Cascades! This was in practice, and the car was hauled out, drained, and started in the race; Wansborough however had to give best to a GTO Ferrari in his class. The Guards 1000 mile race, held in two parts over Saturday and Sunday at Brands Hatch in May, actually saw the E-type of Dean and Banks lead for a while on the Sunday, only to drop out with a broken camshaft. The MGB of Rhodes/Banks eventually won though Jackie Oliver and Chris Craft won Class A with their 4.2 engined E-type ahead of the Hopkirk/Ellice Austin Healey 3000, and were placed third overall.

Peter Lumsden raced the Le Mans E-type at Goodwood on Whit Monday, and finished fourth in the Whitsun Trophy race behind McLaren's Elva-Oldsmobile, Salvadori's Ford GT40, and Roger Mac's Cobra. Phil Scragg continued another successful season on the hills with class wins that included the Diamond Jubilee Shelsley meeting in June, where he beat Thompson's E-type.

On the circuits over the preceeding few months had appeared the fiercesome Jaguar Egal, powered not by six cylinders but by eight, in the form of a Holman and Moody tuned Ford Galaxie engine which had begun life in a power boat. Rob Beck was the original **driver,** and later the car was piloted by Barry Williams who drove it in his usual spectacular style. He also used it on the road, where he found that a cruising speed of about 120mph was about right, as then it wouldn't 'white line' on its racing tyres. He remembers his best lap time around the club Silverstone circuit as being in the region of 1 min 3 secs, and it took five or six years of tyre and engine development before club racing 6-cylinder E-types managed to equal that time. The Jaguar Egal was last seen in use purely as a road car.

THE TWO-PLUS-TWO E-TYPE

The E-type received its first major surgery in March 1966, when the 2-plus-2 E-type was announced. By adding another 9 inches to the wheelbase, and 2 inches to the height, Jaguar had succeeded in producing a car which, if it didn't have all the grace of the original E-type, at least made it possible for a couple of adults to travel in the back with tolerable comfort for a few miles. The rear bench-type seat installed was really more suitable for the owner's children though, so that the car could "extend Dad's youth for another seven years" as *Motor* put it.

The increase in size gave the 2-plus-2 (which at that time was an addition to and not a replacement for the existing E-type range) a wheelbase of 8 feet 9 inches, a height of 4 feet 2 inches, and a 5% increase in frontal area. Weight had risen too of course, to 27.7 cwt kerb, distributed

50/50; this was about 2cwt more than the 4.2 Fixed-head of 1964. Mechanical changes were confined to the necessary higher rear spring rates and damper settings, while cockpit cooling problems were diminished by a better heat shield between the exhaust and the floor of the car. Under the bonnet, a shield was fixed over the alternator and this was carried over to all the E-type range. Headroom in the rear was some 33 inches, while the increase of 1½ inches in the height of the windscreen improved driver visibility a little; as well as the extra ½ inch of headroom this gave, driver comfort was enhanced by it now being possible for the front seats to be pushed further back - so long as the rear passengers had no legs! The doors were widened by 8½ inches to 3 feet 5 inches, and access to the back seats was gained by the normal procedure of tilting the front seat squabs forward; usefully, the rear squabs could be folded forward too providing a much larger luggage space when no rear passengers were being carried. In the front, the facia was given a full-width parcel tray, a bigger glove locker with a lockable lid, improved instrument panel lighting (in green), while the heater now had variable direction outlet nozzles. The doors were given burst proof catches.

An important advance that came with the new lengthened centre section, particularly as regards the North American market, was the option of automatic transmission on the 2-plus-2. When the new car was launched at the New York Show in April 1966, Sir William himself was there to see it. There were high hopes at Jaguar that the availability of automatic transmission on the 2-plus-2 fixed-head E-type (the roadster continued with the short wheelbase chassis and so could only be fitted with the manual box) would help to increase exports to the United States, which had stood at just under 4,000 units the previous year.

Motor tested one of the new automatic 2-plus-2 E-types in April 1966, and found that, as expected, both top speed and acceleration were down. A 10% drop in maximum speed resulted in a figure of 136.2mph, and the new car took 8.9 seconds to reach 60mph, and 19.1 seconds to gain 100mph, using the manual hold device. Leaving the three speed Borg-Warner Model 8 transmission to do all the work resulted in 60mph and 100mph times of 9.1 seconds and 21.3 seconds respectively. The new gearbox took its toll on the car's handling to an extent as well: "The effect of automatic transmission on the E-type's handling is more pronounced than on other cars" remarked *Motor*. "Without the drive line rigidity, it is impossible to vary the attitude of the car on the throttle in the way that you can on the manual car; stability is further enchanced by the use of SP 41HR tyres which further limit slip angles until final rear end breakaway, now rather more sudden but at very high cornering forces".

The E-type's steering remained praiseworthy inspite of some kickback being noticed, displaying "delightful feel and sensitivity"; likewise the brakes seemed immune to fade, although the handbrake only recorded 25% efficiency and barely managed to hold the car on a 1-in-4 hill. Ride was still thought to be "very good by sports car standards" though not as smooth as the S-type saloon (which had started production in 1964 with, of course, a similar independent rear suspension). However, the new 2-plus-2 body shape was effected by side winds, although not enough to force a reduction in speed or even a conscious steering correction. The rear seats were rated as definitely only occasional for adults, but ideal for small children. As for the slightly notorious heating and ventilation system, de-misting was found to be inadequate and there was a call for face-level ventilation.

The automatic gearbox itself was reasonably satisfactory, although the magazine pointed out that it was not quite as smooth as the best American units. As R A B Cook commented in *Motor* some months later after a trip in the automatic 2-plus-2: "Messrs Borg-Warner change gear for you. Warner, by the way, made lovely,

smooth changes but Borg was a bit jerky at times - he took over when the kick-down button was pressed. You dart along like a minnow or like Wordsworth's Reaper - stop here, or gently pass". Home market cars were given a 2.88:1 final drive ratio when the automatic transmission was fitted, torque multiplication giving a range of 2.88 to 5.76:1. Intermediate or 'second gear' gave 87mph (at 4,800rpm), and low or 'first gear' went up to 56mph (at 5,100rpm) though these speeds could be exceeded by the use of the manual hold. The automatic box control lever was set in place of the normal manual gearstick on the transmission hump. The 2-plus-2 manual gearbox car retained the 3.07:1 final drive. For the North American market however, automatic E-types had a 3.31:1 ratio, and manual cars a 3.54:1 rear axle. The price in Great Britain of the new cars were (including purchase tax) £2,245 for the manual transmission E-type, and £2,385 for the automatic - still very good value.

The normal wheelbase 4.2 Roadster and fixed-head continued in production much as before, although some of the detail refinements brought in on the 2-plus-2 were transferred over to them as well. A re-angled clutch pedal was one of these, and all the E-type range now had the later wide-ratio gearboxes.

COMPETITION ACHIEVEMENTS, 1966

Perhaps the most publicised Jaguar competition success of 1966 was Dr. Jorge Burgoa's extraordinary winning of the Gran Premo de Automovilismo, which was rated Bolivia's most important race (though most people would no doubt secretly have confessed, perhaps even at Browns Lane, that until a Jaguar won it, they had never heard of it!). Run in four stages, the race covered over 1,200 miles of roadways that climbed as high as 14,000 feet at times. The first stage was won by a Buick Super Sport, while Shelby Mustangs finished first and second on stage two. But the fixed-head coupe of Dr. Burgoa, who had meanwhile been lying second on aggregate, took the lead on the third section when the road led up through the mountains of Santa Cruz (where the Mustangs retired) and was never headed. The Jaguar's finishing time was 19 hours 31 minutes and 1 second, considerably less than second man Willy Zalles in a surviving Shelby Mustang whose time was 21 hours 10 minutes and 5 seconds; in fact the E-type was the only car to have averaged more than 60mph over the very testing route. A novel and interesting Jaguar victory, at a time when a long distance success by an E-type had become rare.

In the United States, Jaguar was still a prominent name in SCCA production sports car racing, and between 1964 and 1966 one of the most successful cars in this class of racing was Merle Brennan's Huffaker Engineering prepared E-type, which won 39 races out of 42 in which it was entered during those years.

This scarcity of good 'international' results for the E-type was not completely through lack of trying - witness the very amateur but brave entry of John Harper's and Mick Merrick's E-type Roadster in three long distance European events during 1966: the BOAC 500 race at Brands Hatch, the Spa 1000km, and the Nurburgring 1000km. The car was Jack Lambert's early roadster; while still in his hands, a mechanic at the garage where it was being serviced took it out for an unauthorised drive, and virtually wrote it off. It was later rebuilt with a new body shell but left with its wide angle head and other D-type parts. When Harper bought it, the car was returned to Group 3 trim (ie SUs, standard cams and valves, and 5½J wire wheels), in which form it ran in the races mentioned.

In the 'BOAC', the E-type was a non-finisher, blowing a head gasket. But at Spa, things went rather better with Harper and Merrick driving to second place in the GT class despite some relief valve trouble; this position was repeated at the Nurburgring where the only car to finish in front of the Jaguar in its class - by only 2 minutes after 1000 kilometres of racing - was the works 275 GTB Ferrari of 'Elde'. Considering the very 'touring' nature of the car, which was driven to these events with spare wheels and tyres on the hard-top roof, these results were far from disgraceful.

JAGUAR AND BMC

However, by far the most important happening of 1966 so far as the factory was concerned was the joining of Jaguar with the British Motor Corporation. Take-overs and various sorts of mergers had in the past been suggested to Sir William by representatives of a number of different companies, including Leyland, Rolls Royce and Standard; on one occasion, in fact, a suggestion became a threat, and Sir William quickly issued extra stock to defeat a take-over bid. But for some time he had been observing the build up of large combines in Europe and had realised - even encouraged - the inevitability of such happenings in Great Britain. That BMC now owned Pressed Steel, who made Jaguar's bodies, was also a factor he had to take into consideration. An initial and quite serious approach by Sir John Black and Stokes of Leyland in 1965 came to nothing, as the offer did not ensure that Sir William would retain the autocratic control over the company he had founded, and which he had managed so brilliantly ever since 1935. It was Sir George Harriman of BMC who next started serious negotiations, and after an impulsive visit by Harriman to the Browns Lane factory in order to settle the question one way or the other, the deal was agreed in July 1966. The result was the formation of British Motor Holdings, with Sir William still exercising his full freedom to act as he pleased within Jaguar. The story drew to its final conclusion when in May 1968, Leyland, (which had previously taken over the Rover Company) and BMC came together to form British Leyland; though only after considerable drama behind the scenes involving to no small degree Sir William Lyons, who insisted that any such merger should not jeopardize the autonomy of his company and himself within the group. But Stokes was well aware that to lose the individuality of Jaguar would amount to commercial suicide, and so Jaguar was allowed to continue along its own path for a number of years.

Returning to 1967, and the E-type itself, in the April 1967 edition of *Motor Sport* Denis Jenkinson wrote of his two years' experience with a 4.2 Fixed-head Coupe purchased in March 1965. While he had not particularly taken to the 3.8 E-type, which after some ten years of Porsche motoring had seemed too big and possessed of a "lorry like" gearbox and poor seats, a trial run in *Motor Sport's* road test 4.2 had convinced Jenkinson that such a car was what he needed for the extensive, high mileage journeys he undertook on the continent while covering the GP racing scene. In view of the fact that the car would mostly be used abroad, it was ordered with left-hand drive, a kilometer speedometer and 8:1 compression ratio pistons, the latter to take care of the lower grade fuel often encountered away from the British Isles.

The E-type soon became Jenkinson's standard for judging "so called" fast cars, and he found that not many matched up to it, at least so far as acceleration above 90mph was concerned. "This acceleration goes on with a responsive feeling to 135-140mph and after that every mph can be counted, the most I have achieved being 143mph by rev counter reading". As for reliability, the car had a generally good record despite long and hard use over very mixed roads and conditions. "When my friends heard that I was getting an E-type they said: 'A good car, but you will spend all your time picking up little pieces that will fall off.' They were quite wrong, as were those who said everything but the engine would wear out."

The first 20,000 miles were covered with virtually no faults cropping up at all, though sustained use brought about a number of failures during the next 20,000 miles - alternator, exhaust system (the relatively small ground clearance of the E-type was made worse by the low-profile G800 tyres *Motor Sport* had fitted) and brakes had to receive attention. So far as the last were concerned, a rubber seal in a slave cylinder failed, resulting in a non-operative front brake circuit; little retardation was given by the rear brakes alone, partly because an oil leak from the differential housing had effected the discs. At the 40,000 mile mark, the front discs, suspension ball joints and clutch were replaced, as was the final drive unit as a precautionary measure due to a growling noise which had persisted, but grown no worse, for 25,000 miles. "It may seem as though I have had endless trouble but really it has been more a question of maintaining the ravages of hard usage and a rough life" said Jenkinson. "My E-type does not spend much time shut up in a heated garage, nor does it do any quiet commuting...it lives in the mud and roughness of the country and is used consistently for long and short journeys".

Surprisingly perhaps, Denis Jenkinson did not like the car so much when its roadholding was extended to the limit, a "10 mile dash" over a section of the Targa Florio route not engendering a feeling of confidence whatsoevor. Overall though, his verdict after two years of E-type motoring was thus: "Having got used to 250bhp and real acceleration at high speed in an effortless manner, coupled with a docility which Auntie could cope, I would be reluctant to motor in anything less than a 4.2 E-type". True to his word, when the car was eventually sold, it was replaced by a Series 2 E-type.

The Series 2 E-type was the next milestone in the continuing development of Jaguar's sports car. Preceeding its official announcement however, came a car known as the 'Series 1½' E-type; this was made in very small numbers from late 1967 and displayed just a few features that would be seen on the Series 2 car, plus some distinctive characteristics of its own. Thus it displayed open headlights, but retained the small radiator 'grille' and low-mounted bumpers of the early cars.

October 1968 was the launch date for the

Series 2 proper, and when the car was exhibited at Earls Court having just been completed in time for its first public showing, it was at once apparent that there had been a number of exterior modifications. The E-type had been given a considerably larger 'mouth', the intake on the nose having been increased in area by 68%, and two electric fans were now used. These alterations were not done with increased engine cooling in mind so much as to provide a greater capacity for the better air conditioning unit which was now offered as an optional extra. Other new options were power assisted steering, employing the Adwest Engineering Pow-a-Rak system, and bolt-on chromium plated steel wheels; wire wheels were still the standard fitment, and their hubs and spokes came under revision to eliminate further the possibility of spoke breakages.

Up until October 1968 the looks of the 2-plus-2 model E-type had suffered from a rather too upright windscreen angle; with the Series 2 came an alteration in the rake of the screen which went from 46½ degrees to the vertical to 53½, the bottom of the screen being brought further over the scuttle - the contours of the original screen's base could be detected on the new cars by a beading on the top of the facia. This slight reproportioning greatly enhanced the looks of the 2-plus-2 without actually recapturing the elegance of the normal wheelbase car. At the same time, all E-types were altered cosmetically by wrap-round bumpers front and rear, and by changes in their lighting units, partly as a result of United States legislation. Larger sidelight and flasher units were now carried at the front underneath the raised bumpers (with repeater flashers on both sides of the car at either end), and the headlights were brought forwards 2 inches in their scoops to minimise light scatter and cut-off - not from the Perspex covers, however, as they had already been discarded earlier, in mid 1967. At the rear of the car, much larger lamp clusters were housed in satin-finished plinths and mounted underneath the bumper. A new square shaped number plate mounting was provided (no doubt with the shape of United States licence plates in mind) flanked by a reversing light on either side. To clear the new number plate, the exhaust pipes were placed wider apart.

Changes to the E-type's interior were relatively few, although the dashboard was brought up to US Federal Safety Standards, one concession being the substitution of rocker switches for the previous toggle type. Some people liked the new 'modern' combined ignition and starter switch, others thought that a little character had been lost. Heater and choke controls were improved and the wipers (now twin only) were given a new and more powerful electric motor. Mechanical changes were confined to a change in the helix angle of the gear teeth in the manual gearbox to give more silent running, and the incorporation of an energy absorbing expanded metal section in the steering column.

Perhaps the biggest headache caused to Jaguar's development department had been the profusion of the US Federal Safety Regulations that had sprung up, and it had been necessary to allocate nearly a third of the engineering staff to meeting the problem of modifying the E-type so that it met the requirements which came into force in 1968 - the cost of doing this was a quarter of a million pounds. Fortunately the car's braking system, now an updated Girling system with three pistons at the front, two rear, and a larger pad area, and its strong impact resisting centre section, already conformed to legislation on these points (the E-type passed the 30mph barrier test at MIRA with flying colours, no glass being broken even) but a vast number of details still had to be attended to. Outwardly, the only signs of all this work were the 'earless' hub caps on the wire wheels, and the obligatory driver's door exterior mirror. Inside, the facia was replanned to incorporate the rocker switches already mentioned, and the general recessing and rounding of minor controls. The rear view mirror was made to snap off under a 90lb blow, and a wholesale redesign of the doors was necessary to include stronger anti-burst locks, recessed interior door handles, and window winders of a new rounded design. New seats were installed too which complied with the regulations in respect of their adjustable squabs, which were now controlled by a positive locking lever which gave the required resistance to deflection. A new seat belt fitting was standardised as well.

Then there was the pollution side of the story, and much experimentation went on at Jaguar before the best way of meeting the strict requirements regulating the emission of carbon monoxide and hydrocarbons through the exhaust. Petrol injection was immediately thought of, particularly as experience in this field at the works was already quite extensive - apart from racing experiments dating back to 1953, road vehicle applications had been tried with success, a Mk VII saloon having been equipped with a PI system at one time. However, the problem of metering the fuel accurately at low engine speeds and at tickover proved too difficult to be overcome in the time available, and after trying air injection, the final system adopted on the E-type was the use of two specially designed Stromberg CD 'emission' carburettors, which worked in conjunction with a cross-over inlet manifold reaching over the cam covers to one exhaust manifold. At low speeds, the mixture was ducted over to the exhaust manifold where it was turned into a much more readily combustible gas, which was then burnt in the cylinders leaving very little residue. At higher engine speeds, a twin throttle by-pass allowed a full charge of non-heated mixture to enter the cylinders.

This arrangement met the regulations' demands perfectly, and the E-type so equipped passed the 50,000 mile test with no trouble. However, sacrifices in power had been considerable when the emission engine's output was compared to that of the original 4.2 or 3.8 triple SU carburetter engine, and while fuel consumption and low speed acceleration was improved by around 5%, the 'Federal' E-type

was rated at no more than about 177 bhp eventually. For 1968, only the E-type was exported to the United States, the sales target for that year being around 8,000 cars.

The home product had in the meanwhile continued in normal three carburetter form with only a marginal overspill of North American safety devices in its make-up. Inspite of being seven years old, and with radial tyres being virtually the only change in its suspension and running gear, *Motor* could still remark after including an E-type in one of its multi-car group tests that:

"Considering the extra size of the E-type, its wieldy handling, though perhaps not quite so delicately balanced, is perhaps as remarkable as the Elan's and certainly better than any other big-torque road car we can recall. Unexpectedly light and positive steering (those Dunlop SP VRs must have something to do with it) and impeccable manners make it a car you can throw around, drift, even power slide at outrageous angles if you wish, and always feel very much in command. Couple this sort of handling with its tremendous performance and you can understand Jaguar's enthusiasm for a *Motor* group test based on an E-type. Would that all cars commanded such a respect from their makers!"

This group test included the Mercedes Benz 280SL which was very much regarded as a competitor by Jaguar, especially in foreign markets. Although adjudged superb as a grand touring car, a direct comparison between it and the 4.2 E-type Roadster which *Motor's* group test conditions allowed revealed surprisingly few points on which the expensive German car (£4,154 as tested) scored over the (£2,225) Jaguar. Whilst one would not expect the Mercedes' smaller, 2.8 litre, fuel injected six cylinder engine to match the straight line performance of the British car's 4.2 litre XK engine, the E-type was even voted better on ride comfort by four of the six drivers involved.

For the remainder of its production run no fundamental changes took place in the 4.2 E-type. In 1969 a partial re-design of the camshafts did not alter cam profiles but did result in quieter running and increased service intervals. Cold start ballast resister ignition was installed at about the same time, together with a steering lock, gas filled bonnet stay, arm rests on the doors, and re-designed seat backs incorporating apertures for headrests. The clock was now powered by the car's battery. The pressed steel chromium plated wheels became an option on the home market too towards the end of 1969 and the beginning of 1970, and the non-eared hub caps appeared on British cars as well. In fact there was a gradual transference of safety items already used on the North American version of the E-type since 1968 onto the home market product, and eventually rationalisation ensured that there was little difference between the two - even the cars sold in Britain finally wound up with (nearly) the full 'emission' engine, with its twin Zenith-Stromberg carburetters and duplex manifolding. This was to be the final assault on the E-type's performance, already eroded by a gradually increasing frontal area, deteriorating aerodynamics in the form of the open headlights, and weight increases. The last pre-Series 3 E-types could not in fact achieve much more than 130 - 135 mph however ideally they were geared, and the net quoted maximum power was 171 bhp at 4,500 rpm. This was a 'DIN' rating which more honestly reflected the power output of an installed engine, and it was this method of expressing the unit's output which probably accounted for as much 'lost' brake horsepower as all the emission equipment put together.

THE XJ13

A closely kept secret until only quite recently, this mid-engined prototype was built around the originally intended successor to the faithful XK engine, a twin cam per bank V12 engine which began life on the drawing board as far back as 1955. For by then it was becoming clear to Jaguar that if a series of Le Mans wins was to be sustained, a new power unit giving a lot more brake horsepower than the XK engine could

reliably supply would soon become a necessity. Therefore Claude Baily drafted out the basic essentials of a 5-litre over square, 60 degree V12 with four overhead camshafts, working to a rather different brief than that laid down for the XK engine - the V12 was to be built as a competition engine supplying enough power to win at Le Mans, and afterwards to be suitable for use in a road Jaguar in detuned form (the XK engine was on the other hand designed purely as a road unit, and was only afterwards developed into a highly successful racing engine). But as the prospect of Jaguar returning to the race track became ever more remote, the V12 was given a very low priority, being continued for a while almost as a design exercise; the first V12 didn't run until August 1964 in fact, by which time there had been a subtle change in the company's attitude - Le Mans once again appeared attractive.

At first glance the four-cam V12 looks very much as if two XK cylinder heads had been put together on a common crankcase, and indeed the familiar-looking polished aluminium camshaft covers did betray cylinder heads which retained some of the XK's features, like hemispherical combustion chambers and chain driven overhead camshafts. But the inlet porting was downdraught, valve angle was 60 degrees, and the combustion chambers themselves were somewhat shallower than in the six cylinder engine. As built for the XJ13, the V12 featured Lucas mechanical fuel injection driven off a jackshaft at the centre of the vee.

Bore and stroke was 70 by 87mm, and the engine's displacement was 4,994cc; the En40 forged crankshaft with its eight balance weights was carried in seven main bearings, inside an LM8 aluminium alloy sand cast block which was given slip-fit cast iron dry cylinder liners. Brico slipper pistons with Dykes top rings were used, working on forged En16 connecting rods. It was all very strong allowing the engine to run up to 8,500rpm with complete safety. Lubrication on the racing V12 was dry sump, with the oil being circulated by two gear-type scavange and one vane-type pressure pump, driven by their own chain from the crankshaft - the engine had a rather complex triple chain arrangement, for besides the chain driving the oil pumps, two more drove the camshafts. All rather more complicated than the production V12 engine we see today, but then it produced considerably more power - on the test bench, with a 10.4:1 compression ratio, 502bhp at 7,600rpm could be obtained, and 386 lb ft of torque at 6,300rpm.

As for the XJ13 itself (XJ stood for Experimental Jaguar, and bears no relationship to the XJ saloon series), the first thoughts about a mid-engined prototype stirred around 1960. Building however did not commence until June 1965, the car first running in March 1966. It was a very sophisticated machine, and definitely an advance over many designs of its period; its construction was entirely monocoque using mainly 18 gauge aluminium alloy sheet, and consisted in essence of two wide hollow sills running between front and rear pairs of wheels, connected by stressed flooring, a double bulkhead at the front and a single (but boxed at floor level) bulkhead about two-thirds of the way along the floor - to which was connected the V12 engine, also supported by the sills which partially enclosed it. The engine itself was a stressed member, carrying the final drive transaxle and rear suspension which could be removed as a unit with the engine. The front suspension was attached to aluminium boxed extensions projecting from the front bulkhead, the front wings and 'bonnet lid' surround also being stressed - in contrast to the car's tail which was unstressed and removable as a complete unit. The boxed member behind the driver at the base of the rear bulkhead doubled as a container for one of the three fuel bags, the other two flexible bags being located inside the hollow sills.

While much of the chassis work was carried out by the late Derek White, the final body shape was the responsibility of Malcolm Sayer which explains, of course, the car's strong family resemblance to the D-type; it is also the reason why the construction of the XJ13 includes aircraft building techniques, notably the roller seam welding of the sills and floor, and skin-dimpled rivets on the outer nose section - Sayer's background included a period of working for the Bristol Aircraft Corporation.

For expediency (and on cost considerations) the XJ13 was given rather similar suspension to the E-type. Forged wishbones were thus employed at the front, though with the important difference of coil spring/damper units instead of longitudinal torsion bars being used in conjunction with the wishbones. The rear suspension featured the fixed-length drive shafts as part of the top 'wishbone' but differed from the E-type's arrangement by using long tubular trailing links, and not two but one coil spring/damper unit on either side. Anti-roll bars were incorporated at front and rear. The disc brakes all round were originally Dunlop, but were later changed to ventilated Girling; unlike the E-type, they were outboard at the rear. The Dunlop cast magnesium-alloy 15 inch wheels were secured by centre lock fixings.

The XJ13's gearbox was the ZF five-speed unit with its integral final drive, the usual wear for mid-engined cars of the pre-Hewland era; the ratios in this sequential-change box were: first 2.42:1, second 1.61:1, third 1.23:1, fourth 1:1, and fifth, an 'overdrive' 0.846:1. A variety of final drive ratios could of course be fitted, but the car is now medium geared with a 4.2:1 ratio which gives around 170mph.

With the car lying completed in Jaguar's experimental division early in 1966, it was quite feasible that a team could have been built to contest the 1966 or 1967 Le Mans race - but then came the amalgamation with BMC and the attendant disruption of plans; with the future not quite so clear cut, any ideas of racing were shelved and the XJ13 lay idle for over a year before it was even taken out for its first trial. That was at MIRA early one Sunday morning during March 1967, a time chosen to avoid inquisitive eyes. Jaguar's near-terror at the thought of the XJ13's existence becoming public knowledge at that time is, under examination, very understandable. If news of a V12-engined Jaguar had leaked out, it might well have resulted in a lessening of demand for the current six-cylinder E-type (or even the saloon range too), potential customers keeping their money in anticipation of a new V12 road car announcement - which in 1966/67 was still years away. They even went so far as to paint E2A (which was still hanging about at the works) dark green and send it round the banking first for a number of laps, with the idea of persuading any would—be 'spies' that they were merely carrying out tests on an old D-type.

The test session at MIRA went well. With David Hobbs driving (an ex-Daimler apprentice, Hobbs had gained considerable racing experience by 1967 - including with the Mechamatic XK 140 - and was highly rated as a driver by Jaguar) the XJ13 lapped the banked circuit at 161.6mph, reaching 175mph down the straights; and like its C- and D-type forbears, the car needed no drastic modifications to correct serious deficiencies, which were non-existent. Taking even greater courage, as Mr England has said, Jaguar then ran the car at Silverstone a couple of times and got away with that too, Richard Attwood - another ex-Jaguar apprentice - also trying the car. Its lap times were very good considering that tyre and chassis development hadn't stood still while the car had lain unused at Browns Lane, and were only two or three seconds down on such contemporary sports racing cars as the Lola T70. Hobbs has been quoted as saying that the XJ13 could have been competitive up until the arrival of the 5-litre Porsche 917 and Ferrari 512, and certainly in terms of engine power the car's V12 had a definite margin of superiority over even quite highly developed versions of the Ford GT40's V8 engine.

But the fact still remained that the car was too slow - to knock those vital few seconds from the lap times would have required a great deal of work and much testing, involving Jaguar in a commitment that could not be met without its production car activities suffering. Racing had changed since 1956, as Mr. England for one knew:

> We would have to have done a motor racing programme, that is the point. Things have changed and motor racing is now twelve months a year, so you have to be doing a constant development programme to keep up with the Joneses. You can't decide that you'll make a car which gives a certain performance and have your cars all nicely finished in, say, March, in anticipation of doing four major races during the course of the year with the same car unchanged. I don't think you can do that today, development goes ahead too fast.

Then there was the increasingly specialised role of the sports racing car to be considered - it was no longer feasible to build a racing car with an affinity to the road car range such as the C-type and D-types possessed in their time, and thus there would have been that much less identification of the company's racing projects with the Jaguar road sports car in the minds of the customers. So, once and for all, Jaguar Cars turned its back on Le Mans; it wasn't that the XJ13 couldn't have been made to win, but that it simply wasn't worth the effort. And bulging order books amply underlined the fact.

The XJ13 retired under its dust cover in the experimental department once more, not being disturbed until 20th January 1971 - when it kept an almost fatal appointment at MIRA. The idea was to include the XJ13 in a film introducing the new V12 E-type, due to be launched the following April; the script called for an opening shot of the MIRA banking, at first deserted, then with the XJ13 gradually coming into view and finally passing the camera at high speed, the sound track recording the howl of the V12 engine in full song.

That part of the proceedings went extremely well, and some dramatic shots of the XJ13 were soon 'in the can'. However, with the car out of hibernation after so long, the temptation to put in a few more laps after the filming was completed was very strong, and it was during these extra laps that disaster occurred - one of the ageing racing tyres finally decided it couldn't take 160mph any more, and deflated under the extreme loads imposed upon it on the banking. The sequence of events that followed was inevitable - centrifugal force threw the car up to the top of the banking where it hit the retaining wires, bounced down across the track, and turned right over several times on the infield. Luckily the mortified Norman Dewis was unhurt, a tribute in itself to the strength of the car and its stout roll-over bar which took most of the impact, but there wasn't a straight panel left on the XJ13 - a more written-off looking racing car you couldn't imagine. It was a crestfallen party that took the remains back to Browns Lane and pushed it back into its dark corner of the development department.

The story might well have ended there, with the car being broken up in the manner of the C/D prototype in the mid-fifties; but fortunately for posterity it wasn't, merely lying dusty and neglected in exactly the state in which it was pulled from the field on January 20th 1971, for almost two years. Even then, when Mr England finally decided that the car might be rebuilt, it was probably only saved by the fact that due to a lucky chance, the original bodywork formers had survived. Some time after the XJ13 had been completed these had found their way to the redundant stores at Radford, but as the place was packed full inside they were dumped outside amongst other pieces of junk, where they remained half forgotten; had they been taken indoors, the formers would undoubtedly have been broken up during routine scrapping.

The restoration of the mid-engined prototype was carried out beautifully, largely by the men who had been responsible for its original construction both at Jaguar and at Abbey Panels, where the wooden formers were taken once more for new bodywork to be fashioned. Fortunately the strong basic platform of the car formed by the sills and bulkheads had remained almost completely untwisted (it was perhaps a 16th inch out at most) so it was largely a question of completely re-skinning, and

replacing bent suspension parts. The wheels caused problems initially as two appeared to be pretty well destroyed and the original patterns had gone, but in the end the damaged rims were turned off on the lathe, and new rims welded on - after considerable searching, it was found that the outer section of a Concorde undercarriage wheel could be adapted! The car wasn't rebuilt exactly as it had been in 1967, a few extra touches being added including slightly flared wheel arches which would probably have featured anyway had real development been proceeded with. An XJ12 electric fan, twin batteries, ballast resistor ignition and a Lucas OPUS unit were other practical additions or substitutions incorporated during the renovation, aimed at assisting the car to fulfill its new function of 'guest appearances' at race meetings, parades and other public events. The first of these was at the British GP meeting of July 1973, when 'Lofty' England drove the XJ13 round the Silverstone circuit in front of an impressive and impressed crowd. Since then, it has never failed to be a star attraction wherever it has been displayed, usually tended by Phil Weaver who will sometimes start its magnificent engine and send a wave of exciting V12 sound through the ranks of admiring onlookers. The XJ13 is an apt reminder that given the necessity and the right conditions, Jaguar could always produce a potential Le Mans winner.

JAGUAR'S PRODUCTION V12 ENGINE

In view of the gradual dimunition of the XK engined E-type's performance, the Jaguar enthusiast, and no doubt the Jaguar management as well, was relieved when at last the new V12 Jaguar engine could be released, and inserted into the E-type in its new Series 3 form. It had been more or less an open secret for a number of years that the company was steadily pursuing a V12 development programme, although when the engine was finally announced in March 1971, it was not necessarily what everybody had expected - except in terms of engineering excellence and the quality production for which Jaguar has always been known.

The Jaguar V12 engine had its origins in the years when there was a definite possibility that the factory might continue in racing. Under the direction of William Heynes, Claude Baily set about designing a V12 engine which would be capable of supplying the necessary amount of horsepower to win at Le Mans and which in de-tuned form would also make a suitable power unit for Jaguar's planned road cars. This was the reverse procedure to that adopted when the XK engine was evolved back in the forties, when the brief had been purely for a highly efficient road car engine - the XK unit had proved suitable for propelling a Le Mans winner almost by accident. The four ohc, 4,994 cc 502 bhp (gross) V12 which emerged from Claude Baily's design is described, together with the XJ13 sports racing car into which it was fitted, earlier on in this chapter, but not only did it fail to run at Le Mans, it was also never destined to attain production as a road car power unit.

There were a number of good reasons for this change of mind by Jaguar although at the time it caused a great deal of discussion at the works. The four ohc V12 certainly produced ample power even in road tune, but the realisation came that it was too complex and expensive to be put into series production; there was also the slight drawback that it was too bulky for the car it was supposed to fit into - there was no room for the accessories. "Providing space for auxiliaries on the twin-cam engine would have been formidable" stated Harry Mundy in his Institute of Mechanical Engineers paper of October 1971. However, the road car four-cam project (ie twin cams per head) was not finally dropped until around 1967/68, when it was proved that a much cheaper 'flat head' V12 engine with a single ohc to each bank of cylinders actually gave better results up to 5,000 rpm than the twin-cam per bank design, particularly in terms of low-speed torque and exhaust emissions. This comparison test was carried out by fitting one Mk 10 saloon with a road version of the Le Mans V12, and another with a pre-production flat-head V12 engine, and comparing the results.

Involving Heynes, Baily (although he was to suffer a heart attack which unfortunately put him out of action for a while), Mundy and Hassan (after he had come back to Jaguar's engineering department some time after the company had taken over Coventry Climax), the new V12 engine was designed from the outset as a road engine with no thoughts towards a racing application even in the distant future. The chosen V12 configuration had been inevitable from the outset and in fact no other had been considered at all - and certainly not a V8 even as a small sister to the larger engine. When the XK engine had been announced in 1948 one of its main selling points was its sophistication; no other manufacturer offered a twin-overhead camshaft straight-six for general sale to the public. So to make an equal impact with a new engine, Jaguar had again to take one jump ahead. The answer was to leapfrog the V8, so mundane in their largest market, the United States, and go for the V12. It was really the only sensible option open to Jaguar, and it would neatly take advantage of the V12 mystique built up by Ferrari, Lamborghini and other exotic makes (the average American - or European - would not remember, or even be aware of the very unexciting and often side-valve V12 engined cars produced in large numbers before the war by Cadillac, Lincoln, Packard and others). The practical reasons for adopting a V12 were sound too - like the straight six, and unlike the V8, smoothness is an inherent characteristic of the V12 as such an engine is free from either primary or secondary out of balance forces.

When the final production engine arrived, it had a single overhead camshaft on each bank of six cylinders operating in-line valves which worked in a flat cylinder head, with the combustion chamber being formed in the recessed piston crowns - all a bit unexpected to those used to the hemispherical head, twin ohc design used, and indeed loudly proclaimed, by Jaguar since 1948. Although a litre larger than the 4.2 litre XK engine at 5,343 cc, having a bore and stroke of 90 mm x 70 mm, the new V12 was only 80 lbs heavier (at 680 lbs) thanks to its aluminium block and cylinder heads. Needless to say after the less than happy experiences with the make-shift alloy block racing XK engines, the new block combined lightness with rigidity, with a big 4 inch deep skirt below the crankshaft line contributing strength; cast iron cylinder liners were used, these being a light push fit in the block. The crankshaft was supported by seven main bearings, with cast iron being used for the main bearing caps. Because of fears concerning main bearing rumble with the aluminium block, a crankcase of cast iron was built for comparative tests, but there was no detectable difference when the two types were installed in a vehicle; no less than 116 lbs were saved by using the alloy version.

At first a compression ratio of 10.6:1 was used with the engine quite happily running on 99 octane fuel, but this was lowered first to 10:1 and then to 9:1 "to ease the problem of exhaust emission requirements". Carburation was via four emission type Stromberg 175 CD SE carburetters located in pairs outside the 60 degree 'V', the long inlet tracts resulting from this arrangement providing ramm effects which improved mid-range torque. Up until fairly late in the engine's development the use of petrol injection had been envisaged. After initial experiments by the factory with the mechanical Lucas system which was used on the lightweight E-type, (and which turned out to be unsatisfactory because of its inability to meet air pollution demands), Brico Ltd produced an electronic system which met power, torque, cold starting and emission requirements (the latter only after considerable work in conjunction with Jaguar's emission engineers); alas Brico cancelled their plans to go into production with this system and a reversion had to be made to

carburetters. It is a pity on almost all counts that this occured, as not only was the Brico petrol injection a neat installation, but the power developed by the injected engine was some 30 - 40 bhp more than the output of the subsequent carburetted unit; the latter engine developed a quoted 272 bhp DIN at 5,850 rpm, and 304 ft lbs torque at 3,600 rpm. Recently of course, Jaguar have returned to fuel injection for the V12 engine, but only after the E-type had ceased production.

Trouble having been experienced with the twin distributors used on the experimental four-cam engine, Jaguar became the first car company to specify the Lucas Mk II OPUS (Oscillating Pick Up System) ignition, which replaced the conventional make and break mechanism with an electro-magnetic pick up and solid state electronics. The lubrication system of the engine also had a novel aspect, in that it made use of a crescent-type oil pump of the sort used in many automatic transmission (including Borg Warner); an oil cooler was incorporated in the lubrication system, heat being exchanged in a water cooled aluminium die-casting bolted underneath the sump at the front of the engine - this was especially beneficial during high speed cruising, and worked the other way round in assisting a quick warm up of the oil in cold starting.

Jaguar had remained faithful to the well-proven chain drive for the camshafts, a single duplex roller chain being employed which also drove the distributor jackshaft situated between the cylinder heads. The total length of the chain was just over 5½ feet, and it was damped by pads on three of its four runs and tensioned by a Morse long-blade tensioner on the fourth. Toothed belts of the type now in common use were rejected by Jaguar because of insufficient development at the time when the engine was being designed, and because their width would have added to the length of the engine which was not at all desirable.

The new engine was built at the Radford factory in Coventry, where something like £3 million had been spent on a new machine shop and equipment to produce the V12 engine, which was to have an initial production rate of about 9,100 units for the first year. After assembly and a searching bench test, the completed engines were sprayed with a protective coating and taken to Browns Lane, where they were inserted into the Series III frame - from the top, instead of the frame being lowered over the engine as for the six cylinder engine.

THE SERIES 3 E-TYPE

The Series 3 car itself was still basically the same old E-type, which disappointed those who had rather hoped for an all new sports car to come with the V12, though it had undergone its biggest face-lift yet. For the first time the nose aperture was covered by a grille (a "decorative birdcage" as it was rather unkindly described by *Motor Sport*), and the wheel arches front and rear were flared to accommodate both a wider track and bigger tyres; the latter were Dunlop E7OVR 15s mounted on 6 inch rim pressed steel rims (a switch had been made and now the wire wheels were the extras, as in the XK days). The open two-seater was now also on the 2-plus-2 wheelbase although without occasional seats in the back, which meant that the original, normal wheelbase chassis was no longer in production. The prices of the new V12 cars were incredibly competitive; the V12 Roadster retailed at £3,123, and the V12 Fixed-head at £3,369. Catalogued for a time was a Series 3 6-cylinder car powered by the twin Stromberg full emission XK engine (but with a 9:1 compression ratio for the home market) of which only a very few were ever made.

Structually the car was essentially unchanged although the front tubular framework had been redesigned to accommodate the bigger engine, and strengthened by means of triangular plates fixed in the corners of the upper forward tubes; the bulkhead was enlarged and strengthened too, and stresses caused by the V12 engine's greater torque were absorbed by a tie bar under the engine. Front suspension was given the anti-dive characteristics of the XJ6 saloon by repositioning the upper and lower wishbone mountings, and the upper wishbones were given Slip-flex sealed-for-life bearings. Torsion bar adjustment was now by means of a cam plate, and although the same Series 2 dual system, servo assisted brakes were employed, ventilated discs were now used at the front. The inboard, rear brakes were cooled by an under floor air scoop. The new ventilated disc reduced peak temperatures by some 100 deg C, and the ducting helped maintain front and rear brake temperature relationships.

Inside the car largely detail improvements distinguished it from previous models. A greater degree of seat-back recline was provided and the controlling lever was extended so that it could be easily reached by the rear passengers. A full width bar now controlled the seat slide mechanism, and the door trim included a combined arm-rest and door-pull. The throttle pedal was of one-piece manufacture (no hinge as such) and the automatic cars had wider brake pedals. The whole floor area of the car was now brought down to the level of the previous footwells, and the heater/fresh air system was given some much needed help by an extractor ventilator mounted on the rear of the car. A smaller 15 inch Springall steering wheel was fitted, the smaller diameter made possible by the power steering which was now obligatory; the steering rack was modified to reduce compliance in its rubber mountings while retaining their ability to absorb normal road shocks. As the roadster now used the 2-plus-2 chassis for the first time, it became available with automatic transmission - the Borg Warner Model 12 was now used in both roadster and fixed-head automatics, in place of the older Model 8. The same all-synchromesh box was retained on the manual transmission cars, but these were given larger (10½ inch diameter instead of 9½ inch) clutches.

THE V12 E-TYPE ON ROAD TEST

On the road, the Series 3 V12 E-type had certainly regained something of the original straight line performance of its 3.8 XK engined predecessor if not all its agility. The V12 Roadster came up for test by *Motor* in November 1971, a smart red example with a black hard top, and it was the quickest road Jaguar to 100 mph that the magazine had up to then tested, this speed being reached in 15.4 seconds from rest. Sixty miles an hour took 6.4 seconds to attain, compared with the 7.1 seconds taken by the same journal's 3.8 Open Two Seater in 1961, and the 10 seconds it took the 1949 XK 120 to reach the same speed. The V12's standing ¼-mile time was 14.2 seconds, .8 second faster than the 1961 car, and its top speed was 146 mph, some 4 mph slower than the 3.8 car. Running through this road test was a theme which was to be present in all V12 E-type tests - the highest of praise for the new engine, but qualified criticism of a chassis that was becoming outdated.

Autocar tested a V12 Fixed-head Coupe with similar (3.07) gearing which took .4 second longer to get to 60 mph, and 1 second longer to reach 100 mph. The weight of this closed car was 29.5 cwt kerb, and the V12 Roadster turned the scales at 28.8 cwt, which is one explanation for the V12 sports cars' minimal improvement in performance over its 3.8 and early 4.2 six cylinder ancestors. The fixed-head coupe now weighed 22% more than originally, as *Autocar* were quick to point out. Maximum speed was 142 mph which was 4 mph better than that of the 4.2 2-plus-2 which the magazine had tested in 1966 with the same gearing; it was noted that the original road test E-type maximum of 150 mph achieved in 1961 included the use of racing tyres, which absorbed less power and raised the gearing considerably. Other less charitable souls (like Denis Jenkinson of *Motor Sport*) had in any case regarded those early E-type top speed runs with suspicion, particularly as Jenkinson's own 4.2 Fixed-head Coupe (with 8:1 compression ratio but still with the aerodynamic headlight fairings) never managed more than 143 mph, and his replacement 1970 4.2 Roadster had grave difficulty in reaching more than 130 mph. *Autocar's* 142mph was achieved during a run-in of well over 10 miles, but the V12 did not manage to get within 100 rpm of its peak power. The standard UK gearing was in fact 3.31, not the 3.07 ratio fitted to both the V12 road test cars under discussion, and the magazine thought that the former would be best for the UK anyway, as it "should increase the acceleration by a substantial margin". The 3.31 was also the ratio with which the original E-types put up their famous 150 mph maxima! In fact, one can detect just a hint of embarrassment at Jaguar over these figures, and if the 3.8 road test cars were slightly tweaked then the 150 mph gimmick rather back-fired on the company, who up until recently have found it very difficult to match all the 1961 figures with later machinery.

Autocar confirmed *Motor's* feelings about the new engine - superb, smooth power with virtually no mechanical noise at all (rare for a V12) and very little exhaust noise: "from 70 mph to 140 mph wind noise is by far the loudest sound and even that is by no means excessive". A natural cruising speed seemed to be around 125 mph, and though the magazine stated that the V12 E-type was much more of a top-gear car than the old six cylinder E-type, this was only so in terms of smoothness and not acceleration, as a comparison of the figures show. From 20 mph - 40 mph the 'six' (1961 Fixed-head Coupe) and V12 figures are 5.5 seconds and 6.2 seconds respectively, and the older sports car maintains its advantage all the way up the speed range, until the difference over the increment 100 mph - 120 mph is no less than 3.4 seconds in favour of the 3.8 engined car! Admittedly the latter had the lower 3.31 final drive, but as it was also 8 mph faster at the top end too the comparison is surely both valid and fair. Yet another look at the weights of the two road test cars reveals that the original E-type weighed fully laden (ie with two up, and equipment) the same as the V12 empty ; and taking into consideration the effect of a wider air intake, exposed headlights, higher roof line and other changes which all took their toll on the E-type's aerodynamic qualities, it can be seen that there are many reasons why the V12 E-type was no faster than its older sister. In fact, the XJ12 Saloon which was soon to follow had virtually all the performance of the sports car, particularly in terms of maximum speed.

The Series 3 E-types had power steering as a standard fitment, and it was a slightly controversial addition to the car's specification. While *Autocar's* original test of the V12 did not criticise it at all ("delightfully smooth and progressive") other motoring journals considered that it was too light and consequently lacking in 'feel'; certainly many who drove the car much preferred the 'harder' setting used on exactly the same system when it was fitted to the Aston Martin V8 model. Jaguar solidly maintained that theirs was right, though conceded that it sometimes took some getting used to. However, the car was aimed mainly at the North American market and if the steering wasn't strictly to European sporting tastes, then it wasn't too important.

While the V12 E-type was well received in the States, the motoring press there were not unaware of the chassis' relative antiquity, and stated the facts plainly. *Road & Track* even headlined their long-awaited road test of the model "A magnificent engine in an outclassed body" which is certainly not beating about the bush. Under the heading of "outclassed" came the car's heating and ventilation arrangements, although the optional air conditioning plant was highly praised - "Operation is a model of simplicity and a welcome relief from the previously mentioned vent and defroster controls". Inside the car, age was telling as well: "The cockpit, too, lacks the spaciousness and comfort of more modern designs...Seating is another area in which the Jaguar falls behind the times". As previous road testers had found, there was a tendency for the driver to feel he was sliding under the steering wheel, as the seat cushion was not angled backwards enough. Boot

space was supplemented by room behind the seats in the roadster model under test, particularly with the hood erected. It was even found possible to carry an adult behind the roadster's seats for very short periods.

There were still a great many attractions in the E-type on the open road however, as *Road & Track* related: "(although) somewhat disappointing in cornering (the XJ6 corners faster on a skidpan)... the E-type is an easy car to drive and is most at home when driven fast...a very predictable car with excellent balance between ride and handling. The ride is soft but very well controlled and even at high speeds there is no tendency towards front end lift or wander. On rough roads most of the squeaks and rattles we've noted on previous E-types have been eliminated, all the more remarkable when one remembers this is a convertible and not a more rigid coupe... Handling is neutral under all conditions except for extremely heavy applications of power. On such occasions the tail comes out gently and predictably. Such characteristics are forgiving to the inexperienced driver but useful to the more skilful during fast motoring".

However, one not so good point noted was "an extreme display of torque steer, that is, under full power the car points to the left, the driver corrects for the swerve and finds the car pointing to the right when the power stops for, say, a shift into a higher gear". This foible of *Road & Track's* E-type does not seem to be typical of the car though. The gearbox received the magazine's blessing, and so did the brakes, while the power unit was praised without reservation:

"The engine is a sheer delight, by itself almost worth the price of admission, and to some extent it atones for the sins of the outdated car. The V12 is a lovely piece of machinery, lovely to listen to and behold. The exhaust has that hurried sound characteristic of a multiple cylinder engine where the many explosions per revolution make it sound as if it's running faster than an engine with fewer cylinders. The idle is smooth and quiet with none of the busyness one normally experiences from the likes of a Ferrari or Lamborghini V12. And the smoothness lingers throughout the rpm range."

Certainly, an eye on the rev counter was essential when driving the V12 E-type, as the engine was no noisier at 6,500 rpm than at 3,000 rpm. Its smoothness at tickover was such that only the flickering of the rev counter indicated that the engine was running at all. *Road & Track* did not become fond of the car's Dunlop radials, which squealed badly when cornered at normal pressures, and gave a harsher ride when inflated to a higher pressure. Wet grip "wasn't a strong point" either, and rain showed up leaks in the car's hood. "We've been harsh on the car," said the magazine in summary, "but we believe justifiably so. When the same manufacturer can produce such an outstanding car as the XJ6, it not only spoils us for anything he produces thereafter, but makes it exceedingly difficult for us to justify the existence of a car that is not as excellent".

The straight line performance of the American monthly's car was still good, but the extra emission equipment on the engine (which included an air injection pump) resulted in a quoted net bhp of 250, and even with the considerably lower final drive of 3.54 (as opposed to 3.07 for the European market) the car's acceleration figures were noticeably effected. Sixty miles an hour took 7.4 seconds to reach, 100mph 18.5 seconds, and the standing ¼-mile was covered in 15.4 seconds. Speed in top gear at 6,000rpm was 135mph. As for price, the V12 E-type Roadster cost 7599 dollars, which was very reasonable when compared to the Porsche 911E Targa at 9078 dollars, and the Mercedes Benz 350 SL at 10,540 dollars.

The V12 E-type was a thirsty car, and of course drank a lot more petrol than its six cylinder predecessors. Overall consumption figures recorded by *Autocar*, *Motor* and *Road & Track* pretty well coincided, and were, in order: 15.2mpg, 14.5 mpg, and 14.5mpg.

For some interesting comments on the V12 E-type we can turn to Paul Frere, past winner of Le Mans in a Ferrari and at one time a 'works' Jaguar team driver, now one of Europe's most experienced motoring journalists. Early in 1972 Frere completed a 'grand tour' of the exotic car manufacturers around Modena, combining the trip with a road test of a V12 E-type, and reported on his experience in *Motor* week ending March 18 1972:

Three of my four thousand miles were done in this car, and I am pleased to be able to say that none of the exotics I drove during the period - most of them costing nearly twice as much - could claim to have an engine of equal overall merit. More surprisingly, none would accelerate faster, only the Maserati Bora mid-ship engined two-seater Coupe being slightly quicker in top speed. Admittedly, I did not resample a Ferrari Daytona or a Lamborghini Miura, but as far as my note-book goes, these and the 7.4 litre Corvette are about the only three production cars in the world which just won't give the Jaguar a chance... and most people would probably accept this in exchange for the quietness and the flexibility of the Coventry product. Where the Jaguar falls down, however, is on handling which I find much too sloppy and rubbery. Admittedly the low speed ride is good, but the suspension is insufficiently damped for fast driving on mediocre roads such as you find in France, tyre harshness comes through quite badly and the car becomes noisy and rattly on bad roads, where rigidity does not seem to be a strong point.

On Continental motorways, these faults are not felt badly although the rubber in the rear suspension makes the car quite sensitive to side winds.

The trans-Europe journey involved was covered at very high average speeds, including one section in which 128 miles were covered in exactly one hour - and this on a two-lane motorway, and not a very straight one at that! Over the 3,200 miles which Paul Frere drove the Jaguar, its fuel consumption worked out at an average of 11.2mpg, a respectable figure in view of the type of motoring indulged in.

Road & Track, like Paul Frere, also compared the V12 E-type (in roadster form) with some of its contemporaries, although the cars involved in the multi-car test - Mercedes 450SL, Porsche

911 Targa, Chevrolet Corvette, and Ferrari Dino Spyder - were not quite so exotic as those encountered by Paul Frere; but, on the otherhand, they were much more direct rivals to the Jaguar especially on the North American Market. The E-type itself was the latest 1974 full emission control model fitted with the less than beautiful rubber overriders which were then (February 1974) being tacked onto either end of the United States destined Jaguars to meet the 5mph impact tests. Compression ratio was also down to 7.8:1, having been dropped from 9:1 in 1973 to assist the V12 to meet emission requirements, which meant an engine rating of 240bhp (SAE, net) at 5,750rpm - this had the effect of bringing top speed down to 138mph, and increasing the acceleration times considerably. Sixty miles an hour now took 8 seconds to achieve, 100mph 21.2 seconds, and the standing ¼-mile 16.2 seconds to cover. However, the V12 E-type was still marginally faster than the Dino and Porsche in a straight line, considerably faster than the Mercedes, but slower than the Corvette (with its more powerful option, the 5737cc 250bhp engine) in all but top speed.

Handling tests, both subjective and objective, determined, according to *Road & Track* that the E-type came last: "It understeers more than its weight distribution says it should and the power steering is slow to respond, too light and without feel". The Dino "won by a wide margin", the 450SL came second, "on balance", while the Corvette was placed just above the E-type provided the road surface was smooth. On braking the Jaguar stopped second quickest after the Corvette, but the E-type came last again under the heading "Comfort, Controls, Accommodation and Vision". Not mincing their words, *Road & Track* proclaimed: "We said at the outset that the E-type is an outdated design. Nowhere is this more glaringly apparent than inside. The ventilation system is inadequate and the controls maddening. The cockpit, too, lacks the space of more modern designs".

But some good points about the interior was

acknowledged, such as the "large and legible" instruments and the adjustable steering column as a standard feature. When it came to noise at 70mph (top up), the E-type dead-heated with the Mercedes at 80 dBA, being quieter than the Corvette and Dino though noisier than the Porsche at 77 dBA. At least the Jaguar's V12 engine came through without major criticism although it was the only one in the group to suffer from lean surge, and was the thirstiest - the E-type returned 12mpg as opposed to the Corvette's 13.5mpg. And, of course, the car was superb value for money - it cost 8475 dollars, compared with 10,800 dollars for the Porsche, 15,225 dollars for the Dino, and 15,450 dollars for the Mercedes. Only the domestic product was cheaper, at 5499 dollars (all prices basic).

Road & Track didn't seem to think that the V12 E-type was very reliable; the two big circulation weeklies in Britain put this aspect of the car to the test, *Autocar* running a V12 Roadster on extended appraisal, and *Motor* a fixed-head coupe. The latter was the first to report, in August 1973 after some 14,000 miles had been covered by the magazine's editor, Charles Bulmer. Really, there was very little to report if one ignores the comments directed at inherent design features (like the poor seats, over-light steering and inadequate ventilation). Very little oil was used by the engine, and the misfire which earlier units sometimes displayed was easily cured by driving the car hard for a reasonable distance. The exhaust system tended to ground rather easily but didn't seem to suffer any ill effects, the thermostatic switch controlling the twin engine fans failed and left them running all the time, and the interior fan switch stuck in the 'slow' position. A performance check at MIRA with the speedometer reading 13,600 miles showed no deterioration in acceleration, the figures matching the magazine's road-test results "within the limits of experimental error". An overall fuel consumption of 13.5mpg was recorded. In general terms, Charles Bulmer much enjoyed the car, confirming his thoughts after

Motor's 'exoticar' group test of May 1972 when, after sampling the Aston Martin V8, Citroen SM, Lamborghini Espada and V12 E-type Fixed-head under equal conditions, it was the Jaguar that he decided he would want the most. As he said of that occasion:

"Despite the fact that the E-type was by far the cheapest of this group, I thought it was the one which I would choose to live with day in and day out. That just doesn't mean for long fast continental runs, it means for commuting as well, for driving when you feel tired and lethargic, for shopping and for business use when you can't spare much time for servicing and maintenance".

David Thomas also confessed to being a Jaguar enthusiast of long standing too, when he reported on a year's motoring with *Autocar's* red V12 Roadster. Like the editor of *Motor*, who had taken the first road test 3.8 E-type to Italy for its maximum speed runs, his enthusiasm stemmed from 1961 (or even before, having seen the 2½ litre E-type prototype running around MIRA) and the original 3.8 E-type, although he had gone one better and actually bought a 6-cylinder car in 1963, running it for the next three years. The V12 Roadster he took over at 10,757 miles, and ran for a further 9,000 miles. Generally speaking the car was trouble-free but there were snags. One concerned the hood, which a delivery driver had erected without undoing the press studs which secured the material just behind the doors; this had resulted in tearing, which although normally could have been locally repaired, brought to light the cost of a new hood - £170.50, with an extra £13.20 for labour. Both hot air pickup vacuum pipes were renewed at 12,000 miles, and when water was found to collect under the car every time it was parked in sunshine, it was discovered that the length of hose leading to the left hand inlet manifold had split, and that several of the clipped joints were leaking when the cooling system was pressurised. An oil leak at 15,000 miles under the engine was found to be a badly fitting 'O' ring on the oil filter casing, but

another leak at the rear of the car was traced to the final drive unit, a seal having failed allowing oil to spread onto the left hand brake disc. Normally this could have been renewed (at a cost of £5.76 for materials and £17.16 for labour) but Jaguar decided to change the whole final drive unit. Not including this, the cost of attending to the very minor failings listed above, and such other items like a leaking hood at the top of the windscreen, and the screwing-on of various small bits and pieces which had fallen off inside the car, came to £65.46; and as David Thomas pointed out, a lot of this would have been covered under the normal 12,000 mile warranty.

Before the report was concluded, reference was made to the misfiring problems which had been the cause of concern to quite a lot of V12 E-type owners, at least towards the beginning of V12 production. It was noted that "numerous detail changes" had been made over the months including a change of spark plugs from Champion N9Y to N10Y, different plug leads, modification of the distributor pickup module, changes to the transistorised amplifier unit and modifications to the rotor arm (which could become porous). Since *Autocar's* test car was built, further changes had included a higher coil output voltage and a matching of each coil to its amplifier, and it does seem that misfiring troubles no longer occur with the V12 engine.

As for petrol consumption, the roadster managed an overall 14.3mpg, and one pint of oil was used over 750 miles. Tyre life was reckoned to be 24,000 miles for the front pair, and 27,000 miles for the rear; estimated disc pad life was 30,000 miles. The car's performance was checked because at the time of the final drive change at Jaguar, a 3.07:1 ratio was substituted for the previous 3.31:1. Thus the roadster returned acceleration times close to those *Motor* obtained from their similarly geared V12 Roadster on road test. At 18,000 mile odd, acceleration was very much up to scratch with David Thomas's car actually .1 second quicker to 60mph than *Motor's* (at 6.3 seconds), although adrift by exactly one second at 100mph - conceivably because the hardtop on *Motor's* roadster was aerodynamically more efficient than the hood used on the other car.

It is interesting to note that *Autocar* usually came down in favour of the E-type's power steering. "True enough", said David Thomas, "the mechanism is feather light, but it affords quite excellent feel and precision. Moreover, it is quite free from kick-back and fight (the latter being something which I remember disliking in my Series 1)."

NON-INTERNATIONAL RACING, 1964-1975

In attempting a concise review of the E-type's track racing career in British club racing, there is a great danger of presenting the reader with a long list of names and very little else, so many people having taken the wheel of an E-type with reasonable success over the ten years under discussion. One can start with Ken Baker's car, seen in his hands up until about 1964 and re-appearing in 1965 driven by Rob Schroeder, who drove it to many victories between 1965 and 1967 and gaining a number of class lap records in the process; the post office red and white car was a familiar sight at Brands Hatch, and set a Club circuit lap record there which stood for a long while - eventually being beaten during the epic dices between John Quick and Warren Pearce.

Tony Dean was quite a well known name at the beginning of our ten year period, racing his E-type in long-distance events besides the more common Brands Hatch ten-lappers. Robin Sturgess raced Anthony Hopkins' lightweight E-type on occasions and the latter's steel-bodied car more frequently, again around 1964, while Richard Bond (now noted for his Historic drives in Lister and HWM-Jaguars) conducted the Red Rose lightweight E-type in the mid-sixties, together with Brian Redman. John Quick commenced a long and very successful racing E-type career about the same time (with the

famous dark blue WOO 11) as did his arch-rival at Brands Hatch, Warren Pearce. Rhoddy Harvey Bailey was campaigning a Protheroe-prepared E-type at that time (then registered CUT 8), a car which now belongs to one Peter Walker - though not the Walker of XK 120 and C-type fame - and retains its wide-angle cylinder head. Keith Holland was another rapid E-type driver, particularly at Brands Hatch, entering the fray around 1966 along with John Filbee who was still racing his E-type up to a season ago (1973). Brian Spicer and David Plumstead were regular competitors in 1967, Plumstead entering his E-type for the occasional long-distance event at Brands Hatch. John Burbidge, based at Thruxton where he now runs a racing drivers' school, is still one of the most regular E-type drivers, and one of the quickest and most reliable too with his immaculate blue fixed-head - Tony Shaw occasionally drives his car. John Lewis from Wales did well at West Country circuits in the period 1968/69, racing at Thruxton, Castle Combe and on his home circuit Llandow in Wales itself.

Returning again to the Home Counties, Brands Hatch continued to be the happy hunting ground for E-types, such as those driven by Mick Franey, John Wilson and Jenny Tudor-Owen (up to 1969), while Alistair Cowen had a measure of success with his E-type in about the same period; John Scott-Davies raced the ex-Lumsden/Sargent E-type at around that time too. Harry Philips, Brian Mills, and Alan Leeson with a supercharged car, are also names which should be mentioned. By this time, Alan Minshaw had acquired, and virtually written-off, the ex-Ken Baker roadster; after yet another re-build, this old campaigner was purchased by Anthony Hutton in 1971 and, driven by John Harper, was to be about the last consistent race-winning E-type in Modified Sports Car racing. During the 1971 season Harper achieved nine outright wins and 14 second places, plus a class lap record at Oulton Park - as a contrast to some earlier Jaguars, and as an indication of tyre and suspension progress,

Top Peter Taylor's successful championship winning V12 E-type contesting a production sports car race during the 1974 season; the car, incidentally, is the first rhd fixed-head Series 3 E-type built
Centre left Lee Mueller and the Huffaker Engineering V12 winning the Northern Pacific SCCA Divisional Championship for B Production cars
Centre right The Group 44 Jaguar which was also highly successful during 1974, shown on a victory lap with Bob Tullius at the wheel - next to him is Brian Fuerstenau, the Group's chief engineer, and left is Michael H Dale, Vice President Sales, British Leyland Motors Inc.
Bottom The Gran Turismo sponsored 6-cylinder E-type which was driven by Roger Bighouse in the Sports Car Club of America's C Production races in 1973 and 1974, seen here on a victory lap having just won a National round of the championship at Nelson Ledges, Ohio in September 1974

Top The Series 3 V12 E-type. The less steeply raked windscreen helps to smooth out the otherwise rather upright stance of the long wheelbase fixed-head cars

Bottom left Series 3 E-type production line. Up to the end of its run, the building of an E-type included much handwork with panels being welded together and lead-filled individually

Bottom right Series 3 E-type front suspension, little changed from that on the original 1961 cars except for some relocation of wishbone points to introduce an 'anti-dive' movement into its geometry. Note the ventilated disc brake *(photo The Autocar)*

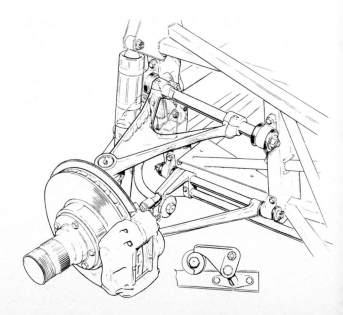

Top The end of an era - the last E-type made, one of the final batch of 50 appropriately finished in black. Jaguar's then Managing Director Geoffrey Robinson is seen right, with Alan Currie, Sales and Marketing Director, Jack Randle of the Radford engine factory and Peter Craig, Plant Director at the Browns Lane assembly plant
Centre The XJ13, as pictured in its original form a few hours before the crash while filming at MIRA in 1968
Bottom XJ13 undergoing its rebuild at Abbey Panels. Note the wooden formers seen in the foreground, which luckily escaped scrapping and enabled Jaguar's only mid-engined car to be rebuilt

Top Public debut for the XJ13 was the British Grand Prix of 1972 at Silverstone; 'Lofty' England took the car on a lap of honour round the circuit, and later drove race winner Ronnie Peterson around too *(photo The Motor)*
Centre Sectional drawing of Jaguar's mid-engined sports racing prototype, the XJ13
Bottom The nearest a mid-engined Jaguar road car got to production was in a series of styling exercises by Malcolm Sayer; shown here is a scale model of one such experiment

Top The XJ-S - the latest generation of sporting Jaguars. The specially designed Cibie lights are prominent in this view, together with the 'impact' bumpers and spoiler. USA versions have a twin headlight system
Centre The XJ-S displays lines that are totally new for Jaguar, and combine elegance with practicality; road wheels are alloy
Bottom Sectional drawing of the XJ-S, showing the fuel injected 5.3 V12 engine, and XJ type suspension; exhaust system is largely stainless steel

VIC BERRIS M.SIA

Top left Instrument panel on the XJ-S, showing the vertical minor indicators (centre) and battery of warning lights (top)

Top right Inside the XJ-S; the fully reclining seats are in leather, the steering column is adjustable, and the handbrake 'drops down' after it has been applied to make getting in and out easier. The (standard) air conditioning plant maintains a cooler temperature at head level than in the footwells, which discourages a 'stuffy' atmosphere

Bottom XJ-S power plant. The now well-tried Jaguar V12 engine, fuel injected and capable of propelling the XJ-S at over 150mph in almost total silence. Bonnet hinges forward on gas-filled struts

Top Perhaps the most easily recognisable engine today - the world famous six cylinder XK engine, shown here in its original 1948 3,442cc form. It has been likened to a typical Grand Prix racing car engine of the thirties but with a little extra weight, and certainly its twin overhead camshaft, cross-flow design has a close affinity to power units of that type

Bottom The four cylinder version of the XK engine, scheduled as an alternative power unit for the XK 120. Of 1,996cc, it gave about 100 bhp at 5,200 rpm but never went into production. This unit was prepared for exhibition at Earls Court at the time of the XK 120's debut *(photo The Motor)*

Top Study in efficiency; an unusual end-elevation view of the 1955 3.4-litre dry-sump D-type engine *(photo The Motor)*

Bottom Awesome in its size and bulk, Jaguar's original V12 with its four overhead camshafts shows its XK ancestry very plainly. Shown here is the proposed road version with SU carburettors. In racing form with fuel injection and other modifications but still of 4,991cc capacity, this unit was capable of 500 bhp at 7,600 rpm - and that was by no means the ultimate brake horsepower figure achieved by the works from this engine, something around 700 bhp having been hinted at in this respect *(photo Jaguar Cars)*

some 20 of these races were run on one set of Dunlop tyres! In 1972 the car appeared, mainly with Anthony Hutton at the wheel, in its new Forward Enterprises' livery of green and yellow (that colour having been adopted by Forward Enterprises in affectionate memory of the works Lister-Jaguars, two of which were also raced by this company - which was formed by Hutton and Harper to facilitate their still very amateur racing activities). Still very fast with its Forward Engineering power unit, 7 CXW was eventually sold during 1973, and crashed at Silverstone that same year by its new owner, during a practice session.

Although there are still many E-types racing in Modified Sports car events at the time of writing, few are truly competitive against such cars as Nick Faure's Porsche Carrera, John N. Pearson's XK 120 Drop-head, and the faster Lotus Elans. Rob Meacham occasionally drives the Forward-Engineering prepared E-type with moderate success, this car running with the 4½-litre XK engine which the Warwickshire company has developed over the past couple of years; but despite having the most powerful Jaguar engine yet seen in Modified Sports car racing, the E-type is only a race-winner when the competition is not fierce, in that particular division of motor sport.

THE V12 E-TYPE IN COMPETITION

The Series 3 E-type is not a common sight on the race track, or really in any form of motor sport. In fact, there are only a few cars actively competing in this country which really need be examined, and they have yet to demonstrate (at the moment of writing) that they can lap a circuit quicker than a similarly modified 6-cylinder E-type. Guy Bedington's petrol injected V12 Fixed-head, which has been running in modified sports car races and in hill climbs and sprints for the past few years, is probably the most developed of the V12 racers in this country to date.

The car started life as an early 1971 standard Series 3 which Guy Bedington occasionally sprinted. Having fuel injected a Mini for autocrossing, he became intrigued by the idea of doing the same with Jaguar's V12 engine. Tecalemit-Jackson took an interest, through employee Bryan Wills, and after much trial and tribulation a PI system was devised that worked, the engine then giving well over 300bhp on the bench compared with an unmodified figure of 230bhp (taken from the output shaft of the gearbox). Piper reprofiled the standard cams, and Janspeed supplied a branch exhaust system.

At first the suspension was left fairly standard, just wider wheels (9 inch rims front, 10 inch rear) being substituted for the 6 inch rim standard items. I drove the car in this form during a track test for *Motor* in 1973 and was surprised at its civilised nature, the V12 engine still remaining beautifully smooth and with a seemingly very wide power band - although maximum torque was developed some 2,000rpm higher than in the standard engine. When it came to the handling, the car was good mannered but obviously lacking in development; the power assisted steering was still connected too, though this was not so disadvantageous as might be expected, the assistance being almost welcome in overcoming the extra effort needed to turn the wide tyres. The Adwest system's servo effect had in fact been lessened, from about 1,000 psi to 800 psi, and the steering was no lighter than on, for instance, an ex-Briggs Cunningham lightweight E-type that I sampled, courtesy of Anthony Bamford, a year later over the same circuit.

Although Tecalemit-Jackson have not proceeded with their original plan to produce a bolt-on PI system for Jaguar's V12 engine, Guy Bedington has since pursued a constant development programme on the V12 E-type, and this very distinctive car acquits itself quite well on the circuit in modified sports car racing; but it is still not a race winner when up against real opposition, and its lap times are a vital two or three seconds down on the fastest XK engined

E-types or John N. Pearson's amazing XK 120 (see Chapter 4). But the potential is certainly there - gross power output is now thought to be about 418bhp and the aforementioned John Pearson, who tried the V12 at Brands Hatch, reckoned that it was as fast as his famous XK in a straight line, even though it was only firing on eight cylinders on that occasion! With further chassis sorting and more weight shedding, this V12 E-type could certainly be made to take the chequered flag consistently.

Potentially the fastest V12 E-type is, however, the car prepared by Kenilworth Motor Racing Services (formerly Forward Engineering Co.) for an American client early in 1975. The engine was taken out from 5.3 to 5980cc, the piston crowns modified, special camshafts fitted and an exhaust system to match the engine's new characteristics installed. Standard size valves were retained as it was found that although larger valves gave a bigger gross bhp output, the original valves provided a more useful torque curve with the loss of only 10 bhp or so. Considerable changes were made to the oil lubrication and cooling systems, which were found to be inadequate at sustained high rpm. The complete bottom end, rods, crankshaft and bearings, were found to be very strong and so were left exactly as they were. The car's owner was Glen Bunch, of Performance Cars, Norfolk, Virginia, who had previously raced an extremely fast 6-cylinder E-type also prepared by the Kenilworth company.

In a different class of racing, another V12 Fixed-Head E-type is already winning - in Production Sports Car racing. This division of British motor sport is for virtually standard series production sports cars, the vehicles being chosen by the RAC (which is fortunate, as if homologation papers had been required the car could not have run, the last Jaguar to be homologated being the S-type saloon). The owner driver of this car was Peter Taylor, a Jaguar development engineer who was very much involved in the test programmes for the V12 E-type and the XJ12; the E-type itself is interesting, as it is the first Series 3 V12 to be built (chassis no EX 100) and was running in late 1969. After a lot of test miles it was returned to production trim before Taylor bought it in 1973.

Little was done to the car before it was raced, bar a top overhaul, the fitting of modified down-pipes as allowed by the regulations, and the substitution of Koni shock absorbers on the rear (and uprated Girling on the front) for the original dampers. Taylor found that fitting the softer torsion bars of the two types used on the Series 3 E-type helped cut down understeer on slow corners (the car has oversteer characteristics on high speed bends), but otherwise the suspension is standard. The 9:1 compression ratio of the home market V12s was of course retained. Reliability has been 100% except for overheating of the brakes, although the use of a new racing brake fluid helped to stop vaporisation.

During 1974 Taylor and his E-type achieved a good measure of success in Production sports car racing, almost always winning their class and sometimes their race - usually giving best only to Chris Meek's de Tomaso Pantera, and running even that exotic piece of machinery close if it should happen to be wet. The car ended the season having won its club championship.

RACING THE E-TYPE IN AMERICA

It came as something of a surprise to many when in August 1974 it was announced that a British Leyland Inc. backed V12 E-type racing programme was being launched in the States, with the aim of winning the Sports Car Club of America's Class B Production championship. This was tantamount to Jaguar re-entering racing, at least in the States, and it aroused widespread interest amongst enthusiasts - especially when the car won first time out, at Seattle International Raceway on 10/11th August 1974 (that occasion also being the first ever race in the United States for a V12 E-type). The driver was Lee Mueller, and the same weekend

Bob Tullius was leading his race in a second V12 E-type when the gearlever broke off in his hand while he was in the lead at Watkins Glen.

The two V12 entries at Seattle and Watkins Glen were in the nature of surprise entries, the cars having been secretly prepared and tested since the preceding May. Two organisations were involved, both of which having a long association with British Leyland in racing MGs, Triumphs or Jaguars. Huffaker Engineering Inc. could boast the closest connections with Jaguar, having modified and prepared 6-cylinder E-types for national racing during the first half of the sixties; though the concern's President, Joe Huffaker, is probably most widely known in the States through the competition equipment for MGs which he has designed and marketed for many years. Huffaker was formerly competition manager for Kjell Qvale's British Motor Car Distributors Ltd of San Fransico. Driving the Huffaker-prepared V12 Roadster during the 1974 season was Lee Mueller, who has a number of national and divisional production sports car racing championships under his belt, driving Austin Healey Sprites, Triumph Spitfires, MGBs and - in 1973 - a Jensen Healey.

Preparing the second V12 to enter racing in the State was Group 44 Inc., the 1974 season being their 10th in association with British Leyland (formerly BMC), Goodyear and Quaker State oil, the team's cars having previously won some 175 races and ten national championships. Group 44 was founded in 1965 by drivers Bob Tullius and Brian Fuerstenau, both past national championship winners themselves; Fuerstenau is in charge of the team's car preparation and development, while Tullius handles the administrative and promotional side of the business, and still finds time to win races. Tullius does, in fact, have an outstanding record in American sports car racing, since he started driving (with a TR3) in 1961, winning four SCCA National Championships in a row from 1962 to 1965 with Triumph production sports cars. He has also driven in Sebring and Daytona long distance racing, and at Le Mans with the Howmet turbine car, and in the Trans-Am saloon car series.

There is no direct equivalent to America's Production sports car racing in Britain, it being mid-way between our own Production racing and Modified Sports car divisions. It is a multi-class formula, divided up according to permance, and B Production was until 1961 the fastest production sports car classification - that year the current A Production class was formed, carrying the really heavy metal with it. In B Production, the V12 E-type contends with such cars as the Ferrari 365 GTB Daytona, the Porsche 911 SC Coupe and Targa, the Shelby 289 Cobra, the Shelby GT 350, the Alfa Montreal, and the AMX sports coupe. But the Jaguar's chief rival is - as it has been for years - the Chevrolet Corvette Stingray, now in V8 5.7 litre form. The Corvette in fact has won 13 of the past 16 national championships in B Production, Allan Barker winning the title four years running with a Stingray being the 1973 champion.

However, it does seem that with the British Leyland sponsored V12 convertibles, "America's only sports car" has met its match, at least in SCCA racing. During the 1974 season the V12s won virtually every race they entered, sometimes lapping the entire field in the process. Indeed, the only comment one can make is that it's a pity, perhaps, that the move to bring the V12 E-type into this sort of competition was not made sooner, as it would appear that it could have made an equally successful debut in say, 1971. This fact rather parallels the delay in producing the lightweight E-type almost ten years earlier, a car which could also have profited by being in action rather sooner that it eventually was. Rather to the dismay of the British Leyland dignitaries watching however, the two V12s failed to win the last round of the 1974 National championships, which was held at Road Atlanta, Georgia on November 3rd. Both Tullius and Mueller were beaten by defending B Production Champion Bill Jobe and his Corvette. Mueller retired with a puncture after an off-course excursion while Tullius was overtaken on the 16th of 18 laps by Jobe, and although the white and green Jaguar set a new class record (at 97.77mph), it could not catch the Corvette, which finished just .8 second in front.

But for a first season try-out, and not a full one at that, the two Jaguars could be said to have acquitted themselves well, and were again campaigned by the same teams in 1975.

While the British Leyland backed V12s took most of the limelight in 1974, it would not come amiss to mention a couple of slightly more amateur efforts at racing the E-type which upheld the marque's name during the 'lean years' leading up to the entry of the BL cars. Peter Schmidt should certainly be mentioned in this context, as 1975 marked more than ten years racing a modified 6-cylinder E-type in the North American Road Racing Championship. His Al Garz tuned car won the 1974 NARRC Championship in fact. Then Jaguar dealers Gran Turismo Jaguar of Eastlake, Ohio, fielded a 6-cylinder E-type in C Production during 1973 and 1974, and by winning at Nelson Ledges in September 1974, gained one of the rare Jaguar wins in National competition with a pre-Series 3 E-type. The driver was Roger Bighouse, who also drove his self-sponsored Formula 5000 racing car that season. There were a number of other E-types which soldiered on too, and it seems that inspite of the retirement from production of the E-type, that car will be around on the race tracks of the world for a good while longer yet.

IN CONCLUSION

It can be said with reasonable confidence that the Jaguar E-type, culminating in the V12 Roadster, was Jaguar's last true sports car - if one defines this as being a strict two-seater with a folding soft-top. It is also a fact that the E-type has become a classic in its own time, as well preserved examples of the early sixties are now emulating the rise in price that was a feature of the XK series a few year ago. The E-type's production run also easily exceeds that of any other Jaguar sports car, including the entire span of XK models from the XK 120 through to the XK 150, and yet the car has still managed to retain much of its exclusivity and emotive appeal.

Nor can it be said that the E-type story ends with a whimper. Quite the contrary in fact, with the 'big cat' unsheathing its racing claws in 1974 to sweep almost all before it in Production sports car racing in the States, and V12 E-type production reaching a climax during the same year. The latter phenomenon is particularly interesting; due to Jaguar's rationalisation of its model line, the injection of extra finance to underwrite greater expansion in production capacity through the resources of British Leyland, and the final overcoming of setbacks caused by the special engineering necessary to meet Federal and State requirements in respect of air pollution and safety, for the first time a customer could order a Jaguar and drive away the same day - or at least, within days or weeks of placing the order instead of months or years as had traditionally been the case. As the *Jaguar Journal* (published in the United States by British Leyland for Jaguar enthusiasts) stated in the summer of 1974: "At last Jaguar dealers have the merchandise and the desired choices of equipment and colour to gain happy customers with the fast open-air V12s". The number of V12 E-types leaving the Coventry factory actually increased by 35% during 1974.

The availability brought about an almost unique situation in the marketing history of Jaguar sports cars - a full advertising and promotion campaign was set in motion to sell the E-type, which included Jaguar television commercials for the first time ever (from April 1974). The same month saw the start of a series of colour advertisements in nearly 20 magazines, depicting the E-type in the beautiful Forest of Arden and carrying headlines such as "Nobody's Pusseycat", and "Prowl Car". There was also a successful tie-up with a famous Fifth Avenue fashion concern, Saks, and its 28 branches throughout the country.

Although the production of the V12 E-type open two seater tailed off in the middle of 1974, the car was kept as a current model until well into 1975, the announcement of its demise not coming from British Leyland's Public Relations Department at Leyland House in Marylebone until 24th February. The car's departure from Jaguar's current model range was indeed the ending of an era which had began in 1935 with the S.S.90, for no direct replacement for the sports car was intended, the XJS being much more 'executive' in its approach than the open E-type.

Fully aware of the classic status which the E-type, particularly the early 3.8 models, had already acquired, Jaguar painted the last 50 right-hand drive roadsters (from chassis number IS 2823) black and gave them chromium plated wheels - a rather uncharacteristicly theatrical flourish this, for a company not traditionally emotional about such things, but then it probably helped sell the last of the old stock! All were painted black that is, except IS 2871 which was ordered in dark green by Jaguar collector Robert Danny of Twickenham, London, who also owns ECD 400, the first E-type to win a race, the first fixed-head E-type, and Dick Protheroe's famous CUT 7, the low-drag coupe experimental E-type. Although Jaguar themselves retained the very last car, IS 2872, body number 4S 8989, for press use and then for display in their Browns Lane exhibition hall, most of the last fifty went overseas, all carrying inscribed dashboard plaques signed by Sir William Lyons identifying them by chassis number. This followed a clearly set precedent as, of course, the majority of E-type production had always been exported - 83% of the E-type's entire production in fact, with the USA taking 49,032, Canada 2,439, and other overseas

countries 8,793. Just 12,320 remained in Great Britain, this figure embracing all types from the original 3.8 model up to the Series 3 cars.

The writer remembers the last black E-type well, as on behalf of *Thoroughbred & Classic Cars* he borrowed IS 2872 to conduct an interesting side-by-side comparison with an early 3.8 'Series 1' roadster. Many people had maintained that the original E-type was the best ever in most respects - we decided to put it to the test.

Interest was added to the experiment by an 3.8 XK 150S open two seater - like the 3.8 E-type, a low mileage mint example - which was representative of the last body-and-chassis Jaguar sports car. This was fast, spacious, rattle free and generally very pleasant to drive, but the altogether more modern feel of the early E-type showed what a great advance Jaguar's new 1961 sports car was. In fact, it was this general up-to-dateness of our resampled 3.8 E-type that was undoubtedly the biggest surprise of the exercise, together with the fact that the early car appeared to ride better than its V12 successor, was slightly quieter (apart from gearbox whine in the lower ratios), and didn't seem to lose anything on cornering. While we expected the 3.8's straight-line performance to be much the same as the V12 (which it was), we had anticipated that the later E-type would have scored in the ride and quietness departments, due to additional development by Jaguar's engineers.

This was not to say that the Series 3 E-type was particularly old-fashioned for a 1975 open two seater, but rather, it emphasised what a truly incredible car the E-type must have seemed when it first burst upon the motoring scene in 1961. The early road-tests were not rapturous without good cause!

So, with the E-type both in 6-cylinder and V12 forms acknowledged as true classics, and with both types still victorious on the race track, the story of the Jaguar roadsters ends on very much a high note - and one that was sustained for forty years.

THE XJ-S

Whether or not the XJ-S can be considered a sports car in the traditional sense of the term, it is indisputably a Jaguar and - like its predecessors - took the company on another big step forward. It is quieter, better riding and faster than virtually any of its rivals, and cheaper too even though it is by far the most expensive car ever to have left Jaguar's production lines.

The XJ-S did not adopt the 'mid-engine' positioning of the power unit which had such a vogue during the early seventies, and in fact this configuration was never seriously considered by Jaguar for a road car - the nearest that the factory got to such a vehicle was by way of a few styling drawings which Malcolm Sayer sketched out in the sixties. Jaguar knew that the benefits in handling qualities accorded by a mid-engine layout are virtually non-existent off the race track compared to a good front-engined design, while the sacrifices in space and silence are apt to be great. Also, it is more difficult to make a mid-engined car meet front crushing tests as the bulk of the engine is not there to absorb or deflect some of the impact.

Perhaps the most significant thing about the XJ-S is the market at which it is aimed - the broad formula of a closed 2-plus-2 based on XJ 5.3 mechanicals was expected, but not, perhaps, Jaguar's attack on the 'exotic' section of the market, which previously had not received all that much interest from the Coventry firm. But with the XJ-S, it was plainly Jaguar's resolve to pursue the type of person who might equally well buy a Ferrari Dino 308 or a Lamborghini. Additionally, in these times of increasing legislation effecting performance and reducing speed limits in most countries of the world, it was possibly surprising that Jaguar heralded the new car with a '150mph' headline.

However, aside from the company's marketing tactics, the XJ-S is a highly interesting car, not the least because it is the last sporting Jaguar to have its basic character and looks moulded by Sir William Lyons and the late Malcolm Sayer. These, in fact, had largely been decided upon by or before 1970, some five or six years before the car was publicly launched in September 1975.

Needless to say the car's looks are totally 'Jaguar'. Wheelbase is some 7 inches shorter than that of the original XJ6 saloon, to whose internal structure the basic monocoque of the XJ-S is related, and the new car's suspension follows the pattern set by the XJ saloon series at both front and rear. The bodyshell itself exceeds all the current and anticipated safety requirements both for Europe and the United States; side intrusion barriers are built into the two (very wide) doors, while the 5mph impact bumpers are an innovation this side of the Atlantic. These use Menasco struts which operate something like telescopic shock absorbers, although a special silicone wax forms the hydraulic medium - this is forced past the piston inside the strut when the bumper meets an obstruction, and its special properties absorb the energy created. After the collision, the strut is forced back to its original position as the wax slowly returns (this takes up to 30 minutes).

The rear suspension of the XJ-S is that developed originally for the E-type of 1961, and gradually refined and improved on the Series 3 E-type and the various XJ saloons; thus the drive shafts still act as upper links, and twin coil spring damper units are featured. With the XJ-S's sporting potential in mind, Jaguar's engineers paid particular attention to the car's total roll stiffness and its distribution front and rear - this resulted in the fitting of a new rear anti-roll bar and an up-rated front one; also, springing/damping relationships, and damper force/velocity interactions were examined closely, so that the whole suspension 'package' resulted in a ride that was probably superior even to that of an XJ saloon, and handling that would be approved of even by the fastest of drivers. Power steering was retained, but at last Jaguar took note of the body of opinion which had for long complained that the effort needed at the wheel was too light for totally confident control under fast driving conditions; so for the XJ-S, steering response was quickened through the use of an 8-tooth pinion which had the effect of reducing the overall ratio. Tyres were specially developed for the car by Dunlop, and are fitted to the Kent Alloy aluminium wheels which had previously been offered as 'extras' on the XJ 5.3 saloons.

The front suspension includes the anti-dive geometry of the XJ saloons, and carries 11.18 inch diameter ventilated cast iron discs with four piston calipers. The rear brakes are inboard mounted of course, the discs being 10.3 inches in diameter and gripped by 3-piston calipers. A Girling in-line tandem servo mounted on the brake pedal box supplies the assistance, using vacuum assistance from a vacuum reservoir tank positioned under the front wing; the hydraulic brake circuit itself is split, with a pressure differential warning actuator shutting off one circuit should there be a failure somewhere. The braking potential of the XJ-S is such that it can be accelerated up to 100mph and braked to a standstill, all in just over 20 seconds.

Needless to say, the only engine offered in the XJ-S is Jaguar's 5343cc V12, and fuel injection is standardised. This injection system is that first seen on the XJ 5.3 saloon and coupe earlier in 1975, and it stems from an original Bendix design which was further developed by Bosch, and adapted for the Coventry product by Lucas and Jaguar. The main reason for dispensing with carburetters was fuel economy, and, indeed, Jaguar originally wanted to use fuel injection on the V12 as already related. The XJ-S engine is rated at 285 bhp DIN at 5,500 rpm, with torque of 294 lbs ft at 3,500 rpm; this is some 30 bhp more than the full emission carburetted V12 engine gave. Its increased efficiency certainly endowed the new car with an overall petrol consumption of nearer 16 - 17mpg rather than the 10 - 13mpg of the original XJ12, or the V12 E-type's 12 - 15mpg. Much work was done to reduce noise in and around the engine bay, which itself was designed to deflect sound waves away from the passenger compartment. Even the wiring which passed through the bulkhead did so via multi-pin plug and socket units, so avoiding holes in the bulkhead through which noise might have been transmitted.

Inside the car, noise suppression was carried out through anti-vibration pads on the floors, door panels, rear seat pan, and through moulded rubber-backed undercarpet mats tailored to fit exactly over the front footwells, bulkhead and transmission tunnel. Felt-backed carpet is used on the floor and on the lower door panels; all the luggage compartment is trimmed in carpet too, and there is a layer of sound insulation sandwiched between the petrol tank and rear seat bulkhead.

Instrumentation in this Jaguar is something of a departure, as the fuel, water temperature, oil pressure and battery condition gauges are a new type of vertically reading indicator, worked by a variation in a magnetic field between three opposing coils; greater accuracy is one of the claimed advantages of this type. All the instruments, including the big speedometer and rev counter, are contained in a binacle together with a battery of no less than 18 warning lights along the top. These monitor safety and mechanical functions, a red light indicating major faults and an amber one covering secondary faults like a side-light failure.

Air conditioning is standard for the XJ-S, and uses the Delanair/Jaguar system already seen in the Series 2 XJ saloons. Operation is simple and extremely effective. New seats add further to comfort, and they are notable in that they are of a new design with the seat cushion made up of two separate parts, centre and outer. The centre section 'gives' under the weight of the occupant while the outer 'ring' provides firm lateral location. Inertia reel seatbelts (the reels are hidden behind trim panels) are standard equipment in front and are also available for the rear seats too. Electrically operated windows and centre door locking are two other standard fitments, and there are five interior lights - one at each end of the facia, one above the driving mirror, and two behind the rear passengers.

Either manual or automatic transmission can be specified, the former box being Jaguar's all-synchro four-speed item used since the 4.2 E-type of 1964. The automatic gearbox is the Borg Warner three-speed Model 12; both versions drive a 3.07:1 rear axle ratio.

A less spectacular but extremely useful improvement over previous Jaguar sporting machinery is the size of the XJ-S's boot, which really has little less capacity than the saloons'. This is besides acting as a storage area for the battery, 20 gallon fuel tank, fuel pump and spare wheel - all out of sight apart from the spare wheel, which has a shaped cover over it. The boot has even been given flap-valves which allows fresh air to circulate and so prevent staleness!

In looks, the XJ-S bears little resemblance to any other Jaguar (although maybe there is something of the XJ saloon in its wheel to bodyline relationship, and in the way it sits squarely on the road). Its general shape was dictated to an extent by Malcolm Sayer's wind tunnel experiments on full-size prototypes at MIRA - it was decided from the outset that the car would not sacrifice aerodynamics for fashion when it came to looks. The car has a spoiler fitted to the front underneath the 'safety' bumpers (standard on all XJ-Ss) and an under-shield below the engine; these two items brought about a dramatic reduction (about 50%) in the car's tendency to lift at high speed, and reduced drag by around 10%. The spoiler was also found to reduce aerodynamic side pressures and to move the centre of pressure further back, which improved stability even further.

Sir William certainly worked closely with Sayer to produce the final main body design; of this collaboration he says:

"We decided from the very first that aerodynamics were the prime concern, and I exerted my influence in a consultative capacity with Malcolm Sayer. Occasionally I saw a feature that I did not agree with and we would discuss it.

"I took my influence as far as I could without interfering with his basic aerodynamic requirements, and he and I worked on the first styling models together. We originally considered a lower bonnet line, but the international regulations on crush control and lighting made us change and we started afresh."

To start with at least, the XJ-S is to be even more exclusive than most new Jaguars are. Although a new 2,000 foot assembly track has been put in for the car, alongside the two lines for the XJ saloons and coupes, and new tooling and press shop equipment installed at British Leyland's Castle Bromwich plant where the bodies are made, only about 60 cars a week are leaving the Browns Lane factory at the time of writing (1975). An eventual total of some 150 cars a week will be achieved however, though it seems certain that a long waiting list for the XJ-S will continue in existence for some time, even in the United States where most of the production is (as ever) scheduled to go.

On the road, the XJ-S is a superb machine. Imagine if you can a car that is perhaps quieter than an XJ 5.3 saloon, considerably faster, with an equally good ride and an additional measure of manoeuverability and fineness of control - that is the XJ-S. Its roadholding is such that its true limits will rarely be reached on closed roads even during very fast driving by an experienced driver, while its ability to cruise at three-figure speeds and in near-total silence matches or exceeds that of every other high-performance car in the world.

While one cannot pretend that the XJ-S is a sports car in the true wind-in-the-hair tradition of the SS 100, XK 120 and E-type Roadsters, as a sporting vehicle to take Jaguar into the 1980s it does not seem as if the XJ-S could be bettered. On the whole, I think that the SS 100 driver of 1936 would totally approve!

Appendix One
Specifications and performance data

SS AND JAGUAR SPORTS CARS 1935 - 1975

NOTES

Only production cars are included in this Appendix. Power outputs are gross and as quoted by the manufacturer; taken under special conditions on the test bench, they should be considered as a comparative guide only and not as an indication of net installed brake horse-power.

Those models which were never independently tested when new, or for which no reliable contemporary performance figures are available, are combined with the nearest similar model for which such data does exist. Where specifications differ, alternative figures will be found in brackets. In this way, it will be found that virtually every model and state of tune has been covered.

As all Jaguar top gears are 'direct', standard final drive ratios are as for the 4th gear ratio. Alternative final drive ratios are noted where applicable.
Prices: these are inclusive of British tax and as quoted at the time of the car's magazine road test from which the performance figures have been taken.

S.S.90

ENGINE

Cubic capacity	2663 cc
Bore and stroke	73 mm x 106 mm
Max. power	70 bhp (approx)
Max. torque	*Not available*
Compression ratio	7 : 1
Cylinder head	Modified Standard 'Six', light alloy casting (side valve)
Carburettors	2 R.A.G.

CHASSIS

Weight and front/rear distribution:			22½ cwt (approx)
Dimensions:	*Wheelbase*		8 feet 8 inches
	Track	*- Front*	4 feet 6 inches
		Rear	4 feet 6 inches
	Length		12 feet 6 inches
	Width		5 feet 3 inches
	Height		4 feet 6 inches (to top of windscreen)
Suspension:	*Front*		Beam axle, flat half-elliptic springs
	Rear		Live axle, flat half elliptic springs
Brakes			Bendix duo-servo, cable operated
Gearing			1st - 15.3 : 1
			2nd - 8.98 : 1
			3rd - 5.83 : 1
			4th - 4.25 : 1 Alternative axle ratio: 3.75 : 1
Tyres and wheels			5.50 x 18 Dunlop tyres on 18 inch knock-off wire wheels

PERFORMANCE

Contemporary data not available but estimated as follows:

0 - 60 mph	17 secs
Standing ¼-mile	20.5 secs
Top speed	89 mph
Overall fuel consumption	19 mpg

PRICE

£395 (GB)

SS 100 2½ litre

ENGINE

Cubic capacity	2663 cc
Bore and stroke	73 mm x 106 mm
Max. power	102 bhp @ 4600 rpm
Max. torque	Not available
Compression ratio	7 : 1
Cylinder head	Weslake ohv, in cast iron
Carburettors	2 1½ inch SU

CHASSIS

Weight and front/rear distribution			23 cwt
Dimensions:	*Wheelbase*		8 feet 8 inches
	Track	*- Front*	4 feet 6 inches
		Rear	4 feet 6 inches
	Length		12 feet 6 inches
	Width		5 feet 3 inches
	Height		4 feet 6 inches (to top of windscreen)
Suspension:	*Front*		Beam axle, half-elliptic springs
	Rear		Live axle, half elliptic springs
Brakes			Girling rod-operated, finned drums
Gearing			1st - 13.6 : 1
			2nd - 6.45 : 1
			3rd - 5.50 : 1
			4th - 4.00 : 1
Tyres and wheels			5.50 or 5.25 x 18 inch on 18 inch knock-off wire wheels

PERFORMANCE
(The Motor, 25.5.37)

Standing start		Top gear acceleration		
0 - 50 mph	8.8 secs	*10 - 30 mph*	8.5 secs
0 - 60	12.8	*20 - 40*	9.0
Standing ¼-mile	18.6 secs	*30 - 50*	10.0
Top speed	94 mph	*40 - 60*	11.5
		50 - 70	13.5

Overall fuel consumption	20 mpg

PRICE

£395 (GB)

SS 100 3½ litre

ENGINE

Cubic capacity	3485 cc
Bore and stroke	82 mm x 110 mm
Max. power	125 bhp @ 4250 rpm
Max. torque	Not available
Compression ratio	7 : 1
Cylinder head	Weslake ohv in cast iron
Carburettors	2 1½ inch SU

CHASSIS

Weight and front/rear distribution			23¼ cwt
Dimensions:	*Wheelbase*		8 feet 8 inches
	Track	*- Front*	4 feet 4½ inches
		Rear	4 feet 6 inches
	Length		12 feet 9 inches
	Width		5 feet 3 inches
	Height		4 feet 6 inches (to top of windscreen)
Suspension:	*Front*		Beam axle, flat half-elliptic springs
	Rear		Live axle, flat half-elliptic springs
Brakes			Girling rod-operated, finned drums
Gearing			1st - 12.04 : 1
			2nd - 7.06 : 1
			3rd - 4.58 : 1
			4th - 3.80 : 1
Tyres and wheels			5.50 or 5.25 x 18 inch on 18 inch knock-off wire wheels

PERFORMANCE
(The Motor, 12.7.38)

Standing start			*Top gear acceleration*		
0 - 30 mph	3.2 secs		*10 - 30 mph*		8.7 secs
0 - 50	7.1		*20 - 40*		7.0
0 - 60	10.9		*30 - 50*		7.3
0 - 70	15.4		*40 - 60*		8.5
Standing ¼-mile	17.1		*10 - 70*		23.6
Top speed	101 mph		*10 - 80*		29.3
Overall fuel consumption	21 mpg				

PRICE

£445 (GB)

XK 120 Open Two Seater

ENGINE

Cubic capacity	3442 cc
Bore and stroke	83 mm x 106 mm
Max. power	160 bhp at 5000 rpm (standard)
	180 bhp at 5300 rpm (Special Equipment)
Max. torque	195 lb ft at 2500 rpm (standard)
	203 lb ft at 4000 rpm (special equipment)
Compression ratio	8 : 1 (7 : 1 or 9 : 1 optional)
Cylinder head	'A-type', alloy twin ohc
Carburettors	2 1¾ inch SU

CHASSIS

Weight and front/rear distribution			25½ cwt alloy car, 26 cwt steel car (48/52)
Dimensions:	*Wheelbase*		8 feet 6 inches
	Track -	*Front*	4 feet 3 inches
		Rear	4 feet 2 inches
	Length		14 feet 6 inches
	Width		5 feet 1½ inches
	Height		4 feet 4½ inches
Suspension:	*Front*		Ind. wish-bone, torsion bar, anti-roll bar
	Rear		Live axle, semi-elliptic leaf springs
Brakes			Drum, Lockheed hydraulic, two leading shoe front, leading and trailing rear
Gearing			1st - 12.29 : 1
			2nd - 7.22 : 1
			3rd - 4.98 : 1
			4th - 3.64 : 1 (ENV axled cars; alternative ENV ratios were 3.27, 3.92 and 4.30. Salisbury axle range was 4.09, 3.77, 3.54 and 3.27)
Tyres and wheels			6.00 x 16 inch on 16 inch x 5K solid wheels (later 5½K); 16 inch x 5K wire wheels optional from March 1951 Chromium plated wire wheels optional from 1953

PERFORMANCE
(Standard version,
The Motor, 16.11.49)
3.64 : 1 final drive

Standing start			Top gear acceleration		
0 - 30 mph	3.2 secs		10 - 30 mph	6.7 secs
0 - 40	5.1		20 - 40	6.7
0 - 50	7.3		30 - 50	6.6
0 - 60	10.0		40 - 60	7.4
0 - 70	12.4		50 - 70	8.1
0 - 80	15.7		60 - 80	8.5
0 - 90	20.1		70 - 90	9.9
0 - 100	27.3		80 - 100	11.3
Standing ¼-mile	17.0 secs			
Top speed	124.6 mph			

Overall fuel consumption   19.8 mpg

PRICE

£1263 (GB)

XK 120 Fixed-head Coupe

ENGINE

Cubic capacity	3442 cc
Bore and stroke	83 mm x 106 mm
Max. power	160 bhp @ 5000 rpm (standard)
	180 bhp @ 5300 rpm (special equipment)
Max. torque	195 lb ft @ 2500 rpm (standard)
	203 lb ft @ 4000 rpm (special equipment)
Compression ratio	8 : 1 (7 : 1 or 9 : 1 optional)
Cylinder head	'A-type', alloy twin ohc
Carburettors	2 1¾ inch SU

CHASSIS

Weight and front/rear distribution		27 cwt (47.5/52.5)
Dimensions:	*Wheelbase*	8 feet 6 inches
	Track - Front	4 feet 3 inches
	Rear	4 feet 2 inches
	Length	14 feet 5 inches
	Width	5 feet 2 inches
	Height	4 feet 5½ inches
Suspension:	*Front*	Ind. wishbone, torsion bar, anti-roll bar
	Rear	Live axle, semi-elliptic leaf springs
Brakes		Drum, Lockheed hydraulic, two leading shoe front, leading and trailing rear
Gearing		1st - 12.73 : 1
		2nd - 7.48 : 1
		3rd - 5.61 : 1
		4th - 3.77 : 1 (Alternative ratios as for open two seater)
Tyres and wheels		6.00 x 16, wheels as for open two seater

PERFORMANCE

(Special Equipment Model, The Autocar, 17.11.52)
3.77 final drive

Standing start			Top gear acceleration		
0 - 30 mph	3.3 secs		10 - 30 mph	7.9 secs
0 - 50	7.5		20 - 40	7.7
0 - 60	9.9		30 - 50	7.3
0 - 70	13.7		40 - 60	7.4
0 - 80	17.1		50 - 70	7.9
0 - 90	22.1		60 - 80	8.1
0 - 100	28.2		70 - 90	9.3
Standing ¼-mile	17.3 secs		80 - 100	10.9
Top speed	120.5 mph			

Overall fuel consumption 17.2 mpg

PRICE

£1,694 (GB)

XK 120 Drop-head Coupe

ENGINE

Cubic capacity	3442 cc
Bore and stroke	83 mm x 106 mm
Max. power	190 bhp at 5500 rpm (standard)
	210 bhp at 5750 (special equipment)
Max. torque	210 ft lbs at 2500 rpm (standard)
	213 ft lbs at 4000 rpm (special equipment)
Compression ratio	8 : 1 (7 : 1 and 9 : 1 optional)
Carburettors	2 1¾ inch SU

CHASSIS

Weight and front/rear distribution			27½ cwt
Dimensions:	*Wheelbase*		8 feet 6 inches
	Track -	*Front*	4 feet 3 inches
		Rear	4 feet 2 inches
	Length		14 feet 5 inches
	Width		5 feet 1½ inches
	Height		
Suspension:	*Front*		Ind. wishbone, torsion bar, anti-roll bar
	Rear		Live axle, semi-elliptic leaf springs
Brakes			Drum, Lockheed hydraulic, two leading shoe front, leading and trailing rear
Gearing			1st - 11.95 : 1
			2nd - 7.01 : 1
			3rd - 4.84 : 1
			4th - 3.54 : 1 (Alternative Salisbury ratios as for open two seater)
Tyres and wheels			6.00 x 16 inch; wheels as for open two seater

PERFORMANCE

(Standard version Autosport, 14.5.54) 3.54 final drive	*Standing start*	
	0 - 30 mph	3.5 secs
	0 - 40	5.3
	0 - 50	7.1
	0 - 60	9.5
	0 - 70	12.5
	0 - 80	16.9
	0 - 90	23.3
	0 - 100	31.0
	0 - 110	40.9
	Standing ¼-mile	17.5 secs
	Top speed	119.5 mph
Overall fuel consumption		14.5 mpg

PRICE

£1,616 (GB)

XK 140 Open Two Seater

ENGINE

Cubic capacity	3442 cc
Bore and stroke	83 mm x 106 mm
Max. power	190 bhp at 5500 rpm (standard)
	210 bhp at 5750 (special equipment)
Max. torque	210 ft lbs at 2500 rpm (standard)
	213 ft lbs at 4000 rpm (special equipment)
Compression ratio	8 : 1 (7 : 1 and 9 : 1 optional)
Carburettors	2 1¾ inch SU

CHASSIS

Weight and front/rear distribution			28 cwt (49.6/50.4)
Dimensions:	*Wheelbase*		8 feet 6 inches
	Track	- *Front*	4 feet 3½ inches
		Rear	4 feet 3 3/8 inches
	Length		14 feet 8 inches
	Width		5 feet 4½ inches
	Height		4 feet 4½ inches
Suspension:	*Front*		Ind. wishbone, torsion bars, anti-roll bar
	Rear		Live axle, semi-elliptic leaf springs
Brakes			Drum, Lockheed hydraulic, two leading shoe front, leading and trailing rear
Gearing			1st - 11.95 : 1
			2nd - 7.01 : 1
			3rd - 4.83 : 1
			4th - 3.54 : 1 Overdrive 3.19 : 1 optional. Alternative final drive ratios: 4.09, 3.77, and 3.27
Tyres and wheels			6.00 x 16 inch, on either 16 inch x 5½K solid wheels or 16 inch x 5K (special equipment) wire wheels

PERFORMANCE

(Special Equipment model, Road & Track, 1955)

	Standing start	
	0 - 30 mph	2.7 secs
	0 - 40	4.2
	0 - 50	6.5
	0 - 60	8.4
	0 - 70	12.1
	0 - 80	15.7
	0 - 100	26.5
	Standing ¼-mile	16.6 mph
	Top speed	121.1 mph
Overall fuel consumption		16 - 18 mpg

PRICE

£1,598 (GB)

XK 140 Fixed-head and Drop-head Coupe

ENGINE

Cubic capacity	3442 cc
Bore and stroke	83 mm x 106 mm
Max. power	190 bhp at 5500 rpm (standard)
	210 bhp at 5750 (special equipment)
Max. torque	210 ft lbs at 2500 rpm (standard)
	213 ft lbs at 4000 rpm (special equipment)
Compression ratio	8 : 1 (7 : 1 and 9 : 1 optional)
Carburettors	2 1¾ inch SU

CHASSIS

Weight and front/rear distribution			28 cwt (50.3/49.7) (Drop-head coupe plus 1 cwt)
Dimensions:	*Wheelbase*		8 feet 6 inches
	Track -	*Front*	4 feet 3½ inches
		Rear	4 feet 3 3/8 inches
	Length		14 feet 8 inches
	Width		5 feet 4½ inches
	Height		4 feet 7 inches
Suspension:	*Front*		Ind. wishbone, torsion bar, anti-roll bar
	Rear		Live axle, semi-elliptic leaf springs
Brakes			Drum, Lockheed hydraulic, two leading shoe front, leading and trailing rear
Gearing			1st - 11.95 : 1
			2nd - 7.01 : 1
			3rd - 4.83 : 1
			4th - 3.54 : 1 Overdrive 3.19 : 1 optional. Alternative final drive ratios: 4.09, 3.77 and 3.27
Tyres and wheels			6.00 x 16 inch, on either 16 inch x 5½K solid wheels or 16 inch x 5K (special equipment) wire wheels

PERFORMANCE

(Fixed-head coupe, Special Equipment model with overdrive, The Autocar, 9.12.55)

Standing start		Top gear (direct) acceleration	
0 - 30 mph	3.2 secs	10 - 30 mph	7.9 secs
0 - 50	7.5	20 - 40	7.5
0 - 60	11.0	30 - 50	7.4
0 - 70	14.2	40 - 60	7.7
0 - 80	16.9	50 - 70	8.3
0 - 90	22.7	60 - 80	9.4
0 - 100	29.5	80 - 100	11.5
0 - 110	37.7		
Standing ¼-mile	17.4 secs		
Top speed	129.25 mph		

Overall fuel consumption   21.7 mpg

PRICE

£1830 (GB), SE fixed-head

XK 150 3.4 Fixed-head and Drop-head Coupe

ENGINE

Cubic capacity	3442 cc
Bore and stroke	83 mm x 106 mm
Max. power	190 bhp at 5500 rpm (standard)
	210 bhp at 5500 rpm (special equipment)
Max. torque	210 lbs ft at 2500 rpm (standard)
	216 lbs ft at 3000 rpm (special equipment)
Compression ratio	8 : 1 (7 : 1 and 9 : 1 optional)
Cylinder head	Uprated 'A-type' (Standard)
	C-type (special equipment)
Carburettors	2 1¾ inch SU

CHASSIS

Weight and front/rear distribution			28¾ cwt (52/43) (Drop-head coupe, add 300 lbs)
Dimensions:	*Wheelbase*		8 feet 6 inches
	Track	- *Front*	4 feet 3¼ inches
		Rear	4 feet 3¼ inches
	Length		14 feet 9 inches
	Width		5 feet 4½ inches
	Height		4 feet 7 inches
Suspension:	*Front*		Ind. wish-bones, torsion bars, anti-roll bar
	Rear		Live axle, semi-elliptic leaf springs

Gearing

1st	-	12.18 : 1
2nd	-	7.16 : 1 O/D ratios Note: non-overdrive cars
3rd	-	4.95 : 1 fitted with 3.54 final drive
4th	-	4.09 : 1 ratio (alternative final
O/D	-	3.18 : 1 drive ratios as for XK 140)

Tyres and wheels   6.00 x 16 inch, on 16 inch x 5K wire wheels, or 16 inch x 5½K solid wheels (basic models)

PERFORMANCE

(Special Equipment fixed-head with overdrive, The Autocar, 21.2.58)

Standing start		Top gear (direct) acceleration		
0 - 30 mph	2.8 secs	10 - 30 mph	7.4 secs
0 - 50	6.5	20 - 40	6.4
0 - 60	8.5	30 - 50	6.2
0 - 70	11.4	40 - 60	6.3
0 - 80	15.0	50 - 70	6.5
0 - 90	19.5	60 - 80	7.1
0 - 100	25.1	70 - 90	8.0
0 - 110	33.5	80 - 100	10.2
Standing ¼-mile	16.9 secs	90 - 110	13.8
Top speed	123.7 mph		

Overall fuel consumption   20.5 mpg

PRICE

£1,939 (GB) SE fixed-head

XK 150S 3.4 Fixed-head and Drop-head Coupe

ENGINE

Cubic capacity	3442 cc
Bore and stroke	83 mm x 106 mm
Max. power	250 bhp @ 5500 rpm
Max. torque	240 lb ft @ 4500 rpm
Compression ratio	9 : 1 (8 : 1 optional)
Cylinder head	Straight port
Carburettors	3 2 inch SU HD 8

CHASSIS

Weight and front/rear distribution			29 cwt (50.5/49.5) (Drop-head coupe, add 300 lbs)
Dimensions:	*Wheelbase*		8 feet 6 inches
	Track - *Front*		4 feet 3¼ inches
	Rear		4 feet 3¼ inches
	Length		14 feet 9 inches
	Width		5 feet 4½ inches
	Height		4 feet 7 inches
Suspension:	*Front*		Ind. wishbone, torsion bar, anti-roll bar
	Rear		Live axle, semi-elliptic leaf spring
Brakes			Dunlop discs, vacuum servo

Gearing

1st - 13.81 : 1 ⎤
2nd - 7.60 : 1   ⎮
3rd - 5.25 : 1   ⎬ O/D ratios   Alternative final drive ratios
4th - 4.09 : 1   ⎮   as for XK 140
O/D - 3.18 : 1   ⎦

Tyres and wheels   Dunlop Road Speed 6.00 x 16 inch, on 16 inch x 5K wire wheels

PERFORMANCE

(The Motor, 19.8.59)

Standing start		Top gear (direct) acceleration	
0 - 30 mph	2.9 secs	*10 - 30 mph*	6.4 secs
0 - 40	4.5	*20 - 40*	6.4
0 - 50	6.1	*30 - 50*	6.1
0 - 60	7.8	*40 - 60*	6.3
0 - 70	10.6	*50 - 70*	6.7
0 - 80	13.2	*60 - 80*	6.3
0 - 90	16.5	*70 - 90*	6.5
0 - 100	20.3	*80 - 100*	7.4
0 - 110	25.6	*90 - 110*	9.1
0 - 120	36.2		
Standing ¼-mile	16.2 secs		
Top speed	132 mph		

Overall fuel consumption   18.6 mpg

PRICE

£2,110 (with overdrive) (GB)

XK 150S 3.4 Open Two Seater

ENGINE

Cubic capacity	3442 cc
Bore and stroke	83 mm x 106 mm
Max. power	250 bhp @ 5500 rpm ⎤ Standard and B-type head versions as
Max. torque	240 lb ft @ 4500 rpm ⎦ for XK 150 3.4 fixed head
Compression ratio	9 : 1
Cylinder head	Straight port
Carburettors	3 2 inch SU HD8

CHASSIS

Weight and front/rear distribution			28.2 cwt (49/51)
Dimensions:	*Wheelbase*		8 feet 6 inches
	Track	*- Front*	4 feet 3¼ inches
		Rear	4 feet 3¼ inches
	Length		14 feet 9 inches
	Width		5 feet 4½ inches
	Height		4 feet 6 inches
Suspension:	*Front*		Ind. wishbone, torsion bars, anti-roll bar
	Rear		Live axle, semi-elliptic leaf springs
Brakes			Dunlop discs, hydraulic vacuum servo
Gearing			1st - 12.2 : 1 ⎤
			2nd - 7.11 : 1 ⎟ O/D
			3rd - 4.94 : 1 ⎬ ratios
			4th - 4.09 : 1 ⎟
			O/D - 3.19 : 1 ⎦ Alternative final drive ratios as for XK 140
Tyres and wheels			6.00 x 16 inch on 16 inch x 5K wire wheels

PERFORMANCE

(Road & Track, 1958)	*Standing start*	
	0 - 30 mph	2.5 secs
	0 - 40	4.0
	0 - 50	5.6
	0 - 60	7.3
	0 - 70	10.0
	0 - 80	13.0
	0 - 100	21.4
	Standing ¼-mile	15.1 secs
	Top speed	136 mph
Overall fuel consumption		14 - 19 mpg

PRICE

$5150 (USA)

XK 150 3.8 and XK 150S 3.8 Fixed-head and Drop-head Coupe

ENGINE

Cubic capacity	3781 cc
Bore and stroke	87 mm x 106 mm
Max. power	220 bhp at 5500 rpm (standard)
	265 bhp at 5500 rpm ('S' version)
Max. torque	240 ft lbs at 3000 rpm (standard)
	260 ft lbs at 4000 rpm ('S' version)
Compression ratio	9 : 1 (8 : 1 optional)
Cylinder head	B-type (standard)
	Straight port ('S' version)
Carburettors	2 1¾ inch SU (standard)
	3 3 inch SU ('S' version)

CHASSIS

Weight and front/rear distribution			29 cwt (50.5/49.5) (Drop-head coupe, add 300 lbs)
Dimensions:	Wheelbase		8 feet 6 inches
	Track -	Front	4 feet 3¼ inches
		Rear	4 feet 3¼ inches
	Length		14 feet 9 inches
	Width		5 feet 4½ inches
	Height		4 feet 7 inches
Suspension:	Front		Ind. wishbone torsion bars, anti-roll bar
	Rear		Live axle, semi-elliptic leaf spring
Brakes			Dunlop disc, hydraulic, vacuum servo

Gearing

1st -	12.2 : 1		Note: standard 3.8 non-overdrive cars fitted with 3.54 final drive ratio. Alternative ratios as for XK 140
2nd -	7.16 : 1		
3rd -	4.95 : 1	O/D ratios	
4th -	4.09 : 1		
O/D -	3.19 : 1		

Tyres and wheels — 6.00 x 16 inch on 16 inch x 5K wire wheels, or 16 inch x 5½K solid wheels (standard version)

PERFORMANCE

(3.8S fixed-head, Autosport, 17.6.60)

Standing start	
0 - 30 mph	3.4 secs
0 - 50	6.2
0 - 60	7.6
0 - 80	12.8
0 - 100	19.0
0 - 110	22.2
0 - 120	27.8
Standing ¼—mile	16.0 secs
Top speed	136.3 mph

Overall fuel consumption — 13 mpg (hard driving)

PRICE

£2,065 (GB) 3.8S Fixed-head

E-Type 'Series 1' 3.8 Open Two Seater

ENGINE

Cubic capacity	3781 cc
Bore and stroke	87 mm x 106 mm
Max. power	265 bhp (gross) at 5500 rpm
Max. torque	260 lb ft @ 4000 rpm
Compression ratio	9 : 1 (8 : 1 optional)
Cylinder head	Straight port
Carburettors	3 2 inch SU HD8

CHASSIS

Weight and front/rear distribution			24 cwt (51/49)
Dimensions:	Wheelbase		8 feet
	Track	- Front	4 feet 2 inches
		Rear	4 feet 2 inches
	Length		14 feet 7½ inches
	Width		5 feet 4¼ inches
	Height		3 feet 11 inches (hood up)
Suspension:	Front		Ind. wishbone, torsion bars, anti-roll bar
	Rear		Ind. lower wishbone, upper driveshaft link, radius arms, coil springs, anti-roll bar
Brakes			Dunlop discs, vacuum servo
Gearing			1st - 11.18 : 1
			2nd - 6.16 : 1
			3rd - 4.25 : 1
			4th - 3.31 : 1 Alternative final drive ratios: 4.09, 3.77, 3.07 and 3.27
Tyres and wheels			Dunlop 6.40 x 15 RS5 (racing tyres optional) on 15 inch x 5K wire wheels (rear 5½K wheels supplied with racing tyres)

PERFORMANCE
(The Motor, 22.3.61)

Standing start			*Top gear acceleration*		
0 - 30 mph	2.6 secs		10 - 30 mph	5.6 secs
0 - 40	3.8		20 - 40	5.6
0 - 50	5.6		30 - 50	5.4
0 - 60	7.1		40 - 60	5.4
0 - 70	8.7		50 - 70	5.3
0 - 80	11.1		60 - 80	5.0
0 - 90	13.4		70 - 90	5.2
0 - 100	15.9		80 - 100	5.7
0 - 110	19.9		90 - 110	6.6
0 - 120	24.2		100 - 120	7.7
0 - 130	30.5		110 - 130	10.4
0 - 140	39.3		120 - 140	15.1
Standing ¼-mile	15.0 secs			
Top speed	149.1 mph			

Overall fuel consumption   19.7 mpg

PRICE

£2,098 (GB)

E-Type 'Series 1' 3.8 Fixed-head Coupe

ENGINE

Cubic capacity	3781 cc
Bore and stroke	87 mm x 107 mm
Max. power	265 bhp (gross) @ 5500 rpm
Max. torque	260 lb ft @ 4000 rpm
Compression ratio	9 : 1 (8 : 1 optional)
Cylinder head	Straight port
Carburettors	3 2 inch SU HD8

CHASSIS

Weight and front/rear distribution			24.1 cwt (49.6/50.4)
Dimensions:	*Wheelbase*		8 feet
	Track	*- Front*	4 feet 2 inches
		Rear	4 feet 2 inches
	Length		14 feet 7.3 inches
	Width		5 feet 5.2 inches
	Height		4 feet
Suspension:	*Front*		Ind. wishbone, torsion bars, anti-roll bar
	Rear		Ind. lower wishbone, upper driveshaft link, radius arms, coil springs, anti-roll bar
Brakes			Dunlop discs, vacuum servo
Gearing			1st - 11.18 : 1
			2nd - 6.16 : 1
			3rd - 4.25 : 1
			4th - 3.31 : 1 Alternative final drive ratios as for **open two-seater**
Tyres and wheels			Dunlop 6.40 x 15 RS5 (racing tyres optional); **wheels as for** open two seater

PERFORMANCE

(The Autocar, 24.3.61)

Standing start			*Top gear acceleration*		
0 - 30 mph	2.8 secs		*20 - 40 mph*	5.5 secs
0 - 40	4.4		*30 - 50*	5.4
0 - 50	5.6		*40 - 60*	5.5
0 - 60	6.9		*50 - 70*	5.4
0 - 70	8.5		*60 - 80*	5.6
0 - 80	11.1		*70 - 90*	5.8
0 - 90	13.2		*80 - 100*	6.1
0 - 100	16.2		*90 - 110*	6.3
0 - 110	19.2		*100 - 120*	7.2
0 - 120	25.9		*110 - 130*	8.5
0 - 130	33.1			
Standing ¼-mile	14.7 secs			
Top speed	150.4 mph			

Overall fuel consumption   17.9 mpg

PRICE

£2,197 (GB)

E-Type 'Series 1' 4.2 Fixed-head Coupe

ENGINE

Cubic capacity	4235 cc
Bore and stroke	92.07 mm x 106 mm
Max. power	265 bhp (gross) @ 5400 rpm
Max. torque	283 lb ft @ 4000 rpm
Compression ratio	9 : 1 (8 : 1 optional)
Cylinder head	Straight port
Carburettors	3 2 inch SU HD8

CHASSIS

Weight and front/rear distribution			25.1 cwt (49½/50½)
Dimensions:	*Wheelbase*		8 feet
	Track	*-* *Front*	4 feet 2 inches
		Rear	4 feet 2 inches
	Length		14 feet 7 inches
	Width		5 feet 6 inches
	Height		4 feet 0¼ inches
Suspension:	*Front*		Ind. wishbone, torsion bar, anti-roll bar
	Rear		Ind. lower wishbone, upper driveshaft link, radius arms, coil springs, anti-roll bar
Brakes			Dunlop discs, vacuum servo
Gearing			1st - 8.23 : 1
			2nd - 5.34 : 1
			3rd - 3.90 : 1
			4th - 3.07 : 1 Alternative final drive ratios as for 3.8 car
Tyres and wheels			Dunlop 6.40 x 16 RS5; wheels as for 3.8 car

PERFORMANCE
(Motor, 31.11.64)
3.07 : 1 final drive

Standing start		*Top gear acceleration*		
0 - 30 mph	2.7 secs	10 - 30 mph	5.8 secs
0 - 40	3.7	20 - 40	5.5
0 - 50	4.8	30 - 50	5.4
0 - 60	7.0	40 - 60	5.3
0 - 70	8.6	50 - 70	6.0
0 - 80	11.0	60 - 80	6.6
0 - 90	13.9	70 - 90	6.6
0 - 100	17.2	80 - 100	7.3
0 - 110	21.0	90 - 110	7.3
0 - 120	25.2	100 - 120	7.8
0 - 130	30.5	110 - 130	10.2
Standing ¼-mile	14.9 secs		
Top speed	150.0 mph		

Overall fuel consumption   18.5 mpg

PRICE

£1,992 (GB)

E-Type 'Series 1' 4.2 2 + 2 Automatic

ENGINE

Cubic capacity	4235 cc
Bore and stroke	92.07 mm x 106 mm
Max. power	265 bhp (gross) @ 5400 rpm
Max. torque	283 lb ft (gross) @ 4000 rpm
Compression ratio	9 : 1
Cylinder head	Straight port
Carburettors	3 2 inch SU HD8

CHASSIS

Weight and front/rear distribution			27.7 cwt (50/50)
Dimensions:	Wheelbase		8 feet 9 inches
	Track	- Front	4 feet 2¼ inches
		Rear	4 feet 2¼ inches
	Length		15 feet 4½ inches
	Width		5 feet 4 inches
	Height		4 feet 2½ inches
Suspension:	Front		Ind. wishbone, torsion bars, anti-roll bar
	Rear		Ind. lower wishbone, upper driveshaft link, radius arms, coil springs, anti-roll bar
Brakes			Dunlop discs with vacuum servo
Gearing			1st - 6.91 : 1
			2nd - 4.20 : 1
			3rd - 2.88 : 1
Tyres and wheels			SP41 185 - 15 inch; wheels as for 3.8 car

PERFORMANCE

(Motor, 30.4.66)

	Standing start		Kickdown (DI) acceleration (Automatic)	
	0 - 30 mph	4.2 secs	20 - 40 mph	2.7 secs
	0 - 40	5.7	30 - 50	2.6
	0 - 50	6.8	40 - 60	3.4
	0 - 60	8.9	50 - 70	4.3
	0 - 70	11.0	60 - 80	4.7
	0 - 80	13.1	70 - 90	6.8
	0 - 90	15.2	80 - 100	7.5
	0 - 100	19.1	90 - 110	8.7
	0 - 110	24.4	100 - 120	10.9
	0 - 120	30.0		
	Standing ¼-mile	16.4 secs		
	Top speed	136.2 mph		
Overall fuel consumption		18.3 mpg		

PRICE

£2,385 (GB)

E-Type V12 Open Two Seater

ENGINE

Cubic capacity	5343 cc
Bore and stroke	90 mm x 70 mm
Max. power	272 bhp (net) @ 5850 rpm
Max. torque	304 lb ft (net) @ 3600 rpm
Compression ratio	9 : 1
Cylinder head	sohc, flat-head
Carburettors	4 Zenith 175CDSE

CHASSIS

Weight and front/rear distribution		28.8 cwt (52/48)
Dimensions:	*Wheelbase*	8 feet 9 inches
	Track - Front	4 feet 6½ inches
	Rear	4 feet 5 inches
	Length	15 feet 4 inches
	Width	4 feet 1 inch
	Height	5 feet 6¼ inches
Suspension:	*Front*	Ind. wishbone, torsion bars, anti-roll bar
	Rear	Ind. lower wishbone, upper driveshaft link, radius arms, coil springs, anti-roll bar
Brakes		Girling discs, vented front, servo assisted
Gearing		1st - 9.00 : 1
		2nd - 5.86 : 1
		3rd - 4.27 : 1
		4th - 3.07 : 1 (3.31 optional)
Tyres and wheels		Dunlop E70VR - 15 inch on 15 inch x 6K wire or solid wheels

PERFORMANCE

(Motor, 27.11.71)
3.07 axle ratio

Standing start			Top gear acceleration		
0 - 30 mph	2.7 secs		*10 - 30 mph*		secs
0 - 40	3.5		*20 - 40*		6.1
0 - 50	4.7		*30 - 50*		6.0
0 - 60	6.4		*40 - 60*		5.6
0 - 70	8.0		*50 - 70*		5.6
0 - 80	9.9		*60 - 80*		5.7
0 - 90	12.7		*70 - 90*		6.0
0 - 100	15.4		*80 - 100*		6.4
0 - 110	19.3		*90 - 110*		7.4
0 - 120	25.8		*100 - 120*		10.4
Standing ¼-mile	14.2 secs				
Top speed	146 mph				
Overall fuel consumption	14.5 mpg				

PRICE

£3,139 (GB)

E-Type V12 2 + 2

ENGINE

Cubic capacity	5343 cc
Bore and stroke	90 mm x 70 mm
Max. power	272 bhp (DIN) @ 5850 rpm
Max. torque	304 lb ft (DIN) @ 3600 rpm
Compression ratio	9 : 1
Cylinder head	sohc, flat-head
Carburettors	4 Zenith Stromberg 175CDSE

CHASSIS

Weight and front/rear distribution			29.5 cwt (50.9/49.1)
Dimensions:	*Wheelbase*		8 feet 9 inches
	Track - *Front*		4 feet 6½ inches
	Rear		4 feet 5 inches
	Length		15 feet 4 inches
	Width		4 feet 1 inch
	Height		4 feet 3 inches
Suspension:	*Front*		Ind. wishbone, torsion bars, anti-roll bar
	Rear		Ind. lower wishbone, upper driveshaft link, radius arms, coil springs, anti-roll bar
Brakes			Girling discs, vented front, servo assisted
Gearing			1st - 9.00 : 1
			2nd - 5.86 : 1
			3rd - 4.27 : 1
			4th - 3.07 : 1 (3.31 optional)
Tyres and wheels			Dunlop E70VR - 15 inch; wheels as for V12 roadster

PERFORMANCE

(Autocar, 18.11.71)
3.07 axle ratio

Standing start			*Top gear acceleration*		
0 - 30 mph	2.7 secs		10 - 30 mph	7.3 secs
0 - 40	3.8		20 - 40	6.2
0 - 50	4.9		30 - 50	5.9
0 - 60	6.8		40 - 60	5.8
0 - 70	8.4		50 - 70	5.8
0 - 80	10.6		60 - 80	6.2
0 - 90	13.7		70 - 90	6.5
0 - 100	16.4		80 - 100	6.9
0 - 110	20.3		90 - 110	8.3
0 - 120	26.5		100 - 120	10.3
Standing ¼-mile	14.6 secs			
Top speed	142 mph			

Overall fuel consumption 15.2 mpg

PRICE

£3,403 (GB)

E-Type V12 Roadster - USA Specification

ENGINE

Cubic capacity	5343 cc
Bore and stroke	90 mm x 70 mm
Max. power	250 bhp @ 6000 rpm (1972 spec.)
	241 bhp @ 5750 rpm (1974 spec.)
Max. torque	288 lb ft @ 3500 rpm (1972 spec.)
	285 lb ft @ 3500 rpm (1974 spec.)
Compression ratio	9 : 1 (1972 spec.), 7.8 : 1 (1974 spec.)
Cylinder head	sohc, flat head
Carburettors	4 Zenith-Stromberg 175CD2SE

CHASSIS

Weight and front/rear distribution			30.1 cwt (53/47); figures variable according to extras fitted
Dimensions:	*Wheelbase*		8 feet 9 inches
	Track -	*Front*	4 feet 6½ inches
		Rear	4 feet 5 inches
	Length		15 feet 4 inches
	Width		4 feet 1 inch
	Height		4 feet 3 inches
Suspension:	*Front*		Ind. wishbone, torsion bar, anti-roll bar
	Rear		Ind. lower wishbone, upper drive shaft link, radius arm, coil springs, anti-roll bar
Brakes			Girling discs, ventilated front, servo assisted
Gearing			1st - 10.37 : 1
			2nd - 6.73 : 1
			3rd - 4.92 : 1
			4th - 3.54 : 1
Tyres and wheels			Dunlop E70VR - 15; wheels as for GB V12 roadster

PERFORMANCE

(Road & Track)

Standing start - 1972 specification (figures in brackets, 1974 specification)

0 - 30 mph	3.3 secs	(3.2)
0 - 40	4.5	
0 - 50	6.0	
0 - 60	7.4	(8.0)
0 - 70	9.2	
0 - 80	11.5	
0 - 90	—	(16.6)
0 - 100	18.5	(21.2)
0 - 110	22.8	
Standing ¼-mile	15.4 secs	(16.2)
Top speed	135 mph at 6000 rpm both specifications	

Overall fuel consumption   14.5 mpg (12 mpg)

PRICE

1972	$ 7599 *USA Basic*
1974	$ 8475 *USA Basic*

XJ-S

ENGINE

Cubic capacity	5343 cc
Bore and stroke	90 mm x 70 mm
Max. power	285 bhp DIN @ 5500 rpm
Max. torque	294 lb ft @ 3500 rpm
Compression ratio	9 : 1
Cylinder head	sohc, flat head
Carburettors	Lucas electronic manifold fuel injection

CHASSIS

Weight			33.1cwt
Dimensions:	*Wheelbase*		8 feet 6 inches
	Track -	*Front*	4 feet 10 inches
		Rear	4 feet 10½ inches
	Length		15 feet 11½ inches
	Width		5 feet 10½ inches
	Height		4 feet 1½ inches
Suspension:	*Front*		Ind. wishbone, coil springs, anti-dive anti-roll bar
	Rear		Ind. lower wishbone, upper drive shaft link, radius arm, coil spring, anti-roll bar
Brakes			Girling discs, ventilated front, servo assisted
Gearing			1st - 9.94 : 1
			2nd - 5.85 : 1
			3rd - 4.26 : 1
			4th - 3.07 : 1
Tyres and wheels			Dunlop SP Super 205/70VR - 15 inch x 6K alloy wheels

PERFORMANCE

(Factory figures)	*Standing start*	
	0 - 60 mph	6.8 secs
	Top speed	153 mph
Overall fuel consumption		16 mpg

PRICE

(Estimated at time of going to press)	£6,500 plus

1952 Production C-Type

ENGINE

Cubic capacity	3442 cc
Bore and stroke	83 mm x 106 mm
Max. power	200 bhp @ 5800 rpm
Max. torque	220 ft lbs @ 3900 rpm
Compression ratio	8 : 1
Cylinder head	C-type
Carburettors	2 2 inch SU

CHASSIS

Weight and front/rear distribution   20 cwt (50/50)

Dimensions: *Wheelbase*   8 feet
    Track - *Front*   4 feet 3 inches
         Rear   4 feet 3 inches
    Length   13 feet 1 inch
    Width   5 feet 4½ inches
    Height   3 feet 6½ inches

Suspension: *Front*   Ind. wishbone, torsion bar, anti-roll bar
     Rear   Torsion bars and rigid axle

Brakes   Lockheed hydraulic drums

Gearing
1st - 9.86 : 1
2nd - 5.78 : 1   Note: full range of Salisbury
3rd - 3.99 : 1   final drives available
4th - 3.31 : 1

Tyres and wheels   6.00 x 16 inch front, 6.50 x 16 inch rear on 16 inch x 5K wire wheels

PERFORMANCE

(The Motor, 10.22.52)

Standing start		Top gear acceleration		
0 - 30 mph	3.2 secs	*10 - 30 mph*		7.3 secs
0 - 40	4.3	*20 - 40*		6.8
0 - 50	6.1	*30 - 50*		7.2
0 - 60	8.1	*40 - 60*		7.5
0 - 70	10.1	*50 - 70*		7.5
0 - 80	12.2	*60 - 80*		7.9
0 - 90	16.2	*70 - 90*		8.0
0 - 100	20.1	*80 - 100*		9.2
0 - 110	24.4			
Standing ¼-mile	16.2 secs			
Top speed	143.7 mph			

Overall fuel consumption   16 mpg

PRICE

£2,327 (GB)

1955 Production D-Type 3.4

ENGINE

Cubic capacity	3442 cc
Bore and stroke	83 mm x 106 mm
Max. power	250 bhp @ 5750 rpm
Max. torque	242 lb ft @ 4000/4500 rpm
Compression ratio	9 : 1
Cylinder head	'Production D-type' (C-type casting, but 1 7/8 inch inlet valves, gas flowed etc. Valve angle 35/35)
Carburettors	3 Weber DCO 3/45 mm

CHASSIS

Weight and front/rear distribution   17 cwt (dry), 53/47

Dimensions: *Wheelbase*   7 feet 6 5/8ths inch

Track - Front   4 feet 2 inches

Rear   4 feet 0 inches

Length   12 feet 10 inches

Width   5 feet 5 3/8ths inches

Height   2 feet 7½ inches (at scuttle)

Suspension: *Front*   Ind. wishbone, torsion bar

Rear   Live axle, trailing links, transverse torsion bar

Brakes   Dunlop discs, triple pad front, twin pad rear

Gearing
(all-synchro gearbox)

			Ratio	mph @ 5750	
1st - 7.61 : 1	Other axle		2.93 : 1	166	in top
2nd - 5.82 : 1	ratios in		3.31 : 1	148	
3rd - 4.52 : 1	use were:-		3.54 : 1	138	
4th - 3.54 : 1			3.92 : 1	124	

Tyres and wheels   Dunlop Racing 6.50 x 16, on 16 inch x 5½K. Dunlop light alloy centre-lock wheels. Similar wheels but of 17 inch diameter could be obtained

PERFORMANCE

(Road & Track,
May 1956)

Standing start (gearing equivalent to 3.54)

0 - 50 mph	3.9 secs
0 - 60	4.7
0 - 70	6.4
0 - 80	8.0
0 - 90	10.1
0 - 100	12.1
Standing ¼-mile	13.7 secs
Top speed	162 mph
Fuel consumption	9 - 14 mpg

PRICE

£3,878 (GB) $ 9875 (USA list)

XKSS

ENGINE

Cubic capacity	3442 cc
Bore and stroke	83 mm x 106 mm
Max. power	250 bhp @ 5750 rpm
Max. torque	242 lb ft @ 4000 / 4500 rpm
Compression ratio	9 : 1
Cylinder head	'Production D-type' (C-type casting, but 1 7/8ths inch inlet valves, gas flowed etc. Valve angle 35/35)
Carburettors	3 Weber DCO 3/45 mm

CHASSIS

Weight and front/rear distribution			18 cwt (53/47) - both no fuel
Dimensions:	*Wheelbase*		7 feet 6 5/8ths inches
	Track - *Front*		4 feet 2 inches
	Rear		4 feet 0 inches
	Length		13 feet 10 inches
	Width		5 feet 5 3/8ths inches
	Height		2 feet 7½ inches (at scuttle)
Suspension:	*Front*		Ind. wishbone, torsion bar, anti-roll bar
	Rear		Live axle, trailing links, transverse torsion bar
Brakes			Dunlop discs, triple pad front, twin pad rear
Gearing			1st - 7.61 : 1 See Production D-type sheet
(all synchro gearbox)			2nd - 5.82 : 1 for alternative axle ratios
			3rd - 4.52 : 1
			4th - 3.54 : 1
Tyres and wheels			Dunlop Racing 6.50 x 16, on 16 inch x 5½K
			Dunlop light alloy centre-lock wheels

PERFORMANCE

Standing start (Road & Track, Aug. 57)		*Top gear acceleration (Autocar, 3.4.57)*	
0 - 50 mph	4.1 secs	*40 - 60 mph*	5.5 secs
0 - 60	5.2	*60 - 80*	6.0
0 - 70	7.3	*80 - 100*	5.0
0 - 80	8.8		
0 - 90	11.2		
0 - 100	13.6		
0 - 110	16.1		
Standing ¼-mile	14.1 secs		
Top speed	149.0 mph (144 mph at 6000 rpm in top gear)		

Overall fuel consumption	10 - 18 mpg according to road/race use

PRICE

£3,878 (GB) $5,600 (USA)

1958 PRODUCTION LISTER-JAGUAR

ENGINE

Jaguar D-type — 3.0, 3.4 or 3.8 litre capacity, (See data sheet for details) Production D-type

CHASSIS

Weight			16 cwt (estimated dry)
Dimensions:	*Wheelbase*		7 feet 6¾ inches
	Track	*Front*	4 feet 4 inches
		Rear	4 feet 5½ inches
	Length		13 feet 6 inches
	Width		5 feet 2½ inches
	Height		2 feet 3 inches at scuttle
			3 feet 3 inches at headrest
Suspension:	*Front*		Ind. equal length wishbones, coil springs
	Rear		De Dion, trailing arms, coil springs
Brakes			Girling quick-change, 12 inch diameter front and rear
Gearing			As for production D-type (all-synchro gearbox)
Final drive			Salisbury
Tyres and wheels			Dunlop Racing 600 x 16 front, 650 x 16 rear, on 16 inch x 5K Dunlop light alloy wheels

PERFORMANCE

(John Bolster,	*0 - 30 mph*	2.0 secs
Autosport, Oct.	*0 - 50*	3.6
1957, works	*0 - 60*	4.6
3.8 litre car)	*0 - 80*	8.0
	0 - 100	11.2
	0 - 120	15.2
	Standing ¼-mile	13.2 secs
	Top speed	140 upwards according to gearing
Fuel consumption		Racing, 10 mpg, Touring 15 mpg (approx)

TOJEIRO-JAGUAR MK 2

ENGINE
Jaguar D-type 3.4 litre capacity, 9 : 1 compression ratio
(See Production D-type data sheet for details)

CHASSIS

Weight			15 cwt
Dimensions:	*Wheelbase*		7 feet 3 inches
	Track	- *Front*	4 feet 2 inches
		Rear	4 feet 2 inches
	Height		2 feet 8 inches (to top of scuttle)
Suspension:	*Front*		Ind. double wishbone, coil springs
	Rear		De Dion axle on parallel trailing arms and central bronze slide block coil springs
Brakes			Discs, inboard at rear
Final drive			Salisbury hypoid and ZF differential
Tyres and wheels			Dunlop Racing 600 x 16 front, 650 x 16 rear, on 16 inch x 5K Dunlop light alloy wheels

PERFORMANCE

(John Bolster,	0 - 30 mph	2.0 secs
Autosport)	0 - 50	3.8
	0 - 60	5.4
	0 - 80	8.2
	0 - 100	12.6
	0 - 120	16.8
	Standing ¼-mile	13.6 secs
	Top speed	152.5 mph
Fuel consumption		15 mpg (approx), road use

HWM JAGUAR

ENGINE
Jaguar D-type

3.4 litre
(See Production D-type data sheet for details)

CHASSIS

Weight			18 cwt (approx)
Dimensions:	*Wheelbase*		7 feet 6 inches
	Track - *Front*		4 feet 1¾ inches
	Rear		4 feet 2½ inches

Suspension: *Front* Independent, transverse spring and wishbone; anti roll bar (later cars, coil spring)

Rear De Dion, torsion bars (later cars, coil spring)

Brakes Finned drum; later cars, disc

Gearing As for Production C- or D-types

Tyres and wheels Dunlop Racing 600 x 16, on 16 inch centre lock wheels

PERFORMANCE

(1955 Works car, C-type			
engine with Weber	*0 - 50 mph*	*5.2 secs*	
carburettors; John	*0 - 60*	*6.5*	
Bolster, Autosport)	*0 - 70*	*8.8*	
	0 - 80	*10.6*	
	0 - 90	*12.8*	
	0 - 100	*17.0*	
	0 - 110	*20.8*	
	Standing ¼-mile	*15.0*	
	Top speed	145.1 mph	

Fuel consumption   15 mpg (touring)

COOPER JAGUAR MK II

ENGINE
> *Jaguar D-type*

3.4 litre
(See Production D-type data sheet for details)

CHASSIS

Weight		17 cwt
Dimensions:	*Wheelbase*	7 feet 7 inches
	Track - Front	4 feet 4 inches
	Rear	4 feet 4 inches
	Length	
	Width	
	Height	
Suspension:	*Front*	Independent transverse leaf, double tubular wishbones
	Rear	Independent transverse leaf, wishbones
Brakes		As for Production D-type
Gearing		As for Production D-type (all-synchro gearbox)
Final drive		ENV or Salisbury
Tyres and wheels		Dunlop Racing on 16 inch x 5K Dunlop light alloy wheels

PERFORMANCE   *Standing ¼-mile*   14.8 seconds

> *Fuel consumption*   10 mpg (racing)

Appendix Two Production figures

NOTES

Production figures have been calculated from factory listings of chassis numbers but should be regarded as a guide only, within the limits of several units either way for the various totals.

Prices given are those which were in force upon the model's first announcement in Great Britain. Post-war prices in sterling are given in three stages - basic GB price, British purchase tax, and total GB price.

The last month in which a model was 'current' is, in most cases, that given by the factory. Sometimes however cars were listed in the new price guides of *Motor* and *Autocar* for a considerable time afterwards, indicating that although out of production, dealers still had new stock to clear.

OTS — Open Two Seater or Roadster
FHC — Fixed-head Coupe
DHC — Drop-head Coupe
2P2 — 2-PLUS-2
SE — Special Equipment

PRODUCTION ROAD CARS

Model	Body Style	Engine	Public Announcement	Current from/to	Price on Introduction	Number Made	Chassis No. Commence	Comments
S.S.90	OTS	2½ litre	Mar 1935	Mar 1935/ Nov 1935	£395	23	In series with SS 1	*Number made includes round-tail prototype*
SS 100	OTS	2½ litre	Sept 1935	Mar 1936/ Mar 1941	£395	190	18001 (1936-1937), 49001 (1938-1940)	*Production as follows: 1936: 31 1937: 94 1938-1941: 65*

Model	Body Style	Engine	Public Announcement	Current from/to	Price on Introduction	Number Made	Chassis No. Commence	Comments
		3½ litre	Sept 1937	Sept 1937/ Nov 1941	£445	118	39001	*Number made includes the 1938 FHC made by Jaguar, and the two chassis supplied to S H Newsome (110 & 112)*
XK 120	OTS	3.4 litre, 150, 160 bhp	22 Oct 1948	Jul 1949/ Sept 1954	£0998 275 £1273	1175 (rhd) 6437 (lhd) 7612 Total	660001 (rhd) 670001 (lhd)	*Aluminium bodies fitted up to 660058 & 670184 inclusive. After Aug 1951, OTS were available with 180 bhp engine to special order, and/or wire wheels. From April 1953, all XK 120s could be ordered with the C-type head, together with 2 inch SU carburettors if required*
	FHC	3.4 litre, 150, 160 bhp	2 Mar 1951	Mar 1951/ Sept 1954	£1088	194 (rhd) 2484 (lhd) 2678 Total	669001 (rhd) 679001 (lhd)	*All SE XK 120s have an 'S' prefix to their chassis numbers. Special Equipment models introduced Sept 1952*
		180, 190 bhp SE, 3.4 litre	Sept 1952	Sept 1952/ Sept 1954	£1265 419 £1684			
	DHC	150/160 bhp 3.4 litre	18 Apr 1953	Apr 1953/ Sept 1954	£1160 480 £1640	294 (rhd) 1471 (lhd) 1765 Total	667001 (rhd) 677001 (lhd)	
		SE, 180/ 190 bhp 3.4 litre	18 Apr 1953	Apr 1953/ Sept 1954				
XK 140	OTS	190 bhp 3.4 litre	15 Oct 1954	Oct 1954/ Feb 1957	£1,127 471 £1,598	73 (rhd) 3281 (lhd) 3354 Total	800001 (rhd) 810001 (lhd)	*SE XK 140s have an 'A' prefix to their chassis numbers when fitted with the 190 bhp engine, or an 'S' prefix when fitted with the 210 bhp engine*
		SE, 210 bhp 3.4 litre	15 Oct 1954	Oct 1954/ Feb 1957	£1,278			

Model	Body Style	Engine	Public Announcement	Current from/to	Price on Introduction	Number Made	Chassis No. Commence	Comments
	FHC	190 bhp 3.4 litre	15 Oct 1954	Oct 1954/ Feb 1957	£1,140 476 £1,616	843 (rhd) 1965 (lhd) 2808 Total	804001 (rhd) 814001 (lhd)	*Automatic transmission available on FHC and DHC XK 140s from Oct 1956*
		SE, 210 bhp 3.4 litre	15 Oct 1954	Oct 1954/ Feb 1957	£1,291 539 £1,830			
	DHC	190 bhp 3.4 litre	15 Oct 1954	Oct 1954/ Feb 1957	£1,160 484 £1,644	479 (rhd) 2310 (lhd) 2889 Total	807001 (rhd) 817001 (lhd)	
		SE, 210 bhp 3.4 litre	15 Oct 1954	Oct 1954/ Feb 1957	£1,311			
XK 150	FHC	190 bhp 3.4 litre	22 May 1957	May 1957 Oct 1961	£1,175 588 £1,763		824001 (rhd) 834001 (lhd)	
		SE, 210 bhp 3.4 litre	22 May 1957	May 1957/ Oct 1961	£1,292 647 £1,939			
		3.4 'S' 250 bhp	18 Feb 1959	Feb 1959/ Oct 1961	£1,457 608 £2,065	1,368 (rhd) 3,094 (lhd) 4,462 Total		*Chassis numbers of 3.4, 3.8 and 'S' models intermixed. Identification by engine number prefix as follows (all body styles):*
		3.8 220 bhp	2 Oct 1959	Oct 1959/ Oct 1961	£1,457 608 £2,065			*V = 3.4* *VS = 3.4S* *VA = 3.8*
		3.8 'S' 265 bhp	2 Oct 1959	Oct 1959/ Oct 1961	£1,535 640 £2,175			*VAS = 3.8S* *Additionally 3.4S models have an 'S' pre-fix to chassis number, and 3.8S models a 'T' prefix to chassis number*
	DHC	190 bhp 3.4 litre	22 May 1957	May 1957 Oct 1960	£1,195 598 £1,793		827001 (rhd) 837001 (lhd)	*Automatic transmission available on all XK 150 models except 'S' ver-sions. Overdrive stan-dard on 'S' models, optional on other versions*
		SE, 210 bhp 3.4 litre	22 May 1957	May 1957/ Oct 1960	£1,292 647 £1,939			

Model	Body Style	Engine	Public Announcement	Current from/to	Price on Introduction	Number Made	Chassis No. Commence	Comments
		3.4 'S' 250 bhp	18 Feb 1959	Feb 1959/ Oct 1960	£1,477 616 £2,093	662 (rhd) 2009 (lhd) 2671 Total		
		3.8 220 bhp	2 Oct 1959	Oct 1959/ Oct 1960	£1,390 580 £1,970			
		3.8 'S' 265 bhp	2 Oct 1959	Oct 1959/ Oct 1960	£1,555 649 £2,204			
	OTS	190 bhp 3.4 litre	28 Mar 1958	Mar 1958/ Oct 1960	£1,175 491 £1,666			
		SE, 210 bhp 3.4 litre	28 Mar 1958	Mar 1958/ Oct 1960			82001 (rhd) 830001 (lhd)	
		3.4 'S' 250 bhp	28 Mar 1958	Mar 1958/ Oct 1960	£1,457 608 £2,065	92 (rhd) 2173 (lhd) 2265 Total		
		3.8 220 bhp	2 Oct 1959	Oct 1959/ Oct 1960	£1,457 608 £2,065			
		3.8 'S' 265 bhp	2 Oct 1959	Oct 1959/ Oct 1960	£1,535 641 £2,176			
E-TYPE	OTS	3.8 265 bhp	15 Mar 1961	Mar 1961/ Oct 1964	£1,480 617 £2,097	942 (rhd) 6885 (lhd) 7827 Total	850001 (rhd) 875001 (lhd)	
	FHC	3.8 265 bhp	15 Mar 1961	Mar 1961/ Oct 1964	£1,550 646 £2,196	1798 (rhd) 5871 (lhd) 7669 Total	860001 (rhd) 885001 (lhd)	
	OTS	4.2 265 bhp	9 Oct 1964	Oct 1964/ Sept 1968	£1,568 328 £1,896	1182 (rhd) 8366 (lhd) 9548 Total	1E1001 (rhd) 1E10001 (lhd)	

Model	Body Style	Engine	Public Announce-ment	Current from/to	Price on Introduc-tion	Number Made	Chassis No. Commence	Comments
	FHC	4.2 265 bhp	9 Oct 1964	Oct 1964/ Sept 1968	£1,648 345 £1,993	1957 (rhd) 5813 (lhd) 7770 Total	1E2001 (rhd) 1E30001 (lhd)	
	2P2	4.2 265 bhp	7 Mar 1966	Mar 1966 Sept 1968	£1,867 378 £2,245	1378 (rhd) 4220 (lhd)	1E50001 (rhd) 1E75001 (lhd)	*Automatic transmission available for 2P2 at £157 total*
SERIES 2 E-TYPE	OTS	4.2	18 Oct 1968	Oct 1968/ Sept 1970	£1,655 508 £2,163	755 (rhd) 7852 (lhd) 8627 Total	1R1001 (rhd) 1R7001 (lhd)	*Power output varied according to emission control equipment fitted*
	FHC	4.2	18 Oct 1968	Oct 1968/ Sept 1970	£1,740 533 £2,273	1070 (rhd) 3785 (lhd) 4855 Total	1R20001 (rhd) 1R25001 (lhd)	
	2P2	4.2	18 Oct 1968	Oct 1968/ Sept 1970	£1,922 590 £2,512	1040 (rhd) 4286 (lhd) 5326 Total	1R35001 1R40001	*Automatic transmission available on 2P2 at £141 total*
SERIES 3 E-TYPE	OTS	5.3 V12	29 Mar 1971	Apr 1971/ Feb 1975	£2,510 629 £3,139	1871 (rhd) 6119 (lhd) 7990 Total	1S1001 (rhd) 1S20001 (lhd)	*OTS now on 2P2 wheelbase. Automatic transmission available on both versions at £161 total*
	2P2	5.3 V12	29 Mar 1971	Apr 1971/ Sept 1973	£2,708 679 £3,387	2115 (rhd) 5182 (lhd) 7297 Total	1S50001 (rhd) 1S70001 (lhd)	

JAGUAR SPORTS RACING CARS

Model	Type	Announcement	Current from/to	Price	Number Made	Comments
C-TYPE	Works Le Mans	June 1951	June 1951/ June 1953		11	
	Production	July 1952	Aug 1952/ Aug 1953	£1,495 832 £2,327	43	
D-TYPE	Works Le Mans	June 1954	June 1954/ July 1956		17	*Total of 'works' cars made up as follows: 6 short nose 1954 5 long nose 1955 6 long nose 1956*
	Production		Aug 1955/ Aug 1956	£1,895 790 £2,685	45	*Fin optional on Production D-types*
XKSS	Road Car	Jan 1957	Jan 1957/ Feb 1957		16	*Two D-types were subsequently converted to XKSS specification by the factory, making a final total of 18*

Appendix Three   *The Jaguar Clubs*

FOR A CAR produced in relatively small numbers, the Jaguar has inspired the formation of a large number of motor clubs devoted to its enjoyment and upkeep, all of which were founded by, or number amongst their membership, sports car owners. Some have branches exclusively for certain Jaguar sports cars, while all are aware of the type's achievements and merits. In this Appendix I intend to outline briefly the major organisations and direct the interested Jaguar owner or enthusiast to the place where he or she can obtain more information.

Great Britain

In commencing with the Jaguar Drivers' Club of Great Britain, one must first acknowledge that it doesn't have the honour of being the first Jaguar club to be formed, even though it is, without doubt, the largest of its kind, having a world-wide membership of about 4,000 - which probably represents something like 5,000 individual cars. Its founding goes back to 1955, with an inaugural meeting being held in May, and formal recognition from the Royal Automobile Club and Jaguar Cars Ltd following some six months later. Whilst being on the friendliest terms with the manufacturer, the club does not have any financial ties with the factory.

Since the late sixties, the club has spawned a number of 'Registers' which look after individual types of car, the three most relevant to this book being the SS Register, XK Register, and E-type Register. The XK Register is the largest having about 1,500 members, and accepts XK 120, 140, 150, C- and D-type cars as well as the XK-engined sports racing variants of the 1950s. The E-type Register, however, is fast catching up as the early 3.8 engined models become accepted as 'classics', though it also caters for the Series 3 V12 cars. The SS Register is the oldest established of the three, its province being all SS and Jaguar cars up to and including the Mk V - the period covered takes in the S.S.90, SS 100 cars of course, and the Register's spares scheme for these cars is noteworthy.

Most of the Registers hold individual events for their own members, while national and international gatherings are organised by the club as a whole. Some 27 local monthly meetings are run by Area Centres at various pubs and inns throughout the country, including Scotland, Wales and Northern Ireland. Motor sport activities include race, sprint, hill climb and 'test day' meetings. All members receive the professionally-produced *Jaguar Driver* magazine each month, while the XK Register publishes its own *XK*

337

Bulletin. The club has a full-time administrative staff and offices at the following address:

Jaguar Drivers' Club Ltd,
The Norfolk Hotel,
Harrington Road,
London SW7,
Great Britain.

United States of America

The publication of this book happily coincides with a boom in Jaguar clubs in the States, where enthusiasm for Jaguar cars has never been greater. There are now well over 30 clubs affiliated to the Jaguar Clubs of North America Incorporated, the British Leyland-sponsored parent body, the oldest established being the Jaguar Associate Group of San Francisco which traces its beginnings to January 21st 1955. None of the individual clubs approach the British JDC's total membership but then they are almost entirely organised on a local basis, and equate more with the British club's Area Centres. As this book went to press, the largest of them was the New England XK Association with 160 members - like the Long Island XK Association, it has a happy association with the British XK Register, and both have founder members who are enthusiastic and knowledgeable XK owners and who, incidentally, own between them some of the top 'concours' XKs in that continent.

Another JCNA affiliate club, the Classic Jaguar Association, should also be singled out for a special mention, as it has acquired a very high reputation amongst SS and early Jaguar owners, chiefly through its authoritative bi-monthly journal, and its painstakingly compiled register of S.S.90 and SS 100 cars which remains the only publication of its kind to date. The CJA is very much a correspondence club and therefore counts amongst its members many owners from overseas.

For obvious reasons, any address listings of individual club secretaries published in this book might quickly become outdated, so interested parties are asked to contact Mr Fred Horner of the JCNA, at 600 Willow Tree Road, Leonia, New Jersey 07605, USA, who will have up-to-date information. However, as a guide I append a list of JCNA-affiliated clubs with their approximate locations:

Jaguar Automobile Club, Inc., San Diego, California
Jaguar Owners Club, Inc., California
Jaguar Associate Group (San Francisco), San Jose, California
Jaguar Owners Club of Oregon, Inc., Oregon
Jaguar Drivers' Club of Northwest America, Inc., Washington
Classic Jaguar Club of Arizona
Jaguar Club of Tulsa, Tulsa, Oklahoma
Jaguar Club of Omaha, Omaha, Nebraska
Jaguar Association of Greater Chicago, Chicago, Illinois
Jaguar Owners Association of the Southwest, Richardson, Texas
The Greater St. Louis Jaguar Association, St Louis, Missouri
Jaguar Affiliates Group of Michigan
New England XK Association, Mass.
Jaguar Club of Southern New England, Connecticut
Empire Division Jaguar Club (New York City), New Jersey
Delaware Valley Jaguar Club, Pennsylvania
Jaguar Club of Pittsburgh, New Kensington, Pa. 15068
The Nation's Capital Jaguar Owners Club, Virginia
Jaguar Owners Club of Virginia
Jaguar Club of Roanoke Valley, Virginia
Carolina Jaguar Club, North Carolina
The Nashville Jags, Tennesse
Greater Memphis Jaguar Club, Tennesse
Classic Jaguar Association, Washington
Jaguar Club of Ohio
The Eastern Jaguar Group, Massachusetts
Jaguar Association of Central Ohio, Bexley, Ohio 43209
Heart of America Jaguar Club, Kansas 66101

Great Plains Jaguar Owners Association, Kansas
67208
Nova Scotia Jaguar Association, Nova Scotia,
Canada
Jaguar Club of Austin, Austin, Texas 78731

Jaguar Drivers Club of Australia (N.S.W.),
Secretary: Ian Hutchinson,
P.O. Box 2,
Drummoyne, N.S.W. 2047.

Jaguar Car Club of Victoria,
Secretary: Maurie Vickerman,
5 Morinda Crescent,
East Doncaster,
Victoria, N.S.W.

The Classic Jaguar Club of W.A. Inc.,
Secretary: Peter Zoontjens,
3 Bower Street,
Langford, W.A. 6155.

Jaguar Drivers Club of S.A.,
Secretary: David Seidel,
8 Templewood Avenue,
Manningham, S.A. 5086.

Jaguar Club of Tasmania,
Secretary: Dave Dungey,
5 Tyndall Court,
Taroona, Tas. 7006.

Jaguar Drivers Club of Canberra,
Secretary: Dick O'Keefe,
15 Kriewaldt Court,
Riggins, A.C.T.

New Zealand

Owing to local reorganisation, the addresses of
the two clubs in New Zealand were not to hand
at the time of publication, and those interested
are asked to contact the British JDC for that
information.

Canada

Two clubs here, both incidentally affiliated to
the JCNA. One of them, the Canadian XK
Register, combines with the Classic MG Club
and very successfully too; both have seperate
meetings besides joint events.

Canadian XK Register,
P.O. Box 48452, Postal Station Bentall Centre,
Vancouver, BC, V7X 1A2,
Canada.

Ontario Jaguar Owners Association,
133 Goulding Avenue,
Willowdale,
Ontario,
Canada M2M 1L5.

South Africa

Initially an offshoot of the British JDC, the
South African XK Register was formed mainly
by XK enthusiasts although now many other
sorts of Jaguar are to be seen at its events. Quite
recently XKs from this club took part in the
historic races now being organised in South
Africa.
Write to:

Keith Paget,
Box 69133,
Bryanston,
Transvaal,
South Africa.

France

The French Jaguar Drivers' Club is an extremely
active organisation, particularly in historic racing
where its members drive such cars as Cooper-and
Lister-Jaguars, and highly modified XK 120s.
Founder member Dr Philip Renault has one of the
largest Jaguar collections in the world.

French Jaguar Drivers' Club,
Dr Philip Renault,
39 Avenue de Laumiere,
Paris 19,
France.

Italy

Another offspring of the British JDC, the Italian XK Register caters for a wider range of Jaguar cars than its title suggests. In this, the land of the Ferrari, there is a small but surprisingly keen Jaguar following; various meetings are organised including an annual 'Jaguar Day' at the Autodromo di Magione.

Italian XK Register,
Roberto Causo,

Via Condotti 91,
00187 Rome,
Italy.

Switzerland

Switzerland has represented quite an important market for Jaguar over the years, and the country can boast of a fair number of well preserved older models including SS and XK sports cars. The membership is predominantly XK at the moment.

Swiss XK Register,
Aldo Vinzio,
34 av. Krieg,
1208 Geneva,
Switzerland.

Appendix Four
List of books from which quoted matter is taken

Challenge Me The Race by Mike Hawthorn, published by William Kimber & Co Ltd, 46 Wilton Place, SW1.

Touch Wood by Duncan Hamilton, published by Barrie & Rockliff, 2 Clement's Inn, London WC2.

Jim Clark At The Wheel by Jim Clark, published by Arthur Barker Ltd, 20 New Bond Street, London W1.

The Leyland Papers by Graham Turner, published by Eyre & Spottiswoode (Publishers) Ltd, 11 New Fetter Lane, London EC4P 4EE.

Index, by model

342

General index

A

Abeccasis, G: 32, 40, 88, 90, 91, 109, 131, 134, 172, 212-216, 228

Abbey Panels: 168, 243, 285

AC: 2-litre 33. Ace 1971cc 201. Cobra 263, 264, 266, 268, 276

Acropolis Rally: 1958: 156

AFN Ltd: 53

Aintree circuit: 1955 GP meeting 171, 1957 GP meeting 219, 1958 April meeting 221, 1959 '200' 224 & 229, 1961 GP meeting 254

Aldington, HJ: 42

Alexander, JMS: 40, 42

Allard, Sydney: 44, 82, 87, 91, 92, 209, 210

Allard V8: 58, 85, 88, 90-92, 99, 120, 130, 210. Palm Beach 193

Allen, Miss M: 18, 238

Alpine International Trial (Rally) 1933: 18, 1934: 19, 1936: 35, 1947: 43, 1948: 88, 1949: 44, 88, 1950: 88, 1951: 95, 99, 1952: 100, 1953: 104, 105, 1954: 110

Alton, D: 233

Alton-Jaguar: 232

American Mountain Rally, 1956: 156

'Ancient Egyption': 106

Anderson, Mrs: 108

Anderson: 270

Appleyard, I: 27, 35, 43, 44, 84, 88, 89, 94-96, 99, 100, 104, 105, 154, 155

Ardmore circuit (NZ): 232

Armstrong-Siddeley 'Jaguar' engine: 23

Ascari, Alberto: 84, 85, 124, 133-135, 160

Ashmore, G: 226

Aston Martin: Type C: 21. 2-litre: 33, 82. DB1: 97. DB2: 58, 87, 88, 90, 91, 94, 96, 97, 119, 121, 151. DB2/4: 58, 155, 156, 193. DB3: 101, 121, 122, 128-130, 219. DB3S: 130, 34, 35, 53, 68, 171, 172, 174, 175, 179, 214. DBR1/300: 180, 181, 183, 184, 219, 224, 225, 254. DBR2: 221. DBR3: 221, 222. DB4: 201, 205. DB4GT: 253, 259. Zagato: 254-256, 258. Project 212: 257.

Aston Martin Owner's Club: 226

Atalanta: 230, 231

Atkins, CT: 263, 264, 269

Attwood, R: 284

Austin: Seven: 14, 106 (monoposto). Seven Swallow Sports 2-seater: 14, saloon: 14. A50: 154. A90: 154.

Australian GP: 233

Autocar: 17, 20-22, 27-32, 34, 40, 60, 61, 69-72, 89, 119, 146, 148-150, 192, 193, 200, 201, 207, 234, 249-251, 289, 290-294

Austro-Union: 233

Automobile Club de France: 94

Automobile Club l'Ouest: 97

Auto Sport (USA): 70, 71

Autosport (GB): 72, 106, 153, 154, 180, 200, 203, 218, 227, 231, 254

Autosport GT Championship 1962: 256

Avon Body Company: 35

B

Bahru circuit: 102

Baillie, Capt. I: 182, 183

Baillie-Hill: 43

Baily, Claude: 48, 271, 282, 286

Baird, R: 135

Bamford, A: 185, 270, 295

Bandini, L: 266

Banks: 275

Barber, D: 40, 44

Bardinau: 263

Barker, M: 232

Barnato-Hassan Special: 38

Barnato, Capt. W: 38

Baron: 39

Bassi, Aldo: 84

Bathurst 100-mile race (Australia): 233

X

Z